Red Hat Enterpris
Desktops
and
Administration

To George, Robert, and Mark

Red Hat Enterprise Linux 7: Desktops and Administration

Richard Petersen

Surfing Turtle Press

Alameda, CA

www.surfingturtlepress.com

Please send inquiries to: editor@surfingturtlepress.com

ISBN 1-936280-62-0

ISBN-13 978-1-936280-62-9

Second Printing

Preface

This book examines Red Hat Enterprise Linux 7 for the desktop user and administrator. This second printing covers RHEL 7.4. Though administrative tools are covered, the emphasis is on what a user would need to know to perform tasks. The focus here is on what users face when using Red Hat Enterprise Linux 7, covering topics like applications, the GNOME and KDE desktops, shell commands, and the administration and network tools. Desktops are examined in detail, including configuration options. Administration topics are also covered including user management, software management, repositories, services, systemd, system monitoring, shell configuration, encryption, network connections, shared resources, authentication, SELinux, firewalls, shell configuration, backups, and printers.

The book is organized into two parts: desktops and administration.

Part 1 covers the desktop. First discussed are basic desktop use and configuration tasks performed by most users. Then the GNOME and KDE desktops are examined in detail covering topics such as the the Nautilus and Dolphin file managers, the GNOME dash, and KDE plasmoids. It also reviews desktop applications available for Red Hat Enterprise Linux including office and Web applications, email clients, graphic tools, databases, editors, video applications, music players, Web browsers, FTP clients, instant messengers, VoIP applications, and sound (PulseAudio) configuration.

Part 2 focuses on administrative tasks such as managing users, monitoring your system, managing software, securing your system, configuring network connections and printers, setting up shared resources (Samba and NFS), and performing backups. Red Hat Enterprise Linux administrative desktop administrative tools are examined. For software management, GNOME Software, PackageKit, and YUM are discussed in detail along with the Red Hat and EPEL repositories. Security issues such as encryption, authorization, and SELinux configuration are covered. system is also examined, including service and template files. The command line shell interface and shell configuration, including system and user shell configuration variables and files are also discussed.

Overview

Contents

Part 2
Administration

Part 1: Desktops

1. Red Hat Enterprise Linux 7 Introduction

Red Hat Enterprise Linux
Red Hat Enterprise Linux Documentation
Red Hat Enterprise Linux 7 Features
Installing Red Hat Enterprise Linux
Open Source Software

Linux is a fast, stable, and open source operating system for laptops, desktops, and servers that feature professional-level Internet services, extensive development tools, desktops, and a massive number of applications including office, multimedia, and social media applications. As an operating system, Linux performs many of the same functions as UNIX, OS/X, and Windows. However, Linux is distinguished by its power and flexibility, along with being freely available. Technically, Linux consists of the operating system program referred to as the kernel, which is the part originally developed by Linus Torvalds. But it has always been distributed with a massive number of software applications, ranging from network servers and security programs to office applications and development tools. Linux has evolved as part of the open source software movement, in which independent programmers joined together to provide free quality software to any user. Linux has become the premier platform for open source software, much of it developed by the Free Software Foundation's GNU project. Many of these applications are bundled as part of the Red Hat Enterprise Linux distribution.

With the both GNOME and KDE desktops, Linux also provides desktop interfaces. Unlike Windows and the Mac, Linux enables you to choose the interface you want and then customize it further, adding panels, applets, virtual desktops, and menus, all with full drag-and-drop capabilities and Internet-aware tools. Red Hat Enterprise Linux uses very stable versions of these desktops.

Companies like Red Hat have taken Linux development a step further by providing a reliable commercial version with high levels of support. Though the source code for Red Hat Enterprise Linux is open source and freely available, Red Hat provides the technical expertise to implement a version of Linux that is commercially reliable. Today commercially supported versions of Linux run a large part of the servers in use around the world.

Red Hat Enterprise Linux

The Red Hat Enterprise Linux release is maintained and developed as an Open Source project for commercial purposes by Red Hat Inc. The project is designed to provide a stable and reliable system, particularly for servers. Releases are timed to extended support intervals, usually about 2 to 3 years, with intermediate refresh releases to incorporate bug fixes and some enhanced software. Though Red Hat Enterprise Linux is open source and its source code freely available, support is commercially contracted, including compiled automatic updates. See the Red Hat Enterprise Linux site for detailed information, **https://www.redhat.com/en/technologies/linux-platforms/enterprise-linux**.

The Red Hat Enterprise Linux versions of Linux work as commercial subscriptions. You can download and install the evaluation version with a 30-day free software update, and then purchase a subscription for continued support.

```
https://access.redhat.com/products/red-hat-enterprise-linux/evaluation
```

Red Hat Enterprise Linux Documentation

Red Hat maintains an extensive library of documentation for Red Hat Enterprise Linux at **https://access.redhat.com/documentation/** (see Table 1-1). The documentation covers topics like storage management, installation, administration, power management, and security. All the Red Hat documentation is freely available under the GNU General Public License.

Web Site	Name
https://www.redhat.com/en	Red Hat home page
https://www.redhat.com/en/technologies/linux-platforms/enterprise-linux	Red Hat Enterprise Linux Website
https://access.redhat.com/home	Red Hat Customer Portal
https://access.redhat.com/documentation/en/	Red Hat Documentation site
https://access.redhat.com/documentation/en-US/Red_Hat_Enterprise_Linux/7/html-single/System_Administrators_Guide/index.html	Red Hat Enterprise Linux 7 Administration Guide
https://access.redhat.com/documentation/en-US/Red_Hat_Enterprise_Linux/7/html-single/Installation_Guide/index.html	Red Hat Enterprise Linux 7 Installation Guide
https://access.redhat.com/documentation/en-US/Red_Hat_Enterprise_Linux/7/html-single/Storage_Administration_Guide/index.html	Red Hat Enterprise Linux 7 Storage Administration Guide
https://access.redhat.com/documentation/en-US/Red_Hat_Enterprise_Linux/7/html-single/Power_Management_Guide/index.html	Red Hat Enterprise Linux 7 Power Management Guide
https://access.redhat.com/documentation/en-US/Red_Hat_Enterprise_Linux/7/html-single/Security_Guide/index.html	Red Hat Enterprise Linux Security Guide
https://access.redhat.com/documentation/en-US/Red_Hat_Enterprise_Linux/7/html-single/SELinux_Users_and_Administrators_Guide/index.html	Red Hat Enterprise Linux 7 Security-Enhanced Linux User Guide
https://www.redhat.com/en/about/newsroom	Red Hat News
https://www.linuxfoundation.org/	The Linux Foundation
https://www.kernel.org/	Latest Linux kernels.

Table 1-1: Red Hat sites

Before installing Red Hat Enterprise Linux on your system, you may want to check the online Installation guide, which provides a detailed description of all install procedures.

```
https://access.redhat.com/documentation/en-US/Red_Hat_Enterprise_Linux/7/html-single/Installation_Guide/index.html
```

The System Administration guide provides detailed information for administrative aspects of your Red Hat Enterprise Linux system ranging from package management to system monitoring. Always check the System Administration Guide before performing an administrative task for the first time. It will have the most up-to-date information.

```
https://access.redhat.com/documentation/en-US/Red_Hat_Enterprise_Linux/7/html-single/System_Administrators_Guide/index.html
```

The System Administration Guide has 8 parts, each with chapters and sub-sections. The parts are listed here:

Part 1: Basic System Configuration

Part 2: Subscription and Support

Part 3: Installing and Managing Software

Part 4: Infrastructure Services

Part 5: Servers

Part 6: Monitoring and Automation

Part 7: Kernel, Module, and Driver Configuration

Part 8: System Backup and Recovery

The Red Hat Enterprise Linux **Storage Administration Guide** covers detailed configuration of storage systems including LVM, hard disk partitions, NFS, and disk quotas.

```
https://access.redhat.com/documentation/en-US/Red_Hat_Enterprise_Linux/7/html-single/Storage_Administration_Guide/index.html
```

Your Firefox Browser will already be configured with bookmarks for accessing Red Hat documentation and support sites. These include the Red Hat home page, the Red Hat documentation site, and the Red Hat Customer Portal page with links for evaluation, product documentation, and subscription support.

For much of the documentation you can also access installed documentation on your system in **/usr/share/doc** folder or the Man and info pages, as well as the context help button for different applications running on your desktop. Web sites for software like those for GNOME, KDE, and Libreoffice.org will provide extensive application documentation.

Linux Documentation

A special Linux project called the Linux Documentation Project (LDP) has developed a complete set of Linux manuals. The documentation is available at the LDP home site at **http://www.tldp.org**. The documentation includes a user's guide, an introduction, and administrative guides, available in various formats. You can also find briefer explanations in HOW-TO documents. The Linux documentation for your installed software will be available in your **/usr/share/doc** folder.

Red Hat-specific documentation is available at **https://access.redhat.com/documentation/**. The **https://help.gnome.org/** site holds documentation for the GNOME desktop, while **https://www.kde.org/** holds documentation for the KDE desktop.

Red Hat Enterprise Linux 7 Features

Red Hat Enterprise Linux 7 (RHEL7) features key updates to critical applications as well as new tools replacing former ones. GNOME 3 is now the default desktop. Consult these notes for detailed information about all new changes. The Red Hat Enterprise Linux 7 release notes are located on the Red Hat documentation site at:

```
https://access.redhat.com/documentation/en-
US/Red_Hat_Enterprise_Linux/7/html/7.4_Release_Notes/index.html
```

Installing Red Hat Enterprise Linux

Red Hat Enterprise Linux uses the Anaconda installation program; it is designed to be easy to use and helpful, while at the same time efficient and brief, installing as many services and applications as possible (see Figure 1-1). A Red Hat Enterprise Linux Installation Guide is available online at:

```
https://access.redhat.com/documentation/en-US/Red_Hat_Enterprise_Linux/7/html-
single/Installation_Guide/index.html
```

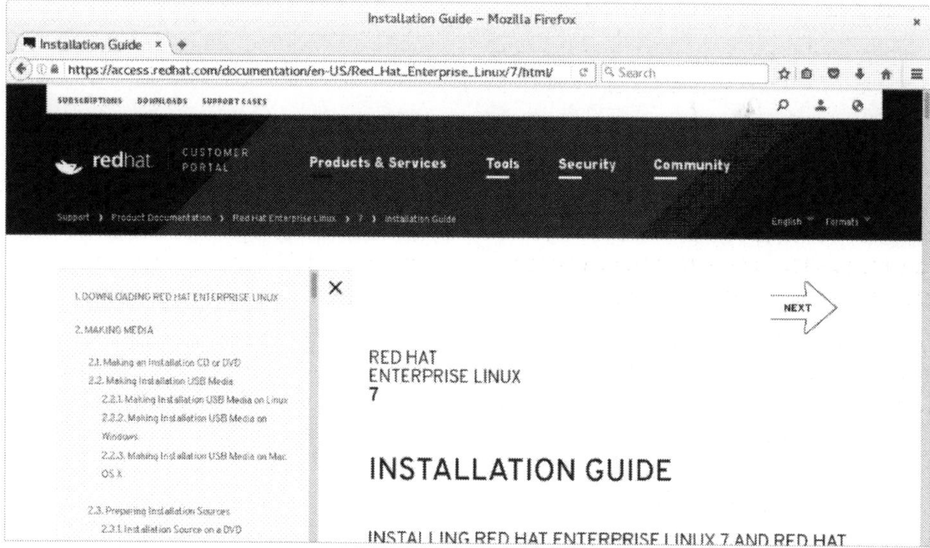

Figure 1-1: Red Hat Enterprise Linux Installation Guide

Red Hat Repositories

To access the full range of Red Hat supported software you need to use the Subscription Manager to register your subscription with Red Hat. You can then configure access to several Red

Hat software repositories. The older Red Hat Network management of repositories has been deprecated. You may also want to enable the Red Hat Supplementary repository which holds the Java software and Adobe Reader and Flash player applications.

Third Party Repositories: EPEL and RPM Fusion

One major third party repository is available for RHEL7, the Extra Packages Enterprise Linux (EPEL) repository. EPEL (**http://fedoraproject.org/wiki/EPEL**) provides popular Fedora supported packages such as BackupPC and Dia. The third-party repositories RPM Fusion (**https://rpmfusion.org**) or Negativo17.org (**https://negativo17.org**) provide most of the third party multimedia applications and codecs like the vlc multimedia player and the DVD video codec. Multimedia codecs with licensing issues can be directly downloaded with PackageKit, once you have configured YUM to use the RPM Fusion (**https://rpmfusion.org**) or Negativo17.org (**https://negativo17.org**) repositories on your system. Use one or the other, not both. These repositories are not configured by default. For the RPM Fusion repository install the configuration package for RHEL 7, which is available from that site at **https://rpmfusion.org/Configuration**.

Obtaining the CDs and DVDs

To obtain the Red Hat Enterprise Linux install CD or DVD, you can either purchase a subscription or apply for a 30-day evaluation subscription. For the evaluation subscription, go to the following site. You will first have to register, verifying your subscription by email. Once registered you can download the Red Hat Enterprise Linux DVD/CDs, and install with a 30 evaluation subscription.

```
https://www.redhat.com/rhel/details/eval/
```

Open Source Software

Linux is distributed freely under a GNU General Public License as specified by the Free Software Foundation, making it available to anyone who wants to use it. GNU (the acronym stands for "GNU's Not Unix") is a project initiated and managed by the Free Software Foundation to provide free software to users, programmers, and developers. Linux is copyrighted, not public domain. However, a GNU public license has much the same effect as the software's being in the public domain. The GNU general public license is designed to ensure Linux remains free and, at the same time, standardized. Linux is technically the operating system kernel and only one official Linux kernel exists.

Most Linux software is developed as Open Source software. This means that the source code for an application is freely distributed along with the application. Programmers over the Internet can make their own contributions to a software package's development, modifying and correcting the source code. Linux is an open source operating system. Its source code is included in all its distributions and is freely available on the Internet. Many major software development efforts are also open source projects, as are the KDE and GNOME desktops along with most of their applications. You can find more information about the Open Source movement at **http://www.opensource.org**.

Open source software is protected by public licenses. These prevent commercial companies from taking control of open source software by adding a few modifications of their own, copyrighting those changes, and selling the software as their own product. The most popular public license is the GNU General Public License provided by the Free Software Foundation. This is the license that Linux is distributed under. The GNU General Public License retains the copyright, freely licensing the software with the requirement that the software and any modifications made to it always be freely available. Other public licenses have also been created to support the demands of different kinds of open source projects. The GNU Lesser General Public License (LGPL) lets commercial applications use GNU licensed software libraries. The Qt Public License (QPL) lets open source developers use the Qt libraries essential to the KDE desktop. You can find a complete listing at **http://www.opensource.org**.

Linux is currently copyrighted under a GNU public license provided by the Free Software Foundation, and it is often referred to as GNU software (see **http://www.gnu.org**). Under the terms of the GNU General Public License, the original author retains the copyright, although anyone can modify the software and redistribute it, provided the source code is included, made public, and provided free. Also, no restriction exists on selling the software or giving it away free. One distributor could charge for the software, while another one could provide it free of charge.

2. Desktop Use and Configuration

Using Linux has become an almost intuitive process, with easy-to-use interfaces, including graphical logins and desktops like GNOME and KDE. Even the standard Linux command line interface has become more user-friendly with editable commands and cursor-based tools. To start using Red Hat Enterprise Linux, you have to know how to access your system and, once you are on the system, how to execute commands and run applications. Access is supported through either the default graphical login or a command line login. For the graphical login, a simple screen appears with menus for selecting login options and dialogs for selecting users and entering your password. Linux is noted for providing easy access to extensive help documentation. It's easy to obtain information quickly about any Linux command and utility while logged into the system.

Accessing Your Linux System

If you have installed the boot loader GRUB, when you turn on or reboot your computer, the bootloader first decides what operating system to load and run. For a few seconds, GRUB will display a short message telling the operating system it will start up. This is usually Red Hat Enterprise Linux by default.

If instead, you press any key on your keyboard, the bootloader displays a menu listing all the operating systems installed on your system, with the default highlighted. If a Windows system is listed, you can choose to start that instead.

Both command line login prompts and graphical login dialogs are supported. Red Hat Enterprise Linux uses the graphical login by default, presenting you with a dialog at which you select a user to log in as and then enter your password. If you choose not to use the graphical login, you are presented with a simple command line prompt to enter your username.

GRUB Start Menu and Boot Problems

When you boot up, the GRUB screen is displayed for a few seconds before the boot procedure begins. Should you want to start a different operating system or add options to your startup, you have to display the GRUB startup menu (see Figure 2-1). Do this by pressing any key on your keyboard. The GRUB menu will be displayed and will list Linux and other operating systems you specified, such as Windows. Your Linux system should be selected by default. If not, use the arrow keys to move to the Linux entry, if it is not already highlighted, and press Enter.

To change a particular line, use the up/down arrow keys to move to the line. You can use the left/right arrow keys to move along the line. The Backspace key will delete characters and, simply by typing, will insert characters. The editing changes are temporary. Permanent changes can be made only by directly editing the GRUB configuration files. RHEL 7 uses GRUB2, which uses the configuration file /etc/default/grub. GRUB2 files are kept in the **/etc/grub.d** directory. Run as root the following grub2-mkconfig to apply changes made in **/etc/default/grub**:

```
grub2-mkconfig -o /boot/grub2/grub.cfg
```

See the GRUB2 page at **http://fedoraproject.org/wiki/GRUB_2** for more information.

When your RHEL operating system starts up, an RHEL logo appears. You can press the ESC key to see the startup messages instead. RHEL uses Plymouth with its kernel-mode setting ability, to display a startup animation. The Plymouth RHEL logo theme is installed by default.

For graphical installations, some displays may have difficulty running the graphical startup display known as the Plymouth boot tool. This tool replaces the Red Hat Graphical Boot tool but still uses the command rhgb. If you have this problem, you can edit your Linux GRUB entry and remove the rhgb term from the Linux line. Press the **e** key to edit a Grub Linux entry (see Figure 2-2). Then move the cursor to the linux line and perform your edit. Use the Backspace key to delete. Then press Ctrl+x to boot the edited GRUB entry.

Your system will start up, initially using the text display for all the startup tasks, then shift to the graphical login.

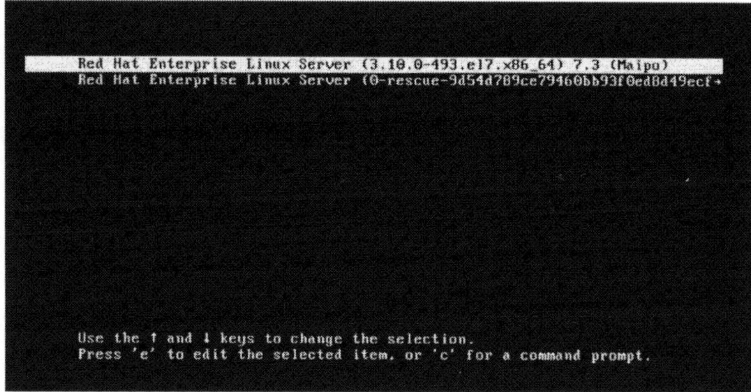

Figure 2-1: GRUB menu

```
        insmod xfs                                                    ↑
        set root='hd0,msdos1'
        if [ x$feature_platform_search_hint = xy ]; then
          search --no-floppy --fs-uuid --set=root --hint-bios=hd0,msdos1 --hin\
t-efi=hd0,msdos1 --hint-baremetal=ahci0,msdos1 --hint='hd0,msdos1'  3977b23a-a\
f64-4c7e-8036-0f2f4eb5e988
        else
          search --no-floppy --fs-uuid --set=root 3977b23a-af64-4c7e-8036-0f2f\
4eb5e988
        fi
        linux16 /vmlinuz-3.10.0-493.el7.x86_64 root=/dev/mapper/rhel-root ro c\
rashkernel=auto rd.lvm.lv=rhel/root rd.lvm.lv=rhel/swap rhgb quiet LANG=en_US.\
UTF-8
        initrd16 /initramfs-3.10.0-493.el7.x86_64.img

      Press Ctrl-x to start, Ctrl-c for a command prompt or Escape to
      discard edits and return to the menu. Pressing Tab lists
      possible completions.
```

Figure 2-2: GRUB Edit window

Should you have difficulty displaying your graphical interface, you can instead choose to boot up the command-line interface. From the command-line interface, you can make any needed configuration changes. To boot to the command-line interface from GRUB, edit the linux line of the Linux GRUB entries, and add a 3 to the end of the line. The 3 indicates the command-line interface. In previous versions of RHEL, the 3 indicated a run level. Now it refers to a systemd target.

The Display Manager: GDM

The graphical login interface displays a login window with a box listing a menu of usernames. When you click a username, a login box replaces the listing of users, displaying the selected username and a text box in which you then enter your password. Upon clicking the Sign In button or pressing Enter, you log in to the selected account, and your desktop starts up.

Graphical logins are handled by the GNOME Display Manager (GDM). The GDM manages the login interface, in addition to authenticating a user password and username, and then starts up a selected desktop. From the GDM, you can shift to the command-line interface with Ctrl+Alt+F2, and then shift back to the GDM with Ctrl+Alt+F1 (from a desktop, you would use the same keys to shift to a command-line interface and to shift back). The keys F2 through F6 provide different command-line terminals, as in Ctrl+Alt+F3 for the third command-line terminal.

When the GDM starts up, it shows a listing of users (see Figure 2-3). A System Status Area at the top right of the screen displays icons indicating the status of the sound and battery. Clicking the icons displays the System Status Area menu, which shows the entries for sound adjustment, network wireless (if supported), and the battery status (if a laptop). A power button at the bottom will display a power off dialog with options to Power Off and Restart. To shut down your RHEL system, click the Power Off button on the dialog.

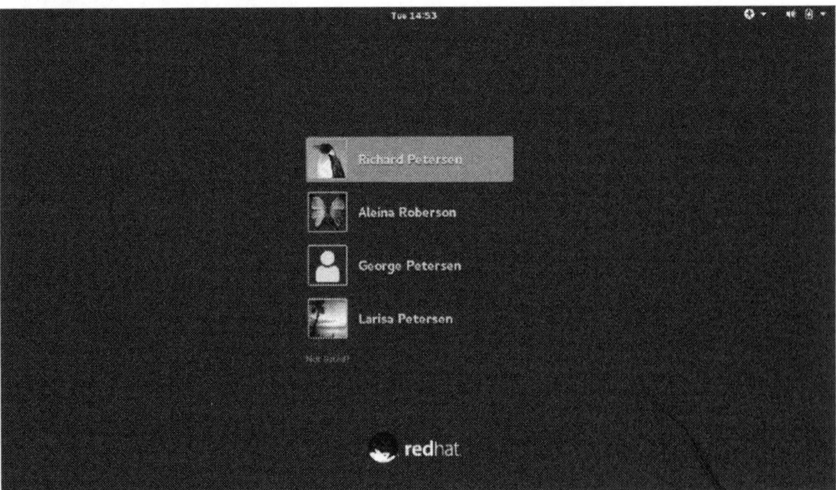

Figure 2-3: The RHEL GDM user listing

The date is displayed at the top center of the screen. Clicking the date displays a calendar.

Next to the System Status Area icons is a menu for accessibility, which displays a menu of switches that let you turn on accessibility tools and such features as the onscreen keyboard, enhanced contrast, and the screen magnifier.

To log in, click a username from the list of users. You are then prompted to enter the user's password (see Figure 2-4). A new dialog replaces the user list, showing the username you selected and a Password text box in which you can enter the user's password. Once you enter the password, click the Sign In button or press Enter. By default, the GNOME desktop starts up. If the name of a user you want to log in as is not listed, click the "Not Listed" entry at the end, to open a text box, which prompts you for a username, and then the password.

Though GNOME is the primary desktop for RHEL, it is possible to install and use other desktops, such as KDE, Xfce, and Mate. Xfce and Mate are available on the EPEL repository. Should you have more than one desktop installed, such as both GNOME and KDE, when you click a username under which to log in, a Session button (gear icon) is displayed below the Password text box next to the "Sign in" button. Click that Session button to open a menu listing the installed desktops, then click the one you want to use (see Figure 2-5).

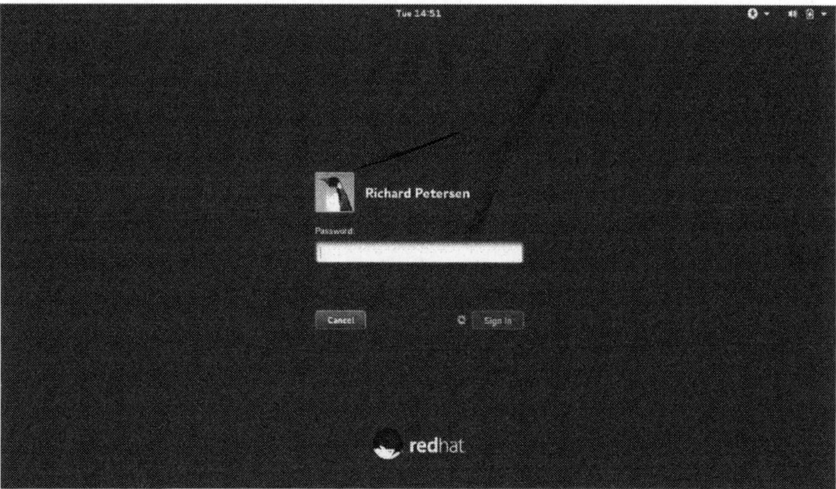

Figure 2-4: GDM login

Figure 2-5: GDM Session menu

The System Status Area

Once logged in, the System Status Area is displayed on the right side of the top bar (see Figure 2-6). The area will include status icons for features such as sound and power. Clicking the button displays the System Status Area menu, with items for sound, brightness, wired and wireless connections, Bluetooth connections, the battery, and the current user, in addition to buttons at the bottom for opening GNOME Settings, activating the lock screen, and shutting down or rebooting the system. The sound and brightness items at the top feature sliding bars with which you can adjust the volume and brightness. The Wired, Wi-Fi, Bluetooth, Battery, and current user entries expand to submenus with added entries (see Figure 2-7). The buttons at the bottom open separate dialogs.

On systems that are not laptops, there will be no brightness slider or Battery entry on the System Status Area menu. If the system also has no wireless device, the Wi-Fi entry will also be missing. A system of this kind will only have a sound slider and a current user entry.

To log out or switch to another user, you click the current user entry to expand the menu to show Switch User and Log Out entries. The Log Out entry returns you to the GDM login screen. The Switch User entry suspends the current user and returns you to the GDM login screen, where you can log in as another user. If only one user is defined, there is no user entry, and, so, no Log Out entry, as there are no other users to log in.

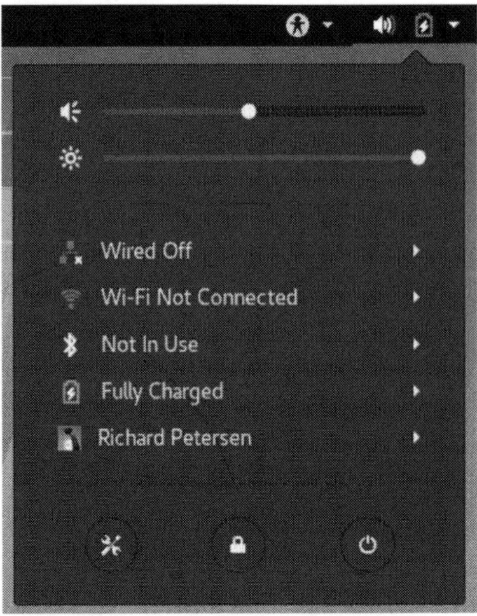

Figure 2-6: System Status Area menu

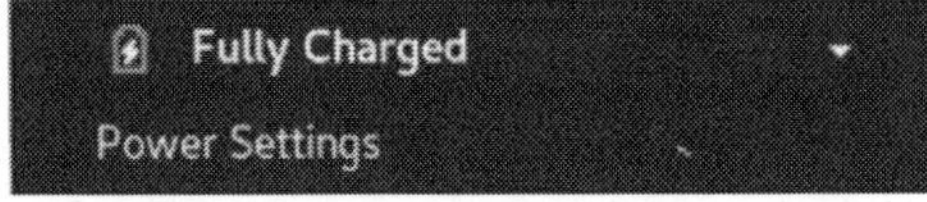

Figure 2-7: System Status Area menu battery entry

For network connections, RHEL uses Network Manager. Network Manager will detect available network connections automatically (see "Network Manager Wireless Connections," later in this chapter). Click the Wi-Fi entry in the System Status Area to expand the menu showing an entry for Select Network. Click this entry to display a dialog showing all possible wireless networks, as well as any wired networks. You can then choose the one you want to use. When you try to connect to an encrypted wireless network, you will be prompted for the password. Wireless networks that you successfully connect to will be added to your Network Manager configuration.

Desktops

Several alternative desktop interfaces, such as GNOME and the K Desktop (KDE), can be installed on RHEL. Each has its own style and appearance. It is important to keep in mind that the GNOME and KDE interfaces are two very different desktop interfaces, with separate tools for selecting preferences.

KDE

The K Desktop Environment (KDE) displays a panel at the bottom of the screen. The file manager operates much the same way as the GNOME file manager. There is a Settings entry in the main menu that opens the KDE Settings window, from which you can configure every aspect of the KDE environment, such as desktop effects, workspace appearance, and devices such as monitors and printers, and networking.

GNOME

RHEL 7 uses the GNOME 3 desktop which is very different from the GNOME 2 desktop use in RHEL 6. It provides easy-to-use overviews and menus, along with a flexible file manager and desktop. GNOME 3 is based on the gnome-shell, which is a compositing window manager. It replaces the GNOME 2 Metacity window manager, gnome-panel, and a notification daemon.

The screen displays a top bar, through which you access your applications, windows, and settings. Clicking the System Status Area button at the right side of the top bar displays the status user area menu, from which you can access buttons at the bottom to display the system setting dialog, lock the screen, and shut down the system (see Figure 2-8).

To access applications and windows, use the Activities overview mode. Click the Activities button at the left side of the top bar (or move the mouse to the left corner, or press the Windows button). The overview mode consists of a dash listing your favorite and running applications, workspaces, and windows (see Figure 2-9). Large thumbnails of open windows are displayed on the windows overview (the desktop area). You can use the Search box at the top to locate an application quickly. Partially hidden thumbnails of your desktop workspaces are displayed on the right side. Initially, there are two. Moving your mouse to the right side displays the workspace thumbnails.

You can manually leave the overview at any time by pressing the ESC key or by clicking a window thumbnail.

The dash is a bar on the left side with icons for your favorite applications. Initially, there are icons for the Firefox web browser, files (the GNOME file manager), GNOME Software, GNOME help, the terminal window, GNOME System Settings, and the Applications overview, as depicted in Figure 2-9. The last icon opens an Applications overview that you can use to start other applications. To open an application from the dash, click its icon or right-click on the icon and choose New Window from the pop-up menu. You can also click and drag the icon to the windows overview or to a workspace thumbnail on the right side.

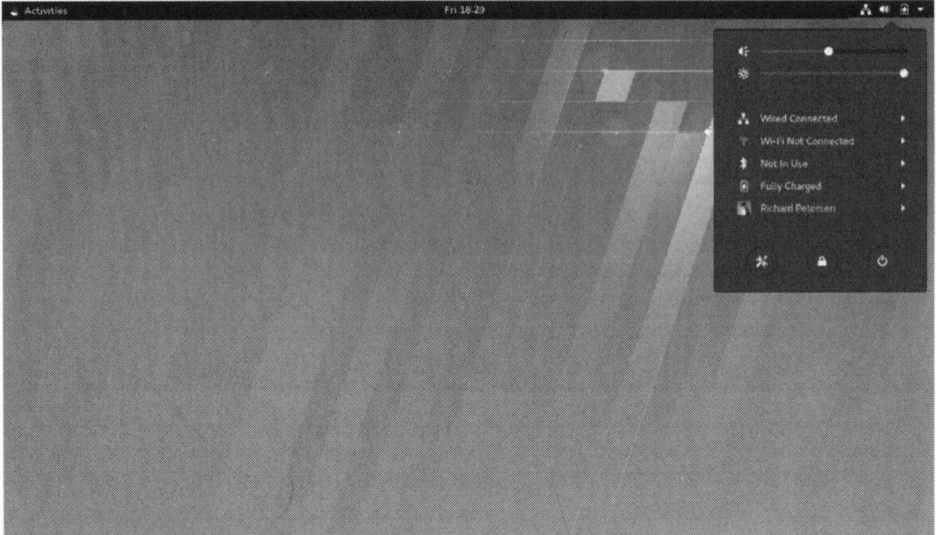

Figure 2-8: The RHEL GNOME desktop

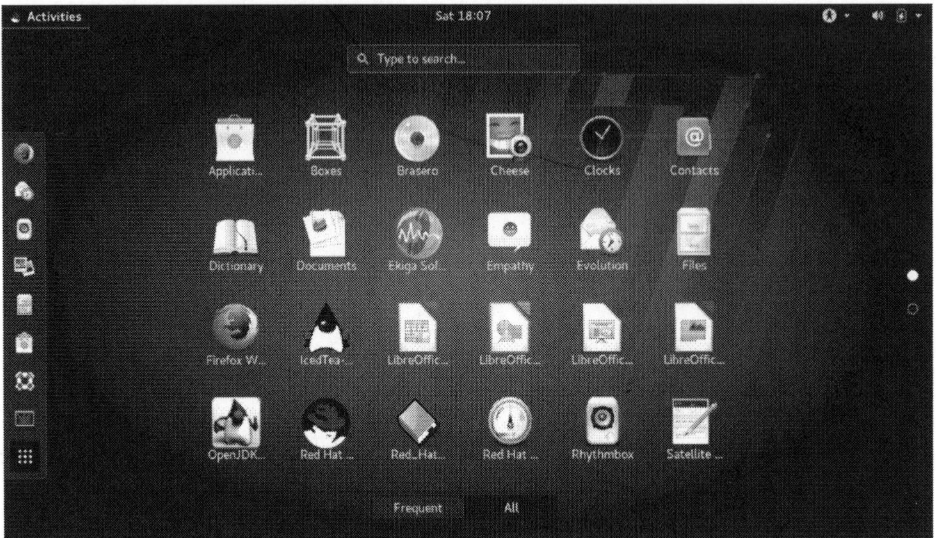

Figure 2-9: GNOME 3 Activities overview mode for applications

You can access windows from the windows overview, which is displayed when you start Activities. The windows overview displays thumbnails of all your open windows. When you pass your mouse over a window thumbnail, a close box appears, at the upper-right corner, with which you can close the window. You can also move the window on the desktop and to another workspace.

To move a window on the desktop, click and drag its title bar. To maximize a window, double-click its title bar or drag it to the top bar. To minimize, double-click the title bar again or drag it away from the top bar. To close a window, click its close box (upper right).

Two sub-overviews are available on the applications overview: Utilities and Sundries. Utilities lists several tools, such as the text editor and system monitor, and Sundries lists older administrative tools, such as system-config-printer and firewall-config. These sub-overviews function like a submenu, overlaying the main overview with a sub-overview.

GNOME File Manager

You can access your home folder from the Files icon on the dash. A file manager window opens, showing your Home folder (see Figure 2-10). Your Home folder will already have default directories created for commonly used files. These include Documents, Downloads, Music, Pictures, and Videos. Your office applications will automatically save files to the Documents folder by default. Image and photo applications place image files in the Pictures directory. The Desktop folder will hold all files and directories saved to your desktop. When you download a file, it is placed in the Downloads directory.

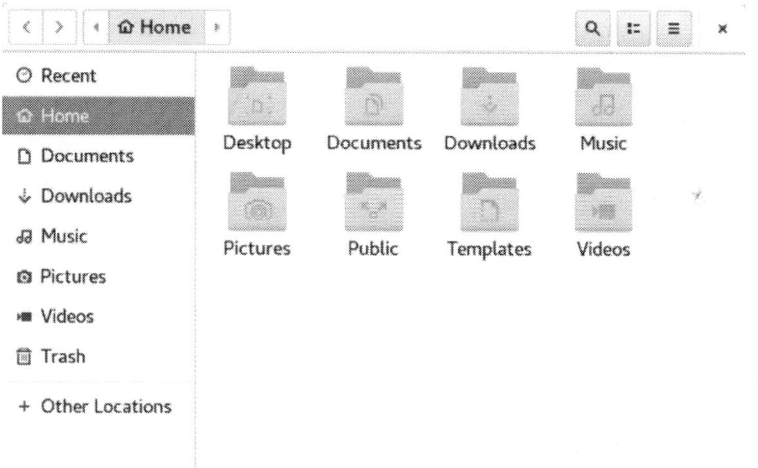

Figure 2-10: File manager for the Home folder

The file manager window displays several components, including a header bar, which combines the title bar and toolbar, and a sidebar. When you open a new directory, the same window is used to display it, and you can use the forward and back arrows to move through previously opened directories. The header bar displays navigation folder buttons that show your current folder and its parent folders. You can click a parent folder to move to it. The GNOME file manager also supports tabs. You can open several folders in the same file manager window.

GNOME Customization with Tweak Tool: Themes, Icons, Fonts, Startup Applications, and Extensions

You can perform common desktop customizations using the GNOME Tweak Tool. Areas to customize include the desktop icons, fonts, themes, startup applications, workspaces, window behavior, and the time display. You can access Tweak Tool from the Applications overview | Utilities. The GNOME Tweak Tool has tabs for Appearance, Desktop, Extensions, Fonts, Keyboard and Mouse, Power, Startup Applications, Top Bar, Typing, Windows, and Workspaces (see Figure 2-11).

The Appearance tab lets you set the theme for your windows, icons, and cursor. GNOME 3 uses the Adwaita Theme. This theme has a light and dark variant. The Global Light Theme is the default, but you can use the switch on the Appearance tab to enable the Global Dark Theme. The Global Dark Theme shades the background of windows to a dark gray, while text and button images appear in white.

As you add other desktops, such as Cinnamon, the available themes increase. There are many window themes to choose from, including Clearlooks, Mist, and Glider. For icons, you can choose among Oxygen (KDE), Mist (Cinnamon), and GNOME.

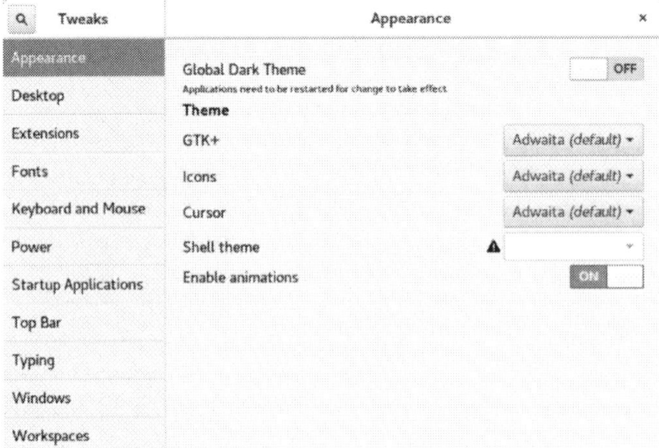

Figure 2-11: GNOME Tweak Tool: Appearance tab (themes)

You may also want to display Home, Trash, and Mounted Volumes like USB drives, on the desktop, as other desktops do. Use the Desktop tab on Tweak Tool to display these icons (see Figure 2-12). Turn on the "Icons on Desktop" switch. Home, Trash, and Mounted Volumes are checked by default. Uncheck them in order not to display the icon. You can also check a Network Servers option to display icons for remotely accessed folders.

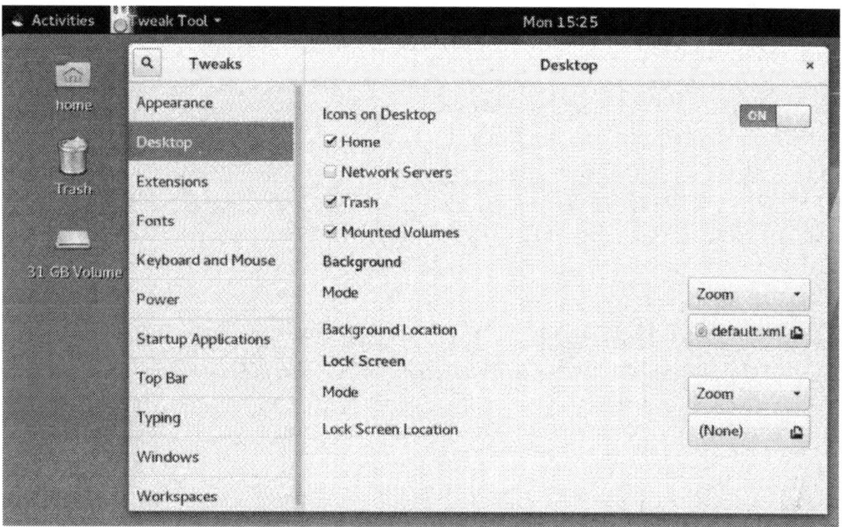

Figure 2-12: GNOME Tweak Tool: Desktop tab (desktop icons)

Desktop fonts for window titles, interface (application or dialog text), documents, and monospace (terminal windows or code) can be changed in the Fonts tab (see Figure 2-13). You can adjust the size of the font or change the font style. Clicking the font name opens a "Pick a Font" dialog from which you can choose a different font. The quality of text display can be further adjusted with Hinting and Antialiasing options. To simply increase or decrease the size of all fonts on your desktop interface, you can adjust the Scaling Factor.

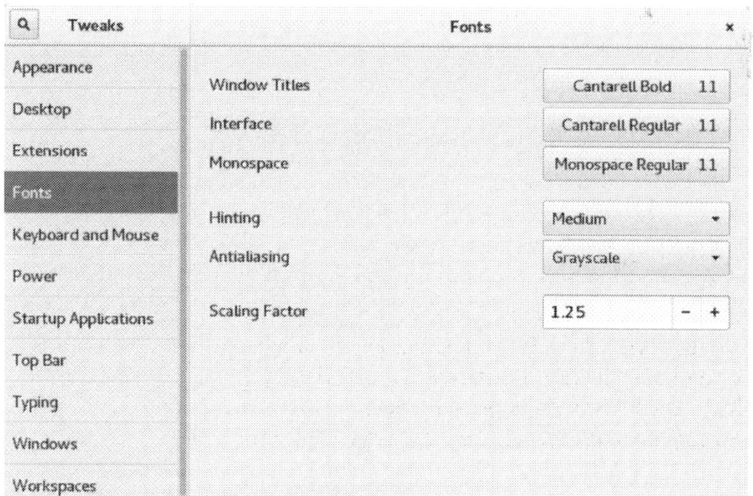

Figure 2-13: GNOME Tweak Tool: Fonts tab

At times, there may be certain applications that you want started up when you log in, such as the Gedit text editor, the Firefox web browser, or the Videos movie player. On the Startup

Applications tab, you can choose the applications to start up (see Figure 2-14). Click the plus (+) button to open an applications dialog from which you can choose an application to start up. Once added, you can later remove the application by clicking its Remove button.

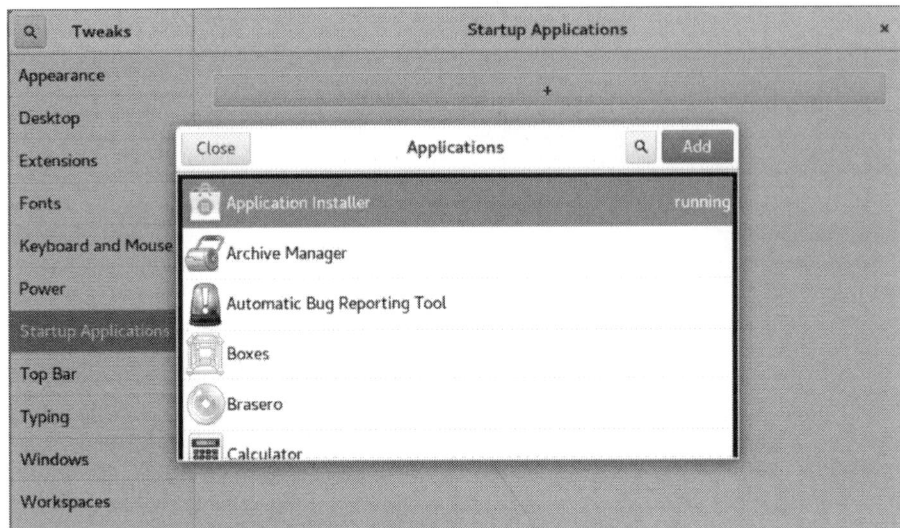

Figure 2-14: GNOME Tweak Tool: Startup Applications tab

Extensions function much as applets did in GNOME 2. They are third-party programs that enhance or modify the GNOME desktop, such as a system monitor, sensors, and applications menu. Extensions appear on the top bar. Installed extensions are listed on the Extensions tab of Tweak Tool, where you can turn them on or off.

Logging Out and Shutting Down from GNOME

If you want to exit your desktop and return to the GDM login screen, or switch to a different user, you click the user entry in the System Status Area menu to expand to a menu with entries for Switch User and Log Out (see Figure 2-15). Click the Log Out entry to display a dialog that shows buttons for Cancel and Log Out. Click Log Out to log out of your account, exiting GNOME and returning to the login screen, where you can log in again as a different user or shut down the system. A countdown will commence in the dialog, showing how much time you have left before it performs the logout automatically.

From the login screen, you can shut down the system: choose Power Off from the System Status Area menu on the lower right of the menu. This displays a power off dialog with options to restart or power off. A countdown will commence in the dialog, showing how much time you have left before it performs the shutdown automatically.

The Switch User entry in the current user submenu switches out from the current user and runs the GDM to display a list of users you can log in as. Click the name to open a password prompt and display a session button. You can then log in as that user. The sessions of users already logged will continue with the same open windows and applications that were running when the user switched off. You can switch back and forth between logged-in users, with all users retaining their session from where they left off. When you switch off from a user, that user's running programs will continue in the background.

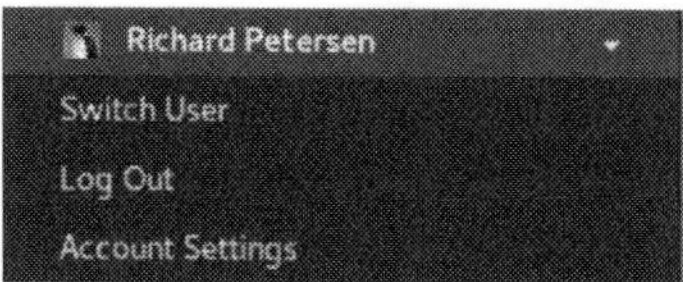

Figure 2-15: GNOME Log Out menu entry

Network Connections

Network connections will be set up for you by Network Manager, which will detect your network connections automatically, both wired and wireless. Network Manager provides status information for your connection and allows you to switch easily from one configured connection to another, as needed. For initial configuration, it detects as much information as possible about the new connection.

Network Manager is user specific. Wired connections will be started automatically. For wireless connections, when a user logs in, Network Manager selects the connection preferred by that user. From a menu of detected wireless networks, the user can select a wireless connection to use.

Network Manager displays active network connections in the System Status Area: Wired for the wired connection and Wi-Fi for a wireless connection. Each entry will indicate its status, as connected or disconnected. The Network Manager icon for these entries will vary according to the connection status: solid for an active connection and faded for a disconnected connection (see Figure 2-16). On wired systems that have no wireless devices, there is no Wi-Fi network entry in the System Status Area menu.

Figure 2-16: Network Manager: wireless

Network Manager Wired Connections

For computers connected to a wired network, such as an Ethernet connection, Network Manager automatically detects and establishes the network connection. Most networks use DHCP to provide such network information as an IP address and DNS server. With this kind of connection, Network Manager can connect automatically to your network whenever you start your system.

Network Manager Wireless Connections

With multiple wireless access points for Internet connections, a system could have several network connections to choose from. This is particularly true for notebook computers that access different wireless connections at different locations. Instead of manually configuring a new connection each time one is encountered, the Network Manager tool can configure and select a connection to use automatically. Click the Wired entry in the System Status Area to expand the menu to show entries from which to connect or disconnect to wired networking, and open the GNOME Network Settings dialog at the Wired tab (Wired Settings).

Network Manager will scan for wireless connections, checking for Extended Service Set Identifiers (ESSIDs). If an ESSID identifies a previously used connection, it is selected. If several are found, the recently used one is chosen. If only new connections are available, Network Manager waits for the user to choose one. A connection is selected if the user is logged in.

Click the Wi-Fi entry in the System Status Area to expand the menu to show entries from which to select a network, turn off wireless networking, and open the GNOME Network Settings dialog at the Wi-Fi tab (Wi-Fi Settings). Click the Select Network item to open a dialog that shows a list of all available wireless connections (see Figure 2-17). Entries display the name of the wireless network and a wave graph showing the strength of its signal. To connect to a network, click its entry, then click the Connect button, to activate the connection. If this is the first time you are trying to connect to that network, you will be prompted to enter the password or encryption key (see Figure 2-18).

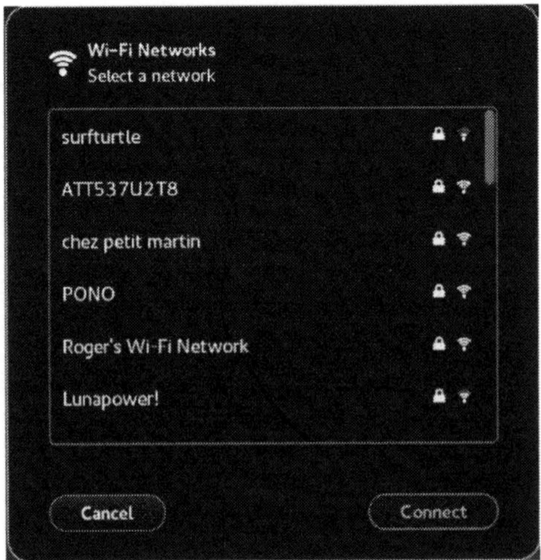

Figure 2-17: Network Manager connections menu: wireless

Figure 2-18: Network Manager wireless authentication

You can turn off wireless by clicking the Turn Off entry in the expanded Wi-Fi section of the System Status Area (see Figure 2-19). When turned off, the entry label changes to Turn On. entry. To reactivate your wireless connection, click the Turn On entry.

Figure 2-19: Network Manager wireless on and off

Settings Network (GNOME and Proxies)

GNOME provides a network dialog for basic information and network connection management, including proxy settings. It is designed to work with Network Manager. Choose Wi-Fi Settings from the expanded Wi-Fi entries in the System Status Area, or click the Network icon in the Settings dialog, to open the Network dialog (see Figure 2-20). Tabs for kinds of network connections are listed to the left. There are tabs for Wi-Fi, Wired, and Network proxy (Wi-Fi is displayed on computers with wireless connections). The Wired tab lets you turn the wired connection on or off. The Wi-Fi tab lets you choose a wireless network and then prompts you to enter a password or encryption key. The connection and security type is automatically detected. Instead of using a wireless network, you can choose an Airplane Mode wireless connection or use your connection as a hotspot. You can also connect to a local hidden network. A switch at the top right lets you turn the wireless connection on or off.

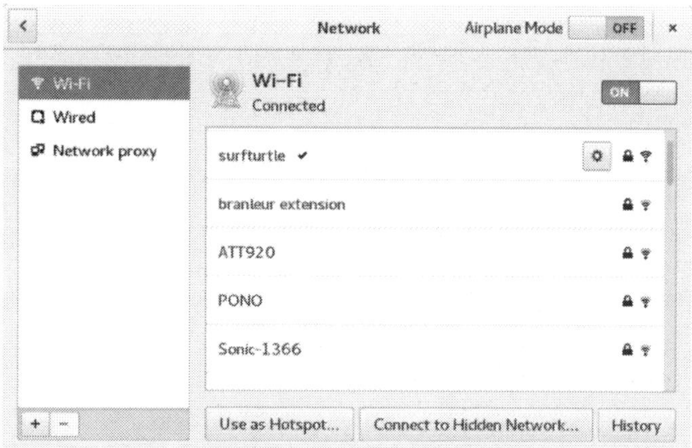

Figure 2-20: Settings Network wireless connections

Your current active connection will have a checkmark next to it and a gear button to the right. Click the gear button to display a dialog with tabs for managing the connection. The Details tab provides information about the connection (see Figure 2-21). The Security, Identity, IPv4, and IPv6 tabs let you perform a detailed configuration of your connection, as described in Chapter 10. The settings are fixed to automatic by default. Should you make any changes, click the Apply button to have them take effect. To remove a network's connection information, open the Reset tab

(Figure 2-22) and click the Forget button. The Reset button on the Reset tab lets you reset the settings.

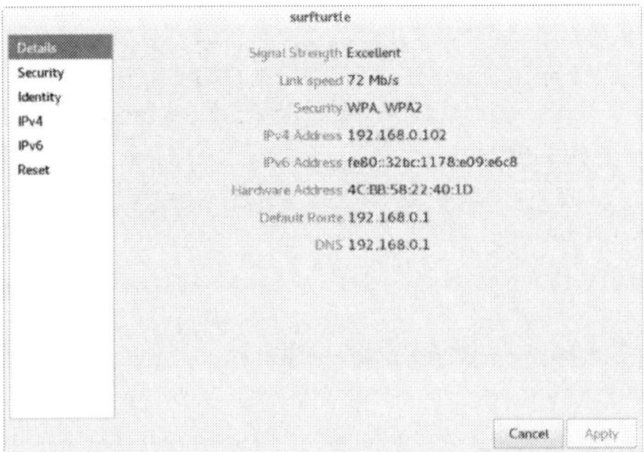

Figure 2-21: Settings Network wireless connection: Details tab

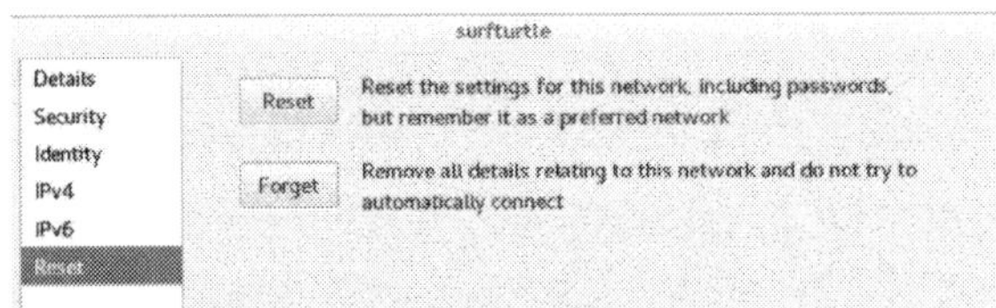

Figure 2-22: Settings Network wireless connection: Reset tab

The Identity tab has options both for connecting automatically and for providing availability to other users. These are set by default. Should you not want to connect to the wireless network automatically, be sure to uncheck this option.

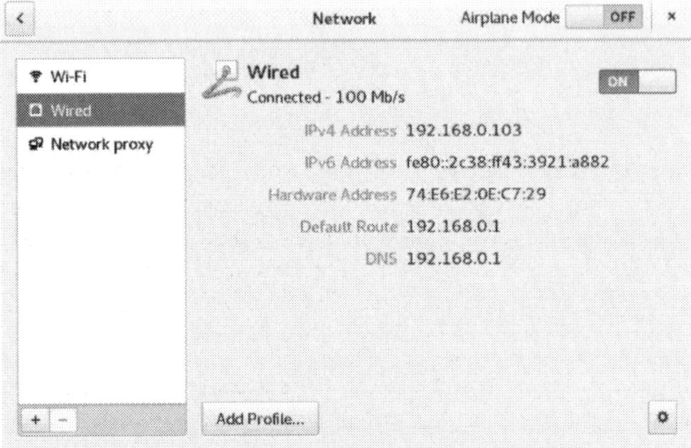

Figure 2-23: Settings Network wired connection

On the Network dialog, the Wired tab (Figure 2-23) shows basic information about the wired connection, including the IP addresses and DNS server. A switch at the top-right corner allows you to disconnect the wired connection, letting you effectively work offline. The gear button at the lower right opens a configuration dialog similar to the wireless configuration dialog, with tabs for Details, Security, Identity, IPv4, IPv6, and Reset. The Profile button to the left lets you add a different set of wired connection information (security, IPv protocols, and identity), should you connect to a different wired network.

The Network proxy tab provides a Method menu with None, Manual, and Automatic options (see Figure 2-24). The Manual option lets you enter address and port information. For the Automatic option, you enter a configuration address.

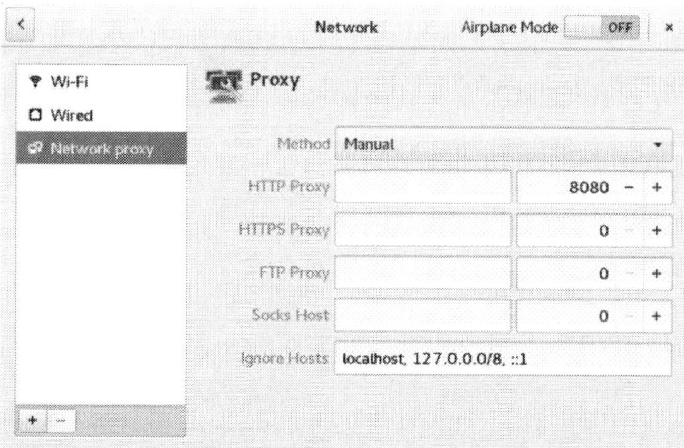

Figure 2-24: Network proxy settings (Settings Network)

To add a new connection, such as a vpn or vlan connection, click the plus (+) button below the network devices listing. You will be prompted to choose the interface types. Then the network configuration dialogs will start up, to let you enter configuration information.

Settings

You can configure desktop settings and perform most administrative tasks using the GNOME configuration tools (see Table 2-1) listed in the GNOME Settings dialog, accessible from the System Status Area dialog (lower left button). Settings organize tools into the Personal, Hardware, and System categories (see Figure 2-25). A few invoke the supported system tools available from previous releases, such as Sound (PulseAudio). Most use the new GNOME 3 configuration and administrative tools such as Background, Privacy, Users, and Power (see Table 2-1).

GNOME 3 tools will open with a back arrow button at the top, which you can click to return to the Settings dialog, and a search button to the right for locating a setting dialog.

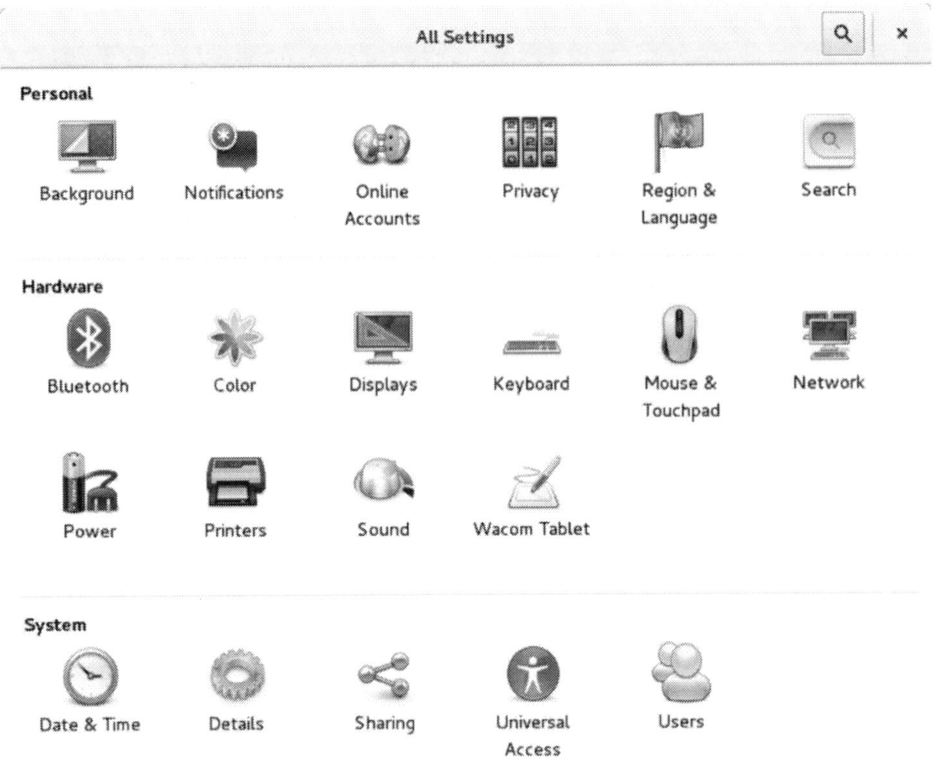

Figure 2-25: GNOME system tools (Settings)

Setting	Description
Personal	
Background	Sets desktop and screen lock backgrounds (wallpaper, color, and image)
Notifications	Turns on notifications for different applications
Online Accounts	Configures online accounts for use by e-mail and browser applications
Privacy	Turns on privacy features, such as screen lock and purging trash
Region & Language	Chooses a language, region (formats), and keyboard layout
Search	Specifies the resources and locations searched by the GNOME overview search box

Hardware	
Bluetooth	Sets Bluetooth detection and configuration
Color	Sets the color profile for a device
Displays	Changes your screen resolution, refresh rate, and screen orientation
Keyboard	Configures repeat key sensitivity and shortcut keys for special tasks, such as multimedia operations
Mouse & Touchpad	Sets mouse and touchpad configuration; selects hand orientation, speed, and accessibility
Network	Lets you turn wired and wireless networks on or off. Allows access to an available wireless network. Also specifies proxy configuration, if needed, manual or automatic
Power	Sets the power options for laptop inactivity
Printers	Turns printers on or off and accesses their print queues
Sound	Configures sound effects, output volume, input volume, and sound application settings
Wacom Tablet	Provides tablet options
System	
Date & Time	Sets the date, time, time zone, and network time
Details	Sets the hostname of your computer, displays hardware information, and assigns default applications for certain basic tasks
Sharing	Turns on sharing for media, remote login, and screen access
Universal Access	Enables features such as accessible login and keyboard screen
Users	Manages accounts

Table 2-1: Settings

Background

With the Background dialog, you can set your background for both the desktop and screen lock backgrounds: wallpaper, picture, or color. You can access the Background dialog from Applications overview or from the Settings dialog (see Figure 2-26). The current backgrounds are shown for the desktop and the screen lock. Click one to open the Select Background dialog, with tabs for Wallpapers, Pictures, and Colors (see Figure 2-27). The dialog is the same for both desktop and screen lock backgrounds. If you choose Wallpapers, the installed backgrounds are displayed.

The Colors tab displays solid color images you can use instead. The Pictures tab displays images in your Pictures folder, which you can scroll through to select one to use for your background. To add your own image, first, add the image to your Pictures folder. Then click the Pictures tab to display all the images in your Pictures folder. Once you make your selection, click the Select button at the upper right. You return to the main Background dialog, showing your new background. The background on your display is updated immediately.

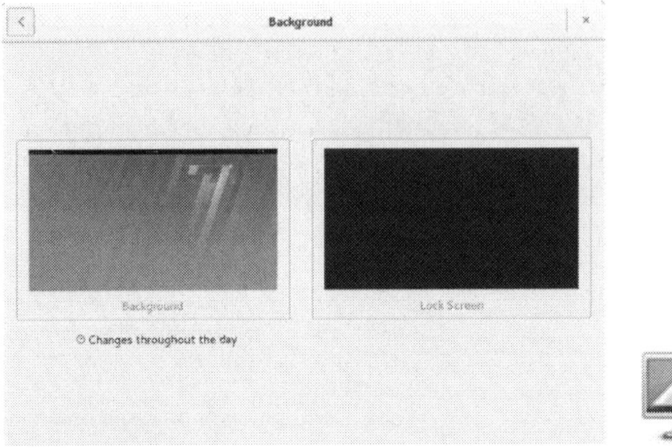

Figure 2-26: Background

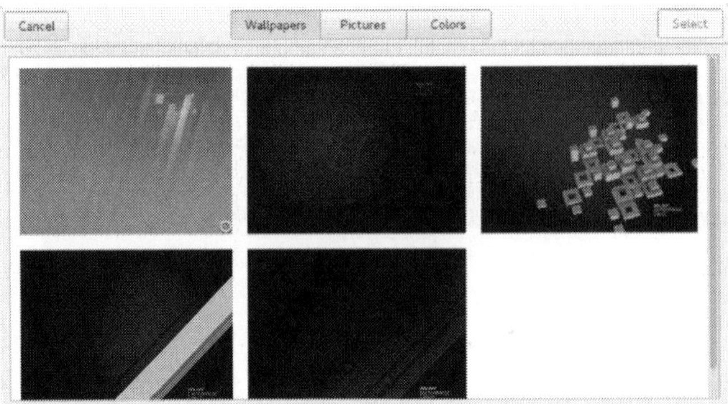

Figure 2-27: Select Background

Install the gnome-background package to add a collection of GNOME backgrounds. You can download more GNOME backgrounds (wallpapers) from **http://gnome-look.org/**.

Date & Time

The Date & Time calendar is located on the top bar at the center (see Figure 2-28). The dialog displays the current time and day of the week but can be modified to display 24-hour or AM/PM time. The calendar shows the current date, but you can move to different months and years using the month scroll arrows at the top of the calendar. On RHEL 7.4, shown here, the left side of the dialog shows your notifications. On RHEL 7.3, the right side of the Date & Time dialog shows your Evolution calendar events for the current and next days. The "Add world clocks" link opens the GNOME Clocks tool for selecting world clocks.

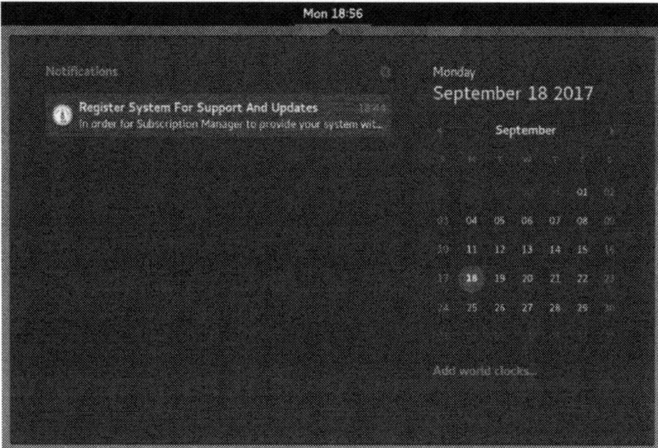

Figure 2-28: Date & Time dialog

You can further adjust the top bar time display using the GNOME Tweak Tool's Top Bar tab (see Figure 2-29). In the Clock section, there are options to show the date and seconds. For the Calendar, you can show week numbers.

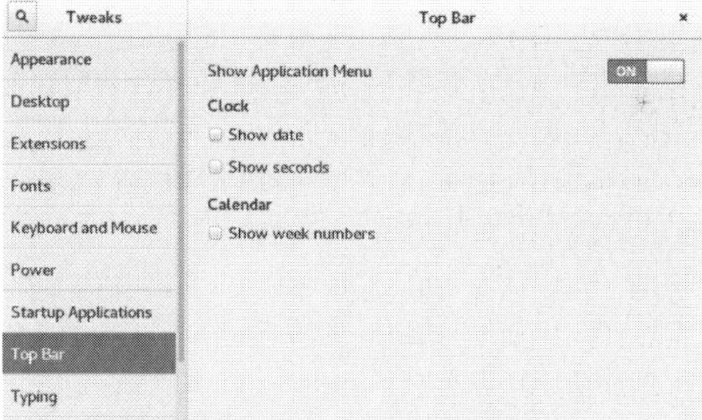

Figure 2-29: GNOME Tweak Tool: Top Bar (clock options)

Date & Time options are set using the Date & Time Settings dialog, which you can access from the Settings dialog or from the Date & Time menu, using the "Date & Time Settings" link at the bottom-left side of the menu. The Date & Time Settings dialog lets you set the time zone and time. Both are configured for automatic settings using Internet time servers (see Figure 2-30). The time zone or the time and date can be set manually by turning off the Automatic switches. Once turned off, the Date & Time and the Time Zone links become active.

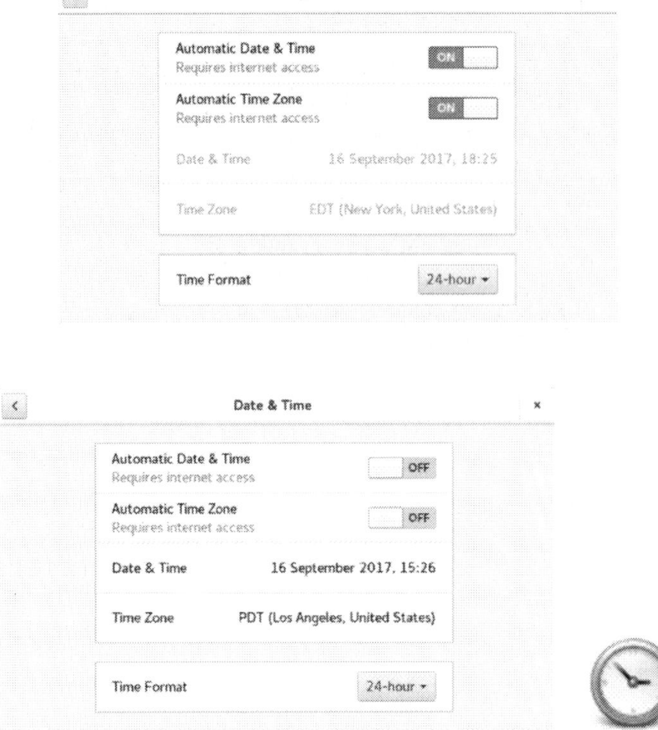

Figure 2-30: Date & Time Settings dialog with automatic settings turned on (top) and off (bottom)

The Date & Time link opens a dialog with settings for the hour, minutes, day, and year, with a menu for the month (see Figure 2-31). You can use the plus (+) and minus (-) buttons to sequentially change the values.

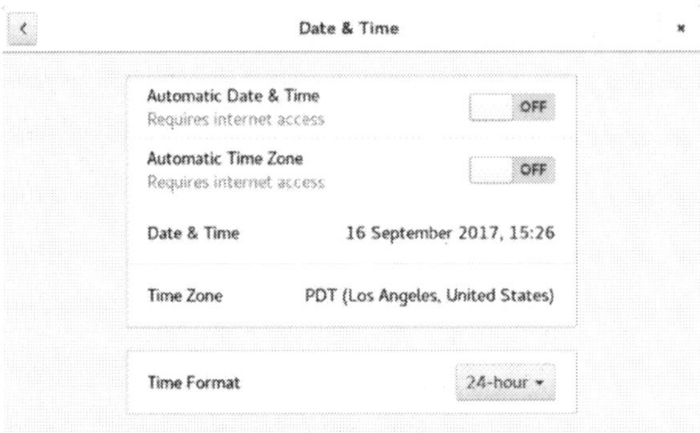

Figure 2-31: Date & Time manual settings

The Time Zone link opens a dialog with a map of the time zones and the current one selected (see Figure 2-32). Click a new time zone to change the zone.

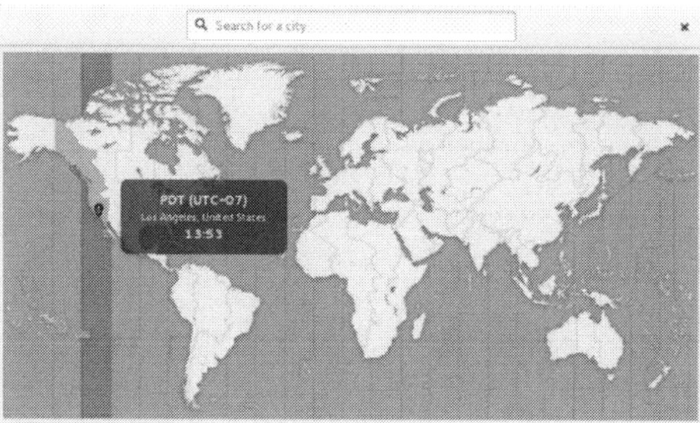

Figure 2-32: Time Zone dialog

Notifications

The Notifications dialog lets you configure notifications for different applications. You can also have the options show pop-up banners at the bottom of the screen or show notices on the lock screen. Both are turned on by default. A listing of supported applications for notifications is displayed (see Figure 2-33).

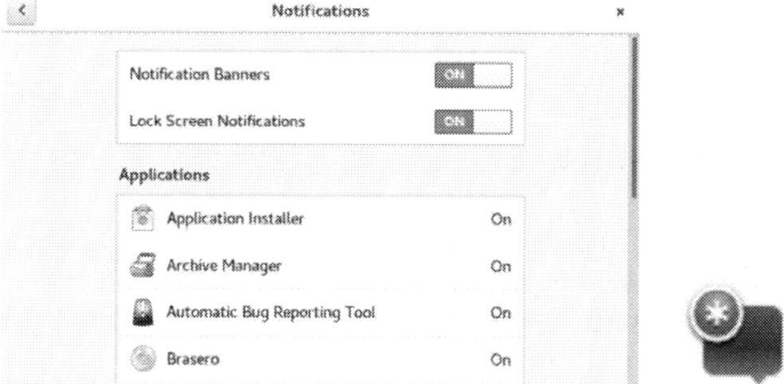

Figure 2-33: Notifications dialog

Click an application to display a dialog from which you can turn notifications for the application on or off, as well as set options such as sound alerts, pop-up banners, and lock screen views (see Figure 2-34).

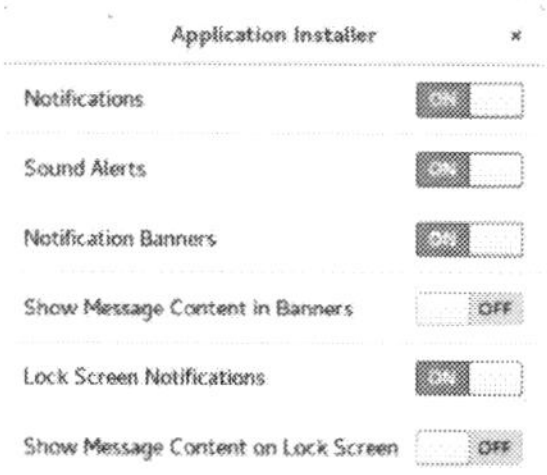

Application Installer

Notifications ON

Sound Alerts ON

Notification Banners ON

Show Message Content in Banners OFF

Lock Screen Notifications ON

Show Message Content on Lock Screen OFF

Figure 2-34: Notification settings for an application

Privacy

The Privacy dialog allows you to turn privacy features, such as the screen lock, usage and history logs, and the purging of trash and temporary files, on or off (see Figure 2-35). Screen Lock and Usage & History are turned on by default. The "Purge Trash & Temporary Files" and Location Services are turned off. Location Services allows your geographical location to be determined.

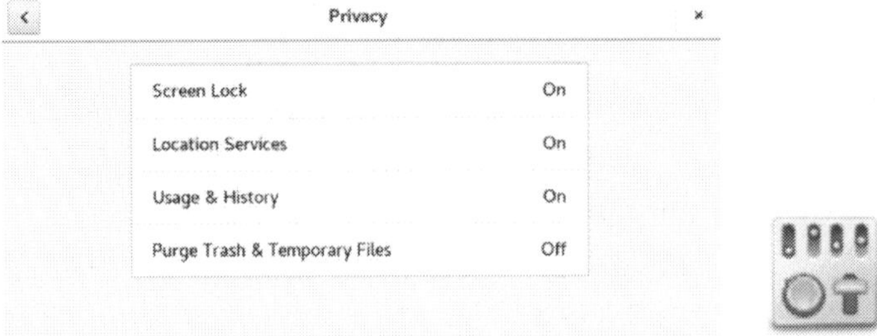

Figure 2-35: Privacy

Clicking the Screen Lock entry opens the Screen Lock configuration dialog, from which you can turn Screen Lock on or off or set it to turn on after a period of idle time and allow or deny notifications on the Screen Lock screen (see Figure 2-36).

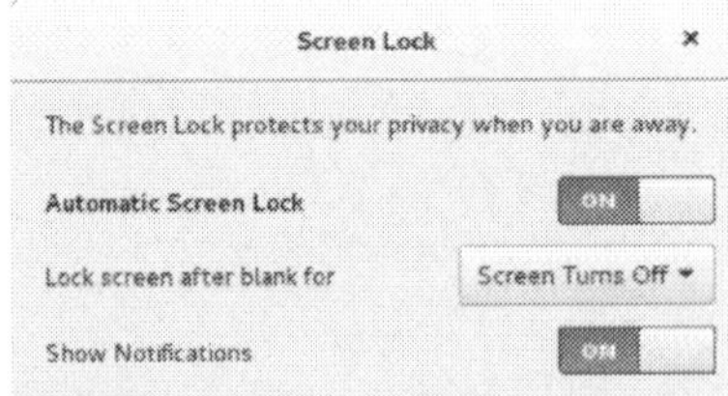

Figure 2-36: Privacy: Screen Lock configuration

Click the Usage & History entry to open a dialog from which you can turn usage history on or off and set how long to keep it. The entry also has a button that allows you to clear recent history (see Figure 2-37).

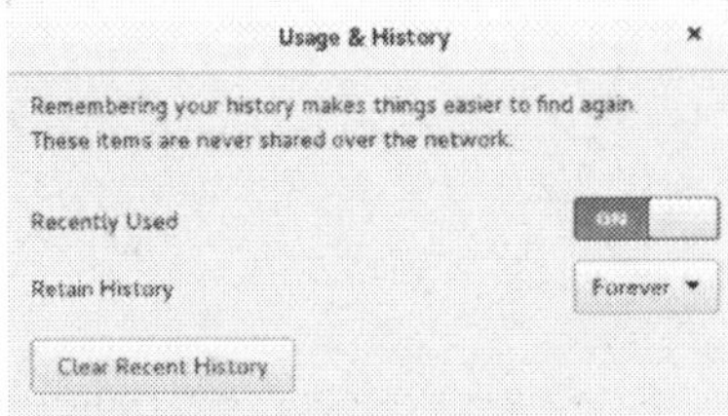

Figure 2-37: Privacy: Usage & History configuration

The Purge Trash & Temporary Files entry has options to automatically empty trash and remove temporary files (see Figure 2-38). You can also set a time limit for purging files. These options are turned off by default. The link also has buttons that allow you to empty trash and purge temporary files immediately.

Figure 2-38: Privacy: Purge Trash & Temporary Files configuration

Details (System Information)

The Details dialog shows system information, using the following three tabs: Overview, Default Applications, and Removable Media. The Overview tab shows your hardware specifications (memory, CPU, graphics card chip, and free disk space), in addition to the hostname (Device name) and the OS type (64- or 32-bit system) (see Figure 2-39). You can change the hostname here if you wish. When you open the dialog, updates are checked, and, if found, an Install Update button is displayed, which opens Software Updates, allowing you to update your system (see Chapter 4).

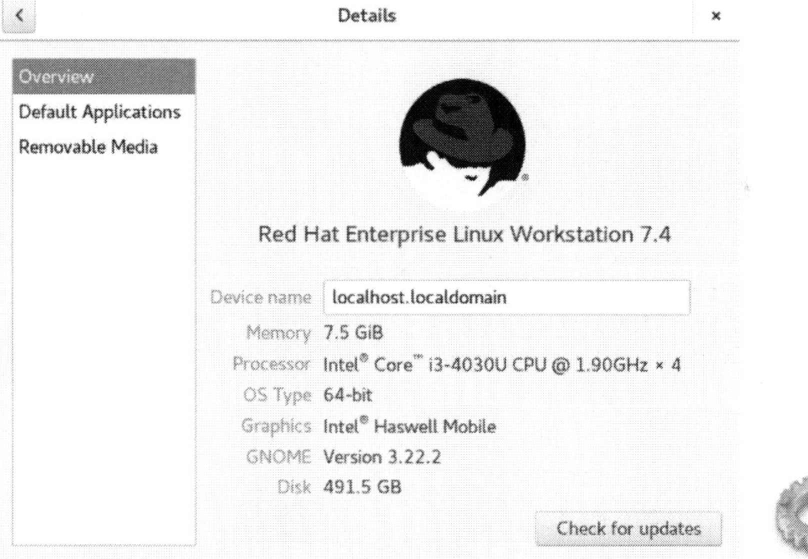

Figure 2-39: Details: Overview

The Default Applications tab lets you set default applications for basic types of files: Web, Mail, Calendar, Music, Video, and Photos (see Figure 2-40). Use the drop-down menus to choose installed alternatives, such as Thunderbird instead of Evolution for Mail or Image Viewer instead of Shotwell for Photos.

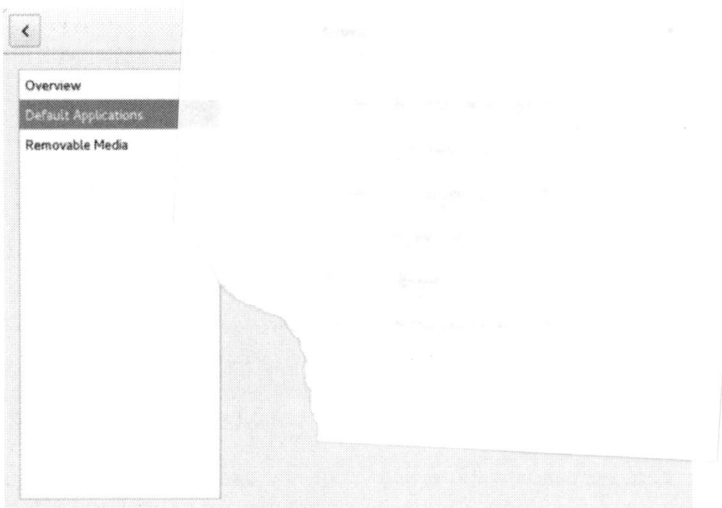

Figure 2-40: Details: Default Applications

Using Removable Devices and Media

RHEL supports removable devices and media, such as digital cameras, PDAs, card readers, and USB printers. These devices are handled automatically with device interfaces set up for them when needed. Removable media, such as CD and DVD discs, USB storage disks, and digital cameras, will be displayed as entries in the message tray Removable Devices menu. On the Overview screen, when you click on the message number notice at the bottom of the screen, the Removable Devices icon is displayed. Clicking this icon displays a menu of all your removable devices, with an Eject button next to each entry. Click an entry to open the device in its associated applications, such as a file manager window for a USB drive. Be sure always to click the Eject button for device entry before removing a drive, such as a USB drive or removable disk drive. Removing the drive before clicking eject can result in incomplete write operations on the disk.

Removable storage devices and media will also appear in the file manager Devices sidebar with eject buttons that you can use instead of the message menu to eject the devices. For example, when you connect a USB drive to your system, it will be detected and can be displayed as a storage device with its own file system by the file manager.

Removable devices and media, such as USB drives and DVD/CD discs, can be ejected using Eject buttons in the Devices section of the file manager sidebar. The sidebar lists all your storage devices, including removable media. Removable devices and media will have an Eject button to the right. Just click the Eject button, and the media is ejected or unmounted. You can right-click the Device entry and, from a pop-up menu, choose the Eject entry.

The Details Removable Media tab lets you specify default actions for CD Audio, DVD Video, Music Player, Photos, and Software media (see Figure 2-41). You can select from drop-down menus the application to use for the different media These menus also include options for Ask What To Do, Do Nothing, and Open Folder. The Open Folder option will open a window displaying the files on the disc. A button labeled “Other Media” opens a dialog that lets you set up an association for less used media such as Blu-Ray discs and Audio DVD. Initially, the Ask What

To Do option is set for all entries. Possible options are listed for the appropriate media, such as Rhythmbox Media Player for CD Audio discs and Videos (Totem) for DVD-Video. Photos can be opened with the Shotwell photo manager.

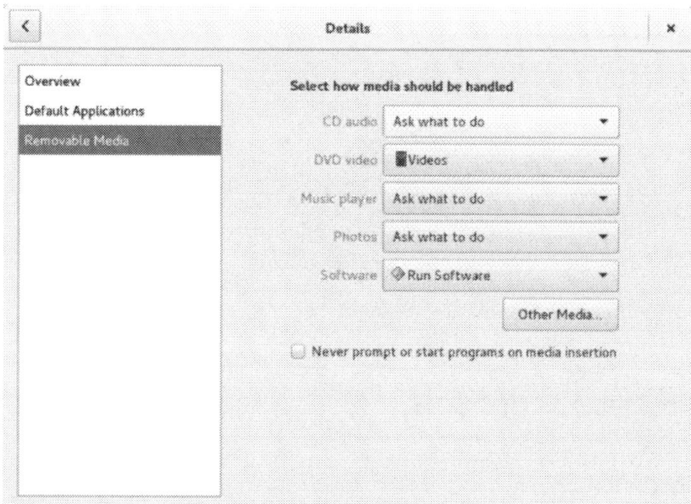

Figure 2-41: Details: Removable Media defaults

When you insert removable media, such as a CD audio disc, its associated application is automatically started, unless you change that preference. If you want to turn off this feature for a particular kind of media, you can select the Do Nothing entry from its application drop-down menu. If you want to be prompted for options, use the Ask What To Do entry. Then, when you insert a disc, a dialog with a drop-down menu for possible actions is displayed. From this menu, you can select another application or select the Do Nothing or Open Folder options.

You can turn the automatic startup off for all media by checking the box labeled "Never prompt or start programs on media insertion," at the bottom of the Removable Media tab.

Sharing

On the Sharing dialog, you can allow access to your account and your screen. A switch lets you turn all sharing on or off (see Figure 2-42).

Figure 2-42: Sharing

Clicking the Screen Sharing entry opens a dialog from which you can allow screen access to other users. You can also require and set a password (see Figure 2-43).

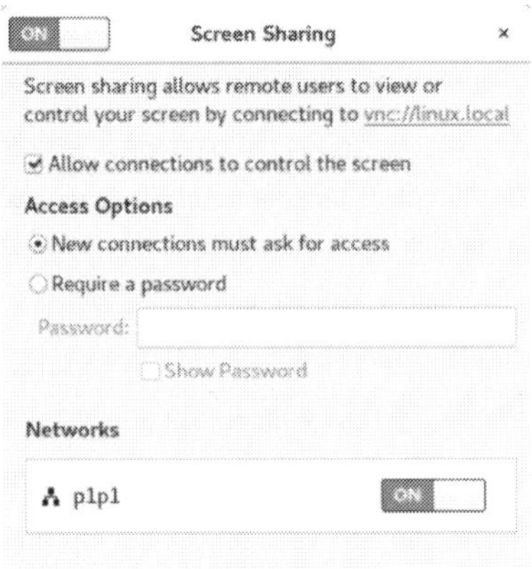

Figure 2-43: Sharing: screen access to other users

Power Management

For laptops and systems with remote battery devices such as mice, a power icon is displayed in the System Status Area (right side of the top bar). The System Status Area menu shows the current strength of the battery (see Figure 2-44). The entry expands to show a Power Settings entry, which you can use to open the Settings Power dialog.

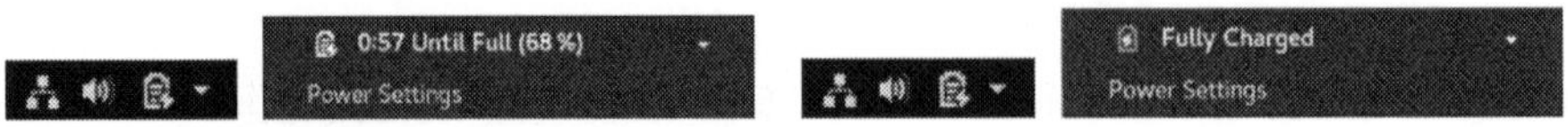

Figure 2-44: GNOME Power Manager menu

The GNOME Power manager is configured with the Power dialog, accessible as Power from Settings (see Figure 2-45). The dialog is organized into four sections: Battery, Devices, Power Saving, and Suspend & Power Off. On laptops, the Battery section shows the battery charge. The Devices section shows the strength of any remote devices, such as a wireless mouse. In the Power Saving section, you can set power saving features for your monitor, wireless devices, and network connections. When inactive for a period of time, you can choose to turn off the screen, as well as dim it whenever it is inactive. For laptops, you can also set the screen brightness. You can also choose to turn off Bluetooth, Wi-Fi, and Mobile broadband. In the Suspend & Power Off section, you can turn on the automatic suspend for when a system remains inactive and, for laptops, hibernate or turn off when the battery is critically low.

Using the GNOME Tweak Tool's Power tab, you can further specify the action to take, such as suspend or shut down, when the Power button is pressed, or to suspend when the laptop lid is closed.

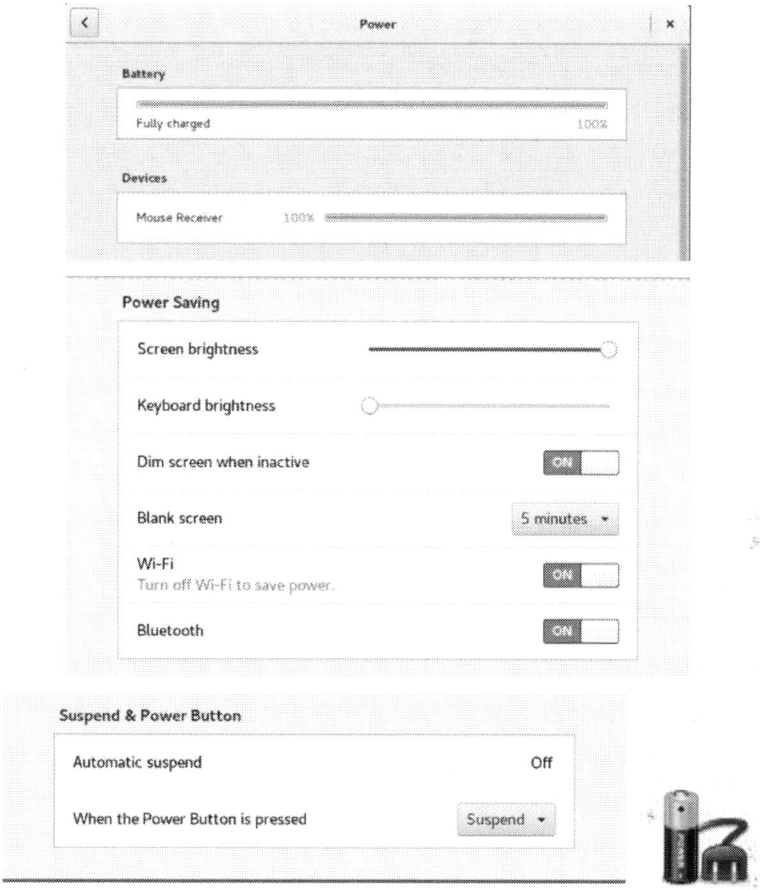

Figure 2-45: GNOME Power manager

powertop, tuned, and BLTK

For more refined power management you can use the powertop and tuned tools. The **powertop** tool runs in a terminal window as the root user. It will detect and display information about the use of the CPU by running applications and connected devices. Recommendations are listed on how to configure the power usage. To display a listing of the powertop results including recommendations, add the **-d** option.

```
su
powertop -d
```

For automatic tuning of hard disk and network devices you can use tuned (**tuned** and **tuned** utils packages). The tuned daemon monitors your system and tunes the settings dynamically. You can use tuned's **diskdevstat** and **netdevstat** tools to monitor your hard disk and network devices.

For laptops, you can use the Battery Life Tool Kit (BLTK) to test and analyze battery performance. Options specify different types of workloads, such as **-O** for office suite use and **-P** for multimedia usage. Depending on the option you specified different applications would be opened and run during the test such as Libreoffice Writer or the Totem multimedia player.

```
bltk -O
```

You can also run the test on desktop systems using an **-a** option.

```
bltk -a -O
```

Mouse and Touchpad

The Mouse & Touchpad dialog is the primary tool for configuring your mouse and touchpad (see Figure 2-46). Mouse preferences allow you to choose the mouse's speed, the primary button, and scrolling. A "Test Your Settings" button lets you check clicks, double-clicks, and scrolling. For laptops, you can configure your touchpad, enabling touchpad clicks and edge scrolling. You can turn the touchpad on or off.

The GNOME Tweak Tool's Keyboard and Mouse tab has options to enable a middle-click paste for the mouse and to show the location of the pointer on the screen.

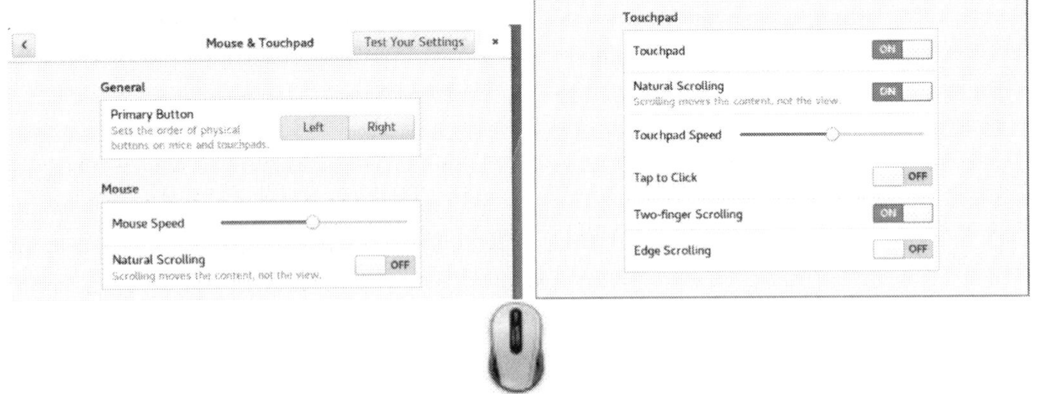

Figure 2-46: GNOME system tools: mouse and touchpad

Display (Resolution and Rotation)

The display drivers for Linux used on RHEL support user-level resolution and orientation changes. Any user can specify a resolution or orientation, without affecting the settings of other users. The Settings Displays dialog provides a simple interface for setting rotation, resolution, and selecting added monitors, allowing for cloned or extended displays across several connected monitors (see Figure 2-47). The dialog displays icons for connected monitors. Click one to open a dialog, which shows the display's size, aspect ratio, and resolution. From the menus, you can set the resolution and refresh rate. Use the arrow buttons below the display image to set the rotation. After you have made your changes, click Apply. The new resolution is displayed with a dialog with buttons that ask you whether to keep the new resolution or return to the previous one. With multiple displays, you can turn a monitor off or mirror displays.

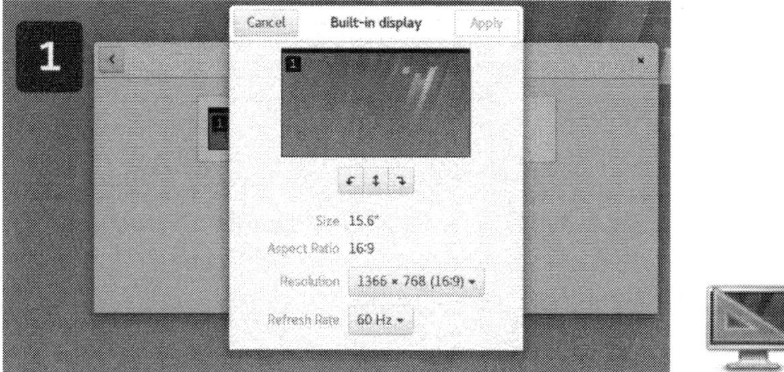

Figure 2-47: Displays

The graphics interface for your desktop display is implemented by the X Window System. The version used on RHEL is X.org (**x.org**). X.org provides its own drivers for various graphics cards and monitors. You can find out more about X.org at **www.x.org**. X.org will automatically detect most hardware. The **/etc/X11/xorg.conf** file is no longer used for the open source drivers (nv and amd). Information such as the monitor used is determined automatically.

Universal Access

The Universal Access dialog in Settings lets you configure alternative access to your interface for your keyboard and mouse actions. Four sections set the display (Seeing), sound properties (Hearing), typing, and point-and-click features. Seeing lets you adjust the contrast and text size, and whether to allow zooming or use of screen reader (see Figure 2-48). Hearing uses visual cues for alert sounds. Typing displays a screen keyboard and adjusts key presses. Pointing and Clicking lets you use the keyboard for mouse operations.

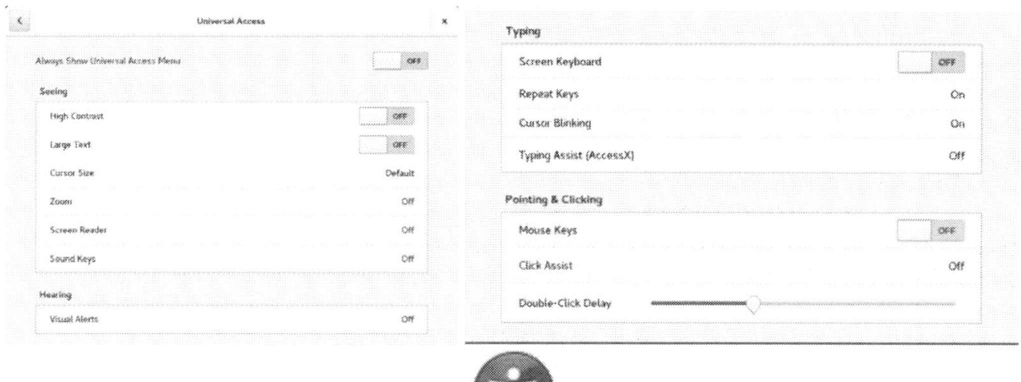

Figure 2-48: Universal Access

Keyboard and Language

The Settings Keyboard dialog shows shortcuts. shortcuts letting you assign keys to perform such tasks as starting the web browser (see Figure 2-49).

On the GNOME Tweak Tool's Typing tab, you can specify the behavior of certain keys, such as the key sequence to stop the X server, the Caps Lock behavior, and the numeric keypad layout.

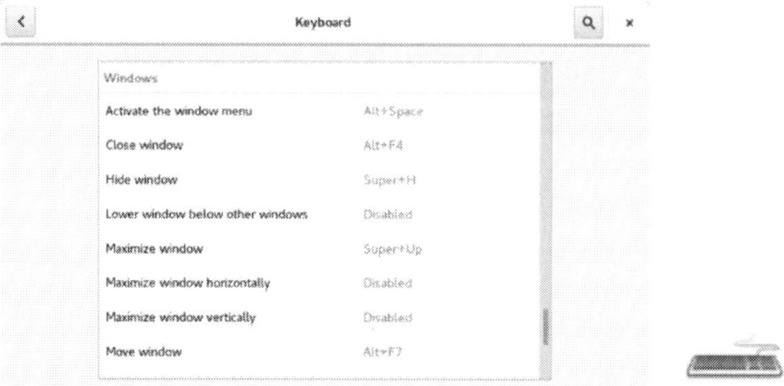

Figure 2-49: Keyboard

The Input Sources link at the bottom of the dialog opens the Region & Language dialog (see Figure 2-50). The current input language source is listed and selected. You can access the Region & Language dialog directly from Settings. Click the plus (+) button to open a dialog listing other language sources, which you can add. Click the Keyboard button to see the keyboard layout of your currently selected input source. You can also allow different language layouts for different windows.

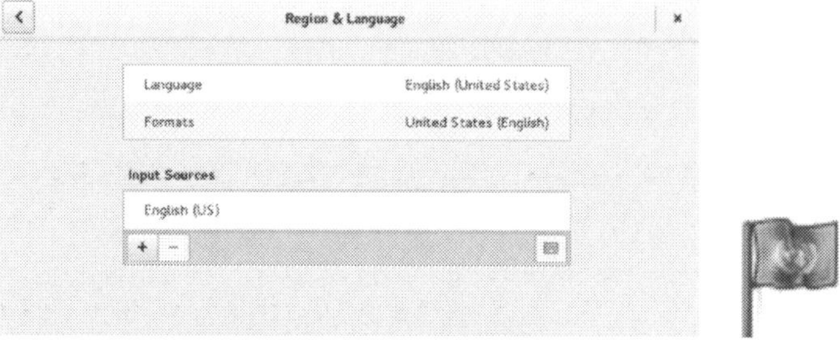

Figure 2-50: Region & Language with Input Sources

Color Profiles (GNOME Color Manager)

You can manage the color for different devices by using color profiles specified with the Color dialog accessible from Settings. The Color dialog lists devices for which you can set color profiles. Click a device to display buttons at the bottom of the screen to Add profile and Calibrate. Your monitor will have a profile set up automatically. Click the Add Profile button to open a dialog with an Automatic Profiles menu from which you can choose a color profile. Click the Add button to add the profile. Available profiles include Adobe RGB, sRGB, and Kodak ProPhoto RGB. You can also import a profile from an ICC profile file of your own.

When you click on a device entry, its Profiles are listed (see Figure 2-51). Click on a profile to display buttons to Set for all users, Remove profile, and View details. Click the View details button for the color profile information.

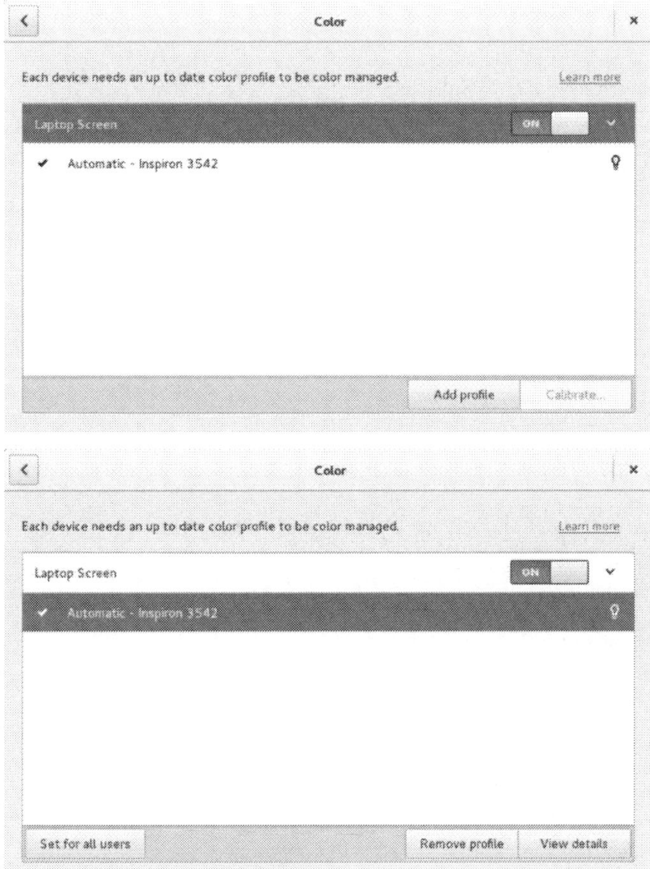

Figure 2-51: Color management dialog

Online Accounts

You can configure your online accounts using the Online Accounts dialog in Settings. Instead of separately configuring mail and chat clients, you can set up access once, using online accounts. Click the plus (+) button at the lower left of the dialog to start the sign-in procedure. You are prompted to sign in using your e-mail and password. Access is provided to Google, Flickr, Microsoft Exchange, ownCloud, and Pocket. Once access is granted, you will see an entry for service. Clicking on the service shows the different kinds of applications that it can be used for such as mail, calendar, contacts, chat, and documents (see Figure 2-52). Switches that you can use to turn access on and off are provided.

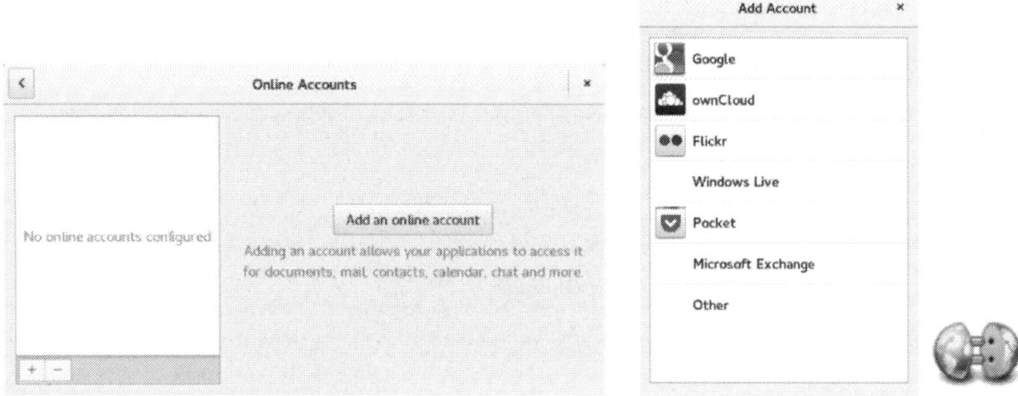

Figure 2-52: Online Accounts

Accessing File Systems, Devices, and Remote Hosts

When you attach an external storage device such as a USB, CD/DVD-ROM, or ESATA drive, it will be mounted automatically, and you will be prompted to open it in a file manager window. Be sure to unmount (Eject) a drive before removing it, so that data will be written.

Your file systems and removable media appear as entries in the file manager sidebar (see Figure 2-53). External devices such as USB drives are mounted automatically and have Eject buttons next to their entries. Internal hard drive partitions not mounted at boot, such as Windows file systems, are not mounted automatically. Double-click the hard drive partition entry to mount them. An Eject button then appears next to the hard drive entry. You are also prompted to open the drive's file system in a new file manager window.

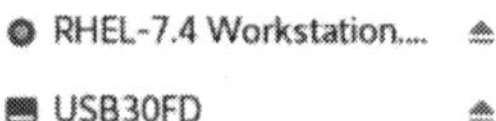

Figure 2-53: Devices sidebar in the file manager window

File systems on removable media will also appear automatically as entries directly on your desktop message tray (lower-right corner of the overview screen; see Figure 2-54). Entries have an Eject button you can use to unmount the drive. Clicking the drive entry opens it in a new file manager window.

To mount Windows NTFS file system, especially external or USB hard drives, you must also install the **fuse-ntfs-3g** package. This package is part of the EPEL repository. It is not provided by Red Hat. You must first configure access to the EPEL repository (see Chapter 8). Once configured use yum or the PackageKit (Packages) software manager to install the **fuse-ntfs-3g** package.

The message tray remains hidden unless you access it manually by pressing the Super key with the **m** key on the keyboard (Super+m, Super is the Windows key), or by clicking the message notice at the center bottom of the overview screen. A DVD/CD-ROM is automatically mounted when you insert it into your DVD/CD-ROM drive, displaying a labeled icon for it. The same kind of access is also provided for card readers, digital cameras, USB drives, and external USB/ESATA hard drives.

Figure 2-54: Removable Devices message tray menu with removable drives mounted

If you have already configured associated applications for video and audio DVD/CDs, or disks with images, sound, or video files, the disk will be opened with the appropriate application; such as Shotwell for images, Rhythmbox for audio, and Movie Player for DVD/video. If you have not yet configured these associations, you will be prompted to specify which application you want to open it with.

From the file manager, you not only have access to removable media, but you also have access to all your mounted file systems, remote and local, including any Windows-shared directories accessible from Samba. You can browse all your file systems directly from GNOME. To see network resources, click the Browse Network entry in the Network section of a file manager sidebar. This network window will list your connected network computers. Opening these networks displays the shares they provide, such as shared directories that you can have access to. Drag-and-drop operations are supported for all shared directories, letting you copy files and folders between a shared directory on another computer with a directory on your system. You first must configure your firewall to accept Samba connections before you can browse Windows systems on GNOME. Opening a network resource may require you to login to access the resource.

GDM Automatic Login

You can configure automatic logins manually using several Timed Login options for the GDM. Edit the **/etc/gdm/custom.conf** file to create a **[daemon]** segment and enter the following TimedLogin options.

```
[daemon]
TimedLoginEnable=true
TimedLogin=myuser
TimedLoginDelay=10
```

First, you enable the TimedLogin feature. Then specify the user you want to have automatically logged in (TimedLogin=). You also have to set up a TimedLoginDelay, usually about 10 seconds; otherwise, if you log out, you will always be logged in to that user immediately, and not have a chance to login to another.

You can only edit this file as the root user. Use **su** command to login as the root user, and then use a line editor like **vi** or **nano** to edit the file, as in **nano /etc/gdm/custom.conf**.

The GDM will show this user specified in the TimedLogin option as automatic login. When logging into another user on the GDM, the automatic login user is initially displayed with the seconds ticking down. Click Cancel to display the list of all users, from which you can choose to log in as.

Video Drivers

Due to the open sourcing of much of both the Nvidia and ATI video drivers, the Xorg and Nouveau open source versions are becoming almost as effective, especially for 2D display support. For normal usage, you may not need vendor driver support. When you installed your system, the correct driver was detected and configured for you automatically.

The name of the Xorg AMD video driver is **ati**. RHEL7 uses the Nouveau drivers for Nvidia, an open source project to provide accelerated drivers, **xorg-x11-drv-nouveau**. These are the default drivers, though the older open source Nvidia drivers are also available, **xorg-x11-drv-nv**.

```
xorg-x11-drv-nouveau
xorg-x11-drv-ati
```

Multimedia Support: MP3, DVD video, and DivX

Due to licensing and other restrictions, the RHEL7 distribution does not include DVD Video or DivX media support. You cannot play DVD-Video discs or DivX files after installing RHEL7. The media restrictions also apply to Fedora, and you can check **http://fedoraproject.org/wiki/ForbiddenItems** for a list of forbidden items. RHEL7 also does not provide many of the popular Linux media players such as vlc and mplayer. However, third-party repositories, such as RPM Fusion (**https://rpmfusion.org**) or Negativo17.org (**https://negativo17.org**), do provide the needed libraries and support files for these media formats, as well as the media players. All packages are RPM packages that you can install with YUM, after first downloading and installing the repository configuration package. DivX support can be obtained using the open source version of DivX, Xvid (xvid-core).

Terminal Window

The Terminal window allows you to enter Linux commands on a command line. It also provides you with a shell interface for using shell commands instead of your desktop. The command line is editable, allowing you to use the backspace key to erase characters on the line. Pressing a key will insert that character. You can use the left and right arrow keys to move anywhere on the line, and then press keys to insert characters, or use backspace to delete characters (see Figure 2-55). Folders, files, and executable files are color-coded: black for files, blue for folders, green for executable files, and aqua for links. Shared folders are displayed with a green background.

The terminal window will remember the previous commands you entered. Use the up and down arrows to have those commands displayed in turn on the command line. Press the ENTER key to re-execute the currently displayed command. You can even edit a previous command before running it, allowing you to execute a modified version of a previous command. This can be helpful if you need to re-execute a complex command with a different argument, or if you mistyped a complex command and want to correct it without having to re-type the entire command. The terminal window will display all your previous interactions and commands for that session. Use the scrollbar to see any previous commands you ran and their displayed results.

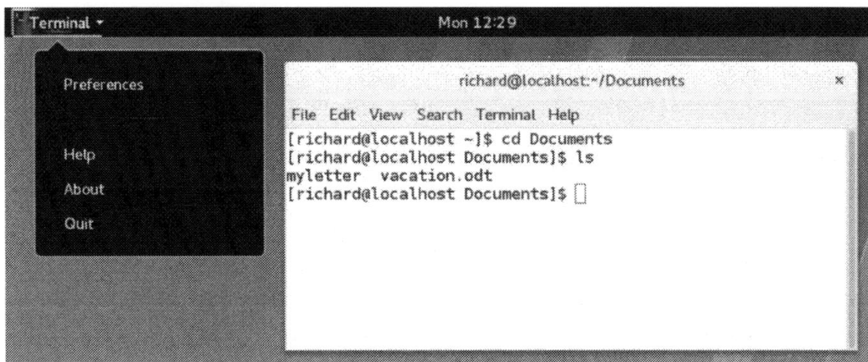

Figure 2-55: Terminal Window

You can open as many terminal windows as you want, each working in its own shell. Instead of opening a separate window for each new shell, you can open several shells in the same window, using tabs. Use the keys **Shift-Ctrl-t** or click the Open Tab item on the File menu to open a new tab. A tab toolbar opens at the top of the terminal window with the folder name and a close button for each tab, with an add tab button and a tab menu to the right. Each tab runs a separate shell, letting you enter different commands in each (see Figure 2-56). You can right-click on the tab's folder name to display a pop-up menu to move to the next tab, or just click on a tab's folder name. Click on the tab menu button (down arrow) at the right to display a list of open tabs, with the current tab selected. You can use the menu to switch to a different tab, or by using the keyboard shortcut shown next to it. You can also use the Tabs menu, or the **Ctrl-PageUp** and **Ctrl-PageDown** keys to move to different tabs. The Tabs menu is displayed if multiple tabs are open.

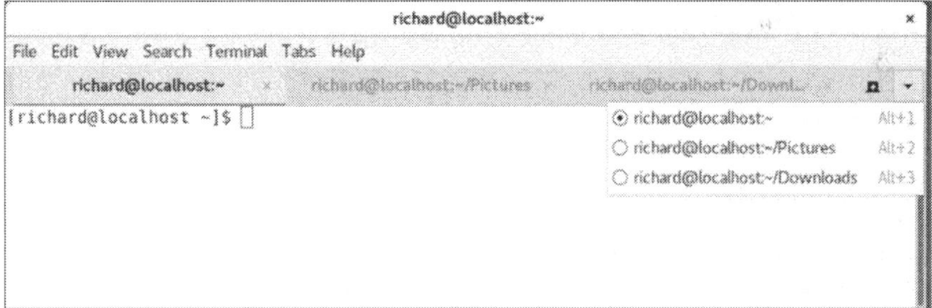

Figure 2-56: Terminal Window with tabs

The terminal window also supports desktop cut/copy and paste operations. You can copy a line from a Web page and then paste it to the terminal window (you can use the Paste entry on the Terminal window's Edit menu or press **Shift-Ctrl-v**). The command will appear and then you can press ENTER to execute the command. This is useful for command line operations displayed on an instructional Web page. Instead of typing in a complex command yourself, just select and copy from the Web page directly, and then paste to the Terminal window. You can also perform any edits on the command, if needed, before executing it. Should you want to copy a command on the terminal window, select the text with your mouse and then use **Shift-Ctrl-c** keys (or the Copy entry on the Terminal window's Edit menu) to copy the command. You can select part of a line or multiple lines, as long as they are shown on the terminal window.

You can customize terminal windows using profiles. A default profile is set up already. To customize your terminal window, select Profile Preferences from the Edit menu. This opens a window for setting your default profile options with tabs for General, Command, Colors, Scrolling, and Compatibility (see Figure 2-57). On the General tab, you can select the default size of a terminal window in text rows and columns.

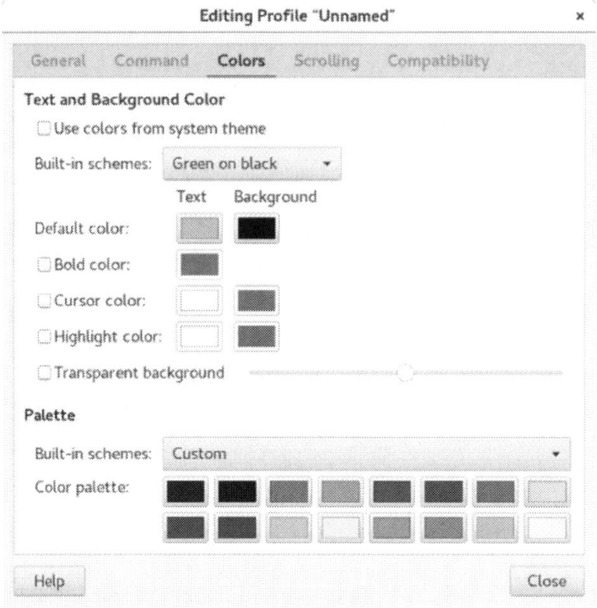

Figure 2-57: Terminal Window Profile configuration

Your terminal window will be set up to use a white background with dark text. To change this, you can edit the profile to change the background and text colors on the Colors tab. De-select the "Use colors from system theme" entry. This enables the "Built-in schemes" menu from which you can select a "Black on white" display. Other color combinations are also listed, such as "Black on light yellow" and "Green on black." The Custom option lets you choose your own text and background colors. The colors on your open terminal window will change according to your selection, allowing you to see how the color choices will look. For a transparent background, choose the "Use transparent background" entry and then set the amount of shading (none is completely transparent and full shows no transparency).

The Scrolling tab specifies the number of command lines your terminal history will keep, as well as other scroll options such as the scroll speed and whether to display the scrollbar. These are the lines you can move back through and select to re-execute. You can de-select the Limit scrollback option to set this to unlimited to keep all the commands.

You can create new profiles with customized preferences. To create a new profile, choose New Profile from the File menu to open the New Profile window where you can enter the profile name and select any profile to base it on. The default profile is chosen initially. Use the Change Profile submenu on the Terminal menu to change profiles.

To edit a particular profile, select Preferences from the Edit menu to open the Preferences window, and then click on the Profiles tab to list your profiles. Choose the one you want to edit and then click the Edit button to open the Editing Profile window for that profile. You can also create new profiles, or delete existing ones. Use the selection menu to at the bottom of the tab to choose which dialog to use.

Command Line Interface

When using the command line interface, you are given a simple prompt at which you type in a command. Even when you are using a desktop like GNOME, you sometimes need to execute commands on a command line. You can do so in a terminal window, which is accessed from the dash.

Linux commands make extensive use of options and arguments. Be careful to place your arguments and options in their correct order on the command line. The format for a Linux command is the command name followed by options, and then by arguments, as shown here:

```
$ command-name options arguments
```

An *option* is a one-letter code preceded by one or two hyphens, which modifies the type of action the command takes. Options and arguments may or may not be optional, depending on the command. For example, the **ls** command can take an option, **-s**. The **ls** command displays a listing of files in your directory, and the **-s** option adds the size of each file in blocks. You enter the command and its option on the command line as follows:

```
$ ls -s
```

If you are uncertain what format and options a command uses, you can check the command syntax quickly by displaying its man page. Most commands have a man page. Just enter the **man** command with the command name as an argument.

An argument is data the command may need to execute its task. In many cases, this is a filename. An argument is entered as a word on the command line that appears after any options. For example, to display the contents of a file, you can use the **more** command with the file's name as its argument. The **less** or **more** command used with the filename **mydata** would be entered on the command line as follows:

```
$ less mydata
```

The command line is actually a buffer of text you can edit. Before you press ENTER to execute the command, you can edit the command on the command line. The editing capabilities provide a way to correct mistakes you may make when typing a command and its options. The **Backspace** key lets you erase the character you just typed (the one to the left of the cursor), and the **Del** key lets you erase the character the cursor is on. With this character-erasing capability, you can backspace over the entire line if you want, erasing what you entered. **Ctrl-u** erases the whole command line and lets you start over again at the prompt.

You can use the **Up Arrow** key to redisplay your last executed command. You can then re-execute that command, or you can edit it and execute the modified command. This is helpful when you have to repeat certain operations, such as editing the same file. It is also helpful when you have already executed a command you entered incorrectly.

Accessing Linux from the Command Line Interface

When accessing Linux from the boot loader directly to the command line interface (or with any of the F1 through F6 keys at the GDM login dialog), you are initially given a login prompt. The login prompt is preceded by the hostname you gave your system. In this example, the hostname is **turtle**. When you finish using Linux, you can log out. Linux then displays exactly the same login prompt, waiting for you or another user to log in again. This is the equivalent of the login window provided by the GDM. You can then log into another account.

```
Red Hat Enterprise Linux Server 7.4 (Maipo)
Kernel 3.18.0-493.e17 on an x86_64

turtle login:
```

Logging into your Linux account involves two steps: entering your username and then entering your password. Type the user name for your user account. If you make a mistake, you can erase characters with the BACKSPACE key. In the next example, the user enters the username **richard** and is then prompted to enter the password:

```
Red Hat Enterprise Linux Server 7.4 (Maipo)
Kernel 3.18.0-493.e17 on an x86_64

turtle login: richard
Password:
```

When you type in your password, it does not appear on the screen. This is to protect your password from being seen by others. If you enter either the username or the password incorrectly, the system will respond with the error message "Login incorrect" and will ask for your username again, starting the login process over. You can then reenter your username and password.

Once you enter your username and password correctly, you are logged into the system. Your command line prompt is displayed, waiting for you to enter a command. Notice the command line prompt is a dollar sign (**$**). The **$** is the prompt for regular users, whereas the **#** is the prompt solely for the root user. In this version of Red Hat Enterprise Linux, your prompt is preceded by the user name, hostname, and the folder you are in, with the home folder represented with a tilde, ~. Both are bounded by a set of brackets.

```
[richard@turtle ~]$
```

To end your session, issue the **logout** or **exit** command. This returns you to the login prompt, waiting for another user to log in.

```
[richard@turtle ~]$ logout
```

Shutting Down Linux from the Command Line

You can shut down your system in either of two ways. First, log into an account and then enter the **poweroff** command. This command will log you out and shut down the system.

```
$ poweroff
```

Alternatively, you can use the **shutdown** command with the **-h** option and a specified time delay. With the **-r** option, it shuts down the system and then reboots it. The time is calculated in minutes. In the next example, the system is shut down after five minutes. To shut down the system immediately, you can use **+0** or the word **now**.

```
# shutdown -h +5
```

To shut down the system immediately, you can use **+0** or the word **now**.

```
# shutdown -h now
```

You can also force your system to reboot at the login prompt, by holding down the CTRL and ALT keys and then pressing the DEL key (CTRL-ALT-DEL). Your system will go through the standard shutdown procedure and then restart your computer.

Help Resources

A great deal of support documentation is already installed on your system, as well as accessible from online sources. Table 2-2 lists Help tools and resources accessible on your Red Hat Enterprise Linux system.

Resource	Description
KDE Help Center	KDE Help tool, desktop interface for documentation on KDE desktop and applications, Man pages, and info documents.
GNOME Help Browser	GNOME Help tool, desktop interface for accessing documentation for the GNOME desktop and applications, Man pages, and info documents
`/usr/share/doc`	Location of application documentation
`man` *`command`*	Linux Man pages, detailed information on Linux commands, including syntax and options
`info` *`application`*	GNU info pages, documentation on GNU applications

Table 2-2: Help Resources

Both the GNOME and KDE desktops feature Help systems that use a browser-like interface to display help files. Both GNOME and KDE, along with other applications, also provide context-sensitive help. Each KDE and GNOME application features detailed manuals that are displayed using their respective Help browsers. Also, many system administrative tools feature detailed explanations for each task.

On your system, the **/usr/share/doc** folder contains documentation files installed by each application. Within each folder, you can usually find HOW-TO, README, and INSTALL documents for that application.

The Man Pages

You can also access the Man pages, which are manuals for Linux commands available from the command line interface. You can access a Man page from a terminal window using the **man** command. Enter **man** with the command on which you want information. The following example asks for information on the **ls** command:

```
$ man ls
```

Pressing the SPACEBAR key advances you to the next page. Pressing the **b** key moves you back a page. When you finish, press the **q** key to quit the Man utility and return to the command line. You activate a search by pressing either the slash (/) or question mark (**?**). The / searches forward, and the **?** searches backward. When you press the /, a line opens at the bottom of your screen, and you then enter a word to search for. Press ENTER to activate the search. You can repeat the same search by pressing the **n** key. You do not need to reenter the pattern.

The Info Pages

Online documentation for GNU applications, such as the gcc compiler and the Emacs editor, also exist as info pages. You can access this documentation by entering the command **`info`**. This brings up a special screen listing different GNU applications.

The info interface has its own set of commands. You can learn more about it by entering **info info**. Typing **m** opens a line at the bottom of the screen where you can enter the first few letters of the application. Pressing ENTER brings up the info file on that application.

Running Windows Software on Linux: Wine

Wine is a Windows compatibility layer that will allow you to run many Windows applications natively on Linux. The actual Windows operating system is not required. Windows applications will run as if they were Linux applications, able to access the entire Linux file system and use Linux-connected devices. Applications that are heavily driver-dependent, like graphic intensive games, may not run. Others that do not rely on any specialized drivers may run very well, including Photoshop and Microsoft Office. For some applications, you may need to use the most recent version of Wine.

Wine is provided by the EPEL repository. It is not a Red Hat supported application. Once installed, a Wine shows applications for Wine configuration, the Wine software uninstaller, and Wine file browser, as well as a regedit registry editor (OLE), a notepad, and a Wine help tool.

To set up Wine, start the Wine Configuration dialog, which displays tabs for Applications, Libraries (DLL selection), Audio (sound drivers), Drives, Desktop Integration, and Graphics. On the Applications tab, you can select the version of Windows an application is designed for. The Drives tab lists your detected partitions, as well as your Windows-emulated drives, such as drive C. The C: drive is actually just a folder, **.wine/drive_c**, not a partition of a fixed size. Your actual Linux file system will be listed as the Z drive.

Once configured, Wine will set up a **.wine** folder in the user's home folder (the folder is hidden, so enable Show Hidden Files in the file manager View menu to display it). Within that folder will be the **drive_c** folder, which functions as the C: drive that holds your Windows system files and program files in the Windows and Program File subfolders. The System and System32 folders are located in the Windows folder. This is where you would place any needed DLL files. The Program Files folder holds your installed Windows programs, just as they would be installed on a Windows Program Files folder.

To install a Windows application with Wine, double-click on the application install icon file on the desktop, or right-click on the application install icon and choose "Open with Wine Windows Program Loader." Alternatively, you can open a terminal window and run the **`wine`** command with the Windows application as an argument.

Icons for installed Windows software will appear on your desktop. Just double-click an icon to start up an application. It will normally run within a Linux window, as would any Linux application.

Installing Windows fonts on Wine is a simple matter of copying fonts from a Windows font folder to your Wine **.wine/drive_c/Windows/fonts** folder. You can copy any Windows **.ttf** file to this folder to install a font. Wine works on both **.exe** and **.msi** files installation files. You may have to make them executable by checking the file's Properties dialog Permissions tab's Execute checkbox.

Tip: Alternatively, you can use the commercial Windows compatibility layer called Crossover Office. This is a commercial product tested to run certain applications like Microsoft Office. Check **http://www.codeweavers.com** for more details. Crossover Office is based on Wine, which CodeWeavers supports directly.

3. GNOME

The GNOME Desktop
GNOME Overview
GNOME Dash
GNOME Windows
GNOME File Manager

The GNU Network Object Model Environment, also known as GNOME, is a powerful and easy-to-use environment consisting primarily of a panel, a desktop, and a set of desktop tools with which program interfaces can be constructed. GNOME is designed to provide a flexible platform for the development of powerful applications. Currently, GNOME is supported by several distributions and is the primary interface for RHEL7. GNOME is free and released under the GNU Public License. GTK+ is the widget set used for GNOME applications. The GTK+ widget set is entirely free under the Lesser General Public License (LGPL). The LGPL enables developers to use the widget set with proprietary software, as well as free software (the GPL is restricted to free software).

For detailed documentation, check the GNOME documentation site at **https://help.gnome.org**. Documentation is organized by users, administrators, and developers. "GNOME Help" provides a complete tutorial on desktop use. For administrators, the "GNOME Desktop System Administration Guide" details how administrators can manage user desktops. Table 3-1 offers a listing of useful GNOME sites.

Web Sites	Description
`http://www.gnome.org`	Official GNOME Web site
`http://help.gnome.org`	GNOME documentation Web site for Users, Administrators, and Developers
`https://wiki.gnome.org/Personalization`	Desktop themes and background art
`http://www.gnomefiles.org`	GNOME Software applications, applets, and tools.
`http://developer.gnome.org`	GNOME developers site, see **http://help.gnome.org** for developer documentation.

Table 3-1: GNOME Resources

GNOME releases new versions on a frequent schedule. RHEL 7.4 uses GNOME 3.22 whereas RHEL 7.3 uses GNOME 3.18. GNOME 3.22 features changes to the file manager and notifications. Both include many features from GNOME 3.0. Key changes with GNOME 3.22, GNOME 3.18, and GNOME 3.0 are described in detail at the following:

```
https://help.gnome.org/misc/release-notes/3.0/
https://help.gnome.org/misc/release-notes/3.18/
https://help.gnome.org/misc/release-notes/3.22/
```

The GNOME 3 Desktop

GNOME 3 is based on the gnome-shell, which is a compositing window manager (see Figure 3-1) . It replaced the GNOME 2 Metacity window manager, gnome-panel, and a notification daemon used in RHEL6. The key components of the gnome-shell are a top bar, an Activities overview, and a notification/message tray feature. The top bar has a dialog for the date and time, a universal access menu, and a status area menu for sound volume, network connections, power information, and user tasks such as accessing settings and logging out. The Activities overview lets you quickly access favorite applications, locate applications, select windows, and change workspaces. The message tray and notification system notifies you of recent events, such as updates and recently attached USB drives. To the right of the Activities button is the Applications menu, which is a menu for the currently selected open application, such as the Files menu for a file manager window. Most applications have only a Quit entry, while others list key tasks.

You can configure desktop settings and perform most administrative tasks using the GNOME configuration tools (see Table 3-1) listed in the GNOME Settings dialog, accessible from the System Status Area menu. Settings organizes tools into Personal, Hardware, and System categories (see Figure 3-25). A few invoke the supported system tools available from previous releases, such as Sound (PulseAudio) and Displays. Most use the GNOME 3 configuration and administrative tools such as Background, Lock Screen, User Accounts, and Power.

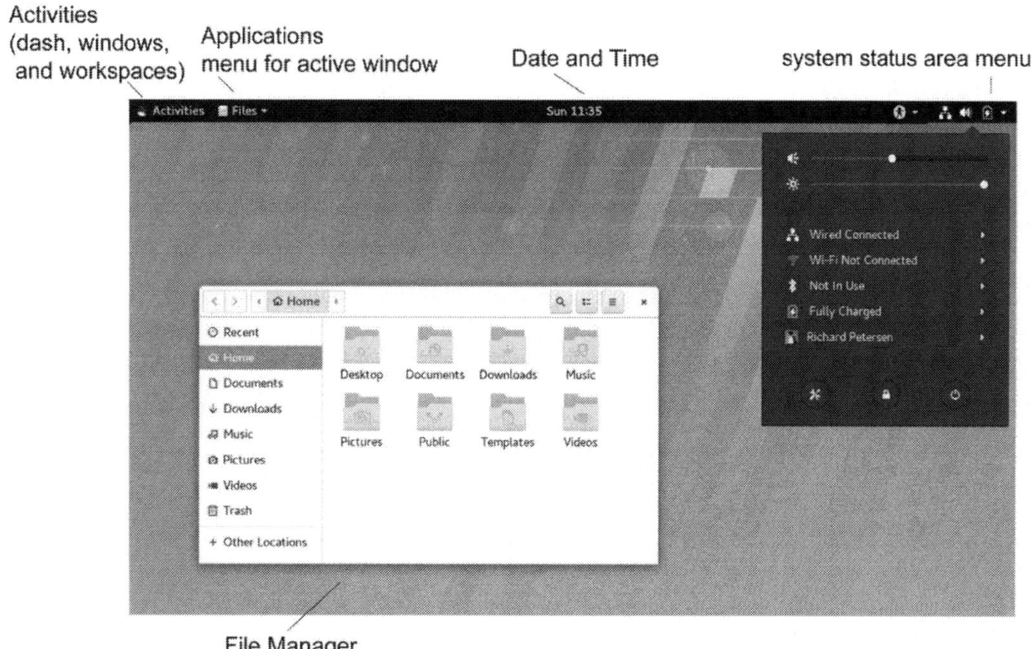

Figure 3-1: GNOME Desktop

Top Bar

The screen displays a top bar, through which you access your applications, windows, and such system properties as sound and networking. Clicking the sound and power icons at the right of the top bar displays a menu with options to set the sound level, screen brightness (laptop), wired and wireless connections, Bluetooth, and to log out (see Figure 3-1). The center of the top bar has a button to display your clock and calendar. To the left is the Activities button, which displays an icon bar for favorite and open applications.

The System Status Area

Once logged in, the System Status Area is displayed on the right side of the top bar (see Figure 3-2) . The area will include status icons for features such as sound and power. Clicking the button showing the sound, power, and down arrow icons displays the System Status Area menu, with items for sound, brightness, wired and wireless connections, the battery, the current user, in addition to buttons at the bottom for opening GNOME Settings, activating the lock screen, and shutting down or rebooting the system. The sound and brightness items feature sliding bars with which you can adjust the volume and brightness. The Wi-Fi, Battery, and current user entries expand to submenus with added entries. The buttons at the bottom open separate dialogs.

On systems that are not laptops, there will be no brightness slider or Battery entry on the System Status Area menu. If the system also has no wireless device, the Wi-Fi entry will also be missing. A system of this kind will only have a sound slider and a user entry.

To log out, you click the current user entry to expand the menu to show Log Out and Account Settings entries. The Log Out returns you to the GDM login screen, where you can log in as another user.

To switch to another user, click the lock button at the bottom of the menu to lock your session. Then, at the unlock screen, click the "Log in as another user" link below the Cancel button. You can then log in as another user. When you log out, you can then select the original user and an unlock screen appears. When you log in, your session is restored.

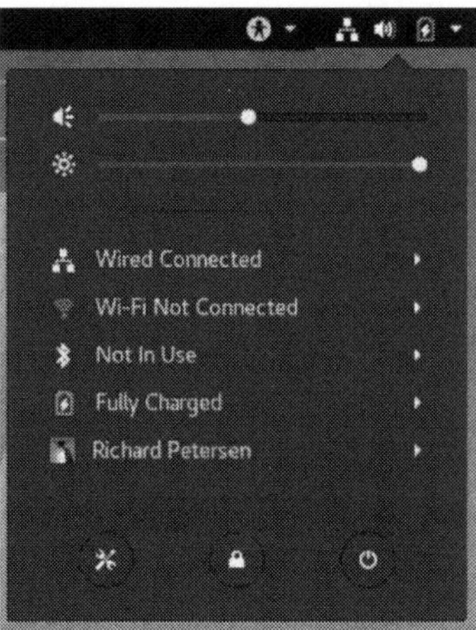

Figure 3-2: System Status Area menu

Activities Overview

To access applications and windows, you use the Activities overview mode. Click the Activities button at the left side of the top bar (or move the mouse to the left corner, or press the super (Windows) button). The Activities overview mode consists of a dash listing your favorite and running applications, thumbnails of open windows, and workspace thumbnails (see Figure 3-3). You can use the search box at the top center to locate applications and files. Partially hidden thumbnails of your desktop workspaces are displayed on the right side. Initially, there are two. Moving your mouse to the right side displays the workspace thumbnails.

You can manually leave the Activities overview mode at any time by pressing the ESC key.

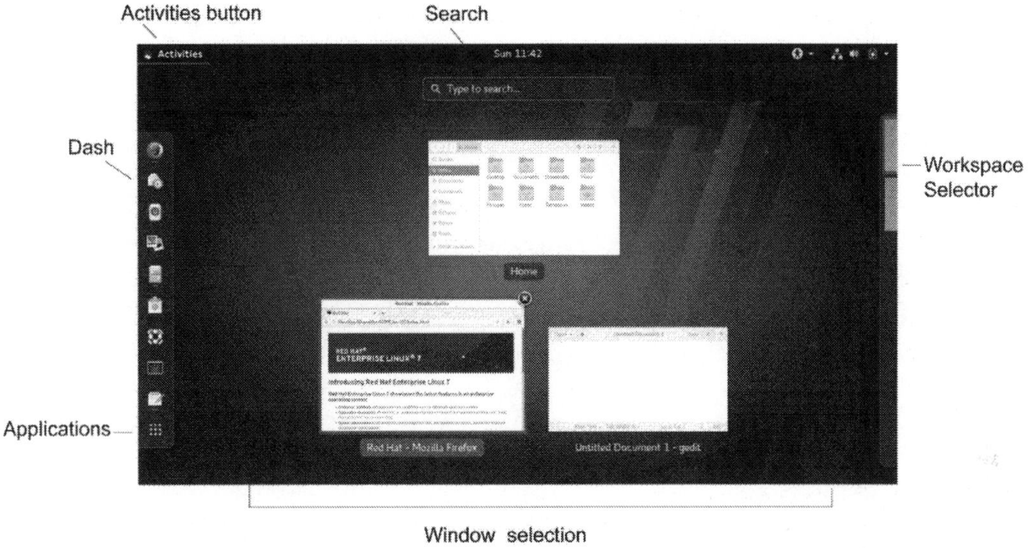

Activities button
Search
Dash
Workspace Selector
Applications
Window selection

Figure 3-3: GNOME 3 Activities Overview

Dash

The dash is a bar on the left side with icons for your favorite applications. Initially, on the RHEL7 server version there are icons for the Firefox web browser, the home folder (the Files file manager), Software, and GNOME Help, the terminal window, Settings, and the Gedit editor (see Figure 3-4). On the RHEL7 Workstation version, there is the Firefox Web browser, the Evolution mail application, the Rhythmbox music player, the Shotwell photo manager, the file manager, Software, GNOME Help, and the terminal window. To open an application from the dash, click its icon, or right-click and choose New Window from the pop-up menu. You can also click-and-drag the icon to the windows thumbnail area or to a workspace thumbnail on the right side.

Favorites are always displayed on the dash. When you run other applications, they are also placed on the dash during the time they are running. To add a running application to the dash as a favorite, right-click the icon and choose Add to Favorites. You can later remove an application as a favorite by choosing Remove from Favorites. You can also add any application to the dash from the Applications overview, by clicking-and-dragging its icon to the dash, or by right-clicking the icon and choosing Add to Favorites from the menu (see Figure 3-4).

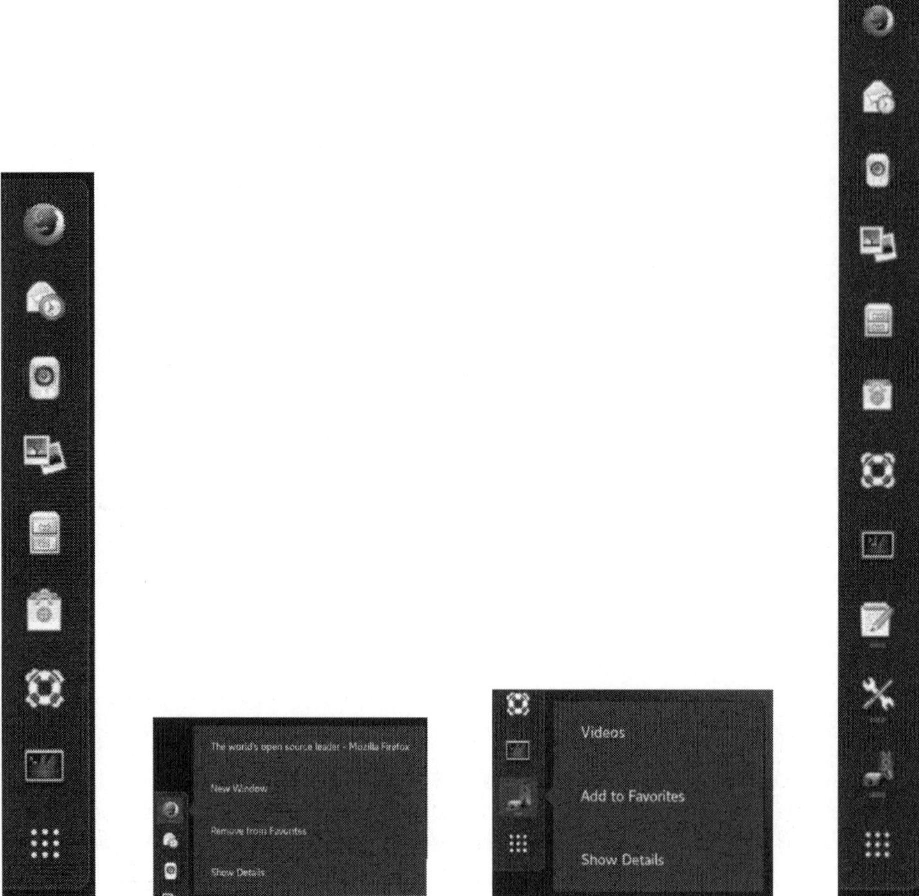

Figure 3-4: Overview dash with favorites and running applications

Window Thumbnails

You access windows using the window thumbnails on the Activities overview. Thumbnails are displayed of all your open windows (see Figure 3-5) . To select a window, move your mouse over the window's thumbnail. The selected window also shows an x (close) button at the top right of the window's thumbnail, which you can use to close the window directly. To access the window, move your mouse over it and click. This displays the window, exiting the overview and returning to the desktop.

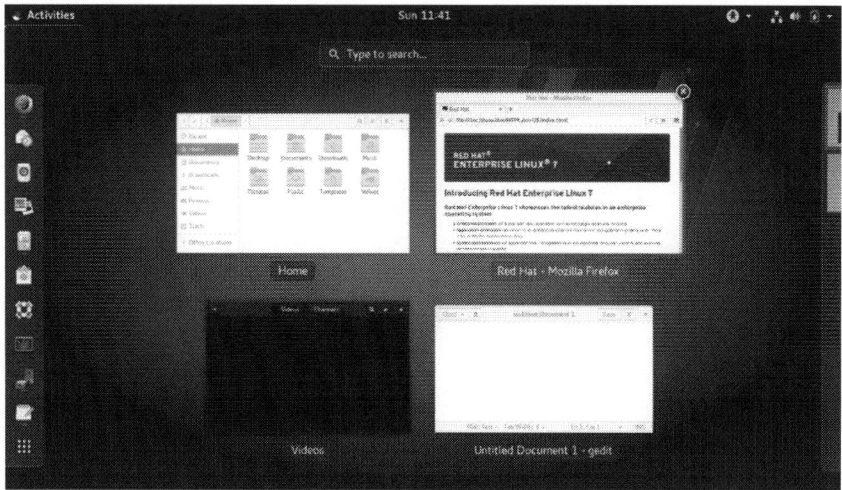

Figure 3-5: Window thumbnails

Moving your mouse to the right side of the screen displays the workspace selector showing workspace thumbnails, with the current workspace highlighted (see Figure 3-6). You can switch to another workspace by clicking its thumbnail. You can also move windows or applications directly to a workspace. If your mouse has a scroll wheel, you can press the Ctrl key and use the scroll wheel to move through workspaces, forward or backward.

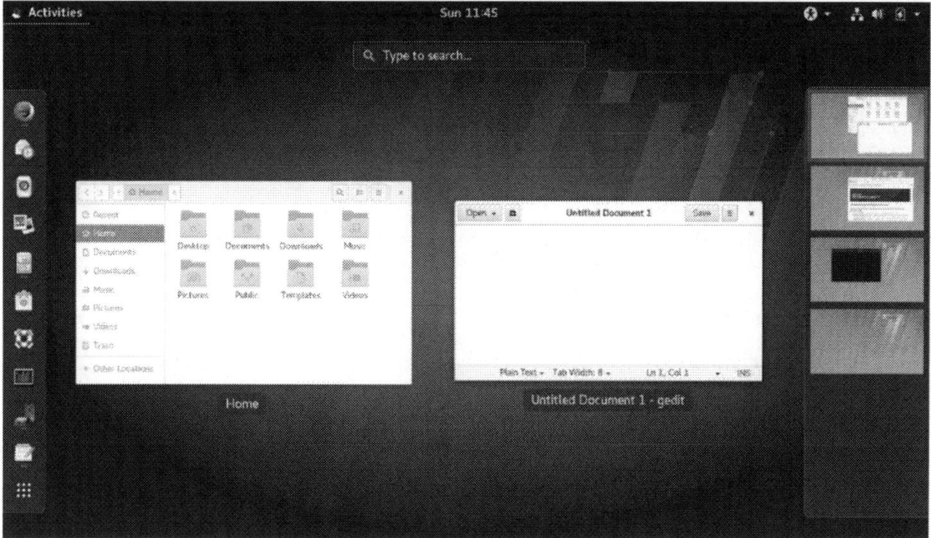

Figure 3-6: Workspace thumbnails

Applications Overview

Clicking the Applications icon (last icon, grid button) on the dash opens the Applications overview, from which you can locate and open applications. Icons for installed applications are displayed (see Figure 3-7) . The Frequent button at the bottom of the overview lets you see only your most frequently used applications. Click the All button to see them all. A pager consisting of buttons, on the right side, lets you move quickly through the list of applications. You can move anywhere to a page in the list using the buttons. There are two special subsections: Utilities and Sundry. Clicking those icons opens another, smaller overview, showing applications in those categories, such as Tweak Tool and Backups in the Utilities overview. Click an application icon to open it and exit the overview. Should you return to the overview mode, you will see its window in the overview. The super key (Windows key) with the **a** key (super+a) will switch automatically from the desktop to the Applications overview. Continuing to press it, switches between the applications overview and the window thumbnails.

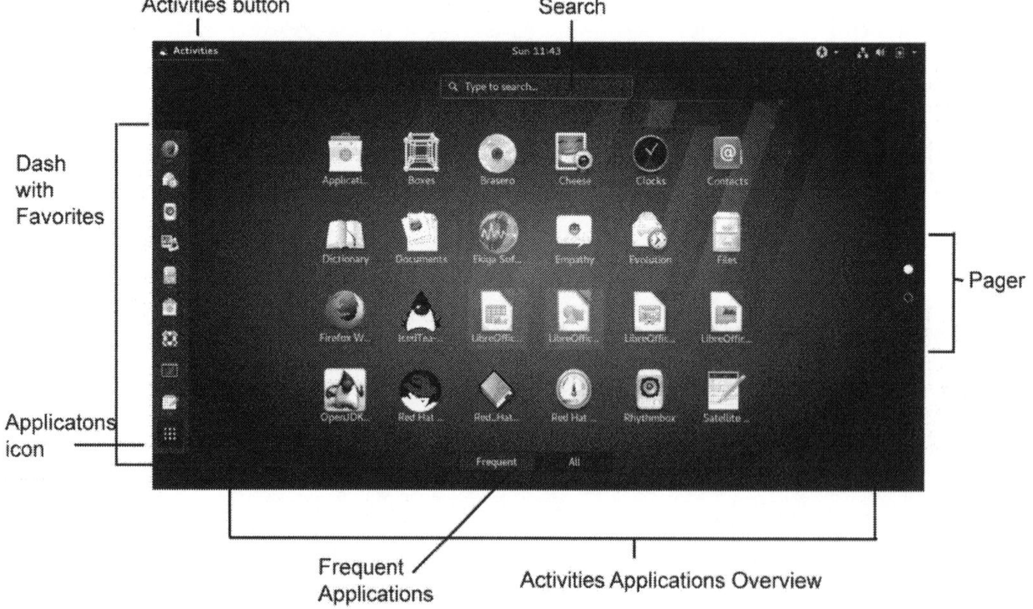

Figure 3-7: Applications overview

You can also open an application by dragging its icon to a workspace thumbnail on the right side, starting it in that workspace.

Also, as previously noted, to add an application as a favorite on the dash, you can simply drag its icon from the Applications overview to the dash directly.

Activities Search

The Activities search will search applications and files. Should you know the name of the application you want, you can simply start typing, and the matching results are displayed (see Figure 3-8). Your search term is entered in the search box as you type. The results dynamically narrow the more you type. The first application is selected automatically. If this is the one you want, just press ENTER to start it. Results will also show Settings tools and recently accessed files.

The search box for the Activities overview can be configured from the Settings Search dialog (see Figure 3-9). Here, you can turn search on or off and specify which applications are to support searches. By default, these include Contacts, Documents, the Files file manager, Passwords and Keys, and the Firefox Web browser. To specify the folders to be searched, click the gear button on the lower right to open the Search Locations Dialog with switches for currently supported folders (see Figure 3-10). Click the plus button to add a folder of your choosing.

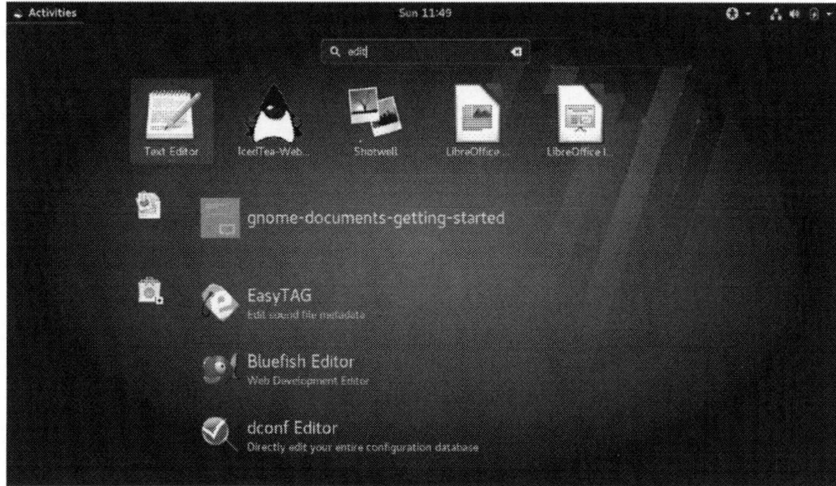

Figure 3-8: Activities: search box

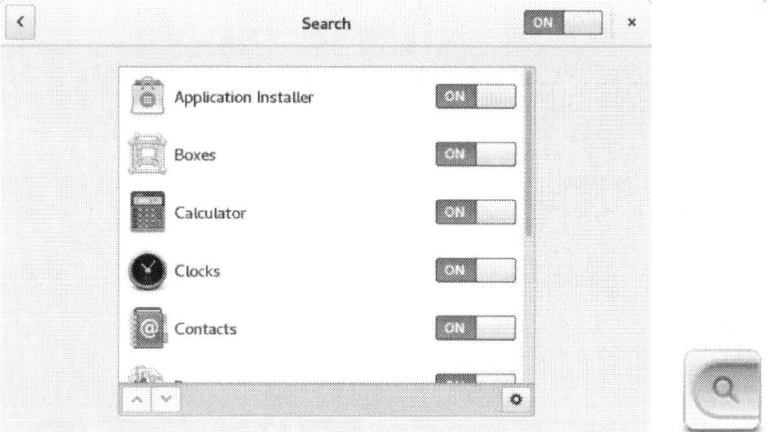

Figure 3-9: Activities: Search configuration

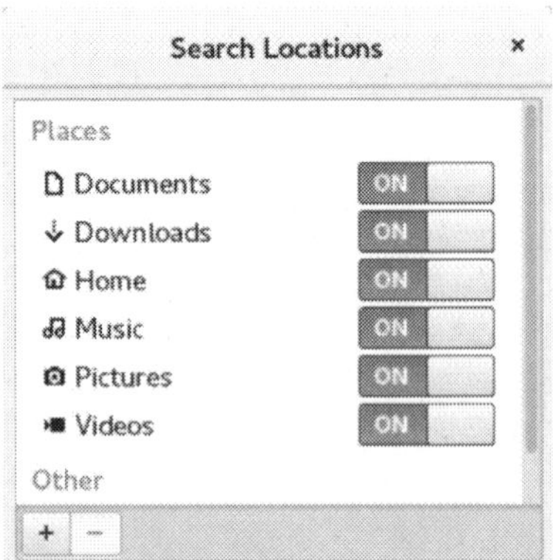

Figure 3-10: Activities: Search Locations

Managing Windows

The title bar and the toolbar for GNOME windows have been combined into a single header bar, as shown in the following for the file manager.

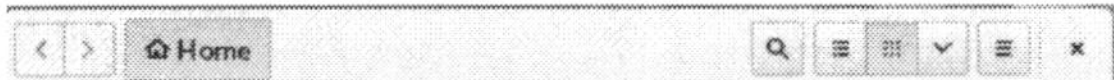

The minimize and maximize buttons have been dropped, and a single close button is always present. You can use Tweak Tool to add the minimize and maximize buttons if you wish. Some applications change the header bar if the function changes, presenting a different set of tools, as shown here for the GNOME Videos application.

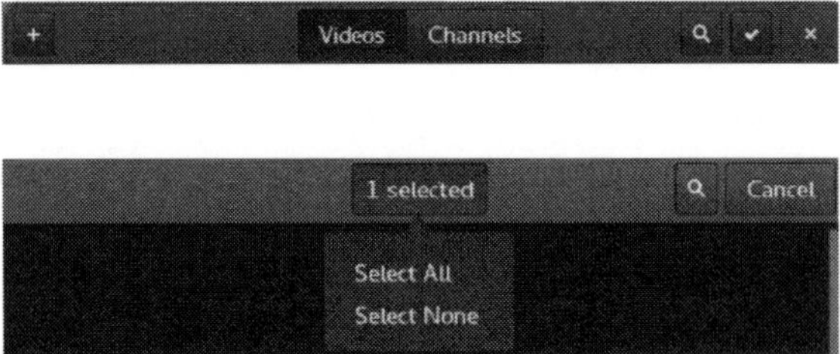

Windows no longer have maximize and minimize buttons. These tasks can be carried out by a dragging operation or by double-clicking the header bar. To maximize a window, double-click its header bar or drag the header bar to the top edge of the screen. To minimize, drag the title away from the top edge of the screen. You can also use a window's menu entries to maximize or minimize it. Right-click the header bar or press Alt+spacebar to display the window menu.

Open application windows also have an Applications menu on the left side of the top bar. For many applications, this menu holds only a Quit entry (see Figure 3-11). Others, such as the file manager, list key tasks, such as Bookmarks, Preferences, and Help. The Firefox web browser only lists a Quit button, whereas the GNOME file manager lists items such as New Window, Bookmarks, Preferences, and Help, as well as Quit.

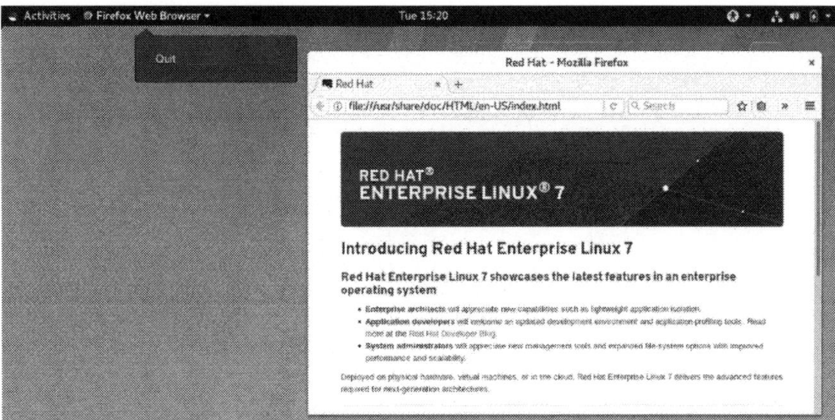

Figure 3-11: Window with Applications menu

To minimize an open window so that it no longer displays on the desktop, right-click the header bar and choose minimize. This will hide the window. You can then maximize the window later, using the window's thumbnails on the activities overview (Activities button).

To close a window, click its close box or choose Close from the Window menu. Many currently selected windows have an Applications menu in the top bar to the left. Should an application not have a close button, you can click the Applications menu button on the top bar and choose the Quit entry (see Figure 3-11).

To tile a window, click-and-drag its header bar to the left or right edge of the screen. When your mouse reaches the edge of the screen, the window is tiled to take up that half of the screen. You can do the same with another window for the other edge, showing two windows side by side.

To resize a window, move the mouse to the edge or corner until it changes to an edge or corner mouse, then click-and-drag.

The scrollbar to the right also features fine scrolling. When scrolling through a large number of items, you can fine scroll to slow the scrolling when you reach a point to search. To activate fine scrolling, click and hold the scrollbar handle, or press the Shift key while scrolling.

You can use the Window Switcher on the desktop to quickly search open windows. Press the Alt+Tab keys to display an icon bar of open windows on the current workspace (see Figure 3-12). While holding down the Alt key, press the Tab key to move through the list of windows. Windows are grouped by application. Instead of the Tab keys, you can use the forward and back arrow keys. For applications with multiple open windows, press the tilde (~) key (above the Tab key) to move through a list of the open windows.

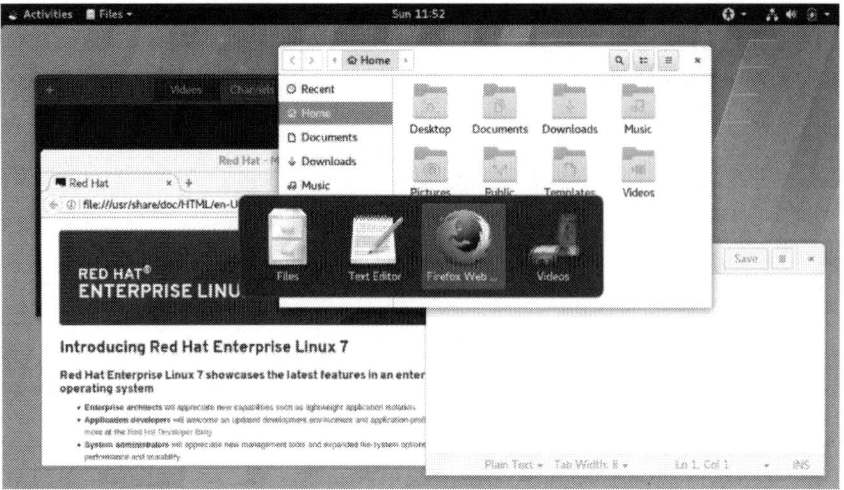

Figure 3-12: Window Switcher (Alt+Tab)

On the GNOME Tweak Tool's Windows tab, you can configure certain windows' actions and components. Attached Modal Dialogs will attach a dialog that an application opens to the application's window (see Figure 3-13). You can use the switch to turn this feature off, allowing you to move a modal dialog away from the application window. Actions on the title bar (Titlebar Actions) are also defined, such as double-click to maximize and secondary-click to display the menu. There are also switches to display the Maximize and Minimize buttons on the title bar.

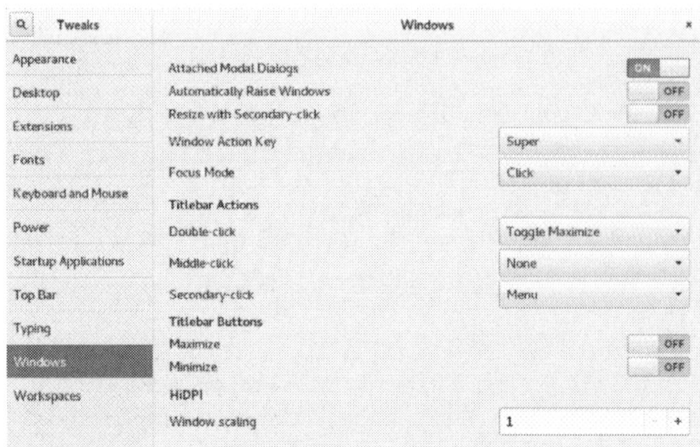

Figure 3-13: GNOME Tweak Tool: Windows (dialogs and title bar)

Workspaces

You can organize your windows into different workspaces. Workspaces are managed using the Workspace selector. In the overview, move your mouse to the right edge of the screen to display the workspace selector, a vertical panel showing thumbnails of your workspaces (see Figure 3-14). Workspaces are generated dynamically. The workspace selector will show an empty workspace as the last workspace (see Figure 3-15). To add a workspace, click-and-drag a window in the overview to the empty workspace on the workspace selector. A new empty workspace appears automatically below the current workspaces.

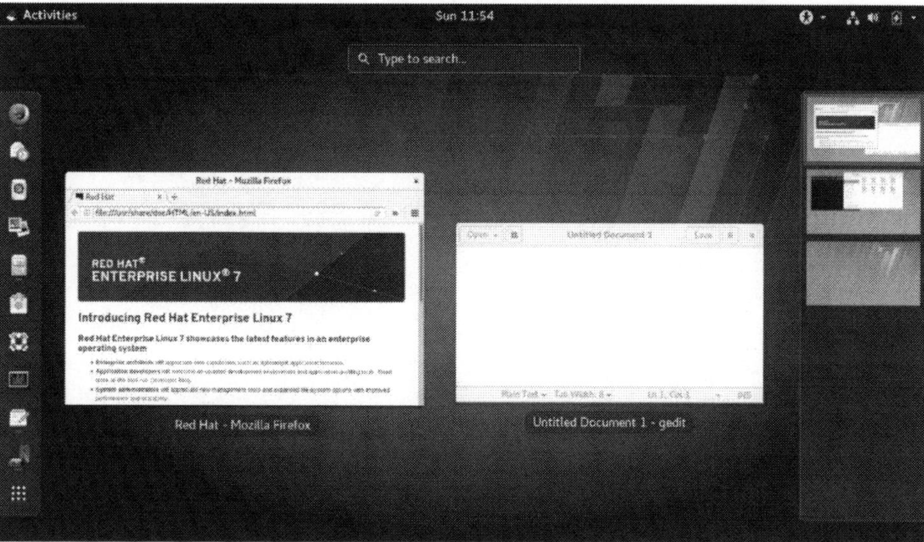

Figure 3-14: Workspace selector

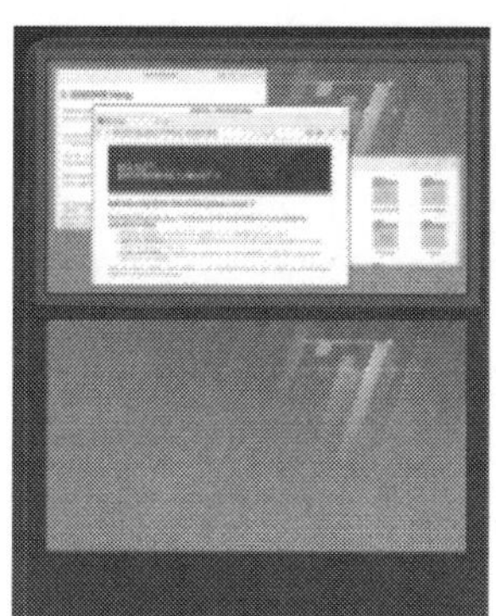

Figure 3-15: Adding workspaces

To remove a workspace, close all its open windows, or move the windows to other workspaces.

To move to another workspace, in the overview mode, move to the right edge to display the workspace selector, then click on the workspace you want. You can also use Ctrl+Alt with the up and down arrow keys to move to the next or previous workspaces.

To move a window to a workspace, on the Windows overview, click-and-drag the window to the workspace selector (right edge) and then to the workspace you want. You can also use the Window menu and choose Move to Workspace Down or Move to Workspace Up. You can also use Ctrl+Alt+Shift and the up or down arrow keys to move the window to the next workspace. Continue pressing the arrow to move it further should you have several workspaces.

You can use the GNOME Tweak Tool's Workspaces tab to change workspace creation from dynamic to static, letting you specify a fixed number of workspaces (see Figure 3-16).

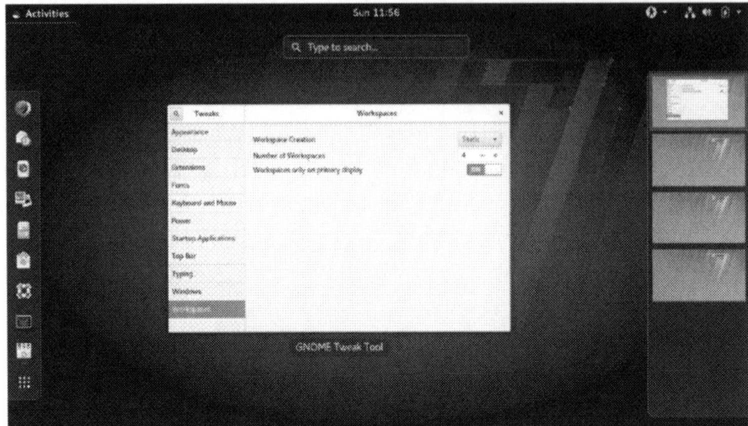

Figure 3-16: GNOME Tweak Tool: Workspaces tab

Notifications and Message Tray

Notifications, such as software updates and removable device activation, are displayed in the notifications area at the left side of the calendar dialog (automatically hidden). Click the time and date button on the middle of the top bar to open it and display your notifications. You can also press the super key with the **m** key to open the notifications area.

When you first attach a removable device such as a USB drive or DVD, a notification is displayed asking you what you want to do, such as open it with the file manager (see Figure 3-17). A notification for the device is also listed in the notifications area. Click on it to open the device.

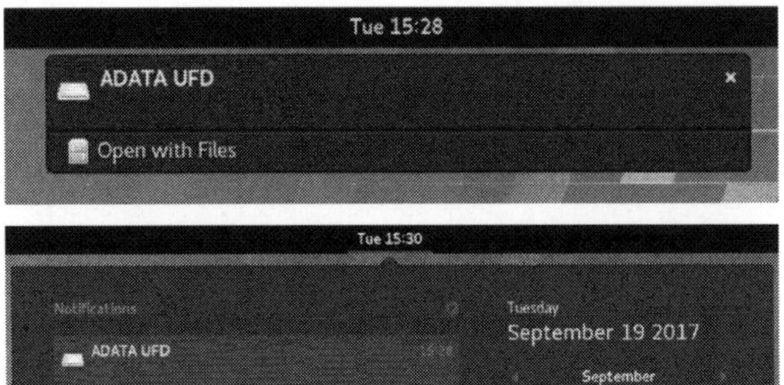

Figure 3-17: Notifications

GNOME Customization with Tweak Tool: Themes, Icons, Fonts, Startup Applications, and Extensions

You can perform common desktop customizations using the GNOME Tweak Tool. Areas to customize include the desktop icons, fonts, themes, startup applications, workspaces, window behavior, and the time display. You can access Tweak Tool from the Applications overview | Utilities. The GNOME Tweak Tool has tabs for Appearance, Desktop, Extensions, Fonts, Keyboard and Mouse, Power, Startup Applications, Top Bar, Typing, Windows, and Workspaces (see Figure 3-18).

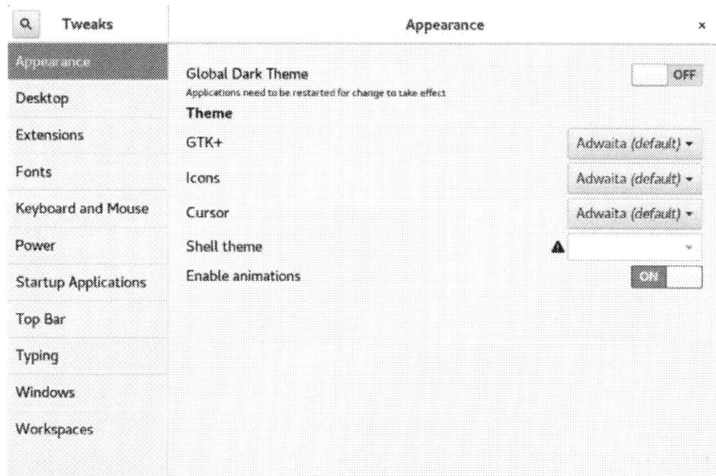

Figure 3-18 GNOME Tweak Tool: Appearance tab (themes)

The Appearance tab lets you set the theme for your windows, icons, and cursor. GNOME 3 uses the Adwaita Theme. This theme has a light and dark variant. The Global Light Theme is the default, but you can use the switch on the Appearance tab to enable the Global Dark Theme. The Global Dark Theme shades the background of windows to a dark gray, while text and button images appear in white.

You may also want to display Home, Trash, and Mounted Volumes like USB drives, on the desktop, as other desktops do. Use the Desktop tab on Tweak Tool to display these icons (see Figure 3-19). Turn on the "Icons on Desktop" switch. Home, Trash, and Mounted Volumes are checked by default. Uncheck an icon in order not to display it. You can also check a Network Servers option to display icons for remotely accessed folders.

Desktop fonts for window titles, interface (application or dialog text), documents, and monospace (terminal windows or code) can be changed in the Fonts tab. You can adjust the size of the font or change the font style. Clicking the font name opens a "Pick a Font" dialog from which you can choose a different font. The quality of text display can be further adjusted with Hinting and Antialiasing options. To simply increase or decrease the size of all fonts on your desktop interface, you can adjust the Scaling Factor.

At times, there may be certain applications that you want started up when you log in, such as the Gedit text editor, the Firefox web browser, or the Videos movie player. On the Startup

Applications tab, you can choose the applications to start up. Click the plus (+) button to open an applications dialog from which you can choose an application to start up. Once added, you can later remove the application by clicking its Remove button.

Extensions function much as applets did in GNOME 2. They are third-party programs that enhance or modify the GNOME desktop, such as a window list, workspace indicator, a removable drive menu, and an applications menu. Extensions appear on the top bar or, in the case of the window list, in an added bottom bar. Installed extensions are listed on the Extensions tab of Tweak Tool, where you can turn them on or off.

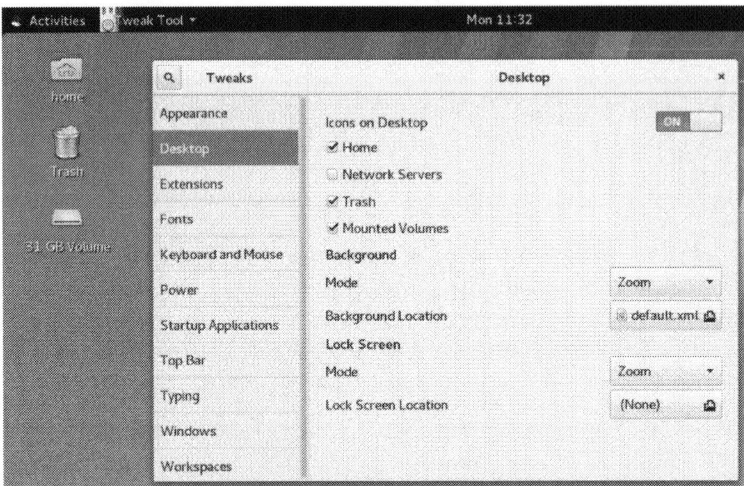

Figure 3-19: GNOME Tweak Tool: Desktop tab (desktop icons)

GNOME Desktop Help

The GNOME Help browser provides a browser-like interface for displaying the GNOME Desktop Help and various GNOME applications, such as Brasero, Evince, and gedit (Utilities | Help) (see Figure 3-20) . It features a toolbar that enables you to move through the list of previously viewed documents. You can even bookmark specific items. You can search for topics using the search box, with results displayed in the drop-down menu. Initially, the Desktop Help manual is displayed. To see other help pages and manuals, choose All Help from the menu next to the close box (see Figure 3-21).

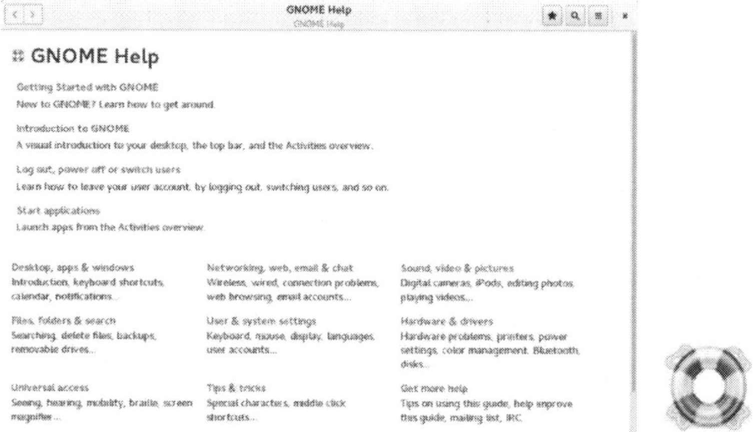

Figure 3-20: GNOME Help browser

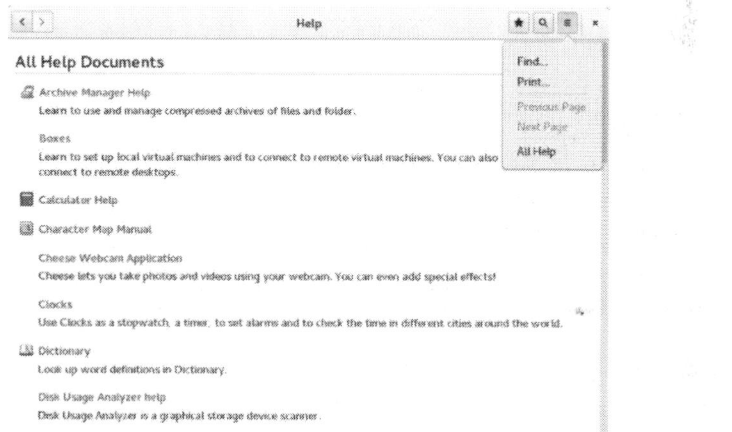

Figure 3-21: GNOME Help: All Documents

The GNOME Files File Manager

The GNOME file manager supports the standard features for copying, removing, and deleting items as well as setting permissions and displaying items. The name used for the file manager is Files, but the actual program name is still nautilus. When you select a file manager window, a Files menu appears as the Applications menu on the top bar to the left (see Figure 3-22). The Files menu has entries for opening a new file manager window, displaying the sidebar, the file manager preferences, displaying the file manager keyboard shorcuts, and help (see Table 3-2).

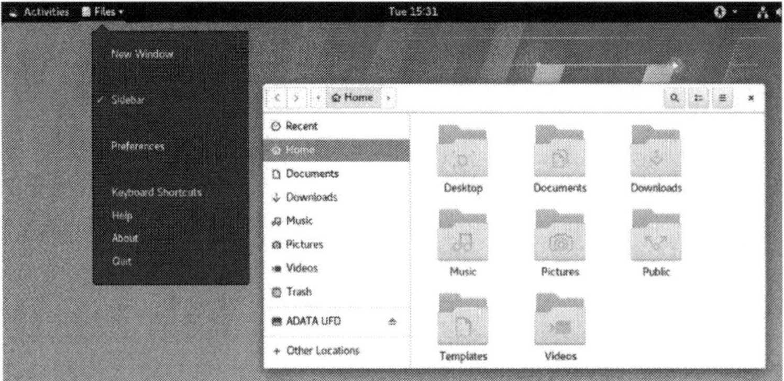

Figure 3-22: File manager with Files applications menu

Menu Item	Description
New Window	Open a new file manager window
Sidebar	Toggle display of the file manager sidebar
Preferences	Open the file manager Preferences dialog
Keyboard Shortcuts	Display a dialog listing keyboard shortcuts
Help	Open GNOME desktop help
About	Current GNOME release
Quit	Close the file manager

Table 3-2: File Manager GNOME Menu

Home Folder Subfolders

GNOME uses the Common User Directory Structure (xdg-user-dirs at **http://freedesktop.org**) to set up subfolders in the user home directory. Folders include Documents, Music, Pictures, Downloads, and Videos. These localized user folders are used as defaults by many desktop applications. Users can change their folder names or place them within each other using the GNOME file browser. For example, Music can be moved into Videos or Documents into Pictures. Local configuration is held in the **.config/user-dirs.dirs** file. System-wide defaults are set up in the **/etc/xdg/user-dirs.defaults** file.

File Manager Windows

When you click the Files icon on the dash, a file manager window opens showing your home folder. The file manager window displays several components, including a toolbar and a sidebar (see Figure 3-23). The sidebar displays sections for folder, device, bookmark, and network items showing your file systems and default home folder subfolders. You can choose to display or hide the sidebar toolbar by selecting its entry in the View and Tools menu. The main pane (to the right) displays the icons or lists files and subfolders in the current working folder. When you select a file and folder, a status section at the bottom right of the window displays the number or name of the file or folder selected and the total size.

When you open a new folder, the same window is used to display it, and you can use the forward and back arrows to move through previously opened folders (top left). As you open subfolders, the main toolbar displays buttons for your current folder and its parent folders, as shown here:

You can click a folder button to move to it directly. It also can display a location URL text box instead of buttons, from which you can enter the location of a folder, either on your system or on a remote one. Press Ctrl+l to display the text bos. Press the ESC key to revert back to the folder location buttons.

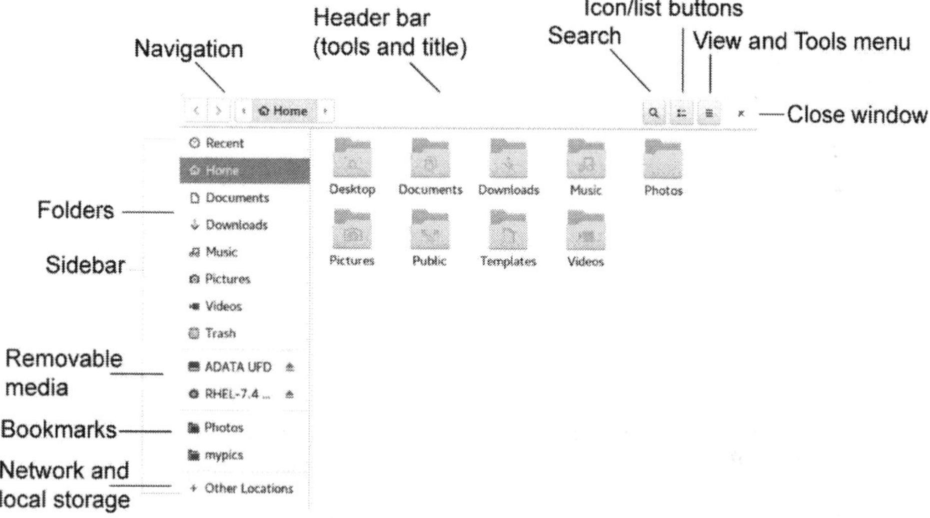

Figure 3-23: File manager with sidebar

The file manager features separate dialogs for folder creation and file renaming (see Figure 3-24). When reaming a file, be sure to click the Rename button once you have entered the new name. You can also change several filenames at once by selecting the files and then right-clicking and choosing Rename. A dialog opens listing the selected files and a text box for specifying the new names, as shown here.

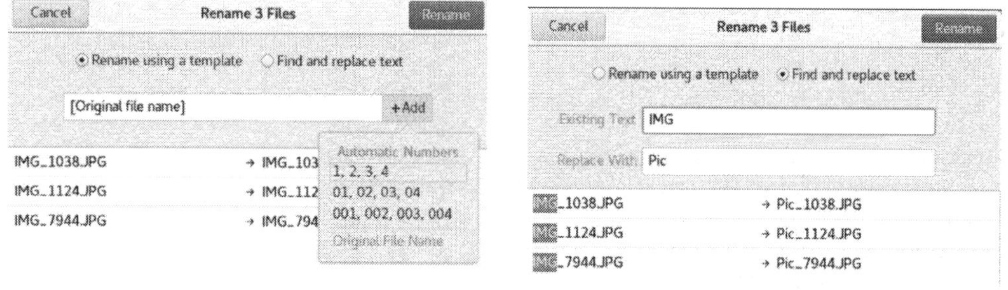

You can add to the name or choose the "Find and replace" option to change a common part of the names. Clicking the Add button lets you choose from a list of possible automatic number formats to add. The added characters are encased in brackets in the text box, separated by commas, one for each file name. The Original File Name entry add the original file name specifier to the text box, should you remove it.

You can also compress files and folders. Select the files or folders to compress, right-click and choose the Compress option. A dialog opens where you can specify the name of the compressed archive, the compression method, and the location for the archive. Clicking on the "Other Options" opens an encryption option, where you can enter a password for the archive.

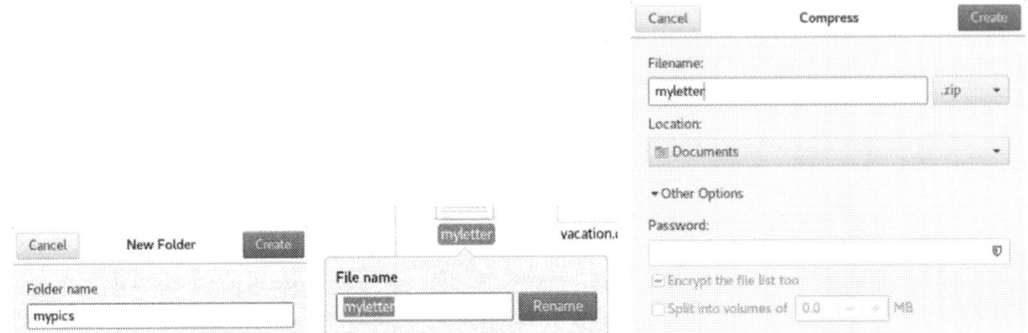

Figure 3-24: File manager New Folder, Rename, and Compress dialogs

You can click anywhere on the empty space on the main pane of a file manager window to display a pop-up menu with entries to create a new folder, open the current folder in a terminal window with a command line prompt, and open the file manager properties dialog (see Table 3-3).

Menu Item	Description
New Folder	Creates a new subfolder in the current folder
Paste	Pastes files that you have copied or cut, letting you move or copy files between folders, or make duplicates
Select All	Select all files and folders in the current folder
Properties	Opens the Properties dialog for the directory
Open in Terminal	Open a terminal window at the current folder

Table 3-3: File Manager Pop-up Menu

File Manager Sidebar

The file manager sidebar shows file system locations that you would normally access: folders, devices, bookmarks, and network folders (See Figure 3-25) . Selecting the Computer entry places you at the top of the file system, letting you move to any accessible part of it. The Recent folder holds links to your recently used files. Should you bookmark a folder (Tools | Bookmark This Location), the bookmarks will appear on the sidebar. To remove or rename a bookmark, right-click its entry on the sidebar and choose Remove or Rename from the pop-up menu. The bookmark's name changes, but not the original folder name.

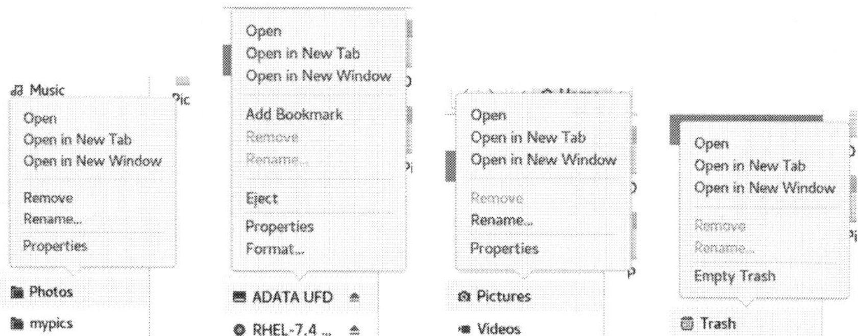

Figure 3-25: File manager sidebar with menus for bookmarks, devices, folders, and trash

Tabs

The GNOME file manager supports tabs with which you can open several folders in the same file manager window. To open a tab, select New Tab from the Tools menu (see Figure 3-24) or press Ctrl+t. You can use the Tabs buttons to move from one tab to another, or to rearrange tabs. You can also use the Ctrl+PageUp and Ctrl+PageDown keys to move from one tab to another. Use the Shift+Ctrl+PageUp and Shift+Ctrl+PageDown keys to rearrange the tabs. To close a tab, click its close (x) button on the right side of the tab (see Figure 3-26), or press Ctrl+w. Tabs are detachable. You can drag a tab out to a separate window.

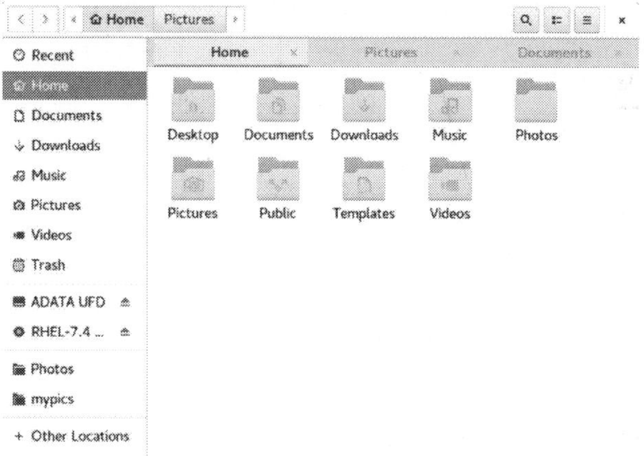

Figure 3-26: File manager window with tabs

Displaying and Managing Files and Folders

You can view a folder's contents as icons or as a detailed list, which you can choose by clicking the icon/list button between the search and menu buttons on the right side of the toolbar as shown here. This button toggles between icon and list views.

Use the Ctrl key to change views quickly: Ctrl+1 for Icons and Ctrl+2 for list (there is no longer a Compact view). The List view provides the name, permissions, size, date, owner, and group. Buttons are displayed for each field across the top of the main pane. You can use these buttons to sort the list according to that field. For example, to sort the files by date, click the Date button; to sort by size, click Size. Click again to alternate between ascending and descending order.

Certain types of file icons display previews of their contents. For example, the icons for image files display a thumbnail of the image. A text file displays in its icon the first few words of its text.

You can click the menu button at the right of toolbar to display the Tools and View menu with entries for managing and sorting your file manager icons (see Table 3-4). The sort entries allow you to sort your icons by name (A-Z and Z-A), size, type, modification date, and access date. You can also reverse the order by name and modification date (see Figure 3-27).

Menu Item	Description
New Folder button	Creates a new subfolder in the current folder
Bookmark button	Creates bookmark for current folder
Tab button	Creates a new tab
Zoom In button	Enlarge icon size
Zoom Out button	Reduce icon size
Undo	Undo the previous operation
Redo	Redo an undo operation
A-Z	Sort in alphabetic order
Z-A	Sort in reverse alphabetic order
Last Modified	Sort by last modified date
First Modified	Sort by recent modified date
Size	Sort by file size
Type	Sort by file type
Show Hidden Files	Shows administrative dot files
Reload	Refreshes file and directory list

Table 3-4: File Manager Tools and View Menu

At the top of the menu is a zoom bar, with zoom in and zoom out buttons, showing the zoom percentage between them. The zoom in button (+ button) enlarges your view of the window, making icons bigger. The zoom out button (- button) reduces your view, making them smaller. You can also use the Ctrl++ and Ctrl+- keys to zoom in and out.

You can also bookmark the folder, create a new folder, create a new tab, and close the file manager window. The top bar of the view menu has buttons to create a new folder, create a bookmark for the current folder, and create a new file manager tab.

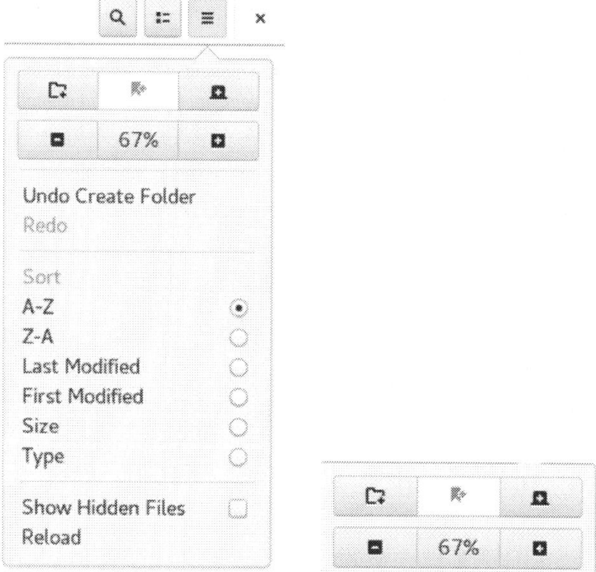

Figure 3-27: File manager View and Tools menu

Previews

The file manager supports previews for many different types of files. Select a file you want to preview, then press the spacebar. A dialog window opens, displaying the contents. Picture files show the image (see Figure 3-28). You can scroll through text and PDF files. Applications files such as LibreOffice files show information about the file. Video files are played, with controls to pause and to expand to full screen.

Figure 3-28: File previews (spacebar)

Menu Item	Description
Open	Opens the file with its associated application. Directories are opened in the file manager. Associated applications are listed.
Open in New Tab	Opens a folder in a new tab in the same window
Open in New Window	Opens a folder in a new file manager window
Open With Other Application	Selects an application with which to open this file. An Open With dialog lists the possible applications
Cut Copy	Cuts or copies the selected file
Copy To	Copies a file to the Home folder, desktop, or to a folder displayed in another pane in the file manager window
Move To	Moves a file to the Home folder, desktop, or to a folder displayed in another pane in the file manager window
Rename (F2)	Renames the file
Move To Trash	Moves a file to the Trash directory, where you can later delete it
Send to	E-mails the file
Compress	Archives the file using File Roller
Properties	Displays the Properties dialog
Open in Terminal	Open a folder in a terminal window

Table 3-5: The File and Folder Pop-up Menu

Navigating in the File Manager

The file manager operates similarly to a web browser, using the same window to display opened folders. It maintains a list of previously viewed folders, and you can move back and forth through that list using the toolbar buttons. The left arrow button moves you to the previously displayed directory, and the right arrow button moves you to the next displayed directory. Use the sidebar to access your storage devices (USB, DVD/CD, and attached hard drives). From the sidebar, you can also access mounted network folders. You can also access your home folders, trash, and recent files. As noted, the Computer entry on the Devices section opens your root (top) system directory.

To open a subfolder, you can double-click its icon or right-click the icon and select Open from the menu (see Table 3-5). To open the folder in a new tab, select Open in New Tab.

You can open any folder or file system listed in the sidebar by clicking it. You can also right-click an entry to display a menu with entries to Open in a New Tab and Open in a New Window (see Table 3-6). The menu for the Trash entry lets you empty the trash. You can also remove and rename the bookmarks.

Entries for removable devices in the sidebar, such as USB drives, also have menu items for Eject and Safely Remove Drive. Internal hard drives have an Unmount option instead.

Menu Item	Description
Open	Opens the file with its associated application. Folders are opened in the file manager. Associated applications are listed.
Open in a New Tab	Opens a folder in a new tab in the same window
Open in a New Window	Opens a folder in a separate window, accessible from the toolbar with a right-click
Remove	Removes the bookmark from the sidebar
Rename	Renames the bookmark

Table 3- 6: The File Manager Sidebar Pop-up Menu

Managing Files and Folders

As a GNOME-compliant file manager, Files supports desktop drag-and-drop operations for copying and moving files. To move a file or directory, drag-and-drop from one directory to another. The move operation is the default drag-and-drop operation in GNOME. To copy a file to a new location, press the Ctrl key as you drag-and-drop.

You can also perform remove, rename, and link-creation operations on a file by right-clicking its icon and selecting the action you want from the pop-up menu that appears (see Table 3-5). For example, to remove an item, right-click it and select the Move To Trash entry from the pop-up menu. This places it in the Trash directory, where you can later delete it. To create a link, right-click the file and select Make Link from the pop-up menu. This creates a new link file that begins with the term "Link."

Renaming Files

To rename a file, you can either right-click the file's icon and select the Rename entry from the pop-up menu or click its icon and press the F2 function key. The name of the icon will be bordered, encased in a small text box. You can overwrite the old one or edit the current name by clicking a position in the name to insert text, as well as by using the Backspace key to delete characters. You can also rename a file by entering a new name in its Properties dialog box (Basic tab).

Grouping Files

You can select a group of files and folders by clicking the first item and then holding down the Shift key while clicking the last item, or by clicking and dragging the mouse across items you want to select. To select separated items, hold the Ctrl key down as you click the individual icons. If you want to select all the items in the directory, choose the Select All entry from the Tools menu (Tools | Select All), or choose Ctrl+a. You can then copy, move, or delete several files at once. To select items that have a certain pattern in their name, choose Select Items Matching from the Tools menu to open a search box from which you can enter the pattern (Ctrl+s). Use the asterisk (*) character to match partial patterns, as in ***let*** to match on all filenames with the pattern let in them. The pattern **my*** would match filenames beginning with the **my** pattern, and ***.png** would match on all PNG image files (the period indicates a filename extension).

Opening Applications and Files MIME Types

You can start any application in the file manager by double-clicking either the application or a data file used for that application. If you want to open the file with a specific application, you can right-click the file and select one of the Open With entries. One or more Open With entries will be displayed for default and possible application, such as Open With gedit for a text file. If the application you want is not listed, you can select Open With | Other Application to access a list of available applications. Drag-and-drop operations are also supported for applications. You can drag a data file to its associated application icon (say, on the desktop) The application then starts up using that data file.

To change or set the default application to use for a certain type of file, you open a file's Properties dialog and select the Open With tab. Here, you can choose the default application to use for that kind of file. Possible applications will be listed, organized as the default, recommended, related, and other categories. Click the one you want, and click the Set As Default button. Once you choose the default, it will appear in the Open With list for this file.

If you want to add an application to the Open With menu, click the Other Applications entry to list possible applications. Select the one you want, and click the Add button. If there is an application on the Open With tab that you do not want listed in the Open With menu items, right-click it and choose Forget Association.

File and Directory Properties

In a file's Properties dialog, you can view detailed information on a file and set options and permissions (see Figure 3-29) . A file's Properties dialog has three tabs: Basic, Permissions, and Open With. Folders will have an additional Local Network Share tab, instead of an Open With tab. The Basic tab shows detailed information, such as type, size, location, accessed, and date modified. The type is a MIME type, indicating the type of application associated with it. The file's icon is displayed at the top, with a text box showing the file's name. You can edit the filename in the Name text box. If you want to change the icon image used for the file or folder, click the icon image (next to the name) to open a Select Custom Icon dialog and browse for the one you want. The **/usr/share/pixmaps** directory holds the set of current default images, although you can select your own images (click the Computer entry to locate the **pixmaps** folder). In the **pixmaps** folder, click an image file to see its icon displayed in the right pane. Double-click to change the icon image.

The Permissions tab for files shows the read, write, and execute permissions for owner, group, and others, as set for this file. You can change any of the permissions here, provided the file belongs to you. You configure access for the owner, the group, and others, using drop-down menus. You can set owner permissions as Read Only or Read and Write. For group and others, you can also set the None option, denying access. Clicking the group name displays a menu listing different groups, allowing you to select one to change the file's group. If you want to execute this as an application, you check the "Allow executing file as program" entry. This has the effect of setting the execute permission.

The Open With tab for files lists all the applications associated with this kind of file. You can select the one you want to use as the default. This can be particularly useful for media files, for which you may prefer a specific player for a certain file or a particular image viewer for pictures.

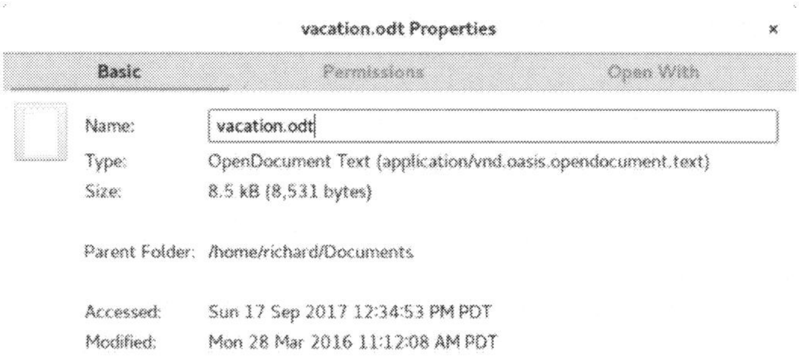

Figure 3-29: File properties

Certain kind of files will have additional tabs, providing information about the file. For example, an audio file will have an Audio tab listing the type of audio file and any other information, such as a song title or the compression method used. An image file will have an Image tab listing the resolution and type of image. A video file will contain an Audio/Video tab showing the type of video file, along with compression and resolution information.

The Permissions tab for folders operates much the same way, with Access menus for Owner, Group, and Others . The Access menu controls access to the folder with options for None, List Files Only, Access Files, and Create and Delete Files. These correspond to the read and execute permissions given to directories. To set the permissions for all the files in the folder accordingly (not just the folder), click the "Change Permissions for Enclosed Files" button to open a dialog where you can specify the owner, group, and others permissions for files and folders in the folder.

File Manager Preferences

You can set preferences for your file manager in the Preferences dialog, accessible by selecting the Preferences item in any file manager window's application menu (Files | Preferences).

The Views tab allows you to select how files are displayed by default, such as a list or icon view. You also can set default zoom levels for icon and list views.

Behavior lets you choose how to select files, manage the trash, and handle scripts.

Display lets you choose what information you want displayed in an icon caption, such as the size or date. You can also choose to have the list view display an expandable tree, showing files and subfolders within and expanded folder.

The List Columns tab lets you choose both the features to display in the detailed list and the order in which to display them. In addition to the already-selected name, size, date, and type, you can add permissions, group, MIME type, location, accessed, and owner.

The Preview tab lets you choose whether you want small thumbnail content displayed in the icons, such as the beginning text for text files.

File Manager Search

Two primary search tools are available for your GNOME desktop: the GNOME dash search and the GNOME file manager search. With GNOME file manager, you enter a pattern to search. You can further refine your search by specifying dates and file types. Click the Search button (looking glass icon) on the toolbar to open a Search box. Enter the pattern to search, then press Enter. The results are displayed (see Figure 3-30). Click the menu button to the right to add file-type (What) and date (When) search parameters. Selecting the When entry opens a dialog where you can specify the recency of the document's last use or modification, by day, week, month, or year. A calendar button to the right of the text box for the date opens a calendar to let you choose a specific date. The What entry displays a menu with different file categories such as music, Documents, folders, picture, and PDF.

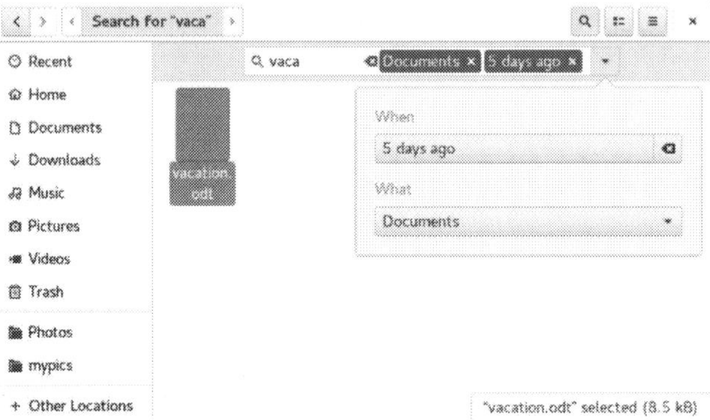

Figure 3-30: GNOME file manager search

GNOME Desktop FTP: Connect to Server

The easiest way to download files from an FTP site is to use the built-in FTP capabilities of the GNOME file manager, GNOME Files. The FTP operation has been seamlessly integrated into standard desktop file operations. Downloading files from an FTP site is as simple as dragging files from one folder window to another, where one of the folders happens to be located on a remote FTP site. Use the GNOME file manager (GNOME Files) to access a remote FTP site, listing files in the remote folder, just as local files are (see Figure 3-31). In a file manager's Location bar (**Ctrl-l** or "Enter Location" from the file manager Files applications menu), enter the FTP site's URL using the prefix **ftp://** and press ENTER. A dialog opens prompting you to specify how you want to connect. You can connect anonymously for a public FTP site, or connect as a user supplying your username and password (private site). You can also choose to remember the password.

Folders on the FTP site will be displayed, and you can drag files to a local folder to download them. You can navigate through the folders as you would with any file manager folder, opening folders or returning to the parent folder. To download a file, just drag it from the FTP window to a local folder window. To upload a file, drag it from your local folder to the window for the open FTP folder. Your file will be uploaded to that FTP site (if you have permission to do so). You can also delete files on the site’s folders if allowed.

You can also use the Connect to Server bar in the file manager (see Figure 3-32) to connect, which remembers your previous FTP connections. To access the Connect to Server bar, click on the "Connect to Server" entry in any file manager sidebar. The Connect to server bar is displayed at the bottom of the file manager window. It shows a text box for the server address, a menu button to display previous addresses, and a Connect button. Enter the server address. The address is remembered and added to the previous servers list. Then click the Connect button. A dialog opens letting you specify an Anonymous login or to enter a username and password. Click the Connect button to access the site.

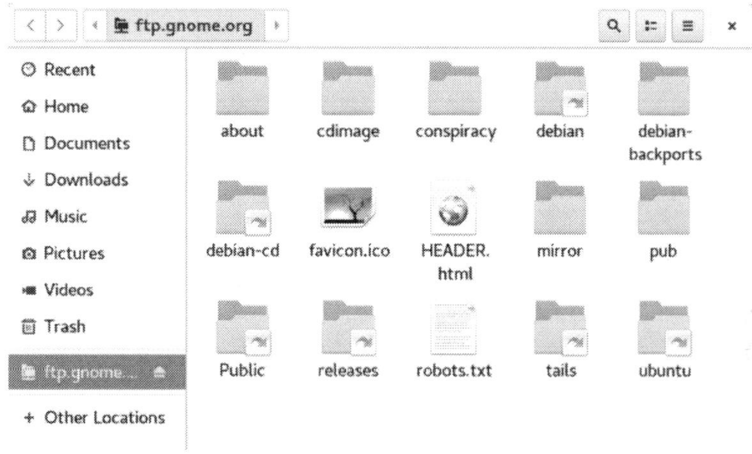

Figure 3-31: GNOME FTP access with the file manager

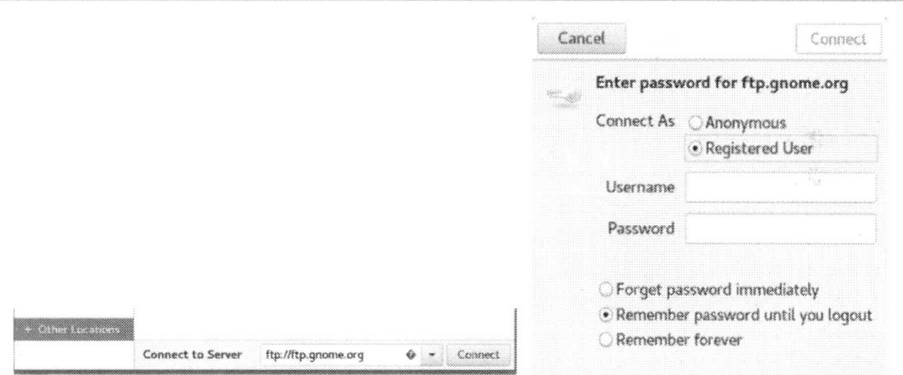

Figure 3-32: GNOME FTP access with Connect to Server and the file manager

The top directory of the remote FTP site will be displayed in a file manager window. Use the file manager to progress through the remote FTP site's directory tree until you find the file you want. Then, open another window for the local directory to which you want the remote files copied. In the window showing the FTP files, select those you want to download. Then click and drag those files to the window for the local folder. As files are downloaded, a dialog appears showing the progress.

The file manager window's sidebar will list an entry for the FTP site accessed. An eject button is shown to the right of the FTP site's name. To disconnect from the site, click this button. The FTP entry will disappear along with the FTP sites icons and file listings.

GNOME Classic

As an alternative to the GNOME desktop, you can use the GNOME Classic desktop, which uses an interface similar to GNOME2 (see Figure 3-33). When you log in, you can choose GNOME Classic from the session menu (gear button next to the Sign In button). GNOME Classic displays a top panel with Applications and Places menus. The System Status Area menu is the same. Also, application menus continue to be displayed on the top panel, after the Places menu. The bottom panel has a taskbar and a workspace switcher menu. Icons for applications can be displayed on the desktop, as are the home folder and trash. The Applications menu is organized into submenus by category, such as Graphics, Office, and Sound & Video. The Activities overview entry at the bottom of the Applications menu starts up the GNOME 3 overview interface.

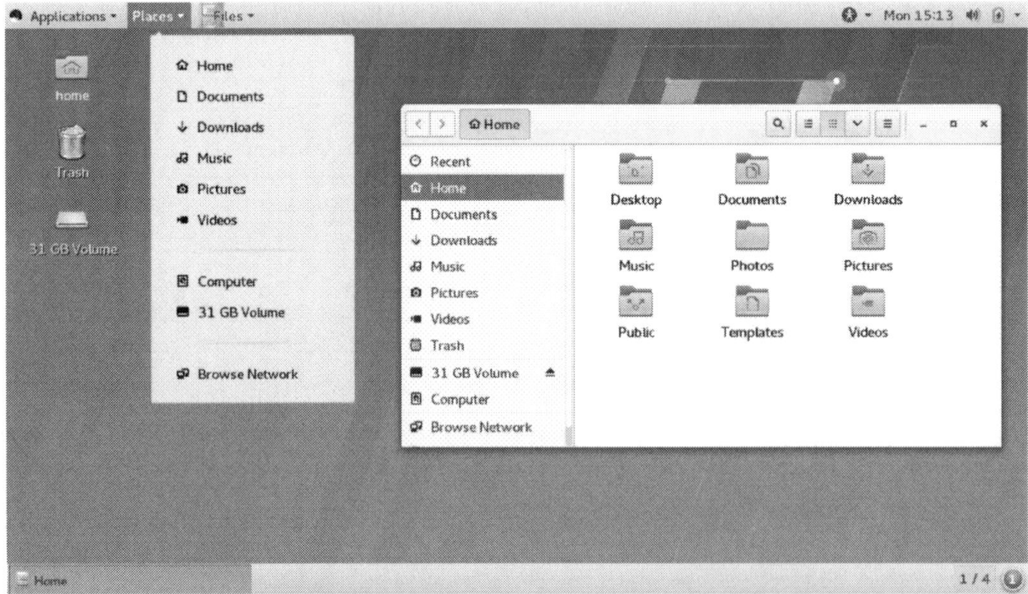

Figure 3-33: GNOME Classic

4. The K Desktop Environment: KDE

KDE 4

Configuration and Administration Access with KDE

Plasma: desktop, panel, and plasmoids

KDE Help Center

KDE Desktop

KDE Panel

KWin Desktop Effects

KDE File Manager: Dolphin

KDE Configuration: KDE Settings

The K Desktop Environment (KDE) is a desktop that includes the standard desktop features, such as a window manager and a file manager, as well as an extensive set of applications that cover most Linux tasks. The KDE desktop is developed and distributed by the KDE Project, which is a large open group of hundreds of programmers. KDE is open source software provided under a GNU Public License and is available free of charge along with its source code. KDE development is managed by the KDE Core Team.

Numerous applications written specifically for KDE are accessible from the desktop. These include editors, photo and paint image applications, sound and video players, and office applications. Such applications usually have the letter *K* as part of their name, such as KMail. On a system administration level, KDE provides several tools for managing your system, such as the kde-config-cron task scheduler and the KDE system monitor. KDE applications also feature a built-in Help application. KDE includes support for the office application suite Calligra, which includes a presentation application, a spreadsheet, an illustrator, and a word processor, among other components (EPEL repository).

Web Site	Description
`http://www.kde.org`	KDE Website
`http://www.kde-apps.org`	KDE software repository
`http://techbase.kde.org`	KDE developer site
`http://www.qt.io`	Site for Qt libraries
`http://www.calligra.org`	Calligra Suite
`http://www.kde-look.org`	KDE desktop themes, select KDE entry
http://`lists.kde.org`	KDE mailing lists

Table 4- 1: KDE Web Sites

KDE, initiated by Matthias Ettrich in October 1996, is designed to run on any Unix implementation, including Linux, Solaris, HP-UX, and FreeBSD. The official KDE website is **https://www.kde.org**, which provides news updates, download links, and documentation. Detailed documentation for the KDE desktop and its applications is available at **https://docs.kde.org**. Several KDE mailing lists are available for users and developers, including announcements, administration, and other topics. A great many additional applications are currently available for KDE at **http://www.kde-apps.org**. Development support and documentation can be obtained at the KDE Techbase site at **http://techbase.kde.org**. Various KDE websites are listed in Table 4-1. KDE uses as its library of GUI tools the Qt library, currently developed and supported by the QT company, owned by Digia (**https://www.qt.io**). It provides the Qt libraries as Open Source software that is freely distributable, though a commercial license is also available.

When you install the RHEL7 workstation, you have the option to install either GNOME or KDE. You can also install KDE as an additional desktop to an RHEL7 workstation that has already installed GNOME. To install KDE as an additional desktop to GNOME, you use a **yum** command with the **group** option in a terminal window. For the group name, you can use variations of KDE such as KDE, kde-desktop, and "KDE Desktop." See Chapter 8.3 "Working with Package Groups" in the System Administration Guide for details on using the group option. First login as the root user with the **su** command.

```
$ su
# yum group install kde-desktop
```

KDE 4

The KDE 4 release is a major reworking of the KDE desktop. KDE 4.14 is included with RHEL7. Check the KDE sites for detailed information on KDE 4, including the visual guide.

```
http://kde.org/announcements/4.0/
```

For features added with KDE 4.5, check:

```
http://kde.org/announcements/4.5/
```

For features added with KDE 4.14, check:

```
http://kde.org/announcements/4.14/
```

Every aspect of KDE has been reworked with KDE4. There is a new file manager, desktop, theme, panel, and configuration interface. KDE Window manager supports advanced compositing effects and Oxygen artwork for user interface theme, icons, and windows.

The primary component of the KDE4 desktop is the Plasma desktop shell. Plasma has containments and plasmoids. Plasmoids operate similarly to applets, small applications running on the desktop or panel. Plasmoids operate within containments. On KDE4, there are two Plasma containments, the panel and the desktop. In this sense, the desktop and the panel are features of an underlying Plasma operation. They are not separate programs. Each has their own set of plasmoids.

Each containment has a toolbox for configuration. The desktop has a toolbox at the top right corner, and panels will have a toolbox on the right side. The panel toolbox includes configuration tools for sizing and positioning the panel. KDE also supports Activities, multiple plasma desktop containments, each with their own set of plasmoids.

Plasma: desktop, panel, and plasmoids (applets)

The primary component of the KDE4 desktop is the Plasma desktop shell. Plasma has containments and plasmoids. Plasmoids are applets that operate within containments. On KDE4 there are two types of Plasma containments, the panel and the desktop. The desktop and the panel are now features of an underlying Plasma operation. They are not separate programs. Both can have plasmoids (applets). For each type, you can have several instances. You can have many different desktop containments, each with its own set of plasmoids installed. You could also have several panels on your desktop, using different collections of plasmoids.

Each containment will have its own toolbox for configuration. The desktop has a toolbox at the top right corner, and panels have a toolbox on the right side. The panel toolbox features configuration tools for sizing and positioning the panel. Keyboard shortcuts are supported for many tasks (see Table 4-2). The desktop toolbox menu has an entry for Shortcut Setting, which opens a Configure Shortcuts dialog where you can configure keys.

RHEL7 KDE 4 also supports the Zoom User Interface (ZUI) with its support for multiple plasma desktop containments (Activities). The desktop toolbox menu shows the Zoom Out entry to access the ZUI interface: adding, removing, and selecting desktop containments.

Keys	Description
ALT-F1	Kickoff menu
ALT-F2	Krunner, command execution, entry can be any search string for a relevant operation, including bookmarks and contacts, not just applications.
UP/DOWN ARROWS	Move among entries in menus, including Kickoff and menus
LEFT/RIGHT ARROWS	Move to submenus menus, including Kickoff and Quick Access submenus menus
ENTER	Select a menu entry, including a Kickoff or QuickAccess
PAGE UP, PAGE DOWN	Scroll up and down fast
ALT-F4	Close current window
ALT-F3	Window menu for current window
CTRL-ALT-F6	Command Line Interface
CTRL-ALT-F8	Return to desktop from command line interface

Table 4-2: KDE Desktop Keyboard Shortcuts

The KDE Help Center

The KDE Help Center provides a browser-like interface for accessing and displaying both KDE Help files and Linux Man and info files (see Figure 4-1). You can start the Help Center by selecting its entry at the bottom of the Kickoff Applications menu. The Help window displays a sidebar that holds three tabs, one listing contents, one providing a glossary, and one for search options (boolean operators, scope, and number of results). The main pane displays currently selected documents. A help tree on the contents tab in the sidebar lets you choose the kind of Help documents you want to access. Here you can choose KDE manuals, Man pages (UNIX manual pages), or info documents (Browse info Pages), or even application manuals (Application Manuals). Online Help provides links to KDE Websites such as the KDE user forum and the KDE tech base sites. The KDE Documentation entry has the KDE System Documentation index, which provides basic configuration and overviews of different topics such as networking, media management, and Office and Productivity. Click the "Table of Contents" button to open a listing of all KDE help documents, which you can browse through and click on to open.

A navigation toolbar enables you to move through previously viewed documents. KDE Help documents contain links you can click to access other documents. The Back and Forward commands move you through the list of previously viewed documents. The KDE Help system provides an effective search tool for searching for patterns in Help documents, including Man and info pages. Click the Find button on the toolbar or choose the Find entry from the Edit menu, to open a search box at the bottom of the Help window where you can enter a pattern to search on the current open help document. The Options menu lets you refine your search with regular expressions, case sensitive queries, and whole words-only matches.

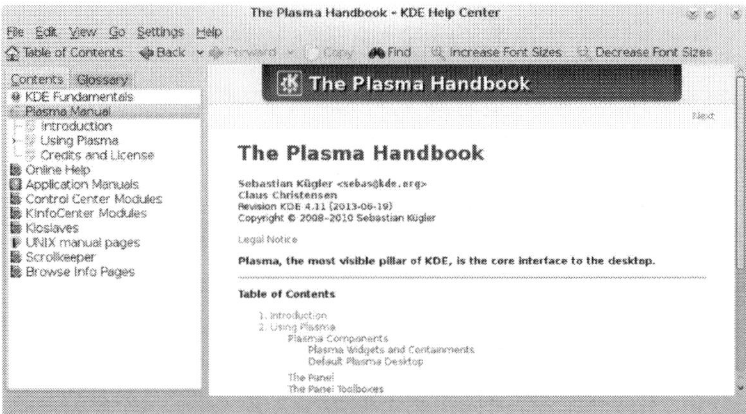

Figure 4-1: KDE Help Center

The KDE Desktop

One of KDE's aims is to provide users with a consistently integrated desktop (see Figure 4-2). KDE provides its own window manager (KWM), file manager (Dolphin), program manager, and desktop and panel (Plasma).

You can run any other X Window System–compliant application, such as Firefox, in KDE, as well as any GNOME application. In turn, you can also run any KDE application, including the Dolphin file manager in GNOME. The KDE 4 desktop features the Plasma desktop shell with panel, menu, and widgets, and adds dashboard and activities functions (see Figure 4-2). As noted, keyboard shortcuts are provided for many desktop operations, as well as plasmoid tasks (see Table 4-3).

The desktop supports drag-and-drop and copy-and-paste operations. With the copy-and-paste operation, you can copy text from one application to another. You can even copy and paste from a Konsole terminal window.

You can place access to any folders on the desktop by simply dragging their icons from a file manager window to the desktop. A small menu will appear with options for Folder or Icon. To create just an icon on the desktop, select the Icon entry. The Folder option sets up a Folder plasmoid for the folder. Items in the folder are displayed within the folder plasmoid as a menu from which you can make a selection.

To configure your desktop, you use the Workspace Appearance and Behavior tools in the Settings window (Favorites | Settings). These include Workspace Appearance, Desktop Effects, Desktop Search, Default Applications, Accessibility, and Window Behavior. Workspace Appearance lets you choose themes and window decorations. Desktop Effects is where you can set window effects and animation. Windows Behavior controls window display features like taskbars, virtual desktops, title bar actions, and screen edge actions. Fonts and Icons are set in the Applications Appearance dialog located in the Common Appearance and Behavior section.

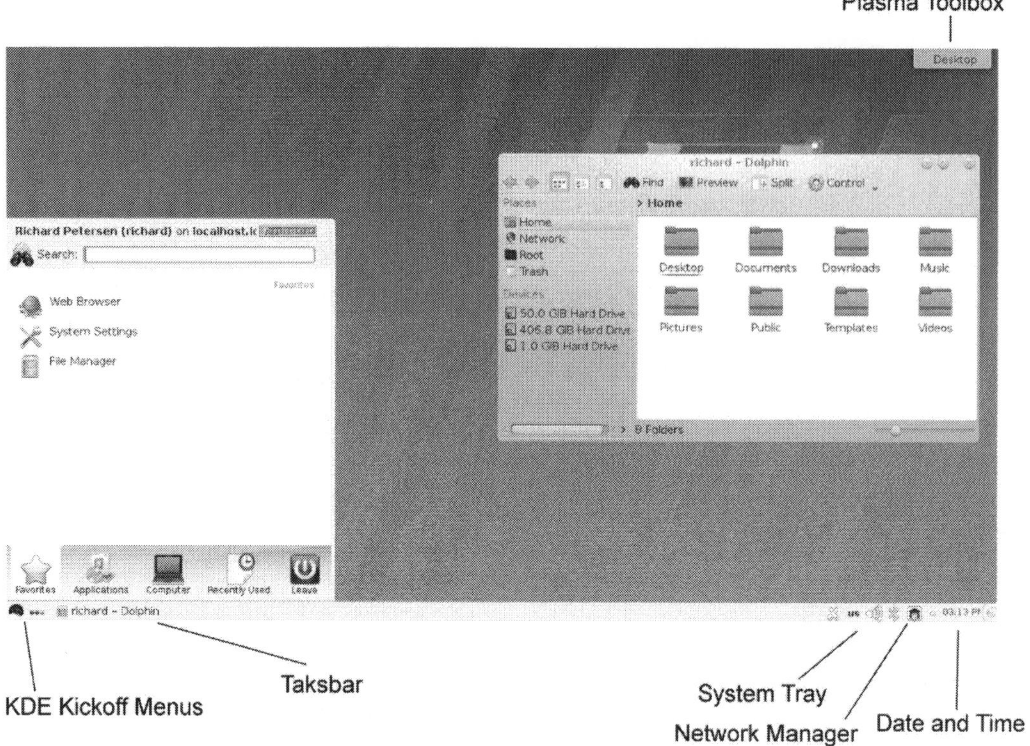

Figure 4-2: The KDE desktop

Key desktop tasks can be accessed directly from the desktop menu. Right-click anywhere on the desktop background to display the menu (see Figure 4-3). There are entries to open a terminal window, run a command, lock the screen, and to leave. The Leave entry displays a dialog with entries to Logout, Turn Off, or Restart the computer. There are also the desktop specific options like adding widgets, add a panel, and configuring the desktop (Default Desktop Settings). The Desktop Settings dialog displays an Appearance tab that lets you configure the wallpaper (background), theme, and the activity name and type.

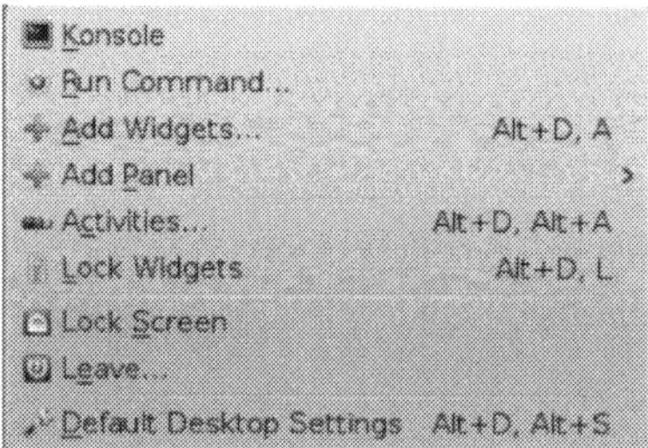

Figure 4-3: The KDE desktop menu

Keys	Description
Alt-F1	Kickoff menu
Alt-F2	Krunner, command execution, entry can be any search string for a relevant operation, including bookmarks and contacts, not just applications.
up/down arrows	Move among entries in menus, including Kickoff and menus
left/right arrows	Move to submenus menus, including Kickoff and Quick Access submenus menus
ENTER	Select a menu entry, including a Kickoff or QuickAccess
PageUp, PageDown	Scroll up fast
Alt-F4	Close current window
Alt-F3	Window menu for current window
Ctrl-Alt -F6	Command Line Interface
Ctrl-Alt -F8	Return to desktop from command line interface
Ctrl-r	Remove a selected plasmoid
Ctrl-s	Open a selected plasmoid configuration settings
Ctrl-a	Open the Add Widgets window to add a plasmoid to the desktop
Ctrl-l	Lock your widgets to prevent removal, adding new ones or changing settings
Alt-Tab	Cover Switch or Box Switch for open windows
Ctrl-F8	Desktop Grid
Ctrl-F9	Present Windows Current Desktop
Ctrl-F10	Present Windows All Desktops
Ctrl-F11	Desktop Cube for switching desktops

Table 4-3: Desktop, Plasma, and KWin Keyboard Shortcuts

Desktop Backgrounds (Wallpaper)

The background (wallpaper) is set from the desktop menu directly, not from the System Settings dialog. Right-click on the desktop background to display the desktop menu and then select Default Desktop Settings to open the Desktop Settings dialog (see Figure 4-4). You can also select Default Desktop Settings from the activities menu in the upper right corner of the desktop. The background is called wallpaper in KDE and can be changed in the View tab. You can select other wallpaper from the wallpaper listing or select your own image by clicking the Open button. You can add more wallpaper by clicking the Get New Wallpaper button to open a "Get Hot New Stuff" dialog, which lists and downloads wallpaper posted on the **www.kde-look.org** site (see Figure 4-5). Each wallpaper entry shows an image, description, and rating. Buttons at the upper right of the dialog let you view the entries in details (list) or icon mode. Click the Install button to download the wallpaper and add it to your Desktop Setting's View tab. The wallpaper is downloaded, and the Install button changes to Uninstall. You can refine the wallpaper listing by size (category), newest, rating, and popularity (most downloads). To remove a wallpaper, you can select installed wallpapers on the "Get Hot New Stuff" dialog to find the entry quickly. You can also search by pattern for a wallpaper, such as baseball or sky.

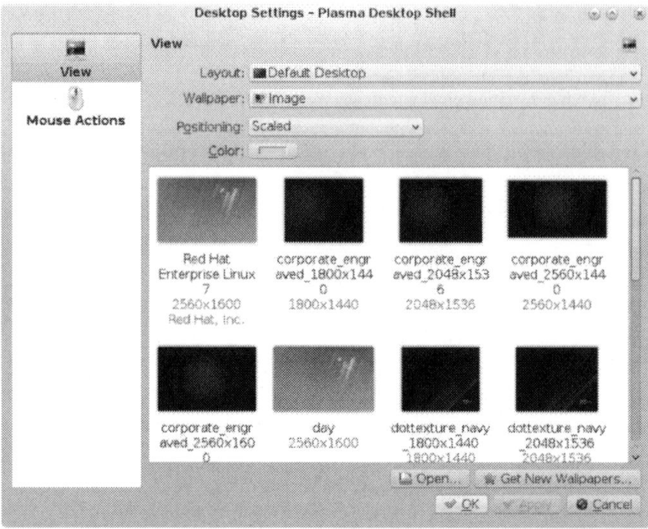

Figure 4-4: Default Desktop Settings, wallpaper

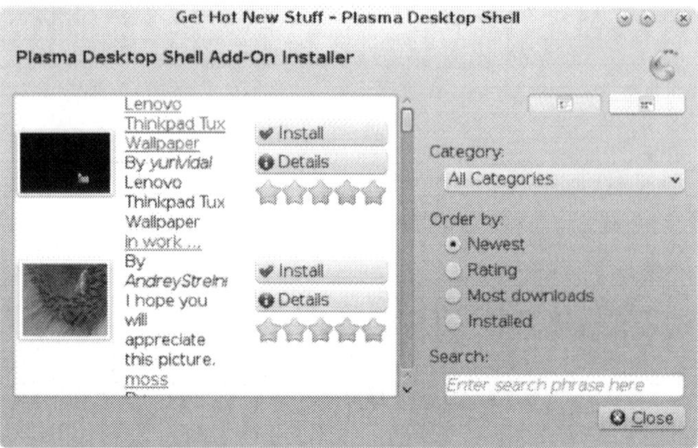

Figure 4-5: Default Desktop Settings, Get New Wallpapers

Themes

For your desktop, you can also select a variety of different themes, icons, and window decorations. A theme changes the entire look and feel of your desktop, affecting the appearance of desktop elements, such as scrollbars, buttons, and icons. Themes and window decorations are provided for workspaces. Access the System Settings dialog from the KDE Favorites menu or the

Applications | Settings menu. On the System Settings dialog, click the Workspace Appearance icon in the "Workspace Appearance and Behavior" section. The Workspace Appearance dialog lets you choose window decorations, cursor themes, desktop themes, and splash screen (startup) themes. The Desktop Themes tab lists installed themes, letting you choose the one you want. Click the Get New Themes button to open a Get Hot New Stuff dialog, listing desktop themes from **http://www.kde-look.org** (see Figure 4-6). Click a theme's Install button to download and install the theme. From the Window Decorations tab, you can select window decoration themes. Click the Get New Decorations button to download new decorations. The Splash Screen tab lists installed splash screen themes to choose. Click the Get New Themes button to install new ones.

Icons styles are chosen using Applications Appearance in System Settings dialog's "Common Appearance and Behavior section", System Settings | Applications Appearance. From the Icons tab, you can select an icon set or click the Get New Themes button to download new sets.

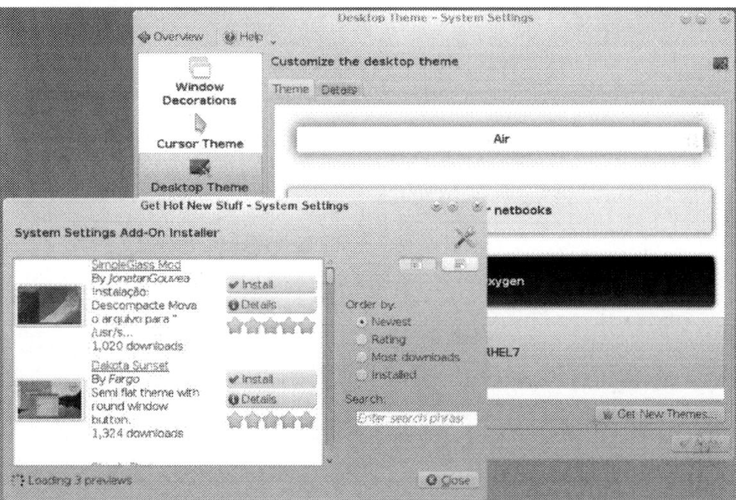

Figure 4- 6: System Settings | Workspace Appearance | Desktop Theme, Get New Themes

Leave KDE

To leave KDE, you first click the Leave tab on the KDE Kickoff menu (see Figure 4-7). Here you will find options to log out, lock, switch user, sleep, shutdown, and restart. There are Session and System sections. The Session section has entries for Logout, Lock, and Switch User. The System section features system-wide operations, including Shutdown, Restart, and Sleep. When you select a leave entry, a dialog for that action appears on the desktop, which you then click. The Shutdown entry will display a Shutdown dialog.

You can also right-click anywhere on the desktop and select the Leave entry from the pop-up menu. If you leave any KDE applications or windows open when you quit, they are restored automatically when you start up again. If you just want to lock your desktop, you can select the Lock entry on the Kickoff Leave menu, and your screensaver will appear. To access a locked desktop, click on the screen and a box appears prompting you for your login password. When you enter the password, your desktop re-appears.

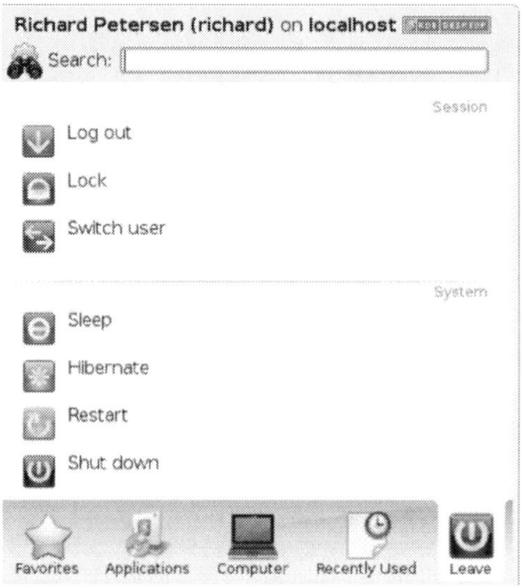

Figure 4-7: The Kickoff menu Leave

KDE Kickoff menus

The KickOff application launcher (see Figure 4-8) organizes menu entries into tabs that are accessed by icons at the bottom of the Kickoff menu. There are tabs for Favorites, Applications, Computer, Recently Used, and Leave. You can add an application to the Favorites tab by right-clicking on the application's Kickoff entry and selecting Add to Favorites. To remove an application from the Favorites menu, right-click on it and select Remove from Favorites. The Applications tab shows application categories. Click the Computer tab to open a window with all your fixed and removable storage. The Recently Used tab shows recently accessed documents and applications. KickOff also provides a Search box where you can search for a particular application instead of paging through menus. As you move through sub-tabs, they are listed at the top of the Kickoff menu, below the search box, allowing you to move back to a previous tab quickly. Click on a sub-tab name to move directly to that menu.

To configure KDE, you use the KDE System Settings referenced by the System Settings item in the Favorites, Computer, or Applications | Settings tabs.

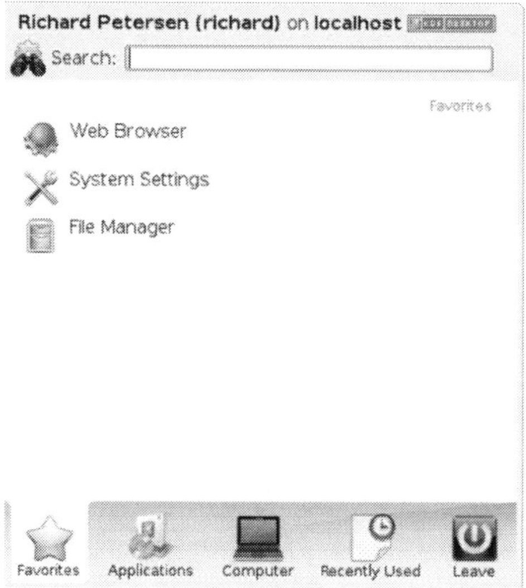

Figure 4-8: The Kickoff menu Favorites

The Computer menu has Applications and Places sections (see Figure 4-9). The Applications section has an entry for System Settings. The Places section is similar to the Places menu in GNOME, with entries for your home folder, root folder, and the trash, as well as removable devices like USB drives and DVD/CD discs. The root folder is the same as the system folder on GNOME, the top level folder in the Linux file system.

Figure 4-9: The Kickoff menu Computer

The Applications menu has most of the same entries as those found on GNOME (see Figure 4-10). You can find entries for categories such as Internet, Graphics, and Office. These menus list both GNOME and KDE applications you can use, should GNOME applications be installed. Some entries will invoke the KDE version of a tool, like the Terminal entry in the System menu, which will invoke the KDE terminal window, Konsole. There is no Preferences menu.

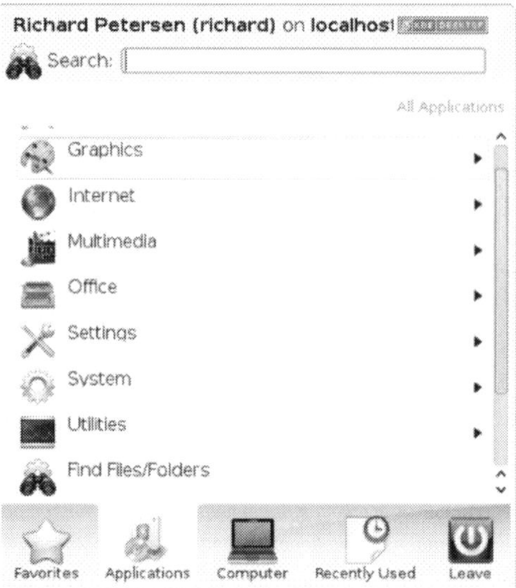

Figure 4-10: The Kickoff menu Applications

Krunner

For fast access to applications, bookmarks, contacts, and other desktop items, you can use Krunner. The Krunner plasmoid operates as a search tool for applications and other items. To find an application, enter a search pattern, and a listing of matching applications is displayed. Click on an application entry to start the application. For applications where you know the name, part of the name, or just its basic topic, Krunner is a very fast way to access the application. To start Krunner, press Alt-F2, or right-click on the desktop to display the desktop menu and select "Run Command." Enter the pattern for the application you want to search for and press enter. The pattern "edit" would display your text editors (see Figure 4-11). Entering the pattern "office" displays entries for all the LibreOffice applications, if installed.

Clicking the wrench button opens tabs for configuring Krunner. The User Interface tab provides position and style options. You can search by command or task. The plugins tab lists the plugins for searching applications, widgets, and bookmarks, as well as providing capabilities such a running shell commands and opening files. The question mark opens a dialog listing search features such a searching for devices, applications, commands, and widgets. You can even search websites you have visited.

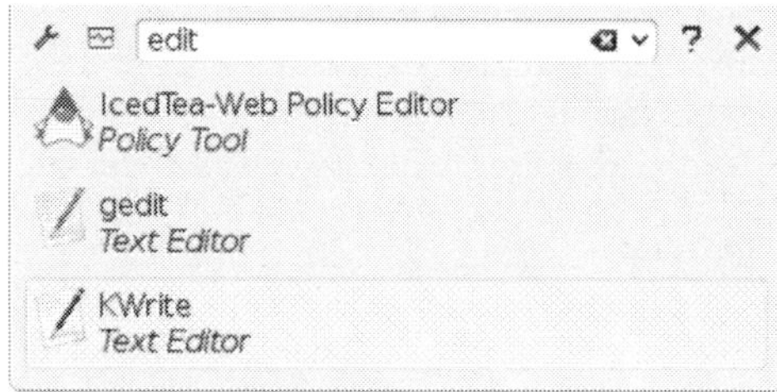

Figure 4-11: Krunner application search

Removable Devices: Device Notifier

Installed on the system tray to the right is the Device Notifier. When you insert a removable device like a CD/DVD disc or a USB drive, the New Device Notifier briefly displays a dialog showing all your removable devices, including the new one. You can click on the New Device Notifier any time to display this dialog. Figure 4-12 shows the New Device Notifier displayed on the panel and its panel icon. The New Device Notifier is displayed if at least one removable device is attached.

Removable devices are not displayed as icons on your desktop. Instead, to open the devices, you use the New Device Notifier. Click on the Device Notifier icon in the panel to open its dialog, as shown here.

The device is unmounted initially with an unmount button displayed. Click on this button to mount the device. An eject button is then displayed which you can later use to unmount and eject the device. Opening the device with an application by clicking on its menu entry will mount the device automatically. Clicking on the eject button for a DVD/CD disc will physically eject it. For a USB drive, the drive will be unmounted and prepared for removal. You can then safely remove the USB drive.

To open a device, click on its entry in the New Device Notifier, like one for your DVD/CD disc or your USB drive. If there is more than one application that can use this device, a menu is displayed showing the options (see Figure 4-12). For a CD/DVD disc, you have the options to open the disc with the file manager, copy it with the K3b application, or download photos from it with Gwenview (should there be photos). You can open a USB drive with either Gwenview (photos) or the file manager, showing its contents. As you install more applications that can use a device, the applications will be added to the menu.

Removable media are also displayed on the File manager window's side pane. You can choose to eject removable media from the file manager instead of from the Device Notifier by right-clicking on the removable media entry and select "Safely remove" from the popup menu.

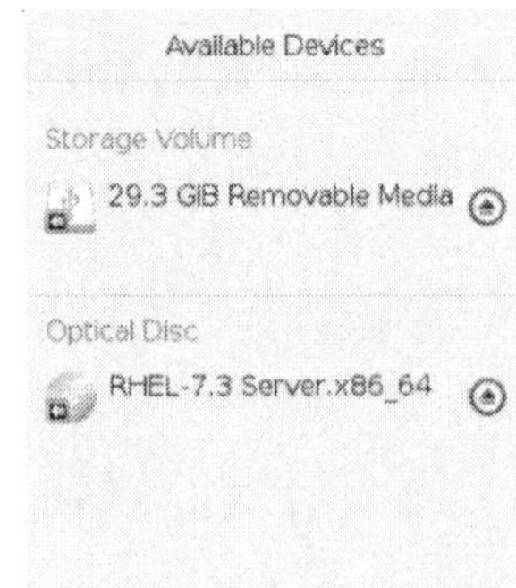

Figure 4-12: Device Notifier and its panel plasmoid icon

Desktop Plasmoids

The KDE desktop features the Plasma desktop that supports plasmoids. Plasmoids are integrated into the desktop on the same level as windows and icons. Just as a desktop can display windows, it can also display plasmoids (see Figure 4-13). Plasmoids can take on desktop operations, running essential operations, even replacing, to a limited extent, the need for file manager windows. The dashboard tool can hide all other desktop items, showing just the plasmoids.

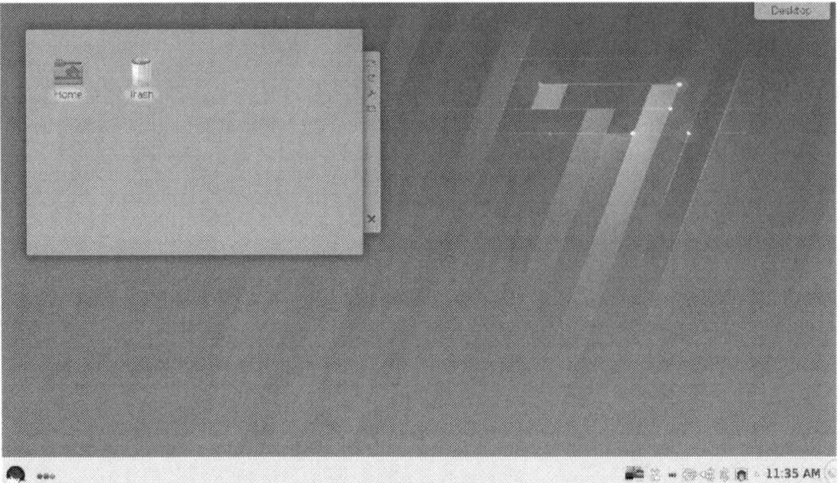

Figure 4-13: KDE screen with Folder plasmoid set to show the Desktop folder

Managing desktop plasmoids

When you pass your mouse over a plasmoid, its sidebar is displayed with buttons for resizing, refreshing, settings, and closing the plasmoid (see Figure 4-14). Click and drag the resize button to change the plasmoid size. Clicking the settings button (wrench icon) opens that plasmoid's settings dialog (see Figure 4-14).

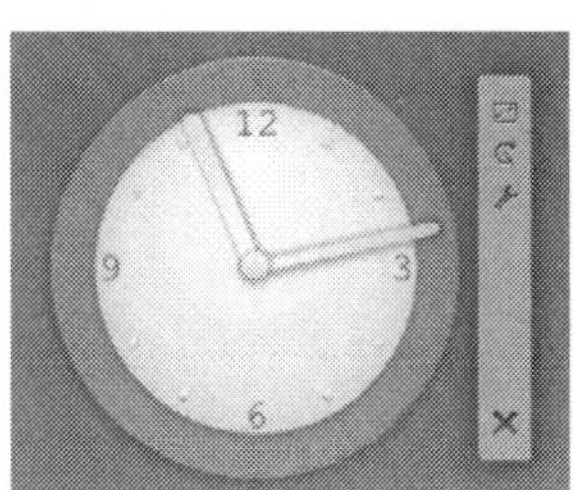

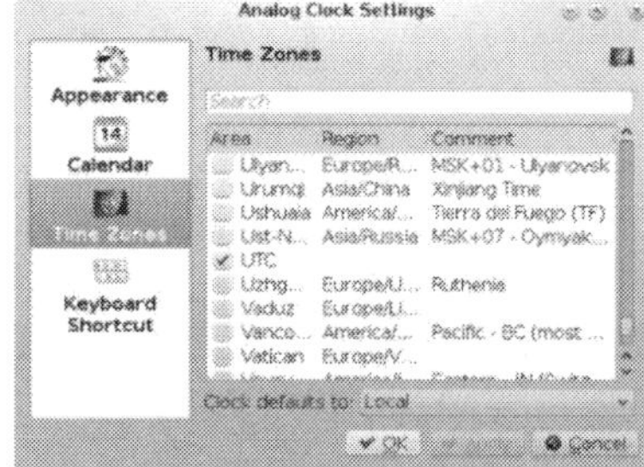

Figure 4-14: Clock Plasmoid with task sidebar and configuration dialog

To add a widget (plasmoid) to the desktop, right-click anywhere on the desktop and select Add Widgets from the pop-up menu. This opens the Add Widgets dialog across the bottom of the desktop that lists widgets you can add (see Figure 4-15). Clicking on the Categories button opens a pop-up menu with different widget categories like Date and Time, Online Services, and Graphics. Use the slider and arrow button below the widgets to move through them. Double-click or drag a widget to add it to the desktop. You can enter a pattern to search for a widget using the search box located to the left of the categories button (top left).

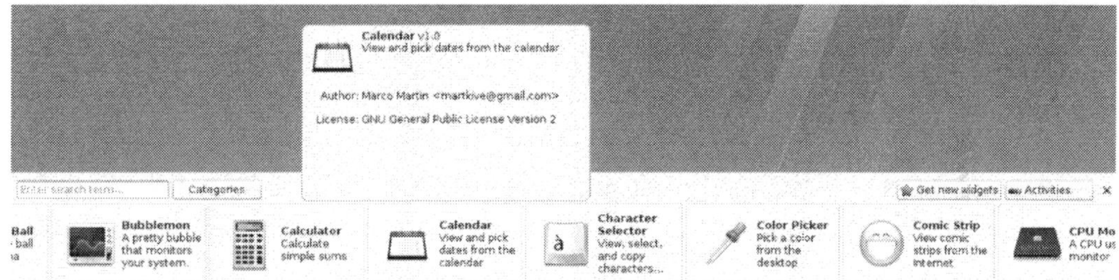

Figure 4-15: Adding a plasmoid: Add Widgets

Figure 4-16 shows the folder view, digital clock, leave a note, calculator, and hardware temperature plasmoids. When you add a Folder View plasmoid, it will default to your home folder.

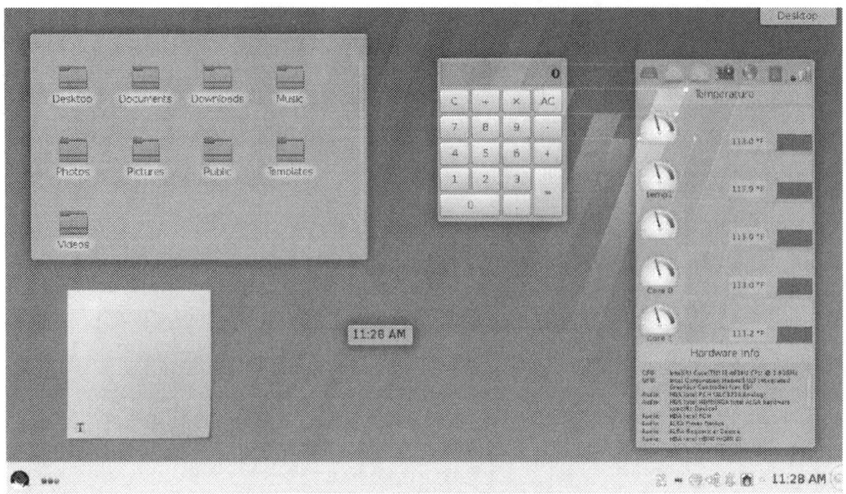

Figure 4-16: Folder View, Calculator, Digital clock, Notes, and System Monitor plasmoids:

Folder and Icon Plasmoids

You can place access to any directories on the desktop (desktop activity) by simply dragging their icons from a file manager window to the desktop. A small menu will appear that includes options for the Icon, Shelf, and Folder View plasmoids. The Folder View option sets up a Folder View plasmoid for the folder showing icons for subfolders and files (see Figure 4-17). The Icon entry creates a desktop icon. The Shelf entry creates a menu of files and folders.

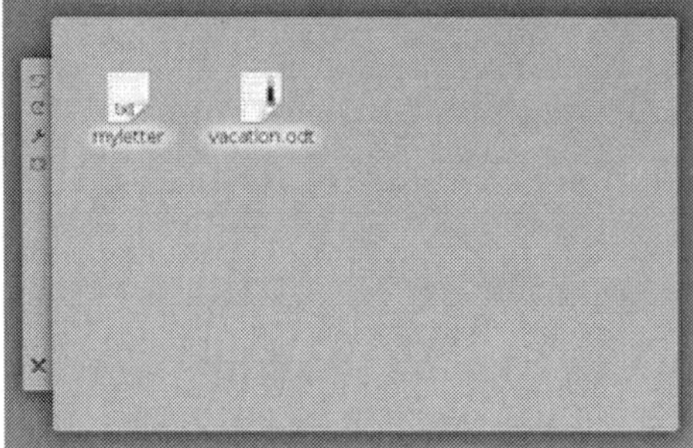

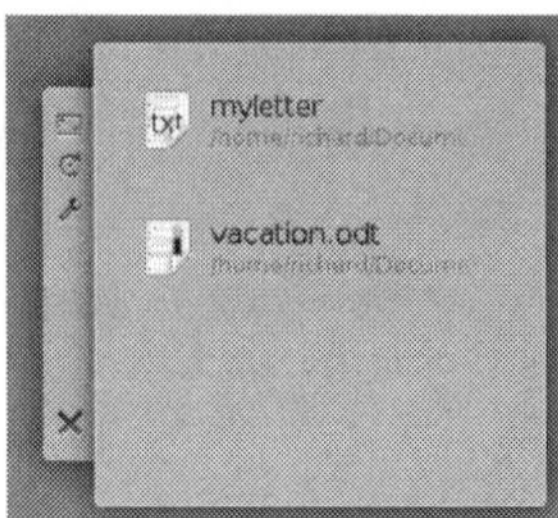

Figure 4-17: Icon, Folder View, and Shelf plasmoids for a folder dragged to the desktop

For any Folder View plasmoid, you can use that plasmoid's settings dialog to change the folder it references. A Folder View plasmoid has options for showing the desktop folder (Location tab), a folder on your Places list, or a specific folder. You can also specify a title (Display tab). You could easily create a Folder View plasmoid for your home folder (Show a place entry in the Location tab).

The settings dialog for the Icon plasmoid shows the configuration dialog for the original folder, with general, permissions, preview, and share tabs.

Dashboard

The dashboard is designed to display plasmoids (applets) only. It hides all windows and icons, showing all your desktop plasmoids. To start the dashboard, press Ctrl-F12. You can also add a "Show Widget Dashboard" widget to your panel or desktop. When in use, the screen will display the Widget Dashboard label at the top (see Figure 4-18). To return to the desktop press Ctrl-F12 again or click the close button on the Widget Dashboard label at the top of the screen. Also, any plasmoid that interacts directly with the desktop, like the opening a folder in the folder plasmoid or clicking a desktop icon, will return you to the desktop automatically.

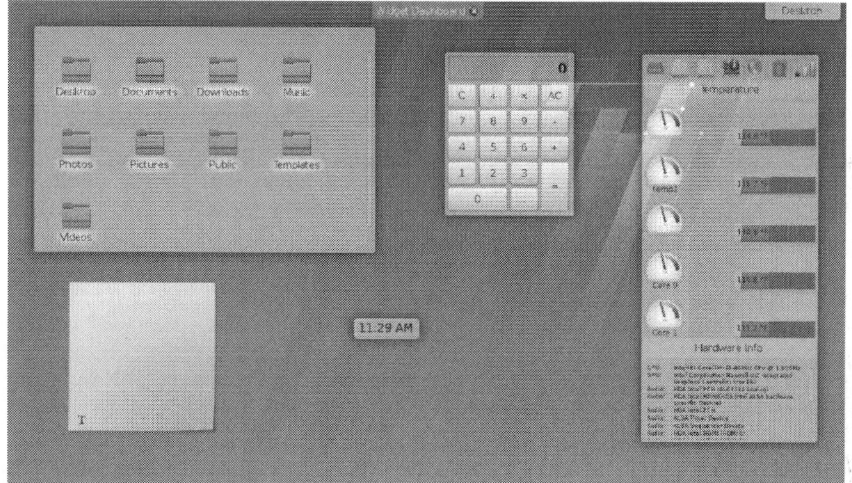

Figure 4-18: The Dashboard (Ctrl-F12, or Show Widget Dashboard)

Activities

KDE is designed to support multiple activities. An activity is not the same as virtual desktop. Virtual desktops affect windows, displaying a different set of windows on each desktop. An activity has its own set of plasmoids (widgets). Technically, each activity is a Plasma containment that has its own collection of plasmoids. You can switch to a different activity (containment) and display a different collection of plasmoids on your desktop.

An activity is a way to set up a set of widgets (plasmoids) for a certain task. You could have one activity for office work, another for news, and yet another for media. Each activity could have its own set of appropriate widgets, like clock, calculator, dictionary, and document folder for an office activity. A media activity might have a Now Playing plasmoid for audio, Picture Frame for photos, and News for the latest news. You can also choose a certain type of activity based on activity templates. KDE provides the desktop, folder, search and launch, photo layout, and newspaper templates, though you can download more. The desktop template provides a desktop interface, the folder is a full-screen view of one folder, "search and launch" displays application and task icons, and the newspaper layout template displays widgets in columns. Your original desktop is already configured as a desktop activity based on the desktop template.

Multiple activities are managed using the Activities toolbar, which is accessed through the Activities entry on the desktop toolbox menu or the Show Activities Manager button on the lower left side of the panel. Both are shown here.

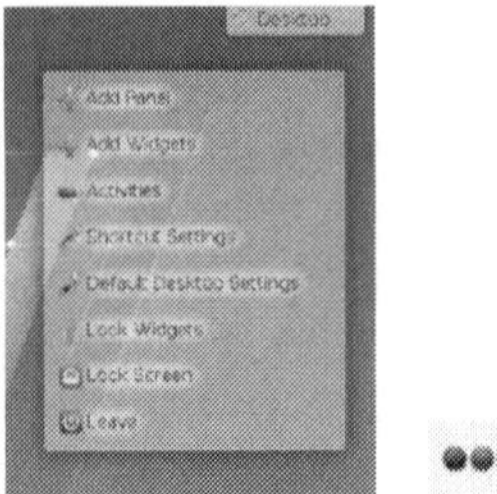

Files and folders can be attached to an activity, displaying them only on that activity. Right-click and choose the Activities submenu to choose an activity for that file or folder. Windows are set by default to display on the activity they are opened on. The setting is configured in the Window Behavior dialog (Workspace Appearance and Behavior section of the System Settings dialog). On the Task Switcher tab, the Filter windows by section has an Activities section checked and Current activity selected.

To add an activity, click the "Activities" entry in the toolbox or desktop menus, or click the Activities button on the left side of the panel. An activities toolbar is displayed listing your activities (see Figure 4-19). An activity icon for your desktop will already be displayed. Click the "Create activity" button to add a new activity. From the pop-up menu, you can choose an empty desktop, a clone of the current activity, or choose from templates of different kinds of activities: Desktop Icons, Grid Desktop, Grouping Desktop, Newspaper Layout, Folder View, Photos Activity, and Search and Launch. The "Get New Templates" entry lets you download additional templates. A New Activity icon then appears on the activity toolbar (see Figure 4-22). To switch to another activity, click its icon.

Figure 4-19: Activity toolbar and icons

Initially, an activity's name is New Activity. To change the name click on the configuration button (wrench icon) to the right of the icon as shown here.

The activity editing mode displays the icon and the name and lets you edit the activity name, with Apply and Cancel buttons to the right (see Figure 4-20). To change the icon image, click on the icon to open a "Icon Source" dialog where you can choose an image. Once you have made your changes, click the Apply button.

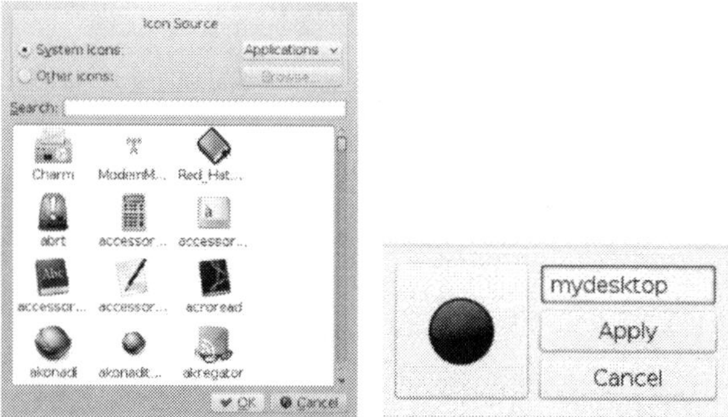

Figure 4-20: Changing an activity

To add widgets (plasmoids) to an activity, first click the activity to make it the current activity, and then click the Add Widgets button to display the Widgets toolbar. Widgets you add are placed in the current activity.

To disable (stop) an activity, click its stop button to the right of its activity icon (a small square next to the wrench icon). A Delete button is then displayed to the right, and a Play button appears in the center of the icon as shown here. To re-activate the activity, click the play button.

To remove an activity, first stop it, and then click Delete button to the right. A remove dialog appears with a Remove button, which you can click to remove the activity.

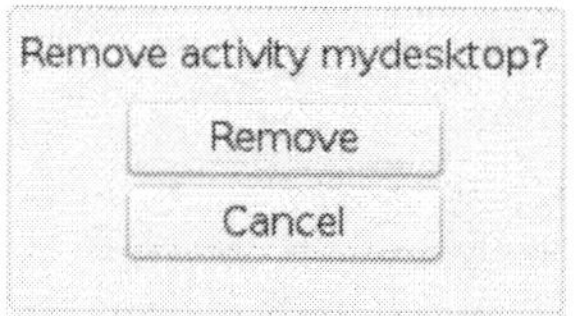

To switch from one activity to another, first, display the Activities toolbar by choosing Activities from the desktop toolbox menu (right-click on desktop) or the Activates button on the panel. Then click on the activity icon you want (see Figure 4-21). The new Activity becomes your screen (see Figure 4-22). To change to another activity, open the Activities toolbar again, and click the activity icon you want.

Figure 4-21: Activity icons

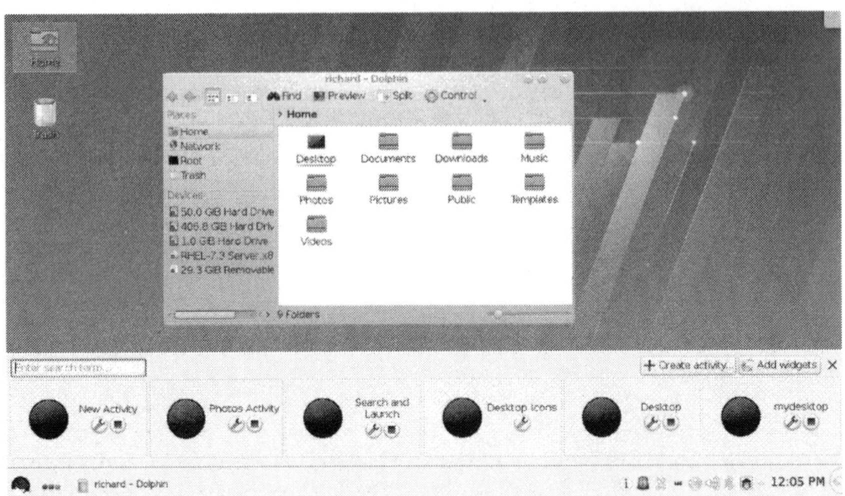

Figure 4-22: Activity toolbar and screen of selected activity

A Folder View activity functions as a file manager window, displaying a particular folder on the desktop. To configure a Folder activity, right-click to display the desktop menu and choose Folder Settings to display the Desktop Settings dialog. Icons are added for Location, Display, and Filter. On the Location tab, you can display the desktop folder, a place like the Home folder, or a folder of your choosing. On the Display tab, you set display features such as arrangement, sorting, and size. The Filter tab lets you display files of certain types or name patterns.

A Search and Launch activity sets up an interface containing icons for tasks and application groups such as Bookmarks, Contacts, Multimedia Graphics, Office, and Internet (see Figure 4-23). To configure a Search and Launch activity, right-click to display the desktop menu and choose Configure Search and Launch to display the Desktop Settings dialog. The Desktop Settings dialog has additional Search plugins and Main Menu tabs. On the Main Menu, you can add or remove application group and task icons.

A Newspaper Layout activity simply displays widgets in two columns. To configure a Newspaper activity, right-click to display the desktop menu and choose Configure Page to display the Desktop Settings dialog.

To move easily between activities, you can add the Activity bar widget, either to the panel or to the desktop. On the panel, the Activity bar displays buttons for each activity. Click to move to a different activity. On the desktop, the Activity bar displays a dialog with an arrow button for moving from one activity to another.

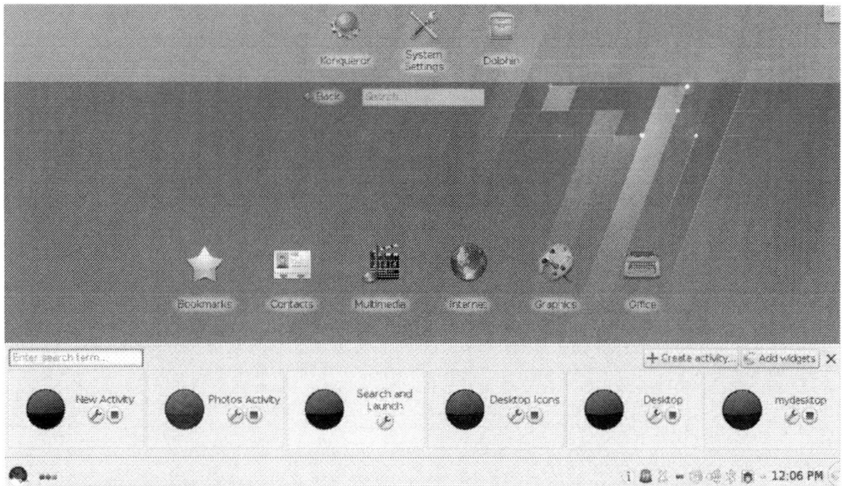

Figure 4-23: Activity search and launch

KDE Windows

A KDE window has the same functionality you find in other window managers and desktops. You can re-size the window by clicking and dragging any of its corners or sides. A click-and-drag operation on a side extends the window in that dimension, whereas a corner extends both height and width at the same time. The top of the window has a title bar showing the name of the window, the program name in the case of applications, and the current folder name for the file manager window. The active window has the title bar highlighted. To move the window, click the title bar and drag it where you want. Right-clicking the window title bar displays a pop-up menu with entries for window operations, such as closing or resizing the window. The "More Actions" entry displays additional options such as Fullscreen and Shade. The Shade option will roll up the window to the title bar. Within the window, menus, icons, and toolbars for the particular application are displayed.

You can configure the appearance and operation of a window by selecting the More Actions | Window Window Manager entry from the Window menu (right-click the title bar). Here you can set the focus policy, such as a mouse-click on the window or just passing the mouse over it (Focus), the titlebar configuration (Actions | Titlebar Actions), button and key operations (Actions | Window Actions), and how the window is displayed when moving it (Moving). All these features can also be configured using the System Setting's Window Behavior dialog's Window Behavior tab in the Workspace Appearance and Behavior section.

Opened windows are shown as buttons on the KDE taskbar located on the panel. The taskbar shows buttons for the different programs you are running or windows you have open. This is essentially a docking mechanism that lets you change to a window or application by clicking its button. When you minimize a window, it is reduced to its taskbar button. You can then restore the window by clicking its taskbar button.

To the right of the title bar are three small buttons for minimizing, maximizing, or closing the window (down, up, and x symbols). You can switch to a window at any time by clicking its taskbar button. You can also maximize a window by dragging it to the top edge of the screen.

From the keyboard, you can use the ALT-TAB key combination to display a list of currently open windows. Holding down the ALT key and sequentially pressing TAB moves you through the list.

A window can be displayed as a tile on one-half of the screen. Another tile can be set up for a different window on the other side of the screen, allowing you to display two windows side by side on the full screen (see Figure 4-24). You can tile a window by dragging it to the side of the screen (over the side edge near the middle of the window). A tile outline will appear. Add a second tile by moving a window to the other side edge. You can add more windows to a tile by moving them to that edge. Clicking on a window's taskbar button will display it on its tile.

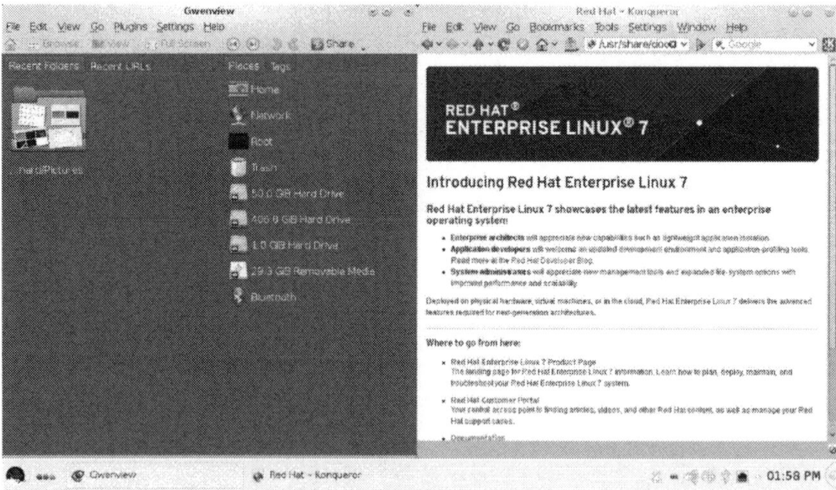

Figure 4-24: Window tiles

Applications

You can start an application in KDE in several ways. If an entry for it is in the Kickoff Applications menu, you can select that entry to start the application. You can right-click on any application entry in the Applications menu to display a pop-up menu with "Add to Panel" and "Add to Desktop" entries. Select either to add a shortcut icon for the application to the desktop or the panel. You can then start an application by single-clicking its desktop or panel icon.

An application icon on the desktop is implemented as a desktop plasmoid. Passing the mouse over the application icon on the desktop displays a sidebar with the wrench icon for the icon settings. This opens a Setting window with tabs for general, permissions, application, and preview. On the general tab, you can select an icon image and set the displayed name. The application tab references the actual application program file with possible options. Permissions set standard access permissions by the owner, group, or others.

You can also run an application by right-clicking on the desktop and selecting the Run Command (or press ALT-F2) which will display the Krunner tool consisting of a box to enter a single command. Previous commands can be accessed from a pop-up menu. You need only enter a pattern to search for the application. Results will be displayed in the Krunner window. Choose the one you want.

Virtual Desktops: Pager

KDE supports virtual desktops, extending the desktop area on which you can work. You could have a Web browser running on one desktop and be using a text editor in another. KDE can support up to 16 virtual desktops. To use virtual desktops, add the Pager widget to your panel. You can use the panel editor (toolbox, right side) to move it to the location you want on the panel. The Pager represents your virtual desktops as miniature screens showing small squares for each desktop. It works much like the GNOME Workspace selector. Initially, there is only one virtual desktop, but you can add more, each represented by a square in the pager widget. To move from one desktop to another, click the square for the destination desktop. The selected desktop will be highlighted. You can also use the CTRL key in combination with a function key to switch to a specific desktop: for example, CTRL-F1 switches to the first desktop and CTRL-F3 to the third desktop.

Just passing your mouse over a desktop square on the pager will open a message displaying the desktop number along with a list of the windows open on that desktop.

If you want to move a window to a different desktop, first open the window's menu by right-clicking the window's title bar. Then select the "Move To Desktop" entry, which lists the available desktops. Choose the one you want.

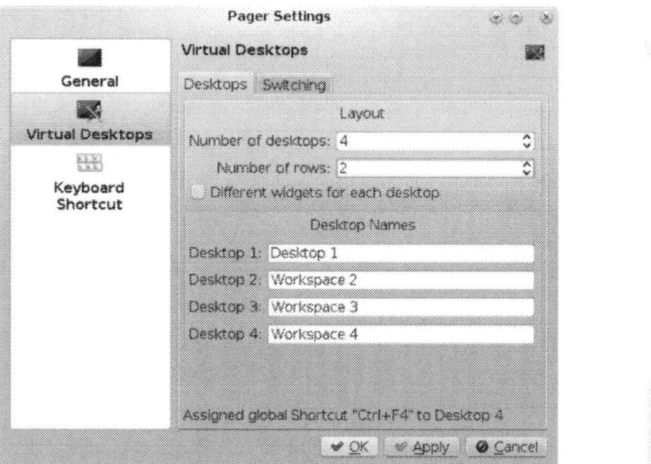

Figure 4-25: Virtual desktop configuration (Workspace Behavior) and Pager widget icon:

You can also configure KDE so that if you move the mouse over the edge of a desktop screen, it automatically moves to the adjoining desktop. You need to imagine the desktops arranged next to each. You enable this feature by enabling the "Switch desktop on edge" feature in the

System Settings | Workspace Behavior | Screen Edges tab. This feature will also allow you to move windows over the edge to an adjoining desktop.

To change the number of virtual desktops, right-click on the Desktop Pager on the panel, select the Pager Settings entry in the pop-up menu to open the Pager Settings window, and choose the Virtual Desktops tab, which displays entries for your active desktops. You can also access the Virtual Desktops tab from System Settings | Workspace Behavior in the "Workspace Appearance and Behavior" section (see Figure 4-25). The text box labeled "Number of Desktops" controls the number of virtual desktops. Use the arrows or enter a number to change the number of desktops.

You can change any of the desktop names by clicking an active name and entering a new one. Choosing to display four desktops in two rows shows then stacked as shown here.

The "Number of rows" entry lets you decide on the number of rows to display. Choosing just one row would display the desktops side by side as shown here.

KDE Panel

The KDE panel, located at the bottom of the screen, provides access to most KDE functions (see Figure 4-26). The panel is a specially configured Plasma containment, just as the desktop is a Plasma containment. The panel includes icons for menus, windows, specific programs, and virtual desktops. These are plasmoids (widgets) that are configured for use on the panel. At the left end of the panel is a button for the Kickoff menu. On RHEL this is the Red Hat icon.

To add an application to the panel, right-click on its entry in the Kickoff menu to open a pop-up menu and select Add to Panel.

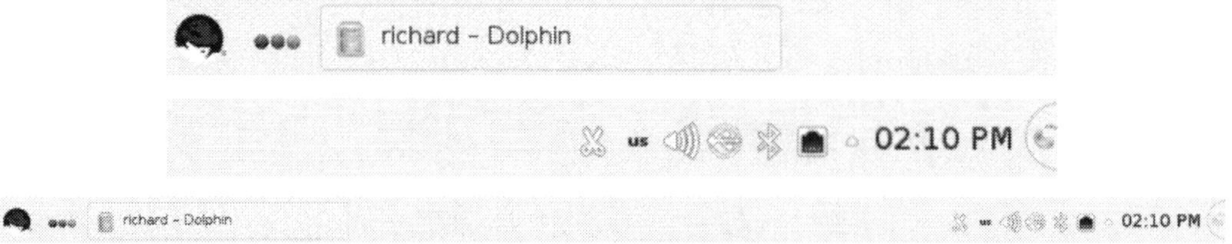

Figure 4-26: KDE panel

To add a widget to the panel, right-click on any panel widget on the panel to open a pop-up menu, and select Panel Options submenu from which you can select the Add Widgets entry. This opens the Add Widgets window that lists widgets you can add to the panel (see Figure 4-27). Use the scrollbar at the bottom to move through the list of widgets. Currently, installed widgets have a green checkmark. As you pass the mouse over a widget, a dialog opens displaying information about it. To add a widget, double-click it or drag it to the right side of the panel. To later remove a widget from the panel, you use the panel toolbox as described in the next section.

Click the Categories button located at the top left to display a menu of different widget categories like Date and Time, Online Services, and Graphics. You can also see currently running widgets. Click the "Get New Widgets" button at the right to open a "Get Hot New Stuff" dialog where you can download new widgets. The Activities button simply switches you to the Activities toolbar.

Note: To open the Add Widgets dialog, you can click on the panel toolbox at the right side of the panel and click the Add widgets button

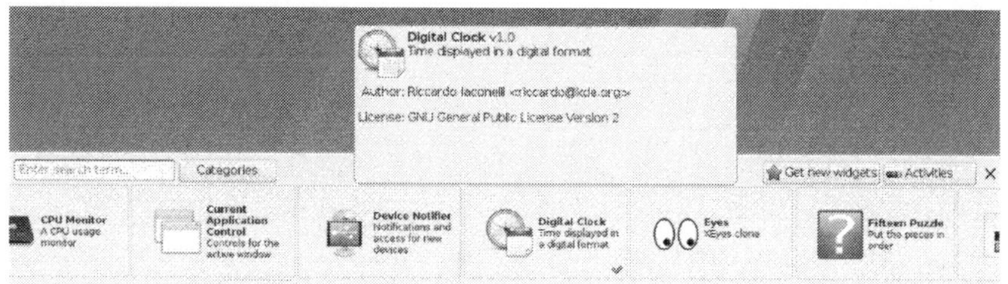

Figure 4-27: KDE Add Widgets for panel

The Plasma panel supports several kinds of Windows and Tasks widgets, including the taskbar (Task Manager) and system tray. To the right of the system tray is the digital clock. To the left are usually added widgets. As shown here, from left to right: show dashboard, show desktop, the system tray (clipboard, keyboard configuration, device notifier, sound volume, Bluetooth, network manager, the pop-up menu for additional system tray icons), and the digital clock.

The system tray holds widgets for desktop operations like update notifier, the clipboard (klipper), power (battery) detection, device notifier, sound settings (kmix), and network manager, as shown here. The right side of the system tray has an arrow for a pop-up menu, as shown here.

The pop-up menu (arrow icon) on the right side of the system tray display widgets that may not be in use, as shown here.

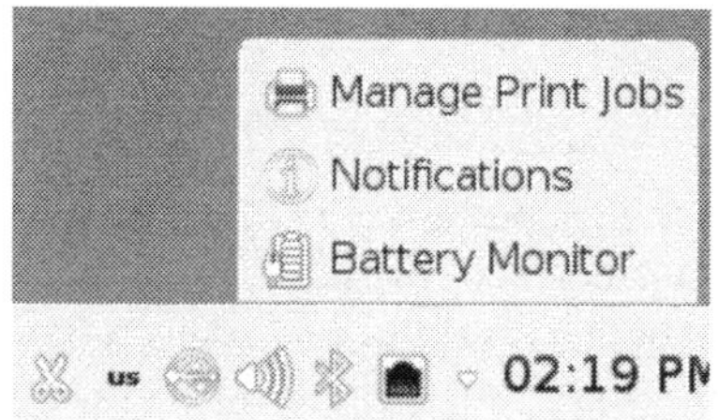

To configure the system tray, right-click on the system tray menu (arrow icon) and choose System Tray Settings to open the system tray configuration dialog at the Display tab, where you can decide what items to display or entries to make visible or remove (see Figure 4-28). In the

"Extra Items" list you can check items that you also want displayed on the system tray, such as Manage Print Jobs and Weather Forecast. When you click the Apply button, the items are displayed. Items not in use are in the menu. The Entries tab shows how selected items are to be displayed (auto, hidden, or always visible).

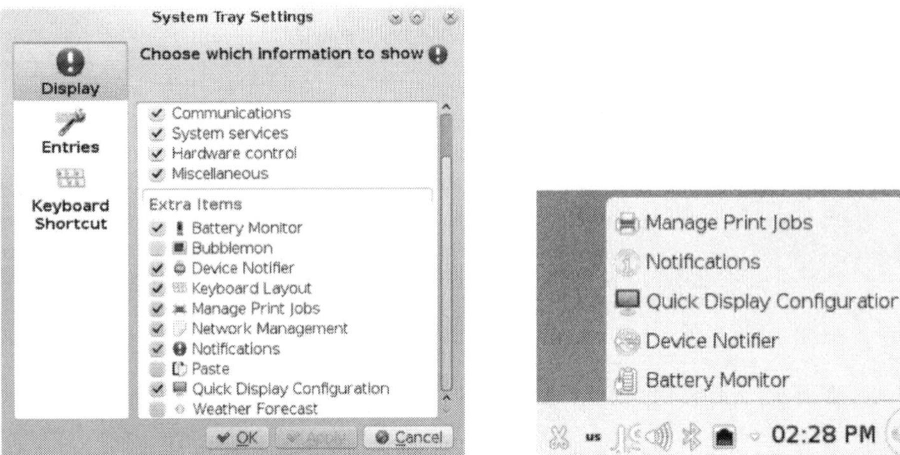

Figure 4-28: KDE panel system tray configuration

KDE Panel Configuration

To configure a panel, changing its position, size, and display features, you use the panel's toolbox, located at the right side of the panel. You also use the panel toolbox to remove widgets. Click on the toolbox icon at the right edge of the panel to open an additional configuration panel with buttons for adding widgets, moving the panel, changing its size and position, and a More Settings menu for setting visibility and alignment features. Figure 4-29 shows the configuration panel as it will appear on your desktop. Figure 4-30 provides a more detailed description, including the More Settings menu entries.

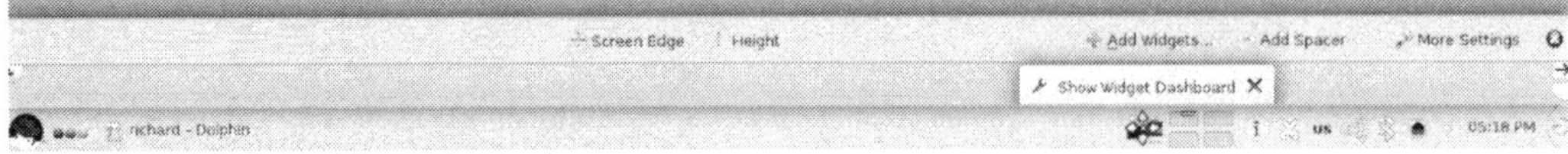

Figure 4-29: KDE Panel Configuration

With the configuration panel activated, the panel itself becomes editable. This means that you can now move or remove widgets on the panel. To move a widget, click on it to overlay a movement icon, letting you then click and drag the plasmoid icon to a different location on the panel. To remove a widget, move your mouse over the widget on the panel to display a small dialog with the widget name and an x button. To remove it, click the x button. There is also wrench button displayed to the left on that small dialog which you can use to display the widget's configuration dialog.

The lower part of the configuration panel is used for panel position settings. On the left side is a slider for positioning the panel on the edge of the screen. On the right side are two sliders for the minimum (bottom) and maximum (top) size of the panel.

The top part of the panel has buttons for changing the location and the size of the panel. The Screen Edge button lets you move the panel to another side of the screen (left, right, top, bottom). Just click and drag. The height button lets you change the panel size, larger or smaller.

The Add Widgets button will open the Add Widgets dialog, letting you add new plasmoids (widgets) to the panel.

The Add Spacer button adds a spacer to separate widgets. Right-click on the spacer to set a flexible size option or to remove the spacer.

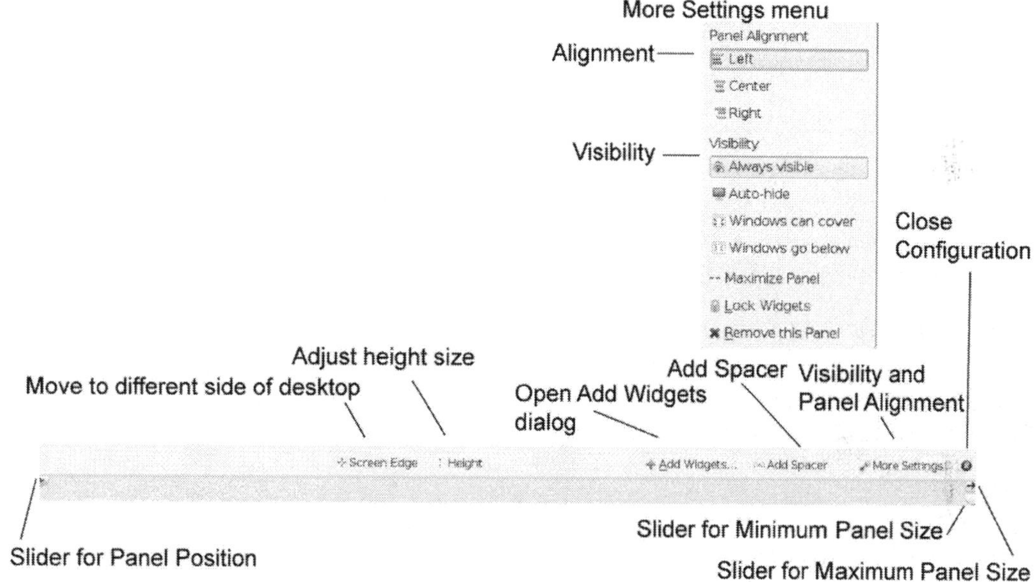

Figure 4-30: KDE Panel Configuration details and display features

The More Setting menu lets you set Visibility and Alignment features. You can choose an AutoHide setting that will hide the panel until you move the mouse to its location. The "Windows can cover" option lets a window overlap the panel. For smaller panels, you can align to the right, left, or center of the screen edge. The More Settings menu also has an entry to remove the panel. Use this entry to delete a panel you no longer want.

When you are finished with the configuration, click the red x icon the upper right side.

KWin - Desktop Effects

KWin desktop effects can be enabled on the System Settings Desktop Effects dialog in the Workspace Appearance and Behavior section (System Settings | Desktop Effects). The switching effects for desktops can be selected on the General tab. For desktop switching, you can choose

Slide, Fade Desktop, and Desktop Cube Animation. The All Effects tab will list all available effects (see Figure 4-31).

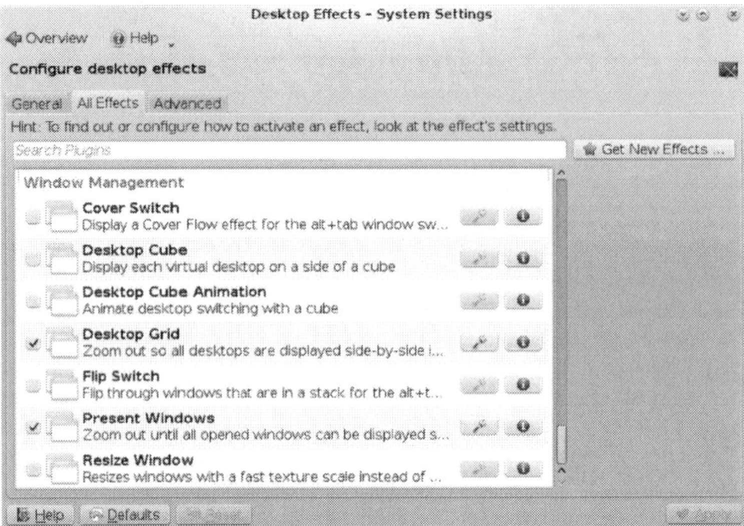

Figure 4-31: Desktop Effects selection and configuration

On the All Effects tab, several window effects are selected by default. A checkmark is placed next to active effects. If there is wrench icon in the effects entry, it means the effect can be configured. Click on the icon to open its configuration dialog. For several effects, you use certain keys to start them. The more commonly used effects are Taskbar Thumbnail, Grid, Present Windows, and Desktop Cube. The keys for these effects are listed in Table 4-4.

Key	Operation
ALT-TAB	Cover Switch or Box Switch for open windows
CTRL-F8	Desktop Grid (use mouse to select a desktop)
CTRL-F9	Present Windows Current Desktop
CTRL-F10	Present Windows All Desktops
CTRL-F11	Desktop Cube (use mouse or arrow keys to move, ESC to exit)

Table 4-4: KWin desktop effects keyboard shortcuts

Window switching using Alt-Tab is controlled on the Windows Behavior dialog's Task Switcher tab, not from Desktop Effects. From the Visualization menu, you can choose effects like Cover Switch, Flip Switch, Grid, and Thumbnails.

Most effects will occur automatically. The Taskbar Thumbnails effect displays a live thumbnail of a window on the taskbar as your mouse passes over it, showing its name, desktop, and image (see Figure 4-32).

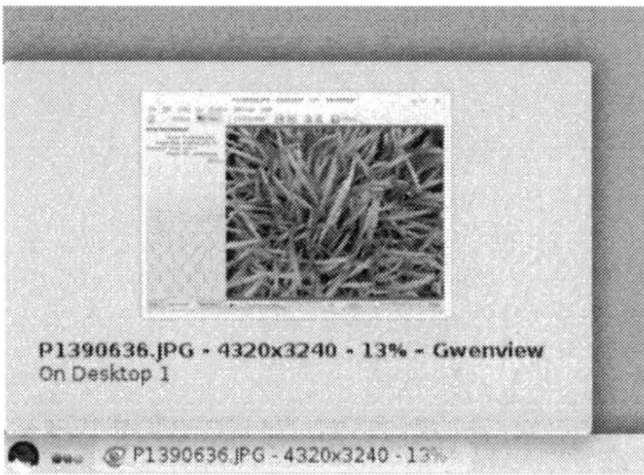

Figure 4-32: Taskbar Thumbnails effect, showing thumbnails of minimized applications

On the Windows Behavior dialog's Task Switcher tab, from the Visualization menu, you can choose the window switching effect you want to use from the drop-down menu. These include Thumbnails, Grid, Small Icons, Cover Switch, and Flip Switch, as well as smaller listings such as informative, compact, text icons, and small icons. The Alt-Tab keys implement the effect you have chosen. Continually pressing the Tab key while holding down the Alt key moves you through the windows. Box Switch displays windows in a boxed dialog, whereas Cover Switch arranges unselected windows stacked to the sides, and Flip Switch arranges the windows to one side (see Figure 4-33 and 4-34).

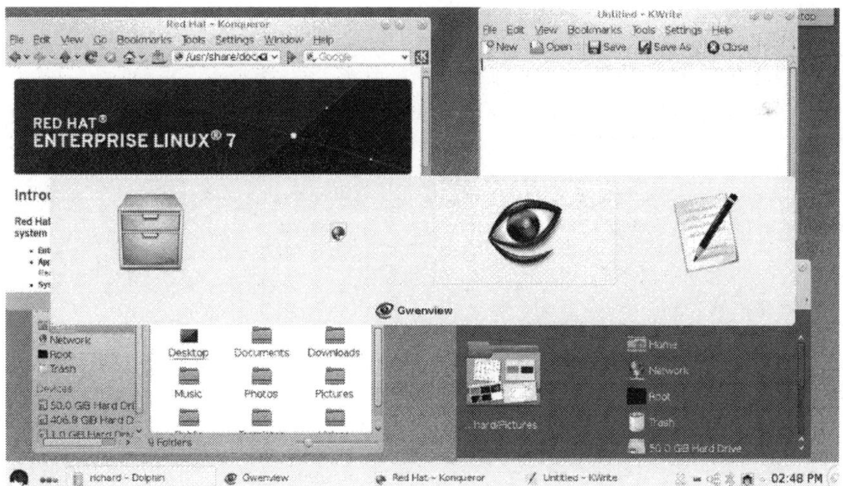

Figure 4-33: Box Switch - Alt-Tab

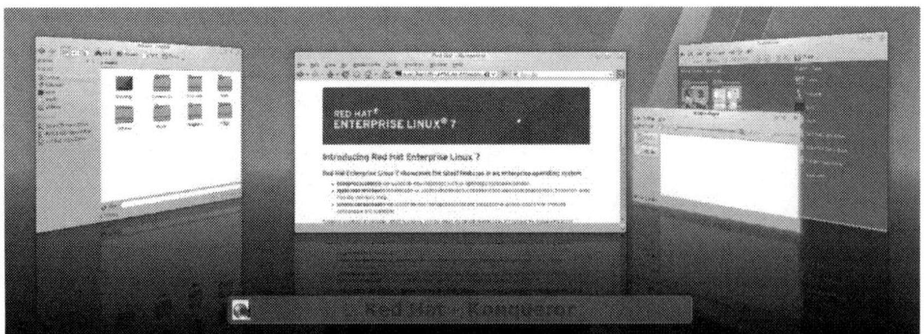

Figure 4-34: Cover Switch - Alt-Tab (Box Switch disabled)

The Present Windows effect displays images of the open windows on your screen with the selected one highlighted (see Figure 4-35). You can use your mouse to select another. This provides an easy way to browse your open windows. You can also use Ctrl-F9 to display windows on your current virtual desktop statically and use the arrow key to move between them. Use Ctrl-F10 to display all your open windows across all your desktops. Press the ESC key to return to the desktop.

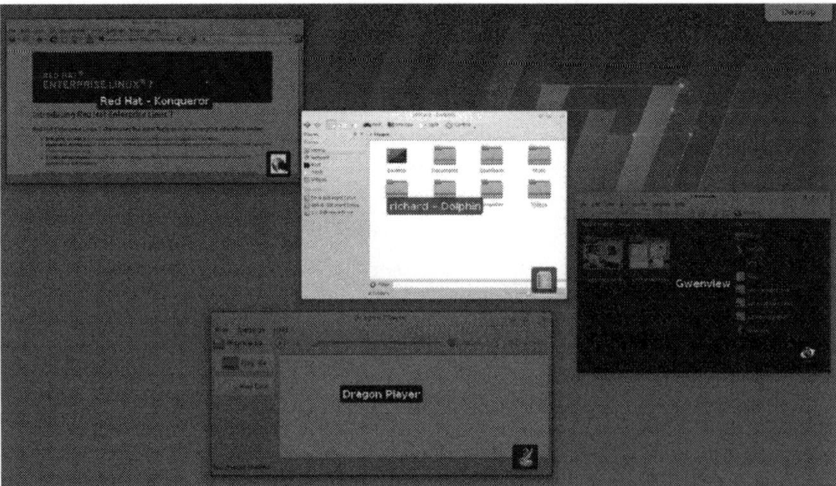

Figure 4-35: Present Windows (Windows effects) Ctrl-F9 for current desktop and Ctrl-f 10 for all desktops

Desktop Grid will show a grid of all your virtual desktops (Ctrl-F8), letting you see all your virtual desktops on the screen at once (see Figure 4-36). You can then move windows and open applications between desktops. Clicking on a desktop makes it the current one. The plus and minus keys allow you to add or remove virtual desktops.

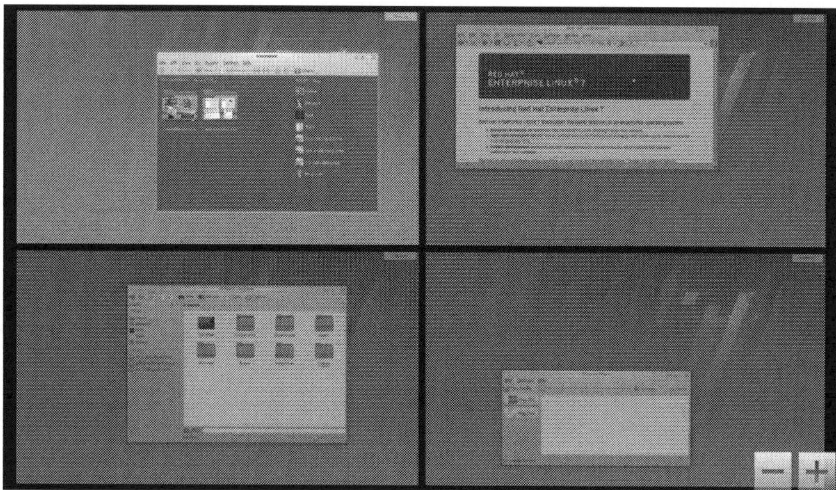

Figure 4-36: Desktop Grid - Ctrl-F8

Desktop Cube will show a cube of all your virtual desktops, letting you move to different desktops around a cube (see Figure 4-37). Stop at the side you want to select. There are as many sides as there are virtual desktops. Press Ctrl-11 to start the Desktop Cube. You can then move around the cube with the arrow keys or by clicking and dragging your mouse. When you are finished, press the ESC key to return you the desktop. Desktop Cube Animation will use cube animation whenever you switch to a different desktop using the Desktop Pager.

Figure 4-37: Desktop Cube - Ctrl-F11, drag-mouse or right/left arrow keys

KDE File Manager: Dolphin

Dolphin is KDE's dedicated file manager (see Figure 4-38). A location bar shows the current folder either in a browser or edit mode. In the browse mode it shows icons for the path of your current folder, and in the edit mode, it shows the path name in a text-editable box. You can use either to move to different folders and their subfolders. Use the **Ctrl-l** key or click to the right of the folder buttons to use the edit mode. You can also choose Control | Location Bar | Editable Location (the **Ctrl-l** key will toggle between the edit and browser modes). Clicking on the checkmark at the end of the editable text box returns you to the browser mode.

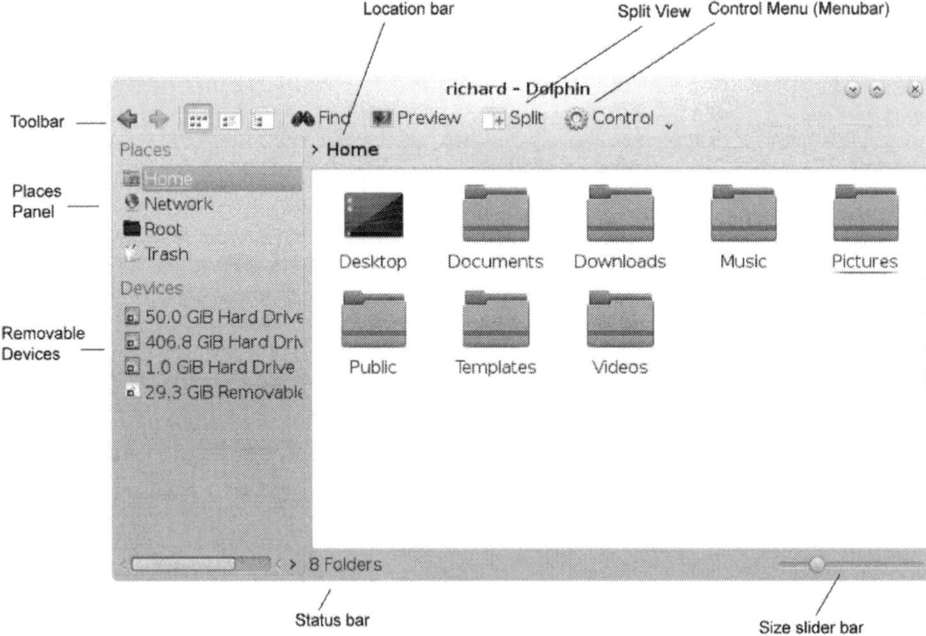

Figure 4-38: The KDE file manager (Dolphin)

The Dolphin menubar has been hidden by default. The menus are displayed when clicking the Control button on the right end of the toolbar (see Figure 4-39). You can redisplay the menubar by choosing "Show Menubar" from the Control menu (**Ctrl-m**). You can hide the menubar again by choosing Show Menubar from the Settings menu (or pressing **Ctrl-m**).

You can choose to display files and subfolders in several different ways: icons (Icons), a detailed listing (Details), and basic listing (Compact). There are buttons for the icons, compact, and details views on the toolbar to the left next to the arrow keys. Click a button to display files and folder with that view. You can also choose a view by from the Control | View Mode menu.

You can open a file either by clicking it or by right-clicking it, and choosing the "Open With" submenu to list applications to open it with. If you want just to select the file or folder, you need to hold down the CTRL key while you click it. A single-click will open the file. If the file is a program, that program starts up. If it is a data file, such as a text file, the associated application is run using that data file. Clicking a text file displays it with the Kate editor, while clicking an image file displays it with the GwenView image viewer. If you want to use a double-click instead to open a file or folder, you can set the Double-click option on the Dolphin Preferences dialog Navigation tab (Control | Configure Dolphin).

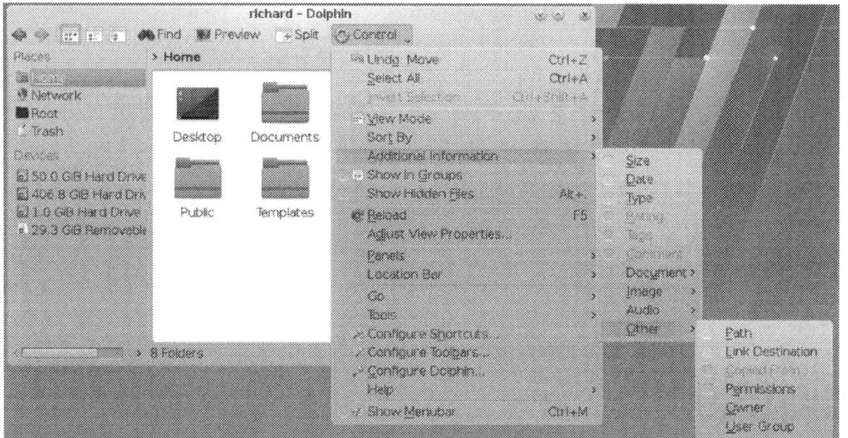

Figure 4-39: The KDE file manager menus

If Dolphin cannot determine the application to use, it opens a dialog box prompting you to enter the application name. You can click the Browse button on this box to use a directory tree to locate the application program you want.

Keys	Description
alt-left arrow, alt-right arrow	Backward and Forward in History
alt-up arrow	One directory up
enter	Open a file/directory
left/right/up/down arrows	Move among the icons
page up, page down	Scroll fast
ctrl-c	Copy selected file to clipboard
ctrl-v	Paste files from clipboard to current directory
ctrl-s	Select files by pattern
ctrl-l	URI text box location bar
ctrl-f	Find files
ctrl-q	Close window

Table 4-5: KDE File Manager Keyboard Shortcuts

Dolphin can display panels to either side (Dolphin refers to these as panels, though they operate more like stand-alone tabs) (see Figure 4-40). The Places panel will show icons for often-used folders like Home, Network, and Trash, as well as removable devices. To add a folder bookmark to the Places panel, just drag the folder to there. To remove the bookmark, right-click and choose the Remove entry. See Table 4-5 for keyboard shortcuts.

The Additional information submenu in the Control menu (or View menu if menubar is displayed) lets you display additional information about files such as the size, date, type, and comments. Type specific information can also be displayed such as album, track, and duration for audio files, and word and line counts for documents. You can also display the full path, permissions, and group information (Other submenu).

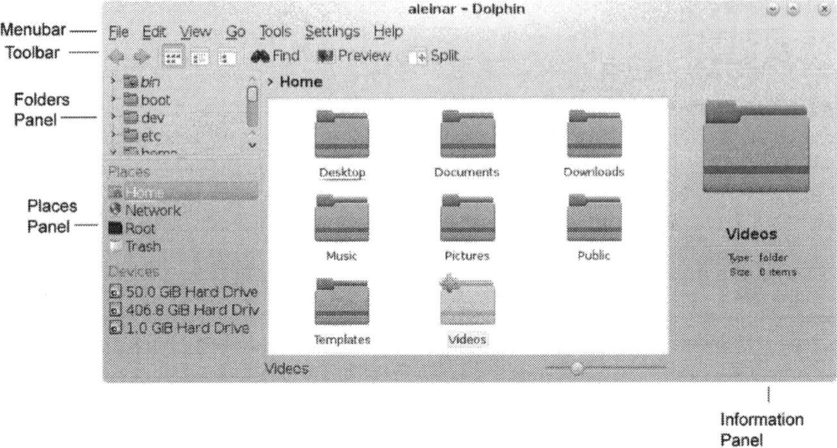

Figure 4-40: The KDE file manager with sidebars

You can display additional panels by selecting them from the Control | Panels submenu. The Information panel displays detailed information about a file or folder, and the Folders panel displays a directory tree for the file system. The panels are detachable from the file manager window. Be sure to choose "Unlock Panels" in the Panels menu to make them detachable. A small detach button (diamond) is then displayed at the top of each panel. Click it to detach the panel, and click it again to re-attach it.

Dolphin supports split views, where you can open two different folders in the same window. Click the Split button in the toolbar. You can then drag folder and files from one folder view to the other (see Figure 4-41).

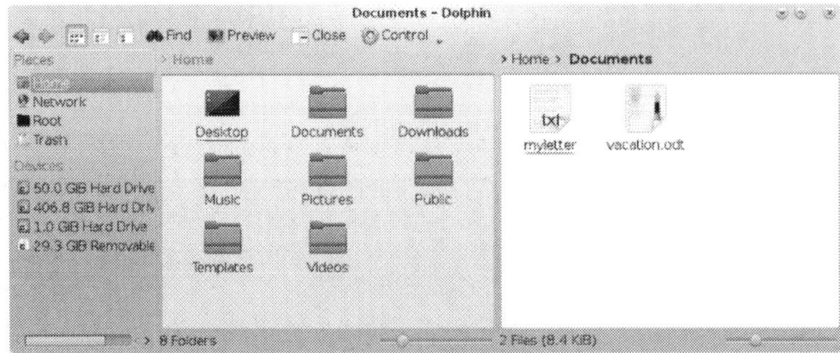

Figure 4-41: The KDE file manager with split views

Dolphin also supports file sharing with Samba. To share a folder, right-click on the folder icon and choose Properties to open the Properties dialog. Then on the Share tab, you can choose to share the folder with Samba (Microsoft Windows). You can also set permissions for users: Read Only, Full Control, and Deny (See Figure 4-42). For the Everyone entry, you would usually set the permission to Read Only.

Figure 4-42: The KDE file manager share dialog for folders

To configure Dolphin, click Configure Dolphin from the Control menu to open the Dolphin Preferences dialog with tabs for Startup, View Modes, Navigation, Services, Trash, and General. On the Startup tab, you can specify features like the split view and the default folder to start up with. On the View Modes tab, you can set display features for the different display modes (Icons, Compact, and Details), like the icon size, font type, and arrangement. The Navigation tab sets features like the double-click for selection. The Services tab is where you specify actions supported for different kinds of files, like play a DVD with Dragon Player, encrypt a file, or archive a folder. The Trash tab lets you configure trash settings like deleting items in the trash after a specified time and setting the maximum size of the trash. The General tab has sub-tabs for Behavior, Previews, Confirmations, and Status Bar. The Behavior tab is where you can enable tooltips and display the selection marker. The Confirmations tab lets you enable confirmation prompts for file deletion, closing multiple tabs, and moving files to the trash. Preview lets you choose which type of files to preview. The image, jpeg, and directories types are already selected.

Navigating Directories

Within a file manager window, a single-click on a folder icon moves to that folder and displays its file and subfolder icons. To move back up to the parent folder, you click the back arrow button located on the left side of the toolbar. A single-click on a folder icon moves you down the folder tree, one folder at a time. By clicking the back arrow button, you move up the tree. The Navigation bar can display either the folder path for the current folder, or an editable location box where you can enter in a pathname. For the folder path, you can click on any displayed folder name to move you quickly to an upper-level folder. To use the location box, click to the right of the folder path. The navigation bar changes to an editable textbox where you can type a path name. To change back to the folder path, click the check mark to the right of the text box.

Like a Web browser, the file manager remembers the previous folder it has displayed. You can use the back and forward arrow buttons to move through this list of prior folders. You can also use several keyboard shortcuts to perform such operations, like Alt-back-arrow to move up a folder, and the arrow keys to move to different icons.

Copy, Move, Delete, Rename, and Link Operations

To perform an operation on a file or folder, you first have to select it by clicking the file's icon or listing. To select more than one file, hold down the **Ctrl** key down while you click the files you want. You can also use the keyboard arrow keys to move from one file icon to another.

To copy and move files, you can use the standard drag-and-drop method with your mouse. To copy a file, you locate it by using the file manager. Open another file manager window to the folder to which you want the file copied. Then drag-and-drop the File icon to that window. A pop-up menu appears with selections for Move Here, Copy Here, or Link Here. Choose Copy Here. To move a file to another directory, follow the same procedure, but select Move Here from the pop-up menu. To copy or move a folder, use the same procedure as for files. All the folder's files and subfolders are also copied or moved. Instead of having to select from a pop-up menu, you can use the corresponding keys: **Ctrl** for copy, **Shift** for move, and **Ctrl-Shift** for link, which are the same as for GNOME.

To rename a file, **Ctrl-click** its icon and press **F2**, or right-click the icon and select Rename from the pop-up menu. A dialog opens where you can enter the new name for the file or folder.

You can delete a file either by selecting it and deleting it, or placing it in the Trash folder to delete later. To delete a file, select it and then choose the Delete entry in the File menu (if menubar is displayed), File | Delete (also SHIFT-DEL key). To place a file in the Trash folder, drag-and-drop it to the Trash icon on the Places panel, or right-click the file and choose "Move To Trash" from the pop-up menu. You can later open the Trash folder and delete the files. To delete all the files in the Trash folder, right-click the Trash icon in Dolphin file manager Places panel, and select Remove Trash from the pop-up menu. To restore files in the Trash bin, open the Trash window and right click on the file to restore and select Restore.

Each file or directory has properties associated with it that include permissions, the filename, and its folder. To display the Properties dialog for a given file, right-click the file's icon and select the Properties entry. On the General tab, you see the name of the file displayed. To change the file name, replace the name there with a new one. Permissions are set on the Permissions tab. Here, you can set read, write, and execute permissions for user, group, or other access to the file. The Group entry enables you to change the group for a file.

Search Bar, Desktop Search, and Filter Bar

KDE has combined the former KFind and Dolphin search tools into one simplified search bar. KDE also supports a filter bar to search files and folders in the current folder.

Search Bar

To search for files, click the Find button on the icon bar to open the search bar, which displays a search text box. You can also choose Find from the Edit menu (if the menubar is displayed) or press Ctrl-f. The search bar displays a search text box where you enter the pattern of the file or folder you are searching for. Click the red x button to the left to close the find bar, and use the black x button in the text box to clear the search pattern.

Buttons below the search box provide options to qualify the search. The Filename button (the default) searches on the file name. The Content button will search the contents of text files for the pattern. The "From Here" button searches the user's home folders, and the Everywhere button (the default) searches the entire file system (see Figure 4-43).

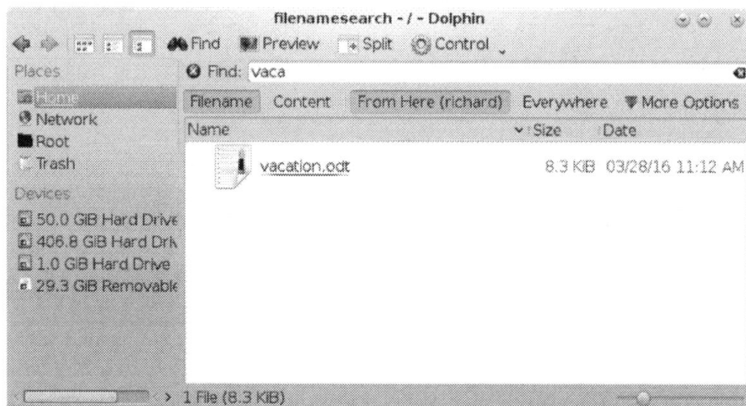

Figure 4-43: The KDE Search Bar

The search results are displayed in the main pane. You can click a file to have it open with its appropriate application. Text files are displayed by the Kate text editor, images by GwenView, and applications are run. The search program also enables you to save your search results for later reference (click the Save button to the right). When you are finished searching, click the Close button.

When you pass your mouse over an icon listed in the Query Results, information about it is displayed on the information panel to the right (should the panel be displayed). Links are shown for adding tags and comments. Right-clicking on this panel lets you open a configure dialog where you can specify what information to display.

Desktop Search (Nepomuk)

Desktop searching can take up computing resources and slow your system. For this reason, it is disabled by default. To configure Desktop search, choose System Settings | Workspace Appearance and Behavior | Desktop Search. This opens the Desktop Search control module where you can enable or disable desktop searching, and choose folders not to search. Click the Enable Nepomuk Semantic Desktop. When desktop searching is enabled, two new sections are displayed on the Places panel: Recently Access and Search For (see Figure 4-44). With all the folder and files on your desktop indexed, these entries provide categories for quickly displaying files based on specified criteria. The Recently Accessed section lets you display files accessed Today, Yesterday, This Month, and Last Month. In the Search For section, you can access files by type: Documents, Images, Audio Files and Videos.

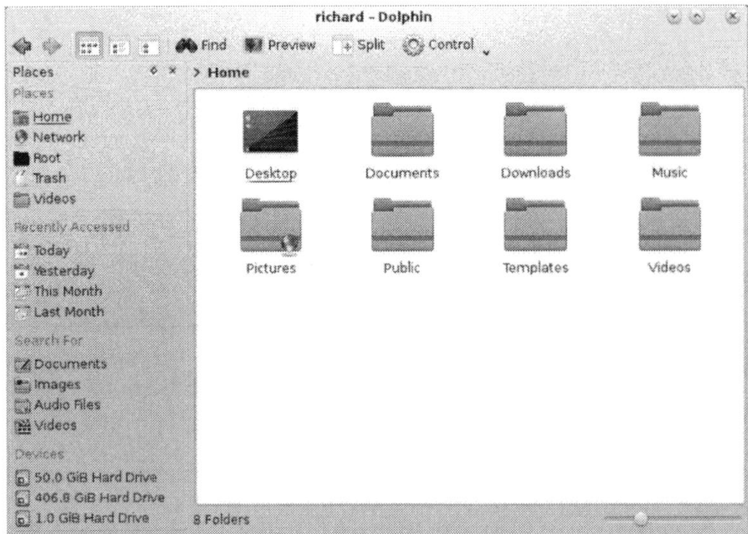

Figure 4-44: Places panel with Desktop Search (Nepomuk) enabled

Filter Bar

For a quick search of the current folder, you can activate the Filter bar (Tools | Show Filter Bar or **Ctrl-i**), which opens a Filter search box at the bottom of the window. Enter a pattern, and only those file and directory names containing that pattern are displayed. Click the x button at the right of the Filter box to clear it (see Figure 4-45).

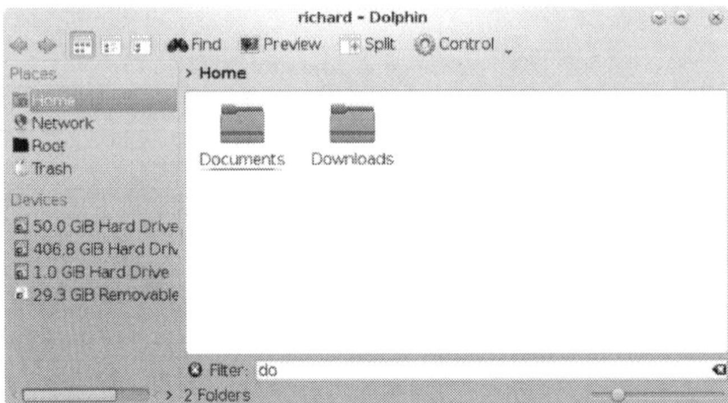

Figure 4-45: The KDE Filter Bar

KDE Configuration: KDE System Settings

With the KDE configuration tools, you can configure your desktop and system, changing the way it is displayed and the features it supports. The configuration dialogs are accessed on the System Settings window (See Figure 4-46). On KDE, you can access System Settings from the System Settings entry in the Kickoff Favorites menu, or from Applications | Settings | System Settings. You should use the KDE System Settings tools to configure your KDE desktop.

The System Settings window shows system dialog icons arranged in several sections: Common Appearance and Behavior, Workspace Appearance and Behavior, Network and Connectivity, Hardware, and System Administration. Click an icon to display a dialog with a sidebar icon list for configuration tabs, with the tab selected shown on the right. The selected tab may also have sub-tabs (see Figure 4-47).

The Network and Connectivity section holds icons for configuring the networking, Bluetooth connections, and sharing. The Common Appearance and Behavior section has icons for personal information, account details, shortcuts, file associations, and your location. Workspace Appearance and Behavior lets you set desktop effects, themes, accessibility, default applications, desktop search, and window features. System Administration lets you set the date and time, install fonts, configure start up and shut down (sessions), and schedule tasks. Hardware lets you set the printer configuration, power management, your display resolution, and input devices (keyboard and mouse).

Alternatively, you can display the System Settings window using the classic tree format. Click the System Settings Configure button to open the configuration dialog, and select Classic tree on the General tab. Setting sections are displayed as expandable trees on the left pane, with packages for a selected section displayed to the right.

Figure 4-46: KDE System Settings

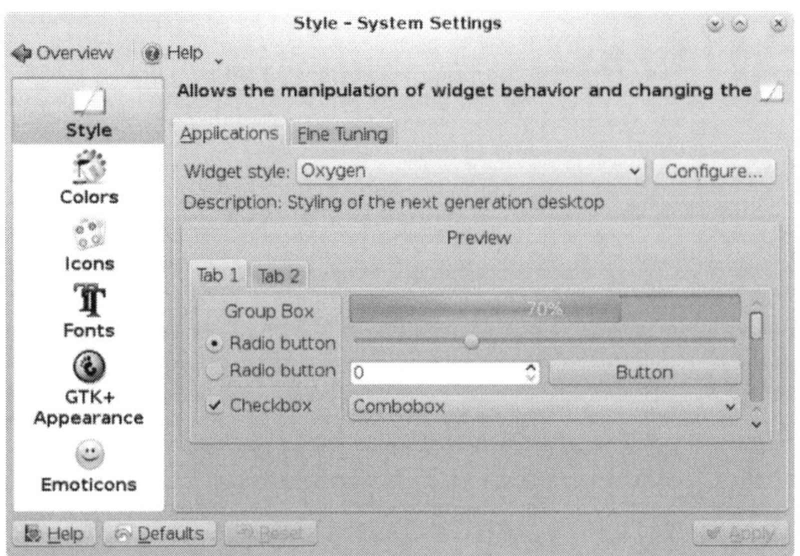

Figure 4-47: KDE System Settings | Application Appearance, Style

KDE Directories and Files

When KDE is installed on your system, its system-wide application, configuration, and support files may be installed in the same system directories as other GUIs and user applications (see Table 4-6). On RHEL, KDE is installed in the standard system directories with some variations, such as **/usr/bin** for KDE program files, **/usr/lib/kde4**, which holds KDE libraries, and **/usr/include/kde**, which contains KDE header files used in application development.

The **.kde** directory holds files and directories used to maintain your KDE desktop. As with GNOME, the **Desktop** directory holds KDE desktop files whose icons are displayed on the desktop. Configuration files are located in the **.kde/share/config** directory. Here you can find the general configuration files for different KDE components: **kwinrc** holds configuration commands for the window manager and **kdeglobals** for keyboard shortcuts, along with other global definitions. The **.kde/share/apps** directory contains files and directories for configuring KDE applications.

The directories located in **share** directory contain files used to configure system defaults for your KDE environment (the system **share** directory is located at **/usr/share**). The **share/apps** directory contains files and directories set up by KDE applications; **share/config** contains the configuration files for particular KDE applications. These are the system-wide defaults that can be overridden by users' own configurations in their own **.kde/share/config** directories. The **share/icons** directory holds the default icons used on your KDE desktop and by KDE applications. The user's home directory, the **.kde** directory holds a user's own KDE configuration for the desktop and its applications.

System KDE Directories	Description
/usr/bin	KDE programs
/usr/include/kde	Header files for use in compiling and developing KDE applications
/usr/share/config	KDE desktop and application configuration files
/usr/share/apps	Files used by KDE applications
/usr/share/icons	Icons used in KDE desktop and applications
User KDE Directories	**Description**
.kde/AutoStart	Applications automatically started up with KDE
.kde/share/config	User KDE desktop and application configuration files for user-specified features
.kde/share/apps	Directories and files used by KDE applications
.kde/share/config/plasma-appletsrc	Plasma applet configuration

Table 4- 6: KDE Installation Directories

5. Applications

Office

Mail

Graphics

Multimedia

Internet

All Linux software for RHEL is currently available from online repositories. You can download applications for desktops, Internet servers, office suites, and programming packages, among others. Software packages are distributed primarily through the official RHEL and EPEL repositories. Downloads and updates are handled automatically by your desktop software manager and updater. During the subscription process, your system is configured to access RHEL repositories. For the EPEL repository, you must download and install the EPEL repository configuration file, **epel-release**, for RHEL7 at **https://fedoraproject.org/wiki/EPEL**. It is a simple automatic procedure.

All software packages in the RHEL repositories are accessible directly with GNOME Software and PackagKit, which provide easy software installation, removal, and searching.

Office Applications

Several office suites are now available for Linux (see Table 5-1). These include professional-level word processors, presentation managers, drawing tools, and spreadsheets. The freely available versions are described in this chapter. All the software are RHEL and EPEL packages. LibreOffice is currently the primary office suite supported by RHEL. Calligra is an office suite designed for use with KDE and is available on the EPEL repository. The GNOME also supports additional office applications, several of which are available on the RHEL and EPEL repositories. CodeWeavers CrossOver Office provides reliable support for running Microsoft Office Windows applications directly on Linux, integrating them with KDE and GNOME. You can also purchase commercial office suites such as Oracle Open Office from Oracle.

Web Site	Description
http://www.libreoffice.org	LibreOffice open source office suite
http://www.calligra.org	Calligra Suite, for KDE
https://wiki.gnome.org/action/show/Projects/GnomeOffice	GNOME Office applications
http://www.codeweavers.com	CrossOver Office (MICROSOFT Office support)

Table 5-1: Linux Office Suites

Several database management systems are also available for Linux, which include high-powered, commercial-level database management systems, such as Oracle, IBM's DB2, and Sybase. Most of the database management systems available for Linux are designed to support large relational databases. RHEL includes both MarisDB (MySQL) and PostgreSQL open source databases in its distribution, which can support smaller databases. Various database management systems available to run under Linux are listed in Table 5-8 later in this chapter.

Note: You can use the GNOME Documents application to access and search for local and cloud-based documents.

Linux also provides several text editors that range from simple text editors for simple notes to editors with more complex features such as spell-checkers, buffers, or complex pattern matching. All generate character text files and can be used to edit any Linux text files. Text editors are often used in system administration tasks to change or add entries in Linux configuration files found in the **/etc** directory or a user's initialization or application configuration files located in a user's home directory (dot files). You can also use a text editor to work on source code files for any of the programming languages or shell program scripts.

LibreOffice

LibreOffice is a fully integrated suite of office applications developed as an open source project and freely distributed to all. It is the primary office suite for Linux. LibreOffice is the open source and freely available office suite derived originally from OpenOffice. LibreOffice is supported by the Document Foundation, which was established after Oracle's acquisition of Sun, the main developer for Open Office. LibreOffice is now the primary open source office software for Linux. Oracle retains control of all the original OpenOffice software and does not cooperate with any LibreOffice development. LibreOffice has replaced OpenOffice as the default Office software for most Linux distributions.

LibreOffice includes word processing, spreadsheet, presentation, and drawing applications (see Table 5-2). Versions of LibreOffice exist for Linux, Windows, and Mac OS. You can obtain information such as online manuals and FAQs as well as current versions from the LibreOffice Web site at **http://www.libreoffice.org**.

Application	Description
Calc (Spreadsheet)	LibreOffice spreadsheet
Draw (Drawing)	LibreOffice drawing application
Writer (Word Processing)	LibreOffice word processor
Math (Formula)	LibreOffice mathematical formula composer
Impress (Presentation)	LibreOffice presentation manager
Base (Database)	Database front end for accessing and managing a variety of different databases.

Table 5-2: LibreOffice Applications

Calligra

Calligra (formerly KOffice) is an integrated office suite for the K Desktop Environment (KDE) consisting of several office applications, including a word processor, a spreadsheet, and graphics applications. Calligra allows components from any one application to be used in another, letting you embed a spreadsheet from Calligra Sheets or diagrams from Karbon in a Calligra Words document. It also uses the open document format (ODF) for its files, providing cross-application standardization. You can obtain more information about Calligra from **https://www.calligra.org**. Calligra is available on the EPEL repository.

Application	Description
Braindump	Whiteboards for notes, images, and charts
Calligra Flow	Flow chart applications
Calligra Stage	Presentation application
Calligra Words	Word processor (desktop publisher)

Calligra Sheets	Spreadsheet
Karbon	Vector graphics program
Kexi	Database integration
Plan	Project management and planning
Kontact (separate project)	Contact application including mail, address book, and organizer

Table 5-3: Calligra Applications

GNOME Office Applications

There are several additional GNOME Office applications available including Evince, Evolution, and GnuCash (see Table 5-4). Evince and Evolution are installed on the RHEL7 Workstation by default. Others such as AbiWord and Gnumeric are not available for RHEL. You can find out more about the GNOME Office applications at **https://wiki.gnome.org/action/show/Projects/GnomeOffice**. All implement the support for embedding components, ensuring drag-and-drop capability throughout the GNOME interface.

Application	Description
Evince	Document Viewer
Evolution	Integrated email, calendar, and personal organizer
GnuCash	Personal finance manager (EPEL repository)

Table 5-4: GNOME Office and Other Office Applications for GNOME

Document Viewers, and DVI)

Though located under Applications lens Graphics filter, PostScript, PDF, and DVI viewers are more commonly used with Office applications (see Table 5-5). Evince (PostScript, PDF and Okular can display both PostScript (**.ps**) and PDF (**.pdf**) files. Okular, Evince, and Xpdf are PDF viewers. They include many of the standard Adobe reader features such as zoom, two-page display, and full-screen mode.

Viewer	Description
Evince	Document Viewer for PostScript, DVI, and PDF files
Okular	KDE application for displaying PDF, DVI, and postscript files
xpdf	X Window System application for displaying PDF files only (EPEL repository)
Scribus	Desktop publisher for generating PDF documents (EPEL repository)
pdfedit	Edit PDF documents (EPEL repository)
Simple Scan	GNOME Scanner interface for scanners (EPEL repository)

Table 5-5: PostScript, PDF, and DVI viewers

Evince is the default document viewer for GNOME. It is started automatically whenever you double-click a PDF file on the GNOME desktop. Its menu entry is Document Viewer in the

Utilities sub-overview menu. Okular is the default document viewer for KDE, with its menu entry as Applications | Graphics | Document Viewer on KDE, but as Okular on GNOME.

Editors

The Linux desktops (GNOME and KDE) support powerful text editors with full mouse support, scrollbars, and menus. These include basic text editors, such as Gedit, Pluma, and Kate, as well as word processors, such as LibreOffice Word and Calligra Words. Linux also provides the cursor-based editors Nano, Vim, and Emacs. Nano is the default cursor-based editor with an easy-to-use interface supporting menus and mouse selection (if run from a terminal window). Vim is an enhanced version of the Vi text editor used on the Unix system. These editors use simple, cursor-based operations to give you a full-screen format. Table 5-6 lists several desktop editors for Linux. Vi and Emacs have powerful editing features that have been refined over the years. Emacs, in particular, is extensible to a full-development environment for programming new applications. Later versions of Emacs and Vi, such as GNU Emacs, XEmacs, and vim provide support for mouse, menu, and window operations.

Application	Description
Kate	Text and program editor
Calligra Words	Desktop publisher, part of Calligra Suite (EPEL repository)
Gedit	Text editor
GNU Emacs	Emacs editor with X Window System support
nano	Easy to use screen-based editor, installed by default
OpenWriter	LibreOffice word processor that can edit text files
Pluma	Text editor (EPEL repository)
vim	Vim version with X Window System support
XEmacs	X Window System version of Emacs editor (EPEL repository)

Table 5-6: Desktop Editors

Database Management Systems

Database software can generally be organized into three categories: SQL and desktop databases. SQL-based databases are professional-level relational databases whose files are managed by a central database server program. Applications that use the database do not access the files directly. Instead, they send requests to the database server, which then performs the actual access. SQL is the query language used on these industrial-strength databases. RHEL7 includes both MariaDB (MySQL) and PostgreSQL databases. Both are open source projects freely available for your use. Table 5-7 lists database management systems currently available for Linux.

SQL databases are relational database management systems (RDBMSs) designed for extensive database management tasks. Many of the major SQL databases now have Linux versions, including Oracle, Informix, Sybase, and IBM. These are commercial and professional database management systems. In addition, free SQL databases are available for Linux that offer much the same functionality.

System	Site
LibreOffice Base	LibreOffice database: **https://www.libreoffice.org/discover/base/**
PostgreSQL	The PostgreSQL database: **www.postgresql.org**
MariaDB	The MariaDB MySQL-derived database: **https://mariadb.org/**
Oracle	Oracle database: **www.oracle.com**
Sybase	Sybase database: **www.sybase.com**
DB2	IBM database: **http://ibm.com/software/data/db2**

Table 5-7: Database Management Systems for Linux

LibreOffice provides a basic database application, LibreOffice Base that can access many database files. You can set up and operate a simple database, as well as access and manage files from other database applications. File types supported include ODBC (Open Database Connectivity), JDBC (Java), MySQL, PostgreSQL, and MDB (Microsoft Access) database files. You can also create your own simple databases. Check the LibreOffice Base page (**https://www.libreoffice.org/discover/base/**) for detailed information on drivers and supported databases.

PostgreSQL is based on the POSTURES database management system, though it uses SQL as its query language. POSTGRESQL is a next-generation research prototype developed at the University of California, Berkeley. Linux versions of PostgreSQL are included in most distributions, including the Red Hat, Fedora, Debian, and Ubuntu. You can find more information on it from the PostgreSQL Web site at **https://www.postgresql.org**. PostgreSQL is an open source project, developed under the GPL license.

MariaDB is derived from MySQL but is a more advanced and fully open-sourced. It is the default MySQL type database for RHEL7 and Fedora Linux. MariaDB is supported and developed by the original MySQL developers. The original MySQL is owned by Oracle and features commercial versions. You can still install the older non-commercial version of MySQL if you wish

MariaDB is designed to be fully compatible with MySQL databases. Like MySQL, MariaDB is structured on a client/server model with a server daemon (**mysqld**) filling requests from client programs. MariaDB is designed for speed, reliability, and ease of use. It is meant to be a fast database management system for large databases and, at the same time, a reliable one, suitable for intensive use. To create databases, you use the standard SQL language. User access can be controlled by assigning privileges. On RHEL7, you can install the MariaDB server and client packages, along with numerous configuration packages for certain services like Postfix, Exim, and Apache. Packages to install are **mariadb** and **mariadb-server**.

Mail (email) and News

Linux supports a wide range of both electronic mail and news clients. Some email clients are designed to operate on a specific desktop interface such as KDE and GNOME. Several older mail clients use a screen-based interface and can be started only from the command line. Table 5-8 lists several popular Linux mail clients. Mail is transported to and from destinations using mail transport agents like Sendmail, Exim, and Postfix. To send mail over the Internet, Simple Mail Transport Protocol (SMTP) is used.

Mail Client	Description
Kontact (KMail, KAddressbook, KOrganizer)	Includes the K Desktop mail client, KMail; integrated mail, address book, and scheduler
Evolution	Email client, **http://projects.gnome.org/evolution/**
Thunderbird	Mozilla mail client and newsreader
Sylpheed	Gtk mail and news client (EPEL repository)
GNUEmacs and XEmacs	Emacs mail clients
Mutt	Screen-based mail client
Mail	Original Unix-based command line mail client
Squirrel Mail	Web-based mail client (EPEL repository)

Table 5-8: Linux Mail Clients

Usenet is an open mail system on which users post messages that include news, discussions, and opinions. It operates like a mailbox to which any user on your Linux system can read or send messages. Users' messages are incorporated into Usenet files, which are distributed to any system signed up to receive them. To access Usenet news, you need access to a news server, which receives the daily Usenet newsfeeds and makes them accessible to other systems. To read Usenet articles, you use a newsreader, a client program that connects to a news server and accesses the articles. On the Internet and in TCP/IP networks, news servers communicate with newsreaders using the Network News Transfer Protocol (NNTP) and are often referred to as NNTP news servers. News transport agent applications can be set up to create such a server.

You read Usenet articles with a newsreader which enable you to select a specific newsgroup and then read the articles in it. Most newsreaders employ a retrieval feature called threads that pulls together articles on the same discussion or topic. Several popular newsreaders are listed in Table 5-9.

Newsreader	Description
Thunderbird	Mail client with newsreader capabilities (X based)
Sylpheed	GNOME Windows-like newsreader (EPEL repository)
Slrn	Newsreader (cursor based) (EPEL repository)
Emacs	Emacs editor, mail client, and newsreader (cursor based)

Table 5-9: Linux Newsreaders

Graphics Applications

The GNOME and KDE desktops support an impressive number of graphics applications, including image viewers, window grabbers, image editors, and paint tools (see Table 5-10). Shotwell provides an easy and powerful way to manage, display, and import, and publish your photos and images. The Eye of GNOME is the GNOME image viewer. GIMP is the GNU Image

Manipulation Program, a sophisticated image application much like Adobe Photoshop. Inkscape is a Gnome based vector graphics application for SVG (Scalable Vector Graphics) images. The KDE desktop features the same variety of graphics applications found on the GNOME desktop.

Tools	Description
Shotwell	GNOME digital camera application and image and video library manager (**https://wiki.gnome.org/Apps/Shotwell**)
Cheese	GNOME Webcam application for taking pictures and videos
Digikam	Digital photo management tool, works with both GNOME and KDE (EPEL repository)
KDE	
Gwenview	Image browser and viewer (default for KDE)
KSnapshot	Screen grabber
KolourPaint	Paint program
GNOME	
Eye of Gnome	GNOME Image Viewer
GIMP	GNU Image Manipulation Program (**https://www.gimp.org/**)
Inkscape	GNOME Vector graphics application (**https://inkscape.org/en/**)
LibreOffice Draw	LibreOffice Draw program
X Window System	
Xfig	Drawing program (EPEL repository)
ImageMagick	Image format conversion and editing tool

Table 5-10: Graphics Tools for Linux

Multimedia

Many applications are available for both video and sound, including sound editors, MP3 players, and video players (see Tables 5-11 and 3-12). Linux sound applications include mixers, digital audio tools, CD audio writers, MP3 players, and network audio support.

Many music applications are currently available for GNOME, including sound editors, MP3 players, and audio players (see Table 5-11). You can use Banshee and Rhythmbox to play music from different sources, and the GNOME Sound Recorder to record sound sources.

Several projects provide TV, video, DivX, DVD, and DVB support for Linux (see Table 5-12). Many GNOME-based applications make use of GStreamer, a streaming media framework based on graphs and filters (**https://gstreamer.freedesktop.org/**). Using a plug-in structure, GStreamer applications can accommodate a wide variety of media types. GStreamer has four different support packages called the base, the good, the bad, and the ugly. The base package is a set of useful and reliable plug-ins. These are in the Ubuntu main repository. The good package is a set of supported and tested plug-ins that meets all licensing requirements. This is also part of the Ubuntu main repository. The bad package is a set of unsupported plug-ins whose performance is not guaranteed and may crash, but still meet licensing requirements. The ugly package contains plug-ins that work fine, but may not meet licensing requirements, like DVD support.

Application	Description
Banshee	Music management (GStreamer) (EPEL repository)
Rhythmbox	Music management (GStreamer), default Music player with iPod support
Amarok	KDE4 multimedia audio player (EPEL repository)
GNOME CD Player	CD player
GNOME Sound Recorder	Sound recorder
XMMS	CD player (EPEL repository)

Table 5-11: Music players

Players	Sites
Videos (Totem)	Videos (formerly Totem) video and DVD player for GNOME using GStreamer.
Dragon Player	Dragon Player video and DVD player for KDE4
VideoLan Media Player (vlc)	Network multimedia streaming. **www.videolan.org** (RPM Fusion repository, third party)
MPlayer	MPlayer DVD/multimedia player **www.mplayerhq.hu** (RPM Fusion repository, third party)
XviD	Open Source DivX, **www.xvid.org** (RPM Fusion repository, third party)

Table 5-12: Video Players

Videos (formerly Totem) is the GNOME movie player and is labeled with the name Videos. It uses GStreamer. To expand Videos capabilities, you may need to install added GStreamer plug-ins. The codec wizard will prompt you to install any needed media codecs and plugins. You can use the dconf editor to modify default settings (org.gnome.totem) (**totem** package).

The Videos movie player uses plugins to add capabilities like Internet video streaming. YouTube support is already installed as part of the desktop, along with the BBC content viewer. Select Preferences from the Videos top bar menu to open the Preferences dialog with a button labeled Plugins. Click on it to open the Configure Plugins window. Choose the plugins you want.

Multimedia Support

Many of the multimedia applications and codecs are third party applications not available on the RHEL or EPEL repositories. These include the vlc media player, the Xvid codec, and ffmpeg sound codec. You can download them from unofficial third party repositories. The third-party repositories RPM Fusion (**https://rpmfusion.org**) or Negativo17.org (**https://negativo17.org**) provide most of the third party multimedia applications and codecs like the vlc multimedia player and the DVD video codec. Multimedia codecs with licensing issues can be directly downloaded with PackageKit, once you have configured YUM to use the RPM Fusion (**https://rpmfusion.org**) or Negativo17.org (**https://negativo17.org**) repositories on your system. Use one or the other, not both. These repositories are not configured by default. For the RPM Fusion repository install the configuration package for RHEL 7, which is available from that site at **https://rpmfusion.org/Configuration**.

MPEG-4 compressed files provide DVD-quality video with relatively small file sizes. They have become popular for distributing high-quality video files over the Internet. When you first try to play an MPEG-4 file, the codec wizard will prompt you to install the needed codec packages to play it. Many multimedia applications like VLC already support MPEG-4 files.

MPEG-4 files using the Matroska wrapper, also known by their file extension **mkv**, can be played on most video players including the VideoLan vlc player and Videos. You will need HDTV codecs, like MPEG4 AAC sound codec, installed to play the high definition **mkv** file files. If needed, the codec wizard will prompt you to install them. To manage and create MKV files you can use the **mkvtoolnix-gui** tools (EPEL repository).

You use the open source version of DivX known as Xvid to play DivX video (**libxvidcore** package. Most DivX files can be run using XviD. XviD is an entirely independent open source project, but it is compatible with DivX files. You can also download the XviD source code from **http://xvid.org**.

CD/DVD Burners

Several CD/DVD writer programs can be used for CD music and MP3 writing. These include Brasero and K3b (See Table 5-13). For burning DVD/CD music and data discs, you can use Brasero CD/DVD burner. For KDE you can use K3b. Brasero, K3b, and dvdauthor can all be used to create DVD-Video discs. All use mkisofs, cdrecord, and cdda2wav DVD/CD writing programs installed as part of your desktop.

Application	Description
Brasero	Full-service CD/DVD burner, for music, video, and data discs
K3b	KDE CD writing interface
dvdauthor	Tools for creating DVDs (EPEL repository)

Table 5-13: CD/DVD Burners

Internet Applications

Linux provides powerful Web and FTP clients for accessing the Internet. Some of these applications are installed automatically and are ready to use when you first start up your system. Linux also includes full Java development support, letting you run and construct Java applets. Web and FTP clients connect to sites that run servers, using Web pages and FTP files to provide services to users.

Popular browsers for RHEL include Firefox (Mozilla), Chromium (Google), Konqueror (KDE), and Elinks (see Table 5-14). Firefox is the default Web browser used on most Linux distributions. Konqueror is the KDE Web browser, accessible from the KDE desktop. Chromium is the open source version of the new Google Web browser. ELinks is a command line based browser with no graphics capabilities, but in every other respect, it is a fully functional Web browser.

Web Site	Description
Firefox	The Mozilla project Firefox Web browser, desktop default browser **http://www.mozilla.org**
Chromium	Open source version of Google Chrome Web browser **http://www.crhomium.org** (EPEL repository)
Konqueror	KDE desktop Web browser
elinks	Text-based command-line Web browser **http://elinks.or.cz**

Table 5-14: Web browsers

Sun (now owned by Oracle) has open sourced Java as the OpenJDK project and supports and distributes Linux versions. The **java-1.8.0-openjdk** package installs the Java runtime environment.

RHEL will install and use the GNOME BitTorrent client, Transmission, accessible from the Internet menu. For KDE you can use the Ktorrent BitTorrent client. To perform a BitTorrent download, you need the BitTorrent file for the file you want to download.

Basic FTP client capabilities are incorporated into the Dolphin (KDE) and Nemo (GNOME) file managers. You can use a file manager window to access an FTP site and drag files to local directories to download them. Effective FTP clients are also now incorporated into most Web browsers, making Web browsers the primary downloading tool. Firefox, in particular, has strong FTP download capabilities.

FTP Clients	Description
Dolphin	KDE file manager
Nemo	GNOME file manager
ftp	Command line FTP client
lftp	Command line FTP client capable of multiple connections
curl	Internet transfer client (FTP and HTTP)
Filezilla	Linux version of the open source Filezilla ftp client (EPEL repository)

Table 5-15: Linux FTP Clients

Although file managers and Web browsers provide effective access to public (anonymous login) sites, to access private sites, you may need a stand-alone FTP client like curl, Filezilla, lftp, or **ftp**. These clients let you enter user names and passwords with which you can access a private FTP site. The stand-alone clients are also useful for large downloads from public FTP sites, especially those with little or no Web display support. Popular Linux FTP clients are listed in Table 5-15.

Linux provides social networking support forIM (Instant Messenger) and VoIP (Voice over Internet). Users can communicate directly with other users on your network (see Table 5-16). These applications are installed automatically and are ready to use when you first start up your system. Instant messenger (IM) clients allow users on the same IM system to communicate anywhere across the Internet. With Voice over the Internet Protocol applications, you can speak over Internet connections.

Clients	Description
Ekiga	VoIP application
empathy	GNOME instant messenger
Pidgin	Older instant messenger client
Jabber	Jabber IM service (gajim, psi, emacs, empathy) (EPEL repository)
Finch	Command line cursor-based IM client (EPEL repository)
Hexchat	IRC client (EPEL repository)

Table 5-16: Instant Messenger and VoIP Clients

Part 2: Administration

6. System Administration Access and Configuration

Red Hat Enterprise Linux Administration Tools

Administrative Access: the root user

Controlled Administrative Access with PolicyKit

Controlled Administrative Access with sudo

Folders

Configuration Folders and Files

System Time and Date

Scheduling Tasks: cron

Grand Unified Bootloader (GRUB)

You may need to configure the operating system in different ways, such as adding new users, devices like printers and scanners, and even file systems. Such operations come under the heading of system administration. The person who performs such actions is referred to as either a system administrator or a superuser. In this sense, there are two types of interaction with Linux: regular users' interactions, and those of the superuser, which performs system administration tasks. For a detailed description of system administration tasks on RHEL, check the RHEL **System Administration Guide**.

```
https://access.redhat.com/documentation/en-
US/Red_Hat_Enterprise_Linux/7/html/System_Administrators_Guide/index.html
```

Red Hat Enterprise Linux Administration Tools

On Red Hat Enterprise Linux, most administration tasks can be handled by a set of separate specialized administrative tools developed and supported by Red Hat, such as those for user management and display configuration. On your GNOME desktop, some of the system administration tools can be found in the Utilities and Sundry sub-overviews. Others are located on the GNOME Settings dialog. If you are logged in as a normal user that has administrative access, you will first be prompted to enter the root user password. Table 6-1 provides a listing of popular administration tools.

Administration Tools	System | Administration	Description
authconfig-gui	Authentication	Sets authentication settings
system-config-date	Date & Time	Changes system time / date
firewall-config	Firewall	Configures your network firewall
system-config-keyboard	Keyboard	Select basic the keyboard type
system-config-printer	Printing	Printer configuration tool
cockpit	Services	Manages services such as starting and stopping servers.
system-config-users	Users and Groups	User and Group configuration tool
system-config-selinux	SELinux Management	SELinux configuration
gpk-application	PackageKit	Software management
nm-connection-editor	Network Connections	Network configuration tool

Table 6-1: Red Hat Enterprise Linux Configuration Tools

Administrative Access: the Root User

To perform some system administration operations, you will have to supply the root user password, making you the superuser (see Figure 6-1). As a superuser, you can perform tasks like starting up and shutting down the system, as well as changing to a different operating mode, such as a single-user mode. You can also add or remove users, add or remove whole file systems, backup and restore files, and even designate the system's name and address.

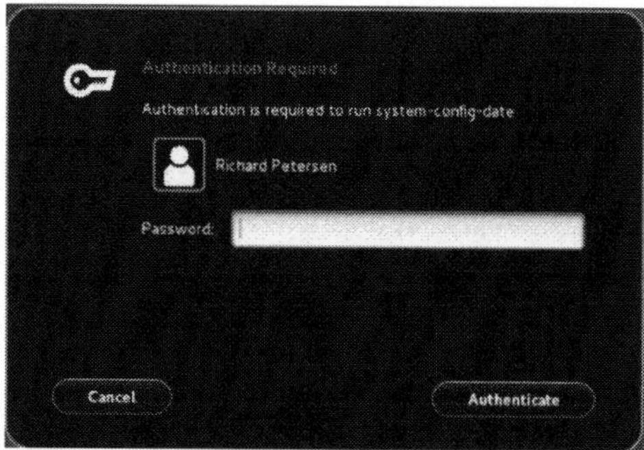

Figure 6-1: Administrative access authentication dialog

Administrative access from normal user accounts

Normally to access an administrative application, you simply log in to an account that has administrative access (an Administrator account type) and then run an administrative application. A dialog is then displayed that prompts you to enter your password. Once you do so, the administrative application you choose will start up, allowing its functions to have full administrative access. Other applications will allow you to browse information, but not changes it. For example, to create a new user, you can log in to any normal account, then choose Users from the Settings dialog. The Users dialog starts up allowing you to browse user information but not change it. To change it, click the Unlock button at the top right to open a dialog prompting you to enter your password. Once you do, the Users dialog Unlock button changes to Lock, and you can now create a new user on the system, as well as modify any other user configurations. The same kind of permission is required for updates. Logged into an account, you will be notified of any new updates. When you try to perform the update, you will be first prompted by the same dialog for your password. For each different administrative application you start up, you will have to enter your password separately. Keep in mind that user accounts can have either an administrator or standard type. Those with a standard type cannot perform administration tasks.

Logging into the root user account directly: su

There are situations where you may want to log in directly to the root user account. This provides total control over the system and is considered to be risky. But if you are performing several administrative tasks at once or if you need to modify configuration files directly, root user account access may work best. The root user is a special account reserved for system management operations with unrestricted access to all components of your Linux operating system. You can log in as the root user from either from a terminal window or the command line login prompt. From the command line and **su** access, you will only be able to use command line command. If you log in from the command line interface, you can run corresponding administrative commands like **yum** to install packages or **useradd** to add a new user. From your desktop, you can also run command line administrative tools using a terminal window. The command line interface for the root user uses a special prompt, the sharp sign, #. In the next example, the user logs into the system as the root user and receives the # prompt.

```
login: root
password:
#
```

su

When logged in as a normal user, you can then log in as a **root** user using a terminal window and the **su** command. This is helpful if you need to run a command as a **root** user. You can use the **su** command with the root username, or just the **su** command alone (the **root** username will be assumed). You will be prompted to enter the **root** user password.

```
su root
password:
```

In the following example, the user logs in as the root user the runs the **nmb** script using the **service** command which requires root user access.

```
su
password:
service nmb start
```

To exit from a **su** login operation, when you are finished on that account, just enter **exit**.

```
exit
```

If you log in as the root user with the **su** command in a terminal window, you cannot run desktop applications from that terminal window as the root user.

Note: The **su** command can actually be used to login to any user, provided you have that user's password.

root password

Because a superuser has the power to change almost anything on the system, the **root** user password is usually a carefully guarded secret, changed very frequently, and given only to those whose job it is to manage the system. With the correct password, you can log into the system as a system administrator and configure the system in different ways. You can also add or remove users, add or remove whole file systems, backup and restore files, and even designate the system's name and address.

To change the root user password, you can use the **passwd** command in a Terminal window, once you have logged in as the **root** user (**su** command). Your password will be checked to see if you have selected one that can be easily cracked.

Controlled Administrative Access with PolicyKit: polkit-1

Designed by the Freedesktop.org project, PolicyKit allows ordinary users and applications access to administrative controlled applications and devices. Currently, it supports several key administrative operations including NetworkManager, Udisks, PackageKit, Firewall, Services, Samba, and the GNOME clock and system monitor. Though this could be done with other operations like group permissions, PolicyKit aims to provide a simple and centralized interface for granting users access to administration controlled devices and tools. PolicyKit is used to grant access to shared devices managed by Udisks. This includes most of the devices on your system including removable ones.

PolicyKit can allow for more refined access. Instead of an all or nothing approach, where a user had to gain full root-level control over the entire system just to access a specific administration tool, PolicyKit can allow access to specific administrative applications. All other access can be denied. Without PolicyKit, this kind of access could be configured for in a limited way for some devices, like mount and unmounting CD/DVD discs, but not for applications. A similar kind of refined control is provided with PAM and **sudo**, allowing access to specific administrative applications, but administrative password access is still required, and root level access, though limited to that application, is still granted. You can find out more about PolicyKit at **http://hal.freedesktop.org/docs/polkit/**.

PolicyKit configuration and support is already set up for you. A new version of PolicyKit, polkit-1, is now used for PolicyKit operations. Configuration files for these operations are held in **/usr/share/polkit-1**. There is, yet, no desktop tool to use to configure these settings. The desktop tool, **polkit-gnome**, only provides GNOME dialogs for providing authentication when required by an application or device.

Changing PolicyKit options

With PolicyKit, administration controlled devices and applications are set up to communicate with ordinary users, allowing them to request certain actions. If the user is allowed to perform the action, then the request is authorized, and the action is performed.

Difficulties occur if you want to change the authorization setting for certain actions, like mounting internal hard drives. Currently, you can change the settings by manually editing the configuration files in the **/usr/share/polkit-1/actions** folder, but this is risky. To make changes you, first, have to know the action to change and the permission to set. The man page for **polkit** will list possible authorizations. The default authorizations can be **allow_any** for anyone, **allow_inactive** for a console, and **allow_active** for an active console only (user logged in). These authorizations can be set to specific values, which are listed here.

auth_admin	Administrative user only, authorization required always
auth_admin_keep	Administrative user only, authorization kept for a brief period.
auth_self	User authorization required
auth_self_keep	User authorization required, authorization kept for a brief period.
yes	Always allow access
no	Never allow access

You will need to know the PolicyKit action to modify and the file to edit. The action files are listed in the **/usr/share/polkit-1/actions** folder. The action files have a **.policy** extension. For example, the action file for mounting internal drives is:

```
org.freedesktop.udisks2.policy
```

It's full path name is:

```
/usr/share/polkit-1/actions/org.freedesktop.udisks2.policy
```

By default, PolicyKit is configured to require authorization using the root password before a user can mount an internal hard drive partition. Should you want to allow users to mount partitions without an authorization request, the **org.freedesktop.udisks2.policy** file in the **/usr/share/polkit-1** folder has to be modified to change the **allow_active** default for **filesystem-mount-system** action from **auth_admin_keep** to **yes**. The **auth_admin_keep** option requires administrative authorization.

Enter the following to edit the **org.freedesktop.udisks2.policy** file in the **/usr/share/polkit-1/actions** folder. First login as the root user, **su**.

```
su
nano /usr/share/polkit-1/actions/org.freedesktop.udisks2.policy
```

If you have enabled the **sudo** command, you can use **sudo** and **gedit** instead of **su** and **nano**.

```
sudo gedit /usr/share/polkit-1/actions/org.freedesktop.udisks2.policy
```

Locate the **action id** labeled as:

```
<action id ="org.feedesktop.udisks2.filesystem-mount-system">
  <description>Mount a filesystem on a system device</description>
```

This is usually the second action id. At the end of that action section, you will find the following entry. It will be located within a defaults subsection, <**defaults**>.

```
<allow_active>auth_admin_keep</allow_active>
```

Replace **auth_admin_keep** with **yes**.

```
<allow_active>yes</allow_active>
```

Save the file. Users will no longer have to enter a password to mount internal partitions.

pkexec

You can use the **pkexec** command in place of **sudo** to run graphical applications with administrative access (see Figure 6-2). The **pkexec** tool is a policykit alternative to **sudo**, and requires that your application has a corresponding policykit action file**.** Applications like user accounts, Udisks, and NetworkManager already have action files. Others, like Gedit, do not. To use **pkexec** with Gedit, you must create a policykit action file for it. This is a simple process, copying most of the entries from the example in the **pkexec** man page.

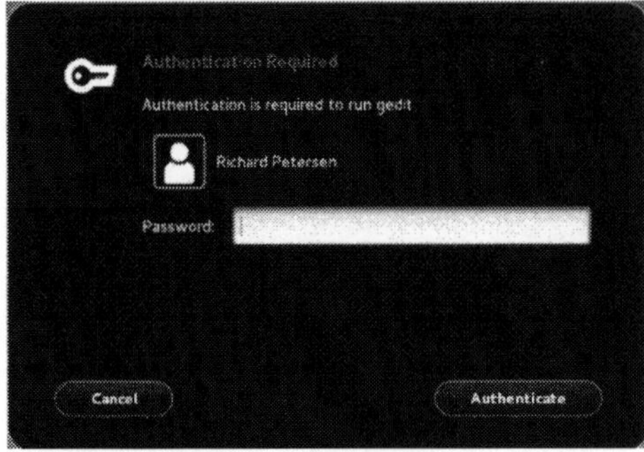

Figure 6-2: pkexec prompt for secure access

To use **gedit** with **pkexec,** you need to add a policy file to the **/usr/share/polkit-1/actions** folder. The file must have the extension **.policy**. You can use a text editor to create the file and then copy it to that folder. The name of the file would be something like **org.freedesktop.policykit.pkexec.gedit.policy**. Be sure to use the **sudo** command with **cp** command in a terminal window to perform the copy. This is an administrative copy. Also, make sure the annotate line at the end for desktop access sets the **exec.allow_gui** option to true.

```
   <annotate key="org.freedesktop.policykit.exec.allow_gui">true</annotate>
```

A sample policy file for Gedit is shown here.

org.freedesktop.policykit.pkexec.gedit.policy

```
<?xml version="1.0" encoding="UTF-8"?>
   <!DOCTYPE policyconfig PUBLIC
     "-//freedesktop//DTD PolicyKit Policy Configuration 1.0//EN"
     "http://www.freedesktop.org/standards/PolicyKit/1/policyconfig.dtd">
 <policyconfig>

  <action id="org.freedesktop.policykit.pkexec.gedit">
    <description>Run the Gedit program</description>
    <message>Authentication is required to run gedit</message>
    <icon_name>gedit</icon_name>
    <defaults>
       <allow_any>auth_admin</allow_any>
       <allow_inactive>auth_admin</allow_inactive>
       <allow_active>auth_self_keep</allow_active>
    </defaults>
    <annotate key="org.freedesktop.policykit.exec.path">/usr/bin/gedit</annotate>
    <annotate key="org.freedesktop.policykit.exec.allow_gui">true</annotate>
   </action>

 </policyconfig>
```

Alternatively, you could simply copy a simple policy file, change the name, and edit it to replace the program names and the message and add the **allow_gui** entry.

You can then enter the **pkexec** command in a terminal window with the application as an argument, or set up an application launcher with **pkexec** as the command. The following example will start up the Gedit editor with administrative access, allowing you to edit system configuration files directly (see Figure 6-3).

```
pkexec gedit
```

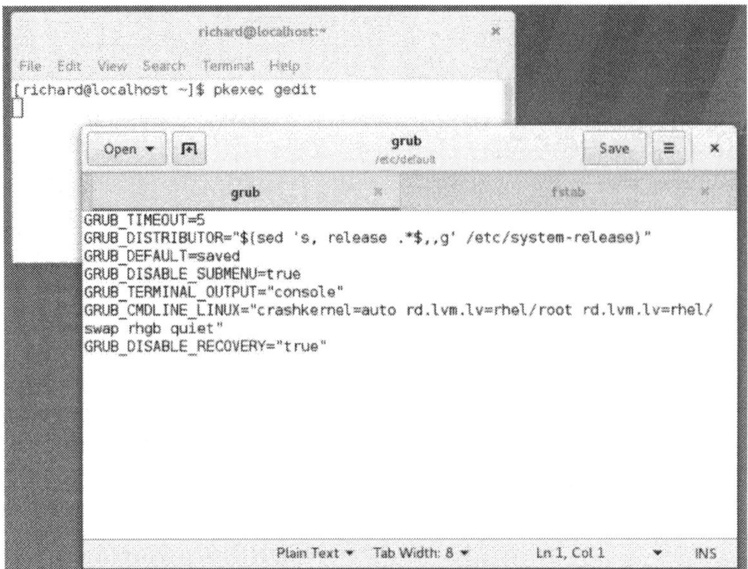

Figure 6-3: Invoking Gedit with pkexec command

Controlled Administrative Access with sudo

With the sudo tool, you can allow ordinary users to have limited root user level administrative access for certain tasks. This allows other users to perform specific superuser operations without having full root level control. You can find more about sudo at **www.sudo.ws**. To use sudo to run an administrative command, the user precedes the command with the **sudo** command. The user is issued a time-sensitive ticket to allow access.

```
sudo date
```

Access is controlled by the **/etc/sudoers** file. This file lists users and the commands they can run, along with the password for access. If the NOPASSWD option is set, then users will not need a password. ALL, depending on the context, can refer to all hosts on your network, all root-level commands, or all users.

To make changes or add entries, you have to edit the file with the special sudo editing command **visudo**. This invokes the Vi editor to edit the **/etc/sudoers** file. Unlike a standard editor, **visudo** will lock the **/etc/sudoers** file and check the syntax of your entries. You are not allowed to save changes unless the syntax is correct. If you want to use a different editor, you can assign it to the EDITOR shell variable.

```
visudo
```

Entries in the sudoers file are technically referred to as specifications, of which there are two kinds: user and alias. The user specification is the primary entry that actually controls user access. The user specification has user, host, runas, and command lists. The user list is the users being controlled in this specification. The hosts are hosts the user can access. The runas list is the list of users the users can access the hosts as (a user with full root user capability should be able to access any user on a host). The command list is the list of commands those users can run. For any of these, you can use **ALL** to indicate all users (user list and runas), hosts, or commands. The user specification has the following syntax:

```
users    hosts=(runas) commands
```

The **(*runas*)** segment is optional and is used to allow a user to access a host as another user. The *runas* segment is simply a list of users. Using ALL for the user gives access to all users.

The host is a host on your network. You can specify all hosts with the **ALL** term. The command can be a list of commands, some or all qualified by options such as whether a password is required. To specify all commands, you can also use the **ALL** term. The following gives the user **george** full root-level access to all commands on all hosts:

```
george  ALL = ALL
```

By default, sudo will deny access to all users but allows access by the root user. The default **/etc/sudoers** file sets full access for the **root** user to all commands using the **ALL=(ALL) ALL** entry.

```
root    ALL=(ALL)    ALL
```

To give a user full administrative access on all hosts (the same a **root** user access), you can copy the **root** user entry and replace root with the name of the user. The following gives full root user level access to the **richard** user.

```
richard  ALL=(ALL)    ALL
```

When editing the **sudoers** file with the **visudo** editor, to copy the line, move to the **root** line, then press the **yy** keys followed by the **p** key to copy and paste the line. Move to the **root** name in the copy and press the **cw** keys to edit the root name, and then type in the new name. Press the **ESC** key when finished, and then the **ZZ** keys to save and exit

You can also let a user run as another user on a given host. Such alternate users are placed within parentheses before the commands. For example, if you want to give **george** access to the **beach** host as the user **robert**, you use the following:

```
george beach = (robert) ALL
```

To let a user run as any user on all hosts, you would use ALL = (ALL), as is done for the root user.

```
george ALL=(ALL) ALL
```

To specify a group name, you prefix the group with a **%** sign, as in **%mygroup**. This way, you can give the same access to a group of users. The **/etc/sudoers** file contains samples for a **%wheel** group.

To give **robert** access on all hosts to the **date** command, you would use

```
robert ALL=/usr/bin/system-config-date
```

If a user wants to see what commands he or she can run, that user would use the **sudo** command with the **-l** option.

```
sudo -l
```

To better control access by different groups and users, sudo also supports alias specifications. See the sudo Man page for more details. You can set up aliases for users, hosts, and commands. Certain aliases are already set up for you. An alias has the following syntax:

```
alias-type   name    list
```

There are three types of aliases, one for each part of a sudo entry: **User_Alias** for users, Runas_Alias for users run as, **Host_Alias** for hosts, and **Cmnd_Alias** for commands. The **Cmnd_Alias** defines groups of commands that can then be easily referenced in a sudo definition. Several are already defined for you (though commented out) like SERVICES for running the **service** and **chkconfig** commands, and STORAGE for running file system operations like **fdisk**, **parted**, and **mount**.

```
Cmnd_Alias SERVICES = /sbin/service, /sbin/chkconfig
```

Certain **User_Alias** and **Host_Alias** entries are already defined in the **/etc/sudoers** file but commented out, like one for **ADMINS**. These are examples you can use to create an entry of your own.

```
# User_Alias ADMINS = jsmith, mkem
```

The following would allow the user robert to use the **service** and **chkconfig** commands on any host.

```
robert ALL=SERVICES
```

If the ADMINS user alias is defined, you could use the following to allow root level access to a group of users designated as administrators.

```
ADMINS  ALL=(ALL)  ALL
```

In addition, sudo also supports tags that provide specialized options. In particular, the **NOPASSWD** tag will allow a user to login without a password. The following would allow a user root level access without having to enter the root password.

```
george ALL = NOPASSWD: ALL
```

There are also options you can set for sudo, including **authenticate** to require a password and **passwd_timeout** for the password prompt timeout. The **rootpw** option would require that users enter the **root** user password, instead of their own user password.

Configuration Folders and Files

Your Linux file system is organized into folders whose files are used for different system functions (see Table 6-2). For basic system administration, you should be familiar with the system program folders where applications are kept, the system configuration folder (**/etc**) where most configuration files are placed, and the system log folder (**/var/log**) that holds the system logs, recording activity on your system.

Folders	Description
/bin	System-related programs
/sbin	System programs for specialized tasks
/lib	System and application libraries
/etc	Configuration files for system and network services and applications
/home	The location of user home folders and server data folders, such as Web and FTP site files
/mnt	The location where removable device file systems are mounted
/var	The location of system folders whose files continually change, such as logs, printer spool files, and lock files
/usr	User-related programs and files. Includes several key subfolders, such as **/usr/bin** and **/usr/doc**
/usr/bin	Programs for users
/dev	Dynamically generated folder for device files
/usr/share	Shared files
/usr/share/doc	Documentation for applications
/tmp	Folder for system temporary files
/var/log/	System logs generated by **rsyslogd**
/var/log/audit	Audit logs generated by **auditd**
/lib/systemd/system	systemd service and target files

Table 6-2: System Folders

Folders with "bin" in the name are used to hold programs. The **/bin** folder holds basic user programs, such as login shells (BASH, TCSH, and ZSH) and file commands (**cp**, **mv**, **rm**, **ln**, and so on). The **/sbin** folder holds specialized system programs for such tasks as file system management (**fsck**, **fdisk**, **mkfs**) and system operations like shutdown. The **/usr/bin** folder holds program files designed for user tasks. The **/usr/sbin** folder holds user-related system operations, such as **useradd** to add new users. The **/lib** folder holds all the libraries your system makes use of, including the main Linux library, **libc**, and subfolders such as **modules**, which holds all the current kernel modules.

When you configure different elements of your system, like users, applications, servers, or network connections, you make use of configuration files kept in certain system folders (see Table 6-3). Configuration files are placed in the **/etc** folder, with more specific device and service configuration located in the **/etc/sysconfig** folder. The systemd user configuration files and folders are located in **/etc/systemd**.

File	Description
/etc/bashrc	Default shell configuration file Bash shell
/etc/group	Contains a list of groups with configurations for each
/etc/fstab	Automatically mounts file systems when you start your system
/etc/profile	Default shell configuration file for users
/etc/motd	System administrator's message of the day
/etc/mtab	Currently mounted file systems
/etc/passwd	Contains user password and login configurations
/etc/services	Services run on the system and the ports they use
/etc/shadow	Contains user-encrypted passwords
/etc/shells	Shells installed on the system that users can use
/etc/sudoers	Sudo configuration to control administrative access
Folders	
/etc/cron.d	Cron scripts
/etc/cups	CUPS printer configuration files
/etc/default	Configuration files for some services
/etc/grub.d	The GRUB configuration files for the GRUB boot loader.
/etc/modprobe.d	Folder with kernel module configuration files specifying modules on your system to be automatically loaded
/etc/openldap	Configuration for Open LDAP server
/etc/skel	Folder that holds the versions of initialization files, such as **.bash_profile**, which are copied to new users' home folders
/etc/sysconfig	Red Hat Enterprise Linux device and service configuration environments
/etc/systemd	Configuration scripts and links for services managed by systemd
/etc/X11	X Window System configuration files
/etc/udev	Rules for generating devices

Table 6-3: Configuration Files and Folders

Configuration Files: /etc

The **/etc** folder holds your system, network, server, and application configuration files. This folder includes various subfolders, such as **/etc/httpd** for the Apache Web server configuration files, **/etc/X11** for the X Window System and window manager configuration files, and **/etc/udev** for rules to generate device files in **/dev**. You can configure many applications and services by directly editing their configuration files, though it is best to use a corresponding administration tool. Table 6-3 lists several commonly used configuration files found in the **/etc** folder.

/etc/sysconfig

On Red Hat Enterprise Linux systems, configuration and startup information is also kept in the **/etc/sysconfig** folder. Here you will find files containing definitions of system variables used to configure devices such as your keyboard and mouse, along with settings for network connections, as well as options for service scripts, covering services such as the Web server or the IPtables firewall. These entries were defined for you when you configured your devices during installation or installed your service software.

A sample of the keyboard file, **/etc/sysconfig/keyboard**, is shown here.

```
KEYBOARDTYPE="pc"
KEYTABLE="us"
```

Several of these files are generated by Red Hat Enterprise Linux administration tools such as system-config-keyboard and system-config-users**.** Table 6-4 lists several commonly used tools and the sysconfig files they control.

Some files provide global or system configuration support for service scripts, like **iptables**, **samba**, **httpd** (Apache), or **SpamAssassin**. Other files provide configuration settings for corresponding tools like system-config-users.

Several folders are included, such as **network-scripts**, which list several startup scripts for network connections, such as **ifup-ppp**, which starts up PPP connections.

Tools	Configuration Files	Description
authconfig	**/etc/sysconfig/authconfig** **/etc/sysconfig/network**	Authentication options, such as enabling NIS, shadow passwords, Kerberos, and LDAP.
system-config-keyboard	**/etc/sysconfig/keyboard**	Selects the keyboard type.
NetworkManager	**/etc/sysconfig/network** **/etc/sysconfig/networking**	Sets your network settings.
system-config-date	**/etc/sysconfig/clock**	Sets the time and date.
system-config-users	**/etc/sysconfig/system-config-users**	Settings for system-config-users.
system-config-httpd	**/etc/sysconfig/httpd**	Settings for Apache Web server.
IPtables	**/etc/sysconfig/iptables**	Firewall rules, IPtables
firewalld	**/etc/sysconfig/firewalld**	Settings for FirewallD.

Table 6-4: Sysconfig Files with Corresponding Red Hat Enterprise Linux System Administration Tools

Some administration tools use more than one **sysconfig** file; for example, NetworkManager places its network configuration information such as the hostname and gateway in the **/etc/sysconfig/network** file. Specific Ethernet device configurations, which would include your IP address and netmask, are placed in the appropriate Ethernet device configuration file in the **/etc/sysconfig/network-scripts** folder. Local host settings are in **/etc/sysconfig/network-scripts/ifcfg-lo**.

System Time and Date

You can set the system time and date using the shell **timedatectl** and **date** commands, the older desktop tool system-config-date, or the GNOME Settings Date & Time dialog. You probably set the time and date when you first installed your system. You should not need to do so again. If you entered the time incorrectly or moved to a different time zone, though, you will have to change your time.

Using the system-config-date Utility

An alternative to the GNOME Settings Date & Time dialog, you can still use the older system-config-date tool to set the system time and date. It is accessible from the Sundry sub-overview. There are two tabs, one for the "Date and Time" and one for the time zone (see Figure 6-4). Use the calendar to select the year, month, and date. Then use the Time box to set the hour, minute, and second. The Time Zone panel shows a map with locations. Select the one nearest you to set your time zone.

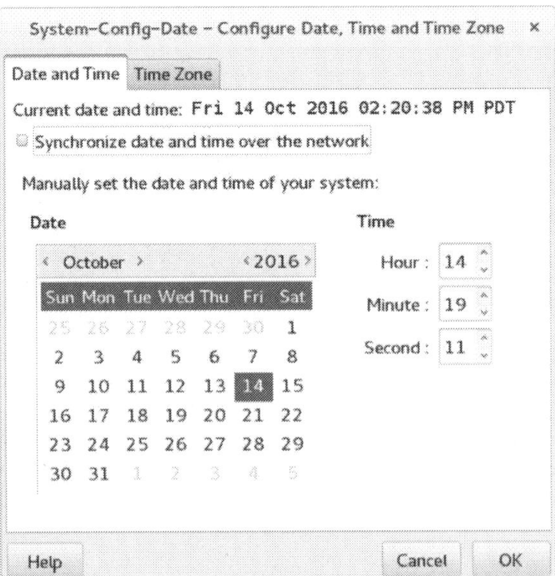

Figure 6-4: Date & Time: system-config-date

The Network Time Protocol (NTP) allows a remote server to set the date and time, instead of using local settings. NTP allows for the most accurate synchronization of your system's clock. It is often used to manage the time and date for networked systems, freeing the administrator from having to synchronize clocks manually. You can download current documentation and NTP software from the **http://www.ntp.org/** site.

On the Date and Time tab, you can choose to enable NTP and select the server to use. Click the "synchronize date and time over the network" checkbox to display the Network Time Protocol settings. NTP servers operate through pools which will randomly select an available server to increase efficiency. A set of pools designated for use by Red Hat Enterprise Linux are already installed up for you, beginning with **0.rhel.pool.ntp.org** (see Figure 6-5). If access with one pool is slow, you change to another. The **pool.ntp.org** pool servers support worldwide access. Pools for specific geographical locations can be found at the NTP Public Services support site (Time Servers link), **http://support.ntp.org/bin/view/Servers/WebHome/**. A closer server could be faster.

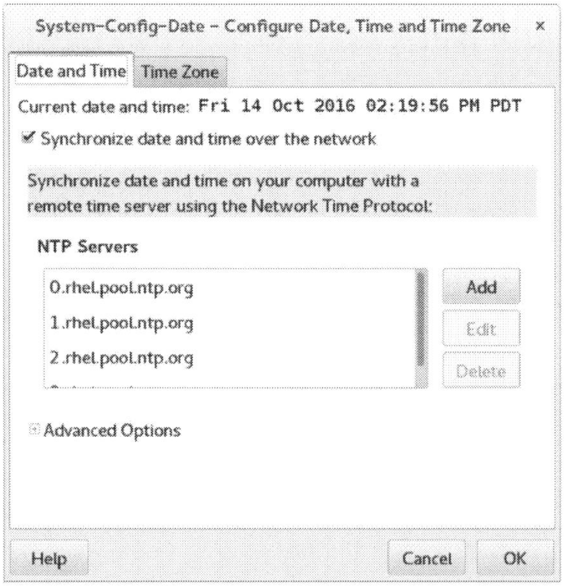

Figure 6-5: Date & Time: system-config-date, Network Time Protocol

Using the date Command

You can also use the older **date** command on your root user command line to set the date and time for the system. As an argument to **date**, you list (with no delimiters) the month, day, time, and year. In the next example, the date is set to 2:59 P.M., April 6, 2016 (04 for April, 03 for the day, 1459 for the time, and 11 for the year 2016):

```
su
date 0403145916
Sun Apr 3 02:59:22 PST 2011
```

Using the timedatectl Command

You can use the **timedatectl** command on your root user command line to set the date and time for the system. As an argument to **timedatectl**, you use the **set-time** option and list the hour, minute, and second separated by colons. In the next example, the date is set to 2:59 P.M.

```
su
timedatectl set-time 14:59:00
```

As an argument to **timedatectl**, you use the **set-time** option and list the year (four digits), month, and day separated by dashes. In the next example, the date is set to December 6, 2016:

```
su
timedatectl set-time 2016:12:06
```

The system clock runs in UTC time. For local time you use the **set-local-rtc** option with the yes argument. Use the no argument to set it back to UTC time.

```
su
timedatectl set-time yes
```

Check the **System Administration Guide**, Section 1: Basic System Configuration, Chapter 2: Configuring the Date and Time for details on using **timedatectl**.

```
https://access.redhat.com/documentation/en-
US/Red_Hat_Enterprise_Linux/7/html/System_Administrators_Guide/chap-
Configuring_the_Date_and_Time.html
```

Scheduling Tasks: cron

Scheduling regular maintenance tasks, such as backups, is managed by the **cron** service and implemented by a **cron** daemon. These tasks are listed in the **crontab** files such as **/etc/crontab**. The **cron** daemon constantly checks the user's **crontab** file to see if it is time to take these actions. Any user can set up a **crontab** file of his or her own. The root user can set up a **crontab** file to take system administrative actions, such as backing up files at a certain time each week or month.

Check the **System Administration Guide** for details on cron, Part **VI. Monitoring and Automation | Chapter 21: Automating System Tasks**.

```
https://access.redhat.com/documentation/en-
US/Red_Hat_Enterprise_Linux/7/html/System_Administrators_Guide/ch-
Automating_System_Tasks.html#s1-autotasks-cron-anacron
```

The crond Service

The name of the **cron** daemon is **crond**. Normally it is started automatically when your system starts up. You can set this feature using **chkconfig**. The following example starts the **crond** service automatically whenever you boot the system.

```
chkconfig crond on
```

You can also start and stop the **crond** service manually, which you may want to do for emergency maintenance or during upgrades. From the command line (or terminal window), you can use the **service** command and the **stop** option to shut down the service, and the **start** option to run it again:

```
service crond stop
```

crontab Entries

A **crontab** file entry has six fields: the first five are used to specify the time for an action, while the last field is the action itself. The first field specifies minutes (0–59), the second field specifies the hour (0–23), the third field specifies the day of the month (1–31), the fourth field specifies the month of the year (1–12, or month prefixes like Jan and Sep), and the fifth field specifies the day of the week (0–6, or day prefixes like Wed and Fri), starting with 0 as Sunday. In each of the time fields, you can specify a range, a set of values, or use the asterisk to indicate all values. For example, **1-5** for the day-of-week field specifies Monday through Friday. In the hour field, **8, 12, 17** would specify 8 A.M., 12 noon, and 5 P.M. An ***** in the month-of-year field indicates every month. The format of a **crontab** field follows:

```
minute  hour  day-month  month  day(s)-week  task
```

The following example backs up the **projects** folder at 2:00 A.M. every weekday using the **tar** command to archive the folder:

```
0 2 * * 1-5   tar cf /home/backp /home/projects
```

The same entry is listed here again using prefixes for the month and weekday:

```
0 2 * * Mon-Fri tar cf /home/backp /home/projects
```

To specify particular months, days, weeks, or hours, you can list them individually, separated by commas. For example, to perform the previous task on Sunday, Wednesday, and Friday, you could use **0,3,5** in the day-of-week field, or their prefix equivalents, **Sun,Wed,Fri**.

```
0 2 * * 0,3,5   tar cf /home/backp /home/projects
```

cron also supports comments. A comment is any line beginning with a # sign.

```
# Weekly backup for Chris's projects
0 2 * * Mon-Fri  tar cf /home/backp /home/projects
```

Environment Variables for cron

In a **crontab** configuration file, the **cron** service lets you define environment variables for use with tasks performed. RHEL defines variables for SHELL, PATH, HOME, and MAILTO. SHELL designates the shell to use tasks, in this case, the bash shell. PATH lists the folders where programs and scripts can be found. This example lists the standard folders, **/usr/bin** and **/bin**, as well as the system folders reserved for system applications, **/usr/sbin** and **/sbin**. MAILTO designates to who the results of a task are to be mailed. By default, these are mailed to the user who schedules it, but you can have the results sent to a specific user, such as the administrator's e-mail address, or an account on another system in a network. HOME is the home folder for a task, in this case, the top folder.

```
SHELL=/bin/bash
PATH=/sbin:/bin:/usr/sbin:/usr/bin
MAILTO=root
HOME=/
```

The cron.d Folder

On a heavily used system, the **/etc/crontab** file can become crowded easily. There may also be instances where certain entries require different variables. For example, you may need to run some task under a different shell. To help better organize your **crontab** tasks, you can place **crontab** entries in files within the **cron.d** folder. The files in the **cron.d** folder all contain **crontab** entries of the same format as **/etc/crontab**. They may be given any name. They are treated as added **crontab** files, with **cron** checking them for tasks to run. For example, Red Hat Enterprise Linux installs a **sysstat** file in the **cron.d** that contains **crontab** entries to run tools to gather system statistics.

The crontab Command

You use the **crontab** command to install your entries into a **crontab** file. To do this, first, create a text file and type your **crontab** entries. Save this file with any name you want, such as **mycronfile**. Then, to install these entries, enter **crontab** and the name of the text file. The **crontab** command takes the contents of the text file and creates a **crontab** file in the **/var/spool/cron** folder, adding the name of the user who issued the command. In the following example, the root user installs the contents of **mycronfile** as the root's **crontab** file. This creates a file called **/var/spool/cron/root**. If a user named **justin** installed a **crontab** file, the action would create a file called **/var/spool/cron/justin**. You can control the use of the **crontab** command by regular users with the **/etc/cron.allow** file. Only users with their names in this file can create **crontab** files of their own. Conversely, the **/etc/cron.deny** file lists those users denied use of the **cron** tool, preventing them for scheduling tasks. If neither file exists, access is denied to all users. If a user is not in a **/etc/cron.allow** file, access is denied. However, if the **/etc/cron.allow** file does not exist, and the **/etc/cron.deny** file does, then all users not listed in **/etc/cron.deny** are automatically allowed access.

```
# crontab mycronfile
```

Editing in cron

Never try to edit your **crontab** file directly. Instead, use the **crontab** command with the **-e** option. This opens your **crontab** file in the **/var/spool/cron** folder with the standard text editor, such as Vi. **crontab** uses the default editor as specified by the **crontab** shell environment variable. To use a different editor for **crontab**, change the default editor by assigning the editor's program name to the **crontab** variable and exporting that variable. Normally, the editor variable is set in the **/etc/profile** script. Running **crontab** with the **-l** option displays the contents of your **crontab** file, and the **-r** option deletes the entire file. Invoking **crontab** with another text file of **crontab** entries overwrites your current **crontab** file, replacing it with the contents of the text file.

Organizing Scheduled Tasks

You can organize administrative **cron** tasks into two general groups: common administrative tasks that can be run at regular intervals, or specialized tasks that need to be run at a unique time. Unique tasks can be run as entries in the **/etc/crontab** file, as described in the next section. Common administrative tasks, though they can be run from the **/etc/crontab** file, are better organized into specialized **cron** folders. Within such folders, each task is placed in its own shell script that will invoke the task when run. For example, there may be several administrative tasks that all need to be run each week on the same day, say if maintenance for a system is scheduled on a Sunday morning. For these kinds of task, **cron** provides several specialized folders for automatic daily, weekly, monthly, and yearly tasks. Each contains a **cron** prefix and a suffix for the time interval. The **/etc/cron.daily** folder is used for tasks that need to be performed every day, whereas weekly tasks can be placed in the **/etc/cron.weekly** folder. The **cron** folders are listed in Table 6-5.

cron Files and Folders	Description
/etc/crontab	System **crontab** file, accessible only by the root user
/etc/cron.d	Folder containing multiple **crontab** files, accessible only by the root user
/etc/cron.hourly	Folder for tasks performed hourly
/etc/cron.daily	Folder for tasks performed daily
/etc/cron.weekly	Folder for tasks performed weekly
/etc/cron.monthly	Folder for tasks performed monthly
/etc/cron.allow	Users allowed to submit **cron** tasks
/etc/cron.deny	Users denied access to **cron**

Table 6-5: Cron Files and Folders

Running cron Folder Scripts

Each folder contains scripts that are all run at the same time. The scheduling for each group is determined by an entry in the **/etc/crontab** file. The actual execution of the scripts is performed by the **/usr/bin/run-parts** script, which runs all the scripts and programs in a given folder. Scheduling for all the tasks in a given folder is handled by an entry in the **/etc/crontab** file. A sample **crontab** file is shown here, with times for running scripts in the different **cron** folders. Here you can see that most scripts are run at about 4 A.M. either daily (4:02), Sunday (4:22), or the first day of each month (4:42). Hourly ones are run one minute after the hour.

```
SHELL=/bin/bash
PATH=/sbin:/bin:/usr/sbin:/usr/bin
MAILTO=root
HOME=/
# run-parts
01 * * * * root run-parts /etc/cron.hourly
02 4 * * * root run-parts /etc/cron.daily
22 4 * * 0 root run-parts /etc/cron.weekly
42 4 1 * * root run-parts /etc/cron.monthly
```

Tip: Scripts within a **cron** folder are run alphabetically. If you need a certain script to run before any others, you may have to alter its name. One method is to prefix the name with a numeral. For example, in the **/cron.weekly** folder, the **anacron** script is named **0anacron** so that it will run before any others.

Keep in mind though that these are simply folders that contain executable files. The actual scheduling is performed by the entries in the **/etc/crontab** file. For example, if the weekly field in the **cron.weekly crontab** entry is entry is changed to ***** instead of **0**, and the monthly field to **1 (22 4 1 * *** instead of **22 4 * * 0**), tasks in the **cron.weekly** file would end up running monthly instead of weekly.

Cron Folder Names

The names used for these folders are merely conventions. They have no special meaning to the **cron** daemon. You could, in fact, create your own folder, place scripts within it, and schedule run-parts to run those scripts at a given time. In the next example, scripts placed in the **/etc/cron.mydocs** folder will run at 12 noon every Wednesday.

```
* 12 * * 3 root run-parts /etc/cron.mydocs
```

Anacron

For a system that may normally be shut down during times that **cron** is likely to run, you may want to supplement **cron** with **anacron**. **anacron** activates only when scheduled tasks need to be executed. For example, if a system is shut down on a weekend when **cron** jobs are scheduled, then the jobs will not be performed; **anacron**, however, checks to see what jobs need to be performed when the system is turned on again and then runs them. It is designed only for jobs that run daily or weekly.

For **anacron** jobs, you place **crontab** entries in the **/etc/anacrontab** file. For each scheduled task, you specify the number of intervening days when it is executed (7 is weekly, 30 is monthly), the time of day it is run (numbered in minutes), a description of the task, and the command to be executed. For backups, the command used would be **tar** operation.

KDE Task Scheduler (Kcron)

On KDE you can use the KDE Task Scheduler (Kcron) to set up user and system-level scheduled tasks (install the **kdeadmin** package). You access the Task Scheduler on the KDE Settings window, System Administration | Task Scheduler. The Task Scheduler window will list your scheduled tasks (see Figure 6-6). Click the New Task button to open a New Task window where you can enter the command to run, add comments, and then specify the time in months, days, hours, and minutes from simple arranged buttons. On the Task Scheduler window, you can select a task and use the side buttons to modify it, delete the task, run it now, or print a copy of it. For tasks using the same complex commands or arguments, you can create a variable, and then use that variable in a command. Variables are listed in the Environment Variables section. To use a variable in a scheduled task, precede its name with the **$** character when you enter the command. Entering just the **$** symbol in the Command text box will display a drop-down list of pre-defined system variables you can use like **$PATH** and **$USER**.

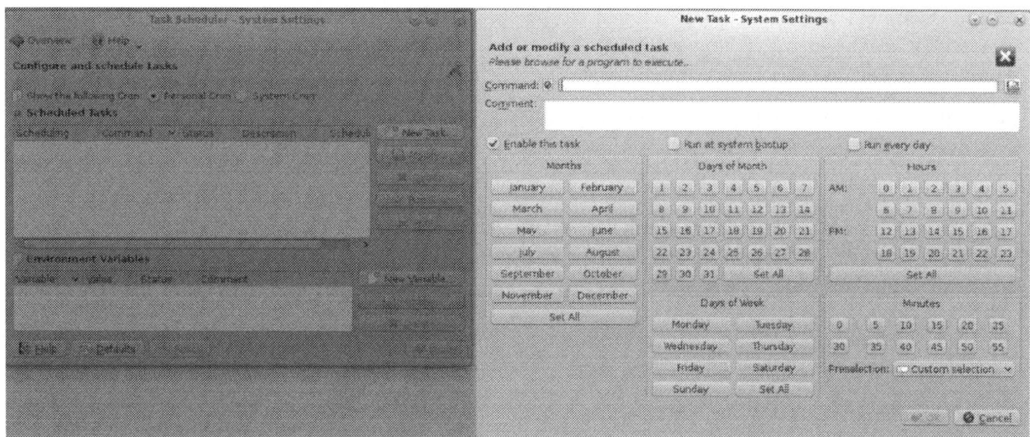

Figure 6-6: KDE Task Scheduler

Grand Unified Bootloader (GRUB)

With Linux, you have the ability to load different versions of the Linux kernel as well as other operating systems that you have installed on your system. The task of selecting and starting up an operating system or kernel is managed by a boot management utility, the Grand Unified Bootloader version 2 (GRUB2). This is a versatile tool, letting you load operating systems installed on your hard drives, as well as letting you choose from different Linux kernels that may be installed on the same Linux system.

With Grub, users can select operating systems to run from a menu interface displayed when a system boots up. Use arrow keys to move to an entry and press ENTER. Linux and Unix operating systems are known as multi-boot operating systems and take arguments passed to them at boot time. Type **e** to edit a command, letting you change kernel arguments or specify a different kernel. The **c** command places you in a command line interface. Provided your system BIOS supports very large drives, GRUB can boot from anywhere on them. Check the grub Man page for Grub options.

```
http://fedoraproject.org/wiki/GRUB_2
```

RHEL uses GRUB2 which uses the configuration file **/etc/default/grub**. GRUB2 files are kept in the **/etc/grub.d** directory. Run as root the following **grub2-mkconfig** to apply changes made in **/etc/default/grub**.

```
grub2-mkconfig -o /boot/grub2/grub.cfg
```

With Grub2, configuration is placed in user-modifiable configuration files held in the **/etc/default/grub** file and in the **/etc/grub.d** directory. There is a Grub2 configuration file called **/boot/grub/grub.cfg**, but this file is generated by Grub each time the system starts up, and should never be edited by a user. Instead, you would edit the **/etc/default/grub** file to set parameters like the default operating system to boot. To create your own menu entries, you create entries for them in the **/etc/grub.d/40_custom** file.

Grub options are set by assigning values to Grub options in the **/etc/default/grub** file. You can edit the file directly to change these options. To edit the file with the Gedit editor, open a terminal window and enter the following command. You will be prompted to enter your password.

```
sudo gedit /etc/default/grub
```

On dual boot systems (those with both RHEL and Windows or Mac), the option that users are likely to change is GRUB_DEFAULT, which sets the operating system or kernel to boot automatically if one is not chosen. The option uses a line number to indicate an entry in the Grub boot menu, with numbering starting from 0 (not 1). First, check your Grub menu when you boot up (press any key on boot to display the Grub menu for a longer time), and then count to where the entry of the operating system you want to make the default is listed. If the Windows entry is at 4th, which would be line 3 (counting from 0), to make it the default you would set the GRUB_DEAULT option to 3.

```
GRUB_DEFAULT=3
```

You can also do a search of the **/boot/grub2/grub.cfg** file for the **menuentry** pattern to display a list of all your menu entries. Use **cut** to display the second column as delimited by single quotes (**-d** "'" **-f2**).

```
grep ^menuentry /boot/grub2/grub.cfg  | cut -d "'" -f2
```

Should the listing of operating systems and kernels change (adding or removing kernels), you would have to edit the **/etc/default/grub** file again and each time a change occurs. A safer way to set the default is to configure GRUB to use the **grub-set-default** command. First, edit the **/etc/default/grub** file and change the option for GRUB_DEFAULT to **saved**, if it is not already set to that option. When installed, the RHEL Workstation will set the GRUB_DEFAULT option to **saved**.

```
GRUB_DEFAULT=saved
```

Then update GRUB.

```
grub2-mkconfig -o /boot/grub2/grub.cfg
```

The **grub2-set-default** command takes as its option the number of the default you want to set (numbering from 0) or the name of the kernel or operating system. The following sets the default to 0, the first kernel entry.

```
sudo grub2-set-default 0
```

For a kernel name or operating system, you can use the name as it appears on the GRUB menu (enclosing the name in quotes), such as:

```
sudo grub2-set-default  'Windows (loader) (on /dev/sda1)'
```

The GRUB_TIMEOUT option sets the number of seconds Grub will wait to allow a user to access the menu, before booting the default operating system. The default options used for the kernel are listed by the GRUB_CMDLINE_LINUX option. Currently, these include the **rhgb** and **quiet** options to display the RHEL emblem on start up, but not the list of startup tasks being performed (**quiet**).

Once you have made your changes, you have to run the **grub2-mkconfig** command. Otherwise, your changes will not take effect. This command will generate a new **/etc/grub/grub.cfg** file, which determines the actual Grub 2 configuration.

```
grub2-mkconfig -o /boot/grub2/grub.cfg
```

You can add your own Grub2 boot entries by placing them in the **/etc/grub.d/40_custom** file. The file is nearly empty except for an initial **exec tail** command that you must take care not to change. After you make your additions to the **40_custom** file, you have to update GRUB to have the changes take effect.

Dracut options (initramfs RAM file system)

RHEL uses the Dracut initramfs RAM file system to speed up the boot process by relying on udev to detect the file system devices so that the root file system can be mounted quickly. Its aim is to rely as little as possible on hard-coded operations. Dracut is installed on RHEL by default (**dracut** package). Check the **dracut** man page for more details, along with a complete set of options. Also, check the Dracut site at **https://sourceforge.net/projects/dracut/** and **http://fedoraproject.org/wiki/Features/Dracut**.

Dracut uses kernel parameters listed on the GRUB kernel command line to configure the initramfs RAM file system on the fly, providing more flexibility and further cutting down on RAM file system code. You also can use the **dracut** command to create an initramfs RAM file system image. Dracut configuration is held in the **/etc/dracut.conf** file and **/etc/dracut.conf.d** folder. See the **dracut.conf** man page for configuration details. A sample **/etc/dracut.conf** file is installed which you can work from.

Puppet

Puppet allows you to configure remote systems automatically, even though they may be running different linux distributions with varying configuration files. Instead of configuring each system on a network manually, you can use Puppet to configure them automatically. Puppet abstracts administration tasks as resources in a resource abstraction layer (RAL). You then specify basic values or operations for a particular resource using a Puppet configuration language. Administration types include services, files, users, and groups. For example, you could use puppet to perform an update for a service (server) on systems using different package managers.

Puppet configuration can become very complex. Once set up though is fully automates configuration changes across all your networked systems. For detailed documentation and guides see the following. The information is not RHEL7 specific.

```
https://docs.puppet.com/
```

Puppet configuration is located in the **/etc/puppet** folder. Puppet operations on resources are specified in manifest files located in the **/etc/puppet/manifests** folder. You can think of puppet as working like a database that specifies values for a resource's fields. A simple example cited in the Puppet documentation are the permissions you want to set for the password file.

```
file { '/etc/passwd':
     owner => root,
     group => root,
     mode  => 644,
}
```

The resource is first defined, in this case, a file, then the resource title, which, for a file, is usually the full file name (/etc/passwd). For a service, it could be the name of the server daemon such as vsftpd. Properties are then specified for the file, owner, group, and mode.

You can also collect resources into aggregates using classes and definition. Classes are defined in the **/etc/puppet/manifest/classes** folder. For example, a class could combine two file resources, letting you reference both with a single class name. As in C++, classes can be inherited by other classes, letting you create complex classes without repeating code. Definitions work similar to classes but do not support inheritance.

On RHEL7, clients use the puppet client (**puppet** package), and the server uses the puppetmaster daemon (**puppet-server** package). These are available from the EPEL repository.

On a puppet clients, be sure to enable the **puppet** service with **chkconfig**. Use the **service** command to manually start and stop. For the server, enable the **puppetmaster** service.

On the firewall add access for the Puppet port, 8140. You can use firewall-config, and on the Other Ports tab, click the Add button to add a port and enter the port 8140. The server uses ports 8141 to 8144. Also, be sure to install the **puppet-firewalld** package.

On SELinux be sure to enable puppet client access (SELinux Management, Boolean tab, **puppet** entry).

The puppet runtime configuration is set in the **/etc/sysconfig/puppet** file. Here you specify the puppet server host, the port to use, and the log file. Default entries are commented out.

The clients will have to know the host that the puppet server is on. For a small network, you can do this manually by setting the **PUPPET_SERVER** variable in the **/etc/sysconfig/puppet** file.

```
PUPPET_SERVER=myserver
```

If your network is running a DNS server, you can set up a CNAME puppet entry for the puppet server. The puppet clients can then use the CNAME to locate the puppet server.

```
puppet   IN   CNAME   turtle.mytrek.com
```

You could also add a host entry for the puppet server in each client's **/etc/host** file.

The puppetmaster configuration in **/etc/sysconfig/puppetmaster** file lets you set port entries and the log service. Default entries are commented out. Remove the comment character, #, to enable.

When you first set up a client server puppet connection, the client and server have to sign the client's SSL certificate. First, run puppet on the client. On the server run the **puppetca --list** command to see the clients certificate request. Then use **puppetca --sign** to sign the certificate.

7. System Tools and Monitoring

Red Hat Enterprise Linux provides system tools, as well as user-specific configuration tools. Information about your system is provided by system logs, performance analysis tools, and network tools. These include the RSyslogd logging application and a variety of performance tools like the GNOME System Monitor, Disk Utility, and the Disk Usage Analyzer.

System Logs: /var/log and rsyslogd

Various system logs for tasks performed on your system are stored in the **/var/log** folder. Here you can find logs for mail, news, and all other system operations, such as server logs. The **/var/log/messages** file is a log of all system tasks not covered by other logs. This usually includes startup tasks, such as loading drivers and mounting file systems. If a driver for a card failed to load at startup, you find an error message for it here. Logins are also recorded in this file, showing you who attempted to log into what account. Check the **System Administration Guide** for details on logs, **Part 6 Monitoring and Automation | Chapter 20. Viewing and Managing Log Files**.

```
https://access.redhat.com/documentation/en-
US/Red_Hat_Enterprise_Linux/7/html/System_Administrators_Guide/ch-
Viewing_and_Managing_Log_Files.html
```

System logging is handled by the Reliable and Extended Syslog service, using the **rsyslogd** daemon. This replaces the older syslogd service. Configuration is held in the **/etc/rsyslog.conf** file. For more information see **http://www.rsyslog.com**.

System Logs, journals, and journald

Various system logs for tasks performed on your system are stored and managed by the journald logging daemon. In effect, logs are now considered to be journals accessible by a systemd daemon, journald. From the command line (terminal window), you can use the **journalctl** command to access messages. The **-f** option displays the last few messages and is equivalent to displaying the last few messages in the old /var/log/messages file. The systemd unit file for logging is **systemd-jounrald.service**. The following command lists the last few messages.

```
journalctl -f
```

To see logs from the last system startup (boot), you use the -b option.

```
journalctl -b
```

To see messages for a particular service, you use the -u option and the name of the unit's service file, such as smb.service. The following lists the messages for the samba server.

```
journalctl -u smb.service
```

With the **--since** and **--until** options you can further specify a time.

```
journalctl -u smb.service --since=12:00
```

If you want, you can still install and run the older rsyslogd, which stores messages in the **/var/log/messages** file.

To view these logs you can use the GNOME Log File Viewer, Utilities | System Log (System Log on GNOME Software and the gnome-system-log package on Packages). A sidebar lists the different logs. Selecting one displays the log in the right pane (see Figure 7-1). A search button on the top right opens a search box where you can search for messages in the selected log. A menu button on the top right lets you perform tasks such as zooming, copying, selecting, and filtering. The Log File Viewer queries the journald daemon for log reports using journalctl.

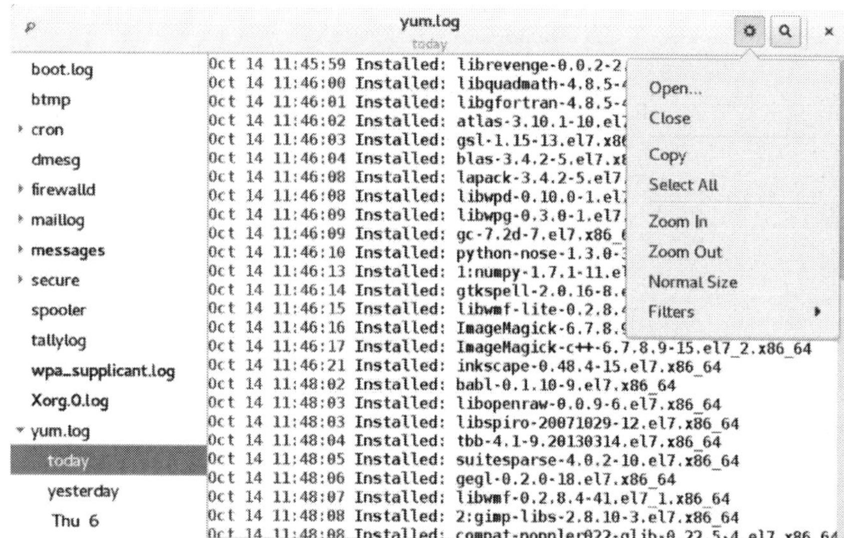

Figure 7-1: GNOME Log File Viewer (System Log)

rsyslogd and /etc/rsyslog.conf

The **rsyslogd** daemon manages the logs on your system, as well as coordinating with any of the logging operations of other systems on your network. Configuration information for **rsyslogd** is held in the **/etc/rsyslog.conf** file, which contains the names and locations for your system log files. Here you find entries for **/var/log/messages** and **/var/log/maillog**, among others. Whenever you make changes to the **rsyslog.conf** file, you need to restart the **rsyslogd** daemon using the following command:

```
service rsyslog restart
```

entries in rsyslogd.conf

An entry in **rsyslog.conf** consists of two fields: a selector and an action (rsyslog uses the same selectors as the older syslog, maintaining compatibility). The selector is the kind of service to be logged, such as mail or news, and the action is the location where messages are to be placed. The action is usually a log file, but it can also be a remote host or a pipe to another program. The kind of service is referred to as a facility. The **rsyslogd** daemon has several terms it uses to specify certain kinds of service (see Table 7-1). A facility can be further qualified by a priority, which specifies the kind of message generated by the facility. **rsyslogd** uses several designated terms to indicate different priorities. A selector is constructed from both the facility and the priority, separated by a period. For example, to save error messages generated by mail systems, you use a sector consisting of the **mail** facility and the **err** priority, as shown here:

```
mail.err
```

Facilities	Description
auth-priv	Security/authorization messages (private)
cron	Clock daemon (cron and at) messages
daemon	Other system daemon messages
kern	Kernel messages
lpr	Line printer subsystem messages
mail	Mail subsystem messages
news	Usenet news subsystem messages
syslog	Syslog internal messages
user	Generic user-level messages
uucp	UUCP subsystem messages
local0 through **local7**	Reserved for local use
priorities	**Description**
debug	7, Debugging messages, lowest priority
info	6, Informational messages
notice	5, Notifications, normal, but significant, condition
warning	4, Warnings
err	3, Error messages
crit	2, Critical conditions
alert	1, Alerts, action must be taken immediately
emerg	0, Emergency messages, system is unusable
Operators	**Description**
*	Matches all facilities or priorities in a sector
=	Restrict to a specified priority
!	Exclude specified priority and higher ones
/	A file to save messages to
@	A host to send messages to
|	A FIFO pipe to send messages to

Table 7-1: rsyslogd Facilities, Priorities, and Operators

To save these messages to the **/var/log/maillog** file, you specify that file as the action, giving you the following entry:

```
mail.err /var/log/maillog
```

The **rsyslogd** daemon also supports the use of ***** as a matching character to match either all the facilities or all the priorities in a sector: **cron.*** would match on all **cron** messages no matter what the priority, ***.err** would match on error messages from all the facilities, and ***.*** would match on all messages. The following example saves all mail messages to the **/var/log/maillog** file and all critical messages to the **/var/log/mycritical** file:

```
mail.* /var/log/maillog
*.crit /var/log/mycritical
```

Priorities

When you specify a priority for a facility, all messages with a higher priority are also included. The **err** priority also includes the **crit**, **alert**, and **emerg** priorities. If you just want to select the message for a specific priority, you qualify the priority with the = operator. For example, **mail.=err** will select only error messages, not **crit**, **alert**, or **emerg** messages. You can also restrict priorities with the ! operator. This will eliminate messages with the specified priority and higher. For example, **mail.!crit** will exclude **crit** messages, as well as the higher **alert** and **emerg** messages. To specifically exclude all the messages for an entire facility, you use the **none** priority; for instance, **mail.none** excludes all mail messages. This is usually used when you're defining several sectors in the same entry.

You can list several priorities or facilities in a given sector by separating them with commas. You can also have several sectors in the same entry by separating them with semicolons. The first example saves to the **/var/log/messages** file all messages with **info** priority, excluding all mail and authentication messages (**authpriv**). The second saves all **crit** messages and higher for the **uucp** and **news** facilities to the **/var/log/spooler** file:

```
*.info;mail.none;news.none;authpriv.none /var/log/messages
uucp,news.crit /var/log/spooler
```

Actions and Users

In the action field, you can specify files, remote systems, users, or pipes. An action entry for a file must always begin with a / and specify its full pathname, such as **/var/log/messages**. To log messages to a remote host, you specify the hostname preceded by an @ sign. The following example saves all kernel messages on **rabbit.trek.com**:

```
kern.* @rabbit.trek.com
```

To send messages to users, you list their login names. The following example will send critical news messages to the consoles for the users **chris** and **aleina**:

```
news.=crit chris,aleina
```

You can also output messages to a named pipe (FIFO). The pipe entry for the action field begins with a |. The following example pipes kernel debug messages to the named pipe **|/usr/adm/debug**:

```
kern.=debug |/usr/adm/debug
```

An Example for /etc/rsyslog.conf

The default rules in the **/etc/rsyslog.conf** file for RHEL systems is shown here. Messages are logged to various files in the **/var/log** folder.

/etc/rsyslog.conf

```
# Log all kernel messages to the console.
kern.*                                  /dev/console
# Log anything (except mail) of level info or higher.
# Don't log private authentication messages!
*.info;mail.none;news.none;authpriv.none;cron.none     /var/log/messages

# The authpriv file has restricted access.
authpriv.*                              /var/log/secure
# Log all the mail messages in one place.
mail.*                                  -/var/log/maillog
# Log cron stuff.
cron.*                                  /var/log/cron
# Everybody gets emergency messages
*.emerg                                 :oumuSrmsg:*
# Save mail and news errors of level err and higher in a special file.
uucp,news.crit                          /var/log/spooler
# Save boot messages also to boot.log
local7.*                                /var/log/boot.log
```

The Linux Auditing System: auditd

The Linux Auditing System provides system call auditing. The auditing is performed by a server called **auditd**, with logs saved to the **/var/log/audit** folder. The primary log file is **/var/log/audit/audit.log**. The audit logging service provides specialized logging for services like SELinux. To refine the auditing, you can create audit rules to check certain system calls like those generated by a specific user or group.

The **/lib/systemd/system/auditd.service** service script is used to manage the **auditd** server. Use the **service** command to start and stop the server.

```
service auditd start
```

Configuration for auditd is located in the **/etc/audit/auditd.conf** file. Primary configuration is handled with **/etc/audit/auditd.conf** where options are specified like the log file name, log format, the maximum size of log files, and actions to take when disk space diminishes. See the **auditd.conf** man page for a detailed description of all options.

The audit package includes the **auditd** server and three commands: **autrace**, **ausearch**, and **auditctl**. You use **ausearch** to query the audit logs. You can search by various ids, process, user, group, or event, as well as by filename or even time or date. Check the **ausearch** man page for a complete listing. **autrace** is a specialized tool that lets you trace a specific process, recording the system calls and actions of a particular process. You can control the behavior of the **auditd** server with the **auditctl** tool. With **auditctl,** you can turn auditing on and off, check its status, and add audit rules for specific events. Check the **auditctl** man page for a detailed description.

Audit rules are organized into pre-determined lists with a specific set of actions for system calls. Currently, there are three lists: task, entry, and exit, and three actions: never, always, and possible. When adding a rule, the list and action are paired, separated by a comma, as in:

```
exit,always
```

To add a rule you use the **-a** option. With the **-S** option you can specify a particular system call, and with the **-F** option specify a field. There are several possible fields you can use such as loginuid (user login id), pid (process id), and exit (system call exit value). For a field, you specify a value, such as **longinuid=510** for the user with a user login id of 510. The following rule, as described in the documentation, checks all files opened by a particular user.

```
auditctl -a exit,always  -S open -F loginuid=510
```

Place rules you want loaded automatically in the **/etc/audit/audit.rules**. Sample rules files are located in the **/usr/share/doc/audit*** folder inside the **rules** folder. You can also create a specific file of audit rules and use **auditctl** with the **-R** option to read the rules from it.

You can use **aureport** and **ausearch** to view messages. With **ausearch**, you can create complex searches. The **aulast** command displays a list of the last logged in users, and the **auvirt** command lists guest user.

Disk Usage Analyzer

The disk usage analyzer lets you see how much disk space is used and available on all your mounted hard disk partitions. You can access it from Utilities | Disk Usage Analyzer. It will also check all LVM and RAID arrays. Usage is shown in a simple graph, letting you see how much overall space is available and where it is. On the scan dialog, you can choose to scan your home folder (Home Folder, your entire file system (disk drive icon), an attached device like a floppy or USB drive, or a specific or remote folder (see Figure 7-2).

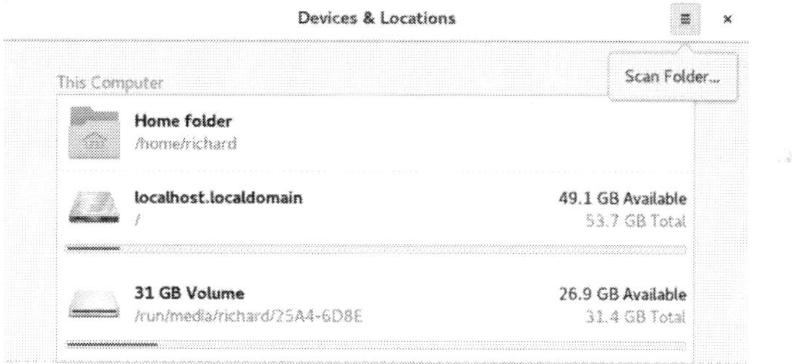

Figure 7-2: Disk Usage Analyzer: Scan dialog

To scan a folder click the gear button (top right) to open a menu with the option "Scan Folder." When you scan a folder or the file system, disk usage for your folder is analyzed and displayed. Each file system is shown with a graph for its usage, as well as its size and the number of top-level folders and files. Then the folders are shown, along with their size and contents (see Figure 7-3).

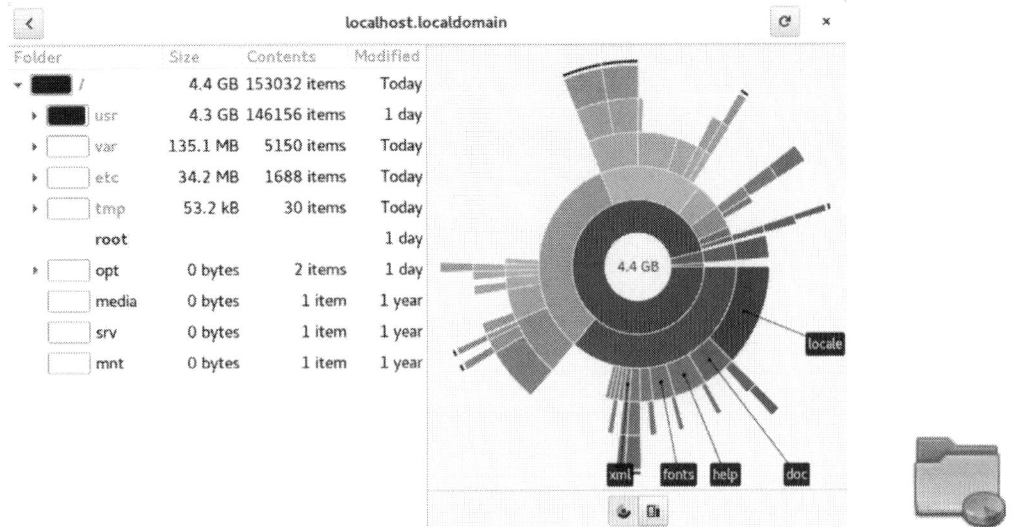

Figure 7-3: Disk Usage Analyzer

A representational graph for disk usage is displayed on the right pane. The graph can be either a Ring Chart or a Treemap. The Ring Chart is the default. Choose the one you want from the buttons on the lower right. For the Ring Chart, directories are shown, starting with the top level directories at the center and moving out to the subfolders. Passing your mouse over a section in the graph displays its folder name and disk usage, as well as all its subfolders. The Treemap chart shows a box representation, with greater disk usage in larger boxes, and subfolders encased within folder boxes.

Disk Utility and Udisks

Disk Utility is a Udisks supported user configuration interface for your storage media, such as hard disks, USB drives, and DVD/CD drives (**gnome-disk-utility** package, installed by default). Tasks supported include disk labeling, mounting disks, disk checks, and encryption. You can also perform more advanced tasks, like managing RAID and LVM storage devices, as well as partitions. Disk Utility is accessible Utilities | Disk Utility. Users can use Disk Utility to format removable media like USB drives. Disk Utility is also integrated into GNOME Files, letting you format removable media directly.

Note: You can use GParted (GNOME Partition Editor) to create and remove your hard disk partitions, and to display information about them. GParted is available from the EPEL repository. Once installed you can access it as the GParted Partition Editor.

The Disk Utility window shows a sidebar with entries for your storage media (see Figure 7-4). Clicking on an entry displays information for the media on the right pane. Removable devices such as USB drives display power and eject buttons, along with a task menu with an entry to format the disk. If you are formatting a partition, like that on removable media, you can specify the file system type to use.

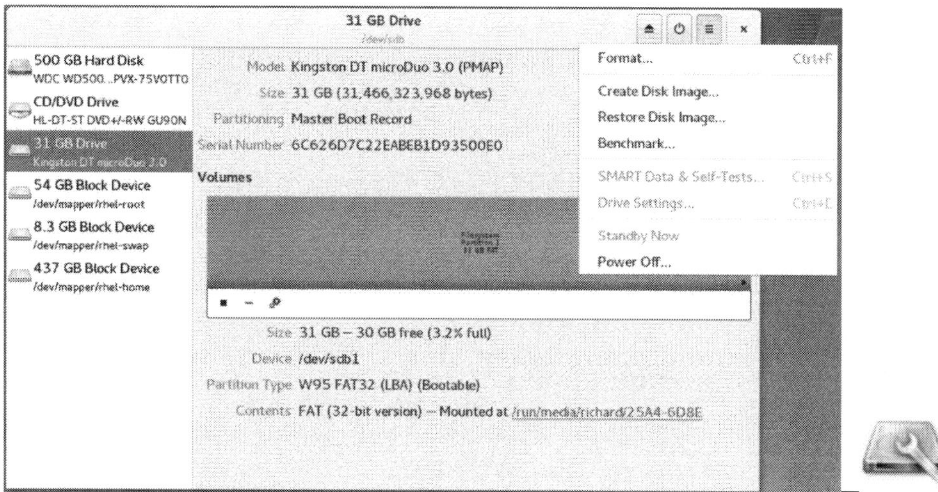

Figure 7-4: Disk Utility

Warning: Disk Utility will list your fixed hard drives and their partitions, including the partitions on which your RHEL system is installed. Be careful not to delete or erase these partitions.

If you select a hard disk device, information about the hard disk is displayed on the right pane at the top, such as the model name, serial number, size, partition table type, and SMART status (Assessment) (see Figure 7-5). Click the menu button to display a menu on the upper right with tasks you can perform on the hard drive: Format, Benchmark, and SMART Data.

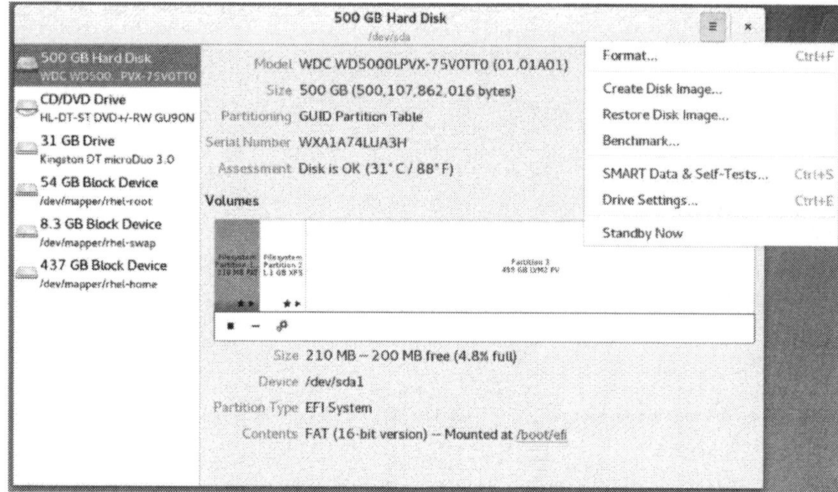

Figure 7-5: Disk Utility, hard drive

The Volumes section on the hard disk pane shows the partitions set up on the selected hard drive (see Figure 7-6). Partitions are displayed in a graphical icon bar, which displays each partition's size and location on the drive.

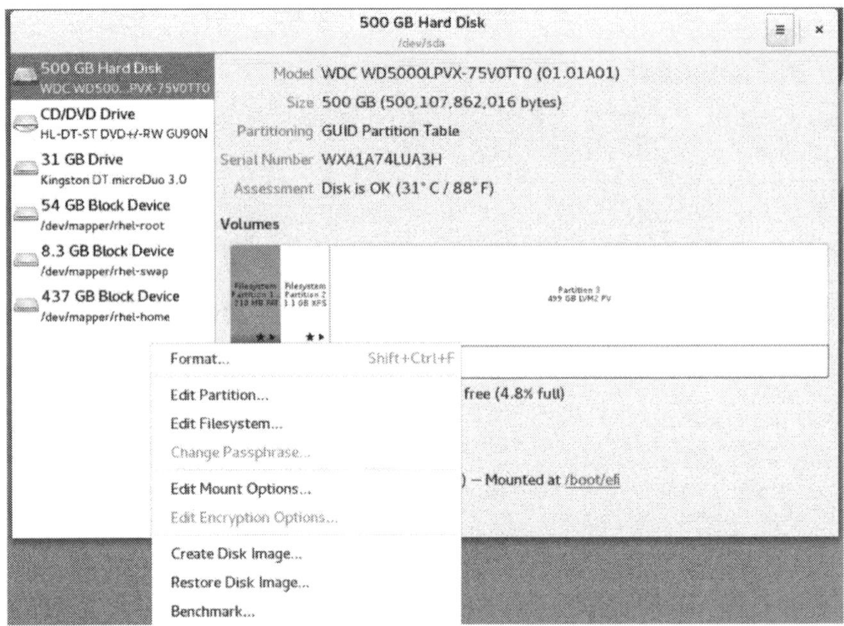

Figure 7-6: Disk Utility, Volumes

Clicking on a partition entry on the graphical icon bar displays information about that partition such as the file system type, device name, partition label, and partition size. The "Contents" entry tells if a partition is mounted. If in use, it displays a "Mounted at:" entry with a link consisting of the path name where the file system is mounted. You can click on this path name to open a folder with which you can access the file system. The button bar below the Volumes images provides additional tasks you can perform, such as unmounting a file system (square button) and deleting a partition (minus button). From the more tasks menu, you can choose entries to change the partition label, type, and mount options. Certain partitions, like extended and swap partitions, display limited information and have few allowable tasks.

For more detailed hardware information about a hard drive, you can click on the "SMART Data and Tests" entry from the task menu in the upper right. This opens a SMART data dialog with hardware information about the hard disk (see Figure 7-7) including temperature, power cycles, bad sectors, and the overall health of the disk. The Attributes section lists SMART details such as the Read Error Rate, Spinup time, temperature, and write error rate. Click the switch on to enable the tests, and off to disable testing. Click the "Refresh" button to manually run the tests. Click the "Start Self-test" button to open a menu with options for short, extended, and conveyance tests.

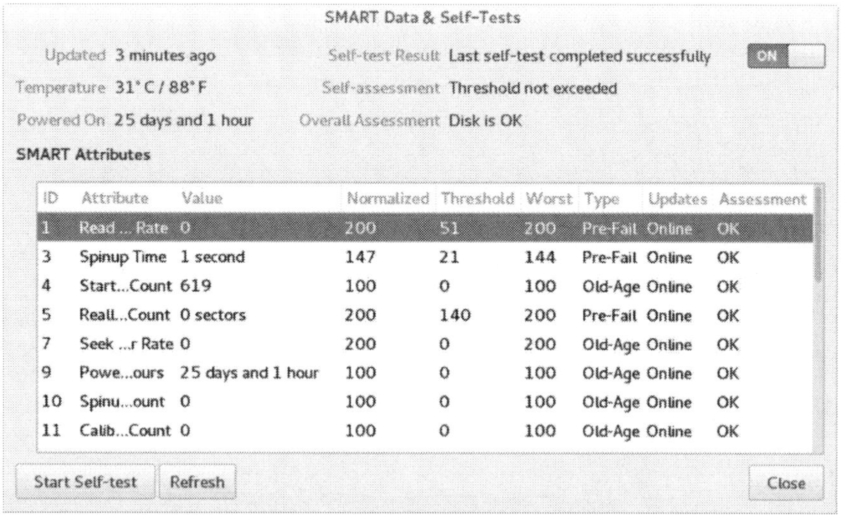

Figure 7-7: Disk Utility: Hard Disk hardware SMART data

Performance Analysis Tools and Processes

Linux treats each task performed on your system as a process, which is assigned a number and a name. You can examine these processes as well as start and stop them. RHEL provides several tools for examining processes as well as your system performance (see Table 7-2). Easy monitoring is provided by the GNOME System Monitor. Other tools are also available, such as KDE System Monitor. Several utilities were designed to be used on a shell command line, displaying output in text lines.

Performance Tool	Description
`vmstat`	Performance of system components
`top`	Listing of most CPU-intensive processes
`free`	Listing of free RAM memory
`sar`	System activity information
`iostat`	Disk usage
GNOME System Monitor	System monitor for processes and usage monitoring (System | Administration | System Monitor)
KDE System Monitor	KDE system monitor for processes and usage monitoring
Frysk	Monitoring tool for system processes
Gnome Power Manager	Manage power efficiency features of your system

Table 7-2: Performance Tools

Check the **System Administration Guide** for details on system monitoring tools, **Part 6 Monitoring and Automation | Chapter 18. System Monitoring Tools**.

```
https://access.redhat.com/documentation/en-US/Red_Hat_Enterprise_Linux/7/html/System_Administrators_Guide/ch-System_Monitoring_Tools.html
```

GNOME System Monitor

RHEL provides the GNOME System Monitor for displaying system information and monitoring system processes, accessible from Utilities | System Monitor. There are three tabs: Processes, Resources, and File Systems (see Figure 7-8). The Resources tab displays graphs for CPU History, Memory and Swap History, and Network History. If your system has a multi-core CPU, the CPU History graph shows the usage for each CPU. The Memory and Swap Memory graph shows the amount of memory in use. The Network History graph displays both the amount of sent and received data, along with totals for the current session. The File Systems tab lists your file systems, where they are mounted, and their type, as well as the amount of disk space used and how much is free. Double clicking on a file system entry will open that file system in a file manager window.

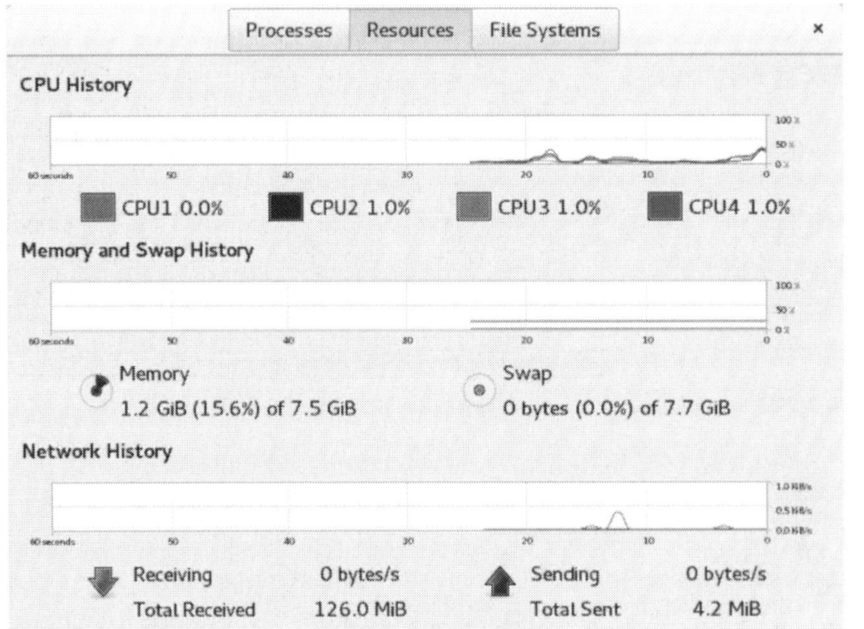

Figure 7-8: GNOME System Monitor: Resources

The Processes tab lists your processes, letting you sort and search processes. You can use field buttons to sort by name (Process Name), process ID (ID), percentage of use (%CPU), and memory used (Memory), among others. The menu (right side of the menu bar) lets you select all processes, just your own (My Processes), or active processes. You can stop any process by selecting it and then clicking the End Process button (lower-right corner) or by right-clicking on it and choosing End. You can right-click a process entry to display a menu with actions you can take on the selected process, such as stopping (Stop), ending (End), killing (Kill), and continuing a process (Continue), as well as changing the priority of the process (Change Priority). The Open Files entry opens a dialog listing all the files, sockets, and pipes the process is using. The Properties entry displays a dialog showing all the details of a process, such as the name, user, status, memory use, CPU use, and priority. Memory Maps display, selected from the Memory Maps entry, shows information on virtual memory, inodes, and flags for a selected process.

Display features such as the colors used for CPU graphs can be set using the dconf editor's gnome-system-monitor keys at org | gnome | gnome-system-monitor.

Managing Processes

Should you have to force a process or application to quit, you can use the Gnome System Monitor Processes tab to find, select, and stop the process. You should be sure of the process you want to stop. Ending a critical process could cripple your system. Application processes will bear the name of the application, and you can use those to force an application to quit. Ending processes manually is usually performed for open-ended operations that you are unable to stop normally. In Figure 7-9, the Firefox application has been selected. Clicking the End Process button on the lower left will then force the Firefox Web browser to end.

The pop-up menu for a process (right-click) provides several other options for managing a selected process: stop, continue, end, kill, and change priority. There are corresponding keyboard keys for most options. The stop and continue operations work together. You can stop (Stop) a process, and then later start it again with the Continue option. The End option stops a process safely, whereas a Kill option forces an immediate end to the process. The End option is preferred, but if it does not work, you can use the Kill option. Change Priority can give a process a lower or higher priority, letting it run faster or slower. The Properties option opens a dialog listing process details such as the name, user, status, different types of memory used, CPU usage, start time, process id, and priority. The Open Files option lists all the files, sockets, and pipes the process is using.

Processes Resources File Systems

Process Name	User	% CPU	ID	Memory	Priority
dconf-service	richard	0	4718	544.0 Ki	Normal
evolution-calendar-factor	richard	0	4465	38.4 MiB	Normal
evolution-source-registry	richard	0	4322	5.6 MiB	Normal
firefox	richard	0	2101	112.0 M	Normal
gam_server	richard	0	2062	168.0 Ki	Normal
gconfd-2	richard	0	4584	560.0 Ki	Normal
gnome-keyring-daemon	richard	0	3530	896.0 Ki	Normal
gnome-screenshot	richard	0	2110	5.3 MiB	Normal
gnome-session	richard	0	3702	3.9 MiB	Normal
gnome-settings-daemon	richard	0	4056	12.9 MiB	Normal
gnome-shell	richard	0	4237	133.5 M	Normal
gnome-shell-calendar-ser	richard	0	4313	2.5 MiB	Normal
gnome-software	richard	0	4427	65.0 MiB	Normal
gnome-system-monitor	richard	0	2094	16.0 MiB	Normal

End Process

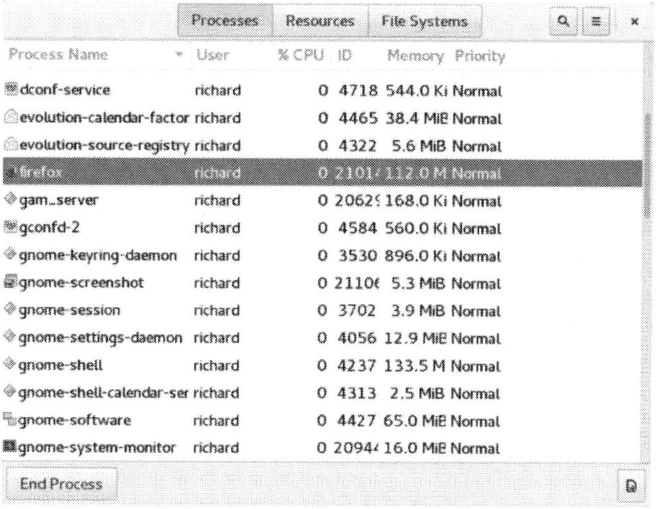

Figure 7-9: GNOME System Monitor: Processes

You can also use the **kill** command in a terminal window to end a process. The **kill** command takes as its argument a process number. Be sure you obtain the correct one. Use the **ps** command to display a process id. Entering in the incorrect process number could cripple your system. The **ps** command with the **-C** option searches for a particular application name. The **-o pid=** option will display only the process id, instead of the process id, time, application name, and tty. Once you have the process id, you can use the **kill** command with the process id as its argument to end the process.

```
$ ps -C firefox -o pid=
5555
$ kill 5555
```

One way to ensure the correct number is to use the **ps** command to return the process number directly as an argument to a **kill** command. In the following example, an open-ended process was started with the **mycmd** command. An open-ended process is one that will continue until you stop it manually.

```
mycmd > my.ts
```

The process is then ended by first executing the **ps** command to obtain the process id for the **mycmd** process (back quotes), and then using that process id in the **kill** command to end the process. The **-o pid=** option displays only the process id.

```
kill `ps -C mycmd -o pid=`
```

KDE System Monitor

The KDE System Monitor is accessible on the KDE desktop from System | System Monitor and on the GNOME desktop from the Applications | System Tools | System Monitor. This tool allows you to monitor the performance of your own system as well as remote systems. KDE System Monitor can provide simple values or detailed tables for various parameters. A System Load tab provides graphical information about CPU and memory usage, and a Process Table tab lists current processes using a tree format to show dependencies. You can design your own monitoring tabs with worksheets, showing different types of values you want to display and the form you want to display them in, like a bar graph or digital meter. The Sensor Browser pane is an expandable tree of sensors for information like CPU System Load or Memory's Used Memory. There is a top entry for each host you are connected to, including your own, localhost. To design your own monitor, create a worksheet and drag and drop a sensor onto it.

vmstat, free, top, iostat, dstat, and Xload

The **vmstat** command outputs a detailed listing indicating the performance of different system components, including CPU, memory, I/O, and swap operations. A report is issued as a line with fields for the different components. If you provide a time period as an argument, it repeats at the specified interval, usually a few seconds. The **top** command provides a listing of the processes on your system that are the most CPU intensive, showing what processes are using most of your resources. The listing is in real time and updated every few seconds. Commands are provided for changing a process's status, such as its priority. The **dstat** command provides a more user-friendly interface for the same operations performed by vmsta, iostat, and netstat, along with added features.

The **free** command lists the amount of free RAM memory on your system, showing how much is used and how much is free, as well as what is used for buffers and swap memory. Xload is an X Window System tool showing the load, CPU, and memory, **iostat** displays your disk usage, and **sar** shows system activity information.

Frysk

Frysk is a specialized complex monitoring tool for system processes. With Frysk you can set up very specific monitoring tasks, focusing on particular applications and selecting from a set of observer processes to provide information about exit notification, system calls, and execution. You can also create your own customized observers for processes. Find out more about Frysk at **http://sourceware.org/frysk**.

Automatic Bug Reporting Tool (ABRT)

The Automatic Bug Reporting Tool (ABRT) detects an application crash and lets you generate a bug report, which you can log or send to Red Hat support. When a crash occurs, the ABRT icon appears on the messages panel (**meta-m**). You can click this to open the ABRT dialog which lists your detected bugs (see Figure 7-10). A description of a selected bug entry is displayed to the right. You can also access the ABRT from Sundry | Automatic Bug Reporting Tool.

To generate a bug report, select the bug entry and click the Report button to start the bug reporting wizard dialogs, beginning with a dialog to choose whether to ask Red Hat for help or to submit a report (see Figure 7-11). The report is processed, and you can then close the window.

Check the **System Administration Guide** for details on ABRT, **Part 6 Monitoring and Automation | Chapter 22. Automatic Bug Reporting Tool (ABRT)**.

```
https://access.redhat.com/documentation/en-
US/Red_Hat_Enterprise_Linux/7/html/System_Administrators_Guide/ch-abrt.html
```

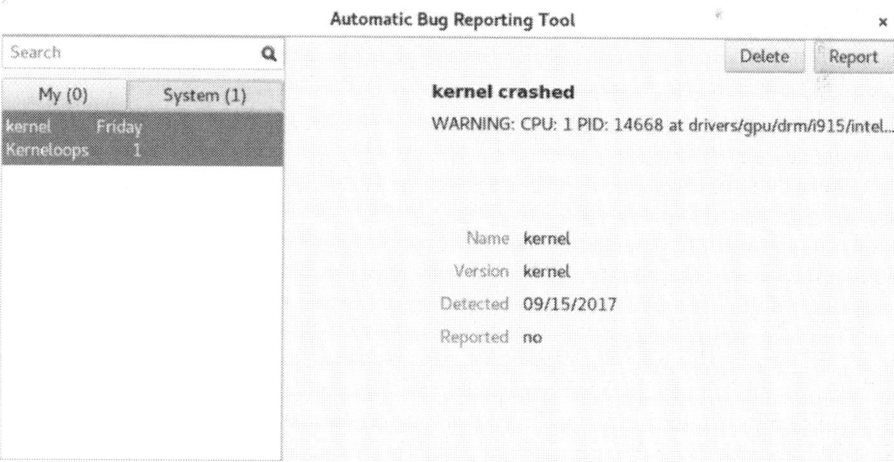

Figure 7-10: Automatic Bug Reporting Tool (ABRT)

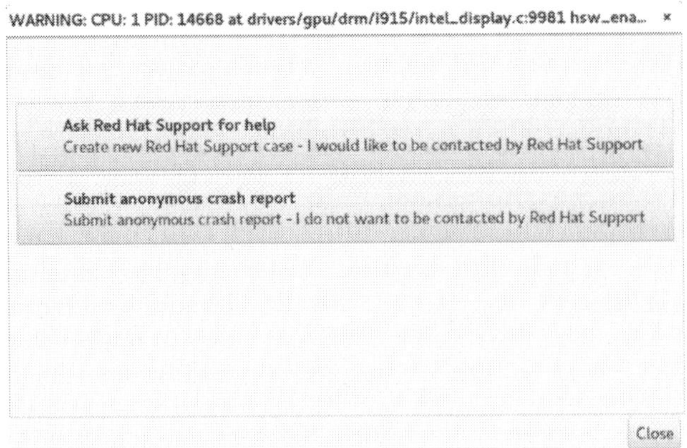

Figure 7-11: Automatic Bug Reporting Tool, sending report

Virus Protection: ClamAV

For virus protection, you can use the Linux version of ClamAV, which provides open source updated virus protection. See **www.clamav.org** for more details. You can install ClamAV from the EPEL repository. ClamAV installs the virus protection software. With ClamAV, you can scan specific files and folders, as well as your home folder (see Figure 7-12). Searches can be recursive, including subdirectories. Infected files are quarantined.

ClamAV command are run from a terminal window (the ClamTK desktop interface for ClamAV is not supported on RHEL7). Use the clamscan command to scan a file or folder. Scan options are set in the ClamAV daemon are located in the **/etc/clam.d/scan.conf** file. Virus updates are configured in the **freshclam.conf** file. Check the Man pages for options.

Hardware Sensors

Disk Utility provides sensor information, including temperatures for hard disks, on the hard disks SMART Data dialog. For CPU, system, fan speeds, and any other motherboard supported sensors, you use the **lm_sensors** service. The **lm_sensors** package is installed on RHEL7 Workstation by default. The GKrellM sensor monitor, available from the EPEL repository, can display CPU, system, fan, and disk information in real time. The older **hddtemp** service for hard disk temperatures is also available from the EPEL repository should you have an application that uses it.

Download and install the **lm_sensors** package. First, you have to configure your sensor detection. In a terminal window login as the root user (**su**) and enter following and answer yes to the prompts:

```
su
sensors-detect
```

This service will detect hardware sensors on your computer.

GKrellM is a set of small stackable monitors for various system, network, and device operations (EPEL repository). A title bar at the top of the stack will display the hostname of your system. By default, GKrellM will display the host name, system time, CPU load, process chart, disk access, network devices, memory use, and a mail check. You can change the chart display of a monitor, like its height, by right-clicking it to show a display options panel.

Each monitor will have a title bar, showing, for instance, CPU for CPU load, Disk for disk access, and Mem for memory. To configure the monitor, right-click its title bar. This will display the GKrellM Configuration dialog at the appropriate tab for that task. For example, the Disk configuration will let you choose particular hard disks and partitions to monitor. The Sensors tab lets you choose temperatures, fans, and voltages to monitor. The full configuration window will be displayed, showing a sidebar with the built-in menu expanded to the selected monitor. To display hard disk temperatures you first have to install **hddtemp**. See the **gkrellm** Man page for a detailed description of all monitor configuration options. The GKrellM site, **www.gkrellm.net**, offers resources for documentation, program support, and themes.

For hard drive temperature detection, you can install the **hddtemp** service (available from the EPEL repository). Keep in mind though that you can easily check the temperature of a hard disk using the Disk Utility's SMART Data dialog for that drive, which does NOT require **hddtemp**. Other sensor applications such as GKrellM do require hddtemp. You will need to enable the **hddtemp** daemon using the **systemctl** and use **chkconfig** command to have it start automatically.

```
systemctl enable hddtemp.service
systemctl start hddtemp.service

chkconfig hddtemp on
```

If your hard disks are not detected, you can to configure the **/etc/sysconfig/hddtemp** file to detect specific hard drives. Add the device name of the drives, using **[abcd]** to match on the last letter, as in **/dev/sd[abcd]** for the sda, sdb, sdc, and sdd hard drives. In the following example, the device names, **/dev/sd[adcd]**, were inserted into the HDDTEMP_OPTIONS entry after **127.0.0.1**, the localhost IP address used to reference your system.

```
HDDTEMP_OPTIONS="-l 127.0.0.1 /dev/sd[abcd]"
```

To edit the **hddtemp** file, you will have to open a terminal window and log in as the root user. Then use an editor like **nano** or **vi**. The **nano** editor is easier to use (**Ctrl-o** to save and **Ctrl-x** to exit, arrow keys to navigate).

```
su
nano /etc/sysconfig/hddtemp
```

Monitoring Your Network: ping, netstat, tcpdump, Wireshark, and Nagios

Several applications are available on Linux to let you monitor your network activity. Graphical applications like Wireshark provide detailed displays and logs to let you analyze and detect network usage patterns. Other tools like **ping**, **netstat**, and **traceroute** offer specific services (see Table 7-3). Tools like **ping**, **traceroute**, and **netstat** can be run individually on a command line (Terminal window).

Network Information Tools	Description
ping	Detects whether a system is connected to the network.
finger	Obtains information about users on the network.
who	Checks what users are currently online.
whois	Obtains domain information.
host	Obtains network address information about a remote host.
traceroute	Tracks the sequence of computer networks and hosts your message passes through.
wireshark	Protocol analyzer to examine network traffic.
netstat	Real time network status monitor
tcpdump	Capture and save network packets
Nagios	Nagios network monitoring, **nagios** packages, **/etc/nagios** configuration folder, **http://localhost/nagios** in browser

Table 7-3: Network Tools

Network Information: ping, finger, traceroute, and host

You can use the **ping**, **finger**, **traceroute**, and **host** commands to find out status information about systems and users on your network. The **ping** command is used to check if a remote system is up and running. You use **finger** to find out information about other users on your network, seeing if they are logged in or if they have received mail; **host** displays address information about a system on your network, giving you a system's IP and domain name addresses; and **traceroute** can be used to track the sequence of computer networks and systems your message passed through on its way to you. Table 7-3 lists various network information tools.

ping

The **ping** command detects whether a system is up and running. **ping** takes as its argument the name of the system you want to check. If the system you want to check is down, **ping** issues a timeout message indicating a connection could not be made. The next example checks to see if **www.redhat.com** is up and connected to the network:

```
$ ping www.redhat.com
PING www.redhat.com (209.132.177.50) 56(84) bytes of data.
64 bytes from www.redhat.com (209.132.177.50):icmp_seq=1 ttl=118 time=36.7ms
64 bytes from www.redhat.com (209.132.177.50):icmp_seq=2 ttl=118 time=36.9ms
--- www.redhat.com ping statistics ---
4 packets transmitted, 3 received, 25% packet loss, time 3000ms
rtt min/avg/max/mdev = 36.752/37.046/37.476/0.348 ms
```

You can also use **ping** with an IP address instead of a domain name. With an IP address, **ping** can try to detect the remote system directly without having to go through a domain name server to translate the domain name to an IP address. This can be helpful for situations where your network's domain name server may be temporarily down, and you want to check if a particular remote host on your network is connected.

```
ping 209.132.177.50
```

who

You can use the **who** command to see what users are currently online on your system. The **who** and **w** commands list all users currently connected, along with when, how long, and where they logged in. The **w** command provides more detailed information. It has several options for specifying the level of detail. The **who** command is meant to operate on a local system or network; **finger** can operate on large networks, including the Internet, though most systems block it for security reasons.

host

With the **host** command, you can find network address information about a remote system connected to your network. This information usually consists of a system's IP address, domain name address, domain name nicknames, and mail server. This information is obtained from your network's domain name server. For the Internet, this includes all systems you can connect to over the Internet.

The **host** command is an effective way to determine a remote site's IP address or URL. If you have only the IP address of a site, you can use **host** to find out its domain name. For network administration, an IP address can be helpful for making your own domain name entries in your **/etc/host** file. That way, you needn't rely on a remote domain name server (DNS) for locating a site.

```
$ host gnomefiles.org
gnomefiles.org has address 74.86.31.159
gnomefiles.org mail is handled by 10 mx.endcrypt.net.

$ host 74.86.31.159
159.31.86.74.in-addr.arpa domain name pointer gnomefiles.org.
```

traceroute

Internet connections are made through various routes, traveling through a series of interconnected gateway hosts. The path from one system to another could take different routes, some of which may be faster than others. For a slow connection, you can use **traceroute** to check the route through which you are connected to a host, monitoring the speed and the number of intervening gateway connections a route takes. The **traceroute** command takes as its argument the hostname or IP addresses for the system whose route you want to check. Options are available for specifying parameters like the type of service (**-t**) or the source host (**-s**). The **traceroute** command will return a list of hosts the route traverses, along with the times for three probes sent to each gateway. Times greater than five seconds are displayed with an asterisk, *.

```
traceroute rabbit.mytrek.com
```

You can also use the mtr or xmtr tools to perform both ping and traces (Traceroute on the System Tools menu).

Wireshark

Wireshark is a network protocol analyzer that lets you capture packets transmitted across your network, selecting and examining those from protocols you want to check. You can examine packets from particular transmissions, displaying the data in readable formats. The Wireshark interface displays three panes: a listing of current packets, the protocol tree for the currently selected packet, a display of the contents of the selected packet. The first pane categorizes entries by time, source, destination, and protocol. There are button headers for each. To sort a set of entries by a particular category, click its header. For example, group entries by protocol, click the Protocol button; for destinations, use the Destination button.

Capture Options

To configure Wireshark, you select the Options entry from the Capture menu. This opens an options window where you can select the network interface to watch. Here you can also select options such as the file to hold your captured information in and a size limit for the capture, along with a filter to screen packets. With the promiscuous mode selected, you can see all network traffic passing through that device, whereas with it off, you will see only those packets destined for that device. You can then click the start button to start Wireshark. To stop and start Wireshark, you select the Stop and Start entries on the Capture menu.

The Capture Files option lets you select a file to save your capture in. If no file is selected, then data is simply displayed in the Wireshark window. If you want to keep a continuous running snapshot of your network traffic, you can use ring buffers. These are a series of files that are used to save captured data. When they fill up, the capture begins saving again to the first file, and so on. Check Use multiple files to enable this option.

Display options control whether packets are displayed in real time on the Wireshark window.

Limits let you set a limit for the capture packet size.

Capture filter lets you choose the type of protocol you want to check.

Name resolution enables the display of host and domain names instead of IP addresses, if possible.

Wireshark Filters

A filter lets you select packets that match specified criteria, such as packets from a particular host. Criteria are specified using expressions supported by the Packet Capture Library and implemented by **tcpdump**. Wireshark filters use similar expressions as those used by the **tcpdump** command. Check the **tcpdump** Man page for detailed descriptions.

You can set up either a Search filter in the Find tab (Edit menu) to search for certain packets, or set up a Capture filter in the Options tab (Capture menu) to select which packets to record. The filter window is the same for both. On the filter window, you can select the protocol you want to search or capture. The Filter name and string will appear in the Properties segment. You can also enter your own string, setting up a new filter of your own. The string must be a filter expression.

To create a new filter, enter the name you want to give it in the Filter Name box. Then in the Filter String box, enter the filter expression, like **icmp**. Then click New. Your new filter will appear in the list. To change a filter, select it and change its expression in the Filter String box, then click Change.

A filter expression consists of an ID, such as the name or number of host, and a qualifier. Qualifiers come in three types: type, direction, and protocol. The type can reference the host, network, or port. The type qualifiers are **host**, **net**, and **port**. Direction selects either source or destination packets, or both. The source qualifier is **src**, and the destination, **dst**. With no destination qualifier, both directions are selected. Protocol lets you specify packets for a certain protocol. Protocols are represented using their lowercase names, such as **icmp** for ICMP. For example, the expression to list all packets coming in from a particular host would be **src host** hostname, where hostname is the source host. The following example will display all packets from the 192.168.0.3 host:

```
src host 192.168.0.3
```

Using just **host** will check for all packets going out as well as coming in for that host. The **port** qualifier will check for packets passing through a particular port. To check for a particular protocol, you use the protocol name. For example, to check for all ICMP packets, you would use the expression

```
icmp
```

There are also several special qualifiers that let you further control your selection. The **gateway** qualifier lets you detect packets passing through a gateway. The **broadcast** and **multicast** qualifiers detect packets broadcast to a network. The **greater** and **less** qualifiers can be applied to numbers such as ports or IP addresses.

You can combine expressions into a single complex Boolean expression using **and**, **or**, or **not**. This lets you create a more refined filter. For example, to capture only the ICMP packets coming in from host 192.168.0.2, you can use

```
src host 192.168.0.3 and icmp
```

tcpdump

Like Wireshark, **v** will capture network packets, saving them in a file where you can examine them. **tcpdump** operates entirely from the command line. You will have to open a terminal window to run it. Using various options, you can refine your capture, specifying the kinds of packets you want. **tcpdump** uses a set of options to specify actions you want to take, which include limiting the size of the capture, deciding which file to save it to, and choosing any filter you want to apply to it. Check the **tcpdump** Man page for a complete listing.

The **-i** option lets you specify an interface to listen to.

With the **-c** option, you can limit the number of packets to capture.

Packets will be output to the standard output by default. To save them to a file, you can use the **-w** option.

You can later read a packet file using the **-r** option and apply a filter expression to it.

The **tcpdump** command takes as its argument a filter expression that you can use to refine your capture. Wireshark uses the same filter expressions as **tcpdump** (see the filters discussion in Wireshark).

netstat

The **netstat** program provides real-time information on the status of your network connections, as well as network statistics and the routing table. The **netstat** command has several options you can use to bring up different sorts of information about your network.

```
$ netstat
Active Internet connections
Proto Recv-Q Send-Q Local Address Foreign Address (State) User
tcp 0 0 turtle.mytrek.com:01 pango1.mytrain.com.:ftp ESTABLISHED dylan
Active UNIX domain sockets
Proto RefCnt  Flags       Type            State         Path
unix    1     [ ACC ]     SOCK_STREAM     LISTENING     /dev/printer
unix    2     [ ]         SOCK_STREAM     CONNECTED     /dev/log
unix    1     [ ACC ]     SOCK_STREAM     LISTENING     /dev/nwapi
unix    2     [ ]         SOCK_STREAM     CONNECTED     /dev/log
unix    2     [ ]         SOCK_STREAM     CONNECTED
unix    1     [ ACC ]     SOCK_STREAM     LISTENING     /dev/log
```

The **netstat** command with no options lists the network connections on your system. First, active TCP connections are listed, and then the active domain sockets are listed. The domain sockets contain processes used to set up communications among your system and other systems. You can use **netstat** with the **-r** option to display the routing table, and **netstat** with the b option displays the uses of the different network interfaces.

Nagios

From the EPEL repository, there are RHEL compatible packages available for Nagios, the enterprise level network monitoring software. You can install Nagios with the **nagios** and **nagios-plugins** packages. The EPEL version provides many more plugin packages such as those for cluster, ldap, and RAID. The **nagios-plugins-all** package will install all plugin packages. You can also choose to install plugins separately, like those for DHCP, DNS, or HTTPD. Configuration files for Nagios are located at **/etc/nagios**. The main configuration file is **nagios.cfg**, an editable text file with detailed comments for each directive.

You will have first to create a nagios administration user and password for accessing the Web interface. Open a terminal window and enter the following. You will be prompted to enter a new password twice. Log in as the root user first, **su** command.

```
htpasswd -c /etc/nagios/passwd nagiosadmin
```

Be sure to enable and run the nagios daemon. Also, configure SELinux to allow Nagios communications. Open the SELinux Management dialog, and on the Boolean tab click the checkbox for the nagios entry.

You then open your browser and access your nagios interface with the following URL (be sure the Apache Web server (**httpd**) is enabled and running.

```
http://localhost/nagios
```

You will be prompted to enter a user and password. Use the user **nagiosadmin** and the password you were prompted to enter when you ran the **htpasswd** command.

```
nagiosadmin
```

The Nagios Web interface is then displayed as shown in Figure 7-12.

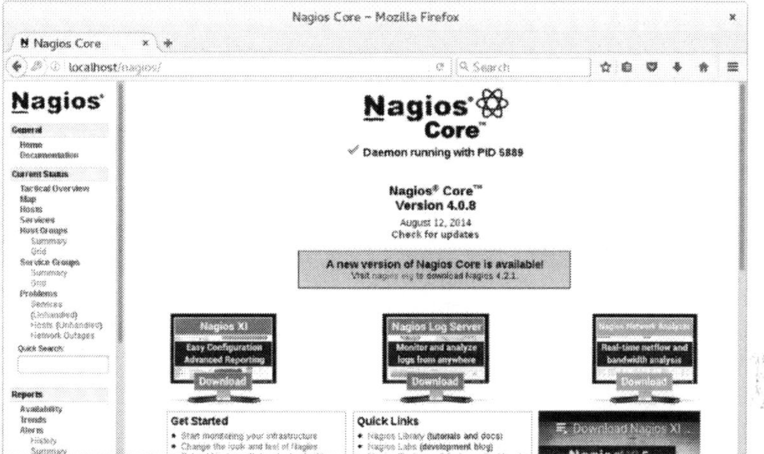

Figure 7-12: Nagios network monitoring Web interface

Using the links listed on the left side panel, you can then display different monitoring information like the service status for hosts on your network (see Figure 7-13).

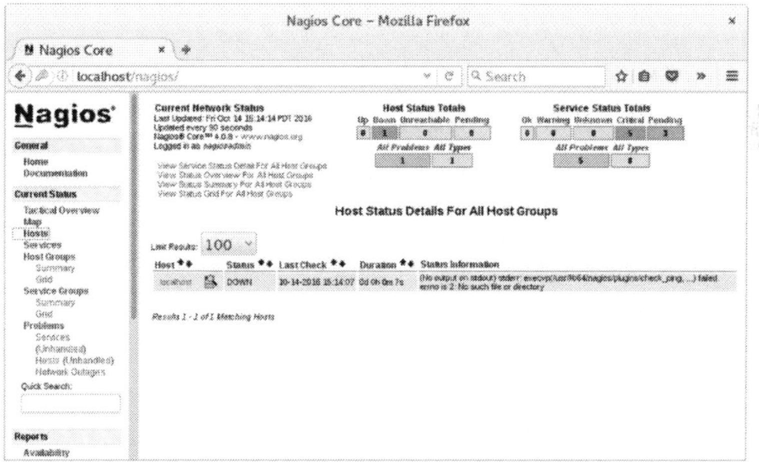

Figure 7-13: Nagios network monitoring Service Status

Nagios also provides a remote plugin server that allows Nagios plugins to run on remote hosts. The Nagios Remote Plugin Executor server (NRPE) is installed with the **nrpe** and the **nagios-plugins-nrpe** packages. The NRPE server script is **nrpe**. The configuration file for the NRPE server is **/etc/nagios/nrpe.cfg**.

```
service nrpe start
```

OpenIPMI

OpenIPMI is an open source version of the Intelligent Platform Management Interface (IPMI), which provides hardware monitoring of local and remote systems. See the following for more information.

```
http://www.intel.com/design/servers/ipmi/index.htm
http://openipmi.sourceforge.net/
```

Install the OpenIPMI (RHEL) and the **ipmiutil** package (EPEL). For Watchdog support install the **watchdog** package (RHEL). With **chkconfig** be sure to enable the **ipmi** drivers. You can use the **service** command to start and stop the drivers.

The ipmiutil project provides an easily used tool for managing IPMI. The project provides an **ipmiutil** meta command and specific commands such as **ihealth** to check the status of a host, **isensor** to check sensor readings and **ialarms** to set front panel alarms.

For **ipmiutil** be sure to enable the **ipmiutil_asy** service (async bridge agent) to enable remote shutdowns, the **impiutil_wdg** service (ipmiutil watchdog timer), **ipmi_port** to reserve an RMCP port, and the **ipmiutil_evt** service (event monitoring).

Bluetooth

RHEL Linux provides Bluetooth support for both serial connections and BlueZ protocol supported devices. Bluetooth is a wireless connection method for locally connected devices such as keyboards, mice, printers, and cell phones. You can think of it as a small local network dedicated to your peripheral devices, eliminating the need for wires. BlueZ is the official Linux Bluetooth protocol and is integrated into the Linux kernel. The BlueZ protocol was developed originally by Qualcomm and is now an open source project, located at **http://www.bluez.org/**. It is included with RHEL in the bluez and bluez-libs packages, among others. Check the BlueZ site for a complete list of supported hardware.

Figure 7-14: Bluetooth Settings (Settings)

If you have Bluetooth devices attached to your system, a Bluetooth entry is displayed on the system status area menu on the top panel. It will display a message showing the number of connected devices if there are any. Click the entry to display items to turn off Bluetooth and for Bluetooth Settings. Should you turn off Bluetooth, Bluetooth will be disabled and its entry removed from the system status area menu. Use the Bluetooth Settings dialog, accessible from the Settings dialog, to turn it on again.

The Bluetooth Settings item opens the Bluetooth dialog (see Figure 7-145). You can also access Bluetooth dialog from the GNOME Settings dialog in the Hardware section. On the Bluetooth settings dialog, a Bluetooth switch at the top right lets you turn Bluetooth on or off. Detected devices are listed in the Devices frame at the center. Initially, devices are disconnected (see Figure 7-15). Click on a device entry to connect it. A dialog opens with a detected pin number, which you confirm. Then the device configuration dialog is displayed, with a switch to connect or disconnect the device (see Figure 7-16). Pair, type, and address information are also displayed. If the device supports sound, a Sound Setting button is shown, which opens the PulseAudio Sound Settings dialog for that device (see Figure 7-17). To remove the device configuration, click the Remove Device button.

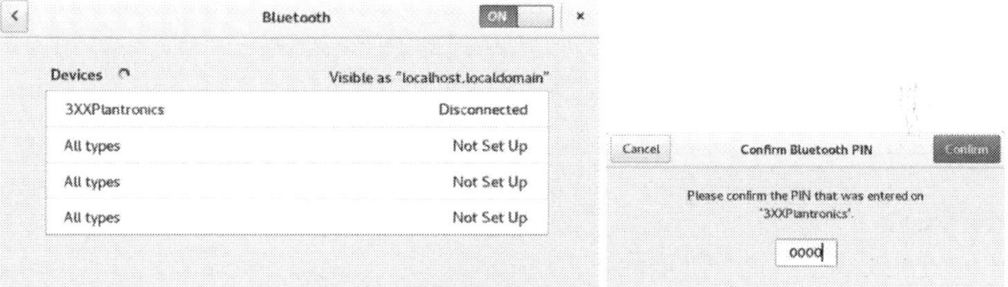

Figure 7-15: Bluetooth Settings: disconnected device

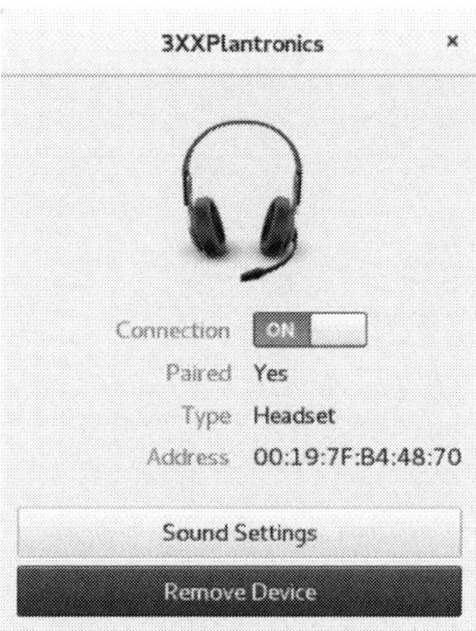

Figure 7-16: Bluetooth Device Configuration

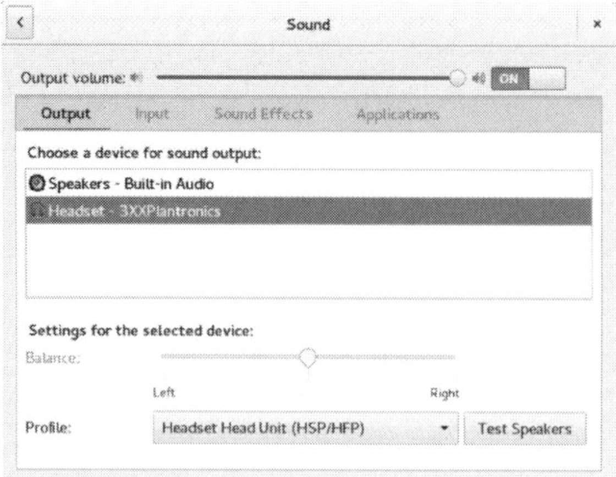

Figure 7-17: Bluetooth Sound

When connecting to a phone (see Figure 7-18), a pin number is detected and displayed. On the configuration dialog, you can choose to connect or disconnect. If you enable a phone to operate as a mobile phone network device (PAN/NAP), then a new entry appears for the device in the system status area menu, which you can expand to list the entries: Use as Internet connection" and "Mobile Broadband Setting." When you click the "Use as Internet connection" entry, it will change to a Turn Off entry, once you have connected.

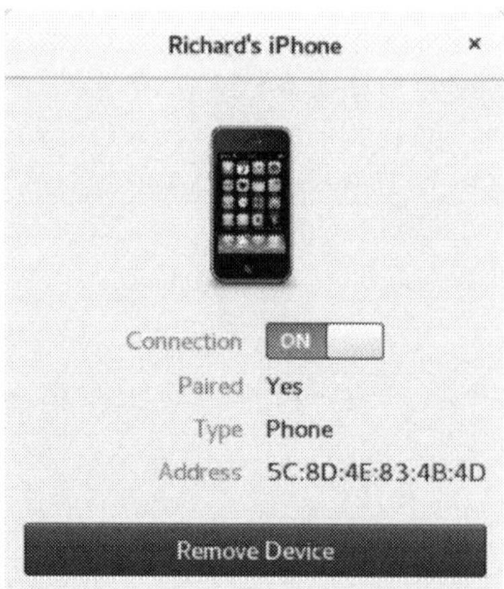

Figure 7-18: Bluetooth Setup Device Wizard: phone

Sound Preferences

Your sound cards are detected automatically for you when you start up your system by ALSA, which is invoked by udev when your system starts up. Removable devices, like USB sound devices, are also detected. See Table 7-4 for a listing of sound device and interface tools.

In addition to hardware drivers, sound systems also use sound interfaces to direct encoded sound streams from an application to the hardware drivers and devices. RHEL7 uses the PulseAudio server for its sound interface. PulseAudio aims to combine and consolidate all sound interfaces into a simple, flexible, and powerful server. The ALSA hardware drivers are still used, but the application interface is handled by PulseAudio. Pulse audio is installed as the default set up for RHEL7 for both GNOME and KDE. PulseAudio provides packages for interfacing with applications like Gstreamer and VLC.

Sound tool	Description
KMix	KDE sound connection configuration and volume tool
Sound	GNOME Settings Sound, used to select and configure your sound interface
PulseAudio	PulseAudio sound interface, the default sound interface for RHEL7. **https://www.freedesktop.org/wiki/Software/PulseAudio/**

Table 7-4: Sound device and interface tools

PulseAudio is a cross-platform sound server, allowing you to modify the sound level for different audio streams separately. See **https://www.freedesktop.org/wiki/Software/PulseAudio/** for documentation and help. PulseAudio offers complete control over all your sound streams, letting you combine sound devices and direct the stream anywhere on your network. PulseAudio is not confined to a single system. It is network capable, letting you direct sound from one PC to another.

As an alternative, you can use the command-line ALSA control tool, **alsamixer** (**alsa-tools** package, RHEL). This will display all connections and allow you to use keyboard commands to select (arrow keys), mute (m key), or set sound levels (Page Up and Down). Press the ESC key to exit. The **amixer** command lets you perform the same tasks for different sound connections from the command line. To actually play and record from the command-line, you can use the **play** and **rec** commands.

Volume Control

Volume control for different applications is displayed on the application's dialog as the speaker icon. You can click it to change your application's output sound volume using a sliding bar. The sliding sound bar on the system status area menu also lets you set the sound volume, as shown here.

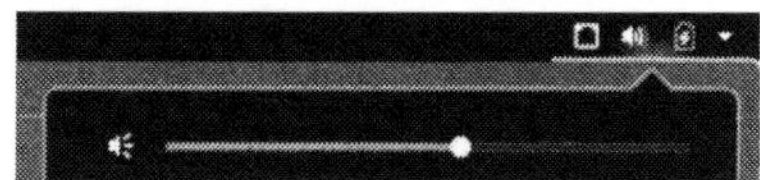

To perform volume control for specific devices like a microphone, you use the GNOME Settings Sound dialog.

Sound: PulseAudio

You configure sound devices and set the volume for sound effects, input, output, and applications using the GNOME Settings Sound dialog. The Sound dialog has four tabs: Output,

Input, Sound Effects, and Applications (see Figure 7-19). Corresponding sound configuration is available on KDE, which also uses PulseAudio.

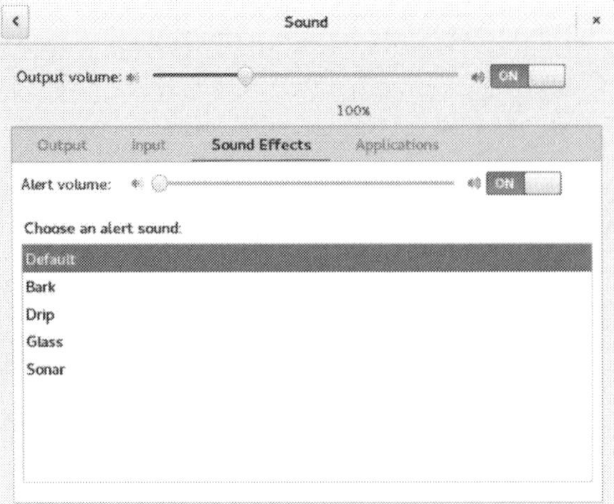

Figure 7-19: Sound Preferences

Volume Control is integrated into the Sound dialog. A sliding bar at the top of the dialog, above the tabs, lets you set the output volume.

The Sound Effects tab lets you select an alert sound, such as Drip or Sonar. A sliding bar lets you set the volume for your sound alerts, or turn them off by clicking the ON/OFF switch.

On the Input tab, you set the input volume for an input device such as a microphone. An ON/OFF switch lets you disable it. When speaking or recording, the input level is displayed (see Figure 7-20). If you have more than one input device, they will be listed in the "Choose a device for sound input" section. Choose the one you want to configure.

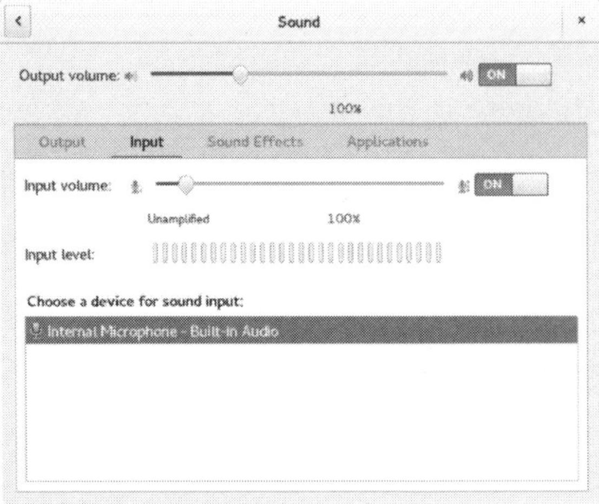

Figure 7-20: Pulse Preferences: Input

On the Output tab, you can configure balance settings for a selected output device. If you have more than one device, it will be listed in the Profile menu. Choose the one you want to configure. The available settings will change according to the device selected. For a simple Analog Stereo Output, there is only a single balance setting (see Figure 7-21).

The Applications tab will show applications currently using sound devices. You can set the sound volume for each (see Figure 7-22).

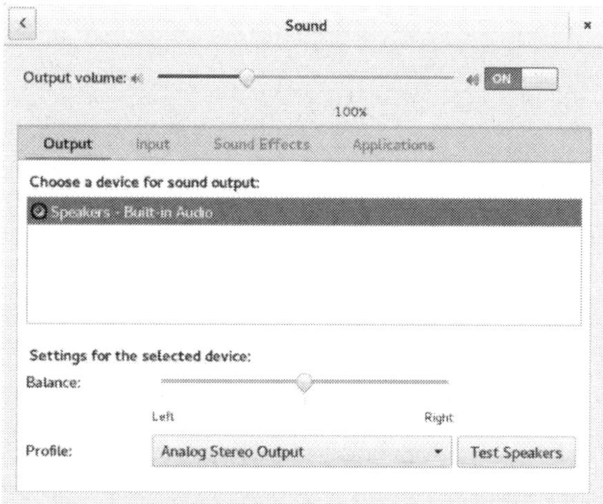

Figure 7-21: Pulse Preferences: Output

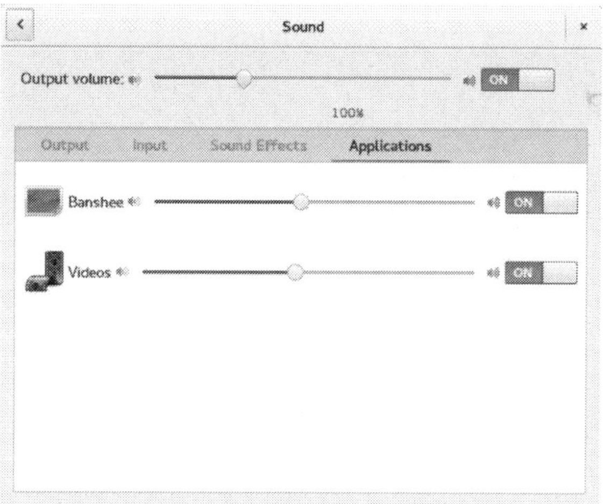

Figure 7-22: Pulse Preferences: Applications

Sound devices that support multiple interfaces like analog surround sound 7.1 and digital SPDIF output, may have an extensive list of interface combinations in the Profile menu. The Input and Output tabs will then display configuration settings for the selected device. With Analog Surround 7.1 Output selected, the Output tab will show settings for Balance, Fade, and Subwoofer.

Configuring digital output for SPDIF (digital) connectors is a simple matter of selecting the digital output entry on the Profiles menu.

Installed with Pulse Audio are the Pulse Audio utilities (**pulseaudio-utils** package) . These are command line utilities for managing Pulse Audio and playing sound files (see Table 7-5). The **paplay** and **pacat** will play sound files, **pactl** will let you control the sound server and **pacmd** lets you reconfigure it. Check the Man pages for each for more details. If you change your sound preferences frequently, you could use these commands in a shell script to make the changes, instead of having to use the sound preferences dialog each time. Some of these commands such as **parec** and **paplay** are links to the **pacat** command, which performs the actual tasks.

Sound tool	Description
`pacat`	Play, record, and configure a raw audio stream
`pacmd`	Generates a shell for entering configuration commands
`pactl`	Control a PulseAudio server, changing input and output sources and providing information about the server.
`padsp`	PulseAudio wrapper for OSS sound applications
`pamon`	Link to pacat
`paplay`	Playback audio. The -d option specifies the output device, the -s option specifies the server, and the --volume option sets the volume (link to pacat)
`parec`	Record and audio stream (link to pacat)
`parecord`	Record and audio stream (link to pacat)
`pasuspender`	Suspend a PulseAudio server
`pax11publish`	Access PulseAudio server credentials

Table 7-5: PulseAudio commands (command-line)

Note: To find the actual name of the SPDIF output is not always obvious. You may need to run **aplay -L** in a terminal window to see what the name of the digital output device is on your system. It will be the entry with Digital in it.

8. Installing and Updating Software

Subscription Manager

Updating Software

GNOME Software

PackageKit (Software)

Installing Packages with the yum command

Yum Configuration

Manually Installing Packages with rpm

Installing Source Code Applications

Installing software is an administrative function performed by a user with administrative access. The primary means of distribution for Red Hat Enterprise Linux software is the online Red Hat Enterprise Linux software repository accessible by a subscription manager. This repository contains an extensive collection of Red Hat Enterprise Linux-compliant software. Software packages are managed by the Yellowdog Updater Modified (YUM) software management system. You can use GNOME Software (Application Installer) or the Packagekit (Software) desktop application, which are front ends for YUM, to install, remove, and update packages on your desktop. Also available are third-party Red Hat compliant repositories, such as Extra Packages Enterprise Linux (EPEL). EPEL provides popular Fedora Linux packages not included on the Red Hat repositories and is officially supported by the Fedora Project (Red Hat's open source non-commercial version of Linux).

Red Hat also offers a Red Hat Network Satellite service, where a Red Hat proxy can be installed on a local network, and updates made directly from the proxy. Client registration and connections to the proxy are similar to the older Red Hat Network (RHN) client. This is a commercial service.

Check the **System Administration Guide** for details on Software Management, **Part 3 Installing and Managing Software**.

```
https://access.redhat.com/documentation/en-
US/Red_Hat_Enterprise_Linux/7/html/System_Administrators_Guide/part-
Installing_and_Managing_Software.html
```

Subscription Manager

For Red Hat Enterprise Linux, you can automatically update your system by registering your Red Hat subscriptions. Registering with and configuring access to the Red Hat repositories is a very simple procedure, using the Red Hat Subscription Manager (RHSM). Registration is restricted to users who have purchased the Red Hat Distribution, though a 30-day free trial is available. Once registered with the Red Hat, you have access to the Red Hat repositories, and you can use Yum to download and install updates automatically. Red Hat operates as a subscription service for which a 30 demo account is freely available. You can purchase a full year-long subscription at any time. The RHSM configuration is held in the **/etc/rhsm** folder. Here you will find RHSM options.

With Yum being RHSM enabled, you can use Yum tools like the **yum** command, GNOME Software, Packages, and Software Update to manage your software. With Software Update, you can automatically locate, download, and install any updates for your Red Hat Enterprise Linux system, and with GNOME Software and Packages you can browse and search for available software packages to install.

Subscription Manager Registration

If you did not register with the subscription manager during setup procedure following installation, then the subscription manager message notice will appear, asking you to register your system (see Figure 8-1). Click the Register Now button to start up the Red Hat Subscription Manager (RHSM). You can also access the RHSM directly as Red Hat Subscription Manager.

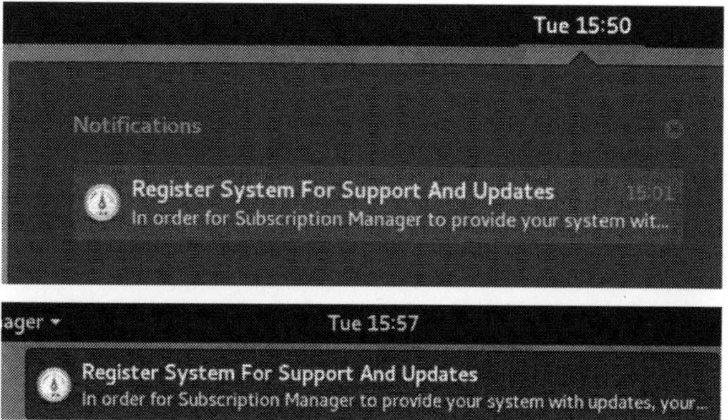

Figure 8-1: Red Hat subscription registration notice

The Subscription Manager initially has two tabs: My Installed Products and My Subscription. On the My Installed Products tab, your system is listed using the name of the installed version of Red Hat Enterprise Linux. Select it and click on the Register button to open the System Registration dialog (see Figure 8-2). The subscription site for registration is shown.

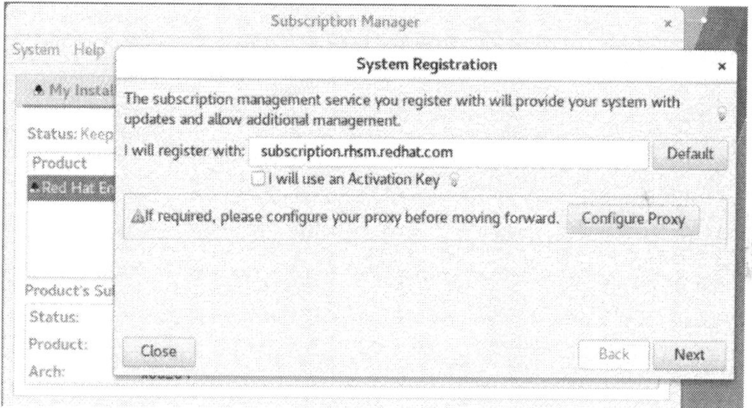

Figure 8-2: Red Hat Subscription Manager System Registration

Click the Next button to enter your login and password for your Red Hat account, as well as the name of your system (see Figure 8-3).

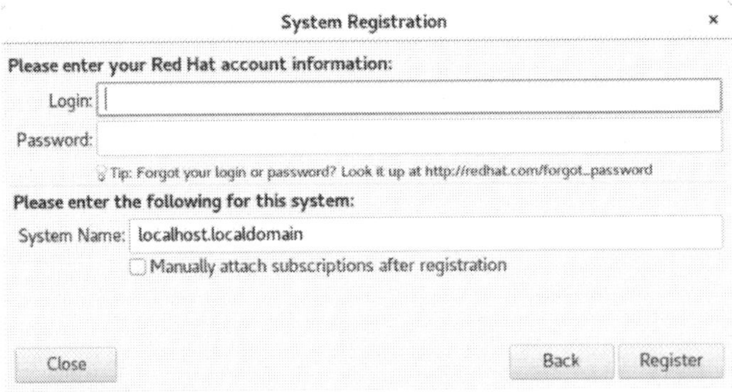

Figure 8-3: Red Hat Subscription Manager Registration

Your registered system is then listed on the My Installed Products tab with a subscribed status and the dates of its activation (see Figure 8-4). Click the Auto-attach button to attach your Red Hat subscription you to this system, in effect, giving your system access to the Red Hat Enterprise Linux repositories. You can also perform the registration and attachment from the command line with the **subscription-manager** command.

```
subscription-manager register --username username --password password --auto-attach
```

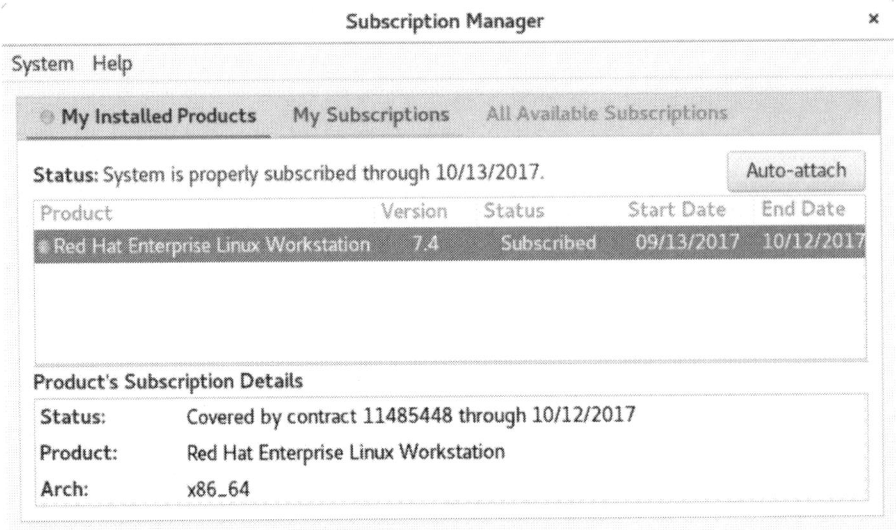

Figure 8-4: Red Hat Subscription Manager Activation

Updating RHEL7: GNOME Software and Software Update

New updates are continually being prepared for particular software packages. These are posted as updates that you can download from software repositories and install on your system. Updating your Linux system has become a very simple procedure. For RHEL, you can update your system by accessing software repositories supporting the YUM update methods. YUM uses RPM headers to determine which packages have to be updated. On RHEL, you can use GNOME Software to perform updates (the default), or you can use the older Software Update. Software Update is part of the PackageKit software manager and is installed with PackageKit. PackageKit is not installed by default. The name used for PackageKit is simply Software. These are graphical update interfaces for YUM, which performs all updates from the desktop. From a command line, you can perform updates using the yum update command.

Updating RHEL with GNOME Software Update

If updates are detected, GNOME Software will display an update message in the notifcations dialog (see Figure 8-5) . Clicking the message opens GNOME Software (Applications Installer) to the Updates tab, from which you can then perform the update. Clicking the Restart & Install button immediately shuts down your system, then restarts, and, as part of the startup process, downloads and installs updates.

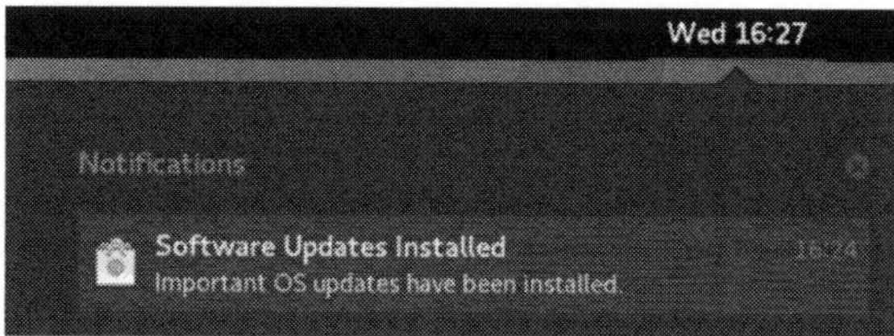

Figure 8-5: Update notification message and icon

GNOME Software (called Application Installer on the desktop) is the primary update tool for RHEL. You can view updates using the Updates tab on GNOME Software (see Figure 8-6). The tab will display the number of updates. Clicking an update opens a dialog showing information about the update. Clicking an entry displays information about the update. Some entries, such as OS Updates, will have several packages that must be updated (see Figure 8-7). When you are ready, click the Restart & Install button on the header bar to shut down your system and install the updates as it restarts.

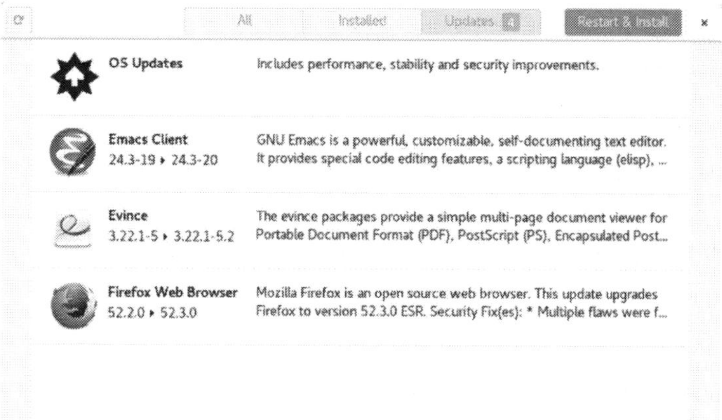

Figure 8-6: GNOME Software (Application Installer): Updates tab

OS Updates

389-ds-base	1.3.6.1-19.el7_4
389-ds-base-libs	1.3.6.1-19.el7_4
bash	4.2.46-29.el7_4
bind	32:9.9.4-51.el7
bind-chroot	32:9.9.4-51.el7
bind-libs	32:9.9.4-51.el7
bind-libs-lite	32:9.9.4-51.el7
bind-license	32:9.9.4-51.el7
bind-utils	32:9.9.4-51.el7
binutils	2.25.1-32.base.el7_4.1
bluez	5.44-4.el7_4
cpio	2.11-25.el7_4
emacs-common	1:24.3-20.el7_4
emacs-filesystem	1:24.3-20.el7_4
evince-nautilus	3.22.1-5.2.el7_4

firefox 52.3.0-2.el7_4

Firefox Web Browser
Browse the Web

Mozilla Firefox is an open source web browser.
This update upgrades Firefox to version 52.3.0 ESR.
Security Fix(es):
* Multiple flaws were found in the processing of malformed web content. A web page containing malicious content could cause Firefox to crash or, potentially, execute arbitrary code with the privileges of the user running Firefox. (CVE-2017-7779, CVE-2017-7798, CVE-2017-7800, CVE-2017-7801, CVE-2017-7753, CVE-2017-7784, CVE-2017-7785, CVE-2017-7786, CVE-2017-7787, CVE-2017-7792, CVE-2017-7802, CVE-2017-7807, CVE-2017-7809, CVE-2017-7791, CVE-2017-7803)
Red Hat would like to thank the Mozilla project for reporting these issues. Upstream acknowledges Mozilla developers and community, Frederik Braun, Looben Yang, Nils, SkyLined, Oliver Wagner, Fraser Tweedale, Mathias Karlsson, Jose María Acuña, and Rhys Enniks as the original reporters.

Figure 8-7: GNOME Software (Application Installer): Update information dialog

Updating RHEL with Software Update (PackageKit)

If you installed PackageKit (Software), the Software Update package is also installed. You can, if you wish, use it to update your system, instead of using GNOME Software. You can open Software Updates from the Applications overview. Software Update displays the Software Update dialog showing your updates (see Figure 8-8).

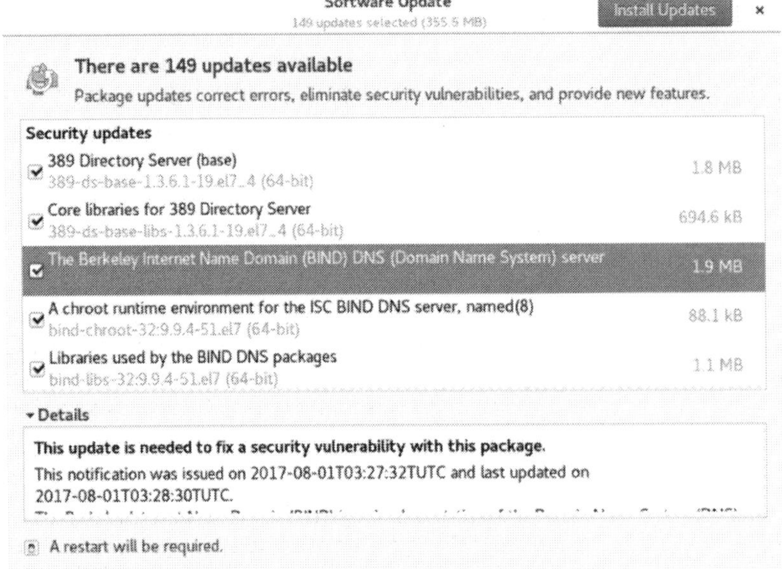

Figure 8-8: Software Update: selected package with displayed description

The number of updates is shown at the top, along with an Install Updates button on the right side of the title bar. To perform the updates, click the Install Updates button. If you want to review the updates, and perhaps deselect certain updates, you scroll through the list of updates, selecting the ones you want more information on. All needed updates are selected automatically when Software Update starts up. The checkboxes for each entry let you deselect particular packages you may not want to update. Should you want to see details about a particular package, click the package entry in the package listing. The lower pane of the window displays the selected package's description. The displayed information includes features such as the version and repository.

Click the Install Updates button to start updating. If additional dependent packages are required, a dialog opens and lists them. Click the Continue button to add the packages to the download list. During the update, a status message is displayed at the bottom of the Software Update dialog showing the update progress (see Figure 8-9).

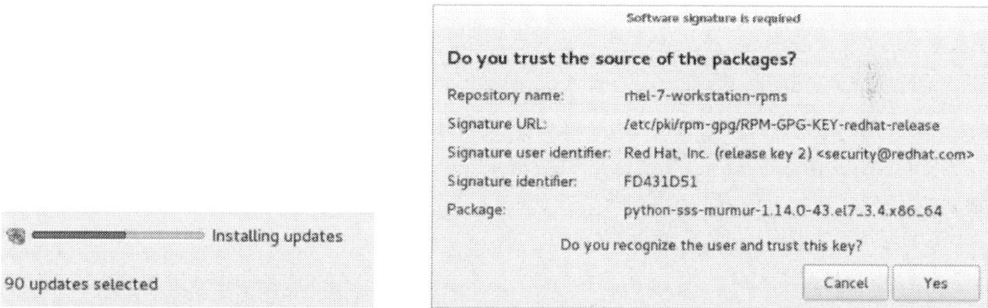

Figure 8-9: Update progress messages

If during the update, if PackageKit has to access a new repository for the first time, you will be prompted to accept the repository's key. Click the Yes button to approve access to that repository. You will then be prompted to authenticate the action by entering the root user (administrative) password.

If a new kernel is installed, you will be prompted to restart your system. If updates to GNOME have been installed, you may have to log out and log back in.

Should a new kernel be installed, when you boot, you will then be using the new kernel. Your old kernel will remain as a GRUB option, should you have difficulties with the new kernel. To choose the old kernel, you must select it from the GRUB boot screen. To make the old kernel the default, you can set the default option in the **/etc/default/grub** file to 1 (the new kernel will be 0).

You can also manually perform updates. From the Software (PackageKit) menu (located on the GNOME top bar), choose Check for Updates. This opens the Software Update dialog with a notice showing how many updates are available. First, a check for updates is performed. Updates are then displayed, with a description of the selected one in the lower pane of the window. You can deselect those you do not want updated. To perform your package updates, click the Install Updates button.

If there are no updates, a message is displayed, notifying you that no updates are available, and then the Software Update dialog closes.

Update with the yum Command

Alternatively, you can update using the yum command and the update option. The following would update an already installed Shotwell package.

```
yum update shotwell
```

You can use the check-update option to see which packages need to be updated.

```
yum check-update
```

To perform a complete update of all your installed packages, you just use the update option. This would have the same effect of updating with Software Update or GNOME Software Updates.

```
yum update
```

In some cases, when you first install a new system from your DVD/CD, there may be incompatibilities or bugs that prevent you from using Software Update to update to the latest system fixes on the RHEL repository. In such cases, you can open a terminal window (Utilities ➤ Terminal) and update directly with the yum command.

```
yum update
```

This can also occur if your display fails and you cannot access your desktop due to bugs in the initial release, which may be fixed with updates. You could then access the command-line interface and, after logging in, enter the yum update command.

A manual update may also become necessary if you have broken dependencies. If among a set of packages to be updated, just one or more have broken dependencies, the entire set will not be updated by GNOME Software. GNOME Software does not always inform you of the packages causing trouble. Otherwise, you could just deselect them from the package listing in Software Update. To exclude such broken dependencies, you can open a terminal window and run **yum update** with the **--skip-broken** option.

```
yum update --skip-broken
```

To exclude a particular package or set of packages, you can run **yum update** with the **--exclude** option. To select several packages with the same prefix, add an asterisk (*****) file-matching operator to the package name. You can add as many exclude options as you want. The following updates all packages except Perl packages:

```
yum update --exclude=perl*
```

Automatic YUM Update with cron

The yum-cron package installs a cron configuration file for YUM. These include yum.cron files in the **/etc/cron.daily** and **/etc/cron.weekly** directories, which will automatically update your system. The cron entry will first update the YUM software, if needed, and then proceed to download and install any updates for your installed packages. It runs yum with the update option.

The automatic update will run if it detects a YUM lock file in the **/var/lock/subsys** directory. By default, this is missing. You can add it using the **yum-cron** service script. The start option creates the lock file, enabling the cron-supported updates, and the stop option removes the file, disabling the automatic update. Be sure first to log in as the root user (**su**).

```
su
service yum-cron start
```

Presto: Efficient Updating with DeltaRPM Packages

Presto updates packages by downloading only those parts of a package that have been modified, instead of the entire package, significantly reducing downloads. The Presto plug-in for YUM (the **yum-presto** package, installed by default) updates packages using DeltaRPM packages, instead of full replacement packages. The DeltaRPM packages are much smaller, containing only changed data that is used to generate an updated package version on your system, which is then used to update your system. Only the changed data for an updated package needs to be downloaded.

Installing Software Packages

Installing software is an administrative function performed by a user with administrative access. Unless you chose to install all your packages during your installation, only some of the many applications and utilities available to Linux users were installed on your system. On RHEL, you can install or remove software from your system with the GNOME Software and PackageKit software managers or the **yum install** command. Alternatively, you can install software as individual packages, with the **rpm** command or by downloading and compiling its source code. The procedure for installing software using its source code has been simplified to just a few commands, though you have a great deal of flexibility in tailoring an application to your specific system.

An RPM software package operates like its own installation program for a software application. A Linux software application often consists of several files that must be installed in different directories. The RPM software packages perform these tasks for you. Also, if you later decide you don't want a specific application, you can uninstall packages to remove all the files and configuration information from your system.

The software packages on your install disk, as extensive as they are, represent only some of the software packages available for RHEL. Most reside on the RHEL Software repository, a repository whose packages are available for automatic download using the GNOME Software and PackageKit applications. Many additional applications and support libraries can be found in the EPEL and RPM Fusion repositories and, once configured, downloaded directly with GNOME Software and PackageKit. A YUM repository configuration file enables you to directly download and install software from that repository using the yum command or the GNOME Software or PackageKit software managers. RHEL repository configuration was performed during the registration procedure for your RHEL system. The EPEL and RPM Fusion repositories provide their own YUM configuration file that you install manually.

Installing with YUM

Downloading RHEL software or software from any configured RHEL YUM repository is a simple matter of using either GNOME Software (Applications Installer) or Software (PackageKit), which provides a desktop interface for YUM. YUM, by default, stops the entire install process if there is any configuration or dependency problem with any a repository or package.

Alternatively, in a terminal window, you can enter the yum command with the install option and the name of the package. YUM will detect the software and any dependencies, and it will prompt you to download and install it. For example, the following command will install Shotwell:

```
yum install shotwell
```

Installing Individual Packages with Your Browser

You can use your browser to download an individual package from a site directly. You should use this method only for packages not already available from YUM-supported repositories. You would also have to install any needed dependent packages manually, as well as check system compatibility. Your Web browser will let you perform both a download and install in one simple operation. A dialog opens that prompts you to open with the package installer, which invokes GNOME Software (Application Installer). The package is downloaded, and you are asked if you want to install the file. Subsequent dialogs show the installation progress.

On a GNOME desktop, packages that have already been downloaded can be installed with a simple right-click, then choose the install selection from the menu invoking GNOME Software to perform the installation. As with the browser download, you are prompted to install the package.

GNOME Software (Application Installer)

GNOME Software (called Application Installer on the desktop) is the software management front end for YUM. GNOME Software is Internet-based, installing from online repositories, using YUM to download and install. It is designed to be a cross-distribution package manager that can be used on any YUM-supported Linux distribution.

GNOME Software performs a variety of different software tasks, including installation, removal, updating, and install of an individual RPM file. The GNOME Software application is **gnome-software**, accessible from the Applications overview as Application Installer.

GNOME Software is currently designed to install client and system applications. It does not install server software, such as the DNS name server or the Apache Web server. To manage such software, you will have to install the PackageKit software manager, which goes by the name "GNOME Packages" on GNOME Software (Application Installer).

To use GNOME Software, click the Application Installer icon on the dash on the left side of the desktop. GNOME Software will start up by gathering information on all your packages. A window opens with three tabs at the top, for All, Installed, and Updates. You can install applications from the All tab, which displays a text box at the top for searching, a featured application, a list of Editor's picks, and a collection of category buttons (see Figure 8-10).

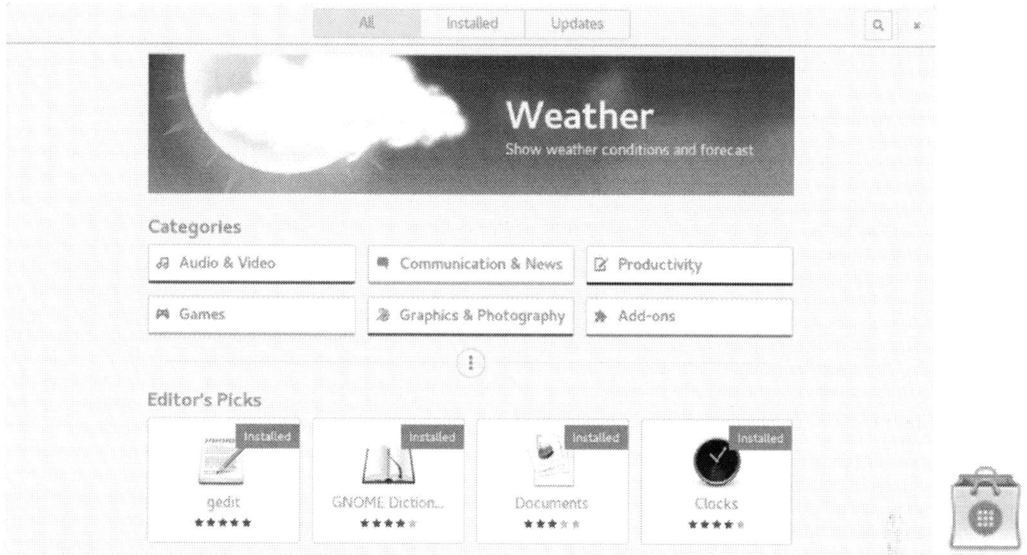

Figure 8-10: GNOME Software

Click any category tab to open a dialog with subcategories. The Graphics category has subcategories such as Vector Graphics, Publishing, and Photography (see Figure 8-11). To the right, the software in each category is listed as icons. Packages already installed are labeled as installed.

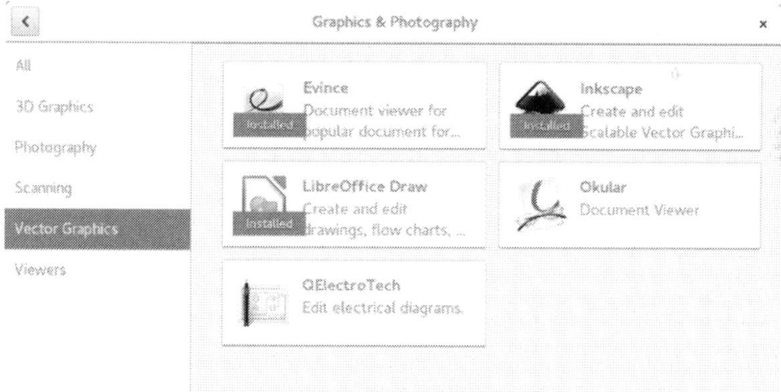

Figure 8-11: GNOME Software: Graphics category

Click a software icon to open a page, which provides a brief description of the software and a link to its related website (see Figure 8-12). Uninstalled software displays an Install button below the software name, and installed software shows a Remove button. The History button displays a dialog showing when it was installed and any updates.

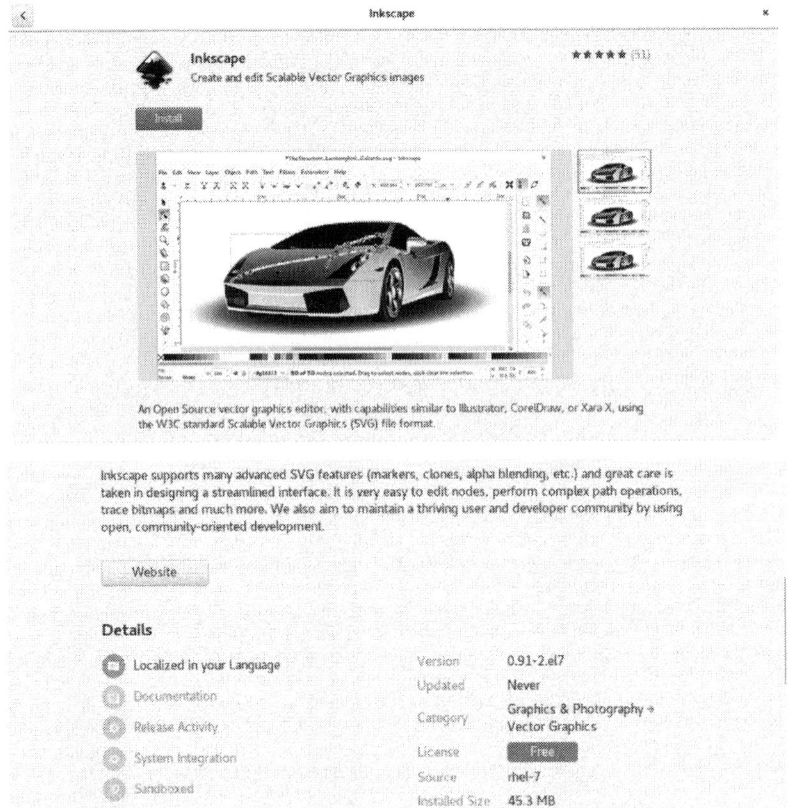

Figure 8-12: GNOME Software: software descriptor page

Click the Install button to install the software. As the software is installed, an "Installing" progress bar appears with a Cancel button (see Figure 8-13). When complete, Launch and red Remove buttons are displayed, which you can use to start or uninstall the software, if you wish.

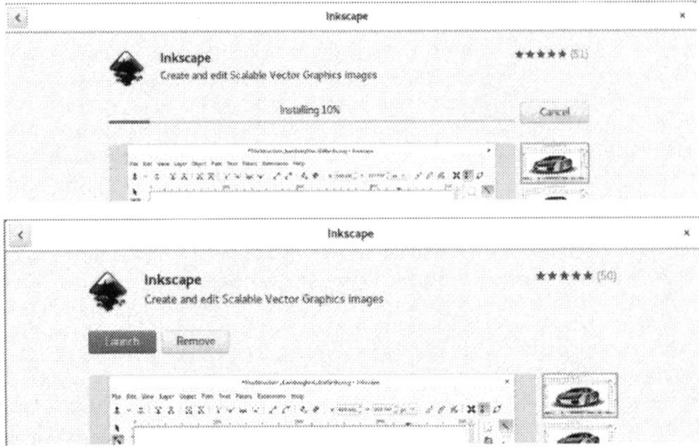

Figure 8-13: GNOME Software: installing software

You can also search for a package using the search box on the All tab. Enter part of the name or a term to describe the package (see Figure 8-14). Results are listed, showing an icon, name and description. An "Installed" label is displayed for installed software. Click an entry to display its descriptor page, where you can perform install or remove tasks.

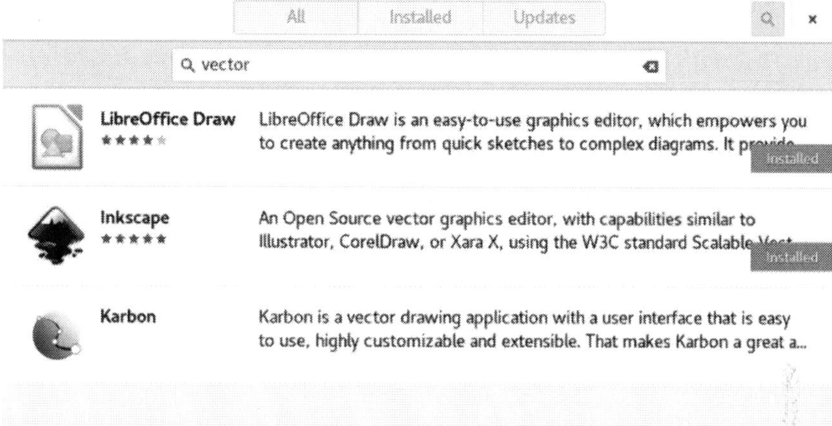

Figure 8-14: GNOME Software: using the search box

The Installed tab lists your installed software (see Figure 8-15). To remove software, click its Remove button.

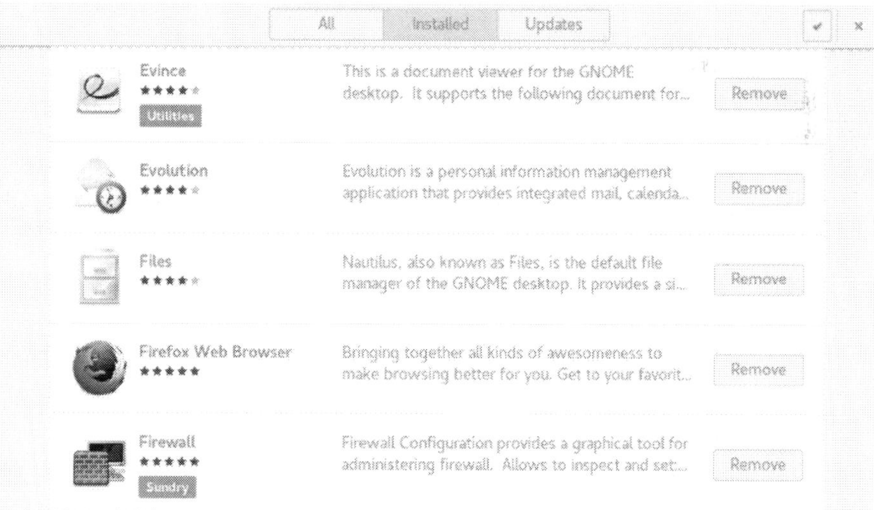

Figure 8-15: GNOME Software: Installed tab

PackageKit (Software)

PackageKit is the software management front end for YUM. It is designed to be a cross-distribution package manager that can be used on any YUM-supported Linux distribution. See **https://www.freedesktop.org/software/PackageKit/** for more information. PackageKit is installed on the RHEL Workstation, but not on the RHEL Server. To install PackageKit, use GNOME Software (Application Installer) and search for GNOME Packages. On GNOME Software, the name for PackageKit is GNOME Packages. To install with the **yum** command use the name **PackageKit**, with the uppercase P and K.

```
yum install PackageKit
```

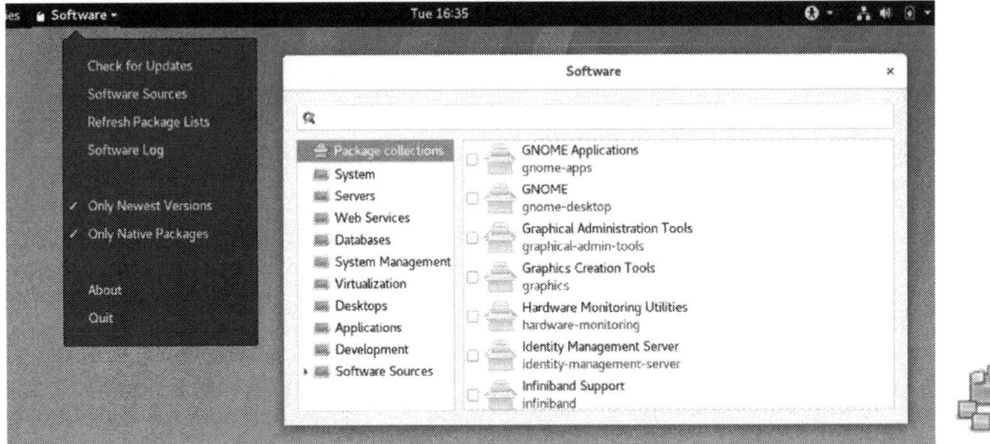

Figure 8-16: PackageKit: Software

To use PackageKit, click the Software icon on the Applications overview. PackageKit will start up by gathering information on all your packages. A Software window opens with a sidebar for searching and a category list (see Figure 8-16). Before you install any packages, it is advisable first to refresh your software lists. This is a listing of software packages available on your enabled repositories. Select Refresh Package Lists from the PackageKit GNOME applications menu (top bar).

You can find packages by category by selecting a category on the sidebar. All the packages in that category are listed. Uninstalled packages have faded package icons with an empty check box, and installed packages have a solid color with a check mark in the checkbox. Categories let you browse through your software, seeing what is available for different kinds of tasks or features. Figure 8-17 shows the packages for the GNOME desktop category.

To install a package, first, click its check box. The box is checked, and a plus sign (+) appears on the package icon (see Figure 8-17).

You can click several packages to select them for installation. Once you are ready to install, click the Apply Changes button (upper right).

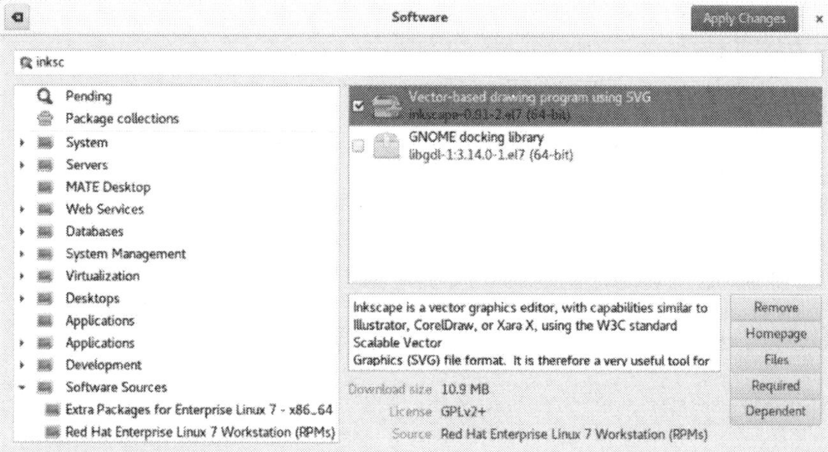

Figure 8-17: Package information

A progress bar will show the install task's progress. The PackageKit task messages are displayed at the top-right corner. At the download phase, a Cancel button becomes active, letting you cancel the install. Once the package is installed, the package icon color will change from faded to a solid color, and a check mark will be displayed in its check box.

If dependent or additional packages are required by the software you want to install, these are listed, and you are prompted to confirm their installation. Click Continue.

Each time you click Apply Changes to install packages, you are prompted to enter the root user password to authorize the installation.

If you choose to remove an installed package, click its check box. The check box becomes empty, and a wastebasket image is displayed on the package icon, as shown in the illustration following. Then click Apply Changes to uninstall. Once the package is removed, the package icon color becomes faded.

To access information about a particular package, select it. A pane then opens at the bottom and displays a description of the software and a button bar to the right, with buttons for the software's website, a list of installed files, required packages, and dependent packages (see Figure 8-17). The Visit Project Website button opens your browser to the package home page where you can find more detailed information about it.

You can also install or remove a selected package using the button bar. Click the package and then, from the button bar to the right of the description, choose Install Package or Remove Package. For an uninstalled package, clicking the Install Package button will place a check mark on the selected package's check box. To actually perform the install, you then click the Apply Changes button. An installed package allows removal, and an uninstalled package allows installation. For installed packages, clicking the Remove Package button will uncheck the package's check box. Clicking Apply Changes will then remove the package. Before you click Apply Changes, you can always change your selections, checking or unchecking a package's check box, as you wish.

The Files, Dependent Packages, and Required Packages buttons open a separate window listing those files and packages (see Figure 8-18). The Files entry opens a window that lists all the files the package can install or has installed. This can be helpful for tracking down the command names and location of the configuration files. The Dependent and Required buttons open windows that show the package's dependencies, those that depend on it as well as those it depends on.

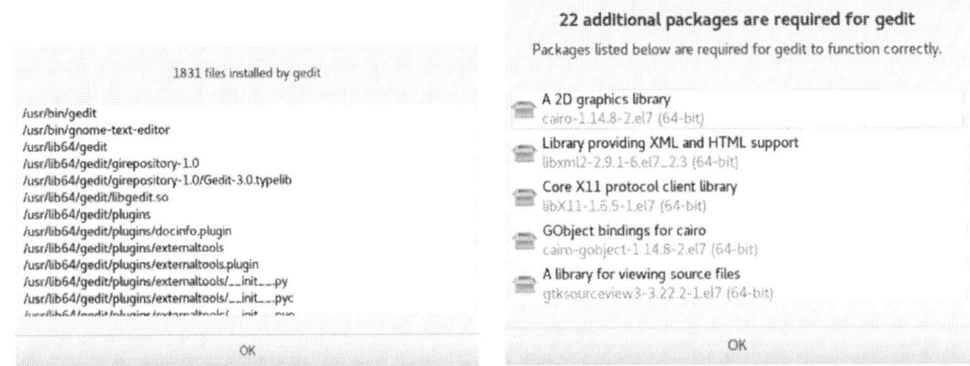

Figure 8-18: Package information

Instead of tracking down a package through categories, you can search for it using its package name. Enter a pattern to search for in the Search box, located at the top of the category sidebar, and press Enter. If you enter a complete package name, like Wine, that package is selected and displayed. You can further refine searched by clicking on the search emblem at the left of the search box to display a menu with entries for "Search by name," "Search by description," and Search by file name."

Instead of showing all your available packages, both installed and uninstalled, you can filter the package listing. Two filter options are available from the PackageKit GNOME applications menu (top bar). You can filter by newest versions and native packages. Native packages are those for your system architecture, such as 68-bit (x86_64) or 32-bit (i686).

Managing Repositories

YUM is the primary package-management tool. When you install a package, YUM is invoked and automatically selects and downloads the package from the appropriate repositoryAfter having installed your system, when you then want to install additional packages, GNOME Software and PackageKit will use YUM to install from online repositories. These will include all active YUM online repositories you have configured, such as sites like EPEL, not just the RHEL and update repositories configured during registration. These are repositories that have YUM configuration files in the **/etc/yum.repos.d** folder, holding information such as URLs, GPG keys, and descriptions.

You can display a list of your configured YUM repositories using the GNOME Software's Software Sources dialog. From the Software GNOME application's menu (top bar), select Software Sources. To remove a (see Figure 8-19). A repository entry will show the number of packages installed on your system from that repository. Clicking on the repository entry displays a dialog listing all the installed packages.

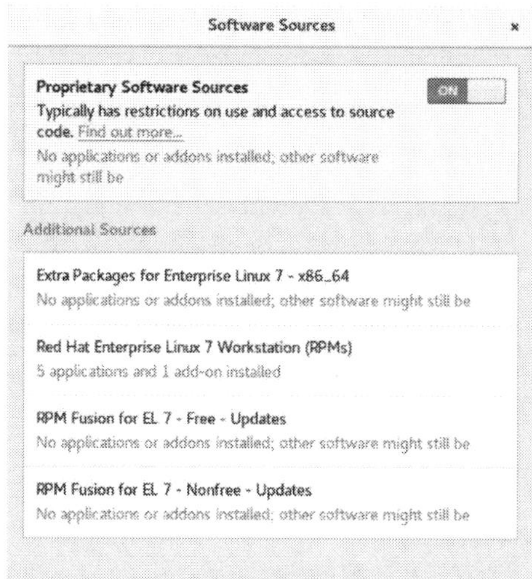

Figure 8-19: Software Sources dialog: GNOME Software

You use PackageKit to enable or disable your configured YUM repositories. From the Software (PackageKit) application's menu (top bar), select Software Sources to open the Software Update Preferences dialog which shows a listing of your configured repositories (see Figure 8-20). Enabled repositories are checked. You can disable a repository by unchecking it. The RHEL repository names include the release number and the platform, such as x86_64 for the 64-bit version.

PackageKit lists the packages available from all the active repositories. If you want to see the package from just one repository, you can deactivate the others. For example, if you wanted to see only the RPM Fusion repository, you could deactivate all others, including RHEL. You can reactivate the other repositories later.

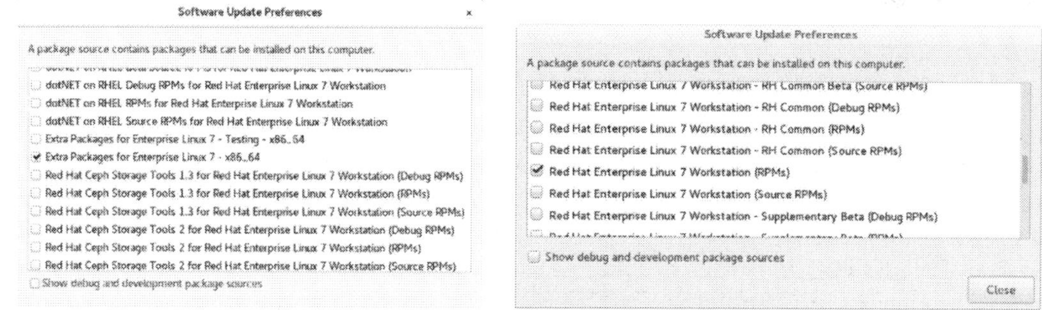

Figure 8-20: Software Sources dialog: PackageKit (Software)

Repositories also have specialized repositories for development, debugging, and source code files. Here you find applications under development that may be useful, as well as the latest revisions. Some will have testing repositories for applications not yet completely validated for the current release. These applications might not work well. Source, Test, and Debug repositories will normally be disabled. Test is the development repository for a future release currently under development. The source repositories hold source code packages. To display the Source, Test, and Debug repositories, check the Show Debug and Development Software Sources checkbox at the bottom of the Software Sources menu.

You can also use the **subscription-manager** command with the **repos** options to manage RHEL repositories. Use the **--list** option to display available repositories, and the **--enable** and **--disable** options to activate and deactivate repositories.

```
subscription-manager repos --list
subscription-manager repos --enable repository
subscription-manager repos --disable repository
```

See the **System Administration Guide**, Part 2**. Subscription and Support**, Chapter **6.2**, **Managing Software Repositories**.

```
https://access.redhat.com/documentation/en-
US/Red_Hat_Enterprise_Linux/7/html/System_Administrators_Guide/sect-
Subscription_and_Support-Registering_a_System_and_Managing_Subscriptions-
Managing_Repositories.html
```

EPEL Repository

A reliable third party repository for RHEL supported software that will run on Red Hat Enterprise Linux is provided by the Extra Packages Enterprise Linux project (EPEL). These packages are popular applications supported on RHEL but not included with Red Hat Enterprise Linux, such as BackupPC, Dia, and Calligra. EPEL is supported and developed by Fedora Linux, the Red Hat development version of Linux. Though not supported as part of RHEL, Red Hat supports the development of the Fedora distribution, along with EPEL. See the EPEL site at **https://fedoraproject.org/wiki/EPEL** for more details.

To access the EPEL repository, you first have to download and install both its YUM configuration file and its GPG authentication key (see Figure 8-21). A YUM repository configuration package (**epel-release-latest-7.noarch.rpm**), which includes the EPEL public key, can be downloaded from:

```
https://dl.fedoraproject.org/pub/epel/epel-release-latest-7.noarch.rpm
```

Check the How to use page for further configuration information

```
https://fedoraproject.org/wiki/EPEL/FAQ#howtouse
```

Be sure to select the one for Red Hat Enterprise Linux 7 and the correct architecture, x86 or x86_64. You can download from Firefox and open it with the GNOME Software to install it directly. A warning may appear that the key is not installed, click Install Anyway. The key is in the package.

You can also use the following command to download the EPEL repo package, **epel-release-7-10.noarch.rpm**. The command is extensive and, instead of typing it on a command line in a terminal window, you could copy and paste the entire command from the **https://fedoraproject.org/wiki/EPEL/FAQ#howtouse** Web page to a terminal window. Click and drag on the command on the Web page to select it, then press **Ctrl-c** to copy it to the clipboard. Open a terminal window and press **Ctrl-Shift-v** to paste the command to the current command line. Specify the correct architecture. Then press ENTER to run the command.

```
su -c 'rpm -Uvh http://download.fedoraproject.org/pub/epel/7/x86_64/e/epel-
release-7-10.noarch.rpm'
```

Once installed, you will have access to all EPEL software packages through PackageKit and **yum**. You can download and install them as you would any Red Hat Enterprise Linux package. The EPEL package names are not distinguished from other packages with any extension. When you select an EPEL package on PackageKit, the Source entry in its description will list "Extra Packages for Enterprise Linux 7 (see Figure 8-22).

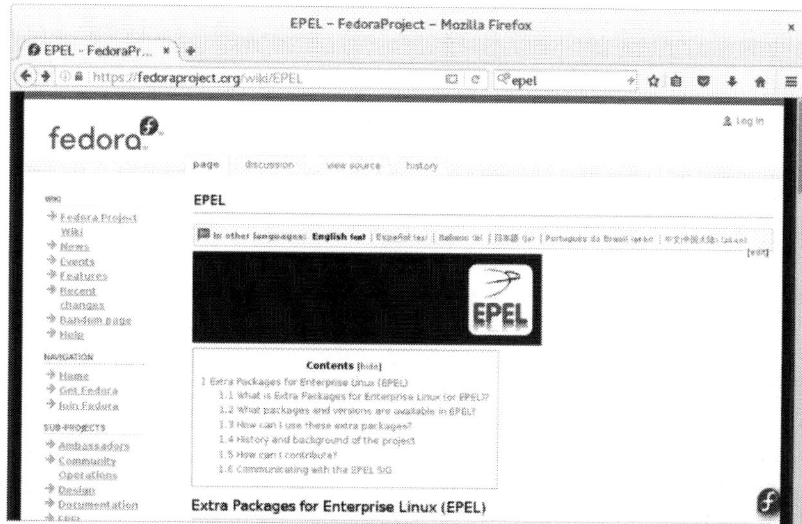

Figure 8-21: EPEL repository

EPEL provides two repositories: epel (the main repository) and epel testing. The testing repository holds packages still being checked though they may work. You can open Software Sources on PackageKit to check that the EPEL repository is enabled.

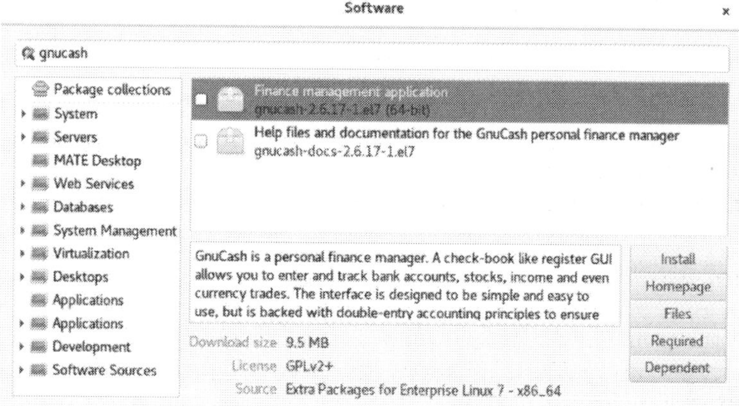

Figure 8-22: Software package accessible from EPEL repository

With the EPEL repository enabled, you can use PackageKit and GNOME Software to search, select, and install any packages on its repository. Both EPEL and the RHEL repositories will have their packages intertwined on the PackageKit and GNOME Software package list. When you first install the repository configuration, be sure to update your PackageKit package lists so that the new repository packages will be listed. From the PackageKit applications menu (top bar), select "Refresh Package Lists."

It is possible to download and install individual RPM packages directly from the **http://download.fedoraproject.org/pub/epel/7/** site, though this is not recommended. You will most likely need to install dependent packages, and to do that you will need YUM and the package managers (PackageKit and GNOME Software).

Third Party Repositories: RPM Fusion

Several third party repositories are available for RHEL which provided applications and codecs that may have licensing issues. It is important when looking for a third-party repository, that it be compliant with the EPEL repository.

The third-party repositories RPM Fusion (**https://rpmfusion.org**) or Negativo17.org (**https://negativo17.org**) provide most of the third party applications and codecs like the vlc multimedia player and the DVD video codec. Multimedia codecs with licensing issues can be directly downloaded with PackageKit, once you have configured YUM to use the RPM Fusion (**https://rpmfusion.org**) or Negativo17.org (**https://negativo17.org**) repositories on your system. Use one or the other, not both. These repositories are not configured by default.

To access the RPM Fusion repository, you first must download and install both its YUM configuration file and its GPG authentication key. These are both included in RPM Fusion's **rpmfusion-free** package for RHEL 7. Simply download and install this package using your web browser. The package is located at **https://rpmfusion.org/Configuration**, which also shows the yum install command to use.

Installing Packages with the yum command

You can also use the **yum** command in a terminal window or command line interface, to access repositories, downloading new software. To use the **yum** command, enter the **yum** command with the **install** option on a command line. The package will be detected, along with any dependent software, and you will be asked to confirm installation. The download and installation will be automatic. You can check the download repository online, as well as the repodata folders, should there be one, to display the available packages on a Web page.

Check the **System Administration Guide** for details on using Yum, Section 3, Installing and Managing Software | chapter **8.2 Working With Packages**.

```
https://access.redhat.com/documentation/en-
US/Red_Hat_Enterprise_Linux/7/html/System_Administrators_Guide/sec-
Working_with_Packages.html
```

The following example installs the Totem video player (Videos):

```
yum install totem
```

You can also remove packages, as well as search for packages and list packages by different criteria, such as those for update, those on the repository not yet installed, and those already installed. The following example lists all installed packages:

```
yum list installed
```

The available option shows uninstalled packages.

```
yum list available
```

To search for a particular package, you can use the search option.

```
yum search totem
```

Use matching operators to match on patterns (file matching characters). Be sure to use single quotes to prevent the shell from expanding the pattern instead of Yum.

```
yum list 'kernel*'
```

Yum Configuration

Yum options are configured in the **/etc/yum.conf** file, the **/etc/yum.repos.d** folder holds repository (repo) files that list accessible Yum repositories, and the **/etc/yum/pluginconf.d** folder. Repositories accessed by plugins such as the subscription manager are configured using the plugin configuration files located in the plugin folder, **/etc/yum/pluginconf.d**. They have a **.conf** extension. Repositories configured by repo files have repos configuration files in the **/etc/yum.repos.d** folder. The repos files have the extension **.repo**.

Check the **yum.conf** Man page for a listing of the different Yum options along with entry formats. The **yum.conf** file consists of different segments separated by bracket-encased headers, the first of which is always the main segment. Segments for different Yum server repo configured repositories can follow, beginning with the repository label encased in brackets. On Red Hat Enterprise Linux, however, these are currently placed in separate repository files in the **/etc/yum.repos.d** folder.

Check the **System Administration Guide** for details on Yum repository configuration, Section 3, Installing and Managing Software | chapter **8.5 Configuring Yum and Yum Repositories**.

```
https://access.redhat.com/documentation/en-
US/Red_Hat_Enterprise_Linux/7/html/System_Administrators_Guide/sec-
Configuring_Yum_and_Yum_Repositories.html
```

/etc/yum.conf

The **yum.conf** file will contain the main segment with settings for Yum options. There are general Yum options like **logfile**, which lists the location of Yum logs. Packages will be downloaded to the folder specified with the **cachdir** option, in this case, **/var/cache/yum**, in subfolders for the architecture and the release. Yum uses the **basearch** special variable to determine the architecture (**i386** for 32 bit and **x86_64** for 64 bit), and the **releaserver** special variable to determine the release (**6Server**). The **distroverpkg** option can be set to reference a specific package for determining the distribution version. On RHEL7 the default is used, **redhat-release**.

The **keepcache** option allows you to keep the downloaded packages (set to 1) or have them removed after they are installed (set to 0, the default). The **tolerant** option allows for package install errors, and the **retries** option specifies the number of times to try to access a package. Both **exactarch** and **obsoletes** apply to Yum updating procedures, invoked with the Yum **update** command. The **tolerant** option will allow package list errors such as those for already installed software, enabling installation of other packages in the list to continue. The **obsoletes** option is used for distribution level updates, and **exactarch** will only update packages in your specific architecture, such as i386 instead of i686.

The **plugins** option (1 or 0) enables or disables yum plugins like presto and search. On RHEL7 this is set to 1. It checks for GPG software signatures **gpgcheck** is a repository option that is set here globally for the **repo** files. It checks for GPG software signatures. The **installonly_limit** is used for certain packages, like the kernel packages, that should be installed and not removed. On RHEL7, this is set to 2. In effect, the number of installed additional kernel packages would be 2. The **metadata_expire** option sets the time for updating package metadata information from repositories, which is used for detecting updates. The default on RHEL7 is 90 minutes (**90m**). A **metadata_expire** entry is included in the **yum.conf** file, though commented out. You can remove the # comment character and set a different value, though it is not recommended.

A sample **yum.conf** file is shown here.

/etc/yum.conf

```
[main]
cachedir=/var/cache/yum/$basearch/$releasever
keepcache=0
debuglevel=2
logfile=/var/log/yum.log
tolerant=1
exactarch=1
obsoletes=1
gpgcheck=1
plugins=1
installonly_limit=3

# metadata_expire=90m

# PUT YOUR REPOS HERE OR IN separate files named file.repo
# in /etc/yum.repos.d
```

Repository repo Files

The repo files in the **/etc/yum.repos.d** folder hold repository options that govern the access to specific software repositories. The repository entries in the repo files begin with a bracket-enclosed server ID, a unique single-word name for the repository such as **[epel]**. Repository-specific options then follow. These usually include **gpgcheck**, which checks for GPG software signatures, **gpgkey**, which specifies the location of the signature, and **mirrorlist**, which references a site holding mirror site addresses. The repository-specific **name** option provides a name for the repository. The repository site address (URL) is then assigned to the **baseurl** option. There should be only one **baseurl** option, but you can list several addresses for it, each on its own line. With the **mirrorlist** option, you can just list a site holding a list of mirrors, instead of listing each mirror separately in the **baseurl** option. The address entries often make use of special variables like **basearch**. The **basearch** variable specifies the architecture you are using as determined by Yum, such as i386. The **gpgcheck** option specifies that you should perform a GPG authentication check to make sure the download is intact. The **enabled** option will enable a repository, allowing Yum to use it. You can set the enable bit to 0 or 1 to turn off or on access to the repository.

The **gpgkey** option provides an authentication check on the package to make sure you have downloaded the appropriate version. Sometimes downloads can be intercepted and viruses inserted. The GPG key check protects against such attacks. It can also check to make sure the download is not corrupt or incomplete. The Red Hat Enterprise Linux public GPG key may already be installed on your system. If you have already used YUM, you will have already downloaded it. The Red Hat Enterprise Linux GPG key allows you to access Red Hat Enterprise Linux packages. Third party repositories such as EPEL and RepoForge will also provide GPG keys. The keys for all repositories are installed in **/etc/pki/rpmgpg** folder.

To see a complete listing of all repositories along with their options and any values set, use the **yum-config-manager** command. Installed YUM plugins are also listed.

```
yum-config-manager
```

Red Hat Enterprise Linux Repository

The Red Hat Enterprise Linux repository is already configured for use by Yum through the subscription manager plugin. There is no RHEL repo file in the **/etc/yum.repos.d** folder. Instead a plugin configuration file is located in the **/etc/yum/pluginconf.d** folder, **/etc/yum/pluginconf.d/subscription-manager.conf**. The configuration file has an **enabled** option set to 1.

Red Hat Enterprise Linux Install DVD Repository,

If you have an RHEL7 Install DVD, you may want to configure it as a repository so that you can use YUM to install packages from it. First, copy the media.repo file on the DVD to the **/etc/yum.repos.d** folder, renaming it. Be sure to do this as the root user.

```
su
cp /run/media/richard/media.repo /etc/yum.repos.d/redhat-dvd.repo
```

The repo file is set up for accessing the Install DVD software packages as the InstallMedia repository. The repo file shown here lists several repository options. The name is Red Hat Enterprise Linux 7.0, with **metadata_expire** option is set to -1 to turn off updating for the repository. The **mediaid** option assigns a media id number located in the Install DVD's **.discinfo** file. The **cost** option sets the relative cost of accessing the repository, with the default set at 1000 if not specified. For the DVD it is set at 500. The **gpgcheck** option is turned off until used.

Use the **yum** command to list and install packages. The **yum repolist** command confirms if the DVD is active as a repository.

```
yum repolist
```

```
[InstallMedia]
name=Red Hat Enterprise Linux 7.4 Install DVD
mediaid=1285191262.134687
metadata_expire=-1
gpgcheck=0
cost=500
enabled=1
baseurl='file:///run/media/richard/RHEL-7.4 Workstation.x86_64/'
```

You will need to add a **baseurl** option, specifying the location where the DVD is mounted. Use the **file:///** prefix. On the RHEL7 Workstation, the DVD is mounted in the **/run/media/** folder, in a subfolder with your user name, and under a further subfolder **RHEL-7.4 Workstation.x86_64**. Enclose the entire reference in single quotes so that the empty space after the RHEL-7.4 can be read, or place a backslash before the space.

```
baseurl='file:///run/media/richard/RHEL-7.4 Workstation.x86_64/'
```

EPEL and RPM Fusion repositories

Access to the EPEL repository is configured with the **/etc/yum.repos.d/epel.repo** file, which configures the main EPEL repository along with the EPEL debugging and source repositories. The repository configurations use the same options. The name is Extra Packages for Enterprise Linux 6, with **basearch** used to determine the architecture part of the name. The **mirrorlist** option specifies the location of the repository mirrors. The **gpgkey** used, RPM-GPG-KEY-EPEL-6, is installed in **/etc/pki/rpm-gpg** folder.

```
[epel]
name=Extra Packages for Enterprise Linux 7 - $basearch
#baseurl=http://download.fedoraproject.org/pub/epel/7/$basearch
mirrorlist=https://mirrors.fedoraproject.org/metalink?repo=epel-7&arch=$basearch
failovermethod=priority
enabled=1
gpgcheck=1
gpgkey=file:///etc/pki/rpm-gpg/RPM-GPG-KEY-EPEL-7
```

Access to the RPM Fusion repository is configured with the **/etc/yum.repos.d/rpmfusion-free-updates.repo** file.

```
[rpmfusion-free-updates]
name=RPM Fusion for EL 7 - Free - Updates
#baseurl=http://download1.rpmfusion.org/free/el/updates/7/$basearch/
mirrorlist=http://mirrors.rpmfusion.org/mirrorlist?repo=free-el-updates-released-
7&arch=$basearch
enabled=1
gpgcheck=1
gpgkey=file:///etc/pki/rpm-gpg/RPM-GPG-KEY-rpmfusion-free-el-7
```

Creating Local Yum Repositories

For local networks where you may have several Red Hat Enterprise Linux systems, each of which may need to update using Yum, you could set up a local repository instead of having each system update from Internet sites directly. In effect, you download those packages on a Yum repository you want and then create from those packages a local repository on one of your local systems. Your local systems then use the local repository to install and update packages. You will have to keep the local repository updated manually. Use the **createrepo** command to create a repository from a folder holding the packages you want in it. Then it is a simple matter of providing a configuration file for it, specifying its location.

Managing Yum Caches

With the **keepcache** option enabled (set to 1), Yum will keep its downloaded packages in the **/var/cache/yum** folder, under subfolders for the architecture and release. Should you want to save or copy any particular packages, you can locate them there. Caching lets you easily uninstall and reinstall packages without having to download them again. The package is retained in the cache. If caching is disabled, then packages are automatically deleted after they are installed.

The size of your cache can increase rapidly, so you may want to clean it out on occasion. If you just want to delete these packages, as they are already installed, you can use the clean packages option.

```
yum clean packages
```

Yum also maintains a list of package headers with information on all packages downloaded. The headers are used to update your system, showing what has already been installed. You can opt to remove the headers with the **clean headers** option.

If you want Yum just to access packages in the cache, you use the **-C** option. The following lists just packages in the cache.

```
yum -C list
```

Manually Installing Packages with rpm

If you are installing a package that is not part of a Yum repository, and you do not have access to the desktop, or you prefer to work from the command line interface, you can use the **rpm** command to manage and install software packages. In most cases, you will not need to use the **rpm** command. Most software now resides on Yum-supported repositories. You would just use the **yum** command or the GNOME Software and PackageKit front ends, to install your package. Yum has the advantage of automatically installing any dependent packages, whereas the **rpm** command, though it will detect dependent packages, will not install them. You will have to install any dependent packages separately in the correct order.

Check the **System Administration Guide** for details on RPM, **Appendix A: RPM, A.2 Using RPM**.

```
https://access.redhat.com/documentation/en-
US/Red_Hat_Enterprise_Linux/7/html/System_Administrators_Guide/s1-rpm-
using.html#sec-Installing_and_Upgrading
```

For packages that are not part of any Yum-supported repository and that have few or no dependent packages, you can use the **rpm** command directly. You could also use the **rpm** command to bypass Yum, forcing the installation of a particular package instead of from Yum repositories (Yum's **localinstall** option will achieve the same purpose). A set of commonly used options is shown in the following table.

Option	Action
`-U`	Updates package
`-i`	Installs package
`-e`	Removes package
`-qi`	Displays information for an installed package
`-ql`	Displays file list for installed package
`-qpi`	Displays information from an RPM package file (used for uninstalled packages)
`-qpl`	Displays file list from an RPM package file (used for uninstalled packages)
`-K`	Authenticates and performs integrity check on a package

The **rpm** command performs installation, removal, and verification of software packages. Each software package is actually an RPM package, consisting of an archive of software files and information about how to install those files. Each archive resides as a single file with a name that ends with **.rpm**, indicating it is a software package that can be installed by the Red Hat Package Manager.

You can use the **rpm** command to either install or uninstall a package. The **rpm** command uses a set of options to determine what action to take. The **-i** option installs the specified software package, and the **-U** option updates a package. With an **-e** option, **rpm** uninstalls the package. A **q** placed before an **i** (**-qi**) queries the system to see if a software package is already installed and displays information about the software (**-qpi** queries an uninstalled package file). The **rpm** command with no options provides a complete list of **rpm** options.

The software package name is usually quite lengthy, including information about the version and release date in its name. All end with **.rpm**. In the next example, the user installs the **lftp** package using the **rpm** command. Notice that the full filename is entered. To list the full name, you can use the **ls** command with the first few characters and an asterisk.

In most cases, you are installing packages with the **-U** option, for update. Even if the package is not already installed, **-U** still installs it.

```
$ rpm -Uvh lftp-4.4.8-8.el7.x86_64.rpm
```

When RPM performs an installation, it first checks for any dependent packages. These are other software packages with programs the application you are installing needs to use. If other dependent packages must be installed first, RPM cancels the installation and lists those packages. You can install those packages and then repeat the installation of the application. To determine if a package is already installed, use the **-qi** option with **rpm**. The **-q** stands for query. To obtain a list of all the files the package has installed, as well as the folders it installed to, use the **-ql** option. To query package files, add the **p** option. The **-qpi** option displays information about a package, and **-qpl** lists the files in it. The following example lists all the files in the **lftp** package:

```
$ rpm -qpl lftp-4.4.8-8.el7.x86_64.rpm
```

To remove a software package from your system, first use **rpm -qi** to make sure it is installed, and then use the **-e** option to uninstall it. As with the **-qi** option, you do not have to use the full name of the installed file. You only need the name of the application. In the next example, the user removes **lftp** from the system:

```
$ rpm -e lftp
```

Package Security Check

If you download a software package, you may want to check its integrity and authentication, making sure the package was not tampered with and that it was obtained from a valid source. Yum is configured to perform this check automatically on all software downloaded from your configured repositories. Each repository configuration file in the **/etc/yum.repos.d** folder will have its **gpgcheck** option set to 1. Should you want to turn off this check for a particular repository, you can set its **gpgcheck** option to 0.

To authenticate a package, you check its digital signature. Packages are signed with encrypted digital keys that can be decrypted using the public key provided by the author of the package. This public key has first to be downloaded and installed on the encryption tool used on your system. Red Hat Enterprise Linux, along with most Linux distributions, uses the GNU Privacy Guard (GPG) encryption tool. To use a public key to authenticate an RPM package, you first have to install it in the RPM key database. For all RPM packages that are part of the Red Hat Enterprise Linux distribution, you can use the Red Hat Enterprise Linux public key, placed in the **/etc/pki/rpm-gpg/RPM-GPG-KEY-redhat-release** file. The key was installed automatically when you registered. In the **/etc/pki/rpm-gpg/** folder you will also find the RPM GPG keys for all your configured repositories.

Alternatively, you can manually import the key as shown here:

```
rpm --import /etc/pki/rpm-gpg/RPM-GPG-KEY-redhat-release
```

If you have downloaded an RPM package from another site, you can also download and install its public key, with which you can authenticate that package.

Once the public key is installed, you can check the package authentication using the **rpm** command with the **--checksig** option.

```
$ rpm --checksig lftp-4.4.8-8.el7.x86_64.rpm
```

You can manually check just a package's integrity with the **rpm** command with the **--checksig** and the **--nosignature** options. A value called the MD5 digest measures the contents of a package. If the value is incorrect, the package has been tampered with. Some packages provide just digest values, allowing only integrity checks. In the next example, the user checks whether the **lftp** package has been tampered with. The **--nosignature** option says not to perform authentication, doing the integrity check only.

```
$ rpm --checksig --nosignature lftp-4.4.8-8.el7.x86_64.rpm
```

Installing Source Code Applications from Red Hat SRPMS

Red Hat packages are also available in source code format. These programs are stored in SRPMS packages that you need to extract to special RPM build folders. The resulting source code can then be configured, compiled, and installed on your system.

The rpmbuild tools

To manage source files, you will also need the supporting **rpmbuild** tools in the **rpm-build** package, as well as additional rpm development tools in the **rpmdevtools** package. Also, make sure the **yum-utils** package is installed.

```
rpm-build
rpmdevtools
yum-utils
```

You can download a source code SRPMS package from a source code repository, SRPMS. You then should make sure that you have all the tools and packages installed that you will need to build a given source code package. To do this, run the **yum-builddep** command on the source code package. You will have to run this command as the root user. You can use the **su -c** command to run just that command as root. In this example, the source code package for freeciv is checked.

```
su -c 'yum-builddep freeciv-2.5.5-1.el7.src.rpm'
```

Then be sure to install the **rpmdevtools** package either with **yum** or PackageKit.

```
su -c 'yum install rpmdevtools'
```

Building the Package Source

RHEL7 RPM source code packages are managed through the Red Hat RPM build folders, not in the traditional **/usr/src** folder. It is always recommended that you **NOT** manage and build from the RPMS source packages as the **root** user. This means that you should not install the RPMS source package directly as the **root** user, which would place the files in a **/usr/src/redhat** folder. This folder should be avoided for use for source packages.

Instead, you should always install the source package in a local user folder as a local user, not the root user (the same is true for archive files extracted from a **tgz** file). You still need to use the **rpmbuild** set of folders like SPECS and BUILD. To set this local build environment up, you use the **rpmdev-setuptree** command (**rpmdevtools** package). Run this command once logged in as the user you want to use for managing the source code file.

```
rpmdev-setuptree
```

This command will create an **rpmbuild** folder with subfolders for SPECS, BUILD, RPMS, SOURCES, and SRPMS. The folder is built at **$(HOME)/rpmbuild**, with **$(HOME)** evaluating to your user home folder.

With the source RPMS package placed in your home folder, run the **rpm** command to extract it, **-ivh**, which will install the source code files to your **rpmbuild** folder. Warning messages will appear saying that it is using root, but it really is not. You can ignore the messages.

```
rpm -ivh freeciv-2.5.5-1.el7.src.rpm
```

The RPM spec file, *filename***.spec**, will be placed in the **SPECS** folder, in this example, it would be **freeciv.spec**. Configuration information, patches, and the compressed archive for the kernel source are placed in the **SOURCES** folder.

To generate the source code, you then use the **rpmbuild** command with the spec file such as **freeciv.spec** file and specify the type of architecture you want. Change to the **SPECS** folder and run **rpmbuild** with the **-bp** option (build) and the **--target** option to specify the architecture. The following command will extract the i686 version of the kernel. For a 64 bit version you would use x86_64:

```
rpmbuild -bp --target=i686  freeciv.spec
```

To ensure compliance with the system you are building on you can use the **uname -m** command to generate the version for the current system's architecture.

```
rpmbuild -bp --target=$(uname -m)  freeciv.spec
```

The extracted package source will be placed in the **BUILD** folder under package name.

Generating RPM Packages for installation

Once you have finished modifying the package source, if you want, you then both generate the binary and package it into an RPM package for installation, using the **rpmbuild** command.

Move to the SPECS folder.

```
cd ~/rpmbuild/SPECS
```

Use the **rpmbuild** command with the **-bb** option. Add the **--target** option to specify a particular hardware platform, **i686** for 32 bit or **x86_64** for 64 bit. The resulting RPM package or packages are placed in the RPMS folder.

```
rpmbuild -bb --target=x86_64 freeciv.spec
```

To guarantee that you generate the correct version for your system's hardware, you can use the **uname -m** command placed within backquotes for the **--target** option. The **-m** option generates the machine name such as **x86_64** or **i686**.

```
rpmbuild -bb --target=`uname -m` freeciv.spec
```

Several RPM packages may be generated in the RPMS folder under the target name subfolder such as **x86_64** and **i686**, as well as the **noarch** subfolder for packages that are not architecture specific.

Installing Source Code Applications from archives

Many programs are available for Linux in source code format. These programs are stored in a compressed archive that you need to decompress and then extract. The resulting source code can then be configured, compiled, and installed on your system. The process has been simplified to the extent that it involves not much more than installing an RPM package. Always check the included README and INSTALL files that come with the source code to check the appropriate method for creating and installing that software.

Be sure that you have installed all development packages onto your system. Development packages contain the key components such as the compiler, GNOME and KDE headers and libraries, and preprocessors. You cannot compile source code software without them.

First, you locate the software, and then you download it to your system. Then decompress and extract the file either with the Archive Manager on the desktop or with the **`tar`** command in a terminal window.

Extracting the Archive: Archive Manager (File Roller)

The easiest way to extract compressed archives is to use the Archive Manager (Utilities | Archive Manager) on GNOME applications overview. Either double-click the compressed archive file or right-click and select Open With "Archive Manager." This displays the top-level contents of the archive, which you can browse if you wish, even reading text files like README and INSTALL files. You can also see what files will actually be installed. Use the button to navigate and double-click a folder to open it. Nothing is extracted at this point. To extract the archive, click Extract. You will be able to select what folder to extract to, The default will be a subfolder in the current one.

Archive Manager will let you actually read text files in the archive directly. Just select and double-click the text file from its listing in the Archive manager window. Archive Manager will extract the file on the fly and display it in a window. The file is not actually extracted anywhere at this point.

You can also use Archive Manager to create your own archives, creating an archive with the New button and then selecting files and folders for it with the Add File and Add Folder buttons.

Alternatively, on a command line, you can use the **tar** command to extract archives. To use the **tar** command, first, open a terminal window. At the prompt, enter the **tar** command with the **xvjf** options (**j** for **bz2** and **z** for **gz**), as shown here:

```
tar xvjf freeciv-2.5.5-1.tar.bz2
```

Configure, Compile, and Install

Extracting the archive will create a folder with the name of the software. Once it is extracted, you have to configure, compile, and install the software. This usually needs to be done from a terminal window.

Change to the software folder with the **cd** command. Issue the command **./configure**. This generates a compiler configuration for your particular system.

```
./configure
```

Compile the software with the **make** command:

```
make
```

Then install the program with the **make install** command:

```
make install
```

Most KDE and GNOME software will also place an entry for the program in the appropriate menus or overview. You could also open a terminal window and enter the program's name.

9. Managing Users

User Accounts
system-config-users (Users and Groups)
Passwords
Managing User Environments
Adding and Removing Users with useradd and userdel
Managing Groups
User Desktop Profiles (sabayon)
Disk Quotas
Lightweight directory Access Protocol

As a system administrator, you can add or remove users, as well as add and remove groups, and you can modify access rights and permissions for both users and groups. You also have access to system initialization files you can use to configure all user shells. And you have control over the default initialization files copied into a user account when it is first created.

Check the **System Administration Guide** for details on Users and Groups, **Part 1. Basic System Configuration | Chapter 3: Managing Users and Groups**

```
https://access.redhat.com/documentation/en-US/Red_Hat_Enterprise_Linux/7/html/System_Administrators_Guide/ch-Managing_Users_and_Groups.html
```

User Accounts: Users, Settings

You can configure and create user accounts using the User Accounts tool accessible from Settings as Users. User Accounts does not provide any way to control groups. If you want group control and more configuration options, you can use the GNOME Users and Groups application (system-config-users package).

The User Accounts dialog displays left scrollable pane for a list of users, showing their icon and login name, and a right pane, showing information about a selected user (see Figure 9-1). An "Add User" button on the right side of the title bar lets you add users, and "Remove Account" button at the bottom right lets you remove a selected user.

When User Accounts is active, the applications menu on the GNOME top bar displays a Settings menu with Help, Keyboard Shortcuts, and Quit options. Choosing the Help entry opens the User Account help pages in GNOME desktop help, with detailed steps for most tasks and an explanation of administrative privileges.

PolicyKit controls administrative access for User Accounts. The User dialog opens initially with read-only access, allowing you to see information about users. To perform any tasks, such as adding or modifying users, you need to click the Unlock button at the top right of the dialog. An Authenticate dialog will open and prompt you to enter your user password. Once authenticated, the Unlock button changes to the "Add User" button.

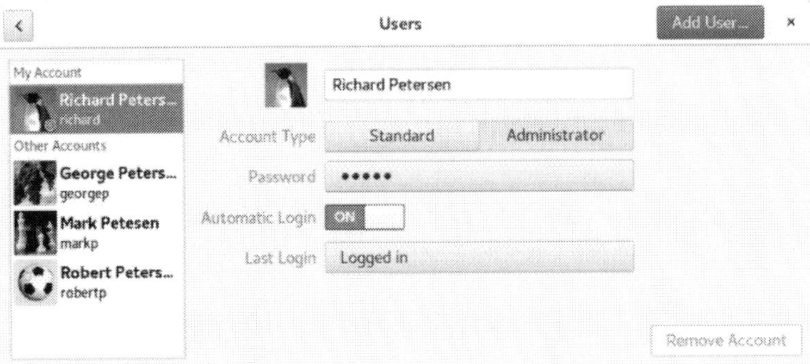

Figure 9-1: User Accounts

To add a new account, click the "Add User" button on the right side of the title bar. A dialog opens, allowing you to set the account type (standard or administrator), the full name of the user, and the username (see Figure 9-2). For the username, you can enter a name or choose from a recommended list of options. You can also choose to set the password at this time. Click the Add button at the top right to create the user. The new account appears on the User Accounts dialog, showing the name, icon, account type, language, password, and an automatic login option.

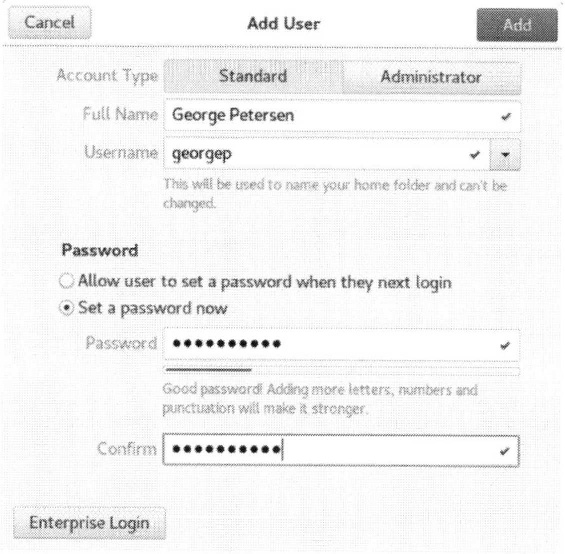

Figure 9-2: Add a new user

The account remains inactive until you specify a password (see Figure 9-3). You can do this when you add the account or later. You can also change the password for an account. Click the password entry to open a dialog in which you can enter the new password. On the right side of an empty Password text box, a password generator button is displayed that will generate a password for you when clicked. Once clicked, a generated password is entered into the textbox and the button disappears, replaced by a checkmark. Deleting the password to show an empty box, once again displays the password generator button. Once the password is selected, the account becomes enabled.

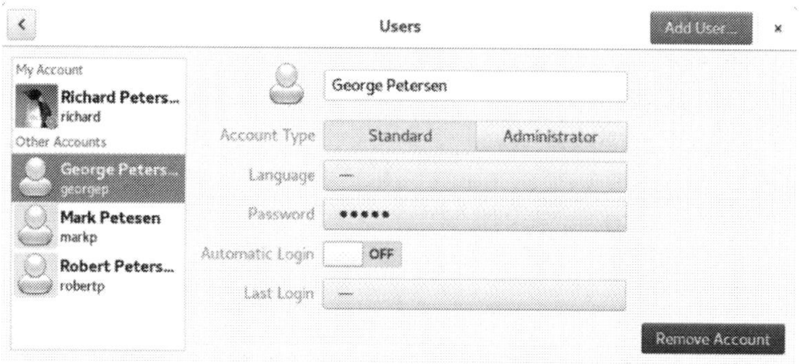

Figure 9-3: Users, inactive user

You can change the account type, language, password, and icon by clicking on their entries. You will be prompted for authorization.

To change the user icon, click the icon image to display a pop-up dialog showing available images you can use (see Figure 9-4). You can also take a photo from your webcam (take a photo entry) or select a picture from your Pictures folder (browse for more pictures).

Currently, group configuration is not supported.

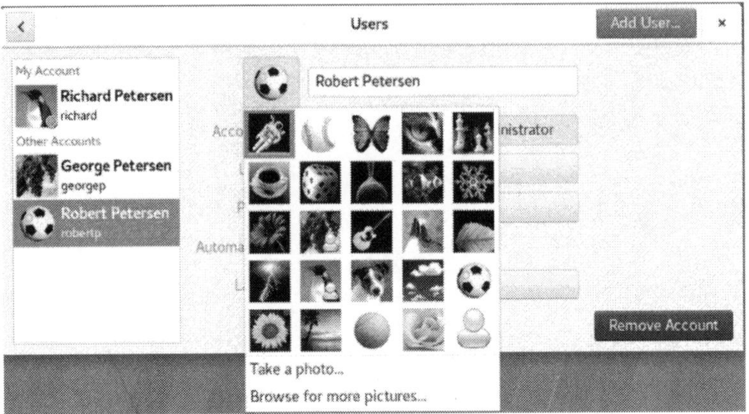

Figure 9-4: Accounts dialog, User Icon

Users and Groups Manager: system-config-users

You can also add and manage users by employing the older system-config-users application known as Users and Groups. It is not installed by default. You can install it using GNOME Software or PackageKit (Software). Once installed, you can access User and Groups from Sundry | Users and Groups. The system-config-users window displays tabs for listing both users and groups (see Figure 9-5). A button bar lists various tasks you can perform, including adding new users or groups, editing current ones (Properties), or deleting a selected user or group. You are prompted for authentication once when you first open Users and Groups. You can then make changes as you wish.

Users and Groups: New Users

To create a new user, click Add User to open a window with entries for the username, password, and login shell, along with options for creating a home directory and a new group for that user (see Figure 9-6).

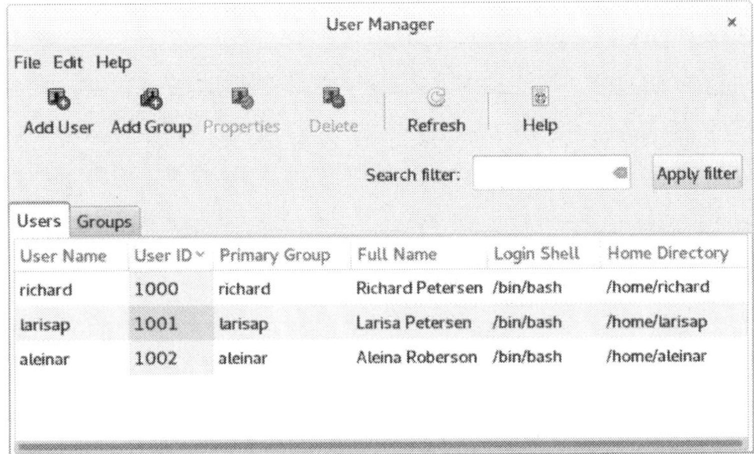

Figure 9-5: Users and Groups: Add New User

Figure 9-6: Users and Groups: Add New User

Once you have created a user, you can edit its properties to add or change features. Select the user's entry and click Properties. This displays a window with tabs for User Data, Account Info, Password Info, and Groups (see Figure 9-7). On the Groups tab, you can select the groups that the user belongs to, adding or removing group memberships (see Figure 9-8). The Accounts Info tab allows you to set an expiration date for the user, as well as lock the local password. Password Info can enable password expiration, forcing users to change their passwords at certain intervals.

Figure 9-7: Users and Groups: User Properties window: User Data tab

Figure 9-8: Users and Groups: User Properties window: Add groups to a user

Users and Groups: Groups

To add a group, click the Add Group button to open a small window in which you can enter the group name. The new group will be listed in the Groups listing (see Figure 9-9). Groups can be used in file and folder permissions to restrict access to a group of users.

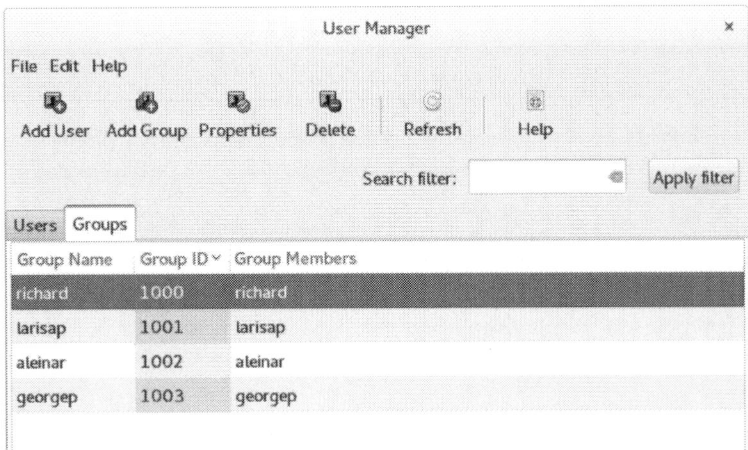

Figure 9-9: Users and Groups: Groups panel

To add users as members of the group, select the group's entry and click the Properties button. This opens a window with tabs for Group Data and Group Users. The Group Users tab lists all current users with check boxes (see Figure 9-10). Click the check boxes of the users you want to become members of this group.

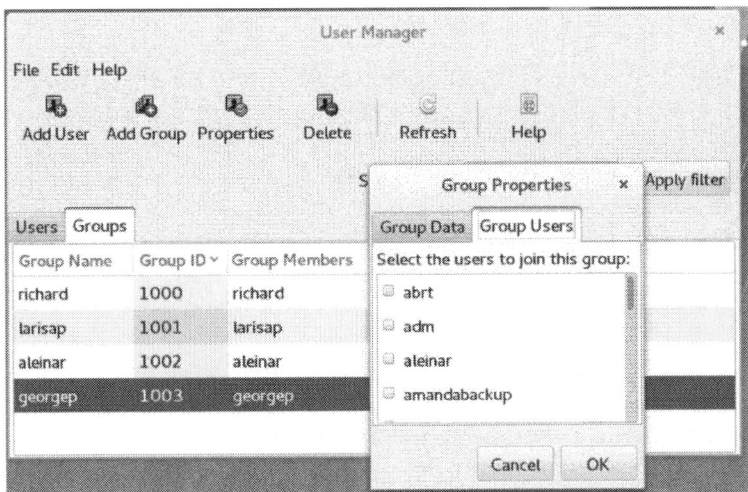

Figure 9-10: Users and Groups: Group Properties: Group Users panel

If you want to remove a user as a member, click the check box to remove its check. Click OK to affect your changes. If you want to remove a group, select its entry in the Groups panel and then click the Delete button.

You can also add groups to a user by selecting a user in the Users tab and opening its Properties window. Then select the Groups tab and select the groups you want that user to belong to.

User Configuration Files

Any utility to manage a user makes use of certain default configuration files and folders to set up a new account. A set of pathnames is used to locate these default files or to indicate where to create certain user folders. For example, **/etc/skel** holds initialization files for a new user. A new user's home folder is created in the **/home** folder. Table 9-1 has a list of the pathnames.

Folder and Files	Description
/home	Location of the user's own home folder.
/etc/skel	Holds the default initialization files for the login shell, such as **.bash_profile**, **.bashrc**, and **.bash_logout**. Includes many user setup folders and files such as **.kde** for KDE and **Desktop** for GNOME.
/etc/shells	Holds the login shells, such as BASH or TCSH.
/etc/passwd	Holds the password for a user.
/etc/group	Holds the group to which the user belongs.
/etc/shadow	Encrypted password file.
/etc/gshadow	Encrypted password file for groups.
/etc/login.defs	Default login definitions for users.

Table 9-1: Paths for User Configuration Files

Passwords

A user gains access to an account by providing a correct login and password. The system maintains passwords in password files, along with login information like the username and ID. Tools like the **passwd** command let users change their passwords by modifying these files; **/etc/passwd** is the file that traditionally held user passwords, though in encrypted form. However, all users are allowed to read the **/etc/passwd** file, which would have allowed access by users to the encrypted passwords. For better security, password entries are kept in the **/etc/shadow** file, which is restricted to the root user.

Tip: Every file is owned by a user who can control access to it. System files are owned by the root user and accessible by the root only. Services like FTP are an exception to this rule. Though accessible by the root, a service's files are owned by their own special user. For example, FTP files are owned by an **ftp** user. This provides users with access to a service's files without also having root user access.

/etc/passwd

When you add a user, an entry for that user is made in the **/etc/passwd** file. Each entry takes up one line that has several fields separated by colons. The fields are as follows:

Username Login name of the user

Password Encrypted password for the user's account

User ID Unique number assigned by the system

Group ID Number used to identify the group to which the user belongs

Comment Any user information, such as the user's full name

Home folder The user's home folder

Login shell Shell to run when the user logs in; this is the default shell, usually /bin/bash

Depending on whether or not you are using shadow passwords, the password field (the second field) will be either an **x** or an encrypted form of the user's password. Red Hat Enterprise Linux implements shadow passwords by default, so these entries should have an **x** for their passwords. The following is an example of an **/etc/passwd** entry. For such entries, you must use the **passwd** command to create a password. Notice also that user IDs in this particular system start at 1000 and increment by one. With Red Hat Enterprise Linux, the group given is not the generic User, but a group consisting uniquely of that user. For example, the **dylan** user belongs to a group named **Dylan**, not to the generic **User** group.

```
dylan:x:1000:1000:Dylan:/home/dylan:/bin/bash
chris:x:1001:1001:Chris:/home/chris:/bin/bash
```

Note: If you turn off shadow password support, entries in your passwd file will display encrypted passwords. Because any user can read the **/etc/passwd** file, intruders can access and possibly crack the encrypted passwords.

Although it is technically possible to edit entries in the **/etc/passwd** file directly, it is not recommended. In particular, deleting an entry does not remove any other information, permissions, and data associated with a user, which opens a possible security breach whereby an intruder could take over the deleted user's ID or disk space.

/etc/shadow and /etc/gshadow

The **/etc/passwd** file is a simple text file and is vulnerable to security breaches. If anyone gains access to the **/etc/password** file, they might be able to decipher or crack the encrypted passwords through a brute-force crack. The shadow suite of applications implements a greater level of security. These include versions of **useradd**, **groupadd**, and their corresponding update and delete programs. Most other user configuration tools, including User Accounts and system-config-users, support shadow security measures. With shadow security, passwords are no longer kept in the **/etc/password** file. Instead, passwords are kept in a separate file called **/etc/shadow**. Access is restricted to the root user.

The following example shows the **/etc/passwd** entry for a user.

```
chris:x:1001:1001:Chris:/home/chris:/bin/bash
```

A corresponding password file, called **/etc/gshadow,** is also maintained for groups that require passwords. Red Hat Enterprise Linux supports shadow passwords by default. You can manually specify whether you want to use shadow passwords with the **authconfig** tool.

Password Tools

To change any particular field for a given user, you should use the user management tools provided, such as the **passwd** command, User Accounts, system-config-users, **adduser**, **usermod**, **useradd**, and **chage**, discussed in this chapter. The **passwd** command lets you change the password only. Other tools, such as system-config-users, not only make entries in the **/etc/passwd** file but also create the home folder for the user and install initialization files in the user's home folder.

These tools also let you control users' access to their accounts. You can set expiration dates for users or lock them out of their accounts. Users locked out of their accounts will have their password in the **/etc/shadow** file prefixed by the invalid string, **!!**. Unlocking the account removes this prefix.

Tip: With the Red Hat Enterprise Linux Authentication tool (**authconfig**) you can enable and configure various authentication tools such as NIS and LDAP servers, as well as enabling shadow passwords, LDAP, and Kerberos authentication (accessible from Sundry | Authentication).

Users changing their own passwords

One common operation performed by users is to change a password. The easiest way to change your password on the GNOME desktop is to use User Accounts (click on a user's Password entry) or Users and Groups (User Properties dialog, User Data tab), as previously described.

Alternatively, you can use the **passwd** command. If you are using GNOME or KDE, you first have to open a terminal window. Then, at the shell prompt, enter the **passwd** command. The command prompts you for your current password. After entering your current password and pressing ENTER, you are then prompted for your new password. After entering the new password, you are asked to re-enter it. This is to make sure you actually entered the password you intended to enter.

```
$ passwd
Old password:
New password:
Retype new password:
$
```

Managing User Environments

Each time a user logs in, two profile scripts are executed, a system profile script that is the same for every user, and a user login profile script that can be customized to each user's needs. When the user logs out, a user logout script is run. In addition, each time a shell is generated, including the login shell, a user shell script is run. There are different kinds of scripts used for different shells. On Red Hat Enterprise Linux, the default shell is the BASH shell. As an alternative, users could use different shells such as TCSH or the Z shell.

Profile Scripts

For the BASH shell, each user has their own BASH login profile script named **.bash_profile** in the user's home folder. The system profile script is located in the **/etc** folder and named **profile** with no preceding period. The BASH shell user shell script is called **.bashrc**. The **.bashrc** file also runs the **/etc/bashrc** file to implement any global definitions such as the **PS1** and **TERM** variables. The **/etc/bashrc** file also executes any specialized initialization files in the **/etc/profile.d** folder, such as those used for KDE and GNOME. The **.bash_profile** file runs the **.bashrc** file, and through it, the **/etc/bashrc** file, implementing global definitions.

As a superuser, you can edit any of these profile or shell scripts and put in any commands you want executed for each user when that user logs in. For example, you may want to modify the default path for commands. Or you may want to notify the user of recent system news or account changes.

/etc/skel

When you first add a user to the system, you must provide the user with skeleton versions of their login, shell, and logout initialization files. For the BASH shell, these would be the **.bash_profile**, **.bashrc**, and **.bash_logout** files. The **useradd** command and other user management tools such as system-config-users add these files automatically, copying any files in the folder **/etc/skel** to the user's new home folder. The **/etc/skel** folder contains a skeleton initialization file for the **.bash_profile**, **.bashrc**, and **.bash_logout** files or, if you are using the TCSH shell as your login shell, the **.login**, **.tcshrc,** and **.logout** files. The **/etc/skel** folder also contains default files and folders for your desktops. These include a **.gnome2** file for the GNOME, a **.mozilla** folder for Firefox.

As a superuser, you can configure the **.bash_profile** or **.bashrc** file in the **/etc/skel** folder. Usually, basic system variable assignments are included that define pathnames for commands and command aliases. The **PATH** and **BASH_ENV** variables are defined in **.bash_profile**. Once users have their own **.bash_profile** or **.bashrc** file, they can redefine variables or add new commands as they choose.

/etc/login.defs

System-wide values used by user and group creation utilities such as **useradd** and **usergroup** are kept in the **/etc/login.defs** file. Here you will find the range of possible user and group IDs listed. **UID_MIN** holds the minimum number for user IDs, and **UID_MAX** the maximum number. Various password options control password controls, such as **PASS_MIN_LEN**, which determines the minimum number of characters allowable in a password. Options such as **CREATE_HOME** can be set to tell user tools like **useradd** to create home folders for new accounts by default. Samples of these entries are shown here:

```
MAIL_DIR /var/spool/mail
PASS_MIN_LEN        5
CREATE_HOME yes
```

/etc/login.access

You can control user login access by remote users to your system with the **/etc/login.access** file. The file consists of entries listing users, whether they are allowed access, and from where they can access the system. A record in this file consists of three colon-delimited fields: a plus (+) or minus (-) sign indicating whether users are allowed access, user login names allowed access, and the remote system (host) or terminal (tty device) from which they are trying to log in. The following enables the user **chris** to access the system from the **rabbit.mytrek.com** remote system:

```
+:chris:rabbit.mytrek.com
```

You can list more than one user or location, or use the **ALL** option in place of either users or locations to allow access by all users and locations. The **ALL** option can be qualified with the

EXCEPT option to allow access by all users except certain specified ones. The following entry allows any valid user to log in to the system using the console, except for the users **larisa** and **aleina**:

```
+:ALL EXCEPT larisa aleina:console
```

Other access control files are used to control access for specific services, such as the **hosts.deny** and **hosts.allows** files used with the **tcpd** daemon.

Controlling User Passwords

Once you have created a user account, you can control the user's access to it. Both the system-config-users and the **passwd** tool let you lock and unlock a user's account. You use the **passwd** command with the **-l** option to lock an account, invalidating its password, and you use the **-u** option to unlock it.

You can also force a user to change his or her password at given intervals by setting an expiration date for that password. Both system-config-users and the **chage** command let you specify an expiration limit for a user's password (see Table 9-2). A user could be required to change his or her password every month, every week, or at a given date. Once the password expires, the user will be prompted to enter a new one. You can issue a warning beforehand, telling the user how much time is left before the password expires. For an account that you want to close, you can permanently expire a password. You can even shut down accounts that are inactive too long. In the next example, the password for the **chris** account will stay valid for only seven days. The **-M** option with the number of days sets the maximum time that a password can be valid.

```
chage -M 7  chris
```

Option	Description
-m	Minimum number of days a user must go before being able to change his password
-M	Maximum number of days a user can go without changing his password
-d	The last day the password was changed
-E	Specific expiration date for a password, date in format in *yyyy-mm-dd* or in commonly used format like *mm/dd/yyyy*
-I	Allowable account inactivity period (in days), after which password will expire
-W	Warning period, number of days before expiration when the user will be sent a warning message
-l	Display current password expiration controls

Table 9-2: Options for the chage Command

To set a particular date for the account to expire, use the **-E** option with the date specified *mm/dd/yyyy*.

```
chage -E 07/30/2011  chris
```

To find out what the current expiration settings are for a given account, use the **-l** option.

```
chage -l chris
```

You can also combine your options into one command,

```
chage -M 7 -E 07/30/2011  chris
```

Adding and Removing Users with useradd, usermod, and userdel

Linux also provides the **useradd**, **usermod**, and **userdel** commands to manage user accounts. All these commands take in all their information as options on the command line. If an option is not specified, they use predetermined default values. These are command line operations. To use them on your desktop you first need to open a terminal window and then enter the commands at the shell prompt.

useradd

With the **useradd** command, you enter values as options on the command line, such as the name of a user, to create a user account. It then creates a new login and folder for that name using all the default features for a new account.

```
useradd chris
```

The **useradd** utility first checks the **/etc/login.defs** file for default values for creating a new account. For those defaults not defined in the **/etc/login.defs** file, **useradd** supplies its own. You can display these defaults using the **useradd** command with the **-D** option. The default values include the group name, the user ID, the home folder, the **skel** folder, and the login shell. Values the user enters on the command line will override corresponding defaults. The group name is the name of the group in which the new account is placed. By default, this is **other**, which means the new account belongs to no group. The user ID is a number identifying the user account. The **skel** folder is the system folder that holds copies of initialization files. These initialization files are copied into the user's new home folder when it is created. The login shell is the pathname for the particular shell the user plans to use.

The **useradd** command has options that correspond to each default value. Table 9-3 holds a list of options you can use with the **useradd** command. You can use specific values in place of any of these defaults when creating a particular account. The login is inaccessible until you do. In the next example, the group name for the **chris** account is set to **intro1,** and the user ID is set to 578:

```
useradd chris -g intro1 -u 578
```

Once you add a new user login, you need to give the new login a password. Password entries are placed in the **/etc/passwd** and **/etc/shadow** files. Use the **passwd** command to create a new password for the user, as shown here. The password you enter will not appear on your screen. You will be prompted to repeat the password. A message will then be issued indicating that the password was successfully changed.

```
$ passwd chris
Changing password for user chris
New UNIX password:
Retype new UNIX password:
```

```
passwd: all authentication tokens updated successfully
```

Options	Description
-d *dir*	Sets the home folder of the new user.
-D	Displays defaults for all settings. Can also be used to reset default settings for the home folder (**-b**), group (**-g**), shell (**-s**), expiration date (**-e**), and password expirations (**-f**).
-e *mm/dd/yy*	Sets an expiration date for the account (none, by default). Specified as month/day/year.
-f *days*	Sets the number of days an account remains active after its password expires.
-g *group*	Sets a group.
-m	Creates user's home folder, if it does not exist.
-m -k *skl-dir*	Sets the skeleton folder that holds skeleton files, such as **.profile** files, which are copied to the user's home folder automatically when it is created; the default is **/etc/skel**.
-M	Does not create user's home folder.
-p *password*	Supplies an encrypted password (crypt or MD5). With no argument, the account is immediately disabled.
-r	Creates a system account (one whose user ID is lower than the minimum set in **logon.defs**). No home folder is created unless specified by **-m**.
-s *shell*	Sets the login shell of the new user. This is **/bin/bash** by default, the BASH shell.
-u *userid*	Sets the user ID of the new user. The default is the increment of the highest number used so far.

Table 9-3: Options for useradd and usermod

usermod

The **usermod** command enables you to change the values for any of these features. You can change the home folder or the user ID. You can even change the username for the account. The **usermod** command takes the same options as **useradd**, listed in Table 9-3.

userdel

When you want to remove a user from the system, you can use the **userdel** command to delete the user's login. With the `-r` option, the user's home folder will also be removed. In the next example, the user **chris** is removed from the system:

```
userdel -r chris
```

Managing Groups

You can manage groups using either shell commands or desktop tools like the User and Groups (system-config-users), as discussed previously. Groups are an effective way to manage access and permissions, letting you control several users with just their group name.

/etc/group and /etc/gshadow

The system file that holds group entries is called **/etc/group**. The file consists of group records, with one record per line and its fields separated by colons. A group record has four fields: a group name, a password, its ID, and the users who are part of this group. The Password field can be left blank. The fields for a group record are as follows:

Group name The name of the group, which must be unique

Password With shadow security implemented, this field is an x, with the password indicated in the /etc/gshadow file.

Group ID The number assigned by the system to identify this group

Users The list of users that belong to the group, separated by commas

Here is an example of an entry in an **/etc/group** file. The group is called **engines**, the password is managed by shadow security, the group ID is 100, and the users who are part of this group are **chris**, **robert**, **valerie**, and **aleina**:

```
engines:x:100:chris,robert,valerie,aleina
```

As in the case of the **/etc/passwd** file, it is best to change group entries using a group management utility like **groupmod**, **groupadd**, or system-config-users. All users have read access to the **/etc/group** file. With shadow security, secure group data such as passwords are kept in the **/etc/gshadow** file, to which only the root user has access.

User Private Groups

A new user can be assigned to a special group set up for just that user and given the user's name. Thus the new user **dylan** is given a default group also called **dylan**. The group **dylan** will also show up in the listing of groups. This method of assigning default user groups is called the User Private Group (UPG) scheme. The supplementary groups are additional groups that the user may want to belong to. Traditionally, users were all assigned to one group named **users** that would subject all users to the group permission controls for the **users** group. With UPG, each user has its own group, with its own group permissions.

Group Folders

As with users, you can create a home folder for a group. To do so, you simply create a folder for the group in the **/home** folder and change its group to that of the group, along with allowing access by any member of the group. The following example creates a folder called **engines** and changes its group to that of the **engines** group:

```
mkdir /home/engines
chgrp engines /home/engines
```

Then the read, write, and execute permissions for the group level should be set with the **chmod** command:

```
chmod g+rwx /home/engines
```

Any member of the **engines** group can now access the **/home/engines** folder and any shared files placed therein. This folder becomes a shared folder for the group. You can, in fact, use the same procedure to make other shared folders at any location on the file system.

Files within the shared folder should also have their permissions set to allow access by other users in the group. When a user places a file in a shared folder, the user needs to set the permissions on that file to allow other members of the group to access it. A read permission will let others display it, write lets them change it, and execute lets them run it (used for scripts and programs). The following example first changes the group for the **mymodel** file to **engines**. Then it copies the **mymodel** file to the **/home/engines** folder and sets the group read and write permission for the **engines** group:

```
$ chgrp engines mymodel
$ cp mymodel /home/engines
$ chmod g+rw /home/engines/mymodel
```

Managing Groups Using groupadd, groupmod, and groupdel

You can also manage groups with the **groupadd**, **groupmod**, and **groupdel** commands. These command line operations let you quickly manage a group from a terminal window.

groupadd and groupdel

With the **groupadd** command, you can create new groups. When you add a group to the system, the system places the group's name in the **/etc/group** file and gives it a group ID number. If shadow security is in place, changes are made to the **/etc/gshadow** file. The **groupadd** command only creates the group category. You need to add users to the group individually. In the following example, the **groupadd** command creates the **engines** group:

```
groupadd engines
```

You can delete a group with the **groupdel** command. In the next example, the **engines** group is deleted:

```
groupdel engines
```

groupmod

You can change the name of a group or its ID using the **groupmod** command. Enter **groupmod -g** with the new ID number and the group name. To change the name of a group, you use the **-n** option. Enter **groupmod -n** with the new name of the group, followed by the current name. In the next example, the **engines** group has its name changed to **trains**:

```
groupmod -n trains engines
```

Disk Quotas

You can use disk quotas to control how much disk space a particular user makes use of on your system. On your Linux system, unused disk space is held as a common resource that each user can access as they need it. As users create more files, they take the space they need from the pool of available disk space. In this sense, all the users are sharing a single resource of unused disk space. However, if one user were to use up all the remaining disk space, none of the other users would be able to create files or even run programs. To counter this problem, you can create disk quotas on particular users, limiting the amount of available disk space they can use.

Check the **Storage Administration Guide** for details on Disk Quotas, **Chapter 16: Disk Quotas**.

```
https://access.redhat.com/documentation/en-
US/Red_Hat_Enterprise_Linux/7/html/Storage_Administration_Guide/ch-disk-
quotas.html
```

Quota Tools

Quota checks can be implemented on the file system of a hard disk partition mounted on your system. The quotas are enabled using the **quotacheck** and **quotaon** programs. Each partition needs to be mounted with the quota options, **usrquota** or **grpquota**. **usrquota** enables quota controls for users, and **grpquota** works for groups. These options are usually placed in the mount entry in the **/etc/fstab** file for a particular partition. For example, to mount the **/dev/sda4** hard disk partition mounted to the **/home** folder with support for user and group quotas, you would require a mount entry like the following:

```
/dev/sda4 /home ext2 defaults,usrquota,grpquota 1 1
```

You also need to create **quota.user** and **quota.group** files for each partition for which you enable quotas. These are the quota databases used to hold the quota information for each user and group. You can create these files by running the **quotacheck** command with the **-a** option or the device name of the filesystem where you want to enable quotas. The following example creates the quota database on the sda1 hard disk partition:

```
quotacheck -a  /dev/sda1
```

edquota

You can set disk quotas using the **edquota** command. With it, you can access the quota record for a particular user and group, which is maintained in the disk quota database. You can also set default quotas that will be applied to any user or group on the file system for which quotas have not been set. **edquota** will open the record in your default editor, and you can use your editor to make any changes. To open the record for a particular user, use the **-u** option and the username as an argument for **edquota** (see Table 9-4). The following example opens the disk quota record for the user **larisa**:

```
edquota -u larisa
```

The limit you set for a quota can be hard or soft. A hard limit will deny a user the ability to exceed his or her quota, whereas a soft limit will just issue a warning. For the soft limit, you can designate a grace period during which time the user has the chance to reduce their disk space below the limit. If the disk space still exceeds the limit after the grace period expires, the user can be denied access to their account. For example, a soft limit is typically 75 megabytes, whereas the hard limit could be 100 megabytes. Users who exceed their soft limit could have a 48-hour grace period.

edquota Option	Description
-u	Edits the user quota. This is the default.
-g	Edits the group quota.
-p	Duplicates the quotas of the typical user specified. This is the normal mechanism used to initialize quotas for groups of users.
-t	Edits the soft time limits for each file system.

Table 9-4: Options for edquota

The quota record begins with the hard disk device name and the blocks of memory and inodes in use. The Limits segments have parameters for soft and hard limits. If these entries are 0, there are no limits in place. You can set both hard and soft limits, using the hard limit as a firm restriction. Blocks in Linux are about 1,000 bytes. The inodes are used by files to hold information about the memory blocks making up a file. To set the time limit for a soft limit, use the **edquota** command with the **-t** option. The following example displays the quota record for **larisa**:

```
Quotas for user larisa:
/dev/sda3: blocks in use: 9000, limits (soft = 40000, hard = 60000)
 inodes in use: 321, limits (soft = 0, hard = 0)
```

quotacheck, quotaon, and quotaoff

The quota records are maintained in the quota database for that partition. Each partition that has quotas enabled has its own quota database. You can check the validity of your quota database with the **quotacheck** command. You can turn quotas on and off using the **quotaon** and **quotaoff** commands. When you start up your system, **quotacheck** is run to check the quota databases, and then **quotaon** is run to turn on quotas.

repquota and quota

As the system administrator, you can use the **repquota** command to generate a summary of disk usage for a specified file system, checking to see what users are approaching or exceeding quota limits. **repquota** takes as its argument the file system to check; the **-a** option checks all file systems.

```
repquota /dev/sda1
```

quota Option	Description
-g	Prints group quotas for the group of which the user is a member.
-u	Prints the user's quota.
-v	Displays quotas on filesystems where no storage is allocated.
-q	Prints information on filesystems where usage is over quota.

Table 9-5: Options for quota

Individual users can use the **quota** command to check their memory use and how much disk space they have left in their quota (see Table 9-5).

Lightweight directory Access Protocol

The Lightweight directory Access Protocol (LDAP) is designed to implement network-accessible folders of information. In this context, the term folder is defined as a database of primarily read-only, simple, small, widely accessible, and quickly distributable information. It is not designed for transactions or updates. It is primarily used to provide information about users on a network, providing information about them such as their e-mail address or phone number. Such folders can also be used for authentication purposes, identifying that a certain user belongs to a specified network. You can find out more information on LDAP at **http://www.openldap.org/**. You can think of an LDAP folder for users as an Internet-accessible phone book, where anyone can look you up to find your e-mail address or other information. In fact, it may be more accurate to refer to such folders as databases. They are databases of user information, accessible over networks like the Internet. Normally, the users on a local network are spread across several different systems, and to obtain information about a user, you would have to know what system the user is on, and then query that system. With LDAP, user information for all users on a network is kept in the LDAP server. You only have to query the network's LDAP server to obtain information about a user. For example, Sendmail can use LDAP to look up user addresses.

Check the **System-Level Authentication Guide** for details on LDAP configuration, **Chapter 3.2: LDAP and IdM**

```
https://access.redhat.com/documentation/en-
US/Red_Hat_Enterprise_Linux/7/html/System-Level_Authentication_Guide/authconfig-
ldap.html
```

Numerous LDAP packages are available on the Red Hat Enterprise Linux repository, which provides specific LDAP support. LDAP support packages include those for Java, Kerberos, Dovecot, Cyrus mail, Mozilla, NSS and PAM, Perl, ProFTP, Samba, and Wine

LDAP Clients and Servers

LDAP folders are implemented as clients and servers, where you use an LDAP client to access an LDAP server that manages the LDAP database. Most Linux distributions use OpenLDAP, an open-source version of LDAP (you can find out more about OpenLDAP at **http://www.openldap.org**). This package includes an LDAP server (**slapd**), an LDAP replication server (**slurpd**), an LDAP client, and tools. **slurpd** is used to update other LDAP servers on your network, should you have more than one. Once the LDAP server is installed, you can start, stop, and restart the LDAP server (**slapd**) with the **ldap** startup script.

```
/etc/init.d/ldap restart
```

Note: On Red Hat Enterprise Linux you can enable LDAP services and select an LDAP server using the Authentication tool (authconfig), accessible from Sundry | Authentication.

LDAP Configuration Files

All LDAP configuration files are kept in the **/etc/openldap** folder. These include **slapd.conf**, the LDAP server configuration file, and **ldap.conf**, the LDAP clients and tools configuration file.

To enable LDAP clients and their tools, you have to specify the correct domain address in the **ldap.conf** file in the BASE option, along with the server's address in the HOST option (domain name or IP address). For clients, you can either edit the **ldap.conf** file directly or use the **authconfig** desktop tool accessible from Sundry | Authentication (see Chapter 15). On the Identity & Authentication tab choose LDAP from the User Account Database menu. You can then enter your domain name and the LDAP server's address. See the **ldap.conf** Man entry for detailed descriptions of LDAP options.

To enable the LDAP server, you have to edit the **slapd.conf** file, and change the domain value (dc) for the suffix and rootdn entries to your own network's domain address. This is the network that will be serviced by the LDAP server.

Tip: Keep in mind that the ***/etc/ldap.conf*** and ***/etc/openldap/ldap.conf*** files are not the same: ***/etc/ldap.conf*** is used to configure LDAP for the Nameservice Switch and PAM support, whereas ***/etc/openldap/ldap.conf*** is used for all LDAP clients.

Red Hat Directory Server

The Red Hat Directory Server (RHDS) is a Red Hat Enterprise Linux implementation of the LDAP server, designed for enterprise level operations. RHDS is undergoing rapid development. It is advisable that you make use of the online documentation for up-to-date reference and instructions. Check the Red Hat Directory Server site and the documentation site for detailed information. You can use the Red Hat documentation to learn how to install and operate your RHDS.

```
https://www.redhat.com/en/technologies/cloud-computing/directory-server
https://access.redhat.com/documentation/en/red-hat-directory-server/
```

The RHDS is comprised of three components: the Directory server, the Directory Server Console, and the Administration server along with its own administration console.

Directory Server The main LDAP server. It includes command-line management tools.

Directory Server Console The Web browser-based interface that allows you to manage LDAP users and groups, as well as manage your server, making backups and setting up security.

Administration Server Administers the folder server, connecting to the Folder Server Console. It communicates with the Folder Server Console and performs operations on the Folder Server instances. Each folder server instance must have its own folder administration server.

RHDS has its own service script called **dirsrv**

```
service dirsrv start
```

10. Network Connections and Firewalls

With Red Hat Enterprise Linux, network configuration is managed primarily by the Network Manager. Network configuration differs depending on whether you are connected to a local area network (LAN) with an Ethernet card or are using a DSL modem, a wireless connection, or a dial-up modem connection. For wireless and dial-up connection configuration from the command line, you can use **wvdial** and **wconfig**. You can control access to your network by setting up a firewall using **firewall-config** (Sundry | Firewall). Table 10-1 lists several different network-related configuration tools.

Network Configuration App	Description
NetworkManager	Automatically configures wireless and wired network connections. Can also manually edit them.
firewall-config	Sets up a network firewall.
wvdial	PPP modem connection, enter on a command line.
wconfig	Wireless connection, enter on a command line.

Table 10-1: RHEL Network Configuration Tools

Network configuration can be found in the **/etc/networking** folder. The devices subfolder holds the **ifcfg** file for your **device**, whereas the **profiles** folder holds the profiles you may have set up. Here you will find the host and nameserver information for your network connection profiles, including the default profile.

Check the **Networking Guide** for details on Network configuration.

```
https://access.redhat.com/documentation/en-
US/Red_Hat_Enterprise_Linux/7/html/Networking_Guide/index.html
```

Network Information: Dynamic and Static

If you are on a network, you may need to obtain certain information to configure your interface. Most networks now support dynamic configuration using either the older Dynamic Host Configuration Protocol (DHCP) or the new IPv6 Protocol and its automatic address configuration. In this case, you need only use the DHCP option in network configuration tools.

If your network does not support DHCP or IPv6 automatic addressing, you will have to provide detailed information about your connection. Such connections are known as static connections, whereas DCHP and IPv6 connections are dynamic. In a static connection, you need to manually enter your connection information such as your IP address and DNS servers, whereas in a dynamic connection this information is automatically provided to your system by a DHCP server or generated by IPv6 when you connect to the network. For DHCP, a DHCP client on each host will obtain the information from a DHCP server serving that network. IPv6 generates its addresses directly from the device and router information such as the device hardware MAC address.

In addition, if you are using a DSL dynamic, ISDN, or modem connection, you will also have to supply provider, login, and password information, whether your system is dynamic or static. You may also need to supply specialized information such as DSL or modem compression methods, dial-up number, or wireless channels to select.

You can obtain most of your static network information from your network administrator or from your ISP (Internet service provider). You would need the following information:

The device name for your network interface For LAN and wireless connections, this is usually an Ethernet card. For a modem, DSL, or ISDN connection, this is a PPP device. Virtual private network (VPN) connections are also supported.

Hostname Your computer will be identified by this name on the Internet. Do not use localhost; that name is reserved for special use by your system. The name of the host should be a simple word, which can include numbers, but not punctuation such as periods and backslashes. The hostname includes both the name of the host and its domain.

Domain name This is the name of your network.

The Internet Protocol (IP) address assigned to your machine This is needed only for static Internet connections. Dynamic connections use the DHCP protocol to assign an IP address for you automatically. Every host on the Internet is assigned an IP address. Traditionally, this address used an IPv4 format consisting of a set of four numbers, separated by periods, which uniquely identifies a single location on the Internet, allowing information from other locations to reach that computer. Most large networks use IP protocol version 6, IPv6, which uses a different format with a much more complex numbering sequence.

Your network IP address This address is usually similar to the IP address, but with one or more zeros at the end.

The netmask This is usually 255.255.255.0 for most networks. If, however, you are part of a large network, check with your network administrator or ISP.

The broadcast address for your network, if available (optional) Usually, your broadcast address is the same as your IP address with the number 255 added at the end.

The IP address of your network's gateway computer This is the computer that connects your local network to a larger one like the Internet.

Name servers The IP address of the name servers your network uses.

NIS domain and IP address for an NIS server Needed if your network uses an NIS server.

User login and password information Needed for dynamic DSL, ISDN, and modem connections.

NetworkManager

Network Manager will automatically detect your network connections, both wired and wireless. It is the default method for managing your network connections. Network Manager makes use the automatic device detection capabilities of udev to configure your connections. Should you instead need to configure your network connections manually, you would use GNOME Network, available from wired and wireless entries on the System Status Area menu, and on the Settings dialog.

Network Manager is user specific. When a user logs in, it selects the network connection preferred by that user. The first time a user runs NetworkManager, the user can choose from a list of current possible connections. For wired connections, a connection can be started automatically, when the system starts up. Initial settings will be supplied from the system-wide configuration.

Configurations can also be applied system-wide to all users. When editing or adding a network connection with GNOME Network, the connection's Identity tab on its configuration dialog displays a "Make available to other users" checkbox. Click this checkbox and then click the Apply button to make the connection configuration available system-wide. If you are using the older nm-connection-editor, its connection configuration dialog displays an "All users may connect to this network" in the General tab which you can check.

Network Manager can configure any network connection. This includes wired, wireless, and all manual connections. Network Interface Connection (NIC cards) hardware is detected using udev. Information provided by Network Manager is made available to other applications over D-Bus.

With multiple wireless access points for Internet connections, a system could have several different network connections to choose from, instead of a single-line wired connection. This is particularly true for notebook computers that could access different wireless connections at different locations. Instead of manually configuring a new connection each time one is encountered, the Network Manager tool can automatically configure and select a connection to use.

Network Manager is designed to work in the background, providing status information for your connection and switching from one configured connection to another as needed. For initial configuration, it detects as much information as possible about the new connection.

Network Manager operates as a daemon with the name NetworkManager. If no Ethernet connection is available, Network Manager will scan for wireless connections, checking for Extended Service Set Identifiers (ESSIDs). If an ESSID identifies a previously used connection, then it is automatically selected. If several are found, then the most recently used one is chosen. If only a new connection is available, then Network Manager waits for the user to choose one. A connection is selected if the user is logged in. If an Ethernet connection is later made, then Network Manager will switch to it from wireless.

The Network Manager daemon can be turned on or off using the service command as the root user.

```
su
service NetworkManager start
service NetworkManager stop
```

The service command simply runs **systemctl**, which you can use directly instead.

```
su
systemctl start NetworkManager
systemctl stop NetworkManager
systemctl restart NetworkManager
```

Networks are actually configured and managed with the lower level tools: ifconfig, route, and netstat. The ifconfig tool operates from your root user desktop and enables you to configure your network interfaces fully, adding new ones and modifying others. The ifconfig and route utilities are lower-level programs that require more specific knowledge of your network to use effectively. The netstat tool provides you with information about the status of your network connections.

Network Manager Manual Configuration using GNOME Network

The GNOME Network utility, available from Settings, can be used to configure all your network connections manually. Automatic wireless and wired connections were also covered in Chapter 2. For detailed manual configuration, Network features the dialogs similar to those used in Network Connections. Network displays a dialog with tabs for Wi-Fi, Wired, and Network proxy (see Figure 10-1).

Check the **Networking Guide | Chapter 2. Configuring IP Networking | 2.5 Using NetworkManager with the GNOME Graphical User Interface** for details on using GNOME network.

```
https://access.redhat.com/documentation/en-US/Red_Hat_Enterprise_Linux/7/html/Networking_Guide/sec-Using_NetworkManager_with_the_GNOME_Graphical_User_Interface.html
```

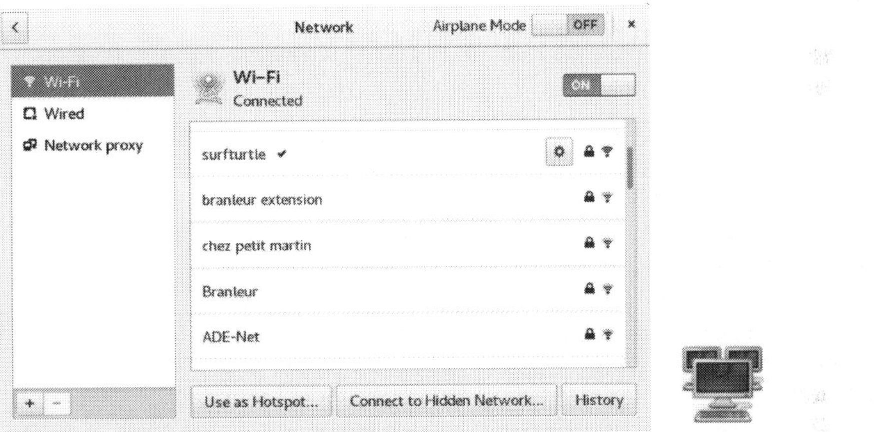

Figure 10-1: Network (Settings): Wi-Fi tab

On the Wi-Fi tab, available wireless connections are listed to the right. Selecting an entry will create a gear button for it, which you can click to open the network configuration dialog with tabs for Details, Security, Identity, IPv4, IPv6, and Reset. The Details tab show strength, speed, security methods, IP and hardware addresses, routes, and the DNS server IP address. To edit the connection manually, you use the Security, Identity, and IP tabs. The Security tab displays a menu from which you can choose a security method and a password (see Figure 10-2).

Figure 10-2: Network wireless configuration: Security tab

On the Identity tab, you can specify the SSID name, choose a firewall zone, and choose to connect automatically when you log in and whether to make the connection system-wide, the "Make available to other users" checkbox. (see Figure 10-3).

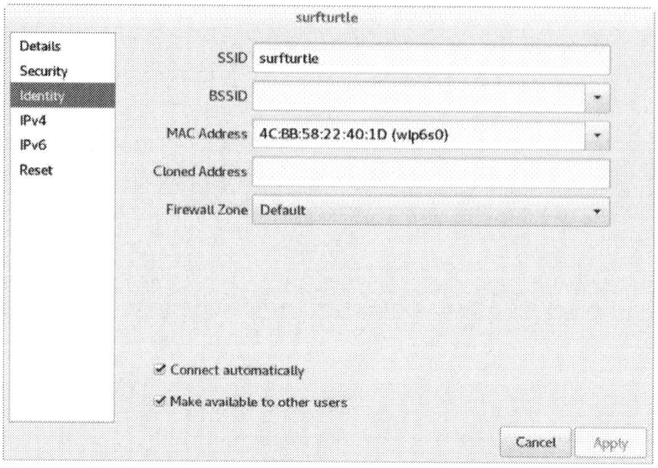

Figure 10-3: Network wireless configuration: Identity tab

On the IPv4 Settings tab, a switch allows you to turn the IP connection on or off. There are sections for Addresses, the DNS servers, and Routes. An Addresses menu lets you choose the type connection you want. By default, it is set to Automatic. If you change it to Manual, new entries appear for the address, netmask, and gateway. On the IPv6 tab, the netmask is replaced by prefix (see Figure 10-4). You can turn off Automatic switches for the DNS and Routes sections to make them manual. The DNS section has a plus button to let you add more DNS servers.

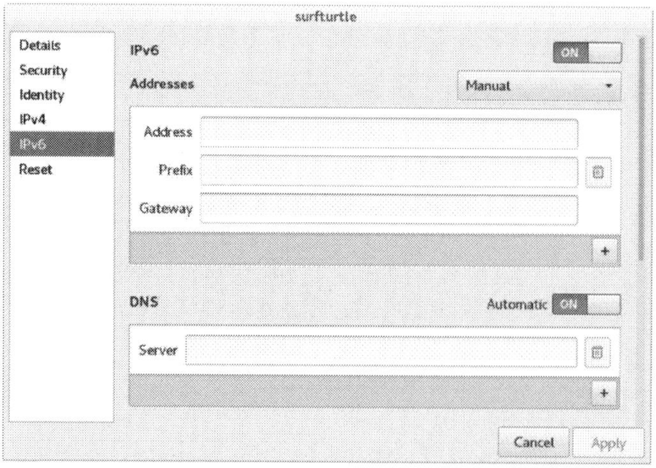

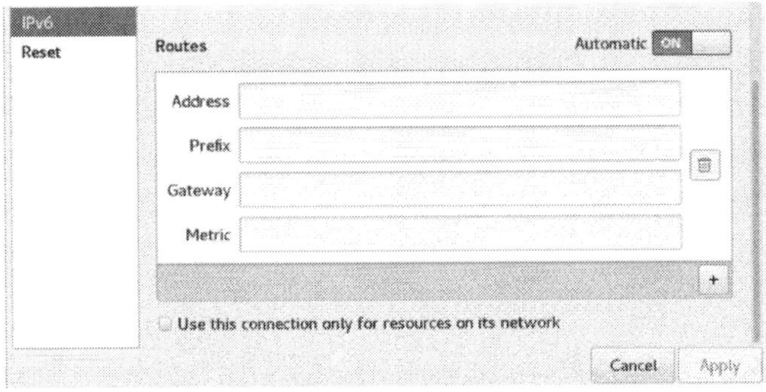

Figure 10-4: Network wireless configuration: IPv6 tab, Manual

On the Wired tab, a gear button is displayed at the lower right. A switch lets you turn the connection on or off (see Figure 10-5). Clicking the gear button opens a configuration dialog with tabs for Details, Security, Identity, IPv4, IPv6, and Reset (see Figure 10-6).

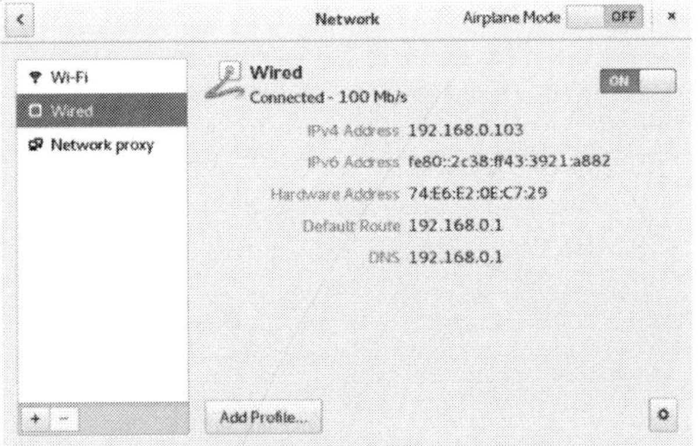

Figure 10-5: Network (Settings): Wired tab

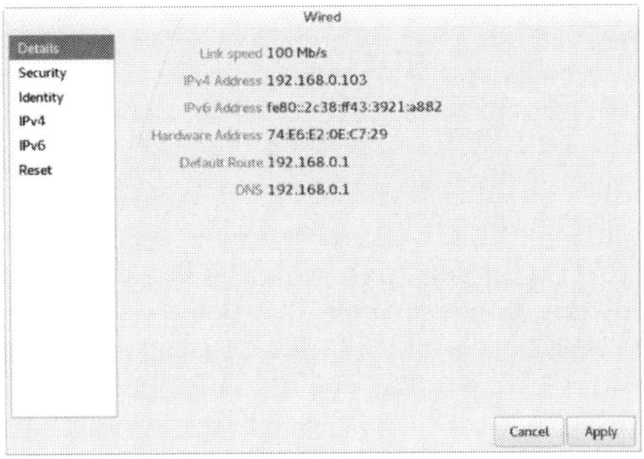

Figure 10-6: Network wired configuration dialog

You can use the Security, Identity, and IP tabs to configure the connection manually. The Security tab lets you turn on 802.1x security and choose an authentication method, as well as provide a username and password (see Figure 10-7).

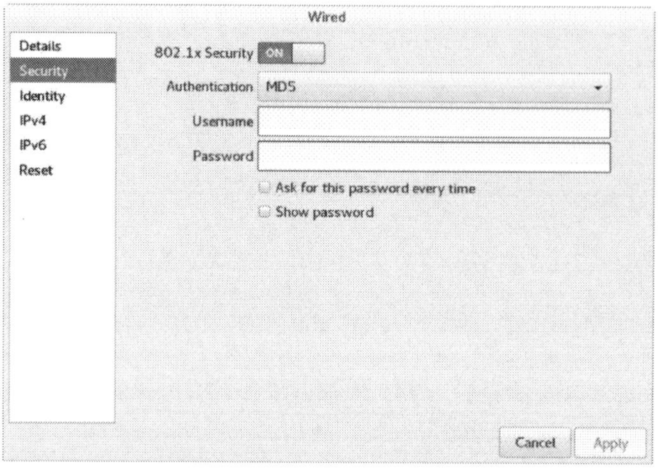

Figure 10-7: Network wired configuration: Security tab

On the Identity tab, you can choose the firewall zone, set the name, choose the hardware address, set the MTU blocks, and choose to connect automatically and whether to make the connection available to other users (see Figure 10-8).

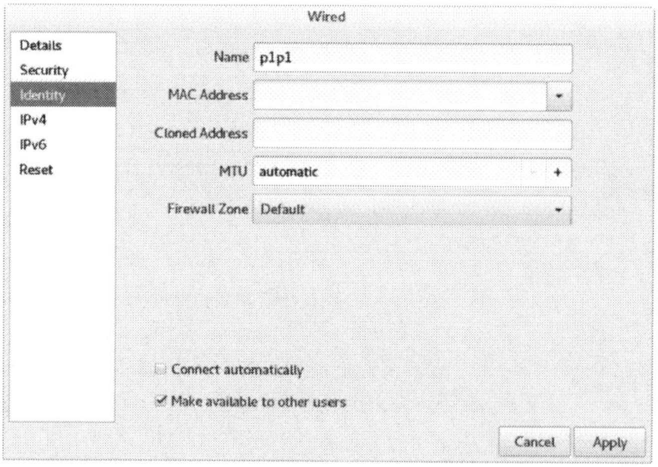

Figure 10-8: Network wired configuration: Identity tab

On the IP tabs, a switch allows you to turn the connection on or off. The tab has sections for Addresses, DNS servers, and Routes. DNS and Routes have a switch for automatic. Turning the switch off allows you to enter a DNS server address or routing information manually. From the Addresses menu, you can also choose to make the connection automatic or manual. When manual, new entries appear that let you enter the address, netmask, and gateway (see Figure 10-9). On the IPv6 tab, the netmask entry is replaced by a prefix entry.

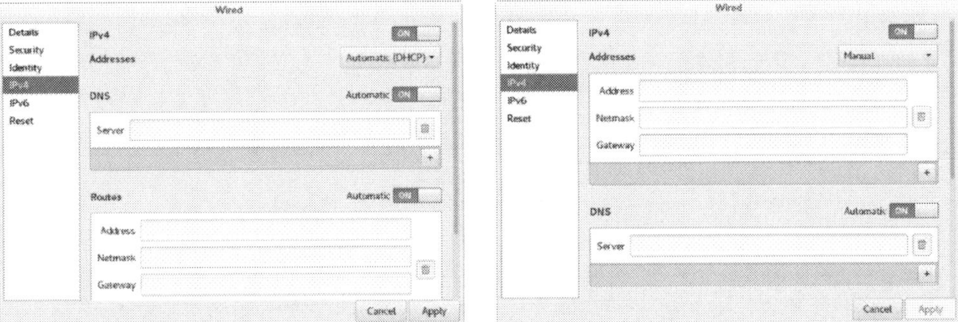

Figure 10-9: Network wired configuration: IPv4 tab, automatic and manual

On the GNOME Network dialog, you can add a new connection by clicking the plus button on the lower-left corner. A dialog opens to let you enter as a VPN, Bond, Bridge, or VLAN connection. A VPN connection opens another dialog listing supported VPN connection types, such as Point-to-Point or OpenVPN (see Figure 10-10). The Bond, Bridge, and VLAN entries open the configuration dialogs for those connections.

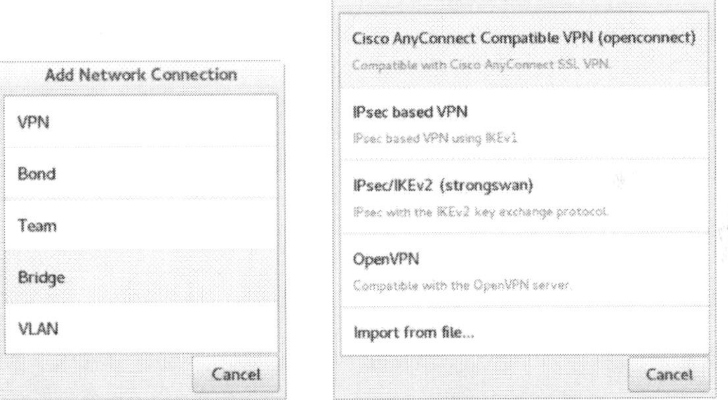

Figure 10-10: Network, new connections and VPN connections

You can then configure the VPN connections in the "Add Network Connection" dialog, which shows three tabs: Identity, IPv4, and IPv6 (see Figure 10-11). The IP tabs are the same as for wireless and wired configuration dialogs. On the Identity tab, you can enter the name, gateway, and authentication information. Click the Advanced button for detailed connection configuration.

Several VPN services are available through the EPEL repository. The PPTP service for Microsoft VPN connections is installed by default. Other popular VPN services include OpenVPN, Cisco Concentrator, and Openswan (IPSec). Network Manager support is installed using the corresponding Network Manager plugin for these services. The plugin packages begin with the name network-manager. To use the openvpn service, first, install the openvpn software along with the network-manager-openvpn plugin. For Cisco Concentrator based VPN, use the network-manager-vpnc plugin. Openswan uses the network-manager-openswan plugin.

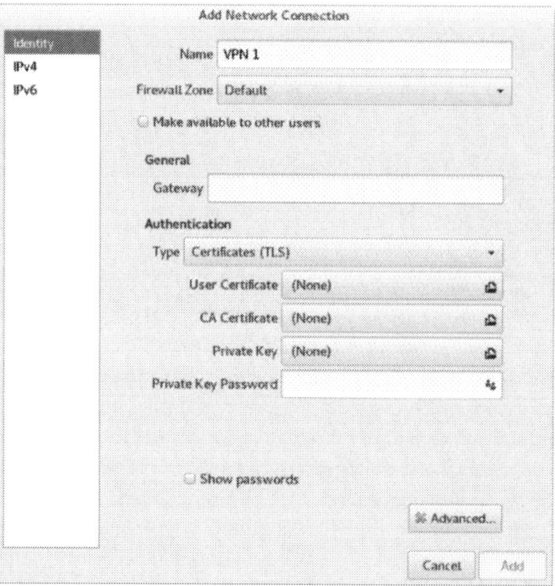

Figure 10-11: Network OpenVPN connection

On the System Status Area menu, the VPN Connection entry submenu will list configured VPN connections for easy access. If you have more than one VPN configured, each will display a switch that allows you to connect or disconnect. The VPN Settings entry will open the GNOME Network to the VPN tab where you can then add, edit, or delete VPN connections.

Network Manager Manual Configuration Using Network Connections (nm-connection-editor)

You can also use the older Network Connections utility (nm-connection-editor) to edit any network connection, accessible from the Sundry | Network Connections on the Applications overview. If not listed in Sundry, you can open a terminal window and enter the command **nm-connection-editor**. On the Network Connections dialog, established connections are listed, with Add, Edit, and Delete buttons for adding, editing, and removing network connections (see Figure 10-12). Your current network connections should already be listed.

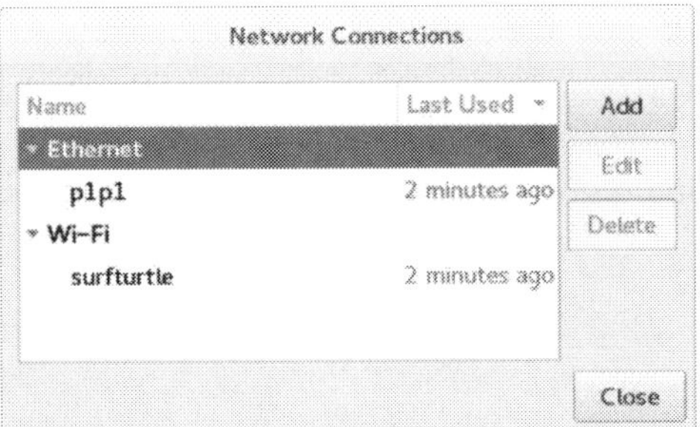

Figure 10-12: Network configuration

When you add a connection, you can choose its type from a drop-down menu (see Figure 10-13). The menu organizes connection types into three categories: Hardware, Virtual, and VPN (Virtual Private Network) (see Figure 10-14). Hardware connections cover both wired (Ethernet, DSL, and InfiniBand) and wireless (Wi-Fi, WiMAX, and Mobile Broadband) connections. VPN lists the supported VPN types, such as OpenVPN, PPTP, and Cisco. You can also import a previously configured connection. Virtual supports VLAN and Bond virtual connections.

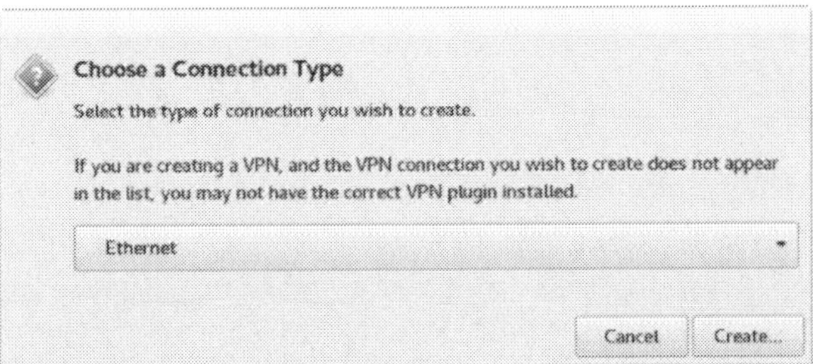

Figure 10-13: Choosing a connection type for a new network connection

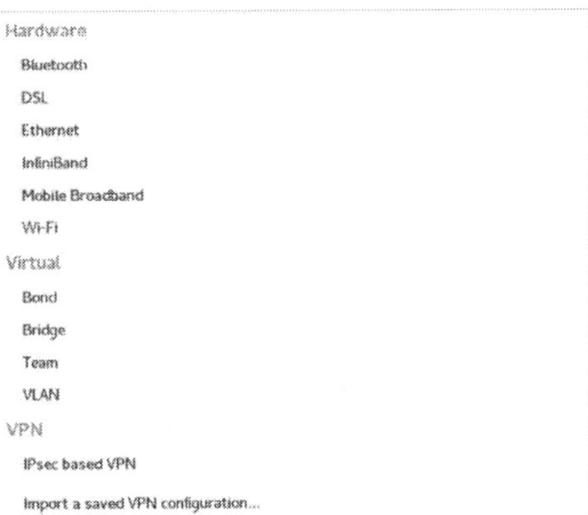

Figure 10-14: New connection types

Editing an Ethernet connection opens an Editing window. The Create button on the "Choose a Connection Type" dialog is used to add a new connection and opens a similar window, with no settings. There are six tabs, General, Ethernet, 8.02.1x Security, DCB, IPv4 Settings, and IPv6 Settings.

All configuration editing dialogs display a General tab from which you can make your configuration available to all users and automatically connect when the network connection is available. You can also choose to use a VPN connection and specify a firewall zone. Figure 10-15 shows the General tab on a wired connection.

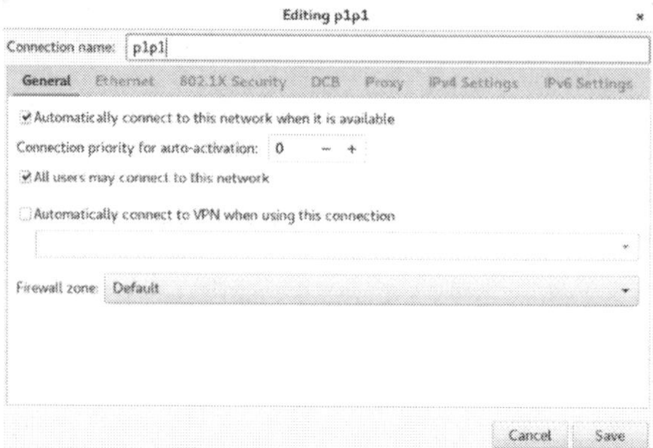

Figure 10-15: Configuration editing dialog: General tab

The Ethernet tab lists the MAC hardware address and the MTU. The MTU is usually set to automatic. The standard default configuration for a wired Ethernet connection uses DHCP.

The IPv4 Settings tab lets you select the kind of wired connection you have. The manual configuration entries for an IPv4 connection are shown in Figure 10-16. Click the Add button to enter the IP address, network mask, and gateway address. Then enter the address for the DNS servers and your network search domains. The Routes button will open a window in which you can manually enter any network routes.

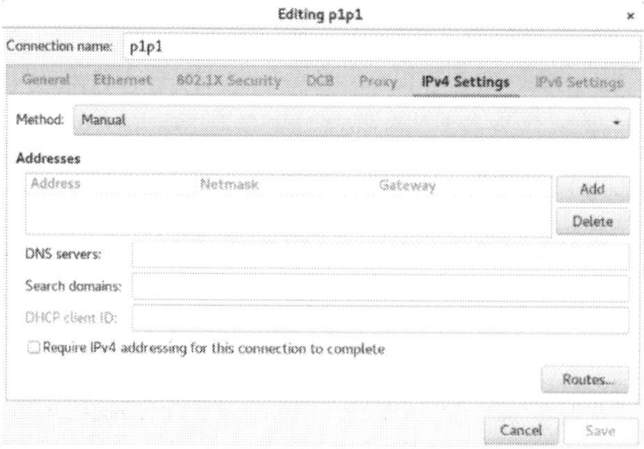

Figure 10-16: IPv4 wired configuration

The DCB tab allows you to configure Data Center Bridging connections, should your network support them. DCB provides extensions to the Internet protocol to manage high-speed connections better, such as storage area network (SAN) connections and data center fiber channels. Connections supported include Fiber Channel over the Ethernet (FCoE and FIP (Fiber Channel Initialization Protocol)) and iSCSI. For each, you can set the flow control priorities (Priority Pause Transmission) and priority groups priorities.

For a wireless connection, you enter wireless configuration data, such as your ESSID, password, and encryption method. For wireless connections, you choose Wi-Fi or WiMAX as the connection type. The Editing Wi-Fi connection window opens with tabs for your wireless information, security, and IP settings (see Figure 10-17). On the Wi-Fi tab, you specify your SSID, along with your mode and MTU.

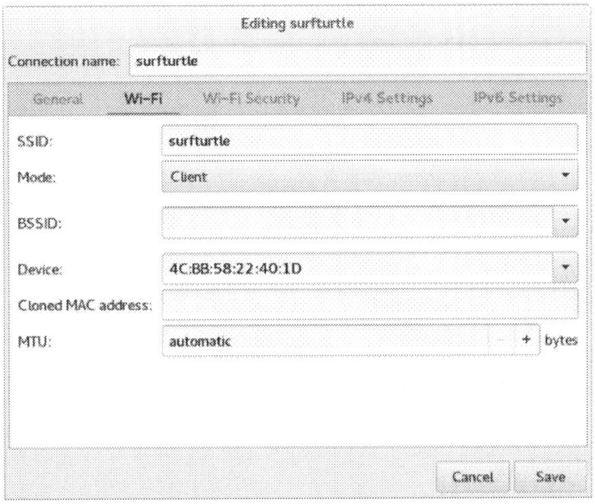

Figure 10-17: Wireless configuration

On the Wi-Fi Security tab, you enter your wireless connection security method. The commonly used method, WEP, is supported, along with WPA personal. The WPA personal method only requires a password. More secure connections, such as Dynamic WEP and Enterprise WPA, are also supported. These will require much more configuration information, such as authentication methods, certificates, and keys.

For a new broadband connection, choose the Mobile Broadband entry in the connection type menu. A setup dialog starts up to help you set up the appropriate configuration for your particular service. Configuration steps are listed on the left pane. If your device is connected, you can select it from the drop-down menu on the right pane.

Once a service is selected, you can further edit the configuration by clicking its entry in the Mobile Broadband tab and clicking the Edit button. The Editing window opens with tabs for Mobile Broadband, PPP, IPv4, and IPv6 settings. On the Mobile Broadband tab, you can enter your number, username, and password. Advanced options include the APN, Network, and PIN. The APN should already be entered.

To add a VPN connection click on the Add button in the Network Connections window VPN tab. You are prompted to choose a VPN Connection Type, which you can select from the drop down menu, such as IPsec or OpenVPN. The "Editing VPN connection" dialog then opens with two tabs: VPN and IPv4 Settings. On the VPN tab, you enter VPN connection information such as the gateway address and any additional VPN information that may be required (see Figure 10-18).

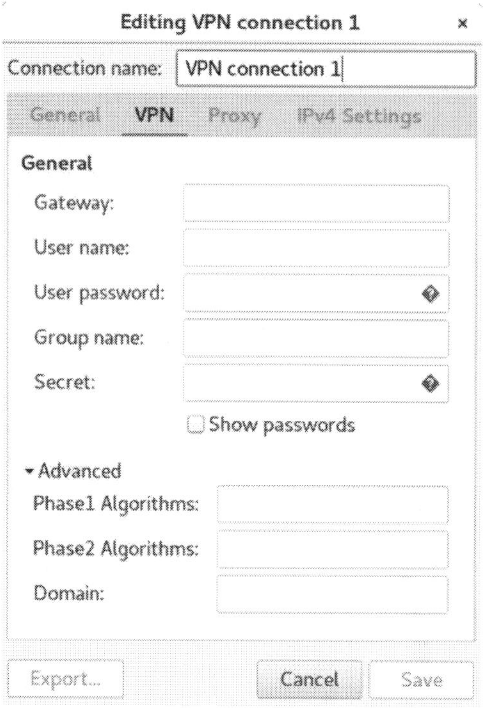

Figure 10-18: VPN configuration (IPsec)

Options will differ depending on the type of VPN connection you choose. For OpenVPN (EPEL repository), on the VPN tab, you enter connection information such as the gateway address and any additional VPN information that may be required. You also have to provide the authentication type, certificates, and keys. Clicking on the Advanced button opens the Advanced Options dialog with tabs for General, Security, and TLS Authentication. On the Security tab, you can specify the cipher to use.

The PPTP connection used on Microsoft networks requires only a gateway address on the VPN tab. Advanced options let you specify the authentication method and security options. The Cisco compatible VPN connection requires a group name and password. You also can specify the encryption method, domain, and username.

Network Manager wireless router and hidden wireless

If you have a wired or other non-wireless connection to the internet, you can set up your wireless connection as a wireless hotspot. The "Use as Hotspot" button on GNOME Network will open a dialog letting you turn on this feature, setting up your computer as a wireless router that other computers can connect to (see Figure 10-19). While operating as a hotspot, you will not be able to use your wireless connection.

You can also access a hidden wireless network by clicking the "Connect to Wi-Fi Network" button on the GNOME Network dialog. This opens the "Hidden wireless network" dialog (see Figure 10-20).

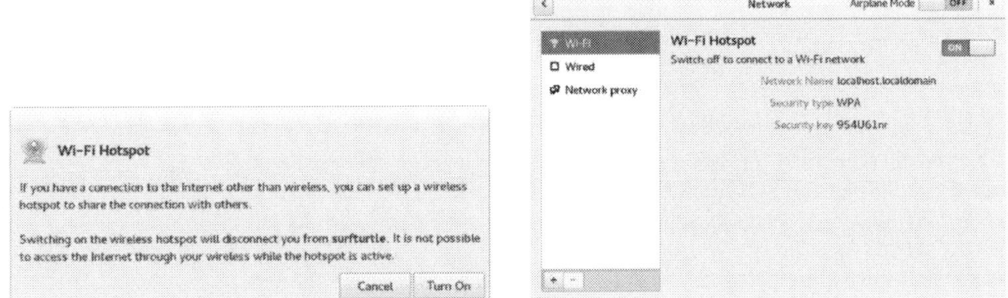

Figure 10-19: Create New Wireless Network

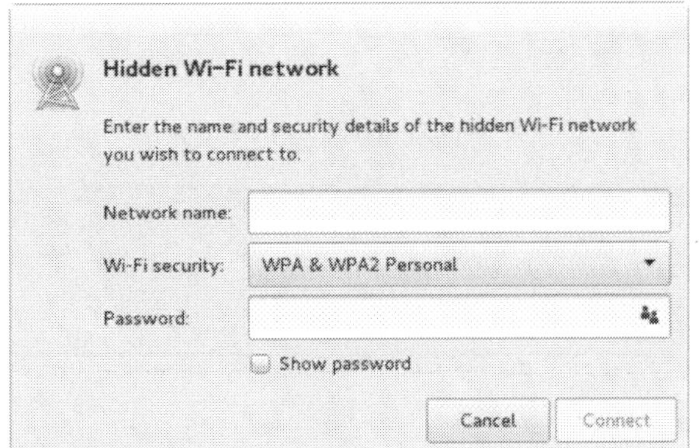

Figure 10-20: Connect as Hidden network

Managing Network Connections with nmcli

The **nmcli** command is NetworkManager Command Line Interface command. Most network configuration tasks can be performed by **nmcli**. The **nmcli** command manages NetworkManager through a set of objects: general (**g**), networking (**n**), radio (**r**), connection (**c**), device (**d**), and agent (**a**). Each can be referenced using the full name or a unique prefix, such as **con** for connection or **dev** for device. The unique prefix can be as short as a single character, such as **g** for general, **c** for connections, or **d** for device. See Table 10-2 for a list of the objects and commonly used options. The **nmcli** man page provides a complete listing with examples.

Object	Description
`general`	NetworkManager status and enabled devices. Use the terse (**-t**) and field (**-f**) option to limit the information displayed.
`networking`	Manage networking, use `on` and `off` to turn networking on or off, and `connectivity` for the connection state.
`radio`	Turns on or off the wireless networking (on or off). Can turn on or off specific kinds of wireless: `wifi`, `wwan` (mobile broadband), and `wimax`. The `all` option turns on or off all wireless.
`connection`	Manage network connections. `show` List connection profiles. With `--active` show only active connections. `up` Activate a connection `down` Deactivate a connection `add` Add a new connection, specifying `type`, `ifname`, `con-name` (profile). `modify` Edit an existing connection, use + and - to add new values to properties `edit` Add a new connection or edit an existing one using the interactive editor `delete` Delete a configured connection (profile) `reload` Reload all connection profiles `load` Reload or load a specific profile (use to load a new or modified connection profile)
`device`	Manage network interfaces (devices). `status` Display device status `show` Display device information `connect` Connect the device `disconnect` Disconnect the device `delete` Delete a software device, such as a bridge. `wifi` Display a list of available wifi access points `wifi rescan` Rescan for and display access points `wifi connect` Connect to a wifi network; specify `password`, `wep-key-type`, `ifname`, `bssid`, and `name` (profile name) `wimax` List available WiMAX networks
`agent`	Run as a Network Manager secret agent or polkit agent. `secret` As a secret agent, nmcli listens for secret requests. `polkit` As a polkit agent it listens for all authorization requests.

Table 10-2: The nmcli objects

Check the **Networking Guide | Chapter 2. Configuring IP Networking | 2.3 Using the NetworkManager Command Line Tool, nmcli** for details on using **nmcli**.

```
https://access.redhat.com/documentation/en-
US/Red_Hat_Enterprise_Linux/7/html/Networking_Guide/sec-
Using_the_NetworkManager_Command_Line_Tool_nmcli.html
```

The general object shows the current status of NetworkManager and what kind of devices are enabled. You can limit the information displayed using the **-t** (terse) and **-f** (field) options. The STATE field show the connection status, and the CONNECTIVITY field the connection.

```
$ nmcli general
STATE      CONNECTIVITY  WIFI-HW  WIFI     WWAN-HW  WWAN
connected  full          enabled  enabled  enabled  enabled

$ nmcli -t -f STATE general
connected
```

The **connection** object references the network connection and the **show** option displays that information. The following example displays your current connection.

```
nmcli connection show
```

You can use **c** instead of **connection** and **s** instead of show.

```
$ nmcli c s
NAME         UUID                                  TYPE             DEVICE
enp7s0       f7202f6d-fc66-4b81-8962-69b71202efc0  802-3-ethernet   enp7s0
AT&T LTE 1   65913b39-789a-488c-9559-28ea6341d9e1  gsm              --
```

As with the general object, you can limit the fields displayed using the **-f** option. The following only list the name and type fields

```
$ nmcli -f name, type c s
NAME         TYPE
enp7s0       802-3-ethernet
AT&T LTE 1   gsm
```

Adding the --**active** option will only show active connections.

```
nmcli c s --active
```

To start and stop a connection (like **ifconfig** does), use the **up** and **down** options.

```
nmcli con up enp7s0.
```

Use the **device** object to manage your network devices. The **show** and **status** options provide information about your devices. To check the status of all your network devices use the **device** object and **status** options:

```
nmcli device status
DEVICE  TYPE      STATE         CONNECTION
enp7s0  ethernet  connected     enp7s0
wlp6s0  wifi      disconnected  --
lo      loopback  unmanaged     --
```

You can abbreviate **device** and **status** to **d** and **s**.

```
nmcli d s
```

You also use the **device** object to connect and disconnect devices. Use the **connect** or **disconnect** options with the interface name (ifname) of the device, in this example, **enp7s0**. With the **delete** option, you can remove a device.

```
nmcli device disconnect enp7s0
nmcli device connect enp7s0
```

To turn networking on or off you use the **networking** object and the **on** and **off** options. Use the **connectivity** option to check network connectivity. The networking object alone tells you if it is enabled or not.

```
$ nmcli networking
enabled

$ nmcli networking on

$ nmcli networking connectivity
full
```

Should you want just to turn on or off the Wifi connection, you would use the **radio** object. Use **wifi**, **wwan**, and **wimax** for a specific type of wifi connection and the **all** option for all of them. The radio object alone shows wifi status of all your wifi connection types.

```
$ nmcli radio
WIFI-HW   WIFI   WWAN-HW  WWAN
enabled  enabled  enabled  enabled

$ nmcli radio wifi on

$ nmcli radio all off
```

nmcli Wired Connections

You can use **nmcli** to add connections, just as you can with the desktop NetworkManager tool. To add a new static connection use the connection object with the **add** option. Specify the connection's profile name with the **con-name** option, the interface name with the **ifname** option, the **type**, such as ethernet. For a static connection you would add the IP address (**ipv4** or **ipv6**), and the gateway address (**gw4** or **gw6**). For a DHCP connection simply do not list the IP address and gateway options. The profile name can be any name. You could have several profile names for the same network device. For example, for your wireless device, you could have several wireless connection profiles, depending on the different networks you want to connect to. Should you connect your Ethernet device to a different network, you would simply use a different connection profile that you have already set up, instead of manually reconfiguring the connection. If you do not specify a connection name, one is generated and assigned to you. The connection name can be the same as the device name as shown here, but keep in mind that the connection name refers to the profile and the device name refers to the actual device.

```
$ nmcli c s
NAME        UUID                                   TYPE              DEVICE
enp7s0      f7202f6d-fc66-4b81-89610-69b71202efc0  8010-3-ethernet   enp7s0
```

For a DHCP connection, specify the profile name, connection type, and ifname. The following example creates an Ethernet connection with the profile name "my-wired."

```
nmcli con add con-name my-wired type ethernet ifname enp7s0
```

For a static connection add the IP (**ip4** or **ip6**) and gateway (**gw4** or **gw6**) options with their addresses.

```
nmcli con add con-name my-wired-static ifname enp7s0 type ethernet ip4
192.168.1.0/24 gw4 192.168.1.1
```

In most cases, the type is Ethernet (wired) or wifi (wireless). Check the **nmcli** man page for a list of other types, such as gsm, infiniband, vpn, vlan, wimax, and bridge.

You can also add a connection using the interactive editor. Use the **edit** instead of the **add** option, and specify the **con-name** (profile) and connection type.

```
nmcli con edit type ethernet con-name my-wired
```

To modify an existing connection, use the **modify** option. For an IP connection, the property that is changed is referenced as part of the IP settings, in this example, **ip4**. The IP properties include addresses, gateway, and method (ip4.addresses, ip4.gateway, and ip4.method).

```
nmcli con mod my-wired ip4.gateway 192.168.1.2
```

To add or remove a value for a property use the + and - signs as a prefix. To add a DNS server address you would use **+ip4.dns**. To remove one use **-ip4.dns**.

```
nmcli con mod my-wired +ip4.dns 192.168.1.5
```

You can also modify a connection using the interactive editor. Use the edit instead of the modify option with the connection name.

```
nmcli con edit enp7s0
```

You are then placed in the interactive editor with an **nmcli>** prompt and the settings you can change are listed. The **help** command lists available commands. Use the **describe** command to show property descriptions.

Use **print** to show the current value of a property and **set** to change its value. To see all the properties for a setting, use the print command and the setting name. Once you have made changes, use the **save** command to effect the changes.

```
print ipv4
print ipv4.dns
print connection
set ipv4.address 192.168.0.1
```

The connection edit command can also reference a profile using the **id** option. The Name field in the connection profile information is the same as the ID. Also, each profile is given a unique system UUID, which can also be used to reference the profile.

Once you are finished editing the connection, enter the **quit** command to leave the editor.

nmcli Wireless Connections

To see a list of all the available wifi connections in your area, you use the **wifi** option with the **device** object. You can further qualify it by interface (if you have more than one) by adding the **ifname** option, and by BSSID adding the **bssid** option.

```
nmcli device wifi
```

To connect to a new Wifi network, use the **wifi connect** option and the SSID. You can further specify a password, wep-key-type, key, ifname, bssid, name (profile name), and if it is private. If you do not provide a name (profile name), nmcli will generate one for you.

```
nmcli dev wifi connect surfturtle password mypass wep-key-type wpa ifname wlp6s0
name my-wireless1
```

To reconnect to a Wifi network for which you have previously set up a connection, use the **connection** object with the **up** command and the **id** option to specify the profile name.

```
nmcli connection up id my-wireless1
```

You can also add a new wireless connection using the **connection** object and the **wifi** type with the **ssid** option.

```
nmcli con add con-name my-wireless2 ifname wlp6s0 type wifi ssid ssidname
```

Then, to set the encryption type use the **modify** command to set the **sec.key-mgmt** property, and for the passphrase set the **wifi-sec.psk** property.

```
nmcli con mod my-wirless2 wifi-sec.key-mgmt wpa-psk
nmcli con modify my-wireless2 wifi-sec.psk mypassword
```

Predictable and unpredictable network device names

Network devices now use a predictable naming method that differs from the older naming method. Names are generated based on the specific device referencing the network device type, its hardware connection and slot, and even its function. The traditional network device names used the **eth** prefix with the number of the device for an Ethernet network device. The name **eth0** referred to the first Ethernet connection on your computer. This naming method was considered unpredictable as it did not accurately reference the actual Ethernet device. The old system relied on probing the network driver at boot, and if you're your system had several Ethernet connections, the names could end up being switched, depending on how the startup proceeded. With the current version of systemd udev, the naming uses a predictable method that specifies a particular device. The predictable method references the actual hardware connection on your system.

The name used to reference predictable network device names has a prefix for the type of device followed by several qualifiers such as the type of hardware, the slot used, and the function number. Instead of the older unpredictable name like **eth0**, the first Ethernet device is referenced by a name like **enp7s0**. The interface name **enp7s0** references an Ethernet (en) connection, at pci slot 7 (p7) with the hotplug slot index number 0 (s0). **wlp6s0** is a wireless (wl) connection, at pci slot 6 (p6) with the hotplug slot index number 0 (s0). **virvb0** is a virtual (vir) bridge (vb) network interface. Table 10-3 lists predictable naming prefixes.

Unlike the older unpredictable name, the predictable name will most likely be different for each computer. Predictable network names, along with alternatives, are discussed at:

```
https://www.freedesktop.org/wiki/Software/systemd/PredictableNetworkInterfaceName
s/
```

The naming is carried out by the kernel and is describe in the comment section of the kernel source's **systemd/src/udev/udev-bultin-net_id.c** file (see Table 10-3).

Network device path names

The directory **/sys/devices** lists all your devices in subdirectories, including your network devices. The path to the devices progresses through subdirectories named for the busses connecting the device. To quickly find the full path name, you can use the **/sys/class** directory instead. For network devices use **/sys/class/net**. Then use the **ls -l** command to list the network devices with their links to the full pathname in the **/sys/devices** directory (the **../..** path references a **cd** change up two directories (**class/net**) to the /sys directory).

```
$ cd /sys/class/net
$ ls
enp7s0  lo  wlp6s0
$ ls -l
total 0
lrwxrwxrwx 1 root root 0 Feb 19 12:27 enp7s0 ->
../../devices/pci0000:00/0000:00:1c.3/0000:07:00.0/net/enp7s0
lrwxrwxrwx 1 root root 0 Feb 19 12:27 lo -> ../../devices/virtual/net/lo
lrwxrwxrwx 1 root root 0 Feb 19 12:28 wlp6s0 ->
../../devices/pci0000:00/0000:00:1c.2/0000:06:00.0/net/wlp6s0
```

So the full path name in the **/sys/devices** directory for **enp7s0** is:

```
/sys/devices/pci0000:00/0000:00:1c.3/0000:07:00.0/net/enp7s0
```

You can find the pci bus slot used with the **lspci** command. This command lists all your pci connected devices. In this example, the pci bus slot used 7, which is why the pci part of the name enp7s0 is **p7**. The **s** part refers to a hotplug slot, in this example **s0**.

```
$ lspci
06:00.0 Network controller: Qualcomm Atheros QCA9565 / AR9565 Wireless Network
Adapter (rev 01)
07:00.0 Ethernet controller: Realtek Semiconductor Co., Ltd. RTL8101/2/6E PCI
Express Fast/Gigabit Ethernet controller (rev 07)
```

Name	Description
`en`	Ethernet
`sl`	serial line IP (slip)
`wl`	wlan, wireless local area network
`ww`	wwan, wireless wide area network (mobile broadband)
`p`	pci geographical location (pci-e slot)
`s`	hotplug slot index number
`o`	onboard cards
`f`	function (used for cards with more than one port)
`u`	USB port
`i`	USB port interface

Table 10-3: Network Interface Device Naming

Devices have certain properties defined by udev, which manages all devices. Some operations, such as systemd link files, make use these properties. The ID_PATH, ID_NET_NAME_MAC, and INTERFACE properties can be used to identify a device to udev. To display these properties, you use the **udevadm** command to query the udev database. With the **info** and **-e** options, properties of all active devices are displayed. You can pipe (|) this output to a **grep** command to display only those properties for a given device. In the following example, the properties for the **enp7s0** device are listed. Preceding the properties for a given device is a line, beginning (^) with a "P" and ending with the device name. The **.*** matching characters match all other intervening characters on that line, **^P.*enp7s0**. The **-A** option displays the specified number of additional lines after that match, **-A 22**.

```
$ udevadm info -e | grep -A 22 ^P.*enp7s0
P: /devices/pci0000:00/0000:00:1c.3/0000:07:00.0/net/enp7s0
E: DEVPATH=/devices/pci0000:00/0000:00:1c.3/0000:07:00.0/net/enp7s0
E: ID_BUS=pci
E: ID_MM_CANDIDATE=1
E: ID_MODEL_FROM_DATABASE=RTL8101/2/6E PCI Express Fast/Gigabit Ethernet
controller
E: ID_MODEL_ID=0x8136
E: ID_NET_DRIVER=r8169
E: ID_NET_LINK_FILE=/lib/systemd/network/99-default.link
E: ID_NET_NAME_MAC=enx74e6e20ec729
E: ID_NET_NAME_PATH=enp7s0
E: ID_OUI_FROM_DATABASE=Dell Inc.
E: ID_PATH=pci-0000:07:00.0
E: ID_PATH_TAG=pci-0000_07_00_0
E: ID_PCI_CLASS_FROM_DATABASE=Network controller
E: ID_PCI_SUBCLASS_FROM_DATABASE=Ethernet controller
E: ID_VENDOR_FROM_DATABASE=Realtek Semiconductor Co., Ltd.
E: ID_VENDOR_ID=0x10ec
E: IFINDEX=2
E: INTERFACE=enp7s0
E: SUBSYSTEM=net
E: SYSTEMD_ALIAS=/sys/subsystem/net/devices/enp7s0
E: TAGS=:systemd:
E: USEC_INITIALIZED=1080179
```

For certain tasks, such as renaming, you many need to know the MAC address. You can find this with the **ip link** command, which you can abbreviate to **ip l**. The MAC address is before the brd string. In this example, the MAC address for **enp7s0** is **74:e6:e2:0e:c7:29**. The ip link command also provides the MTU (Maximum Transmission Unit) and the current state of the connection.

```
$ ip link
1: lo: <LOOPBACK,UP,LOWER_UP> mtu 65536 qdisc noqueue state UNKNOWN mode DEFAULT
group default qlen 1 link/loopback 00:00:00:00:00:00 brd 00:00:00:00:00:00
2: enp7s0: <BROADCAST,MULTICAST,UP,LOWER_UP> mtu 1500 qdisc fq_codel state UP
mode DEFAULT group default qlen 1000 link/ether 74:e6:e2:0e:c7:29 brd
ff:ff:ff:ff:ff:ff
3: wlp6s0: <BROADCAST,MULTICAST> mtu 1500 qdisc noop state DOWN mode DEFAULT
group default qlen 1000 link/ether 4c:bb:58:22:40:1d brd ff:ff:ff:ff:ff:ff
```

Renaming network device names with udev rules

If you should change your hardware, like your motherboard with its Ethernet connection, or, if you use an Ethernet card and simply change the slot it is connected to, then the name will change. For firewall rules referencing a particular Ethernet connection, this could be a problem. You can, if you wish, change the name to one of your own choosing, even using the older unpredictable names. This way you would only have to update the name change, rather than all your rules and any other code that references the network device by name.

You can change device name by adding a user udev rule for network device names. Changes made with udev rules work for both NetworkManager and systemd-networkd. In the **/etc/udev/rules.d** directory, create a file with the **.rules** extension and prefixed by a number less than 80, such as **70-my-net-names.rules**.The **.rules** files in **/etc/udev/rules.d** take precedence over those in the udev system directory, **/lib/udev/rules.d**.

In the udev rule, identify the subsystem as net (SUBSYSTEM=="net"), the action to take as add (ACTION=="add)), then the MAC address (ATTR[address}, the address attribute). Use **ip link** to obtain the mac address. The MAC address is also listed as the ID_NET_NAME_MAC entry in the **udevadm info** output (be sure to remove the prefix and add intervening colons). Use the NAME field to specify the new name for the device. Use the single = operator to make the name assignment.

/etc/udev/rules.d/70-my-net-names.rules

```
SUBSYSTEM=="net", ACTION=="add", ATTR{address}=="74:e6:e2:0e:c7:29", NAME="eth0"
```

To further specify the device you can add the kernel name (KERNEL) of the device. The kernel name is the INTERFACE entry.

```
SUBSYSTEM=="net", ACTION=="add", ATTR{address}=="74:e6:e2:0e:c7:29",
KERNEL=="enp7s0", NAME="eth0"
```

Command Line PPP Access: wvdial

If for some reason, you have been unable to set up a modem connection on your Desktop, you may have to set it up from the command line interface. For a dial-up PPP connection, you can use the wvdial dialer, which is an intelligent dialer that not only dials up an ISP service but also performs login operations, supplying your username and password.

/etc/wvdial.conf

```
[Modem0]
Modem = /dev/ttyS0
Baud = 57600
Init1 = ATZ
SetVolume = 0
Dial Command = ATDT

[Dialer Defaults]
Modem = /dev/ttyS0
Baud = 57600
Init1 = ATZ
SetVolume = 0
Dial Command = ATDT
```

The wvdial program first loads its configuration from the **/etc/wvdial.conf** file. In here, you can place modem and account information, including modem speed and serial device, as well as ISP phone number, username, and password. The **wvdial.conf** file is organized into sections, beginning with a section label enclosed in brackets. A section holds variables for different parameters that are assigned values, such as **username = chris**. The default section holds default values inherited by other sections, so you needn't repeat them. Table 10-4 lists the wvdial variables.

Variable	Description
Inherits	Explicitly inherits from the specified section. By default, sections inherit from the [Dialer Defaults] section.
Modem	The device wvdial should use as your modem. The default is /dev/modem.
Baud	The speed at which wvdial communicates with your modem. The default is 57,600 baud.
Init1...Init9	Specifies the initialization strings to be used by your modem; wvdial can use up to 9. The default is "ATZ" for Init1.
Phone	The phone number you want wvdial to dial.
Area Code	Specifies the area code, if any.
Dial Prefix	Specifies any needed dialing prefix—for example, 70 to disable call waiting or 9 for an outside line.
Dial Command	Specifies the dial operation. The default is "ATDT".
Login	Specifies the username you use at your ISP.
Login Prompt	If your ISP has an unusual login prompt, you can specify it here.
Password	Specifies the password you use at your ISP.
Auto Reconnect	If enabled, wvdial attempts to reestablish a connection automatically if you are randomly disconnected by the other side. This option is on by default.

Table 10-4: Variables for wvdial

You can use the **wvdialconf** utility to create a default **wvdial.conf** file for you automatically. The **wvdialconf** utility will detect your modem and set default values for basic features. You can then edit the **wvdial.conf** file and modify the Phone, Username, and Password entries with your ISP dial-up information. Remove the preceding semicolon (;) to unquote the entry. Any line beginning with a semicolon is ignored as a comment.

```
$ wvdialconf
```

You can also create a named dialer. This is helpful if you have different ISPs you log in to.

To start wvdial, enter the command **wvdial**, which then reads the connection configuration information from the **/etc/wvdial.conf** file; wvdial dials the ISP and initiates the PPP connection, providing your username and password when requested.

```
$ wvdial
```

You can set up connection configurations for any number of connections in the **/etc/wvdial.conf** file. To select one, enter its label as an argument to the **wvdial** command, as shown here:

```
$ wvdial Modem0
```

Manual Wireless Configuration with Wireless Tools

NetworkManager will automatically detect and configure your wireless connections for both GNOME and KDE desktops. You can manually configure your connections with wireless tools on Network Manager and ifwconfig. Wireless configuration using Network Manager was discussed in the previous sections.

Wireless configuration makes use of the same set of Wireless Extensions. The Wireless Tools package is a set of network configuration and reporting tools for wireless devices installed on a Linux system (**wireless-tools**, EPEL repository). They are currently supported and developed as part of the Linux Wireless Extension and Wireless Tools Project. Wireless Tools includes the configuration and report tools listed here:

Tool	Description
iwconfig	Sets the wireless configuration options basic to most wireless devices.
iwlist	Displays current status information of a device.
iwspy	Sets the list of IP addresses in a wireless network and checks the quality of their connections.
iwpriv	Accesses configuration options specific to a particular device.

iwconfig

The **iwconfig** command works much like **iwconfig**, configuring a network connection. You can run **iwconfig** directly on a command line, specifying certain parameters. Added parameters let you set wireless-specific features such as the network name (nwid), the frequency or channel the card uses (freq or channel), and the bit rate for transmission (rate). See the **iwconfig** Man page for a complete listing of accepted parameters. Some of the commonly used parameters are listed in Table 10-5.

The wireless LAN device will have a predictable device name. For example, to set the channel used for the wireless device installed as the wireless device **wlp6s0**, you would use the following, setting the channel to 2:

```
iwconfig wlp6s0 channel 2
```

You can also use **iwconfig** to display statistics for your wireless devices, just as **iwconfig** does. Enter the **iwconfig** command with no arguments or with the name of the device. Information such as the name, frequency, sensitivity, and the bit rate is listed. Check also **/proc/net/wireless** for statistics.

Instead of using **iwconfig** directly to set parameters, you can specify them in the wireless device's configuration file. The wireless device configuration file will be located in the **/etc/sysconfig/network-scripts** folder and given a name like **ifcfg-surfturtle**, depending on the name of the connection. This file will already contain many **iwconfig** settings. Any further setting can be set by assigning **iwconfig** values to the IWCONFIG parameter as shown here.

```
IWCONFIG="rate 11M"
```

Option	Description
essid	A network name
freq	The frequency of the connection
channel	The channel used
nwid or domain	The network ID or domain
mode	The operating mode used for the device, such as Ad Hoc, Managed, or Auto. Ad Hoc = one cell with no access point, Managed = network with several access points and supports roaming, Master = the node is an access point, Repeater = node forwards packets to other nodes, Secondary = backup master or repeater, Monitor = only receives packets
sens	The sensitivity, the lowest signal level at which data can be received
key or **enc**	The encryption key used
frag	Cut packets into smaller fragments to increase better transmission
bit or rate	Speed at which bits are transmitted. The auto option automatically falls back to lower rates for noisy channels
ap	Specify a specific access point
power	Power management for wakeup and sleep operations

Table 10-5: iwconfig: commonly used parameters

iwpriv

The **iwpriv** command works in conjunction with **iwconfig**, allowing you set options specific to a particular kind of wireless device. With **iwpriv**, you can also turn on roaming or select the port to use. The following example sets roaming on:

```
iwpriv wlp6s0 roam on
```

iwspy

Your wireless device can check its connection to another wireless device it is receiving data from, reporting the quality, signal strength, and noise level of the transmissions. Your device can maintain a list of addresses for different devices it may receive data from. You use the **iwspy** tool to set or add the addresses that you want checked. You can list either IP addresses or the hardware versions. A **+** sign will add the address, instead of replacing the entire list:

```
iwspy wlp6s0 +192.168.2.5
```

To display the quality, signal, and noise levels for your connections, you use the **iwspy** command with just the device name:

```
iwspy wlp6s0
```

iwlist

To obtain more detailed information about your wireless device, such as all the frequencies or channels available, you use the **iwlist** tool. Using the device name with a particular parameter, you can obtain specific information about a device, including the frequency, access points, rate, power features, retry limits, and encryption keys used. You can use **iwlist** to obtain information about faulty connections. The following example will list the frequencies used on the **wlp6s0** wireless device.

```
iwlist wlp6s0 freq
```

Firewalls

Most systems currently connected to the Internet are open to attempts by outside users to gain unauthorized access. Outside users can try to gain access directly by setting up an illegal connection, by intercepting valid communications from users remotely connected to the system, or by pretending to be a valid user. Firewalls, encryption, and authentication procedures are ways of protecting against such attacks. A firewall prevents any direct unauthorized attempts at access, encryption protects transmissions from authorized remote users, and authentication verifies that a user requesting access has the right to do so. The current Linux kernel incorporates support for firewalls using the Netfilter (IPtables) packet filtering package (the previous version, IP Chains, is used on older kernel versions). To implement a firewall, you provide a series of rules to govern what kind of access you want to allow on your system. If that system is also a gateway for a private network, the system's firewall capability can effectively help protect the network from outside attacks.

You can run your firewall on a stand-alone system directly connected to the Internet, or on a gateway system that connects a local network to the Internet. Most networks now use dedicated routers for Internet access which have their own firewalls. If instead, you decide to use a Linux system as a gateway, it will have at least two network connections, one for the local network and an Internet connection device for the Internet. Make sure that the firewall is applied to the Internet device, not to your local network.

Web Site	Security Application
www.netfilter.org	Netfilter project, Iptables, and NAT
www.netfilter.org/ipchains	IP Chains firewall
www.openssh.org	Secure Shell encryption
http://fedoraproject.org/wiki/FirewallD	FirewallD
www.squid-cache.org	Squid Web Proxy server
http://web.mit.edu/Kerberos	Kerberos network authentication

Table 10-6: Network Security Applications

To provide protection for remote communications, transmission can be simply encrypted. For Linux systems, you can use the Secure Shell (SSH) suite of programs to encrypt any transmissions, preventing them from being read by anyone else. Kerberos authentication provides another level of security whereby individual services can be protected, allowing the use of a service only to users who are cleared for access. Outside users may also try to gain unauthorized access through any Internet services you may be hosting, such as a Web site. In such a case, you can set up a proxy to protect your site from attack. Table 10-6 lists several network security applications commonly used on Linux.

Check the **Security Guide | Chapter 4. Hardening Your System with Tools and Services | 4.5 Using Firewalls** for details on using **firewalld**.

```
https://access.redhat.com/documentation/en-
US/Red_Hat_Enterprise_Linux/7/html/Security_Guide/sec-Using_Firewalls.html
```

For clarity, the examples in this chapter use the traditional network device name (like **eth0** and **eth1**) instead of the predictable device names (like **enp7s0**). Keep in mind, that, unless you rename your network devices, the actual devices on your system will use a predictable device name (like **enp7s0**).

Dynamic and Static Firewalls: FirewallD and the iptables command

Traditionally firewalls were static. You modified firewall rules and then restarted your firewall to load the rules. RHEL has adopted a dynamic firewall, called FirewallD, which can apply modified rules without restarting the firewall. Rules, however, have to be managed directly by the FirewallD daemon. You cannot use the **iptables** command to add firewall rules for the firewalld daemon. In fact, FirewallD does not user netfilter rules in the traditional sense. You do not list a set of rules that the firewall then reads, as you do with static firewalls like iptables. Instead, you use to **firewall-config** and **firewall-cmd** tools to directly configure your firewall.

FirewallD is managed by systemd using the **firewalld.service** unit file. It is started before networking (Before) and conflicts with the static iptables managed firewall (Conflicts). Runtime configuration is read from **/etc/sysconfig/firewalld** (EnvironmentFile). Communication with the FirewallD daemon is handled over Dbus. FirewallD is started by the basic target (WantedBy), which means it starts for all start-up targets.

firewalld.service

```
[Unit]
Description=firewalld - dynamic firewall daemon
Before=network.target
Before=libvirtd.service
Before=NetworkManager.service
After=dbus.service
After=polkit.service
Conflicts=iptables.service ip6tables.service ebtables.service ipset.service
Documentation=man:firewalld(1)

[Service]
EnvironmentFile=-/etc/sysconfig/firewalld
ExecStart=/usr/sbin/firewalld --nofork --nopid $FIREWALLD_ARGS
ExecReload=/bin/kill -HUP $MAINPID
# suppress to log debug and error output also to /var/log/messages
StandardOutput=null
StandardError=null
Type=dbus
```

```
BusName=org.fedoraproject.FirewallD1

[Install]
WantedBy=basic.target
Alias=dbus-org.fedoraproject.FirewallD1.service
```

If you wish, you can still use iptables instead of FirewallD to manage firewalls. Older customized firewall configurations may still want to use the older iptables static firewall. IPtables **systemd** unit files manage static IPtables rules, much like System V scripts did in previous releases. The iptables command keeps firewall rules in **/etc/sysconfig/iptables**, which is checked for (ConditionPathExists). The iptables operation runs an **iptables.service** script to start and stop the firewall. The script reads runtime configuration from **/etc/sysconfig/iptables-config**.

iptables.service

```
[Unit]
Description=IPv4 firewall with iptables
After=syslog.target
ConditionPathExists=/etc/sysconfig/iptables

[Service]
Type=oneshot
RemainAfterExit=yes
ExecStart=/usr/libexec/iptables/iptables.init start
ExecStop=/usr/libexec/iptables/iptables.init stop
Environment=BOOTUP=serial
Environment=CONSOLETYPE=serial
StandardOutput=syslog
StandardError=syslog

[Install]
WantedBy=basic.target
```

Dynamic Firewall with FirewallD

FirewallD is the default firewall used in RHEL and runs as a daemon implementing a dynamic firewall. Instead of loading rules offline from a file, you add them directly to the FirewallD daemon. For documentation see:

```
http://fedoraproject.org/wiki/FirewallD
```

FirewallD sets up network zones to define the level of trust for different kinds of network connections (see Table 10-7). Each zone can have several connections, but a connection can belong only to one zone. FirewallD defines several zones, most of which you can change (mutable). The drop and block zones are immutable and designed to stop all incoming packets. The public, external, and dmz zones are designed for untrusted networks, exposing only part of your system. The work, home, and internal zone are used for trusted networks. The trusted zone (also immutable) allows all network connections.

Zone	Description
drop (immutable)	Deny all incoming connections; outgoing ones are accepted.
block (immutable)	Deny all incoming connections, with ICMP host prohibited messages issued.
trusted (immutable)	Allow all network connections
public	Public areas, do not trust other computers
external	For computers with masquerading enabled, protecting a local network
dmz	For computers publicly accessible with restricted access.
work	For trusted work areas
home	For trusted home network connections
internal	For internal network, restrict incoming connections

Table 10-7: FirewallD zones

Zone configurations are located in **/etc/firewalld/zones**. You can use **firewall-config** or **firewall-cmd** to manage your zones and add new ones. The default zone is set in the **/etc/firewalld.conf** configuration files by the DefaultZone variable. Initially, it is set to public. The default and fallback zones are saved in **/lib/firewalld/zones**.

Zone files are saved as XML files which list the zone name and the services and ports allowed. Also any masquerade, ICMP, and port forwarding options.

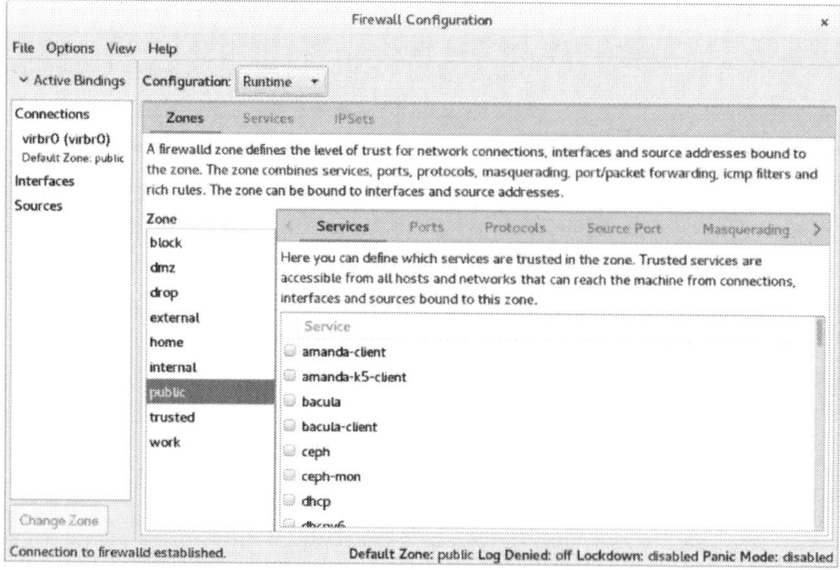

Figure 10-21: firewall-config: Runtime Configuration

firewall-config

RHEL uses the Firewalld firewall daemon. To configure Firewalld, you use the **firewall-config** graphical interface. You can also use **firewall-cmd** command from the command line. To set up your firewall, run firewall-config (Sundry | Firewall) (see Figure 10-21). The firewall is configured using zones displayed on the Zones tab. To configure a particular service you use the Services tab. Additional tabs can be displayed from the View menu for configuring ICMP types, whitelists, and for adding firewall rules directly (Direct Configuration).

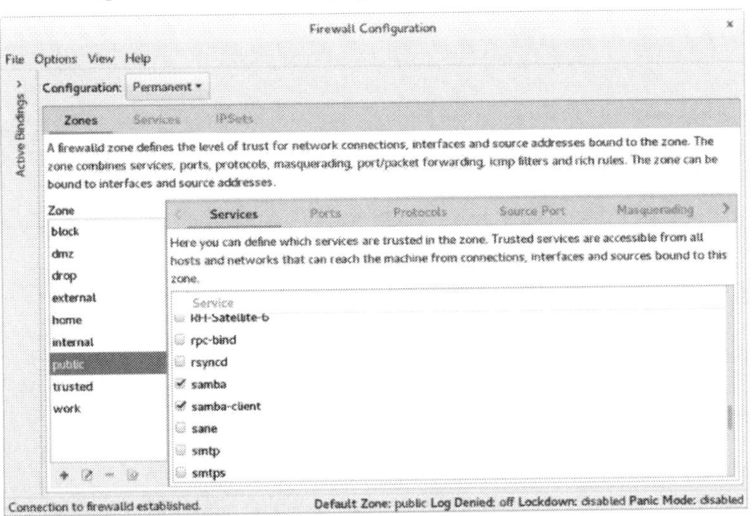

Figure 10-22: firewall-config: Permanent Configuration

With firewall-config, you can configure either a Runtime Configuration or Permanent Configuration. Select one from the Configuration. The Runtime Configuration shows your current runtime set up, whereas a Permanent configuration does not take effect until you reload or restart. If you wish to edit your zones and services, you need to choose the Permanent Configuration (see Figure 10-22). This view displays a zone toolbar for editing zones at the bottom of the zone scroll box.

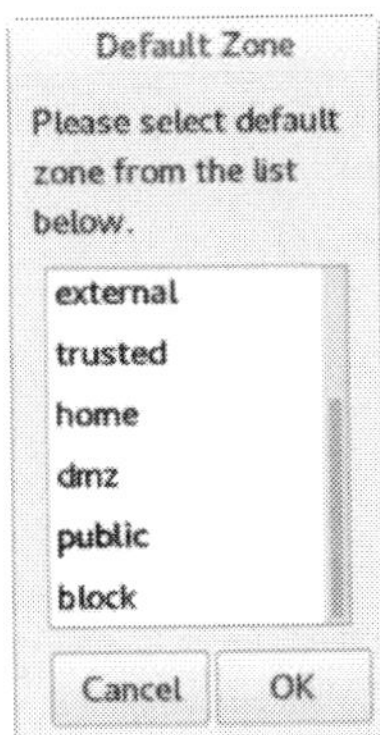

Figure 10-23: Default Zone

A firewall configuration is set up for a given zone, such as a home, work, internal, external, or public zone. Each zone can have its own configuration. Zones are listed in the Zone scroll box on the left side of the firewall-config window (see Figure 10-23). Select the one you want to configure. The firewall-config window opens to the default. You can choose the default zone from the System Default Zone dialog (see Figure 10-4), which you open from the Options menu as "Change Default Zone."

If you choose Permanent Configuration from the Configuration Menu, a toolbar for zones is displayed below the Zone scroll box, as shown here.

The plus button lets you add a zone, minus removes a zone. The pencil/page button lets you edit a zone. The add and edit buttons open the Base Zone Settings dialog, where you enter or edit the zone name, version, description, and the target (see Figure 10-24). The default target is ACCEPT. Other options are REJECT and DROP. The Load Zone Defaults button (yellow arrow) loads default settings, removing any you have made.

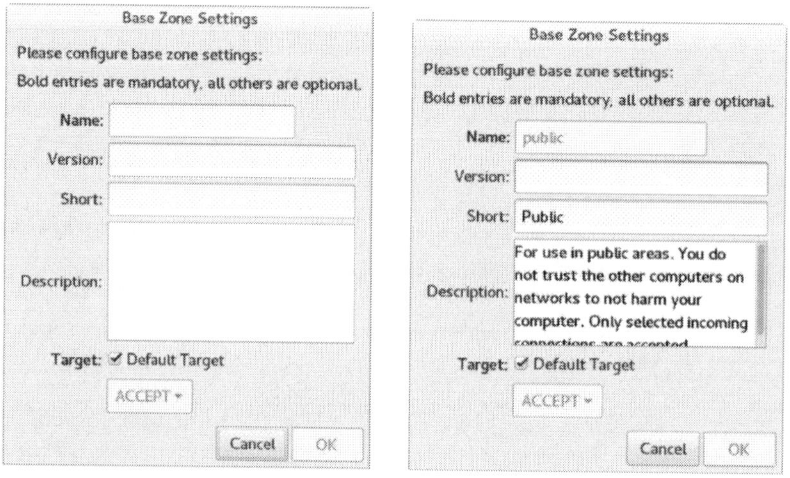

Figure 10-24: Base Zone Settings

Each zone, in turn, can have one or more network connections. From the Options menu choose "Change Zones of Connections" which lists available connections which you can select to open a dialog where you choose the connection's zone.

For a given zone you can configure services, ports, masquerading, port forwarding, and ICMP filter (see Figure 10-25). The feature many users may want to change are the services. A Linux system is often used to run servers for a network. If you are creating a strong firewall but still want to run a service such as a Web server, an FTP server, Samba, or SSH encrypted connections, you must specify them in the Services tab. Samba lets you access your Samba shares, like remote Windows file systems, from your GNOME or KDE desktops.

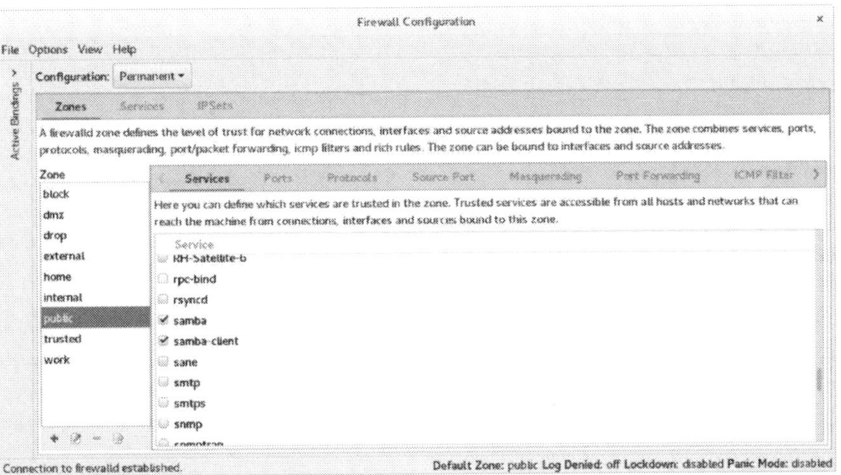

Figure 10-25: Service Settings

For a selected service, you can specify service settings such as ports and protocols it uses, any modules, and specific network addresses. Default settings are already set up for you such as port 139 for Samba, using the TCP protocol. To modify the settings for service, click the Services tab on the Firewall Configuration window to list your services. Choose the service you want to edit from the Service scroll box at the left. For a given service you can then use the Ports and Protocols, Modules, and Destination tabs to specify ports, protocols, modules, and addresses. On the Ports and Protocols tab click the Add button to open the Port and/or Protocol dialog where you can add a port or port range, and choose a protocol from the Protocol menu (see Figure 10-26). On the Destination tab, you can enter an IPv4 or IPv6 destination address for the service.

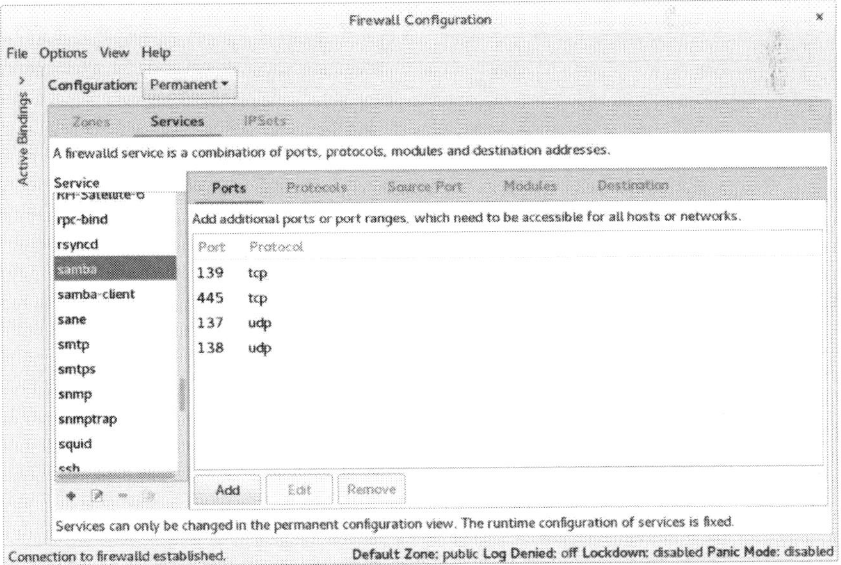

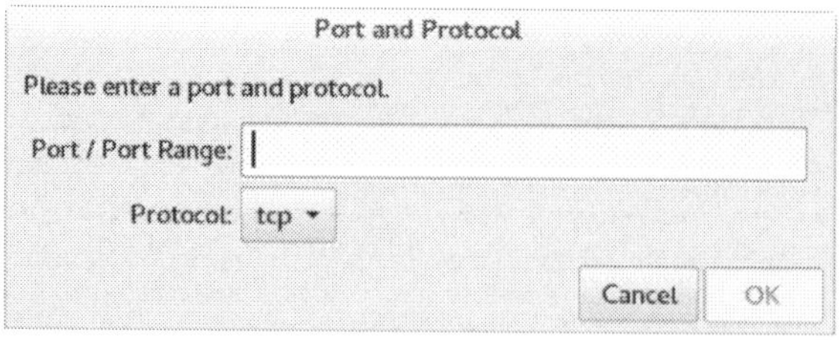

Figure 10-26: Service Protocols and Ports

The Ports tab lets you specify ports that you may want opened for certain services, like BitTorrent. Click the Add button to open a dialog where you can select the port number along with the protocol to control (tcp or udp), or enter a specific port number or range.

If your system is being used as a gateway to the Internet for your local network, you can implement masquerading to hide your local hosts from outside access from the Internet (Zone Masquerading tab). This, though, also requires IP forwarding which is automatically enabled when you choose masquerading. Local hosts will still be able to access the Internet, but they will masquerade as your gateway system. You would select for masquerading the interface that is connected to the Internet. Masquerading is available only for IPv4 networks, not IPv6 networks.

The Port Forwarding tab (Zones) lets you set up port forwarding, channeling transmissions from one port to another, or to a different port on another system. Click the Add button to add a port, specifying its protocol and destination (see Figure 10-27).

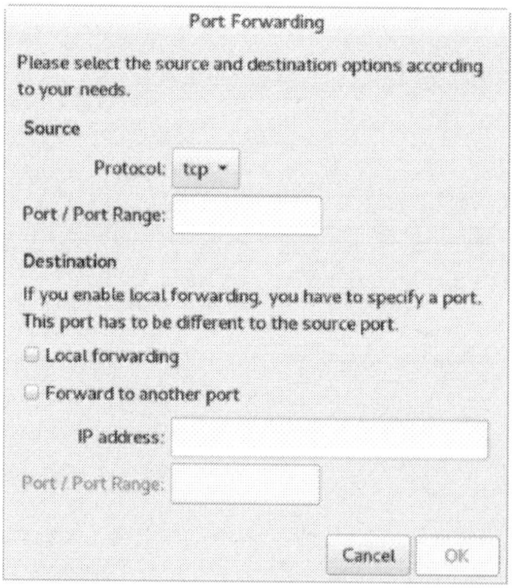

Figure 10-27: Port Forwarding

The ICMP Filters tab allows you to block ICMP messages. By default, all ICMP messages are allowed. Blocking ICMP messages makes for a more secure system. Certain types of ICMP messages are often blocked as they can be used to infiltrate or overload a system, such as the ping and pong ICMP messages (see Figure 10-28).

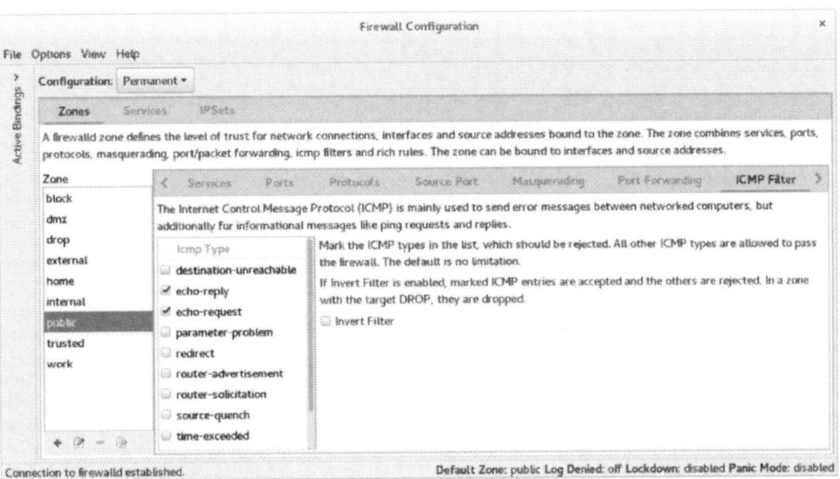

Figure 10-28: ICMP Filters

If you have specific firewall rules to add, use the Direct Configuration tab (displayed from the View | Direct Configuration menu).

firewall-cmd

The **firewall-cmd** command works on a command line interface, using options to set features for different zones. Zone modification options such as **--add-service**, can be either runtime or permanent. Runtime changes are gone after a restart or reload. To make the changes permanent you add the **--permanent** option, making changes for a permanent configuration, instead of a runtime one.

Use the get options to display information about the firewall. The **--get-zones** option lists your zones, the **--get-services** option list services supported by the current zone, and the **--get-icmptypes** lists the ICMP types.

```
firewall-cmd --get-zones
firewall-cmd --get-services
firewall-cmd --get-icmptypes
```

The **--get-default-zone** option lists the default zone, and **--set-default-zone** sets up a new default zone.

```
firewall-cmd --set-default-zone  home
```

To find out what features have been enabled for a zone, use the **--list-all** option with a **--zone=** option to specify the zone.

```
firewall-cmd home --zone=home  --list-all
```

Zone are assigned network interfaces. There are interface options to add, remove, or change an interface. Use the query option to check if an interface belongs to a zone.

```
firewall-cmd --zone=home  --query-interface=eth0
```

The service, port, masquerade, icmp, and forwarding options can be either runtime or permanent. The **--service** options can add and remove services to a zone.

```
firewall-cmd -add-service=vsftp
```

To make the change permanent, add the **--permanent** option.

```
firewall-cmd --permanent -add-service=vsftp
```

The **--query-service** option checks to see if a service is enabled for a zone.

```
firewall-cmd --zone=home -query-service=http
```

The **--port** options are used to add, remove, or query ports.

```
firewall-cmd --zone=home --add-port=22
```

Add the **--permanent** option to make it permanent.

```
firewall-cmd --permanent --zone=home --add-port=22
```

The **--masquerade** option add, removes, and queries zones for masquerading.

```
firewall-cmd --zone=work --add-masquerade
```

The **--icmp-block** options add, remove, and query ICMP types.

```
firewall-cmd --zone=work --add-icmp-block=echo-reply
```

Should your firewall needs to use custom firewall rules, you can add, remove, and list them using the **--direct** option. These are rules written in the IPtables syntax. You have to specify the protocol, table, chain, and arguments. The following lists the rules you added to the netfilter table. The rules are not saved and have to be added again each time you restart or reload. You could have a script of firewall-cmd rules to do this.

```
firewall-cmd --direct --get-rules ipv4 netfilter
```

The following adds a simple netfilter rule.

```
Firewall-cmd --direct -add-rule ipv4 netfilter INPUT  Deny
```

11. Shared Resources: Samba, NFS, and NIS

With Samba, you can connect your Windows clients on a Microsoft Windows network to services such as shared files, systems, and printers controlled by the Linux Samba server and, at the same time, allow Linux systems to access shared files and printers on Windows systems. Samba is a collection of Linux tools that allow you to communicate with Windows systems over a Windows network. In effect, Samba allows a Linux system or network to act as if it were a Windows server, using the same protocols as used on a Windows network.

Whereas most Unix and Linux systems use the TCP/IP protocol for networking, Microsoft networking with Windows uses a different protocol, called the Server Message Block (SMB) protocol that implements a local area network (LAN) of computers running Windows. SMB makes use of a network interface called Network Basic Input Output System (NetBIOS) that allows Windows systems to share resources, such as printers and disk space. One Windows systems on such a network can access part of another Windows system's disk drive as if it were its own. SMB was originally designed for small LANs. To connect it to larger networks, including those with Unix systems, Microsoft developed the Common Internet File System (CIFS). CIFS still uses SMB and NetBIOS for Windows networking.

Wanting to connect his Linux system to a Windows PC, Andrew Tridgell wrote an SMB client and server that he called Samba. Samba allows Unix and Linux systems to connect to such a Windows network; as if they were Windows systems. Unix systems can share resources on Windows systems as if they were just another Windows system. Windows systems can also access resources on Unix systems as if they were Windows systems. Samba, in effect, has become a professional-level, open source, and free version of CIFS. Samba effectively enables you to use a Linux or Unix server as a network server for a group of Windows machines operating on a Windows network. You can also use it to share files on your Linux system with other Windows systems or to access files on a Windows systems from your Linux system, as well as between Windows systems.

You can obtain extensive documentation and current releases from the Samba Web and FTP sites at **http://www.samba.org**. Samba HOW-TO documentation is also available at **http://www.tldp.org**. Samba software is incorporated into several packages. By selecting the samba server package, needed supporting packages like smbclient and samba-common are automatically selected.

Check the **System Administration Guide** for details on Samba, **Part 5 Servers | Chapter 14. File and Print Servers | 14.1. Samba**.

```
https://access.redhat.com/documentation/en-US/Red_Hat_Enterprise_Linux/7/html/System_Administrators_Guide/ch-File_and_Print_Servers.html#sect-Samba
```

Samba Applications

The Samba software package consists of two server daemons and several utility programs (see Table 11-1). One daemon, **smbd**, provides file and printer services to SMB clients and other systems, such as Windows, that support SMB. The **nmbd** is a daemon that provides NetBIOS name resolution and service browser support. Configuration files are kept in the **/etc/samba** directory. The **smbclient** tool provides FTP-like access by Linux clients to Samba services. The **mount.cifs** and **umount.cifs** tools enable Linux clients to mount and unmount Samba shared directories (used by the **mount** command with the **-t samba** option). The **smbstatus** utility displays the current status of the SMB server and who is using it. You use **testparm** to test your Samba configuration. **smbtar** is a shell script that backs up SMB/CIFS-shared resources directly to a Unix archive. You can use **nmblookup** to map the NetBIOS name of a Windows system to its IP address.

Application	Description
smbd	Samba server daemon that provides file and printer services to SMB clients
nmbd	Samba daemon that provides NetBIOS name resolution and service browser support
winbindd	Uses authentication services provided by Windows domain
smbclient	Provides FTP-like access by Linux clients to Samba services
mount.cifs	Mounts Samba share directories on Linux clients (used by the `mount` command with the `-t cifs` option)
smbpasswd	Changes SMB-encrypted passwords on Samba servers
smbstatus	Displays the current status of the SMB network connections
smbrun	Interface program between **smbd** and external programs
testparm	Tests the Samba configuration file, **smb.conf**
smbtar	Backs up SMB/CIFS-shared resources directly to a Unix tape drive
nmblookup	Maps the NetBIOS name of a Windows PC to its IP address
smb.service	The systemd service script for the Samba server

Table 11-1: Samba Applications

Samba provides four main services: file and printer services, authentication and authorization, name resolution, and service announcement. The SMB daemon, **smbd**, provides the file and printer services, as well as authentication and authorization for those services. This means users on the network can share files and printers. You can control access to these services by requiring users to provide a password. When users try to access a shared directory, they are prompted for a password. Control can be implemented in share mode or user mode. The share mode sets up one password for the shared resource and then enables any user who has that password to access it. The user mode provides a different password for each user. Samba maintains its own password file for this purpose.

Name resolution and service announcements are handled by the **nmbd** server. Name resolution resolves NetBIOS names with IP addresses. Service announcements, also known as browsing, are the way a list of services available on the network is made known to the connected Windows PCs (and Linux PCs connected through Samba).

Samba also includes the **winbind** service, which allows Samba servers to use authentication services provided by a Windows domain. Instead of a Samba server maintaining its own set of users to allow access, it can make use of a Windows domain authentication service to authenticate users.

Setting Up Samba

To allow Windows to access a Linux system, as well as Linux to access a Windows system, you use the Samba server. First be sure that Samba is installed. Selecting **samba** for installation will automatically select any needed dependent packages

Be sure that the firewall on your Windows system is not blocking Samba (see Figure 11-1). Run **firewall-config** (Sundry | Firewall) and choose the Services tab. Make sure that the Samba service and Samba client entries are checked, allowing Samba to operate on your system, along with Multicast-DNS (**mdns**). Click Apply to make the changes.

The Samba server consists of two daemons: **smbd** and **nmbd**. You may have to first enable and then start these daemons using the **service** or **systemctl** commands as the **root** user and the **smb** and **nmb** service names (the server names without the **d** character). Open a terminal window, access the root user with the **su** command, and then enter a **systemctl** command for the **smb** and **nmb** servers with the **enable** command to enable the server, and then use the **service** command with the **start** command to start it. Once enabled, the server should start automatically whenever your system starts up. Samba is managed by **systemd** (see Chapter 14).

```
su
systemctl nmb enable
systemctl smb enable
service nmb start
service smb start
```

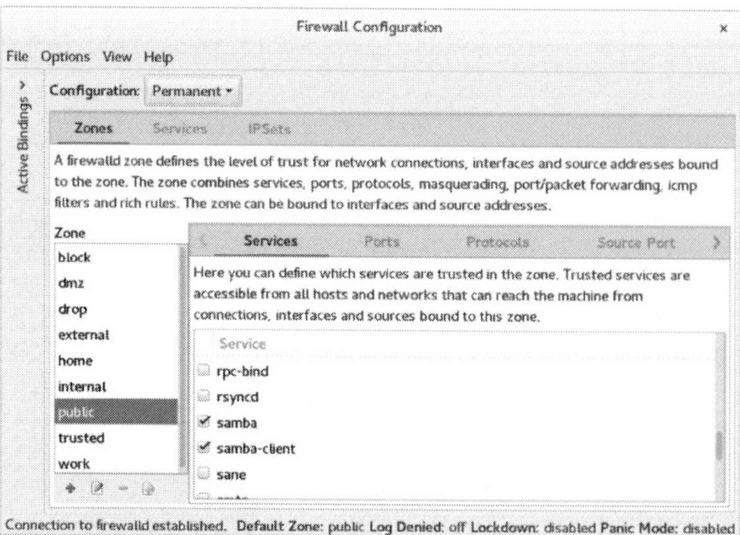

Figure 11-1: Allowing Samba on Firewall

Also, make sure that Samba access is permitted by SELinux (system-config-selinux). Open the SELinux Management tool, and on the Boolean tab, enable Samba access (see Figure 11-2). To share folders, Windows folders, and NFS folders you would check the samba and samba-client entries.

Should you receive a security alert, you can change the Samba SELinux file context manually using the **chcon** and **semanage** commands. The commands to enter will be listed in the Fix Command section of the security alert's "Show full error output" scroll window. The Samba share directory's SELinux file context is set to **samba_share_t**. The **semanage** command preserves the change through relabelings. In the following example, the SELinux file context for the **/mymedia** share is set.

```
chcon -R -t samba_share_t '/mymedia'
semanage fcontext -a  -t samba_share_t '/mymedia'
```

Note: If SELinux continues to block your connections, you could disable SELinux by placing it in the Permissive mode, system-config-selinux (Status tab).

Samba has two methods of authentication, shares and users. User authentication requires that there be corresponding accounts in the Windows and Linux systems. They can have the same name, though a Windows user can be mapped to a Linux account. A share can be made open to any user and function as an extension of the user's storage space. The user method is recommended.

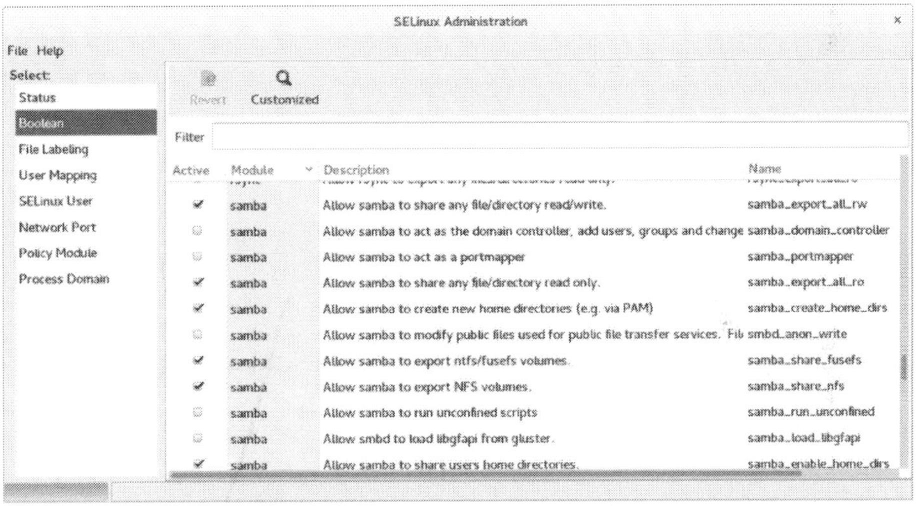

Figure 11-2: Allowing Samba on SELinux: system-config-selinux

To set up simple file sharing on a Linux system, you first need to configure your Samba server. You can do this by directly editing the **/etc/samba/samba.conf** file.

Samba is managed by **systemd** using the **smb.service** and **nmb.service** unit files in **/etc/systemd/system**. The **smb.service** file is shown here. Samba is started after the system log, networking, nmb, and the Winbind service (After). It is started for the **multi-user.target** (runlevels 2, 3, 4, and 5) (WantedBy). Runtime configuration is read from the **/etc/sysconfig/samba** file (EnvironmentFile).

smb.service

```
[Unit]
Description=Samba SMB Daemon
After=syslog.target network.target nmb.service winbind.service

[Service]

Environment=KRB5CCNAME=FILE:/run/samba/krb5cc_samba
Type=notify
NotifyAccess=all
PIDFile=/run/smbd.pid
LimitNOFILE=16384
EnvironmentFile=-/etc/sysconfig/samba
ExecStart=/usr/sbin/smbd $SMBDOPTIONS
ExecReload=/usr/bin/kill -HUP $MAINPID

[Install]
WantedBy=multi-user.target
```

The NMB daemon is started after system logging and networking (After). It also reads runtime configuration from **/etc/sysconfig/samba** (EnvironmentFile). It starts the nmbd server (ExecStart) for the multi-user target (WantedBy).

nmb.service

```
[Unit]
Description=Samba NMB Daemon
After=syslog.target network.target
[Service]
Type=forking
Environment=KRB5CCNAME=FILE:/run/samba/krb5cc_samba
Type=notify
NotifyAccess=all
PIDFile=/run/nmbd.pid
EnvironmentFile=-/etc/sysconfig/samba
ExecStart=/usr/sbin/nmbd $NMBDOPTIONS
ExecReload=/usr/bin/kill -HUP $MAINPID
[Install]
WantedBy=multi-user.target
```

User Level Security

Samba primarily provides user level security, requiring users on remote systems to log in using Samba registered passwords. Samba still provides share and server level access, but these methods have been deprecated and are not recommended. User level security requires the use of Windows encrypted passwords. Windows uses its own methods of encryption. For Samba to handle such passwords, it has to maintain its own Windows compatible password database. It cannot use the Linux password databases. Windows also uses additional information for the login process like where the user logged in.

User level security requires that each user that wants to login to a Samba share from a Windows system has to have a corresponding user account on the Samba server. In addition, this account has to have a separate Samba password with which to log in to the Samba share. In effect, they become Samba users.

The account on the Samba server does not have to have the same name as the one on the Windows system. A Windows user name can be specified for a Samba user. This mapping of windows users to Samba (Linux) users is listed in the **/etc/samba/smbusers** file. The following maps the Windows user **rpetersen** to the Samba (Linux) user **richard**.

```
richard = rpetersen
```

When the Windows user in Windows tries to access the Samba share, the user will be prompt to login. The Windows user would then enter **rpetersen** as the user name and the Samba password that was set up for **richard**.

User level security is managed by password backend databases. By default, the **tdbsam** back-end database is used. This is a **tdb** database file (trivial database) that stores Samba passwords along with Windows extended information. The tdbsam database is designed for small networks. For systems using LDAP to manage users, you can use the LDAP enabled back end, **ldbsam**. The **ldbsam** database is designed for larger networks. The **smbpasswd** file previously used, is still available, but included only for backward compatibility. The default configuration entries for user access in the **smb.conf file** are shown here.

```
security = user
passdb backend = tdbsam
```

The **username map** option specifies the file used to associate Windows and Linux users. Windows users can use the Windows user name to log in as the associated user. The username map file is usually **/etc/samba/smbusers**.

```
username map = /etc/samba/smbusers
```

Be sure to enable PAM in the **smb.conf** file:

```
obey pam restrictions = yes
```

If you are using an LDAP-enabled Samba database, ldbsam, you would use special LDAP Samba tools to manage users. These are provided in the smbldap-tools package. They are prefixed with the term smbldap. There are tools for adding, modifying, and deleting users and groups like **smbldap-useradd**, **smbldap-userdelete**, and **smbldap-groupmod**. You use the **smbldap-passwd** command to manage Samba passwords with LDAP. The **smdbldap-userinfo** obtains information about a user. You configure your LDAP Samba tools support using the **/etc/smbldap-tools/smbldap.conf** file.

Samba also provides its own Samba authentication PAM module for domain logons, **pam_smb_auth.so (pam_smb** package). Configuration is set up in the **/etc/pam_smb.conf** file where you specify your domain and login servers.

smbpasswd

With user-level security, access to Samba server resources by a Windows client is allowed only to users on that client. The username and Samba password used to access the Samba server has to be registered in the Samba password database.

To manage users, you can use the **smbpasswd** command, or the **pdbedit** tool. The **smbpasswd** command will work on both the older smbpasswd files and the backend databases like **tdbsam**. The **pdbedit** command works only on the backend databases.

Alternatively, you can use the **smbpasswd** command in a terminal window to add, or later change, passwords. The **smbpasswd** command with the **-a** option with add a user and the **-x** option will remove one. To enable or disable users you would use the **-e** and **-d** options.

```
smbpasswd -a aleina
```

Users can use **smbpasswd** to change their own password. The following example shows how you would use **smbpasswd** to change your Samba password. If the user has no Samba password, that user can just press the ENTER key.

```
smbpasswd
Old SMB password: old-password
New SMB Password: new-password
Repeat New SMB Password: new-password
```

Should you want to use no passwords, you can use smbpasswd with the **-n** option. The **smb.conf** file will have to have the **null passwords** option set to yes. Note: If you are using the older smbpasswords file, be sure that Samba is configured to use encrypted passwords. Set the **encrypt passwords** option to **yes** and specify the SMB password file.

pdbedit

pdbedit is a command line tool with options for adding and removing users, as well as features like changing the password and setting the home directory. You can also import or export the user entries to or from other backend databases. It operates just on the backend database files like **tdbsam**, not on the older **smbpasswd** files.

To add a user, you would use the **-a** option and to remove a user you use the **-x** option.

```
pdbedit -a larisa
```

The **pdbedit** command lets you display more information about users. To display users from the backend database, you could use the **-L** option. Add the **-v** option for detailed information. For a particular user add the username.

```
pdbedit -Lv richard
```

For domain policies like minimum password length or retries, you use the -P option.

```
pdbedit -P
```

You use the **-i** and **-e** options to import and export database entries. The following will import entries from the old **smbpasswd** file to the new **tdbsam** backend database.

```
pdbedit -i smbpasswd -e tdbsam
```

If your system is using LDAP enabled Samba database, then use the smbldap tools to manage users and groups.

The Samba smb.conf Configuration File

Samba configuration is held in the **smb.conf** file located in the **/etc/samba** directory. Alternatively, you can manually edit the file directly, creating your own Samba configuration. You may have to do this if your Samba configuration proves to be very complex. Direct editing can also provide more refined control over your shares.

You use the **testparm** command to check the syntax of any changes you have made to the **/etc/samba/smb.conf** file. Run the following in a terminal window.

```
testparm
```

The file is separated into two basic parts: one for global options and the other for shared services. A shared service, also known as *shares*, can either be file space services (used by clients as an extension of their native file systems) or printable services (used by clients to access print services on the host running the server). The file space service is a directory to which clients are given access; they can use the space in it as an extension of their local file system. A printable service provides access by clients to print services, such as printers managed by the Samba server.

The **/etc/samba/smb.conf** file holds the configuration for the various shared resources, as well as global options that apply to all resources. Linux installs a **smb.conf** file in your **/etc/samba** directory. RHEL installs both a basic configuration in the **smb.conf** file and a detailed sample configuration in the **smb.conf.example** file. The **smb.conf.example** file is described here. You should consult this file for detailed descriptions of key options. The file contains default settings used for your distribution. You can edit the file to customize your configuration to your own needs. Many entries are commented with either a semicolon or a # sign, and you can remove the initial comment symbol to make them effective. For a complete listing of the Samba configuration parameters, check the Man page for **smb.conf**.

In the **smb.conf** file, global options are set first, followed by each shared resource's configuration. The basic organizing component of the **smb.conf** file is called a section. Each resource has its own section that holds its service name and definitions of its attributes. Even global options are placed in a section of their own, labeled **global**. For example, each section for a shared directory consists of the directory and the access rights allowed to users of the directory. The section of each share is labeled with the name of the shared resource. Special sections called **printers** and **homes**, provide default descriptions for user directories and printers accessible on the Samba server. Following the special sections, sections are entered for specific services, namely access to specific directories or printers.

A section begins with a section label consisting of the name of the shared resource encased in brackets. Other than the special sections, the section label can be any name you want to give it. Following the section label, on separate lines, different parameters for this service are entered. The parameters define the access rights to be granted to the user of the service. For example, for a directory, you may want it to be browseable, but read-only, and to use a certain printer. Parameters are entered in the format *parameter name = value*. You can enter a comment by placing a semicolon at the beginning of the comment line.

A simple example of a section configuration follows. The section label is encased in brackets and followed by two parameter entries. The **path** parameter specifies the directory to which access is allowed. The **writeable** parameter specifies whether the user has write access to this directory.

```
[mysection]
 path = /home/chris
 writeable = true
```

A printer service has the same format but requires certain other parameters. The path parameter specifies the location of the printer spool directory. The **read-only** and **printable** parameters are set to `true`, indicating the service is read-only and printable. The **guest ok** option indicates anyone can access it.

```
[myprinter]
 path = /var/spool/samba
 read only = yes
 printable = yes
 guest ok = yes
```

Parameter entries are often synonymous but different entries that have the same meaning. For example, **read only** = **no**, **writeable** = **yes**, and **write ok** = **yes** all mean the same thing, providing write access to the user.

Hint: The **writeable** option is an alias for the inverse of the **read only** option. The **writeable = yes** entry is the same as **read only = no** entry.

Global Section

The Global section determines the configuration for the entire server, as well as specifying default entries to be used in the home and directory sections. In this section, you find entries for the workgroup name, password configuration, and directory settings. The Global section begins with the **[global]** label.

```
[global]
```

Several of the more important entries are discussed here. The Global section is organized into several segments, each with a commented heading, like Network Related Options. All are part of the **[global]** section.

Samba provides support for the **SMB2** protocol used by Windows. Enable it by setting the **max protocol** option to **SMB2**.

```
max protocol = SMB2
```

Network related options

The Network related options begin with a commented section describing each option followed by the option entries. Comments are commented with a preceding **#**, and actual options are commented with a preceding **;**.

```
# ---------------------- Network Related Options -------------------------
#
# workgroup = NT-Domain-Name or Workgroup-Name, eg: MIDEARTH
#
# server string is the equivalent of the NT Description field
#
# netbios name can be used to specify a server name not tied to the hostname
#
# Interfaces lets you configure Samba to use multiple interfaces
```

```
# If you have multiple network interfaces then you can list the ones
# you want to listen on (never omit localhost)
# interface (lo).
#
# hosts allow = the hosts allowed to connect. This option can also be used on a
# per-share basis.

# hosts deny = the hosts not allowed to connect. This option can also be used on
# a per-share basis.
#
# max protocol = used to define the supported protocol. The default is NT1. You
# can set it to SMB2 if you want experimental SMB2 support.
#
     workgroup = MYGROUP
     server string = Samba Server Version %v

;     netbios name = MYSERVER

;     interfaces = lo eth0 192.168.12.2/24 192.168.13.2/24
;     hosts allow = 127. 192.168.12. 192.168.13.

:     max protocol = SMB2
```

The Workgroup entry specifies the workgroup name you want to give to your network. This is the workgroup name that appears on the Windows client's Network window. The default Workgroup entry in the **smb.conf** file is shown here:

```
# workgroup = NT-Domain-Name or Workgroup-Name
 workgroup = WORKGROUP
```

The workgroup name has to be the same for each Windows client that the Samba server supports. On a Windows client, the workgroup name is usually found in the System tool located in the Control Panel window. On many clients, this is defaulted to WORKGROUP. If you want to change this name, you have to change the Workgroup entry in the **smb.conf** file accordingly. The Workgroup entry and the workgroup name on each Windows client have to be the same. In this example the workgroup name is **mygroup**.

```
workgroup = mygroup
```

The server string entry, shown here, holds the descriptive name you want displayed for the server on the client systems. On Windows systems, this is the name displayed on the Samba server icon.

```
# server string is the equivalent of the NT Description field
     server string = Samba Server Version %v
```

The default is Samba Server, but you can change this to any name you want. Here the **%h** variable is used to display the server's host name.

```
    server string = %h server (Samba, RHEL)
```

As a security measure, you can restrict access to SMB services to certain specified local networks. For the **hosts allow** option, enter the network addresses of the local networks for which you want to permit access. To deny access to everyone in a network except a few particular hosts, you can use the EXCEPT option after the network address with the IP addresses of those hosts. The localhost (127) is always automatically included. The next example allows access to two local networks:

```
hosts allow = 127. 192.168.1. 192.168.2.
```

To use the new SMB2 protocol, you can set **max protocol** to SMB2.

Note: You can also configure Samba to be a Primary Domain Controller (PDC) for Windows NT networks. As a PDC, Samba sets up the Windows domain that other systems will use, instead of participating in an already established workgroup.

Logging Options

This section has directives for setting up logging for the Samba server. The log file directive is configured with the **%m** substitution symbol so that a separate log file is set up for each machine that connects to the server. Logging is managed by the **journald** daemon.

```
log file = /var/log/samba/log.%m
```

The maximum size of a log file is set to 1000 lines.

```
max log size = 50
```

Standalone Server Options

```
# ---------------------- Standalone Server Options -----------------------
#
# security = the mode Samba runs in. This can be set to user, share
# (deprecated), or server (deprecated).
#
# passdb backend = the backend used to store user information in. New
# installations should use either tdbsam or ldapsam. No additional configuration
# is required for tdbsam. The "smbpasswd" utility is available for backwards
# compatibility.
#

    security = user
    passdb backend = tdbsam
```

Samba resources are normally accessed with either share or user-level security. On a share level, any user can access the resource without having to log in to the server. On a user level, each user has to log in, using a password. Windows clients use encrypted passwords for the login process. Passwords are encrypted by default and managed by the password database. In the following entries, the **security** is set to the user level (**user** option), and the password database file (**passdb backend**) uses **tdbsam**.

```
security = user
passdb backend = tdbsam
```

If you want share-level security, specify **share** as the security option. However, this option is deprecated. User level security is considered the standard:

```
security = share
```

Domain Members Options

If your network handles authentication centrally through a domain server, then your Samba server needs to become a domain member. Domain membership is normally handled by an Active Directory Server (**ads** option) or a specific PDC server (**domain** option). To configure the **smb.conf** file for domain membership, the **security** option is set to **domain** or **ads**. If you choose **domain**, then the **workgroup** option is set to the name of the domain.

```
security = domain
workgroup = mydomain
```

In the Domain Members Options section of the **smb.conf** file, you can set the **realm** or **password server** options. If **security** is set to **ads**, you can set the **realm** option (Active Directory Realm). If you set **security** to **domain** you use the **password server** option to specify the Windows PDC server your network uses. Using an asterisk (*) instead of the PDC name lets Samba detect the PDC server automatically.

```
;       realm = MY_REALM
;       password server = <NT-Server-Name>
```

Name Resolution

Name service resolution is normally provided by the WINS server (Windows NetBIOS Name Service, **nmbd**), which is started by a samba systemd dependency. If your local network already has a WINS server, you can specify that instead. The commented default entry is shown here. Replace w.x.y.z with your network's WINS server name.

```
;   wins server = w.x.y.z
```

WINS server support by your Samba **nmbd** server is commented out to avoid conflicts, turning your Samba name resolution server into just a client. The commented entry to turn on WINS support is shown here.

```
;   wins support = yes
```

```
#------------------------------ Name Resolution --------------------------------
# This section details the support for the Windows Internet Name Service (WINS).
#
# Note: Samba can be either a WINS server or a WINS client, but not both.
#
# wins support = when set to yes, the NMBD component of Samba enables its WINS
# server.
#
# wins server = tells the NMBD component of Samba to be a WINS client.
#
# wins proxy = when set to yes, Samba answers name resolution queries on behalf
# of a non WINS capable client. For this to work, there must be at least one
# WINS server on the network. The default is no.
#
# dns proxy = when set to yes, Samba attempts to resolve NetBIOS names via DNS
# nslookups.

;       wins support = yes
```

```
;       wins server = w.x.y.z
;       wins proxy = yes

;       dns proxy = yes
```

If you network also has its own DNS server that it wants to use for name resolution, you can enable that instead. By default, this is commented out as shown here. Remove the comment symbol to allow the use of your network's DNS server for Windows name resolution. Also, WINS server support would have to be turned off.

```
;  dns proxy = yes
```

Name resolution can also be instructed to check the **lmhosts** and **/etc/hosts** files first. The commented default entry is shown here.

```
;    name resolve order = lmhosts host wins bcast
```

Printing Options

```
# --------------------------- Printing Options -----------------------------
#
#
# The options in this section allow you to configure a non-default printing
# system.
#
# load printers = when set you yes, the list of printers is automatically
# loaded, rather than setting them up individually.
#
# cups options = allows you to pass options to the CUPS library. Setting this
# option to raw, for example, allows you to use drivers on your Windows clients.
#
# printcap name = used to specify an alternative printcap file.
#
     load printers = yes
     cups options = raw

;     printcap name = /etc/printcap
     #obtain list of printers automatically on SystemV
;     printcap name = lpstat
;     printing = cups
```

To enable printing, set the **load printers** option to yes.

```
load printers = yes
```

Other options like **printing** let you specify a different printing server (CUPS is the default).

```
printing = cups
```

File System Options

The File System Options segment lists options for file systems that support extended attributes and support for guest accounts. Normally access to certain types of files can be blocked such as archive, hidden files, read only files, and system files. Access to extended attributes can be enabled.

```
;      map archive = no
;      map hidden = no
;      map read only = no
;      map system = no
;      store dos attributes = yes
```

You can use a guest user login to make resources available to anyone without requiring a password. A guest user login would handle any users who log in without a specific account. On Linux systems, by default Samba will use the **nobody** user as the guest user. Alternatively, you can set up and designate a specific user to use as the guest user. Be sure to add the guest user to the password file. You designate the guest user with the **guest account** entry in the **smb.conf** file.

```
guest account = nobody
```

Homes Section

The Homes section specifies default controls for accessing a user home directory through the SMB protocols by remote users. Setting the **browseable** option to **no** prevents the client from listing the files in a file browser. The **writable** option specifies whether users have read and write control over files in their home directories. The **create mask** and **directory mask** options set maximum default permissions for new files and directories. The **valid users** option uses the **%S** macro to map to the current service.

```
[homes]
 comment = Home Directories
 browseable = no
 writable = yes
 valid users = %S
 valid users = MYDOMAIN\%S
 create mask = 775
 directory mask = 775
```

The printer and print$ Sections

The printers section specifies the default controls for accessing printers. These are used for printers for which no specific sections exist. Setting **browseable** to `no` simply hides the Printers section from the client, not the printers. The **path** entry specifies the location of the spool directory Samba will use for printer files. To enable printing at all, the **printable** entry must be set to yes. To allow guest users to print, set the **guest ok** entry to **yes**. This specifies the command the server actually uses to print documents. The standard implementation of the Printers section is shown here:

```
[printers]
 comment = All Printers
 path = /var/spool/samba
 browseable = no
 guest ok = yes
 writable = no
 printable = yes
```

Shares

Sections for specific shared resources, such as directories on your system, are usually placed after the Homes and Printers sections. For a section defining a shared directory, enter a label for the system. Then, on separate lines, enter options for its pathname and the different permissions you want to set. For the **path** option, specify the full pathname for the directory. The **comment** option holds the label to be given the share. You can make a directory writable, public, or read-only. For those options not set, the defaults entered in the Global, Homes, and Printers segments are used. For more examples, check those in the original **smb.conf** file. The following example is the **myprojects** share. Here the **/myprojects** directory is defined as a shared resource that is open to any user with guest access.

```
[myprojects]
    comment = Great Project Ideas
    path = /myprojects
    read only = no
    guest ok = yes
```

To allow complete public access, set the **guest ok** option to **yes**, with no valid user's entry (use this instead of the **public** option).

```
[newdocs]
 comment =  New Documents
 path = /home/newdocs
 guest ok = yes
 read only = no
```

To limit access to certain users, you can list a set of valid users with the **valid users** option. Setting the **guest ok** option to `no` closes it off from access by others. The **invalid users** option denies access to certain users.

```
[mynewmusic]
  comment =  New Music
  path = /home/specialprojects
  valid users = robert george larisa aleina
  invalid users = richard mark
  guest ok = no
  read only = no
```

You can use the **read list** and **write list** options to control read and write access to certain users. The **read list** option allow read only access to files and the **write list** option permits read/write access. In the following example, **robert** and **george** have read only access whereas **larisa** and **aleina** have read/write access. Groups can be specified by preceding the group name with an @ symbol, **@mygroup**. Keep in mind that write permissions would still have to be enabled on the Linux system for those files **(chmod)**.

```
[mynewpics]
  comment =  New Music
  path = /home/specialprojects writable = yes
  valid users = robert george larisa aleina
  read list = robert george
  write list = larisa aleina
```

To set up a directory that can be shared by more than one user, where each user has control of the files he or she creates, simply list the users in the Valid Users entry. Permissions for any created files are specified in the Advanced mode by the Create Mask entry (same as create mask). In this example, the permissions are set to 765, which provides read/write/execute access to owners, read/write access to members of the group, and only read/execute access to all others (the default is 744, read-only for group and other permissions):

```
[myshare]
 comment = Writer's projects
 path = /usr/local/drafts
 valid users = justin chris dylan
 writable = yes
 guest ok = no
 read only = no
 create mask = 0765
```

Printers

Access to specific printers is defined in the Printers section of the **smb.conf** file. For a printer, you need to include the Printer and Printable entries, as well as specify the type of Printing server used. With the Printer entry, you name the printer, and by setting the Printable entry to yes, you allow it to print. You can control access to specific users with the valid users entry and by setting the Public entry to no. For public access, set the public entry to yes. For the CUPS server, set the printing option cups.

The following example sets up a printer accessible to guest users. This opens the printer to use by any user on the network. Users need to have write access to the printer's spool directory, located in **/var/spool/samba**. Keep in mind that any printer has first to be installed on your system. The following printer was already installed as **myhp**. You use the CUPS administrative tool to set up printers for the CUPS server. The Printing option can be inherited from general Printers share.

```
[myhp]
      path = /var/spool/samba
      read only = no
      guest ok = yes
      printable = yes
      printer = myhp
      oplocks = no
      share modes = no
      printing = cups
```

As with shares, you can restrict a printer's use to certain users, denying it to public access. The following example sets up a printer accessible only by the users **larisa** and **aleina** (you could add other users if you want). Users need to have write access to the printer's spool directory.

```
[larisalaser]
      path = /var/spool/samba
      read only = no
      valid users = larisa aleina
      guest ok = no
      printable = yes
      printing = cups
      printer = larisalaser
      oplocks = no
      share modes = no
```

Variable Substitutions

For string values assigned to parameters, you can incorporate substitution operators. This provides greater flexibility in designating values that may be context-dependent, such as usernames. For example, suppose a service needs to use a separate directory for each user who logs in. The path for such directories could be specified using the `%u` variable that substitutes in the name of the current user. The string **path = /tmp/%u** would become **path = /tmp/justin** for the **justin** user and **/tmp/dylan** for the **dylan** user. Table 11-2 lists several of the more common substitution variables.

Variable	Description
`%S`	Name of the current service
`%P`	Root directory of the current service
`%u`	Username of the current service
`%H`	Home directory of the user
`%h`	Internet hostname on which Samba is running
`%m`	NetBIOS name of the client machine
`%L`	NetBIOS name of the server
`%M`	Internet name of the client machine
`%I`	IP address of the client machine

Table 11-2: Samba Substitution Variables

Testing the Samba Configuration

After you make your changes to the **smb.conf** file, you can then use the **testparm** program to see if the entries are correctly entered. **testparm** checks the syntax and validity of Samba entries. By default, **testparm** checks the **/etc/samba/smb.conf** file. If you are using a different file as your configuration file, you can specify it as an argument to **testparm**. You can also have **testparm** check to see if a particular host has access to the service set up by the configuration file.

To check the real-time operation of your Samba server, you can log in to a user account on the Linux system running the Samba server and connect to the server.

Samba Public Domain Controller: Samba PDC

Samba can also operate as a Public Domain Controller (PDC). The domain controller will be registered and advertised on the network as the domain controller. The PDC provides a much more centralized way to control access to Samba shares. It provides the netlogon service and a NETLOGON share. The PDC will set up machine trust accounts for each Windows and Samba client. Though you can do this manually, Samba will do it for you automatically. You can find out more about Samba PDC at:

```
http://us1.samba.org/samba/docs/man/Samba-HOWTO-Collection/samba-pdc.html
```

Microsoft Domain Security

As noted in the Samba documentation, the primary benefit of Microsoft domain security is single-sign-on (SSO). In effect, logging into your user account also logs you into access to your entire network's shared resources. Instead of having to be separately authenticated anytime you try to access a shared network resource, you are already authenticated. Authentication is managed using Security IDs (SID) that consists of a network ID (NID) and a relative ID (RID). The RID references your personal account. A separate RID is assigned to every account, even those for groups or system services. The SID is used to set up access control lists (ACL) the different shared resources on your network, allowing a resource to identify you automatically.

Note: You can enable and configure the Samba PDC controller using system-config-authentication (Applications overview, Other filter). On the Identity & Authorization tab, choose Winbind from the User Account Database drop down menu to display entries where you can enter the workgroup and the domain controller URL (PDC).

Essential Samba PDC configuration options

To configure your PDC edit the Domain Control Options section in the **smb.conf** file. Here you will find entries for configuring your Samba PDC.

The essential PDC options are shown here.

```
netbios name = mysystem
workgroup = myworkgroup
domain logons = yes
domain master = yes
security = user
```

Basic configuration

The netbios name is the name you want to give to the PDC server.

```
netbios name = MYSERVER
```

Like most Samba configurations, the PDC requires a Samba backend. The **tdbsam** is already configured for you. The security level should be **user**. This is normally the default and should already be set. The **smb.conf** entries are shown here:

```
security = user
passdb backend = tdbsam
```

Domain Logon configuration

Samba PDC uses domain logons service whereby a user can log on to the network. The domain logon service is called the netlogon service by Microsoft. The samba share it uses is also called netlogon. To configure the domain logon service you set the domain logons entry to yes. The PDC must also be designated the domain master. These are located in the **[global]** section of your **smb.conf** file, in the Domain Controller Options segment. The entries are commented with preceding semicolon, ;. Remove the semi-colon to uncomment them, making them active. The entries are already set to yes.

```
domain master = yes
domain logons = yes
```

The login script can be one set by the system or by users. The logon path references the profile used for a user.

```
# the login script name depends on the machine name
logon script = %m.bat
# the login script name depends on the unix user used
logon script = %u.bat
logon path = \\%L\Profiles\%u
```

You can then enable user add and delete operations for adding and removed users from the PDC. The **add machine** entry allows Samba to automatically add trusted machine accounts for Windows systems when they first join the PDC controlled network.

```
add user script = /usr/sbin/useradd "%u" -n -g users
add group script = /usr/sbin/groupadd "%g"
add machine script = /usr/sbin/useradd -n -c "Workstation (%u)" -M -d /nohome -s
/bin/false "%u"
delete user script = /usr/sbin/userdel "%u"
delete user from group script = /usr/sbin/userdel "%u" "%g"
delete group script = /usr/sbin/groupdel "%g"
```

You then need to set up a netlogon share in the **smb.conf** file. Find the section labeled **[netlogon]**. This share holds the `netlogon` scripts, in this case, the **/var/lib/samba/netlogon** directory, which should not be writable but should be accessible by all users (Guest OK). In the share definitions section of the **smb.conf** file, you will find the `[netlogon]` section commented. Remove the semi-colon comments from the entry, as shown here.

```
# Un-comment the following and create the netlogon directory for Domain Logon
[netlogon]
comment = Network Logon Service
path = /var/lib/samba/netlogon
guest ok = yes
writable = no
share modes = no
```

If you are using profiles, you should add the roving profile share (**[Profiles]** label). Add the following to provide a specific roving profile share, located just after the netlogon shares. The profile share is where user netlogon profiles are stored.

```
# the default is to use the user's home directory
[Profiles]
path = /var/lib/samba/profiles
```

```
browseable = no
guest ok = yes
```

Master Browser configuration

The PDC has browser functionality, with which it locates systems and shares on your network. Browser features are set in the Browser Control Options section of the **smb.conf**. The local master option is used if you already have another PDC that you want to operate as the local master. Normally you would leave the entry commented, as shown here. You could have several domain controllers operating on your network. Your Microsoft network holds an election choose which should be the master. The **os level** sets the precedence for this PDC. It should be higher than 32 to gain preference over other domain controllers on your network, ensuring this PDC's election as the primary master controller. The preferred master option starts the browser election on startup.

```
;      local master = no
;      os level = 33
;      preferred master = yes
```

Accessing Samba Services with Clients

Client systems connected to the SMB network can access the shared services provided by the Samba server. Windows clients should be able to access shared directories and services automatically on a Windows desktop. For Linux systems connected to the same network, Samba services can be accessed using the GNOME file manager or the KDE file manager, as well as special Samba client programs.

With the Samba **smbclient,** a command line client, a local Linux system can connect to a shared directory on the Samba server and transfer files, as well as run shell programs (**samba-clients** package). Using the **mount** command with the **-t cifs** option, directories on the Samba server can be mounted to local directories on the Linux client. The **cifs** option invokes **mount.cifs** to mount the directory.

Accessing Windows Samba Shares from GNOME

You can use Nautilus (the GNOME file manager) to access your Samba shares. On the GNOME file manager choose Network to open a Network window, which displays the icons for your network. The Windows Network icon will hold the Windows workgroups that your Windows hosts are part of. Opening up the Windows Network icon will list your Windows network groups, like WORKGROUP. Opening up the Windows group icon will list the hosts in that group. These will show host icon for your shared Windows hosts. Clicking a host icon will list all the shared resources on it.

Alternatively, you can open a location entry in a file manager window and enter the **smb:** protocol to display all the Samba and Windows networks, from which you can access the Samba and Windows shares.

smbclient

The smbclient utility operates like FTP to access systems using the SMB protocols. Whereas with an FTP client you can access other FTP servers or Unix systems, with smbclient you can access SMB-shared services, either on the Samba server or on Windows systems. Many smbclient commands are similar to FTP, such as **mget** to transfer a file or **del** to delete a file. The smbclient program has several options for querying a remote system, as well as connecting to it. See the **smbclient** Man page for a complete list of options and commands. The **smbclient** program takes as its argument a server name and the service you want to access on that server. A double slash precedes the server name, and a single slash separates it from the service. The service can be any shared resource, such as a directory or a printer. The server name is its NetBIOS name, which may or may not be the same as its IP name. For example, to specify the **myreports** shared directory on the server named **turtle.mytrek.com**, use **//turtle.mytrek.com/myreports**.

```
//server-name/service
```

You can also supply the password for accessing the service. Enter it as an argument following the service name. If you do not supply the password, you are prompted to enter it.

You can then add several options to access shares, such as the remote username or the list of services available. With the **-I** option, you can specify the system using its IP address. You use the **-U** option and a login name for the remote login name you want to use on the remote system. Attach **%** with the password if a password is required. With the **-L** option, you can obtain a list of the services provided on a server, such as shared directories or printers. The following command will list the shares available on the host **turtle.mytrek.com**:

```
smbclient -L turtle.mytrek.com
```

To access a particular directory on a remote system, enter the directory as an argument to the **smbclient** command, followed by any options. For Windows files, you use backslashes for the pathnames, and for Unix/Linux files, you use forward slashes. Once connected, an SMB prompt is displayed, and you can use smbclient commands such as **get** and **put** to transfer files. The **quit** or **exit** commands quit the smbclient program. In the following example, smbclient accesses the directory **myreports** on the **turtle.mytrek.com** system, using the **dylan** login name:

```
smbclient //turtle.mytrek.com/myreports -I 192.168.0.1 -U dylan
```

In most cases, you can simply use the server name to reference the server, as shown here:

```
smbclient //turtle.mytrek.com/myreports -U dylan
```

If you are accessing the home directory of a particular account on the Samba server, you can simply specify the **homes** service. In the next example, the user accesses the home directory of the **aleina** account on the Samba server, after being prompted to enter that account's password:

```
smbclient //turtle.mytrek.com/homes -U aleina
```

You can also use smbclient to access shared resources located on Windows clients. Specify the computer name of the Windows client along with its shared folder. In the next example, the user accesses the **windata** folder on the Windows client named **lizard**. The folder is configured to allow access by anyone, so the user just presses the ENTER key at the password prompt.

```
smbclient //lizard/windata
```

Once logged in, you can execute smbclient commands to manage files and change directories. Shell commands can be executed with the **!** operator. To transfer files, you can use the **mget** and **mput** commands, much as they are used in the FTP program.

mount.cifs: mount -t cifs

Using the **mount** command with the **-t cifs** option, a Linux client can mount a shared directory onto its local system. The **cifs** option invokes the **mount.cifs** command to perform the mount operation. The syntax for the **mount.cifs** command is similar to that for the **smbclient** command, with many corresponding options. The **mount.cifs** command takes as its arguments the Samba server and shared directory, followed by the local directory where you want to mount the directory. T

Instead of using **mount.cifs** explicitly, you use the `mount` command with the file system type **cifs**. This will then run the **/sbin/mount.cifs** command, which will invoke **smbclient** to mount the file system:

```
mount -t cifs //turtle.mytrek.com/myreports /mnt/myreps -U dylan
```

To unmount the directory, use the **cifs.umount** command with the local directory name, as shown here:

```
cifs.umount /mnt/myreps
```

To mount the home directory of a particular user on the server, specify the **homes** service and the user's login name. The following example mounts the home directory of the user **larisa** to the **/home/chris/larisastuff** directory on the local system:

```
mount -t samba //turtle.mytrek.com/homes /home/chris/larisastuff -U larisa
```

You can also mount shared folders on Windows clients. Just specify the computer name of the Windows client along with its folder. If the folder name contains spaces, enclose it in single quotes. In the following example, the user mounts the **windata** folder on **lizard** as the **/mylinux** directory. For a folder with access to anyone, just press **ENTER** at the password prompt:

```
$ mount -t cifs //lizard/windata  /mylinux
Password:
$ ls /mylinux
_hi_mynewdoc.doc_myreport.txt
```

To unmount the shared folder when you are finished with it, use the `cifs.umount` command.

```
cifs.umount /mylinux
```

You could also specify a username and password as options if user-level access is required:

```
mount -t cifs -o username=chris passwd=mypass //lizard/windata /mylinux
```

You can also use the cifs type in an **/etc/fstab** entry to have a Samba file system mounted automatically:

```
//lizard/windata /mylinux cifs defaults 0 0
```

Network File System (NFS)

NFS enables you to mount a file system on a remote computer as if it were local to your own system. You can then directly access any of the files on that remote file system. This has the advantage of allowing different systems on a network to access the same files directly, without each having to keep its own copy. Only one copy will be on a remote file system, which each computer can then access. You can find out more about NFS at its website at **http://nfs.sourceforge.net**.

Check the **Storage Administration Guide** for details on NFS configuration, **Chapter 8: Network File System (NFS)**.

```
https://access.redhat.com/documentation/en-
US/Red_Hat_Enterprise_Linux/7/html/Storage_Administration_Guide/ch-nfs.html
```

For information on how to configure access to NFS with SELinux, check the **SELinux User's and Administrator's Guide | Part 2. Managing Confined Services | Chapter 16. Network File System**.

```
https://access.redhat.com/documentation/en-
US/Red_Hat_Enterprise_Linux/7/html/SELinux_Users_and_Administrators_Guide/chap-
Managing_Confined_Services-Network_File_System.html
```

NFS Daemon	systemd unit file	Description
rpc.nfsd	**nfs-server.service**	Receives NFS requests from remote systems and translates them into requests for the local system.
rpc.mountd	**nfs-mountd.service**	Performs requested mount and unmount operations.
rpc.statd	**nfs-lock.service** **rpc-statd.service**	Provides locking services when a remote host reboots.
rpc.idmapd	**nfs-idmapd.service**	Maps user and group IDs to names.
rpc.gssd	nfs-secure.service rpc-gssd.service	Client support for the rpcsec_gss protocol for gss-api security in NFSv4.
rpc.svcgssd	**nfs-secure-server.service**	Server support for the rpcsec_gss protocol for gss-api security in NFSv4.

Table 11-3: NFS daemons and systemd unit files

NFS Daemons

NFS operates over a TCP/IP network. The remote computer that holds the file system makes it available to other computers on the network. It does so by exporting the file system, which entails making entries in an NFS configuration file called **/etc/exports**, as well as by running several daemons to support access by other systems. These include **rpc.mountd**, **rpc.nfsd**, and **rpc.gssd**. Access to your NFS server can be controlled by the **/etc/hosts.allow** and **/etc/hosts.deny** files. The NFS daemons are managed by **systemd** using several service unit files located in **/lib/systemd/system**. The NFS daemons and their **systemd** unit files are listed in Table 11-3.

The **nfs-server.service** file is shown here. Runtime configuration information is read from **/etc/sysconfig/nfs-utils** (EnvironmentFile).

nfs-server.service

```
[Unit]
Description=NFS Server and services
DefaultDependencies=no
Requires= network.target proc-fs-nfsd.mount rpcbind.target
Requires=nfs-mountd.service
Wants=rpc-statd.service  nfs-idmapd.service
Wants=rpc-statd-notify.service

After=local-fs.target
After=network.target proc-fs-nfsd.mount rpcbind.target nfs-mountd.service
After=nfs-idmapd.service nfs-statd.service
Before=rpc-statd-notify.service

# GSS services dependencies and ordering
Wants=auth-rpcgss-module.service
After=rpc-gssd.service gssproxy.service rpd-svcgssd.service

Wants=nfs-config.service
After=nfs-config.service

 [Service]
EnvironmentFile=-/etc/sysconfig/nfs-utils

Type=oneshot
RemainAfterExit=yes
ExecStartPre=/usr/sbin/exportfs -r
ExecStart=/usr/sbin/rpc.nfsd $RPCNFSDARGS
ExecStop=/usr/sbin/rpc.nfsd 0
ExecStopPost=/usr/sbin/exportfs -au
ExecStopPost=/usr/sbin/exportfs -f
ExecReload=/usr/sbin/exportfs -r

[Install]
WantedBy=multi-user.target
```

You can start up and shut down the NFS daemons using the **nfs.service** file and **systemd,** which you can invoke with the **service** command.

```
service nfs start
```

To have NFS is started automatically for the **multi-user.target** . You can use **chkconfig** or cockpit to turn NFS on or off.

```
chkconfig nfs on
```

The corresponding **systemd** unit files for the **nfsd**, **mountd**, **idmapd**, **statd**, and **svcgssd** daemons, will run these daemons.

The RHEL NFS server and support tools are located in the following packages.

nfs-utils	NFS server and supporting tools
nfs4-acl-tools	Access control list commands for NFS4 supported security
nfswatch	Monitor NFS usage

Make sure that your firewall allows NFS access, make sure that NFS4 is checked. Also be sure to allow SELinux to permit NFS access. Using system-config-selinux select Boolean on the sidebar, and then locate NFS and make sure "Support NFS home directories" is checked.

NFS Configuration: /etc/exports

An entry in the **/etc/exports** file specifies the file system to be exported and the hosts on the network that can access it. For the file system, enter its mountpoint, the directory to which it was mounted on the host system. This is followed by a list of hosts that can access this file system along with options to control that access. A comma-separated list of export options placed within a set of parentheses may follow each host. For example, you might want to give one host read-only access and another read and write access. If the options are preceded by an * symbol, they are applied to any host. A list of options is provided in Table 11-4. The format of an entry in the **/etc/exports** file is shown here:

```
directory-pathname   host-designation(options)
```

NFS Host Entries

You can have several host entries for the same directory, each with access to that directory:

```
directory-pathname   host(options) host(options)  host(options)
```

You have a great deal of flexibility when specifying hosts. For hosts within your domain, you can just use the hostname, whereas, for those outside, you need to use a fully qualified domain name. You can also use just the host's IP address. Instead of a single host, you can reference all the hosts within a specific domain, allowing access by an entire network. A simple way to do this is to use the * for the host segment, followed by the domain name for the network, such as ***.mytrek.com** for all the hosts in the **mytrek.com** network. Instead of domain names, you can use IP network addresses with a CNDR format where you specify the netmask to indicate a range of IP addresses.

You can also use an NIS netgroup name to reference a collection of hosts. The NIS netgroup name is preceded by an @ sign.

```
directory      host(options)
directory      *(options)
directory      *.domain(options)
directory      192.168.1.0/255.255.255.0(options)
directory      @netgroup(options)
```

General Option	Description
`secure`	Requires that requests originate on secure ports, those less than 1024. This is on by default.
`insecure`	Turns off the `secure` option.
`ro`	Allows only read-only access. This is the default.
`rw`	Allows read/write access.
`sync`	Performs all writes when requested. This is the default.
`async`	Performs all writes when the server is ready.
`no_wdelay`	Performs writes immediately, not checking to see if they are related.
`wdelay`	Checks to see if writes are related, and if so, waits to perform them together. Can degrade performance. This is the default.
`hide`	Automatically hides an exported directory that is the subdirectory of another exported directory.
`subtree_check`	Checks parent directories in a file system to validate an exported subdirectory. This is the default.
`no_subtree_check`	Does not check parent directories in a file system to validate an exported subdirectory.
`insecure_locks`	Does not require authentication of locking requests. Used for older NFS versions.
User ID Mapping	**Description**
`all_squash`	Maps all UIDs and GIDs to the anonymous user.
`no_all_squash`	The opposite option to `all_squash`. This is the default setting.
`root_squash`	Maps requests from remote root user to the anonymous UID/GID. This is the default.
`no_root_squash`	Turns off root squashing. Allows the root user to access as the remote root.
`anonuid`	Sets explicitly the UID and GID of the anonymous account used for `all_squash` and `root_squash` options.

Table 11-4: The /etc/exports Options

NFS Options

Options in **/etc/exports** operate as permissions to control access to exported directories. Read-only access is set with the `ro` option, and read/write with the **rw** option. The **sync** and **async** options specify whether a write operation is performed immediately (**sync**) or when the server is ready to handle it (**async**). By default, write requests are checked to see if they are related, and if so, they are written together (**wdelay**). This can degrade performance. You can override this default with **no_wdelay** and have writes executed as they are requested. If two directories are exported, where one is the subdirectory of another, the subdirectory is not accessible unless it is explicitly mounted (**hide**). In other words, mounting the parent directory does not make the subdirectory accessible. The subdirectory remains hidden until also mounted. You can overcome this restriction with the **no_hide** option (though this can cause problems with some file systems). If an exported directory is actually a subdirectory in a larger file system, its parent directories are checked to make sure that the subdirectory is the valid directory (**subtree_check**). This option works well with read-only file systems but can cause problems for write-enabled file systems, where filenames and directories can be changed. You can cancel this check with the **no_subtree_check** option.

NFS User-Level Access

Along with general options, there are also options that apply to user-level access. As a security measure, the client's root user is treated as an anonymous user by the NFS server. This is known as squashing the user. In the case of the client root user, squashing prevents the client from attempting to appear as the NFS server's root user. Should you want a particular client's root user to have root-level control over the NFS server, you can specify the **no_root_squash** option. To prevent any client user from attempting to appear as a user on the NFS server, you can classify them as anonymous users (the **all_squash** option). Such anonymous users only have access to directories and files that are part of the anonymous group.

Normally, if a user on a client system has a user account on the NFS server, that user can mount and access his or her files on the NFS server. However, NFS requires the User ID for the user be the same on both systems. If this is not the case, he or she is considered to be two different users. To overcome this problem, you can use an NIS service, maintaining User ID information in just one place, the NIS password file.

NFS /etc/exports Example

Examples of entries in an **/etc/exports** file are shown here. Read-only access is given to all hosts to the file system mounted on the **/pub** directory, a common name used for public access. Users, however, are treated as anonymous users (**all_squash**). Read and write access is given to the **lizard.mytrek.com** computer for the file system mounted on the **/home/mypics** directory. The next entry allows access by **rabbit.mytrek.com** to the NFS server's CD-ROM, using only read access. The last entry allows anyone secure access to **/home/richlp**.

/etc/exports

```
/pub              *(ro,insecure,all_squash,sync)
/home/mypics     lizard.mytrek.com(rw,sync)
/media/cdrom      rabbit.mytrek.com(ro,sync)
/home/richlp      *(secure,sync)
```

Applying Changes

Each time your system starts up the NFS server (usually when the system starts up), the **/etc/exports** file will be read and those directories specified will be exported. When a directory is exported, an entry for it is made in the **/var/lib/nfs/xtab** file. It is this file that NFS reads and uses to perform the actual exports. Entries are read from **/etc/exports** and corresponding entries made in **/var/lib/nfs/xtab**. The **xtab** file maintains the list of actual exports.

If you want to export added entries in the **/etc/exports** file immediately, without rebooting, you can use the **exportfs** command with the **-a** option. It is helpful to add the **-v** option to display the actions that NFS is taking. Use the same options to effect any changes you make to the **/etc/exports** file.

```
exportfs -a -v
```

If you later make changes to the **/etc/exports** file, you can use the **-r** option to re-export its entries. The **-r** option will re-sync the **/var/lib/nfs/xtab** file with the **/etc/exports** entries, removing any other exports or any with different options.

```
exportfs -r -v
```

To both export added entries and re-export changed ones, you can combine the **-r** and **-a** options.

```
exportfs -r -a -v
```

Manually Exporting File Systems

You can also use the **exportfs** command to manually export file systems instead of using entries for them in the **/etc/exports** file. Export entries will be added to the **/var/lib/nfs/xtab** file directly. With the **-o** option, you can list various permissions and then follow them with the host and file system to export. The host and file system are separated by a colon. For example, to manually export the **/home/myprojects** directory to **golf.mytrek.com** with the permissions **ro** and **insecure**, you use the following:

```
exportfs -o rw,insecure golf.mytrek.com:/home/myprojects
```

You can also use **exportfs** to un-export a directory that has already been exported, either manually or by the **/etc/exports** file. Just use the **-u** option with the host and the directory exported. The entry for the export will be removed from the **/var/lib/nfs/xtab** file. The following example will un-export the **/home/foodstuff** directory that was exported to **lizard.mytrek.com**:

```
exportfs -u lizard.mytrek.com:/home/foodstuff
```

NFSv4

NFS version 4 is the new version of the NFS protocol with enhanced features like greater security, reliability, and speed. It is the default NFS server for RHEL. The NFS client (**nfs-utils** package) supports both NFSv3 and NFSv4. When you mount an NFSv4 file system, you use still use the **nfs** file type. See the **nfs** man page for more details.

In the **/etc/exports** file, you can use the **fsid=0** option to specify the root export location.

```
/home/richlp          *(fsid=0,ro,sync)
```

The preceding entry lets you mount the file system to the **/home/richlp** directory without having to specify it in the mount operation.

```
mount -t nfs  rabbit.mytrek.com:/  /home/dylan/projects
```

NFSv4 also supports the RPCSEC_GSS (Remote Procedure Call Security, Generic Security Services) security mechanism which provides for private/public keys, encryption, and authentication with support for Kerberos.

Tip: To see what file systems are exported currently by an NFS server, you can use the **showmount** command with the **-e** option, **showmount -e** *nfserver*. To see what client hosts mount file systems on the NFS server, you use **showmount** with no options.

NFS File and Directory Security with NFS4 Access Lists

With NFS4 you can set up access control lists (ACL) for particular directories and files. You use the NFS4 ACL tools to manage these lists (**nfs4-acl-tools** package). The NFS4 file system ACL tools include **nfs4_getfacl**, **nfs4_setfacl**, and **nfs4_editfacl**. Check the Man page for each for detailed options and examples. **nfs4_getfacl** will list the access controls for a specified file or directory. **nfs4_setfacl** will create access controls for a directory or file, and **nfs4_editfacl** will let you change them. **nfs4_editfacl** simply invokes **nfs_setfacl** with the **-e** option. When editing access controls, you are placed in an editor where you can make your changes. For setting access controls, you can read from a file, the standard input, or list the control entries on the command line.

The file and directory access controls are more refined that the standard permissions. The ACL entries follow the syntax described in detail on the **nfs4_acl** Man page. An ACL entry begins with an entry type such as an accept or deny entry (**A** or **D**); followed by an ACL flag, which can specify group or inheritance capability and then the principal to which the ACL is applied; and finally, the list of access options, such as **r** for read or **w** for write. The principal is usually a user URL that is to be permitted or denied access. You can also specify groups, but you need to set the **g** group flag. The special URLs OWNER@, GROUP@, and EVERYONE@ correspond to the owner, group, and other access used on standard permissions. The following example provides full access to the owner but gives only read and execute access to the user **george@rabbit.com**. Group write and execute access is denied.

```
A::OWNER@:rwadtTnNcCy
A::george@rabbit.com:rxtncy
D:g:GROUP@:waxtc
```

In addition to read, write, and execute permissions (**r**,**w**,**x**), ACL lists also provide attribute reads (**t**,**n**) and attribute writes (**T**,**N**), as well as ACL read (**c**) and write (**C**) access. NFS read and write synchronization is enabled with the **y** option. The ability to delete files and directories is provided by the **d** option and for subdirectories with the **D** option. The **a** option lets you append data and create subdirectories. Keep in mind that **rtncy** are all read options, whereas **wadDTNC** are write options, while **x** remains the execute option. You will need **y** for any synchronized access. The **C** option, in particular, is very powerful as it allows the user to change the access controls (lowercase **c** allows only reading of the access controls).

Controlling Accessing to NFS Servers

You can use several methods to control access to your NFS server, such as using **hosts.allow** and **hosts.deny** to permit or deny access, as well as using your firewall to intercept access.

/etc/hosts.allow and /etc/hosts.deny

The **/etc/hosts.allow** and **/etc/hosts.deny** files are used to restrict access to services provided by your server to hosts on your network or on the Internet (if accessible). For example, you can use the **hosts.allow** file to permit access by certain hosts to your FTP server. Entries in the

hosts.deny file explicitly deny access to certain hosts. For NFS, you can provide the same kind of security by controlling access to specific NFS daemons. The entries in the hosts.allow file are the same you specified in the **shares-admin** tool's Add Allow hosts window (Share Folder).

Portmapper Service

The first line of defense is to control access to the portmapper service. The portmapper tells hosts where the NFS services can be found on the system. Restricting access does not allow a remote host even to locate NFS. For a strong level of security, you should deny access to all hosts except those that are explicitly allowed. In the **hosts.deny** file, you place the following entry, denying access to all hosts by default. ALL is a special keyword denoting all hosts.

```
portmap:ALL
```

In the **hosts.allow** file, you then enter the hosts on your network, or any others that you want to permit access to your NFS server. Again, you specify the portmapper service and then list the IP addresses of the hosts you are permitting access. You can list specific IP addresses or a network range using a netmask. The following example allows access only by hosts in the local network, 192.168.0.0, and to the host 10.0.0.43. You can separate addresses with commas:

```
portmap: 192.168.0.0/255.255.255.0, 10.0.0.43
```

The portmapper is also used by other services such as NIS. If you close all access to the portmapper in **hosts.deny**, you will also need to allow access to NIS services in **hosts.allow**, if you are running them. These include ypbind and ypserver. In addition, you may have to add entries for remote commands like `ruptime` and `rusers`, if you are supporting them.

It is also advisable to add the same level of control for specific NFS services. In the **hosts.deny** file, you add entries for each service, as shown here:

```
mountd:ALL
rquotad:ALL
statd:ALL
lockd:ALL
```

Then, in the **hosts.allow** file, you can add entries for each service:

```
mountd:  192.168.0.0/255.255.255.0, 10.0.0.43
rquotad: 192.168.0.0/255.255.255.0, 10.0.0.43
statd:   192.168.0.0/255.255.255.0, 10.0.0.43
lockd:   192.168.0.0/255.255.255.0, 10.0.0.43
```

Netfilter Rules

You can further control access using Netfilter to check transmissions from certain hosts on the ports used by NFS services. portmapper uses port 111, and nfsd uses 2049. Netfilter is helpful if you have a private network that has an Internet connection and you want to protect it from the Internet. Usually, a specific network device, such as an Ethernet card, is dedicated to the Internet connection. The following examples assume that device **eth1** is connected to the Internet. Any packets attempting access on port 111 or 2049 are refused.

```
iptables -A INPUT -i eth1 -p 111 -j DENY
iptables -A INPUT -i eth1 -p 2049 -j DENY
```

To enable NFS for your local network, you will have to allow packet fragments. Assuming that **eth0** is the device used for the local network, you could use the following example:

```
iptables -A INPUT -i eth0 -f -j ACCEPT
```

Mounting NFS File Systems: NFS Clients

Once NFS makes directories available to different hosts, those hosts can then mount those directories on their own systems and access them. The host needs to be able to operate as an NFS client. Current Linux kernels all have NFS client capability built in. This means that any NFS client can mount a remote NFS directory that it has access to by performing a simple mount operation.

Mounting NFS Automatically: /etc/fstab

You can mount an NFS directory either by an entry in the **/etc/fstab** file or by an explicit `mount` command. You have your NFS file systems mounted automatically by placing entries for them in the **/etc/fstab** file. An NFS entry in the **/etc/fstab** file has a mount type of NFS. An NFS file system name consists of the hostname of the computer it is located on, followed by the pathname of the directory where it is mounted. The two are separated by a colon. For example, **rabbit.trek.com:/home/project** specifies a file system mounted at **/home/project** on the **rabbit.trek.com** computer. The format for an NFS entry in the **/etc/fstab** file follows. The file type for NFS versions 1 through 3 is **nfs**, whereas for NFS version 4 it is **nfs4**.

```
host:remote-directory    local-directory      nfs    options    0   0
```

You can also include several NFS-specific mount options with your NFS entry. You can specify the size of datagrams sent back and forth and the amount of time your computer waits for a response from the host system. You can also specify whether a file system is to be hard-mounted or soft-mounted. For a *hard-mounted* file system, your computer continually tries to make contact if for some reason the remote system fails to respond. A soft-mounted file system, after a specified interval, gives up trying to make contact and issues an error message. A hard mount is the default. A system making a hard-mount attempt that continues to fail will stop responding to user input as it tries continually to achieve the mount. For this reason, soft mounts may be preferable, as they will simply stop attempting a mount that continually fails. Table 11-5 and the Man pages for `mount` contain a listing of these NFS client options. They differ from the NFS server options indicated previously.

An example of an NFS entry follows. The remote system is **rabbit.mytrek.com**, and the filesystem is mounted on **/home/projects**. This file system is to be mounted on the local system as the **/home/dylan/projects** directory. The **/home/dylan/projects** directory must already be created on the local system. The type of system is NFS, and the **timeo** option specifies the local system waits for up to 20 tenths of a second (two seconds) for a response. The mount is a soft mount and can be interrupted by NFS.

```
rabbit.mytrek.com:/home/projects /home/dylan/projects  nfs  soft,intr,timeo=20
```

Mounting NFS Manually: mount

You can also use the `mount` command with the **-t nfs** option to mount an NFS file system explicitly. For an NFSv4 file system you use **-t nfs4**. To mount the previous entry explicitly, use the following command:

```
mount -t nfs -o soft,intr,timeo=20 rabbit.mytrek.com:/home/projects \
/home/dylan/projects
```

You can, of course, unmount an NFS directory with the `umount` command. You can specify either the local mountpoint or the remote host and directory, as shown here:

```
umount /home/dylan/projects
umount  rabbit.mytrek.com:/home/projects
```

Option	Description
`rsize=`*n*	The number of bytes NFS uses when reading files from an NFS server. The default is 1,024 bytes. A size of 8,192 can greatly improve performance.
`wsize=`*n*	The number of bytes NFS uses when writing files to an NFS server. The default is 1,024 bytes. A size of 8,192 can greatly improve performance.
`timeo=`*n*	The value in tenths of a second before sending the first retransmission after a timeout. The default value is seven-tenths of a second.
`retry=`*n*	The number of minutes to retry an NFS mount operation before giving up. The default is 10,000 minutes (one week).
`retrans=`*n*	The number of retransmissions or minor timeouts for an NFS mount operation before a major timeout (default is 3). At that time, the connection is canceled or a "server not responding" message is displayed.
`soft`	Mount system using soft mount.
`hard`	Mount system using hard mount. This is the default.
`intr`	Allows NFS to interrupt the file operation and return to the calling program. The default is not to allow file operations to be interrupted.
`bg`	If the first mount attempt times out, continues trying the mount in the background. The default is to fail without backgrounding.
`tcp`	Mounts the NFS filesystem using the TCP protocol, instead of the default UDP protocol.

Table 11-5: NFS Mount Options

Mounting NFS on Demand: autofs

You can also mount NFS file systems using the automount service, autofs. This requires added configuration on the client's part. The autofs service will mount a file system only when you try to access it. A directory change operation (**cd**) to a specified directory will trigger the mount operation, mounting the remote file system at that time.

The autofs service is configured using a master file to list map files, which in turn lists the file systems to be mounted. The **/etc/auto.master** file is the autofs master file. The master file will list the root pathnames where file systems can be mounted along with a map file for each of those pathnames. The map file will then list a key (subdirectory), mount options, and the file systems that can be mounted in that root pathname directory. On some distributions, the **/auto** directory is already implemented as the root pathname for file systems automatically mounted. You can add your own file systems in the **/etc/auto.master** file along with your own map files, if you wish. You will find that the **/etc/auto.master** file contains the following entry for the **/auto** directory, listing **auto.misc** as its map file:

```
/auto     auto.misc    --timeout 60
```

Following the map file, you can add options, as shown in the preceding example. The `timeout` option specifies the number of seconds of inactivity to wait before trying to automatically unmount.

In the map file, you list the key, the mount options, and the file system to be mounted. The key will be the subdirectory on the local system where the file system is mounted. For example, to mount the **/home/projects** directory on the **rabbit.mytrek.com** host to the **/auto/projects** directory, you use the following entry:

```
projects  soft,intr,timeo=20   rabbit.mytrek.com:/home/projects
```

You can also create a new entry in the master file for an NFS file system, as shown here:

```
/myprojects    auto.myprojects   --timeout 60
```

You then create an **/etc/auto.myprojects** file and place entries in it for NFS files system mounts, like the following:

```
dylan    soft,intr,rw   rabbit.mytrek.com:/home/projects
newgame  soft,intr,ro   lizard.mytrek.com:/home/supergame
```

Network Information Service: NIS

On networks supporting NFS, many resources and devices are shared by the same systems. Normally, each system needs its own configuration files for each device or resource. Changes entail updating each system individually. However, NFS provides a special service called the Network Information System (NIS) that maintains such configuration files for the entire network. For changes, you need only to update the NIS files. NIS works for information required for most administrative tasks, such as those relating to users, network access, or devices. For example, you can maintain user and password information with an NIS service, having only to update those NIS password files.

Note: NIS+ is a more advanced form of NIS that provides support for encryption and authentication. However, it is more difficult to administer.

NIS was developed by Sun Microsystems and was originally known as Sun's Yellow Pages (YP). NIS files are kept on an NIS server (NIS servers are still sometimes referred to as YP servers). Individual systems on a network use NIS clients to make requests from the NIS server. The NIS server maintains its information on special database files called *maps*. Linux versions exist for both NIS clients and servers. Linux NIS clients easily connect to any network using NIS.

Note: Instead of NIS, many networks now use LDAP to manage user information and authentication.

The NIS client is installed as part of the initial installation with the **ypbind** and **yp-tools** packages. The NIS server can be installed from the **ypserv** package. NIS client programs are ypbind (the NIS daemon, **ypbind** package), ypwhich, ypcat, yppoll, ypmatch, yppasswd, and ypset (**yp-tools** package). Each has its own Man page with details of its use. The NIS server programs are ypserv (the NIS server package, **ypserv**), ypinit, yppasswdd, yppush, ypxfr, and netgroup, each also with its own Man page.

You can start and stop the **ypbind** client daemon and the **ypserv** NIS server with the **service** command. Alternatively, you can use cockpit to start and stop the NIS client and server daemons.

```
service ypbind start
service ypserv start
```

The NIS server is managed by **systemd** using the **ypbind.service** and **ypserv.service** unit file. Runtime configuration is read from /etc/sysconfig/ypbind (EnvironmentFile). SELinux (**setsebool**) is configured to allow access (ExecStartPre).

ypbind.service

```
[Unit]
Description=NIS/YP (Network Information Service) Clients to NIS Domain Binder
Requires=rpcbind.service
After=syslog.target network.target rpcbind.service ypserv.service NetworkManager-
wait-online.service
Before=systemd-user-sessions.service

[Service]
Type=notify
NotifyAccess=all
EnvironmentFile=-/etc/sysconfig/network
EnvironmentFile=-/etc/sysconfig/ypbind
ExecStartPre=/usr/libexec/ypbind-pre-setdomain
ExecStartPre=-/usr/sbin/setsebool allow_ypbind=1
ExecStart=/usr/sbin/ypbind -n $OTHER_YPBIND_OPTS
ExecStartPost=/usr/libexec/ypbind-post-waitbind
PrivateTmp=true

[Install]
WantedBy=multi-user.target
```

The **ypserv.service** file simply starts the NIS server (/usr/sbin/ypserv) .

ypserv.service

```
[Unit]
Description=NIS/YP (Network Information Service) Server
Requires=rpcbind.service
After=syslog.target network.target rpcbind.service

[Service]
Type=notify
NotifyAccess=all
EnvironmentFile=-/etc/sysconfig/network
ExecStart=/usr/sbin/ypserv -f $YPSERV_ARGS
PrivateTmp=true
```

```
[Install]
WantedBy=multi-user.target
```

Note: You can use system-config-authentication to specify the remote NIS server on your network.

NIS Servers

You have significant flexibility when setting up NIS servers. If you have a small network, you may need only one NIS domain, for which you would have one NIS server. For larger networks, you can divide your network into several NIS domains, each with its own server. Even if you only have one domain, you may want several NIS slave servers. For an NIS domain, you can have a master NIS server and several NIS slave servers. The slave servers can act as backups, in case the master server goes down. A slave server only contains copies of the configuration files set up on the NIS master server.

Configuring an NIS server involves several steps, listed here:

1. Define the NIS domain name that the NIS server will work for.
2. Start the **ypserv** daemon.
3. In the **/var/yp/Makefile** file, set any NIS server options and specify the configuration files to manage.
4. Use `/usr/lib/ypinit` to create the NIS versions of the configuration files.

Defining NIS Domain

You first have to define an NIS domain name. You can have the NIS domain defined whenever you start up your system, by defining the NIS_DOMAIN variable in the **/etc/sysconfig/network** file. To this variable, you assign the name you want to give your NIS domain. The following example defines the NIS domain called **myturtles.nis:**

```
NIS_DOMAIN=myturtles.nis
```

When first setting up the server, you may want to define your NIS domain name without having to restart your system. You can do so with the `domainname` command, as shown here:

```
domainname myturtles.nis
```

NIS server options are kept in the **/etc/ypserv.conf** file. Check the man page for that file for details. You can start the NIS server with the `ypserv` startup script:

```
service ypserv start
```

Setting NIS Server Options

Next edit the **/var/yp/Makefile** file to select the configuration files that the NIS server will maintain, along with setting any NIS server options. Standard options as well as most commonly used configuration files are usually already set up.

NIS server options are listed first. The **NOPUSH** option will be set to true, indicating that there are no slave NIS servers. If you are setting up any slave NIS servers for this domain, you will have to set this option to false:

```
NOPUSH = true
```

The minimum user and group IDs are set to 500. These are set using the **MINUID** and **MINGID** variables:

```
MINUID=500
MINGID=500
```

Most distributions use a shadow password and shadow group files to encrypt passwords and groups; the **MERGE_PASSWD** and **MERGE_GROUP** settings will be set to true. NIS will merge shadow password information into its password file:

```
MERGE_PASSWD=true
MERGE_GROUP=true
```

The directories where NIS will find password and other configuration files are then defined using the **YPSRCDIR** and **YPPWDIR** variables. Normally, the **/etc** directory holds your configuration files:

```
YPSRCDIR = /etc
YPPWDDIR = /etc
```

Then the configuration files that NIS can manage are listed. Here, you will find entries like **PASSWD** for password, **GROUP** for your groups, and **PRINTCAP** for your printers. A sample of the entries are shown here:

```
GROUP       = $(YPPWDDIR)/group
PASSWD      = $(YPPWDDIR)/passwd
SHADOW      = $(YPPWDDIR)/shadow
GSHADOW     = $(YPPWDDIR)/gshadow
ALIASES     = /etc/aliases
ETHERS      = $(YPSRCDIR)/ethers     # ethernet addresses (for rarpd)
BOOTPARAMS  = $(YPSRCDIR)/bootparams # for booting Sun boxes (bootparamd)
HOSTS       = $(YPSRCDIR)/hosts
NETWORKS    = $(YPSRCDIR)/networks
PRINTCAP    = $(YPSRCDIR)/printcap
PROTOCOLS   = $(YPSRCDIR)/protocols
```

Specifying Shared Files

The actual files that are shared on the network are listed in the **all:** entry, which follows the list of configuration files. Only some of the files defined are listed as shared, those listed in the first line after **all:**. The remaining lines are automatically commented out (with a preceding **#** sign). You can add files by removing the **#** sign or moving their entries to the first line.

```
all:  passwd group hosts rpc services netid protocols mail \
      # netgrp shadow publickey networks ethers bootparams printcap \
      # amd.home auto.master auto.home auto.local passwd.adjunct \
      # timezone locale netmasks
```

Be sure not to touch the remainder of the Makefile.

Creating the NIS Database

You then enter the **ypinit** command with the **-m** option to create the NIS database consisting of the NIS configuration files. Your NIS server will be detected, and then you will be asked to enter the names of any slave NIS servers used on this NIS domain. If there are any, enter them. When you are finished, press CTRL-D. The NIS database files are then created.

```
ypinit -m
```

For an NIS slave server, you would use

```
ypinit -s masterhost
```

Should you receive the following error, it most likely means that your NIS server was not running. Be sure to start ypserv before you run **ypinit**.

```
failed to send 'clear' to local ypserv: RPC: Program not registeredUpdating
```

If you later need to update your NIS server files, you would change to the **/var/yp** directory and issue the **make** command.

```
cd /var/yp
make
```

Controlling Access

The **/var/yp/securenets** file enables access by hosts to your NIS server. Hosts can be referenced by network or individually. Entries consist of a subnet mask and an IP address. For example, you could give access to all the hosts in a local network with the following entry:

```
255.255.255.0  192.168.1.0
```

For individual hosts, you can use the mask 255.255.255.255 or just the term "host," as shown here:

```
host   192.168.1.4
```

Controlling how different hosts access NIS shared data is determined in **/etc/ypserv.conf**.

Netgroups

You can use NIS to set up netgroups, which allow you to create network-level groups of users. Whereas normal groups are created locally on separate hosts, an NIS netgroup can be used for network-wide services. For example, you can use NIS netgroups to control access to NFS file systems. Netgroups are defined in the **/etc/netgroup** file. Entries consist of a netgroup name followed by member identifiers consisting of three segments: the host, the user, and the NIS domain:

```
group    (host, user, NIS-domain) (host, user, NIS-domain) ...
```

For example, in the NIS domain **myturtles.nis**, to define a group called **myprojects** that consist of the user **chris** on the host **rabbit**, and the user **george** on the host **lizard.mytrek.com**, you would use the following:

```
myprojects (rabbit, chris, myturtles.nis) \
                          (lizard.mytrek.com, george, myturtles.nis)
```

A blank segment will match on any value. The following entry includes all users on the host **rabbit**:

```
newgame (rabbit,,myturtles.ni)
```

If your use of a group doesn't need either a user or a host segment, you can eliminate one or the other using a hyphen (-). The following example generates a netgroup consisting just of hostnames, with no usernames:

```
myservers (rabbit,-,) (turtle.mytrek.com,-,)
```

You can then reference different netgroups in various configuration files by prefixing the netgroup name with an @ sign, as shown here:

```
@newgame
```

NIS Clients

For a host to use NIS on your network, you first need to specify your NIS domain name on that host. In addition, your NIS clients need to know the name of your NIS server. If you installed Linux on a network already running NIS, you may have already entered this information during the installation process. NIS client applications are installed with the **yp-tools** package.

Specifying the NIS Domain and Server

You can specify your NIS domain name and server with the authconfg-gtk tool, which you can access from the Settings window. In that window, select Authentication. This opens the Authentication Configuration window. On the User Information panel, click the Configure NIS button to open a dialog where you can enter the name of the NIS domain as well as the NIS server. Be sure also to enable NIS on the User Information panel. The NIS domain will be saved in the **/etc/sysconfig/network** file, and the NIS server, in the **/etc/yp.conf** file.

Accessing the Server

Each NIS client host on your network then has to run the ypbind NIS client to access the server. In the client's **/etc/yp.conf** file, you need to specify the NIS server it will use. The following entry would reference the NIS server at 192.168.1.1:

```
ypserver 192.168.1.1
```

Alternatively, you can specify the NIS domain name and the server it uses:

```
domain mydomain.nis  server servername
```

The authconfg-gtk tool will make the following entry in **/etc/yp.conf** for the **myturtle.nis** NIS domain using the **turtle.mytrek.com** server:

```
domain myturtles.nis server turtle.mytrek.com
```

To start the NIS client, you run the `ypbind` script:

```
service ypbind start
```

Then, to check that all is working, you can use `ypcat` to try to list the NIS password file:

```
ypcat passwd.
```

You can use **ypcat** to list any of the NIS configuration files. The **ypwhich** command will display the name of the NIS server your client is using. **ypmatch** can be used to find a particular entry in a configuration file.

```
ypmatch cecelia passwd.
```

Users can change their passwords in the NIS **passwd** file by using the **yppasswd** command. It works the same as the **passwd** command. You will also have to have the **yppasswdd** daemon running.

Specifying Configuration Files with nsswitch.conf

To ensure that the client accesses the NIS server for a particular configuration file, you should specify **nisplus** in file's entry in the **/etc/nsswitch.conf** file. The `nisplus` option refers to the NIS version 3. The **nis** option refers to the older NIS version 2. The **/etc/nsswitch.conf** file specifies where a host should look for certain kinds of information. For example, the following entry says to check the local configuration files (**files**) first and then the NIS server (**nisplus**) for password data:

```
passwd:    files nisplus
```

12. Print Services

Print services have become an integrated part of every Linux system. They allow you to use any printer on your system or network. Once treated as devices attached to a system directly, printers are now treated as network resources managed by print servers. In the case of a single printer attached directly to a system, the networking features become transparent, and the printer appears as just one more device. On the other hand, you could easily use a print server's networking capability to let several systems use the same printer. Although printer installation is almost automatic on most Linux distributions, it helps to understand the underlying process. Printing sites and resources are listed in Table 12-1.

The Common UNIX Printing System (CUPS) provides printing services. It is freely available under the GNU Public License. Though it is now included with most distributions, you can also download the most recent source code version of CUPS from **https://www.cups.org/**, which provides detailed documentation on installing and managing printers. CUPS is based on the Internet Printing Protocol (IPP), which was designed to establish a printing standard for the Internet (for more information, see **www.pwg.org/ipp**). Whereas the older line printer (LPD) based printing systems focused primarily online printers, an IPP-based system provides networking, PostScript, and web support. CUPS works like an Internet server and employs a configuration setup much like that of the Apache web server. Its network support lets clients directly access printers on remote servers, without having to configure the printers themselves. Configuration needs to be maintained only on the print servers.

If you cannot find the drivers for your printer, you may be able to download them from OpenPrinting database at **http://linux-foundation.org/en/OpenPrinting**. The site maintains an extensive listing of drivers. The RHEL **system-config-printer** tool can now download the most recent drivers from the OpenPrinting site.

Resource	Description
www.cups.org	Common Unix Printing System
www.pwg.org/ipp	Internet Printing Protocol
http://linux-foundation.org/en/OpenPrinting	OpenPrinting, print drivers

Table 12-1: Print Resources

Printer Services: CUPS

CUPS is the primary print server for most Linux distributions. GNOME provides integrated support for CUPS, allowing GNOME-based applications to access CUPS printers directly. Once you have installed your printers and configured your print server, you can print and manage your print queue using print clients. There are a variety of printer clients available for the CUPS server: the GNOME print manager, system-config-printer, the CUPS configuration tool, and various line printing tools like **lpq** and **lpc**. These are described in further detail later in this chapter. The CUPS configuration tool is a web-based configuration tool that can also manage printers and print jobs (open your browser and enter the URL **http://localhost:631**). A web page is displayed with entries for managing jobs, managing printers, and administrative tasks. Select the Manage Jobs entry to remove or reorder jobs you have submitted.

CUPS is managed by systemd using an on demand socket implementation with **cups.service**, **cups.socket**, and **cups.path** files. In addition, a special **printer.target** unit detects when a printer is connected to your system. The **cups.service** file runs the CUPS server,

/usr/sbin/cupsd (ExecStart). It is run when the **printer.target** is activated, which happens when a user connects a printer (WantedBy). The **cups.socket** unit file has CUPS listen for request at the CUPS socket, **/var/run/cups/cups.sock** (ListenStream). In effect, CUPS runs like the old inetd daemons, activated only when requested. The **cups.path** unit sets up CUPS print directories at **/var/spool/cups** (PathExistsGlob) when the system starts up (WantedBy=multi-user.target).

cups.service

```
[Unit]
Description=CUPS Printing Service
Documentation=man:cupsd(8)
After=network.target

[Service]
ExecStart=/usr/sbin/cupsd -l
Type=notify

[Install]
Also=cups.socket cups.path
WantedBy=printer.target
```

cups.socket

```
[Unit]
Description=CUPS Printing Service Sockets

[Socket]
ListenStream=/var/run/cups/cups.sock

[Install]
WantedBy=sockets.target
```

cups.path

```
[Unit]
Description=CUPS Printer Service Spool

[Path]
PathExistsGlob=/var/spool/cups/d*

[Install]
WantedBy=multi-user.target
```

Note: Line Printer, Next Generation (LPRng) was the traditional print server for Linux and UNIX systems, but it has since been dropped from RHEL. You can find out more about LPRng at **http://sourceforge.net/projects/lprng**.

Printer Configuration Files

Before you can use any printer, you first have to install it on a Linux system on your network. A local printer is installed directly on your own system. This involves creating an entry for the printer in a printer configuration file that defines the kind of printer it is, along with other features such as the device file and spool directory it uses. On CUPS, the printer configuration file is **/etc/cups/printers.conf**. Installing a printer is fairly simple: determine which device file to use for the printer and the configuration entries for it.

When your system prints a file, it makes use of special directories called spool directories. A print job is a file to be printed. When you send a file to a printer, a copy of it is made and placed in a spool directory set up for that printer. The location of the spool directory is obtained from the printer's entry in its configuration file. On Linux, the spool directory is located at **/var/spool/cups** under a directory with the name of the printer. For example, the spool directory for the **myepson** printer would be located at **/var/spool/cups/myepson**. The spool directory contains several files for managing print jobs. Some files use the name of the printer as their extension. For example, the **myepson** printer has the files **control.myepson**, which provides printer queue control, and **active.myepson** for the active print job, as well as **log.myepson,** which is the log file.

You can start, stop, and restart CUPS using the **service** command and the **cups** script, cockpit. When you make changes or install printers, be sure to restart CUPS to have your changes take effect. You can use the following command:

```
service cups restart
```

Printer Install and Configuration

There are several tools available for installing CUPS printers. The easiest method is to use the GNOME Printers tool (Settings). You can also use the older RHEL system-config-printer tool. Alternatively, you can use the CUPS Web browser-based configuration tools, included with the CUPS software. Finally, you can just edit the CUPS printer configuration files directly.

Automatic printer detection

When you attach a local printer to your system for the first time, the GNOME 3 printers tool automatically detects the printer and installs the appropriate driver. The printer is then listed in both the GNOME 3 printer tool and in the older system-config-printer. If the detection fails, you can use the GNOME 3 printer tool, accessible from Settings, to set up your printer.

Printer URI (Universal Resource Identifier)

Printers can be local or remote. Both are referenced using Universal Resource Identifiers (URI). URIs support both network protocols used to communicate with remote printers, and device connections used to reference local printers.

Remote printers are referenced by the protocol used to communicate with it, like **ipp** for the Internet Printing Protocol used for Unix network printers, **smb** for the Samba protocol used for Windows network printers, and **lpd** for the older LPRng Unix servers. Their URIs are similar to a Web URL, indicating the network address of the system the printer is connected to.

```
ipp://mytsuff.com/printers/queue1
smb://guest@lizard/myhp
```

For attached local printers, the URI will use the device connection and the device name. The **usb:** prefix is used for USB printers, **parallel**: for older printers connected to a parallel port, **serial:** for printers connected to a serial port, and **scsi:** for SCSI connected printers. For a locally attached USB printer, the URI would be something like this.

```
usb://Canon/S330
```

Settings Printers: GNOME 3 Printers tool

The GNOME 3 Printers tool, accessible from the Settings dialog as Printers, lists installed printers, letting you turn them on or off and access their job queues (see Figure 12-1). If no printers are detected, an "Add new printer" button is displayed which you can use to detect your printer. Select a printer to displays the printer name, model, location, and number of jobs. Click the Show Jobs button to list the current jobs for this printer. To make the printer the default, click the Default check box. You can also print a test page.

You can use the GNOME 3 Printers tool to configure your printer. Click the Options button to open the printer's options dialog. From the options dialog, you can configure printer features such as page setup, image, quality, and color. The Advanced tab lets you set specialized options such as contrast, ink type, and saturation.

Figure 12-1: GNOME 3 Printers tool

system-config-printer: Print Settings

To edit a printer configuration or to add a remote printer, you can also use system-config-printer, accessible as Printing (Sundry | Print Settings). This utility enables you to select the appropriate driver for your printer, as well as set print options such as paper size and print resolutions. You can configure a printer connected directly to your local computer or a printer on a remote system on your network. A printer configuration window is displayed showing icons for installed printers. As you add printers, icons for them are displayed in the Printer configuration window (see Figure 12-2).

Check the **System Administration Guide** for details on Print Settings, **Part 5 Servers | Chapter 14. File and Print Servers | 14.3. Print Settings**.

```
https://access.redhat.com/documentation/en-US/Red_Hat_Enterprise_Linux/7/html/System_Administrators_Guide/sec-Printer_Configuration.html
```

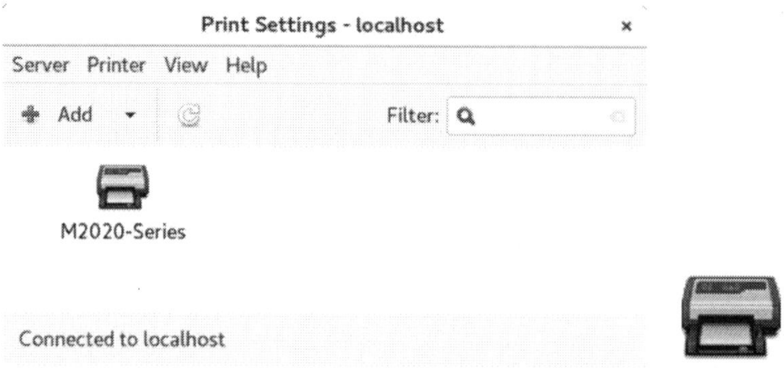

Figure 12-2: system-config-printer tool: multiple printers

To see the printer settings such as printer and job options, access controls, and policies, double-click on the printer icon or right-click and select Properties. The Printer Properties window opens up with five tabs: Settings, Policies, Access Control, Printer Options, and Job Options (see Figure 12-3).

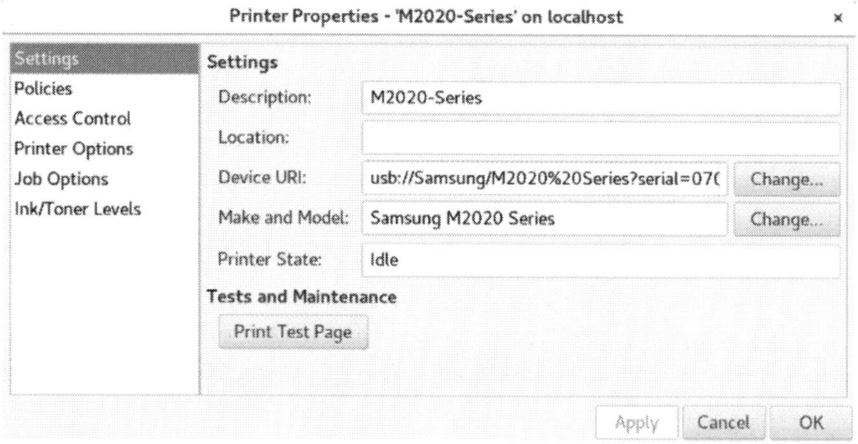

Figure 12-3: Printer properties window

CUPS Web Configuration Interface

One of the easiest ways to configure and install printers with CUPS is to use the CUPS configuration Web interface, a web browser–based tool. The CUPS configuration interface is a web-based tool that can also manage printers and print jobs. A web page is displayed with tabs for managing jobs and printers and performing administrative tasks.

You access the CUPS configuration tool using the **localhost** address and specifying port **631**. Enter the following URL into your web browser:

```
http://localhost:631
```

Entering the **localhost:631** URL in your Web browser opens the Home screen for the CUPS Web interface. There are tabs for various sections, as well as links for specialized tasks like adding printers or obtaining help (see Figure 12-4). Tabs include Administration, Classes, Help, Jobs, and Printers. You can manage and add printers on the Administration tab. The Printers tab will list installed printers with buttons for accessing their print queues, printer options, and job options, among others. The Jobs tab lists your print jobs and lets you manage them.

When you try to make any changes for the first time during the session, you will first be asked to enter the administrator's username (your username) and password (your user password), just as you would for the **sudo** command.

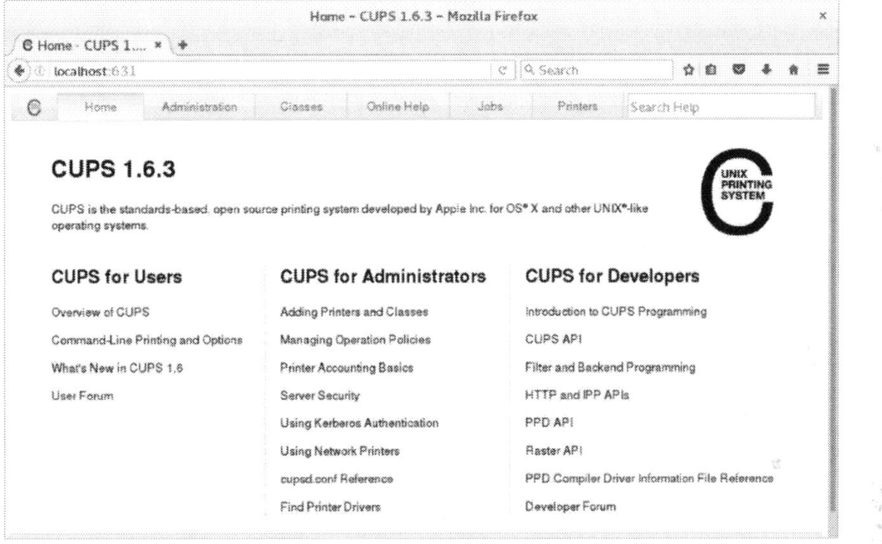

Figure 12-4: CUPS Web-based Configuration: Home tab

The Administration tab displays segments for Printers, Classes, Jobs, and the Server). The server section is where you allow printer sharing. Buttons allow you to view logs and change settings.

With the CUPS configuration tool, you install a printer on CUPS through a series of Web pages, each of which requests different information. To install a printer, click the Add Printer button either on the Home page or the Administration page. You first specify the protocol. On the next screen, you enter a URI to use for the printer. For a local printer, this is the protocol and the hostname. A page is displayed where you enter the printer name and location. A Sharing entry lets you choose to share the printer. The location is the host to which the printer is connected. The procedure is similar to **system-config-printer**. Subsequent pages will prompt you to enter the make and model of the printer, which you select from available listings. You can also load a PPD driver file instead if you have one. Click the Add Printer button when read. On the following page, you then set default options for your printer, like paper size and type, color, print quality, and resolution.

Configuring Remote Printers

To install a remote printer that is attached to a Windows system or another Linux system running CUPS, you specify its location using special URL protocols. For another CUPS printer on a remote host, the protocol used is **ipp**, for Internet Printing Protocol, whereas for a Windows printer, it would be **smb**. Older Unix or Linux systems using LPRng would use the **lpd** protocol.

Be sure your firewall is configured to allow access to remote printers. On the Trusted Services tab in system-config-firewall (Sundry | Firewall), be sure that the Samba and IPP services are checked. Samba allows access to Windows printers, and IPP allows access for Internet Printer Protocol printers usually found on other Linux systems. There will be entries for the Samba client and server, as well as IPP client and server.

To access an SMB shared remote printer, you need to install Samba and have the Server Message Block services enabled using the smb and nmb daemons. The Samba service should be enabled by default. If not, you can enable it using the **service** command as the **root** user. Open a terminal window (Utilities| Terminal), access the root user with the **su** command, and then enter a **service** command for the **smb** and **nmb** servers with the **enable** command.

```
su
service nmb enable
service smb enable
```

Configuring Remote Printers with system-config-printer

You can use system-config-printer to set up a remote printer on Linux, UNIX, or Windows networks. When you add a new printer or edit one, the New Printer/Select Connection dialog will list possible remote connection types. When you select a remote connection entry, a pane will be displayed where you can enter configuration information.

The location is specified using special URI protocols. For another CUPS printer on a remote host, the protocol used is **ipp**, for Internet Printing Protocol, whereas for a Windows printer, it would be **smb**. Older UNIX or Linux systems using LPRng would use the **lpd** protocol

To access an SMB shared remote printer, you need to install Samba and have the Server Message Block services enabled using the **smb** and **nmb** daemons. The Samba service will be enabled by default. The service is enabled using the **service** command as the **root** user. Open a terminal window (Utilities| Terminal), access the root user with the **su** command, and then enter a **service** command for the **smb** and **nmb** servers with the **enable** command.

```
su
service nmb enable
service smb enable
```

Configuring Remote Printers with CUPS Web-based Configuration

To use the CUPS configuration tool to install a remote printer, you specify the remote printer network protocol on the initial Add Printer page. You can choose from Windows, Internet Printing Protocol (other UNIX or Linux systems), Apple and HP JetDirect connected printers and the older LPD line printers. If a network printer is connected currently, it may be listed in the Discovered Network Printers list.

Configuring remote printers manually

In the **cupsd.conf** file, for a remote printer, the DeviceURI entry, instead of listing the device, will have an Internet address, along with its protocol. For example, a remote printer on a CUPS server (**ipp**) would be indicated as shown here (a Windows printer would use an **smb** protocol):

```
DeviceURI ipp://mystuff.com/printers/queue1
```

For a Windows printer, you first need to install, configure, and run Samba. (CUPS uses Samba to access Windows printers.) When you install the Windows printer on CUPS, you specify its location using the URL protocol **smb**. The user allowed to log in to the printer is entered before the hostname and separated from it by an `@` sign. On most configurations, this is the **guest** user. The location entry for a Windows printer called **myhp** attached to a Windows host named **lizard** is shown here. It's Samba share reference would be **//lizard/myhp**:

```
DeviceURI smb://guest@lizard/myhp
```

To enable CUPS on Samba, you also have to set the printing option in the **/etc/samba/smb.conf** file to **cups**, as shown here:

```
printing = cups
printcap name = cups
```

Note: To configure a shared Linux printer for access by Windows hosts, you need to configure it as an SMB shared printer. You do this with Samba.

CUPS Configuration files

CUPS configuration files are placed in the **/etc/cups** directory. These files are listed in Table 12-2. The **classes.conf**, **printers.conf**, and **client.conf** files can be managed by the web interface. The **printers.conf** file contains the configuration information for the different printers you have installed. Any of these files can be edited manually if you wish.

cupsd.conf

The CUPS server is configured with the **cupsd.conf** file located in **/etc/cups**. You must edit configuration options manually; the server is not configured with the web interface. Your installation of CUPS installs a commented version of the **cupsd.conf** file with each option listed, though most options will be commented out. Commented lines are preceded with a **#** symbol. Each option is documented in detail. The server configuration uses an Apache web server syntax consisting of a set of directives. As with Apache, several of these directives can group other directives into blocks.

For a detailed explanation of **cupsd.conf** directives check the CUPS documentation for **cupsd.conf**. You can also reference this documentation from the Online Help page | References link on the CUPS browser-based administration tool, **http://localhost:631**.

```
http://www.cups.org/documentation.php/doc-2.1/man-cupsd-conf.html
```

Filename	Description
classes.conf	Contains configurations for different local printer classes
client.conf	Lists specific options for specified clients
cupsd.conf	Configures the CUPS server, **cupsd**
printers.conf	Contains printer configurations for available local printers
cups-files.conf	File and directories used by CUPS
cups-browsed.conf	Access to remote and local printers
subscriptions.conf	Subscription controls for printer and print job information

Table 12-2: CUPS Configuration Files

For a detailed explanation of **cupsd.conf** directives check the CUPS documentation for **cupsd.conf**. You can also reference this documentation from the Online Help page | References link on the CUPS browser-based administration tool, **http://localhost:631**.

```
http://www.cups.org/documentation.php/doc-2.1/man-cupsd-conf.html
```

The **cupsd.conf** file begins with setting the log level to **warn** for warning.

```
LogLevel warn
```

The Listen directives are sets the machine and socket on which to receive connections. These are set by default to the local machine, localhost port 631. If you are using a dedicated network interface for connecting to a local network, you would add the network card's IP address, allowing access from machines on your network.

```
# Only listen for connections from the local machine.
Listen localhost:631
Listen /var/run/cups/cups.sock
```

Browsing directives allow your local printers to be detected on your network, enabling them to be shared. For shared printing, the Browsing directive is set to on (it is set to Off by default). A BrowseOrder of allow, deny will deny all browse transmissions, then first check the BrowseAllow directives for exceptions. A reverse order (deny, allow) does the opposite, accepting all browse transmissions, and then first check for those denied by BrowseDeny directives. The default **cupsd.conf** file has a BrowseOrder allow, deny directive followed by a BrowseAllow directive which is set to **all**. To limit this to a particular network, use the IP address of the network instead of **all**. The BrowseLocalProtocols lists the network protocols to use for advertising the printers on a local network. The BrowseAddress directive will make your local printers available as shared printers on the specified network. It is set to @LOCAL to allow access on your local network. You can add other BrowseAddress directives to allow access by other networks.

```
# Show shared printers on the local network.
Browsing On
BrowseOrder allow,deny
BrowseAllow all
BrowseLocalProtocols CUPS dnssd
BrowseAddress @LOCAL
```

CUPS supports both Basic and Digest forms of authentication, specified in the **AuthType** directive. Basic authentication uses a user and password. For example, to use the web interface, you are prompted to enter the root user and the root user password. Digest authentication makes use of user and password information kept in the CUPS **/etc/cups/passwd.md5** file, using MD5 versions of a user and password for authentication. In addition, CUPS also supports a BasicDigest and Negotiate authentication. BasicDigest will use the CUPS md5 password file for basic authentication. Negotiate will use Kerberos authentication. The default authentication type is set using the DefaultAuthType directive, set to Basic.

```
# Default authentication type, when authentication is required...
DefaultAuthType Basic
```

Location Directives

Certain directives allow you to place access controls on specific locations. These can be printers or resources, such as the administrative tool or the spool directories. Location controls are implemented with the **Location** directive. There are several Location directives that control access. The first controls access to the server root directory, /. The Order allow, deny entry activates restrictions on access by remote systems. If there are no following Allow or Deny entries, then the default is to deny all. There is an implied Allow localhost with the Order allow, deny directive, always giving access to the local machine. In effect, access here is denied to all system, allowing access only by the local system.

```
# Restrict access to the server...
<Location />
  Order allow,deny
</Location>
```

Another **Location** directive is used to restrict administrative access, the **/admin** resource, adding a requirement for encryption. The **Order allow,deny** directive denies access to all systems, except for the local machine.

```
# Restrict access to the admin pages...
<Location /admin>
  Order allow,deny
</Location>
```

Allow from and **Deny from** directives can permit or deny access from specific hosts and networks. If you wanted just to allow access to a particular machine, you would use an Allow from directive with the machine's IP address. CUPS also uses **@LOCAL** to indicate your local network, and **IF(*name*)** for a particular network interface (*name* is the device name of the interface) used to access a network. Should you want to allow administrative access by all other systems on your local network, you can add the **Allow from @LOCAL**. If you add an **Allow** directive, you also have to explicitly add the **Allow localhost** to ensure access by your local machine.

```
# Restrict access to the admin pages...
<Location /admin>
  Allow from localhost
  Allow from @LOCAL
  Order allow,deny
</Location>
```

The following entry would allow access from a particular machine.

```
  Allow From 192.168.0.5
```

The next location directive restricts access to the CUPS configuration files, **/admin/conf**. The **AuthType default** directive refers to the default set by DefaultAuthType. The **Require user** directive references the **SystemGroup** directive, **@SYSTEM** (defined in the **cups-files.conf** file). Only users from that group are allowed access.

```
# Restrict access to configuration files...
<Location /admin/conf>
  AuthType Default
  Require user @SYSTEM
  Order allow,deny
</Location>
```

Default Operation Policy: Limit Directives

A default operation policy is then defined for access to basic administration, printer, print job, and owner operations. The default operation policy section begins with the **<Policy default>** directive. Limit directives are used to implement the directives for each kind of operation. Job operations covers tasks like sending a document, restarting a job, suspending a job, and restarting a job. Administrative tasks include modifying a printer configuration, deleting a printer, managing printer classes, and setting the default printer. Printer operations govern tasks like pausing a printer, enable or disable a printer, and shutting down a printer. The owner operations consist of just canceling a job and authenticating access to a job. Subscriptions are defined in the **/etc/cups/subscriptions.conf** file.

See the CUPS documentation on managing operations policies for more details.

```
http://www.cups.org/documentation.php/doc-2.1/policies.html
```

On all the default **Limit** directives, access is allowed only by the local machine (localhost), **Order allow,deny**.

The policy section begins with access controls for user and job information. The default for **JobPrivateAccess** limits access to owner, system, and access control lists. **JobPrivateValues** specifies values made private, such as the job name, originating host, and originating user. **SubscriptionPrivateAccess** and **SubscriptionPrivateValues** specify access for subscription attributes such notifications of printer events like job completed or job stopped.

Both the administrative and printer **Limit** directives are set to the **AuthType default** and limited to access by administrative users, **Require user @SYSTEM**. The administrative directive is shown here.

```
  # All administration operations require an administrator to authenticate...
  <Limit CUPS-Add-Modify-Printer CUPS-Delete-Printer CUPS-Add-Modify-Class CUPS-
Delete-Class CUPS-Set-Default CUPS-Get-Devices>
    AuthType Default
    Require user @SYSTEM
    Order deny,allow
  </Limit>
```

Both the job related and owner Limit directives require either owner or administrative authentication, **Require user @OWNER @SYSTEM**. The **Owner Limit** directive is shown here.

```
# Only the owner or an administrator can cancel or authenticate a job...
<Limit Cancel-Job CUPS-Authenticate-Job>
  Require user @OWNER @SYSTEM
  Order deny,allow
</Limit>
```

For all other tasks, **<Limit All>**, access is restricted to the local machine (localhost).

```
<Limit All>
 Order deny,allow
</Limit>
```

The **AuthClass** directive can be used within a **Limit** directive to specify the printer class allowed access. The **System** class includes the root, sys, and system users.

An authenticated set of policy directives follows the default policy, with similar entries and an added Limit directive to create and print jobs.

```
<Limit Create-Job Print-Job Print-URI Validate-Job>
  AuthType Default
  Order deny,allow
</Limit>
```

cupsctl

You can use the **cupsctl** command to modify your cupsd.conf file, rather than editing the file directly. Check the **cupsctl** Man page for details. The **cupsctl** command with no options will display current settings.

```
cupstctl
```

The changes you can make with this command are limited turning off remote administration or disabling shared printing. The major options you can set are:

remote-admin Enable or disable remote administration

remote-any Enable or disable remote printing

remote-printers Enable or disable the display of remote printers

share-printers Enable or disable sharing of local printers with other systems

printers.conf

Configured information for a printer will be stored in the **/etc/cups/printers.conf** file. You can examine this file directly, even making changes. Here is an example of a printer configuration entry. The **DeviceURI** entry specifies the device used, in this case, a USB printer. It is currently idle, with no jobs. The **OpPolicy** entry specifies the policy defined in the **cupsd.conf** file to be used for this printer.

```
# Printer configuration file for CUPS
# Written by cupsd
<Printer mycannon>
UUID urn:uuid:72f4abc6-9afe-35f6-47e3-35ae26e3fdc1
Info Cannon S330
Location
MakeModel Canon S300 - CUPS+Gutenprint v5.2.9 Simplified
DeviceURI usb://Canon/S330
State Idle
StateTime 1166554036
Accepting Yes
Shared Yes
JobSheets none none
QuotaPeriod 0
PageLimit 0
KLimit 0
OpPolicy default
ErrorPolicy stop-printer
</Printer>
```

subscriptions.conf

Configured information for printer and job information is located in the **/etc/cups/subscriptions.conf** file. Those receiving the information are specified by the **SubscriptionPrivateAccess** and **SubscriptionPrivateValues** directives in the policy section of the **cupd.conf** file. The **Events** directive specifies notifications of events to be sent, events such as job-completed, printer-stopped, and server-started. The **Owner** directive lists the users for this subscription. **LeaseDuration** is the time the subscription remains valid (0 value is the life of the print job or forever). **Interval** is the time between notifications. **Recipient** is the recipient URI for the notification. In the following example it is dbus:// (your desktop). You can find a complete list of directives and events at:

```
https://www.cups.org/documentation.php/doc-1.7/ref-subscriptions-conf.html
```

A sample **subscriptions.conf** file is shown here:

```
# Subscription configuration file for CUPS v1.6.3
# Written by cupsd on 2016-10-26 11:24
NextSubscriptionId 42
<Subscription 41>
Events printer-state-changed printer-restarted printer-shutdown printer-stopped
printer-added printer-deleted job-state-changed job-created job-completed job-
stopped
Owner richard
Recipient dbus://
LeaseDuration 3600
Interval 0
ExpirationTime 1477509828
NextEventId 1
</Subscription>
```

cups-files.conf

The files and directories that CUPS uses to manage print jobs can be configured in the **/etc/cups/cups-files.conf** file. The ErrorLog directive specified the CUPS error log output.

```
ErrorLog  /var/log/cups/error_log
```

The SystemGroup directive defines the users referenced by @SYSTEM in **cupsd.conf**.

```
SystemGroup sys root
```

cups-browsed.conf

The cups-browsed.conf file configures the cups-browsed daemon, used for browsing remote and local printers. The BrowseRemoteProtocoals defines the protocols to use.

```
BrowseRemoteProtocols  dnssd cups
```

The BrowseAllow directive can be used to restrict browsing to specified servers or networks.

```
BrowseAllow 192.168.1.0/24
```

The CreateIPPPritnerQueues directive allows the detection of non-CUPS IPP printers.

CUPS Command Line Print Clients

Once a print job is placed in a print queue, you can use any of several print clients to manage the printing jobs on your printer or printers, such as Klpq, the GNOME Print Manager, and the CUPS Printer Configuration tool for CUPS. You can also use several command line print CUPS clients. These include the **lpr**, **lpc**, **lpq**, and **lprm** commands. With these clients, you can print documents, list a print queue, reorder it, and remove print jobs, effectively canceling them. For network connections, CUPS features an encryption option for its commands, **-E**, to encrypt print jobs and print information sent on a network. Table 12-3 shows various printer commands.

Note: The command line clients have the same name, and much the same syntax, as the older LPR and LPRng command line clients used in Unix and older Linux systems.

lpr

The **lpr** client submits a job, and `lpd` then takes it in turn and places it on the appropriate print queue; **lpr** takes as its argument the name of a file. If no printer is specified, then the default printer is used. The **-P** option enables you to specify a particular printer. In the next example, the user first prints the file **preface** and then prints the file **report** to the printer with the name **myepson**:

```
$ lpr preface
$ lpr -P myepson report
```

lpc

You can use **lpc** to enable or disable printers, reorder their print queues, and re-execute configuration files. To use **lpc**, enter the command **lpc** at the shell prompt. You are then given an

lpc> prompt at which you can enter **lpc** commands to manage your printers and reorder their jobs. The **status** command with the name of the printer displays whether the printer is ready, how many print jobs it has, and so on. The **stop** and **start** commands can stop a printer and start it back up. The printers shown depend on the printers configured for a particular print server. A printer configured on CUPS will only show if you have switched to CUPS.

```
$ lpc
lpc> status myepson
myepson:
 printer is on device 'hal' speed -1
 queuing is enabled
 printing is enabled
 1 entry in spool area
```

Printer Management	Description
`lpr` *options file-list*	Prints a file, copies the file to the printer's spool directory, and places it on the print queue to be printed in turn. `-P` *printer* prints the file on the specified printer.
`lpq` *options*	Displays the print jobs in the print queue. `-P` *printer* prints the queue for the specified printer. `-l` prints a detailed listing.
`lpstat` *options*	Displays printer status.
`lprm` *options printjob-id* `or` *printer*	Removes a print job from the print queue. You identify a particular print job by its number as listed by `lpq`. `-P` *printer* removes all print jobs for the specified printer.
`lpc`	Manages your printers. At the `lpc>` prompt, you can enter commands to check the status of your printers and take other actions.

Table 12-3: CUPS Command Line Print Clients

lpq and lpstat

You can manage the print queue using the **lpq** and **lprm** commands. The **lpq** command lists the printing jobs currently on the print queue. With the `-P` option and the printer name, you can list the jobs for a particular printer. If you specify a username, you can list the print jobs for that user. With the **-l** option, **lpq** displays detailed information about each job. If you want information on a specific job, simply use that job's ID number with **lpq**. To check the status of a printer, use **lpstat**.

```
$ lpq
myepson is ready and printing
Rank    Owner  Jobs  File(s)           Total Size
active  chris    1   report            1024
```

lprm

The **lprm** command enables you to remove a print job from the queue, erasing the job before it can be printed. The **lprm** command takes many of the same options as **lpq**. To remove a specific job, use **lprm** with the job number. To remove all printing jobs for a particular printer, use the **-P** option with the printer name. **lprm** with no options removes the job printing currently. The following command removes the first print job in the queue (use **lpq** to obtain the job number):

```
lprm 1
```

CUPS Command Line Administrative Tools

CUPS provides command-line administrative tools like **lpadmin**, **lpoptions**, **lpinfo**, **cupsenable**, **cupsdisable**, **accept**, and **reject**. The **cupsenable** and **cupsdisable** commands start and stop print queues directly, whereas the **accept** and **reject** commands start and stop particular jobs. The **lpinfo** command provides information about printers, and **lpoptions** lets you set printing options. The **lpadmin** command lets you perform administrative tasks like adding printers and changing configurations. CUPS administrative tools are listed in Table 12-4.

Administration Tool	Description
`lpadmin`	CUPS printer configuration
`lpoptions`	Sets printing options
`cupsenable`	Activates a printer
`cupsdisable`	Stops a printer
`accept`	Allows a printer to accept new jobs
`reject`	Prevents a printer from accepting print jobs
`lpinfo`	Lists CUPS devices available

Table 12-4: CUPS Administrative Tools

lpadmin

You can use the **lpadmin** command to either set the default printer or configure various options for a printer. You can use the **-d** option to specify a particular printer as the default destination. Here **myepson** is made the default printer:

```
lpadmin -d myepson
```

The **-p** option lets you designate a printer for which to set various options. The following example sets printer description information:

```
lpadmin -p myepson  -D  Epson550
```

Certain options let you control per-user quotas for print jobs. The **job-k-limit** option sets the size of a job allowed per user, **job-page-limit** sets the page limit for a job and **job-quota-period** limits the number of jobs with a specified time frame. The following command set a page limit of 100 for each user:

```
lpadmin -p myepson  -o job-page-limit=100
```

User access control is determined with the **-u** option with an **allow** or **deny** list. Users allowed access are listed following the **allow:** entry and those denied access are listed with a `deny:` entry. Here access is granted to **chris** but denied to **aleina** and **larisa**.

```
lpadmin -p myepson -u allow:chris  deny:aleina,larisa
```

Use **all** or **none** to permit or deny access to all or no users. You can create exceptions by using **all** or `none` in combination with user-specific access. The following example allows access to all users except **justin**:

```
lpadmin -p myepson  -u allow:all   deny:justin
```

lpoptions

The **lpoptions** command lets you set printing options and defaults that mostly govern how your print jobs will be printed. For example, you can set the color or page format to be used with a particular printer. Default settings for all users are maintained by the root user in the **/etc/cups/lpoptions** file, and each user can create their own configurations, which are saved in their **.lpoptions** files. The **-l** option lists current options for a printer, and the **-p** option designates a printer (you can also set the default printer to use with the **-d** option).

```
lpoptions -p myepson -l
```

Printer options are set using the **-o** option along with the option name and value, **-o** *option=value.* You can remove a printer option with the **-r** option. For example, to print on both sides of your sheets, you can set the b option to **two-sided:**

```
lpoptions -p myepson -o sides=two-sided
```

To remove the option, use **-r**.

```
lpoptions -p myepson -r sides
```

To display a listing of available options, check the standard printing options in the CUPS Software Manual at **www.cups.org**.

cupsenable and cupsdisable

The **cupsenable** command starts a printer, and the **cupsdisable** command stops it. With the **-c** option, you can cancel all jobs on the printer's queue, and the **-r** option broadcasts a message explaining the shutdown.

```
cupsdisable myepson
```

accept and reject

The **accept** and **reject** commands let you control access to the printer queues for specific printers. The **reject** command prevents a printer from accepting jobs, whereas **accept** allows new print jobs.

```
reject myepson
```

lpinfo

The **lpinfo** command is a handy tool for letting you know what CUPS devices and drivers that are available on your system. Use the **-v** option for devices and the **-m** option for drivers.

```
lpinfo -m
```

13. Security Tools: Authorization, Encryption, and SELinux

authconfig
Pluggable Authentication Modules
Encryption
SELinux

Authorization, encryption, and permissions are all methods for controlling access. Authorizations can control access to administrative tools, making sure only valid and trusted users make changes to your system setup. Certain security packages control access to resources such as devices, messages, folders, and file systems. Pluggable Authentication Modules (PAM) is an authentication service that lets a system determine the method of authentication to be performed for users such as passwords, LDAP servers, or NIS servers.

For detailed information on Red Hat Enterprise Linux security check the **Security Guide** at:

```
https://access.redhat.com/documentation/en-
US/Red_Hat_Enterprise_Linux/7/html/Security_Guide/index.html
```

authconfig

To confirm that user identities are valid, your network may provide several authentication services. These can be enabled on your system using **authconfig**. Install both the **authconfig** and **authconfig-gtk** packages.

Check the **System-Level Authentication Guide** for details on authentication configuration, **Part 1. System Logins | Chapter 2: Configuring System Authentication | 2.2 Using Authconfig**

```
https://access.redhat.com/documentation/en-
US/Red_Hat_Enterprise_Linux/7/html/System-Level_Authentication_Guide/authconfig-
install.html
```

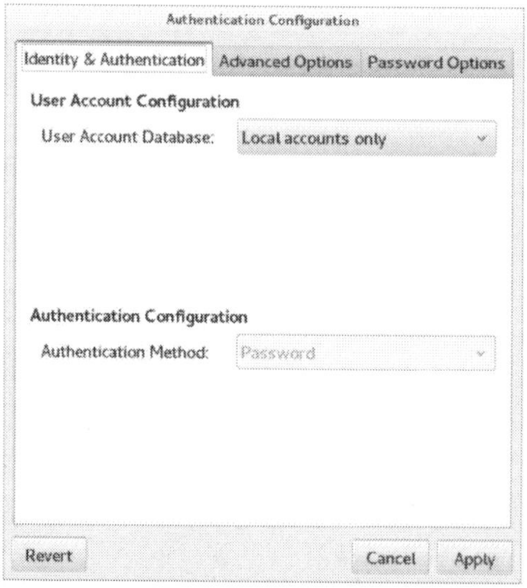

Figure 13-1: authconfig (System | Administration | Authentication)

You can invoke **authconfig** from Sundry as Authentication. The authconfig tool consists of three tabs, Identity & Authentication, Advanced Options, and Password Options (see Figure 13-1). On the Identity & Authentication tab, the User Account Database drop-down menu is used to specify a service like NIS and LDAP which maintain configuration information about systems and users on your network. If your network maintains LDAP, NIS, and Winbind authentication servers, you can enable support for them here, specifying their servers and domains. Entries available on the Identity and Authentication dialog will change according to the database you choose (see Figure 13-2). The LDAP and FreeIPA databases display a textbox where you can enter the address for your LDAP server. When you select a service from the User Account Database menu, the Identity and Authentication tab expands to list Authentication Configuration options. From the Authentication Method drop-down menu, you can select a Kerberos or password method. Kerberos is the default and will display entries for specifying the Kerberos KDC and administration server addresses.

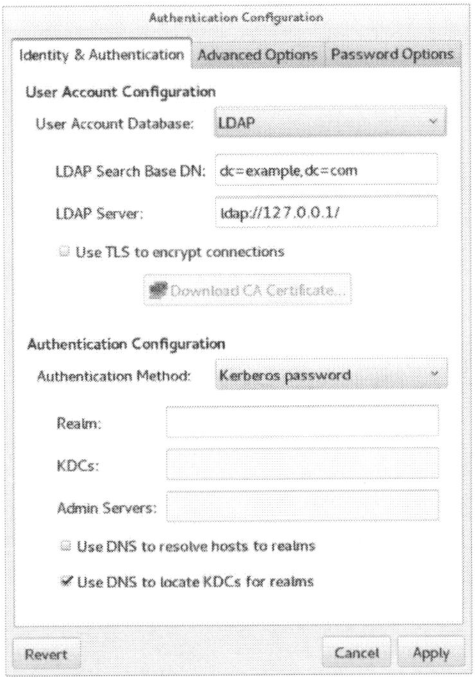

Figure 13-2: authconfig: LDAP entries

The Advanced Options tab lets you set authentication options like password hashing algorithm (see Figure 13-3). From a pop-up menu, you can select the password encryption codec, SHA512 is the default. Other options provide for more controlled access, like not creating user home folders until the user first logins, or checking **/etc/security/access.conf** for users to deny or allow access. You can also enable fingerprint reader support.

The Password Options tab lets you set conditions of possible passwords, including length, required characters such as uppercase and digits, and possible repeated characters.

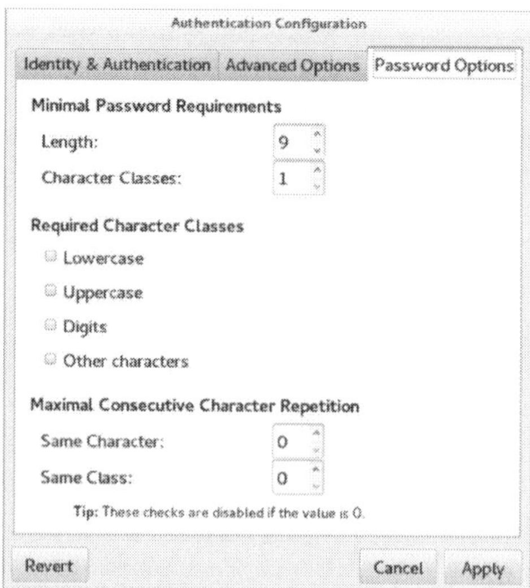

Figure 13-3: authconfig: Advanced Options and Password Options tabs

Pluggable Authentication Modules

Pluggable Authentication Modules (PAM) is an authentication service that lets a system determine the method of authentication to be performed for users. In a Linux system, authentication has traditionally been performed by looking up passwords. When a user logs in, the login process looks up their password in the password file. With PAM, users' requests for authentication are directed to PAM, which in turn uses a specified method to authenticate the user. This could be a simple password lookup or a request to an LDAP server, but it is PAM that provides authentication, not a direct password lookup by the user or application. In this respect, authentication becomes centralized and controlled by a specific service, PAM. The actual authentication procedures can be dynamically configured by the system administrator. Authentication is carried out by modules that can vary according to the kind of authentication needed. An administrator can add or replace modules by simply changing the PAM configuration files. See the PAM Web site at **http://www.kernel.org/pub/linux/libs/pam** for more information and a listing of PAM modules.

System Security Services Daemon

The System Security Services Daemon (SSSD) provides offline access for users relying on remote authentication such as an LDAP server. The SSSD will cache the authentication method, allowing you to still login offline. Without SSSD, users had to maintain a corresponding local account with which to gain access when offline. SSSD is installed by default. You start it using the **sssd** daemon. Configuration is integrated into authconfig. Configuration files are located at **/etc/sssd**. See **https://fedorahosted.org/sssd/** for more details.

Check the **System-Level Authentication Guide** for details on authentication configuration, **Part 2. Identity and Authentication Stores | Chapter 7: Using and Caching Credentials with SSSD**

```
https://access.redhat.com/documentation/en-
US/Red_Hat_Enterprise_Linux/7/html/System-Level_Authentication_Guide/SSSD.html
```

Encryption

You can use encryption, integrity checks, and digital signatures to protect data transmitted over a network. For example, the GNU Privacy Guard (GPG) encryption as supported by Seahorse encryption management lets you encrypt your e-mail messages or files you want to send, as well as letting you sign them with an encrypted digital signature authenticating that the message was sent by you. The digital signature also includes encrypted modification digest information that provides an integrity check, allowing the recipient to verify that the message received is the original and not one that has been changed or substituted.

Check the **Security Guide** for details on Encryption configuration, **Chapter 4.10: Encryption**.

```
https://access.redhat.com/documentation/en-
US/Red_Hat_Enterprise_Linux/7/html/Security_Guide/sec-Encryption.html
```

Encrypting data is the only sure way to secure data transmitted over a network. Encrypt data with a key, and the receiver or receivers can later decrypt it. To fully protect data transmitted over a network, you should not only encrypt it, but also check that it has not been modified, as well as confirm that it was actually created by the claimed author. An encrypted message could still be intercepted and modified and then re-encrypted. Integrity checks such as modification digests make sure that the data was not altered. Though encryption and integrity checks protect the data, they do not authenticate it. You also need to know that the person who claimed to send a message actually is the one who sent it, rather than an imposter. To authenticate a message, the author can sign it using a digital signature. This signature can also be encrypted, allowing the receiver to validate it. Digital signatures ensure that the message you receive is authentic.

This type of encryption was originally implemented with Pretty Good Privacy (PGP). Originally a privately controlled methodology, it was handed over to the Internet Engineering Task Force (IETF) to support an open standard for PGP called OpenPGP, **http://www.openpgp.org/**. Any project can use OpenPGP to create encryption applications, such as GnuPG, **http://www.gnupg.org/**. Commercial products for PGP are still developed by Symantec, which also uses the OpenPGP standard.

Public-Key Encryption

Encryption uses a key to encrypt data in such a way that a corresponding key can decrypt it. In the past, older forms of encryption used the same key to both encrypt and decrypt a message. This, however, involved providing the receiver with the key, opening up the possibility that anyone who obtained the key could decrypt the data. Public-key encryption uses two keys to encrypt and decrypt a message, a private key and a public key. The private key you always keep and use to decrypt messages you have received. The public key you make available to those who send messages to you. They then use your public key to encrypt any message they want to send to you. The private key decrypts messages and the public key encrypts them. Each user has a set of private and public keys, securely kept in keyrings. Reciprocally, if you want to send messages to another user, you first obtain the user's public key and use it to encrypt the message you want to send to the user. The user then decrypts the messages with their private key. In other words, your public key is used by others to encrypt the messages you receive, and you use other users' public keys to encrypt messages you send to them. All the users on your Linux system can have their own public and private keys. They will use the **gpg** program to generate them and keep their private key in their own keyrings.

Digital Signatures

A digital signature is used to both authenticate a message and provide an integrity check. Authentication guarantees that the message has not been modified, that it is the original message sent by you, and the integrity check verifies that it has not been changed. Though usually combined with encrypted messages to provide a greater level of security, digital signatures can also be used for messages that can be sent in the clear. For example, you would want to know if a public notice of upgrades of a Red Hat release was actually sent by Red Hat and not by someone trying to spread confusion. Such a message still needs to be authenticated and checked to see if it was actually sent by the sender or, if sent by the original sender, was not somehow changed en route. Verification like this protects against modification or substitution of the message by someone pretending to be the sender.

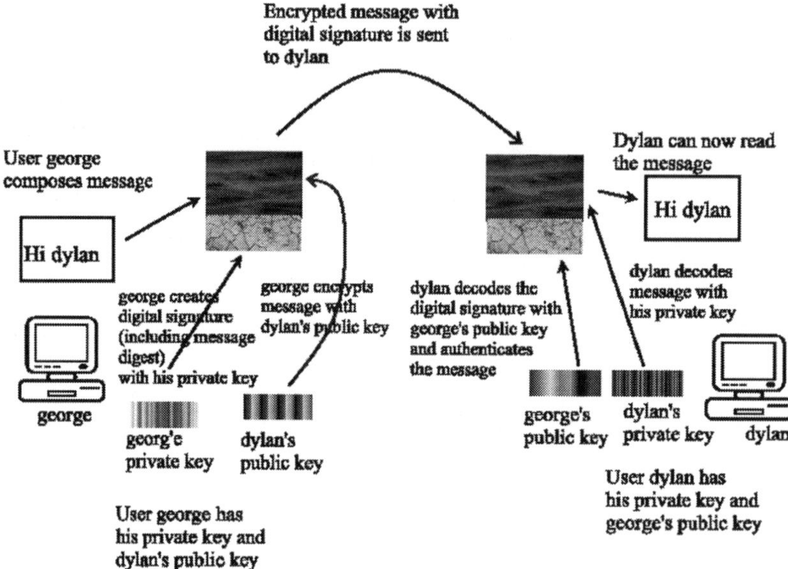

Figure 13-4: Public-key encryption and digital signatures

Integrity Checks

Digitally signing a message involves generating a checksum value from the contents of the message using an encryption hash algorithm such as the SHA2 modification digest algorithm. This is a unique value that accurately represents the size and contents of your message. Any changes to the message of any kind will generate a different value. Such a value provides a way to check the integrity of the data. The value is commonly known as the MD5 value, reflective of the MD5 hash algorithm that was used encrypt the value. The MD5 algorithm has since been replaced by the more secure SHA2 algorithms.

The MD5 value is then itself encrypted with your private key. When the user receives your message, they decrypt your digital signature with your public key. The user then generates an MD5 value of the message received and compares it with the MD5 value you sent. If they are the same, the message is authenticated, it is the original message sent by you, not a false one sent by a user pretending to be you. The user can use GnuPG to decrypt and check digital signatures.

Combining Encryption and Signatures

Normally, digital signatures are combined with encryption to provide a more secure level of transmission. The message is encrypted with the recipient's public key, and the digital signature is encrypted with your private key. The user decrypts both the message (with their private key) and then the signature (with your public key). The user then compares the signature with one that user generates from the message to authenticate it. When GnuPG decodes a message, it will also decode and check a digital signature automatically. Figure 13-4 shows the process for encrypting and digitally signing a message.

Managing keys with Seahorse

For GPG and SSH encryption, signing, and decryption of files and text, GNOME provides Seahorse. With Seahorse you can manage your encryption keys stored in keyrings as well as SSH keys and passphrases. You can import keys, sign keys, search for remote keys, and create your own keyrings, as well as specify keyserver to search and publish to. All these operations can also be performed using the **gpg** command. Seahorse is not installed by default. Install the **seahorse** and **seahorse-gnome** packages.

Passwords and Keys

To import, sign, and locate keys you use the Password and Keys utility (Utilities | Passwords and Keys). The Passwords and Keys window displays a sidebar with four sections: Passwords, Certificates, Secure Shell, and PGP Keys.

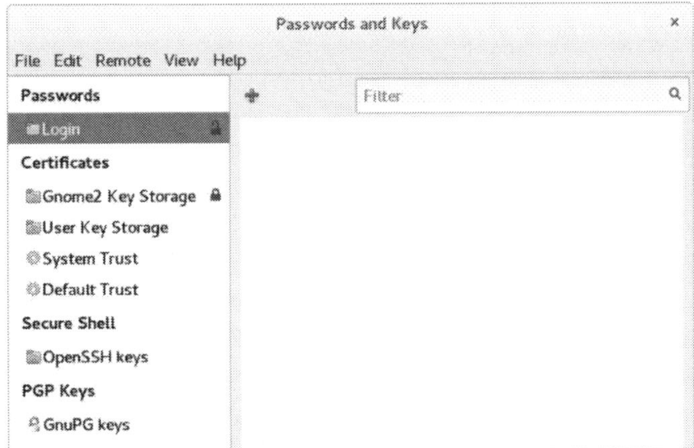

Figure 13-5: Seahorse Passwords and Keys

Keyrings

The Passwords section lists your keyrings. Keyrings store network and application passwords. A login keyring is set up for you (see Figure 13-5). You can create new keyrings by choosing File | New to open the Create New dialog and selecting Password Keyring. An "Add Password Keyring" dialog prompts you for the name of the keyring, and then a "New Keyring Password" dialog prompts you to enter the keyring password. The strength of the password is indicated. The new keyring is listed in the Passwords tab. To make a keyring the default, right-click its entry and select "Set as default" from the pop-up menu.

Creating a new key

Your personal encryption keys are displayed on the PGP Keys section. The link for GnuPG keys displays your GPG keys. Choose File | New to create your own private/public keys. Keep in mind that before you can perform any encryption, you first have to set up your own GPG key pair, private and public. You can choose whether to set up a PGP, Private, or Secure Shell key. The PGP entry sets up a GPG key (GPG is the GNU version of PGP). Choose the PGP Key entry and click Continue (see Figure 13-6).

Figure 13-6: Choose Encryption key type

This opens a New PGP Key window where you enter your name and email address. Click the Advanced key options drop-down arrow to set Encryption type (DSA, RSA, or the signature only for each), Key strength, and Expiration Date (see Figure 13-7). You can choose to never have it expire. Then click the Create button.

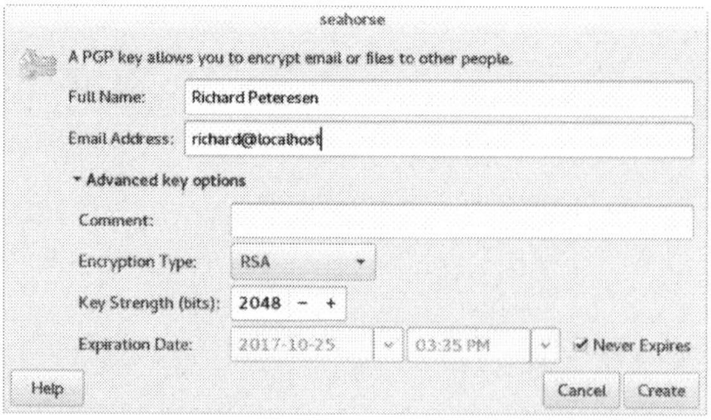

Figure 13-7: Create Encryption key

You are then asked to enter a passphrase (password) for the encryption key (see Figure 13-8). This passphrase will allow you to decrypt any data encrypted by your key.

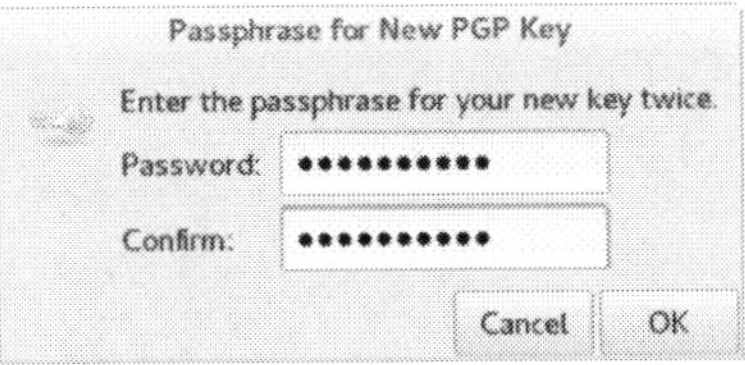

Figure 13-8: Passphrase for encryption key

The key is then generated. This can take some time.

Once you key is created, it will appear in the GnuPG keys tab of the Passwords and Keys dialog (see Figure 13-9).

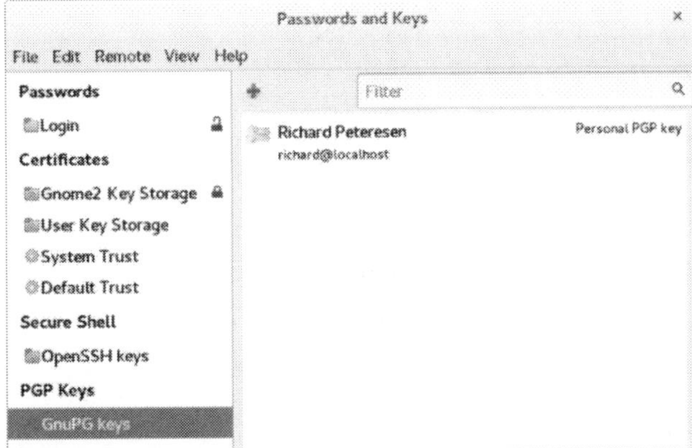

Figure 13-9: My Personal Keys

Clicking on an entry displays a dialog titled with the name of the key and showing three tabs: Owner, Names and Signatures, and Details. The Owner tab shows the key type and ID, as well as a photo for the key and a button to allow you to change the passphrasse for the key (see Figure 13-10). The Names and Signatures tab lets you add users to the key, sign the key, and to delete it.

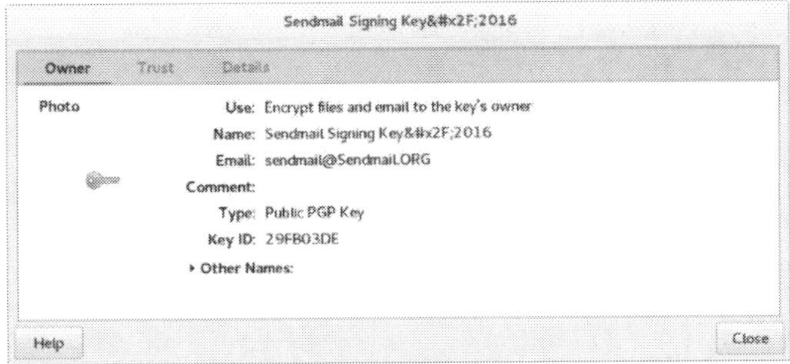

Figure 13-10: GnuPGP key dialog: Owner tab

The Details tab shows technical details such as the key id, type, and strength (see Figure 13-11). It also shows the creation and expiration date (if any). In the Actions section, the Override Owner Trust menu lets you set the level of trust for the key. You can also export the private (secret) key to a file. Any subkeys are also listed, which you can expire, revoke, or delete. You can add new subkeys.

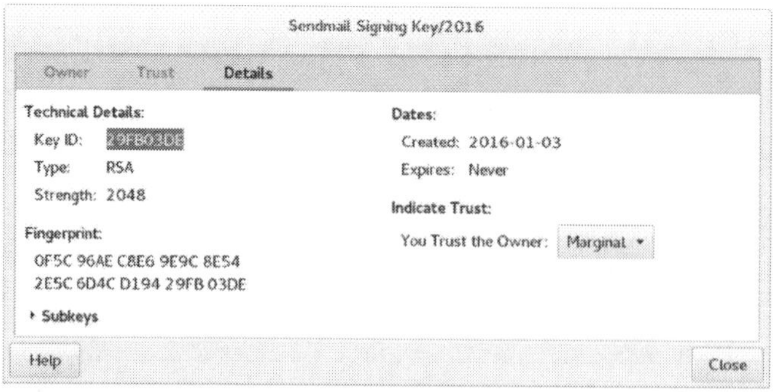

Figure 13-11: GnuPGP key dialog: Details tab

Importing Public Keys

In the Passwords and Keys window, choose File | Import (or press Ctrl-i) to import any public keys you have already downloaded. If you know the name of the key file, you can try searching the key servers for it. Choose Remote | Find Remote Keys to open the Find Remote Keys dialog where you can enter a search string for the key (see Figure 13-12). The search term is treated as a prefix, matching on all possible completions. An expandable tree lists available key servers, letting you choose which ones to search.

Results are listed in a new window labeled Remote Keys Containing (see Figure 13-13). Select the one you want, and then either click the Import button at the top left to import the key directly. To see information about a key, double click the entry (see Figure 13-14). Information about the owner (Owner tab), the trust level (Trust tab), and details about the key such as type and strength are displayed (Details tab).

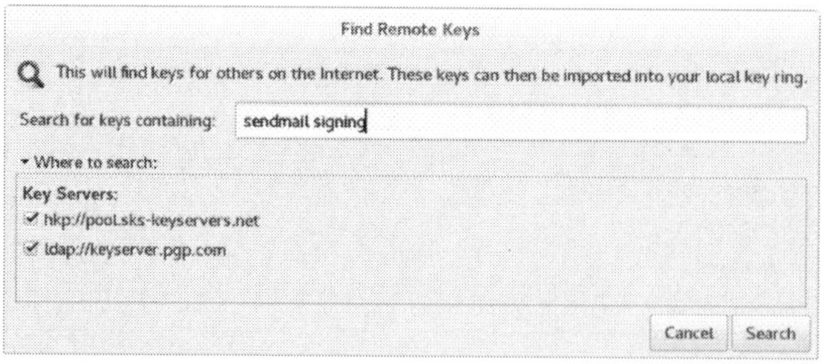

Figure 13-12: Searching for keys

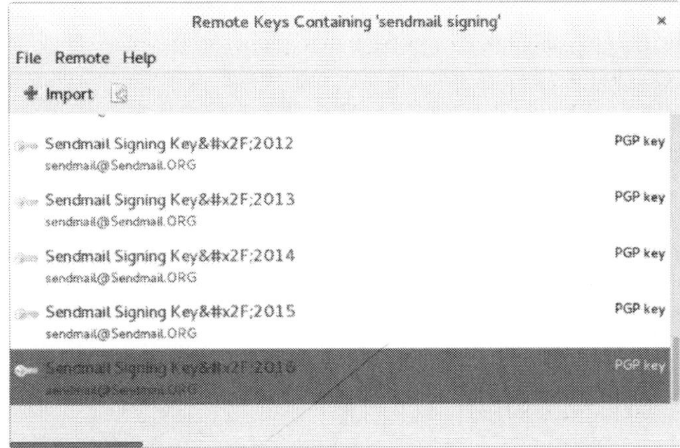

Figure 13-13: Importing keys

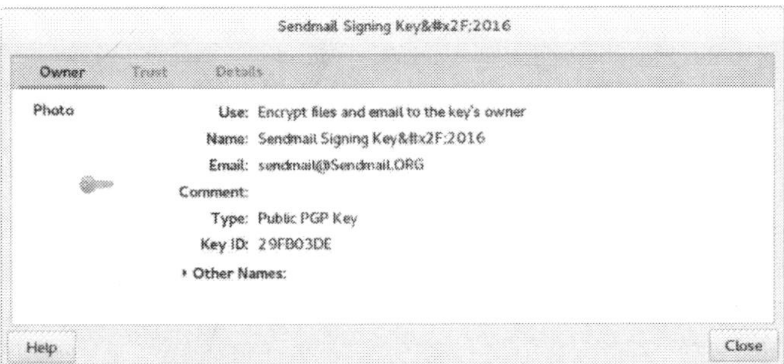

Figure 13-14: Key information

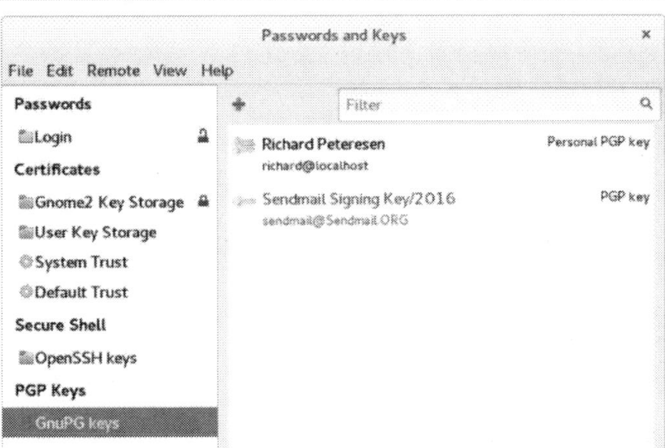

Figure 13-15: Imported keys

Once you have imported the key, it will appear in the PGP Keys tab in the Passwords And Keys window (see Figure 13-15). The View menu list the types of keys to display in the PGP Keys tab: Show Personal, Show Trusted, and Show Any. For newly imported keys, be sure to choose the Show Any option otherwise the new entry will not be displayed.

If you know that you can trust the key, you can sign it, making it a valid key. Double click on its entry to open its dialog, and choose the Trust tab (see Figure 13-16). Click the checkbox for trusting the key signatures. Then click the "Sign this Key" button to open the Sign key dialog (see Figure 13-17). You are asked how carefully you have checked the key: Not at all, Casually, or Very Carefully. You also choose whether others can see your signature and if you can revoke it later. Then click the Sign button. A dialog appears prompting you to enter your PGP passphrase. The key will now appear with the View | Show Trusted options set.

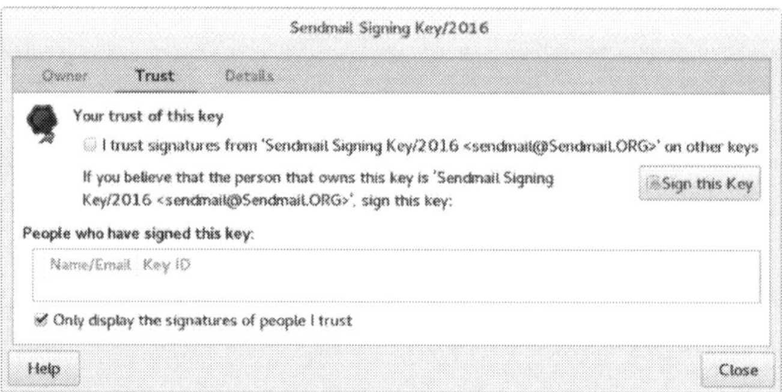

Figure 13-16: Imported key Trust tab for an unsigned key

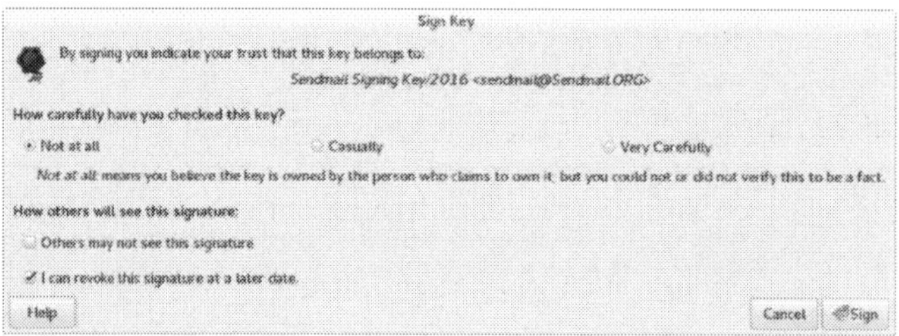

Figure 13-17: Signing a key

Sharing Keys

When you created your own private key, you also generated a corresponding public key that others can use to encrypt data they send to you and decrypt signatures of messages you send to them. To make you public key available to others, you can export it to a file to send directly other users, automatically share it with other users on your system, or publish on a keyserver. To export your public key to a file, select your key in the "My Personal Keys" tab, and click the "Export to a file" button. You can do this for your public keys also.

You configure key sharing on the Preferences window. Choose Edit | Preferences to open the Preferences window, displaying two tabs, Key Servers and Key Sharing (see Figure 13-18). On the Key Servers tab, you specify the keyservers to access. Two default servers are specified:

hkp://pool.sks-keyservers.net and **ldap://keyserver.pgp.com**. Click the Add button to add more, opening a dialog where you enter the keyserver type and host. From the "Publish Keys to:" drop down menu you can choose the keyserver to publish to or choose not to publish (the default). You also have the options to automatically retrieve keys and synchronize modified keys. To publish a key choosing Remote | Sync and Publish Keys to open the Sync Keys dialog and click the Sync button. The Key Servers button opens the Preferences dialog to the Key Servers tab.

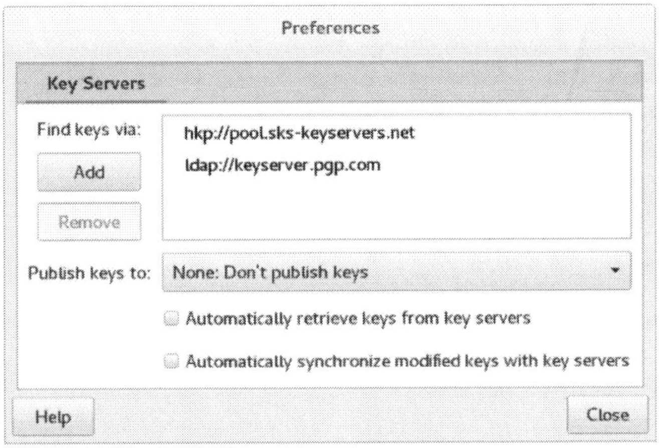

Figure 13-18: Seahorse Preferences

Seahorse integrates support for GPG. Should you import a key with the **gpg** command, it will appear in the GnuPG keys tab. Also, you can sign a key using the **gpg** command with the --**sign-key** option and the key is validated.

Encrypting and decrypting data with gpg command

The **gpg** command provides several options for managing secure messages. The **e** option encrypts messages, the **a** option generates an armored text version, and the **s** option adds a digital signature. Email applications will use this option. You will need to specify the recipient's public key, which you should already have imported into your **pubring** file. It is this key that is used to encrypt the message. The recipient will then be able to decode the message with their private key. Use the --**recipient** or -**r** option to specify the name of the recipient key. You can use any unique substring in the user's public key name. The e-mail address usually suffices. You use the **d** option to decode received messages. In the following example, the user encrypts (**e**) and signs (**s**) a file generated in armored text format (**a**). The -**r** option indicates the recipient for the message (whose public key is used to encrypt the message).

```
gpg e -s -a -o myfile.asc -r george@rabbit.mytrek.com myfile
mail george@rabbit.mytrek.com < myfile.asc
```

You can leave out the ASCII armor option if you want to send or transfer the file as a binary attachment. Without the --**armor** or -**a** option, **gpg** generates an encoded binary file, not an encoded text file. This is the method used for encryption by Nautilus. A binary file can be transmitted through e-mail only as an attachment. As noted previously, ASCII armored versions usually have an extension of **.asc**, whereas binary version use **.gpg**.

When the other user receives the file, they can save it to a file named something like **myfile.asc** and then decode the file with the **-d** option. The **-o** option will specify a file to save the decoded version in. GPG will automatically determine if it is a binary file or an ASCII armored version.

```
gpg -d -o myfile.txt myfile.asc
```

To check the digital signature of the file, you use the **gpg** command with the **--verify** option. This assumes that the sender has signed the file.

```
gpg --verify myfile.asc
```

Note: You can use **gpgsplit** to split a GPG message into its components to examine them separately.

As you perform GPG tasks, you will need to reference the keys you have using their key names. Bear in mind that you need only a unique identifying substring to select the key you want. GPG performs a pattern search on the string you specify as the key name in any given command. If the string matches more than one key, all those matching will be selected.

Encrypting and decrypting files with Nautilus

The GNOME Nautilus file manager can generate an encrypted copy of a file, giving that copy the extension **.gpg**. It operates like gpg with just the **-e** option, and no **-a** option. To encrypt a file from Nautilus, select the file and then right-click to open the Nautilus pop-up menu. On this menu select the Encrypt option. The Choose Recipients window then opens letting you select the encryption keys and digital signature to use. Select the encryption key. You will be prompted to enter the key's passphrase. Then an encrypted copy of the file will be generated with the extension **.pgp**. The original is left untouched.

If you just want to sign a file, you can right-click on the filename/icon and choose Sign from the pop-up menu. This opens a dialog with a drop-down menu listing digital signatures you can use.

To decrypt the encrypted **.pgp** file, simply double-click on it or right-click and choose Open With to select Decrypt File. This opens the file with the decrypt tool which will generate a decrypted copy of the file. A "Choose decrypted file name" dialog will then open where you can enter the name for the copy and the folder to save it in. You are then prompted for the passphrase.

Decrypting a Digital Signature

You will need to have the signer’s public key to decode and check the digital signature. If you do not have the key, you will receive a message saying that the public key was not found. In this case, you will first have to obtain the signer’s public key. You can access a keyserver that you think may have the public key or request the public key directly from a website or from the signer. Then import the key as described earlier.

SELinux

Although numerous security tools exist for protecting specific services, as well as user information and data, no tool has been available for protecting the entire system at the administrative level. Security-Enhanced Linux is a project to provide built-in administrative protection for aspects of your Linux system. Instead of relying on users to protect their files or on a specific network program to control access, security measures would be built into the basic file management system and the network access methods. All controls can be managed directly by an administrator as part of Linux system administration.

Security-Enhanced Linux (SELinux) is a project developed and maintained by the National Security Agency (NSA), which chose Linux as its platform for implementing a secure operating system. Most Linux distributions have embraced SELinux and have incorporated it as a standard feature. Detailed documentation is available from resources listed in Table 13-1, including sites provided by the NSA and SourceForge.

Resource	Location
Red Hat Enterprise Linux 7 SELinux User Guide	**https://access.redhat.com/documentation/en-US/Red_Hat_Enterprise_Linux/7/html/SELinux_Users_and_Administrators_Guide/index.html**
NSA SELinux	**http://www.nsa.gov/selinux**
NSA SELinux FAQ	**http://www.nsa.gov/selinux/info/faq.cfm**
SELinux at sourceforge.net	**http://selinux.sourceforge.net**
Writing SELinux Policy HOWTO	Accessible from "SELinux resources at sourceforge" link at **http://selinux.sourceforge.net**
NSA SELinux Documentation	**http://www.nsa.gov/selinux/info/docs.cfm**
Configuring SELinux Policy	Accessible from NSA SELinux Documentation
SE Linux Reference Policy Project	**http://oss.tresys.com/projects/refpolicy**

Table 13-1: SELinux Resources

Check the **Security-Enhanced Linux User Guide** for details at the Red Hat documentation site.

```
https://access.redhat.com/documentation/en-US/Red_Hat_Enterprise_Linux/7/html/SELinux_Users_and_Administrators_Guide/index.html
```

For information on how to configure access to network servers under a targeted policy such as the Apache Web servers, NFS, DHCP, Samba, Squid, rsync, DNS, and Postfix, check **Part 2. Managing Confined Services** section in the **Security-Enhanced Linux User Guide.**

```
https://access.redhat.com/documentation/en-US/Red_Hat_Enterprise_Linux/7/html/SELinux_Users_and_Administrators_Guide/part_II-Managing_Confined_Services.html
```

Linux and Unix systems normally use a discretionary access control (DAC) method for restricting access. In this approach users and the objects they own, such as files, determine permissions. The user has completed discretion over the objects it owns. The weak point in many Linux/Unix systems has been the user administrative accounts. If an attacker managed to gain access to an administrative account, they would have complete control over the service the account managed. Access to the root user would give control over the entire system, all its users, and any network services it was running. To counter this weakness, the NSA set up a mandatory access control (MAC) structure. Instead of an all-or-nothing set of privileges based on accounts, services and administrative tasks are compartmentalized and separately controlled with policies detailing what can and cannot be done. Access is granted not just because one is an authenticated user, but when specific security criteria are met. Users, applications, processes, files, and devices can be given just the access they need to do their job, and nothing more.

Flask Architecture

The Flask (Flux Advanced Security Kernel) architecture organizes operating system components and data into subjects and objects. Subjects are processes: applications, drivers, system tasks that are currently running. Objects are fixed components such as files, folders, sockets, network interfaces, and devices. For each subject and object, a security context is defined. A security context is a set of security attributes that determine how a subject or object can be used. This approach provides a very fine-grained control over every element in the operating system as well as all data on your computer.

The attributes designated for the security contexts and the degree to which they are enforced are determined by an overall security policy. The policies are enforced by a security server. Distributions may provide different pre-configured policies from which to work. For example, Red Hat provides three policies each in its own package, minimum, targeted, and mls, which are all variation of a single reference policy.

SELinux uses a combination of the Type Enforcement (TE), Role Based Access Control (RBAC), and Multi-Level Security (MLS) security models. Type Enforcement focuses on objects and processes like folders and applications, whereas Role Based Access Enforcement controls user access. For the Type Enforcement model, the security attributes assigned to an object are known as either domains or types. Types are used for fixed objects such as files, and domains are used for processes such as running applications. For user access to processes and objects, SELinux makes use of the Role Based Access Control model. When new processes or objects are created, transition rules specify the type or domain they belong to in their security contexts.

With the RBAC model, users are assigned roles for which permissions are defined. The roles restrict what objects and processes a user can access. The security context for processes will include a role attribute, controlling what objects it can assess. The Multi-Level Security (MLS) adds a security level, containing both a sensitivity and capability value.

Users are given separate SELinux user identities. Normally these correspond to the user IDs set up under the standard Linux user creation operations. Though they may have the same name, they are not the same identifiers. Standard Linux identities can be easily changed with commands like **setuid** and **su**. Changes to the Linux user ID will not affect the SELinux ID. This means that even if a user changes its ID, SELinux will still be able to track it, maintaining control over that user.

SE Linux Policy Packages

RHEL7 Linux provides several SELinux policy packages (see Table 13-2). The targeted policy is installed by default. You can use PackageKit to download and install the others. The source code, along with the source code documentation, is kept in separate RPMS packages, which you download and manually install.

Package	Description
selinux-policy-targeted	SELinux targeted policy configuration, /etc/selinux/targeted
selinux-policy-minimum	SELinux minimum policy configuration, /etc/selinux/minimum
selinux-policy-mls	SELinux MLS policy configuration, /etc/selinux/mls
selinux-policy	man pages and development modules in /usr/share/selinux/devel
selinux-policy-*version*-src.rpm	SELinux Reference Policy source files
selinux-doc	Module and policy documentation in /usr/share/doc/selinux-doc
selinux-doc-*version*-src.rpm	SELinux Reference Policy documentation

Table 13-2: SELinux packages

Note: You can also use **setroubleshoot** to check and locate problems you may be having with SELinux.

Each policy installs its configuration files in **/etc/selinux**. The **selinux-policy** package installs the main development module headers in **/usr/share/selinux/devel**. Other packages, such as targeted-policy, then install their own module **.pp** files, with links to the **devel** folder.

Configuration with system-config-selinux

With system-config-selinux (**policycoreutils.gui** package) you can manage and configure your SELinux policies, though you cannot create new policies (see Figure 13-18). You can access system-config-selinux on your desktop as SELinux Management.

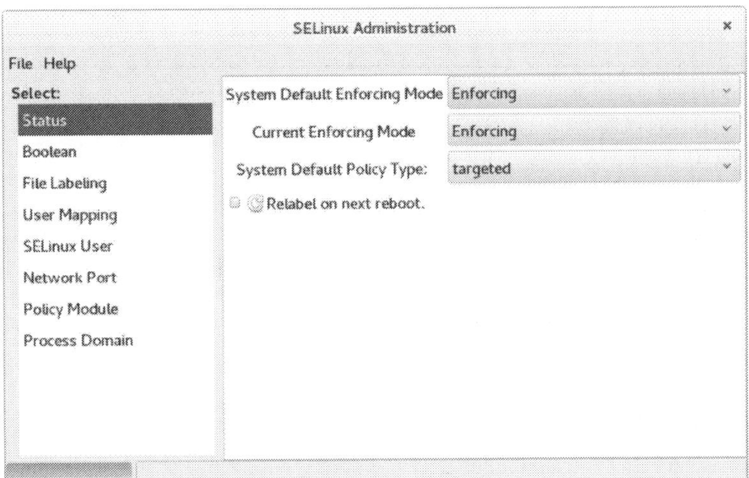

Figure 13-19: The system-config-selinux: Status

The system-config-selinux window lists several tabs with a sidebar menu for Status, Boolean, File Labeling, User Mapping, SELinux User, Translation, Network Port, and Policy

Module. The system-config-selinux tool will invoke the SELinux management tools like **sestatus** and **semanage** with appropriate options to make configuration changes.

The Status tab lists pop-up menus for selecting policy and enforcement defaults, as well as the current enforcing mode. A check box to relabel on reboot lets you force relabeling of your file security contexts when you reboot (see Figure 13-19).

The Boolean tab lists various options for targeted services like Web and FTP servers, NFS, and Samba (see Figure 13-20). With these, you can further modify how each service is controlled. There are expandable menus for different services like FTP, Apache Web server, and Samba. For example, the FTP entries let you choose whether to allow access to home folders or to allow NFS file transfers. The number of boolean entries is extensive. To see just the ones you have activated, you can click the Customized button. Only selected boolean options will be displayed. When you click the Customized button, it changes to the All button and the Revert button becomes active. Revert will restore system boolean defaults. The Lockdown button will start the Lockdown wizard, opening a new window with Booleans displayed in an expandable tree in a left pane, and the right pane gives you a choice of Enable, Disable, and Default option for the selected boolean. Forward and Backward buttons move you sequentially through the list of Booleans. The Lockdown wizard will lock down an SELinux system, preventing any modification to the boolean configuration. From the File menu, you can select Apply to apply the configuration directly, or save the configuration as a different file.

The File Labeling tab will list your system folders and files, showing their security contexts and types. You can edit a file's properties by selecting the entry and then clicking Properties. This displays a dialog with the File Name, Type, SELinux Type, and MLS Level. You can change the SELinux type or the MLS level. For a permissive policy, the MLS level will be s0, allowing access to anyone. You can also add or delete entries.

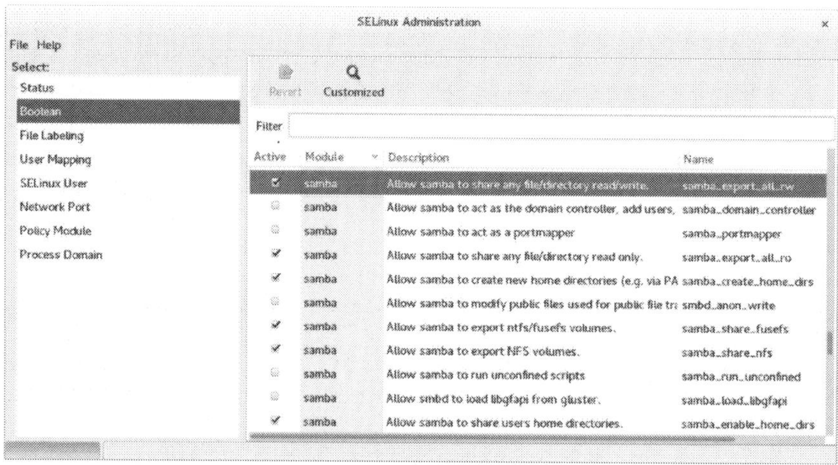

Figure 13-20: The system-config-selinux: Boolean pane

The User Mapping tab shows the mapping of user login names to SELinux users. Initially, there will be two mappings: the root user and the default user.

The SELinux User tab shows the different kinds of SELinux users. Initially, there will be three user types: root, system_u, and user_u (see Figure 13-21). The root user is the root user, which has full and total administrative access to the entire system. The system_u user allows users to take on administrative access where needed. The user_u user is used for normal users. Each entry lists its SELinux User, SELinux prefix, MLS (Multi-level Security) level, MLS range, and SELinux roles. MLS level is the access level (s0 on a permissive policy), and MLS range is the range of access from SystemLow to SystemHigh.

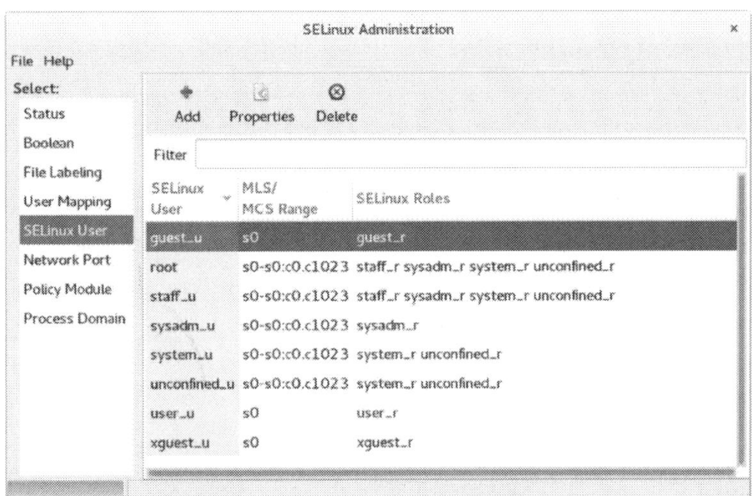

Figure 13-21: system-config-selinux SELinux User pane

A given user has certain roles available. The root user has the system_r, sysadm_r, and user_r roles, allowing it system access, administration capability, and standard user access. The same roles are applied to user_u, allowing the user to perform system administration if that user has the root user password. The system_u role has only system access and cannot perform system administration.

The Translation tab lets you set MLS symbols. Initially, you will have symbols for SystemHigh and the SystemLow–SystemHigh range. You change the MLS levels for a mapping, changing security level access across the system.

The Network Port tab lists the network protocol, the SELinux type, and the MLS security level for ports on your system. Select an entry and click Properties to change the SELinux type or the MLS level for the port. The Group View button will display the SELinux type along with a list of the ports they apply to. This view does not display the MLS level, as these apply to ports individually.

The Policy Module tab lists the different SELinux policy modules. Here you will see modules for different applications like Thunderbird and Evolution, as well as device services like USB and HAL. Listed also are desktops like GNOME. The pane allows you to add or remove a module. You can also enable or provide additional audit rules for a module for logging.

SELinux Troubleshooting and audit2allow

RHEL7 includes the SELinux troubleshooter . which notifies you of problems that SELinux detects. Whenever SELinux denies access to a file or application, the kernel issues an AVC notice. These are analyzed by the SELinux troubleshooter to detect problems that users may have to deal with. When a problem is detected, an SELinux troubleshooter notification is displayed in the desktop notification area along with the troubleshooter icon. Clicking on the icon or notice will open the SELinux troubleshooter window. You can also access it at any time from Sundry | SELinux Troubleshooter. You can find out more information about SELinux troubleshooter at **https://fedorahosted.org/setroubleshoot/**.

The SELinux troubleshooter window displays the current notice (see Figure 13-22). Use the Next and Previous buttons to page through notices. The number of the displayed notice is shown at the top right next to a Show all button.

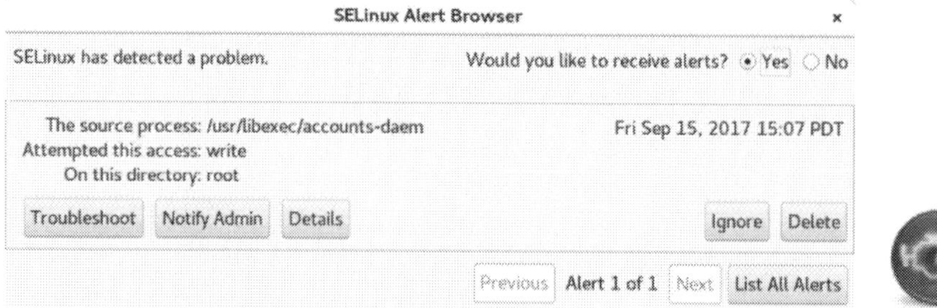

Figure 13-22: SELinux troubleshooter

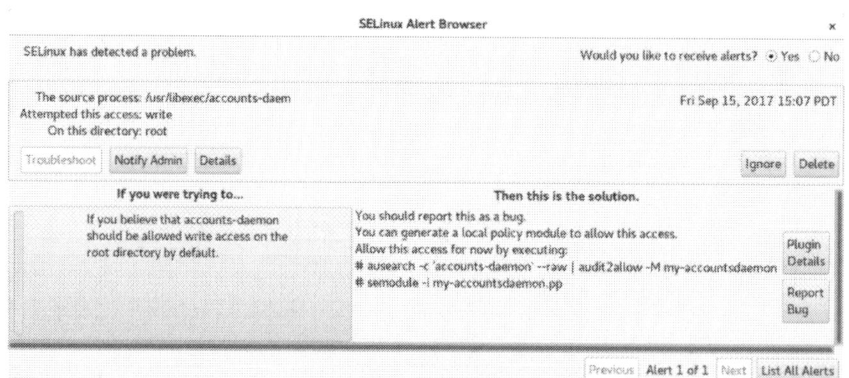

Figure 13-23: SELinux troubleshooter: Troubleshoot listing

Clicking on the expand arrow for "Show full error output" displays detailed information about the notice in four sections: Summary, Detailed Description, Allowing Access, and Additional Information (see Figure 13-23). To copy the full description of the problem and solution as text, click the Copy to Clipboard button. You could then open a text editor and paste the error report to a file (see Figure 13-24).

To see a full listing of error messages at once, click the List All Alerts button to display a list of alert notices, along with their date, the number of times it has occurred, its category, and brief explanation (see Figure 13-25). The Delete button lets you delete alerts.

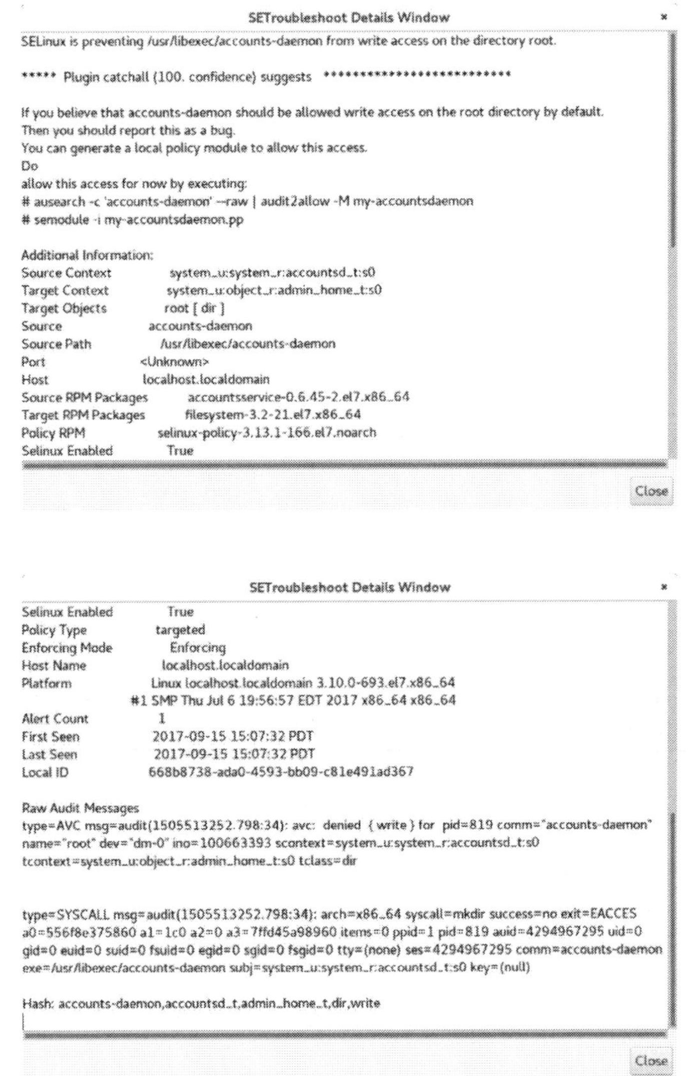

Figure 13-24: SELinux troubleshooter: Full details window

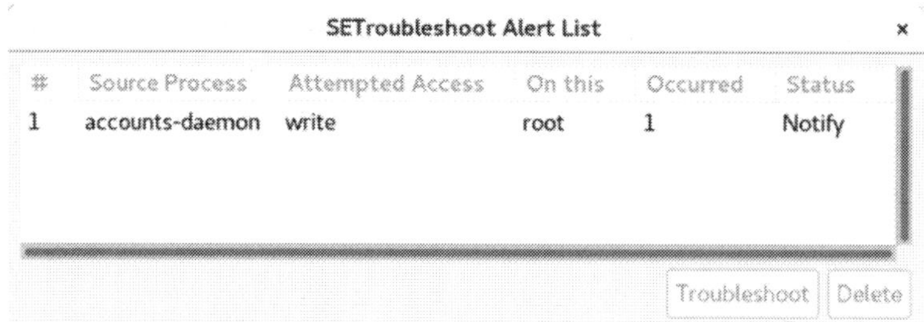

Figure 13-25 SELinux troubleshooter full list

You could also use the SELinux Management tool to make the changes, in this case, the Network Port tab and clicking the Add button to open the Add Network Port dialog (see Figure 13-26).

In many cases, the problem may be simple to fix. Often, the security context of a file has to be renamed to allow access, or access set up to a particular port. In this example, SELinux needs to set up port access for the puppetmaster service on port 8141. A **semanage** operation is listed as the solution. You could open a terminal window, log in as the root user (**su**), and run the command.

```
semanage port -a -t puppet_port_t -p tcp 8141
```

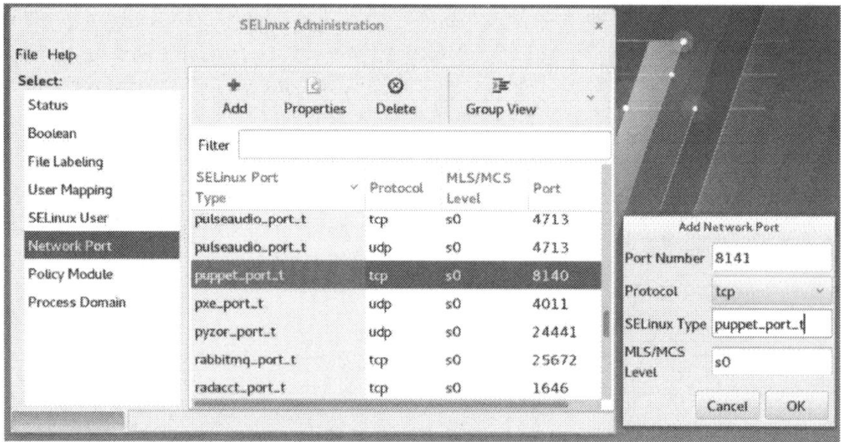

Figure 13-26: SELinux Management: network port

Allowing access: chcon and audit2allow

Whenever SELinux denies access to a file or application, the kernel issues an AVC notice. In many cases, the problem can be fixed by just renaming the security context of a file to allow access. You use the **chcon** command to change a file's security context. Access needs to be granted to the Samba server for a **log.richard3** file in the **/var/lib/samba** folder. The SELinux troubleshooter will take no action of its own. Instead, it recommends possible actions. In this example, the user just issues the following **chcon** command.

```
chcon -R -t samba_share_t log.richard3
```

More complicated problems, especially ones that are unknown, may require you to create a new policy module using the AVC messages in the audit log. To do this, you can use the **audit2allow** command. The command will take an audit AVC messages and generate commands to allow SELinux access. The audit log is **/var/log/audit/audit.log**. This log is output to **audit2allow** which then can use its **-M** option to create a policy module. I

```
cat /var/log/audit/audit.log | audit2allow -M local
```

You then use the **semodule** command to load the module.

```
semodule -i local.pp
```

If you want first to edit the allowable entries, you can use the following to create a **.te** file of the local module, **local.te**, which you can then edit.

```
audit2allow -m local -i  /var/log/audit/audit.log   >  local.te
```

Once you have edited the **.te** file, you can then use **checkmodule** to compile the module, and then **semodule_package** to create the policy module, **local.pp**. Then you can install it with **semodule**. You first create a **.mod** file with **checkmodule**, and then **.pp** file with **semodule_package**.

```
checkmodule -M -m -o local.mod local.te
semodule_package -o local.pp  -m local.mod
semodule -i local.pp
```

In this example, the policy module is just called **local**. If you later want to create a new module with **audit2allow**, you should either use a different name or just append the output to the **.te** file using the **-o** option.

SELinux Policy Generation Tool

The SELinux Policy Generation tool generates policy frameworks to allow SELinux to control specific applications or users. On the initial screen, you select the type of application, user, or the root user (system administrator), see Figure 13-27.

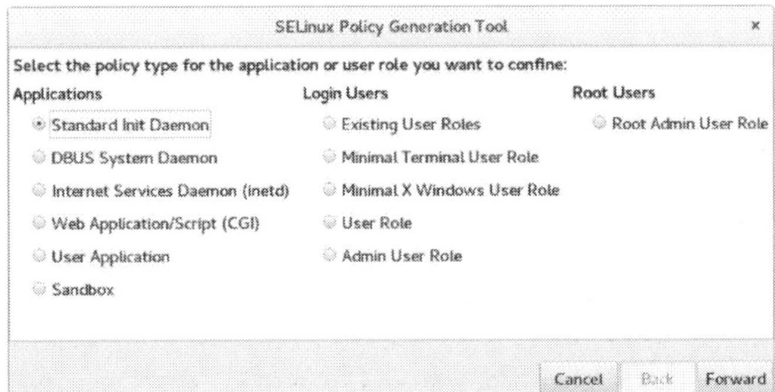

Figure 13-27: SELinux Policy Generation Tool: policy type

For an application, you are then prompted to enter the application name and the location of its executable file. For the executable file, you can click on a file manager button to the right of the text box to open a selection window for the **/usr/sbin** folder.

On the following screens you enter the ports the application listens on and the ones it connects to. Then you select common traits like sending email or using PAM authentication. Then select the files and folders the application uses, along with the Booleans it may use. Choose where to save the policy file. The rules generated will then be listed. When you click Apply, the policy files will be generated (**.te**, **.fc**, **.sh**, and **.if**).

After clicking Apply and saving your configuration files, you can click the Back button until you return to the first window. Then you can select another type of role for another policy.

For users, when you select Exiting User Roles, a list of existing user roles will be displayed, like guest_u or user_u. On the next screen, you can choose addition domains the user can access like Wine, polkit, or games. You can then select additional roles for the user, like sysadm and webadm. You then enter the ports the user can listen and connect to, as well as any Booleans that may apply. Choose where to save the policy file. If you have already selected one, it will be displayed. The rules generated will then be listed. When you click Apply, the policy files will be generated (**.te**, **.fc**, **.sh**, and **.if**).

For User Role, you will be prompted to enter a name for the role, then select the domains it can access, followed the ports used, and any booleans you want to apply. Upon clicking Apply, the policy files will be generated and saved.

For the Root Admin User Role, you first enter a name for the name for the user role, and then you select the domains this user role can administer, like bind, cups, and ntp. Use the Ctrl key to select more than one. Then select the user roles that can transition to this domain. Again select the ports listened and connected to, if any, along with any Boolean. Click Apply to generate the configuration files.

SELinux Policy Management Tool

You can edit your current policy using the SELinux Policy Mangement Tool. Use the Select menu to display options to search for an application, display and edit file equivalances, and to modify users (see Figure 13-28). Click the help icon to the right to display an explanation of the current dialog. When you perform a search for an application, matches are automatically displayed as you type a pattern. Choose the one you want. The Advanced Search button opens a dialog where you can choose from all the available applications.

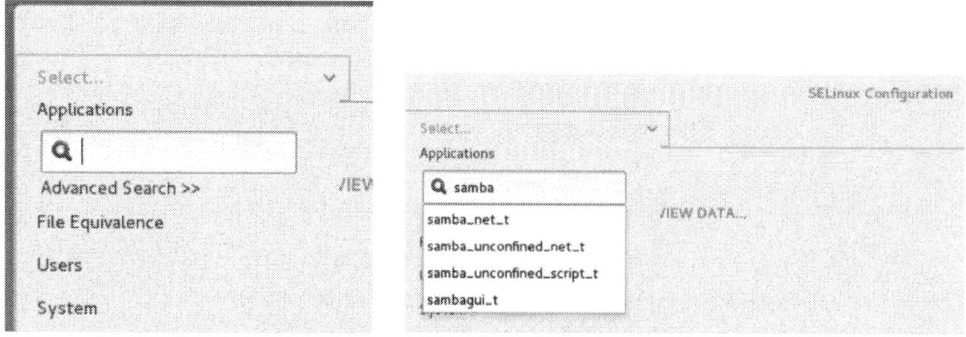

Figure 13-28: SELinux Policy Management Tool: menu

Selecting an application opens a dialog with tabs for application Booleans, Files, Network, and Transitions (see Figure 13-29). On the Booleans tab, you can specify SELinux options for that application. The Files tab show files used by the applications: executable, writeable, and file types. The Network tab lists the ports being used for the application. The Transitions tab shows other SELinux domains that become activated with the application when it runs or is run by other applications.

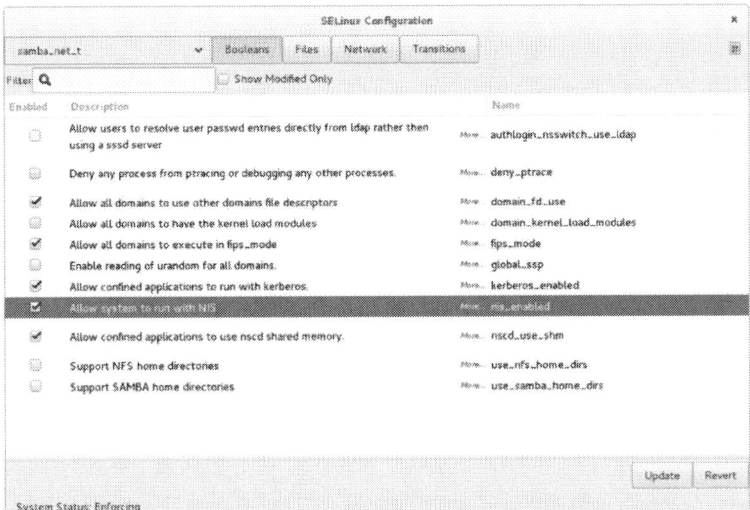

Figure 13-29: SELinux Policy Management Tool: application

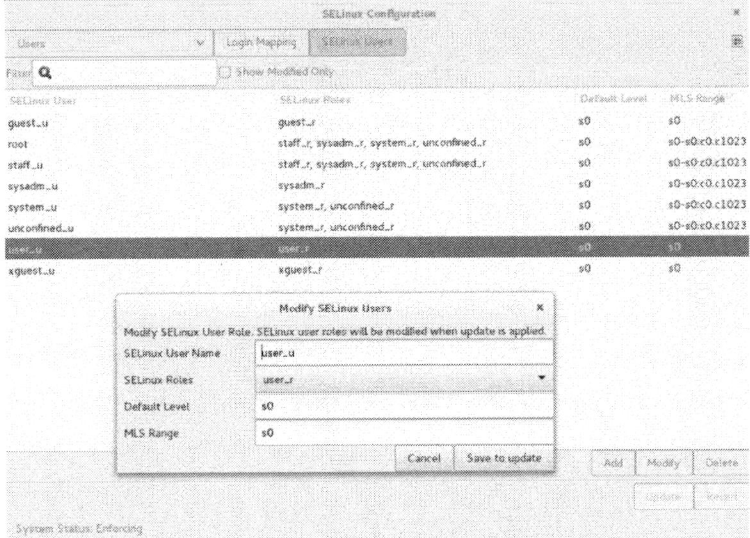

Figure 13-30: SELinux Policy Management Tool: SELinux Users

The Users option on the menu opens a dialog with Login Mapping and SELinux Users tabs (see Figure 13-30). The Login Mapping tab lets you map an SElinux user to a login user. The SELinux Users tab lists SELinux users. Selecting a user and clicking the Modify button opens a dialog where you can modify user roles and levels.

The File equivalance entry opens a dialog listing folder locations. The System entry opens a dialog where you can set a permanent or temporary enforcing mode, as well as import or export a configuration.

semanage

semanage lets you change your SELinux configuration without having to edit selinux source files directly. It covers several major categories including users, ports, file contexts, and logins. Check the man page for semanage for detailed descriptions. Options let you modify specific security features such as **-s** for the username, **-R** for the role, -t for the type, and -r for an MLS security range. The following example adds a user with role user_r.

```
semanage user -a -R user_r  justin
```

semanage is configured with the **/etc/selinux/semanage.conf** file where you can configure semanage to write directly on modules (the default) or work on the source.

Checking SELinux Messages: seaudit

SELinux AVC messages are now saved in the **/var/log/audit/audit.log** file. These are particularly important if you are using the permissive mode to test a policy you want to enforce later. You need to find out if you are being denied access where appropriate and afforded control when needed. To see just the SELinux messages, you can use the seaudit tool (SELinux Audit Log Analysis). Start up messages for the SE Linux service are still logged in **/var/log/messages**.

14. systemd: unit files and server management

systemd
systemd unit files: /lib/systemd/system
special targets (runlevels)
managing services
Cockpit

A single Linux system can provide several different kinds of services, ranging from security to administration and including more obvious Internet services like web and FTP sites, e-mail, and printing. Security tools such as SSH and Kerberos run as services, along with administrative network tools such as DHCP and LDAP. The network connection interface is itself a service that you can restart at will. Each service operates as a continually running daemon looking for requests for its particular services.

System startup is managed by the **systemd** service. The original System V init system for starting individual services has been phased out. The Upstart service used in previous RHEL releases has been deprecated.

systemd

Linux systems traditionally used the Unix System V init daemon to manage services by setting up runlevels at which they could be started or shutdown. RHEL has since replaced the SystemV init daemon with the **systemd** init daemon. Whereas the System V init daemon would start certain services when the entire system started up or shut down using shell scripts run in sequence, **systemd** uses sockets for all system tasks and services. **systemd** sets up sockets for daemons and coordinates between them as they start up. This allows **systemd** to start daemons at the same time (in parallel). Should one daemon require support from another, **systemd** coordinates the data from their sockets (buffering), so that one daemon receives the information from another daemon that it needs to continue. This parallel start up compatibility allows for very fast boot times.

In effect, you can think of **systemd** as a combination of System V init scripts and the inetd daemon (xinetd), using socket activation applied to all system startup tasks and to network servers. The socket activation design was originally inspired by the inetd service that used sockets (AT_INET) to start internet daemons when requested. The socket activation design was used by in Apple's OS X system to apply to all sockets (AF_UNIX). This allowed all start up processes to start at the same time in parallel, making for very fast boot times. Sockets are set up and managed by **systemd**. When D-BUS needs to write to journald (logging), it writes to the systemd-journald socket set up and managed by **systemd**. It does not have to communicate directly with journald. This means that services no longer have to be started and shutdown in a particular sequence as they were under System V. They can all start and stop at the same time. Also, as **systemd** controls the socket, if a service fails, its socket remains in place. The service can be restarted using the same socket with no loss of information. **systemd** manages all types of sockets including UNIX (system), INET (network), NETLINK (devices), FIFO (pipes), and POSIX (messages). See the following for more details:

```
http://fedoraproject.org/wiki/systemd
```

systemd sets up sockets for all system tasks and services. Configurations for systemd tasks are defined in unit files in **/lib/systemd/system** directory. In this respect, **systemd** files replace the entries that used to be in the Sys V init's **/etc/inittab** file. **systemd** also has its own versions of **shutdown**, **reboot**, **halt**, **init**, and **telinit**, each with their own man page. These versions are used on RHEL, instead of the original Linux versions.

systemd is entirely compatible with both System V scripts and **/etc/fsta**b. The SystemV scripts and **/etc/fstab** are treated as additional configuration files for **systemd** to work with. If System V scripts are present it will use them to generated a corresponding unit configuration file, if there are no corresponding **systemd** unit configuration files already. **systemd** configuration always takes precedence. **systemd** will also, if needed, use the start and stop priority files in the System V init **/etc/rc.d** directory to determine dependencies. Entries in **/etc/fstab** are used to generate corresponding **systemd** unit files that are then used to manage file systems. **systemd** also supports snapshots that allow restoring services to a previous state.

systemd basic configuration files

You can configure **systemd** for system, login manager, users, and, journal service using the configuration files located in the **/etc/systemd** directory. When run for a system service, systemd uses the **system.conf** file, otherwise it uses the **user.conf** file. You can set options such as the log level (LogLevel) and resource size limits. See the man page for **systemd.conf** (system.conf and user.conf), **logind.conf**, and **journald.conf** for details on the options available.

units

systemd organizes tasks into units, each with a unit configuration file. There are several types of units (see Table 14-1). A unit file will have an extension to its name that specifies the type of unit it is. Service types have the extension **.service**, and mount types have the extension **.mount**. The service type performs much the same function as System V init scripts. Services can be stopped, started and restarted. The **systemctl** command will list all units, including the ones it generates.

Units can also be used for socket, device, and mount tasks. The socket type implements the kind of connection used for inetd and xinetd, allowing you to start a service on demand. The device type references devices as detected by udev. The mount type manages a file system's mount point, and automount activates that mount point should it be automounted. An automount unit file has a corresponding mount unit file, which it uses to mount a file system. Similarly, a socket type usually has a corresponding service type used to perform a task for that socket.

Within each unit are directives that control a service, socket, device, or mount point. Some directives are unique to the type of unit. These are listed in the man page for that service, such as **systemd.service** for the service unit, or **systemd.mount** for a mount unit (see Table 14-1).

```
man systemd.service
```

Options common to units are listed in the **systemd.exec** and **systemd.unit** pages. The **systemd.unit** page lists directives common to all units such as Wants, Conflicts, Before, SourcePath, and Also. The **systemd.exec** pages list options for the execution of a program for a unit, such as the starting of a server daemon. These include options such as User, group, WorkingDirectory, Nice, Umask, and Environment. The **systemd.exec** page covers options for service, socket, mount, and swap units. The **systemd.directives** man page provides a listing of all systemd unit options and the man page for each option.

The target unit is used to group units. For example, targets are used to emulate runlevels. A multi-user target groups units (services) together that, in System V, would run on runlevel 3. In effect, targets group those services that run on a certain runlevel for a certain task. The printer target activates the CUPS service, and the graphical target emulates runlevel 5. A target can also be used to reference other targets. A default target designated the default runlevel.

Unit Type	Unit Man page	Description
`service`	systemd.service	Services such as servers, which can be started and stopped
`socket`	systemd.socket	Socket for services (allows for inetd like services, AF_INET)
`device`	systemd.device	Devices
`mount`	systemd.mount	File system mount points
`automount`	systemd.automount	Automount point for a file system. Use with mount units.
`target`	systemd.target	Group units
`path`	systemd.path	Manage directories
`snapshot`	systemd.snapshot	Created by systemd using the **systemctl snapshot** command to save runtime states of systemd. Use **systemctl isolate** to restore a state.
`swap`	systemd.swap	Swap unit file generated by systemd for the swap file system.
`timer`	systemd.timer	Time-based activation of a unit. Corresponds to a service file. Time formats are specified on the **systemd.time** man page.
	systemd.unit	Man page with configuration options common to all units
	systemd.exec	Man page for execution environment options for service, socket, mount, and swap units
	systemd.special	Man page for systemd special targets such as multi-user.target and printer.target.
	systemd.time	Time and date formats for **systemd**
	systemd.directives	Listing of all systemd options and the man page they are described on.

Table 14-1: systemd unit types and man pages

Some unit files are automatically generated by **systemd**. For example, operations specified in the **/etc/fstab** are performed by mount units, which are automatically generated from the fstab entries.

Units can be dependent on one another, where one unit may require the activation of other units. This dependency is specified using directories with the **.wants** extension. For example, the **poweroff.target** is dependent on the **plymouth-poweroff** service. The directory **poweroff.target.wants** has a symbolic link to this service. Should you want a service dependent on your graphical desktop, you can add symbolic links to it in the **graphical.target.wants** directory.

It is important to distinguish between the wants directories in the **/etc/systemd/system** directory and those in the **/lib/systemd/system** directory. Those in the **/lib/systemd** directory are set up by your system and should be left alone. To manage your own dependencies, you can set up corresponding wants directories in the **/etc/systemd/system** directory. The **/etc/systemd** directory always takes priority. For example, in the **/etc/systemd/system/multi-user.target.wants** directory you can place links to services that you want started up for the **multi-user.target** (runlevel 3). Your system automatically installs links for services you enable, such as **smb.service** and **httpd.service**. These are all links to the actual service files in the **/lib/systemd/system** directory. The **basic.target.wants** directory holds a link to **firewalld.sevice**, starting up the firewall for all runlevels. The **printer.target.wants** directory has a link to the cups service.

Disabling a service removes its link from its wants directory in **/etc/systemd/system**. For example, disabling the httpd service removes its link from the **/etc/systemd/system/multi-user.target.wants** directory. The original service file, in this case, **httpd.service**, remains in the **/lib/systemd/system** directory. If you enable the service again, a link for it is added to the **/etc/systemd/system/multi-user.target.wants** directory.

The **/etc/systemd/system directory** also hold links to services. The **/etc/systemd/system/default.target** file is a link to the **/lib/systemd/system/multi-user.target.** The **/etc/systemd/system/dbus-org.freedesktop.NetworkManager.service** link references **/lib/systemd/system/NetworkManager.service.**

To manage **systemd** you can use **systemctl** or cockpit. Older service management tools, such as **service** and **chkconfig** have been modified to use **systemctl** to perform actions on services such as starting and stopping.

unit file syntax

A unit file is organized into sections designated by keywords enclosed in brackets. All units have a unit section, **[Unit]**, and an install section, **[Install]**. The options for these sections are descript in the **systemd.unit** Man page. Comments can be written by beginning a line with # or **;** character. See Table 14-2 for a listing of commonly used Unit and Install section options.

The Unit section of a unit file holds generic information about a unit. The Description option provides information about the task the unit manages, such as the Samba server as shown here.

```
Description=Samba SMB Daemon
```

The Documentation option lists URIs for the application's documentation.

```
Documentation=man:dhcpd(8) man:dhcpd.conf(5)
```

Note: The syntax for unit files is base on **.desktop** files, which in turn are inspired by Windows ini files. The .desktop type of file conforms to the XDB Desktop Entry Specification.

Types of dependencies can be specified using the Before, After, Requires, Wants, and Conflicts options in the unit section. After and Before configure the ordering of a unit. In the following After option in the **smb.service** file, the smb service is started after system logging, networking, the nmbd server, and the Winbind server.

```
After=syslog.target network.target nmb.service winbind.service
```

The Requires option sets up a dependency between units. This is a strong dependency. If one fails so does the other. In the following Requires option from the **graphical.target** unit file, the graphical target can only be started if the multi-user target is activated.

```
After=multi-user.target
```

The Wants option sets up a weaker dependency, requiring activation, but not triggering failure should it occur. This is the case with the graphical target and the display manager service like GDM.

```
Wants=display-manager.service
```

Unit options	Description
`[Unit]`	
`Description`	Description of the unit.
`Documentation`	URIs referencing documentation.
`Requires`	Units required by the service. This is a strict requirement. If the required units fail, so will the unit.
`Wants`	Units wanted by the service. This is not a strict requirement. If the required units fail, the unit will still start up. Same functionality as the wants directories.
`Conflicts`	Negative unit dependency. Starting the unit stops the listed units in the Conflicts option.
`Before`	Unit ordering. Unit starts before the units listed.
`After`	Unit ordering. Unit waits until the units listed start.
`OnFailure`	Units to be run if the unit fails.
`SourcePath`	File the configuration was generated from, such as the mount unit files generated from **/etc/fstab**.
`[Install]`	
`WantedBy`	Sets up the unit's symbolic link in listed unit's .wants subdirectory. When the listed unit is activated, so is the unit. This is not a strict requirement.
`RequiredBY`	Sets up the unit's symbolic link in listed unit's .requires subdirectory. When the listed unit is activated, so is the unit. This is a strong requirement.
`Alias`	Additional names the unit is installed under. The aliases are implemented as symbolic links to the unit file.
`Also`	Additional units to install with this unit.

Table 14-2: systemd Unit and Install section options (common to all units, systemd:unit)

Several condition options are available such as ConditionACPower which, if true, checks to see if a system is using AC power. ConditionPathExists checks for the existence of file for static firewall rules.

```
ConditionPathExists=/etc/sysconfig/iptables
```

Some unit files are automatically generated by systemd, allowing you to use older configuration methods. For example, the unit file used to manage the mounting of your file systems is generated from the configuration information in the **/etc/fstab** file. The SourcePath option specifies the configuration file used to generate the unit file. The SourcePath option for the **boot.mount** unit file is shown here.

```
SourcePath=/etc/fstab
```

The Install section provides installation information for the unit. The WantedBy and RequiredBy options specify units that this unit wants or requires. For service units managing servers like Samba and the Apache Web server, the install section has a WantedBy option for the **multi-user.target**. This has the effect of running the server at runlevels 2, 3, 4, and 5. When the multi-user target becomes activated so does that unit.

```
WantedBy=multi-user.target
```

The WantedBy option is implemented by setting up a link to the unit in a wants subdirectory for the wanted by unit. For the **multi-user.target** unit, a subdirectory called **multi-user.target.wants** has symbolic links to all the units that want it, such as **smb.service** for the Samba service. These wants symbolic links are set up in the **/etc/systemd/system** directory, which can be changed as you enable and disable a service. Disabling a service removes the link. RequiredBy is a much stronger dependency.

The Alias option lists other unit names that could reference this unit. This is the case for the **default.target**, which is used to reference a startup target (runlevel). In the **multi-user.target** and the **graphical.target** files you will find an Alias option for **default.target**. When the system starts up, it activates a **default target** which is a symbolic link to the target you want.

```
Alias=default.target
```

The Also option lists other units that should be activated when this unit is started. The Sendmail service has an Also option to start the sendmail client service.

```
Also=sm-client.service
```

Different types of units have their own options. Service, socket, target, and path units all have options appropriate for their tasks.

special targets

A target file groups units for services, mounts, sockets, and devices. **systemd** has a set of special target files designed for specific purposes (see Table 14-3). Some are used for on-demand services such as bluetooth and printer. When a bluetooth device is connected the bluetooth target becomes active. When you connect a printer, the printer target is activated which, in turn, activates the CUPS print server. The sound target is activated when the system starts and runs all sound-related units. See the **special.target** Man page for more details.

There are several special target files that are designed to fulfill the function of runlevels in System V (see Table 14-4). These include the rescue, multi-user, and graphical targets. On boot, **systemd** activates the default target, which is a link to a special target, such as **multi-user.target** and **graphical.target**. You can override the default target with a **systemd.unit** kernel command line option in the GRUB.

The following will start up the rescue target.

```
systemd.unit=rescue.target
```

On the GRUB startup menu, you could edit the kernel boot line and add the following option to boot to the command line instead of the desktop.

```
systemd.unit=multi-user.target
```

The following will start up the rescue target.

```
systemd.unit=rescue.target
```

Special units	Description
`basic.target`	Units to be run at early boot
`bluetooth.target`	Starts when a bluetooth device becomes active
`printer.target`	Starts printer service when a printer is attached.
`sound.target`	Starts when sound device is detected, usually at boot.
`ctrl-alt-del.target`	Activated when the user presses Ctrl-Alt-Del keys, this is a link to the reboot.target which reboots the system.
`system-update.target`	Implements an offline system update. After downloading, the updates are performed when your system reboots, at which time it detects the presence of the target.

Table 14-3: special units

On the GRUB startup menu, you could edit the kernel boot line and add the following option to boot to the command line instead of the desktop.

```
systemd.unit=multi-user.target
```

You could also simply add a 3 as in previous releases, as runlevel links also reference the special targets in **systemd**. The 3 would reference the runlevel 3 target, which links to the multi-user target.

Special RunlevelTargets	Description
`default.target`	References special target to be activated on boot
`rescue.target`	Starts up base system and rescue shell
`emergency.target`	Starts base system, with option to start full system
`multi-user.target`	Starts up command line interface, multi-user and non-graphical (similar to runlevel 3)
`graphical.target`	Start graphical interface (desktop) (similar to runlevel 5)

Table 14-4: special runlevel targets (boot)

A copy of the **multi-user.target** file follows. The multi-user target requires the basic target which loads the basic system (Requires). It conflicts with the rescue target (Conflicts), and it is run after the basic target. It can be isolated allowing you to switch special targets (AllowIsolate). The default.target is an alias for it (Alias), letting that target start it.

multi-user.target

```
[Unit]
Description=Multi-User System
Documentation=man:systemd.special(7)
Requires=basic.target
Conflicts=rescue.service rescue.target
After=basic.target rescue.service rescue.target
AllowIsolate=yes
```

The **graphical.target** depends on the **multi-user.target**. A copy of the **graphical.target** unit file follows. It requires that the **multi-user.target** be activated (Requires). Anything run for the multi-user target, including servers, is also run for the graphical target, the desktop. The desktop target is run after the **multi-user.target** (After). It is not run for the **rescue.target** (Conflicts). It also wants the display-manager service to run (GDM or KDM) (Wants). You can isolate it to switch to another target (AllowIsolate).

graphical.target

```
[Unit]
Description=Graphical Interface
Documentation=man:systemd.special(7)
Requires=multi-user.target
Wants=display-manager.service
Conflicts= rescue.service rescue.target
After=multi-user.target rescue.service rescue.target display-manager.service
AllowIsolate=yes
```

Modifying unit files: /etc/systemd/system

systemd uses unit files to manage devices, mounts, and services. These are located in the **/lib/systemd/system** directory and are considered system files that you should not modify. Instead, to modify a unit file, you should copy it to the **/etc/systemd/system** directory. Unit files in this directory take precedence over those in the **/lib/systemd/system** directory. You can then modify the unit file version in **/etc/systemd/system**. Use a **cp** command to copy the file. The following command copies the Samba service unit file.

```
cp /lib/systemd/system/smb.service   /etc/systemd/system/smb.service
```

If you just want to add unit options to a unit file, not changing the original options in the **/lib/systemd/system** version, you do not have to copy the original unit file. Instead, you can set up a corresponding new unit file in **/etc/systemd/system** that has an include option that reads in the original unit file from **/lib/systemd/system**. Then, in the new **/etc/systemd/system** file, you can add the new systemd options.

Alternatively, you can create a corresponding configuration directory in the /lib/systemd/system directory, where you can place configuration files to be read in by the service or socket file. For example, for the **httpd.service** file, there is a corresponding **httpd.service.d** directory, both in the **/lib/systemd/system** directory. Configuration files have a **.conf** extension, such as **local.conf**. The **/lib/systemd/system/httpd.service.d/local.conf** file will be read in by the **/lib/systemd/system/httpd.service** file and will take priority.

Keep in mind that most runtime options for a service application, such as the Samba server, are still held in the appropriate **/etc/sysconfig** file, such as **/etc/sysconfig/samba**. This file is read by the service when it is activated.

The actual enabling or disabling of services such as Samba or vsftpd is handled through symbolic links set up or removed from the **multi-user.target.wants** directory in the **/etc/systemd/system** directory. This is considered a user based modification appropriate for **/etc/systemd/system**.

Execution Environment Options

The unit files of type service, sockets, mount, and swap share the same options for the execution environment of the unit (see Table 14-5). These are found in the unit section for that type such as **[Service]** for service units or **[Socket]** for socket unit. With these options, you can set features such as the working directory (WorkingDirectory), the file mode creation mask (UMask), and the system logging level (SysLogLevel). Nice sets the default scheduling priority level. User specifies the user id for the processes the unit runs.

```
User=mysql
```

Exec options	Description
`WorkingDirectory`	Sets the working directory for an application.
`RootDirectory`	Root directory for an application
`User, Group`	Application's user and group ids.
`Nice`	Sets priority for an application
`CPUSchedulingPriority`	CPU Scheduling priority for the applications.
`UMask`	File mode creation mask, default is 022.
`Environment`	Set environment variables for an application.
`StandardOutput`	Direct standard output a connection such as log, console, or null.
`SysLogLevel`	System logging level such as warn, alert, info, or debug.
`DeviceAllow, DeviceDeny`	Control applications access to a device.
`ControlGroup`	Assign application to a control group.

Table 14-5: systemd exec options (Service, Socket, Mount, Swap) (systemd:exec)

service unit files

A service unit file is used to run applications and commands such as the Samba (smb) and Web (httpd) servers. They have a **[Service]** section with options specified in the **systemd.service** Man page. See Table 14-6 for a listing of several common service options. A service unit file has the extension **.service** and the prefix is the name of the server program, such as **httpd.service** for the Apache Web server and **vsftpd.service** for the Very Secure FTP server. Table 14-7 lists several popular servers.

Service options	Description
`ExecStart`	Commands to execute when service starts, such as running an application or server.
`Type`	Startup type such as simple (the default), forking, dbus, notify, or idle
`ExecStartPre`, `ExecStartPost`	Commands executed before and after the ExecStart command.
`TimeStartSec`	Time to wait before starting the ExecStart command.
`Restart`	Restart when the ExecStart command end.
`PermissionsStartOnly`	Boolean value, If true the permission based options are applied, such as User.
`RootDirectoryStartOnly`	Boolean value, if true, the RootDirectory option applies only to the ExecStart option.

Table 14-6: systemd service options [Service] (systemd:service)

Service unit files	Description
`NetworkManager`	Operations to start up or shut down your network connections.
`cups`	The CUPS printer daemon
`dhcpd`	Dynamic Host Configuration Protocol daemon
`httpd`	Apache Web server
`iptables`	Controls the IPtables daemon for static firewall
`ip6tables`	IPtables for IP protocol version 6 for static firewall
`krb5kdc`	Kerberos kdc server
`nfs-server`	Network Filesystem
`postfix`	Postfix mail server
`sendmail`	The Sendmail MTA daemon
`smb`	Samba for Windows hosts
`squid`	Squid proxy-cache server
`sshd`	Secure Shell daemon
`systemd-journald`	System logging daemon
`vsftpd`	Very Secure FTP server
`ypbind`	Network Information Service (NIS)

Table 14-7: Collection of Service unit files in /lib/systemd/system

A copy of the Samba service unit file, **smb.service**, follows. The Samba service is started after the system log, network, nmb, and Winbind services have started. It is of type forking (Type). An environment variable for Kerberos is defined (Environment). The process ID file is specified (PIDFile). A limit set to the number of files (LimitNOFILE). The configuration file for environment variables is located in the **/etc/sysconfig** directory, **/etc/sysconfig/samba** (EnvironmentFile). The server program to run is specified, **/usr/sbin/smbd** (ExecStart). The service is installed by the **multi-user.target** (WantedBy), in effect at runlevel 2, 3, 4, and 5, when the system starts up.

smb.service

```
[Unit]
Description=Samba SMB Daemon
After=syslog.target network.target nmb.service winbind.service
[Service]
Environment=KRB5CCNAME=/run/samba/krb5cc_samba
Type=notify
NotifyAccess=all
PIDFile=/run/smbd.pid
LimitNOFILE=16384
EnvironmentFile=-/etc/sysconfig/samba
ExecStart=/usr/sbin/smbd $SMBDOPTIONS
ExecReload=/usr/bin/kill -HUP $MAINPID

[Install]
WantedBy=multi-user.target
```

A copy of the **httpd.service** unit file follows. It is run after network, remote file system mounts, and name service lookup. The service is of type notify (Type). It uses the **/etc/sysconfig/httpd** file for runtime environment options (EnvironmentFile). The server program run is **/usr/sbin/httpd** (ExecStart). The same program is used to reload and stop the server but with different options (ExecReload and ExecStop). It is started by the **multi-user.target** (WantedBy), which is the equivalent of runlevels 2, 3, 4, and 5.

httpd.service

```
[Unit]
Description=The Apache HTTP Server
After=network.target remote-fs.target nss-lookup.target
[Service]
Type=notify
EnvironmentFile=-/etc/sysconfig/httpd
ExecStart=/usr/sbin/httpd $OPTIONS -DFOREGROUND
ExecReload=/usr/sbin/httpd $OPTIONS -k graceful
ExecStop=/bin/kill -WINCH ${MAINPID}
KillSignal=SIGCONT
KillMode=mixed
PrivateTmp=true
[Install]
WantedBy=multi-user.target
```

Some service files are very simple such as the **hddtemp.service** file for monitoring hard drive temperatures. It is run after the system log starts (After). An environment variable is set for the system to access, localhost (Environment). Its runtime environment options are in the **/etc/sysconfig/hddtemp** file. The program it starts is **/usr/sbin/hddtemp (**ExecStart). It is started by the **multi-user.target** when the system starts (WantedBy).

hddtemp.service

```
[Unit]
Description=Hard drive temperature monitor daemon
Documentation=man:hddtemp(8)

[Service]
Environment=HDDTEMP_OPTIONS=--listen=127.0.0.1
EnvironmentFile=-/etc/sysconfig/hddtemp
ExecStart=/usr/sbin/hddtemp -dF $HDDTEMP_OPTIONS

[Install]
WantedBy=multi-user.target
```

The **dhcpd.service** file is even simpler, incorporating configuration references into the program command. It is run after the network and time services and is started by the **multi-user.target**.

dhcpd.service

```
[Unit]
Description=DHCPv4 Server Daemon
Documentation=man:dhcpd(8) man:dhcpd.conf(5)
Wants-network-online.target
After=network.target
After=time-sync.target

[Service]
Type=notify
ExecStart=/usr/sbin/dhcpd -f -cf /etc/dhcp/dhcpd.conf -user dhcpd -group dhcpd --
no-pid
StandardError=null

[Install]
WantedBy=multi-user.target
```

On Demand and Standalone Services (socket)

The On Demand activation of services, formerly implemented by inetd, is the default in systemd. Should you want a standalone service, you can specify that it is wanted by a special target so that it will be started up at boot time, instead of when it is first activated. In the Install section of a service unit file, a WantedBy option specifying the multi-user target will start the service at boot, making it a standalone service. In the following, the service is wanted by the multi-user.target. To put it another way, the service starts at runlevels 2, 3, 4, and 5. Note that the graphical target (5) is dependent on (Requires) the multi-user target (2, 3, and 4), so by specifying the multi-user target, the service is also started with the graphical target.

```
[Install]
WantedBy=multi-user.target
```

The Bluetooth service only wants the **bluetooth.target** which is only activated if a bluetooth device is present. It is not started at boot.

```
[Install]
WantedBy=bluetooth.target
```

Should you want the service started at all runlevels, you would use the **basic.target**, as is done for iptables (**iptables.service**).

```
[Install]
WantedBy=basic.target
```

To emulate an on-demand server service, as inetd used to do, you would use a **.socket** file to compliment a **.service** file. This is the case with CUPS, which has a cups service file and corresponding cups socket file. The WantedBy option for **sockets.target** ties the socket to the special target **sockets.target**, which makes the unit socket-activated.

The Socket section lists options for the socket, usually what socket to listen on (ListenStream). The **systemd.socket** Man page lists socket options. Table 14-8 lists common options.

Socket options	Description
`ListenStream`	Address to listen on for a stream. The address can be a port number, path name for a socket device, or an IPv4 or IPv6 address with a port number.
`Accept`	If true, service instance is set up for each connection; if false, only one service instance is set up for all connections
`MaxConnections`	Maximum number of connections for a service
`Service`	Service unit to run when the socket is active. Default is a service name that is the same as the socket name.

Table 14-8: systemd socket file options [Socket] (systemd:socket)

cups.socket

```
[Unit]
Description=CUPS Printing Service Sockets

[Socket]
ListenStream=/var/run/cups/cups.sock

[Install]
WantedBy=sockets.target
```

cups.service

```
[Unit]
Description=CUPS Printing Service
Documentation=man:cupsd(8)
After=network.target

[Service]
ExecStart=/usr/sbin/cupsd -f
Type=notify

[Install]
Also=cups.socket cups.path
WantedBy=multi-user.target printer.target
```

Path units

systemd uses path units to monitor a path. Sometimes a service unit has a corresponding path unit to monitor directories, as is the case with **cups.path** and **cups.service**. Options for the Path section are listed in Table 14-9 and on the **systemd.path** Man page. The **cups.path** unit file is shown here. The PathExistsGlob option checks if the printer spool files exist.

cups.path

```
[Unit]
Description=CUPS Printer Service Spool

[Path]
PathExistsGlob=/var/spool/cups/d*

[Install]
WantedBy=multi-user.target
```

path options	Description
PathExists	Activates if a file exists
PathExistsGlob	Activates if there exists a file matching a pattern, such as any file in a specified directory.
PathModified	Activates if a file has been modified

Table 14-9: path option (systemd:path)

Template unit files

There is a special type of unit file called a template file, which allow for the generation of several unit files at runtime using one template file. Templates are used for services that generate instances of a service such as a getty terminal, an OpenVPN connection, and an rsync connection. A template file name ends with an **@** sign. If a corresponding unit file is not found for a service, **systemd** will check to see if there is a template file that can be applied to it. **systemd** matches the service name with the template name. It then generates an instance unit for that particular service.

For example, a terminal uses the getty service (get TTY). As you do not know how many terminals you may use, they are generated automatically using the **getty@.service** unit file.

In the configuration file, the **%I** specifier is used to substitute for the service name. Given the service name **getty@tty3**, the **%I** specifier substitutes for **tty3**. The uppercase **%I** uses the argument literally, making no changes in the filename (the literal name).

```
ExecStart=-/sbin/agetty --noclear %I $TERM
```

The **getty@.service** template file is shown here.

getty@.service

```
[Unit]
Description=Getty on %I
Documentation=man:agetty(8) man:systemd-getty-generator(8)
Documentation=http://0pointer.de/blog/projects/serial-console.html
After=systemd-user-sessions.service plymouth-quit-wait.service
After=rc-local.service
# If additional gettys are spawned during boot then we should make
# sure that this is synchronized before getty.target, even though
# getty.target didn't actually pull it in.
Before=getty.target
IgnoreOnIsolate=yes
# On systems without virtual consoles, don't start any getty. (Note
# that serial gettys are covered by serial-getty@.service, not this
# unit
ConditionPathExists=/dev/tty0
[Service]
# the VT is cleared by TTYVTDisallocate
ExecStart=-/sbin/agetty --noclear %I $TERM
Type=idle
Restart=always
RestartSec=0
UtmpIdentifier=%I
TTYPath=/dev/%I
TTYReset=yes
TTYVHangup=yes
TTYVTDisallocate=yes
KillMode=process
IgnoreSIGPIPE=no
SendSIGHUP=yes
# Unset locale for the console getty since the console has problems
# displaying some internationalized messages.
Environment=LANG= LANGUAGE= LC_CTYPE= LC_NUMERIC= LC_TIME= LC_COLLATE=
LC_MONETARY= LC_MESSAGES= LC_PAPER= LC_NAME= LC_ADDRESS= LC_TELEPHONE=
LC_MEASUREMENT= LC_IDENTIFICATION=
[Install]
WantedBy=getty.target
DefaultInstance=tty1
```

The lowercase **%i** specifier escapes characters in the argument to make sure the file name is valid. The OpenVPN service uses the uppercase **%i** for the description and a lowercase **%i** for execution.

openvpn@.service

```
 [Unit]
Description=OpenVPN Robust And Highly Flexible Tunneling Application On %I
After=network.target
[Service]
PrivateTmp=true
Type=forking
PIDFile=/var/run/openvpn/%i.pid
ExecStart=/usr/sbin/openvpn --daemon --writepid /var/run/openvpn/%i.pid --cd
/etc/openvpn/ --config %i.conf
```

```
[Install]
WantedBy=multi-user.target
```

Runlevels and Special Targets

Under the old System V, a Linux system could run in different levels, called **runlevels**, depending on the capabilities you want to give it. Under System V, Linux had several runlevels, numbered from 0 to 6. When you power up your system, you enter the default runlevel. Runlevels 0, 1, and 6 are special runlevels that perform specific functions. Runlevel 0 was the power-down state. Runlevel 6 was the reboot state—it shuts down the system and reboots. Runlevel 1 was the single-user state, which allowed access only to the superuser and does not run any network services.

systemd uses special targets instead of runlevels create the same effect as runlevels, grouping services to run for specified targets. Runlevels are no longer directly implemented. There are two major special targets: multi-user and graphical. The multi-user target is similar to runlevel 3, providing you with a command line login. The graphical target is similar to runlevel 5, providing you with a graphical login and interface.

You set the default target (runlevel) by linking a target's **systemd** service file to the **systemd** default target file. This operation replaces the way inittab was used to specify a default runlevel in previous releases. The **inittab** file is no longer used. The following makes the graphical interface the default (runlevel 5).

```
ln -s /lib/systemd/system/graphicl.target  /etc/systemd/system/default.target
```

systemd does provide compatibility support for runlevels. Runlevel compatibility is implemented using symbolic links in **/lib/system/systemd** directory to **systemd** targets. The **runlevel0.target** link references the **systemd poweroff.target**. Runlevel 2, 3, and 4 targets all link to the same **multi-user.target** (command line interface). The **runlevel6.target** links to the reboot target, and **runlevel5.target** links to **graphical.target** (desktop interface). The runlevels and their targets are listed in Table 14-10.

System Runlevel links	systemd targets
runlevel0	poweroff.target
runlevel1	rescue.target
runlevel2	multi-user.target
runlevel3	multi-user.target
runlevel4	multi-user.target.
runlevel5	graphical.target.
runlevel6	reboot.target

Table 14-10: System Runlevels (States)

You can still use the **runlevel** command to see what state you are currently running in. It lists the previous state followed by the current one. If you have not changed states, the previous state will be listed as N, indicating no previous state. This is the case for the state you boot up in. In the next example, the system is running in state 3, with no previous state change:

```
# runlevel
N 3
```

Changing runlevels can be helpful if you have problems at a particular runlevel. For example, if your video card is not installed properly, then any attempt to start up in runlevel 5 (graphical.target) will likely fail, as this level immediately starts your graphical interface. Instead, you should use the command line interface, runlevel 3 (multi-user.target), to fix your video card installation.

No matter what runlevel you start in, you can change from one runlevel to another with the **telinit** command. If your default runlevel is 3, you power up in runlevel 3, but you can change to, say, runlevel 5 with **telinit 5**. The command **telinit 0** shuts down your system. In the next example, the **telinit** command changes to runlevel 1, the administrative state:

```
telinit 1
```

Before **systemd** was implemented, you could also use **init** to also change runlevels. With **systemd**, both **telinit** and **init** are now **systemd** emulation versions of the original UNIX commands. The **telinit** command is always used to change runlevels. If you use **init** with a runlevel number, it now merely invokes **telinit** to make the change.

Alternatively, you can use the systemctl command directly to change runlevels (targets). The **systemctl** command with the isolate option and the name of the target file changes to that target (runlevel). The following command changes to the multi-user target.

```
systemctl isolate multi-user.target
```

You could also use the runlevel link instead.

```
systemctl isolate runlevel3.target
```

This is what the telinit command actually does.

systemd and automatically mounting file systems: /etc/fstab

The **systemd** unit files with the extension **.mount** can be used to mount file systems automatically. Normally systemd will read the **/etc/fstab** for mount information. If a mount unit file exists in the **/etc/systemd** directory, it takes precedence, but **/etc/fstab** takes precedence over any unit mount files in the **/lib/systemd** directory. Currently, on RHEL, the **/etc/fstab** file is used for mount configuration information. Most of the options for a mount unit file correspond to those of the **/etc/fstab** file, specifying the device path name, the mount point, file system type, and mount options (see Table 14-11). In fact, the entries in the **/etc/fstab** file are converted to mount unit files at boot, which are then used by systemd to perform the actual mount operations. These mount unit files are created by the systemd-fstab-generator and can be found in the **/run/systemd/generator** directory.

The following fstab file entries have corresponding mount files created in the **/run/systemd/generator** directory: **boot.mount** for the boot file system, **home.mount** for the home file system, and **-.mount** for the fedora root file system. For the swap file system a swap unit file is generated, **dev-mapper-rhel\x2dswap.swap.** For the **rhel-home** and **rhel-root** partitions, the RHEL Workstation uses **ext2** formatting, and RHEL Server uses **xfs**.

mount options	Description
What	Path of the device
Where	Directory of the mount point.
Type	File system type
Options	Mount options
DirectoryMode	Permissions for created file system mount directories
TimeoutSec	Time to wait for a mount operation to finish
automount options	**Description**
Where	Mount point for the file system. If it does not exist, it will be created.
DirectoryMode	Permissions for any directories created.

Table 14-11: systemd mount and automount file options [Mount] [Automount]

```
/dev/mapper/rhel-root /         xfs    defaults    0 0
UUID=e759aa59-4a86-4072-982e-000717229b4a /boot    ext4   defaults    0 0
UUID=F075-3DA4 /boot/efi    vfat   umask=0077,shortname=winnt 0 0
/dev/mapper/rhel-home /home     xfs    defaults    0 0
/dev/mapper/rhel-swap swap      swap    defaults    0 0
```

For this example, the **-.mount** file used for the root file system will have the following mount options. The root directory is represented in the mount file name as a dash, -, instead of a slash, /. The mount options are listed in a **[Mount]** section. The RHEL Workstation uses **ext2** formatting, and RHEL Server uses **xfs**.

```
[Mount]
What=/dev/mapper/rhel-root
Where=/
Type=xfs
```

The **home.mount** file references **/dev/mapper/rhel-home** file system and mounts it to the **/home** directory. The RHEL Workstation uses **ext2** formatting, and RHEL Server uses **xfs**.

```
[Mount]
What=/dev/mapper/rhel-home
Where=/home
Type=xfs
```

The **boot.mount** file mounts the ext4 file system that holds the kernel in the **/boot** directory.

```
[Mount]
What=/dev/disk/by-uuid/e759aa59-4a86-4072-982e-000717229b4a
Where=/boot
Type=xfs
```

The EFI partition (required by UEFI motherboards) uses a **vfat** partition, **boot-efi.mount**.

```
[Mount]
What=/dev/disk/by-uuid/F075-3DA4
Where=/boot/efi
```

```
Type=vfat
options=umask=0077,shortname=winnt
```

All the unit files will designate the **/etc/fstab** file as the SourcePath, the file from which the configuration was generated from.

```
SourcePath=/etc/fstab
```

All are mounted before any local file systems.

```
Before=local-fs.target
```

Local and remote file systems are distinguished by Wants options in their unit files for **local-fs.target** or **remote-fs.target**.

A mount unit file has to be named for the mount point it references. The path name slashes are replaced by dashes in the unit name. For example, the **proc-fs-nfsd.mount** file references the mount point **/proc/fs/nfsd**. The root path name, /, becomes simple a dash, -.

For file systems to be automatically mounted when accessed you can use the automount unit type. An automount unit must have a corresponding mount unit of the same name.

systemd slice and scope units

The slice and scope units are designed to group units to more easily control their processes and resources. The scope units are generated by systemd to manage a process and its subprocesses. An example of a scope unit is a user session scope that groups the processes for a user session together. A slice is used to manage resources for processes, such as the machine slice for virtual machines, the system slice for system services, and the user slice for usr sessions.

System V: /etc/rc.d/init.d

The SysVinit support for services is no longer implemented. There are no **rc.d** scripts for starting services. **systemd** manages all services directly. Check the README file in the **/etc/init** directory. For a very few system tasks, you may find System V scripts in the **/etc/rc.d/init.d** directory. **systemd** will read these scripts as configuration information for a service, generating a corresponding unit configuration file for it. Should there be a unit file already in existence, that unit file is used and the System V script is ignored. An **rc-local.service** unit file in the **/lib/systemd/system** directory will run a **/etc/rc.d/rc.local** file, if present. This is to maintain compatibility with older System V configuration.

Shutdown and Poweroff

You can use the **shutdown** and **poweroff** commands to power down the system. The **shutdown** command provides more options. Keep in mind that the **shutdown** command used is the **systemd** version, which will use **poweroff.target** to actually shut down the system. The **poweroff** command with the **-f** option forces a shutdown, with the **--reboot** option, it reboots the system.

```
poweroff
```

The **shutdown** command has a time argument that gives users on the system a warning before you power down. You can specify an exact time to shut down, or a period of minutes from the current time. The exact time is specified by *hh*:*mm* for the hour and minutes. The period of time is indicated by a + and the number of minutes.

The **shutdown** command takes several options with which you can specify how you want your system shut down. The `-h` option, which stands for halt, simply shuts down the system, whereas the `-r` option shuts down the system and then reboots it. In the next example, the system is shut down after ten minutes:

```
shutdown -h +10
```

To shut down the system immediately, you can use `+0` or the word `now`. The shutdown options are listed in Table 14-12. The following example shuts down the system immediately and then reboots:

```
shutdown -r now
```

Command	Description
`shutdown [-rkhncft]` *time* `[`*warning*`]`	Shuts the system down after the specified time period, issuing warnings to users; you can specify a warning message of your own after the time argument; if neither `-h` nor `-r` is specified to shut down the system, the system sets to the administrative mode, runlevel state 1.
Argument	
Time	Has two possible formats: it can be an absolute time in the format *hh*:*mm,* with *hh* as the hour (one or two digits) and *mm* as the minute (in two digits); it can also be in the format +*m,* with *m* as the number of minutes to wait; the word `now` is an alias for `+0`.
Option	
`-t` *sec*	Tells `init` to wait *sec* seconds between sending processes the warning and the kill signals, before changing to another runlevel.
`-k`	Doesn't actually shut down; only sends the warning messages to everybody.
`-r`	Reboots after shutdown, runlevel state 6.
`-h`	Halts after shutdown, runlevel state 0.
`-n`	Doesn't call `init` to do the shutdown; you do it yourself.
`-f`	Skips file system checking (fsck) on reboot.
`-c`	Cancels an already running shutdown; no time argument.

Table 14-12: System Shutdown Options

With the **shutdown** command, you can include a warning message to be sent to all users currently logged in, giving them time to finish what they are doing before you shut them down.

```
shutdown -h +5 "System needs a rest"
```

If you do not specify either the `-h` or the `-r` options, the **shutdown** command shuts down the multi-user mode and shifts you to an administrative single-user mode. In effect, your system state changes from 3 (multi-user state) to 1 (administrative single-user state). Only the root user is active, allowing the root user to perform any necessary system administrative operations with which other users might interfere.

Note: the halt command now merely halts the system, it does not turn it off.

Managing Services

You can select certain services to run and the special target (runlevel) at which to run them. Most services are servers like a Web server or FTP server. Other services provide security, such as SSH or Kerberos. You can decide which services to use with the **chkconfig**, **systemctl**, or cockpit tools.

Enabling services: starting a service automatically at boot

Most services are servers like a Web server or proxy server. Other services provide security, such as SSH or Kerberos. Services such as the Apache Web server, Samba server, and the FTP server are now handled by the **systemd** daemon. You can decide which services to start when the system boots using the **systemctl** command. The older **chkconfig** command and the cockpit tool are simply front ends to the **systemctl** command.

To have a service start up at boot, you need to first enable it using the **systemctl** tool as the root user. Use the **enable** command to enable the service. The following command enables the vsftpd server and the Samba server (**smb**). The **systemctl** command uses the service's service configuration file located in the **/lib/systemd/system** directory.

```
su
systemctl enable vsftpd.service
systemctl enable smb
```

You can also use the **chkconfig** command to enable or disable a service, using the on and off option. **chkconfig** is only a front end for **systemctl**.

```
chkconfig vsftpd on
```

Managing services manually

Use the start, stop, and restart command with systemctl to manually start, stop, and restart a service. The enable command only starts up a service automatically. You could choose to start it manually when you wish using the **start** command. You can stop and restart a service any time using the **stop** and **restart** commands. The **condrestart** command only starts the server if it is already stopped. Use the **status** command to check the current status of service.

```
systemctl start vsftpd
systemctl restart vsftpd
systemctl condrestart vsftpd
systemctl stop vsftpd
systemctl status vsftpd
```

You can also use **service** and cockpit to start, stop, or restart a service. These are simply front ends for the **systemctl** command which performs the actual operation using **systemd**.

```
service start vsftpd
```

Cockpit

The Cockpit management console (available from the RHEL7 Extras repository) provides a Web interface for managing both system administration and internet servers on your system, as well as servers on your network (**http://cockpit-project.org**). The Web interface works best on a desktop system. You can use it to manage your system resources, including services, storage, and networking. Cockpit dynamically updates with systemctl. Should you make changes in a terminal window using systemctl, the changes are immediately shown on Cockpit.

Once you install cockpit, be sure to enable it with **systemd**, and then allows access by your firewall for both cockpit and https. The package name is **cockpit**.

```
yum install cockpit
systemctl start cockpit
firewall-cmd --permanent --add-service=cockpit
```

You can access cockpit using a Web browser and accessing port 9090 on your local system. If you install on the workstation, a Cockpit icon is displayed on the applications overview that you can click to open cockpit with your default browser. The cockpit page initially prompts you for your username and password. It then shows a listing of the systems on your network. Upon clicking one, you will see links on the left side for administration categories such as System administration, services, networking, and storage (see Figure 14-1). The System link shows system information and resource usage.

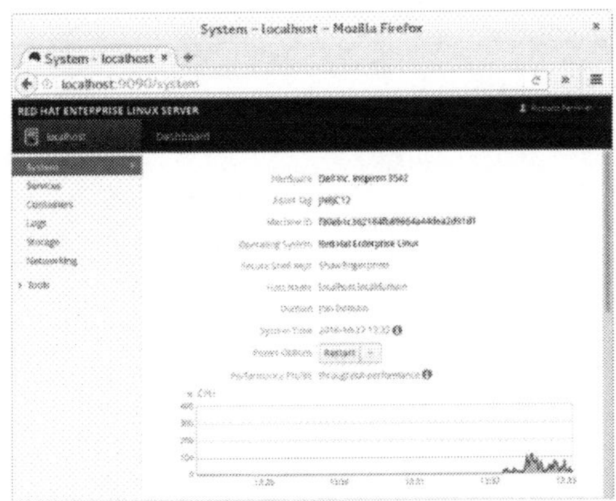

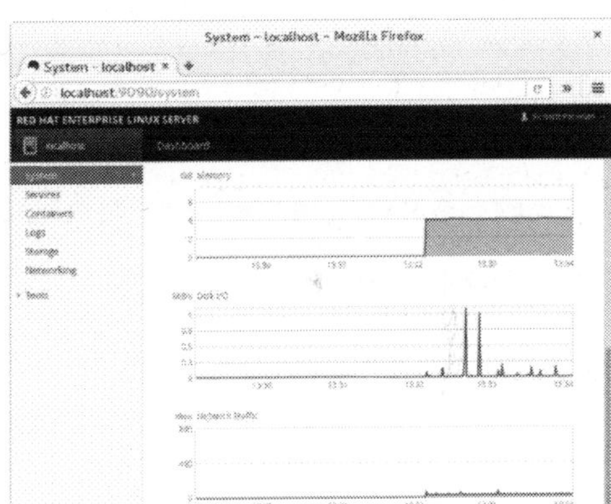

Figure 14-1: System Information: cockpit

Click on the Services link to manage your services. Then click the System Services tab to list the enabled and disabled services, including the network services such as the Apache Web server and the vsftpd FTP server (see Figure 14-2).

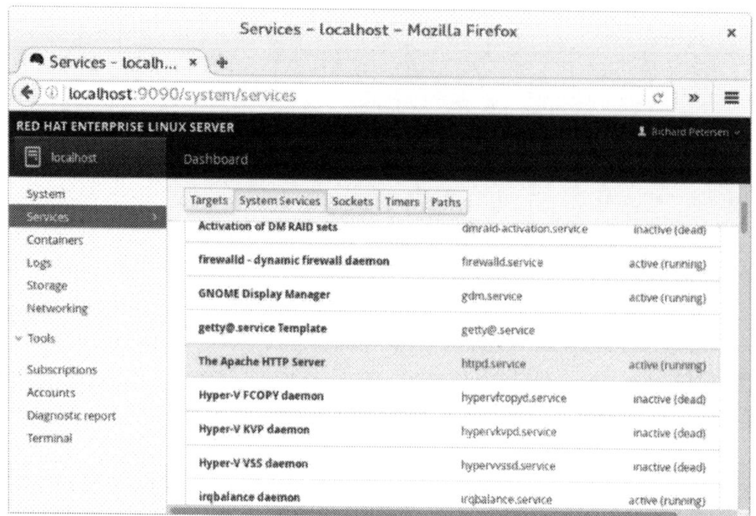

Figure 14-2: Services: cockpit

Click on a service entry to open a dialog where you can manage the service (see Figure 14-3). The dialog is labeled with the systemd service name of the service, such as **httpd.service** for the Apache Web server. Buttons to the right show the current status. A disabled service will show Enable and Start buttons, and an inactive status. An enabled service shows a Disable button and either a Start or Stop button.

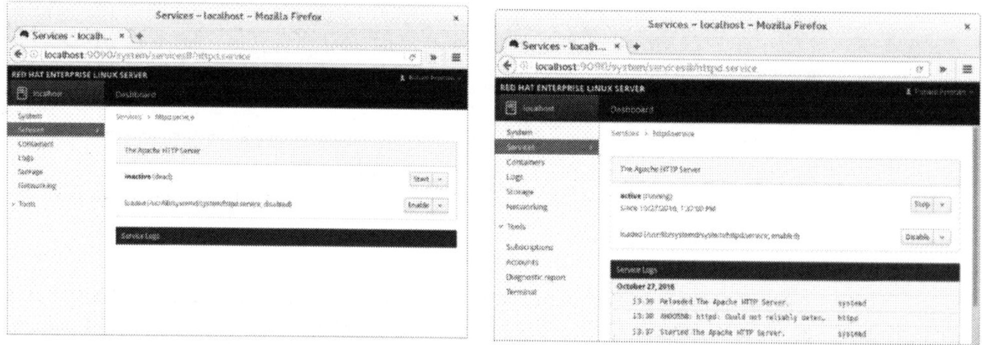

Figure 14-3: Managing a service: cockpit

Clicking on a menu button to the right displays a menu for actions you may want to take, such as stopping or restarting a service (see Figure 14-4). The menus are different for disabled and enabled services.

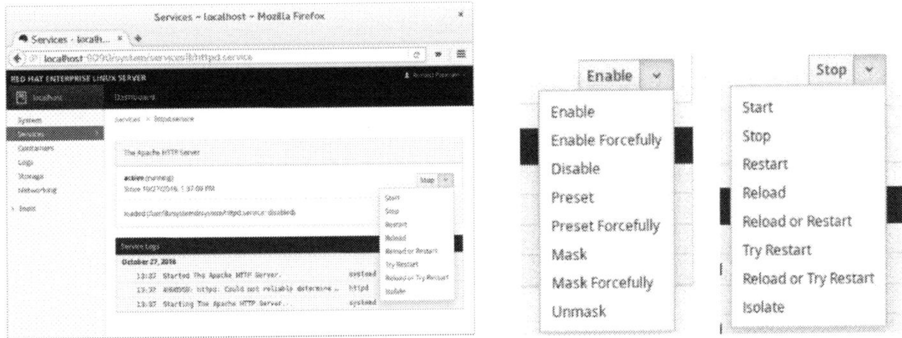

Figure 14-4: Menus for disabled and enabled services: cockpit

When you are finished managing a service, you can click on the Services link at the left or the Services item at the top of the dialog to return to the Services list.

If you disable a service, it is moved down to the disabled list (see Figure 14-5). Enabling a service moves it up to the enabled list. To enable a disabled service, locate it in the Disabled list and click on it to open its management tab, where you can enable it.

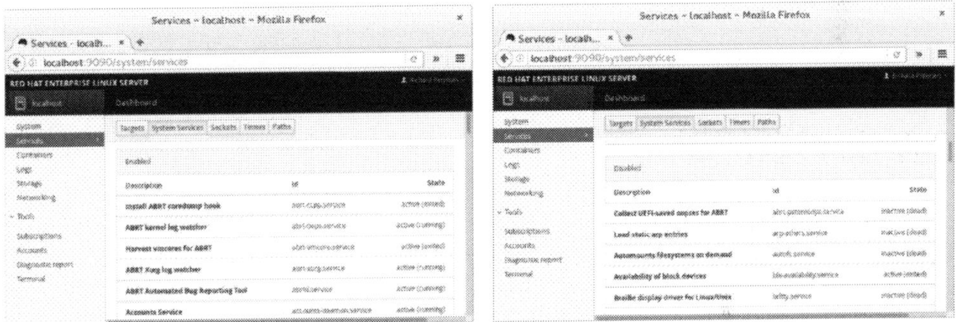

Figure 14-5: Enabled and Disabled Service lists: cockpit

chkconfig

To configure a service to start up automatically when the system boots, you also can use the `chkconfig` tool, which is run on a command line. The `chkconfig` command uses the `on` and `off` options to select and deselect services for startup.

```
chkconfig smb on
```

The chkconfig tool has been modified to work with **systemd**. You can use chkconfig to turn services on or off (enable or disable).However, runlevels are no longer supported.

Though chkconfig can turn **systemd** service on or off, it was still designed for use by System V services. chkconfig with the **--list** option lists only System V services, which may not be valid. The **--level** option is also no longer valid, as **systemd** no longer supports runlevels for services. You can enter it, but it is ignored. The **reset** command does not work with **systemd** services.

You use the `on` option to have a service enabled, and the `off` option to disable it.

```
chkconfig httpd on
```

The `off` option disables a service:

```
chkconfig httpd off
```

The service Command

The **service** command is now simply a front end for the **systemctl** command which performs the actual operation using **systemd**. The **service** command cannot enable or disable services. It only performs management operations such as stop, restart, and status. To start and stop services manually, you can use cockpit or the `service` command. With the `service` command, you enter the service name with the `stop` argument to stop it, the `start` argument to start it, and the `restart` argument to restart it. The `service` command is run from a Terminal window. You will have first to log in as the **root** user, using the **su** command, or use the **sudo** command if configured. The following will start the **smb** Samba service.

```
service smb start
```

In RHEL, the **systemd** version of the **service** command actually invokes the **systemctl** command to run the service's **systemd .servic**e unit file in **/lib/systemd/system**. If a service is not enabled, **systemd** will enable it. You can perform the same operations as the **service** command, using the **systemctl** command. The following is the equivalent of the previous command.

```
systemctl start smb
```

Extended Internet Services Daemon (xinetd)

Xinetd functionality is now performed by **systemd**. Only a few older applications still make use of it. The xinetd package is not installed by default. You should install it only if an older package requires it. Use **chkconfig** to turn a xinetd service on. The service is started up or shut down, and the disable line in its xinetd configuration script in the **/etc/xinetd.d** directory is edited accordingly.

15. Backups

Individual Backups: archive and rsync

Amanda

Backups with dump and restore

Backup operations have become an important part of administrative duties. Several backup tools are provided on Linux systems, including Anaconda and the traditional dump/restore tools, as well as the **rsync** command for making individual copies. Anaconda provides server-based backups, letting different systems on a network back up to a central server. The dump tools let you refine your backup process, detecting data changed since the last backup. Table 15-1 lists Web sites for Linux backup tools.

Web Site	Tools
http://rsync.samba.org	rsync remote copy backup
http://www.amanda.org	Amanda network backup
http://dump.sourceforge.net	dump and restore tools

Table 15-1: Backup resources

Note: You can also use BackupPC and Duplicity for backups which are available from the EPEL repository.

Individual Backups: archive and rsync

You can back up and restore particular files and folders with archive tools like **tar**, restoring the archives later. For backups, **tar** is usually used with a tape device. To automatically schedule backups, you can schedule appropriate **tar** commands with the **cron** utility. The archives can also be compressed for storage savings. You can then copy the compressed archives to any medium, such as a DVD disc, a floppy, or tape. On GNOME you can use File Roller to create archives easily (Archive Manager under System Tools). The Kdat tool on KDE will back up to tapes, a front end to **tar**.

If you want to remote-copy a folder or files from one host to another, making a particular backup, you can use **rsync**, which is designed for network backups of particular folders or files, intelligently copying only those files that have been changed, rather than the contents of an entire folder. In archive mode, it can preserve the original ownership and permissions, providing corresponding users exist on the host system. The following example copies the **/home/george/myproject** folder to the **/backup** folder on the host **rabbit**, creating a corresponding **myproject** subfolder. The **-t** specifies that this is a transfer. The remote host is referenced with an attached colon, **rabbit:**.

```
rsync -t /home/george/myproject   rabbit:/backup
```

If instead, you wanted to preserve the ownership and permissions of the files, you would use the **-a** (archive) option. Adding a **-z** option will compress the file. The **-v** option provides a verbose mode.

```
rsync -avz  /home/george/myproject   rabbit:/backup
```

A trailing slash on the source will copy the contents of the folder, rather than generating a subfolder of that name. Here the contents of the **myproject** folder are copied to the **george-project** folder.

```
rsync -avz  /home/george/myproject/   rabbit:/backup/george-project
```

The **rsync** command is configured to use SSH remote shell by default. You can specify it or an alternate remote shell to use with the **-e** option. For secure transmission, you can encrypt the copy operation with ssh. Either use the **-e ssh** option or set the **RSYNC_RSH** variable to ssh.

```
rsync -avz -e ssh  /home/george/myproject   rabbit:/backup/myproject
```

As when using **rcp**, you can copy from a remote host to the one you are on.

```
rsync -avz  lizard:/home/mark/mypics/  /pic-archive/markpics
```

You can also run rsync as a server daemon. This will allow remote users to sync copies of files on your system with versions on their own, transferring changed files rather than entire folders. Many mirror and software FTP sites operate as rsync servers, letting you update files without have to download the full versions again. Configuration information for rsync as a server is kept in the **/etc/rsyncd.conf** file. On Linux, rsync as a server is managed through systemd, using the **rsyncd** service and socket files, which starts **rsync** with the --**daemon** option. It is off by default, but you can enable it with the **systemctl** tool.

Tip: Though it is designed for copying between hosts, you can also use **rsync** to make copies within your own system, usually to a folder in another partition or hard drive. There are different ways of using **rsync**. Check the **rsync** Man page for detailed descriptions.

Amanda

To back up hosts connected to a network, you can use the Advanced Maryland Automatic Network Disk Archiver (Amanda) to archive hosts. Amanda uses **tar** tools to back up all hosts to a single host operating as a backup server. Backup data is sent by each host to the host operating as the Amanda server, where they are written out to a backup medium such as tape. With an Amanda server, the backup operations for all hosts become centralized in one server, instead of each host having to perform their own backup. Any host that needs to restore data simply requests it from the Amanda server, specifying the file system, date, and filenames. Backup data are copied to the server's holding disk and from there to tapes. Detailed documentation and updates are provided at **http://www.amanda.org**. For the server, be sure to install the amanda-server package, and for clients, you would use the amanda-clients package.

Amanda is designed for automatic backups of hosts that may have very different configurations, as well as operating systems. You can back up any host that supports GNU tools, including Mac OS X and Windows systems connected through Samba.

Amanda Commands

Amanda has its own commands corresponding to the common backup tasks, beginning with "am," such as **amdump**, **amrestore**, and **amrecover**. The commands are listed in Table 15-2. The **amdump** command is the primary backup operation.

The **amdump** command performs requested backups; it is not designed for interactive use. For an interactive backup, you would use an archive tool like **tar** directly. The **amdump** is placed within a cron instruction to be run at a specified time. If for some reason, **amdump** cannot save all its data to the backup medium (tape or disk), it will retain the data on the holding disk. The data can then later be directly written with the with the **amflush** command. You can restore particular files as well as complete systems with the **amrestore** command. With the **amrecover** tool, you can select from a list of backups.

Command	Description
amdump	Perform automatic backups for the file systems listed in the disklist configuration file.
amflush	Used to directly back up data from the holding disk to a tape.
amcleanup	Clean up if there is a system failure on the server.
amrecover	Select backups to restore using an interactive shell.
amrestore	Restore backups, either files or complete systems.
amlabel	Label the backup medium for Amanda.
amcheck	Check the backup systems and files as well as the backup tapes before backup operations.
amadmin	Backup administrative tasks.
amtape	Manage backup tapes, loading and removing them.
amverify	Check the format of tapes.
amverifyrun	Check the tapes from the previous run, specify the configuration folder for the backup.
amrmtape	Remove a tape from the Amanda database, use for damaged tapes.
amstatus	Show the status of the current Amanda backup operation.

Table 15-2: Amanda Commands

Amanda Configuration

Configuration files are placed in **/etc/amanda**, and log and database files in **/var/lib/amanda**. These are created automatically when you installed Amanda. You will also need to create a folder to use as a holding disk where backups are kept before writing to the tape. This should be on a file system with very large available space, enough to hold the backup of your largest entire host.

/etc/amanda

Within the **/etc/amanda** folder are subfolders for the different kind of backups you want to perform. Each folder will contain its own **amanda.conf** and **disklist** file. By default, a daily backup folder is created called **DailySet1**, with a default **amanda.conf** and a sample **disklist** file. To use them, you will have to edit them to enter your system's own settings. For a different backup configuration, you can create a new folder and copy the **DailySet1/amanda.conf** and **disklist** files to it, editing them as appropriate. When you issue Amanda commands like **amdump** to perform backups, you will use the name of the **/etc/amanda** subfolder to indicate the kind of backup you want performed.

```
amdump DailySet1
```

The **/etc/amanda** folder also contains a sample cron file, **crontab.sample** that shows how a cron entry should look.

amanda.conf

The **amanda.conf** file contains basic configuration parameters such as the tape type and logfile as well as holding file locations. In most cases, you can just use the defaults as listed in the **DailySet1/amanda.conf** file. The file is commented in detail, telling you what entries you will have to change. You will need to set the tapedev entries to the tape device you use, and the tape type entry for your tape drive type. In the holding disk segment, you will need to specify the partition and the folder for the holding disk you want to use. See the amanda Man page and documentation for detailed information on various options.

disklist

The **disklist** file is where you specify the file systems and partitions to be backed up. An entry lists the host, the partition, and the dump-type. The possible dump-types are defined in **amanda.conf**. The dump-types set certain parameters such as the priority of the backup and whether to use compression or not. The comp-root type will back up root partitions with compression and low priority, whereas the always-full type will back up an entire partition with no compression and the highest priority. You can define other dump-types in **amanda.conf** and use them for different partitions.

Backups will be performed in the order listed; be sure to list the more important ones first. The **disklist** file in **DailySet1** provides detailed examples.

Enabling Amanda on the Network

To use Amanda on the network, you need to run two servers on the Amanda server as well as an Amanda client on each network host. Access must be enabled for both the clients and the server.

Amanda Server

The Amanda server runs through systemd, using Amanda systemd service files located in **/lib/systemd/system**. The Amanda systemd template file, allowing for multiple instances of the Amanda server, **amanda@.service.** The template file uses the TCP protocol.

amanda@.service

```
[Unit]
Description=Amanda Backup System
After=local-fs.target

[Service]
User=amandabackup
Group=disk
ExecStart=/user/sbin/amandad -auth=bsdtcp amdump
StandardInput=socket
```

For the UDP protocol, use the **amanda-udp.service** file, and enable and start the Amanda server directly with **systemctl**.

```
systemctl enable amanda-udp
systemctl start amanda-udp
```

For clients to be able to recover backups from the server, the clients' host names must be placed in the **.amandahosts** file in the server's Amanda users' folder. This is **/var/lib/amanda**. On the server, **/var/lib/amanda/.amandahosts** will list all the hosts that are backed up by Amanda.

Amanda Hosts

Each host needs to allow access by the Amanda server. To do this, you place the host name of the Amanda server in each client's **.amandahosts** dot file. This file is located in the client's Amanda user home folder, **/var/lib/amanda**.

Tip: If your server and hosts have firewalls, you will need to allow access through the ports that Amanda uses, usually 10080, 10082, and 10083.

Using Amanda

Backups are performed by the **amdump** command.

```
amdump DailySet1
```

An **amdump** command for each backup is placed in the Amanda **crontab** file. It is helpful to run an **amcheck** operation to make sure that a tape is ready.

```
0 16 * * 1-5 /usr/sbin/amcheck -m DailySet1
45 0 * * 2-6 /usr/sbin/amdump DailySet1
```

Before you can use a tape, you will have to label it with **amlabel**. Amanda uses the label to determine what tape should be used for a backup. Log in as the Amanda user (not root) and label the tape so that it can be used.

```
amlabel DailySet DailySet1
```

A client can recover a backup using **amrecover**. This needs to be run as the root user, not as the Amanda user. The **amrecover** command works through an interactive shell much like **ftp**, letting you list available files and select them to restore. Within the **amrecover** shell, the **ls** command will list available backups, the **add** command will select one, and the extract operation will restore it. The **lcd** command lets you change the client folder; **amrecover** will use **DailySet1** as the default, but for other configurations, you will need to specify their configuration folder with the **-C** option. Should you have more than one Amanda server, you can list the one you want with the **-t** option.

```
amrecover -C DailySet1
```

To restore full system backups, you use the **amrecover** command, specifying the tape device and the host name.

```
amrestore  /dev/rmt1  rabbit
```

To select certain files, you can pipe the output to a recovery command such as **restore** (discussed in the next section).

```
amrestore -p /dev/rmt1  rabbit mydir  | restore  -ibvf 2 -
```

Backups with dump and restore

You can back up and restore your system with the dump and restore utilities. dump can back up your entire system or perform incremental backups, saving only those files that have changed since the last backup. The dump operation supports several options for managing the backup operation, such as specifying the size and length of storage media (see Table 15-3).

The dump Levels

The dump utility uses dump levels to determine to what degree you want your system backed up. A dump level of 0 will copy file systems in their entirety. The remaining dump levels perform incremental backups, backing up only files and folders that have been created or modified since the last lower-level backup. A dump level of 1 will back up only files that have changed since the last level 0 backup. The dump level 2, in turn, will back up only files that have changed since the last level 1 backup (or 0 if there is no level 1), and so on up to dump level 9.

You could run an initial complete backup at dump level 0 to back up your entire system, and then run incremental backups at certain later dates, having to back up only the changes since the full backup.

Using dump levels, you can devise certain strategies for backing up a file system. It is important to keep in mind that an incremental backup is run on changes from the last lower-level backup. For example, if the last backup was 6 and the next backup was 8, then the level 8 would back up everything from the level 6 backup. The sequence of the backups is important. If there were three backups with levels 3, then 6, and then 5, the level 5 backup would take everything from the level 3 backup, not stopping at level 6. Level 3 is the next-lower-level backup for level 5, in this case. This can make for some complex incremental backup strategies. For example, if you want each succeeding incremental backup to include all the changes from the preceding incremental backups, you could run the backups in descending dump level order. Given a backup sequence of 7, 6, and 5, with 0 as the initial full backup, 6 would include all the changes to 7, because its next lower level is 0. Then 5 would include all the changes for 7 and 6, also because its next lower level is 0, making all the changes since the level 0 full backup. A simpler way to implement this is to make the incremental levels all the same. Given an initial level of 0, and then two backups both with level 1, the last level 1 would include all the changes from the backup with level 0, since level 0 is the next lower level, not the previous level 1 backup.

Recording Backups

Backups are recorded in the **/etc/dumpdates** file. This file will list all the previous backups, specifying the file system they were performed on, the dates they were performed, and the dump level used. You can use this information to restore files from a specified backup. Recall that the **/etc/fstab** file records the dump level as well as the recommended backup frequency for each file system. With the **-W** option, dump will analyze both the **/etc/dumpdates** and **/etc/fstab** files to determine which file systems need to be backed up. The **dump** command with the **-w** option just uses **/etc/fstab** to report the file systems ready for backup.

Option	Description
-0 through **-9**	Specifies the dump level. A dump level 0 is a full backup, copying the entire file system (see also the **-h** option). Dump level numbers above 0 perform incremental backups, copying all new or modified files new in the file system since the last backup at a lower level. The default level is 9.
-B *records*	Lets you specify the number of blocks in a volume, overriding the end-of-media detection or length and density calculations that dump normally uses for multivolume dumps.
-a	Lets dump bypass any tape length calculations and write until an end-of-media indication is detected. Recommended for most modern tape drives and is the default.
-b *blocksize*	Lets you specify the number of kilobytes per dump record. With this option, you can create larger blocks, speeding up backups.
-d *density*	Specifies the density for a tape in bits per inch (default is 1,600 BPI).
-h *level*	Files that are tagged with a user's nodump flag will not be backed up at or above this specified level. The default is 1, which will not back up the tagged files in incremental backups.
-f *file/device*	Backs up the file system to the specified file or device. This can be a file or tape drive. You can specify multiple filenames, separated by commas. A remote device or file can be referenced with a preceding hostname, *hostname:file.*
-M *file/device*	Implements a multivolume backup, where the *file* written to is treated as a prefix and the suffix consisting of a numbered sequence from 001 is used for each succeeding file, *file*001, *file* 002, etc. Useful when backup files need to be greater than the Linux **ext3** 2GB file size limit.
-n	Notifies operators if a backup needs operator attention.
-s *feet*	Specifies the length of a tape in feet. dump will prompt for a new tape when the length is reached.
-S	Estimates the amount of space needed to perform a backup.
-T *date*	Allows you to specify your own date instead of using the **/etc/dumpdates** file.
-u	Writes an entry for a successful update in the **/etc/dumpdates** file.
-W	Detects and displays the file systems that need to be backed up. This information is taken from the **/etc/dumpdates** and **/etc/fstab** files.
-w	Detects and displays the file systems that need to be backed up, drawing only on information in **/etc/fstab**.

Table 15-3: Options for dump

Operations with dump

The **dump** command takes as its arguments the dump level, the device it is storing the backup on, and the device name of the filesystem that is being backed up. If the storage medium (such as a tape) is too small to accommodate the backup, **dump** will pause and let you insert another. **dump** supports backups on multiple volumes. The **u** option will record the backup in the **/etc/dumpdates** file. In the following example, an entire backup (dump level 0) is performed on the file system on the **/dev/sda3** hard disk partition. The backup is stored on a tape device, **/dev/tape**.

```
dump -0u -f /dev/tape /dev/sda5
```

Note: You can use the **mt** command to control your tape device; **mt** has options to rewind, erase, and position the tape. The **rmt** command controls a remote tape device.

The storage device can be another hard disk partition, but it is usually a tape device. When you installed your system, your system most likely detected the device and set up **/dev/tape** as a link to it (just as it did with your CD-ROMs). If the link was not set up, you have to create it yourself or use the device name directly. Tape devices can have different device names, depending on the model or interface. SCSI tape devices are labeled with the prefix **st**, with a number attached for the particular device: **st0** is the first SCSI tape device. To use it in the **dump** command, just specify its name.

```
dump -0u -f /dev/st0 /dev/sda5
```

Should you need to back up to a device located on another system on your network, you would have to specify that hostname for the system and the name of its device. The hostname is entered before the device name and delimited with a colon. In the following example, the user backs up file system **/dev/sda5** to the SCSI tape device with the name **/dev/st1** on the **rabbit.mytrek.com** system:

```
dump -0u -f rabbit.mytrek.com:/dev/st0 /dev/sda5
```

The **dump** command works on one file system at a time. If your system has more than one file system, you will need to issue a separate **dump** command for each.

Tip: You can use the system **cron** utility to schedule backups using dump at specified times.

Recovering Backups

You use the **restore** command either to restore an entire file system or to retrieve particular files. **restore** will extract files or folders from a backup archive and copy them to the current working folder. Make sure you are in the folder you want the files restored to when you run **restore**. **restore** will also generate any subfolders as needed. **restore** has several options for managing the restore operation (see Table 15-4).

To recover individual files and folders, you run **restore** in an interactive mode using the **-i** option. This will generate a shell with all the folders and files on the tape, letting you select the ones you want to restore. When you are finished, **restore** will then retrieve from a backup only those files you selected. This shell has its own set of commands that you can use to select and extract files and folders (see Table 15-5). The following command will generate an interactive interface listing all the folders and files backed up on the tape in the **/dev/tape** device:

```
restore -ivf /dev/tape
```

This command will generate a shell encompassing the entire folder structure of the backup. You are given a shell prompt and can use the **cd** command to move to different folders, and the **ls** command to list files and subfolders. You use the **add** command to tag a file or folder for extraction. Should you later decide not to extract it, you can use the **delete** command to remove from the tagged list. Once you have selected all the items you want, you enter the **extract** command to retrieve them from the backup archive. To quit the restore shell, you enter **quit**. The **help** command will list the restore shell commands.

Operation	Description
-C	Lets you check a backup by comparing files on a file system with those in a backup.
-i	The interactive mode for restoring particular files and folders in a backup. A shell interface is generated where the user can use commands to specify file and folders to restore (see Table 15-5).
-R	Instructs **restore** to request a tape that is part of a multivolume backup, from which to continue the restore operation. Helpful when multivolume restore operations are interrupted.
-r	Restores a file system. Make sure that a newly formatted partition has been mounted and that you have changed to its top folder.
-t	Lists the contents of a backup or specified files in it.
-x	Extracts specified files or folders from a backup. A folder is restored with all its subfolders. If no file or folder is specified, the entire file system is restored.
Additional Option	**Description**
-b *blocksize*	Use a specific block size; otherwise, restore will dynamically determine it from the block device.
-f *file/device*	Restores the backup on the specified file or device. Specify a hostname for remote devices.
-F *script*	Runs a script at the beginning of the restore.
-k	Uses Kerberos authentication for remote devices.
-h	Extracts only the specified folders, without their subfolders.
-M *file/device*	Restores from multivolume backups, where the *file* is treated as a prefix and the suffix is a numbered sequence, *file*001, *file*002.
-N	Displays the names of files and folders, does not extract them.
-T *folder*	Specifies a folder to use for the storage of temporary files. The default value is **/tmp**.
-v	The verbose mode, where each file and its file type that **restore** operates on is displayed.
-y	By default, **restore** will query the operator to continue if an error occurs, such as bad blocks. This option suppresses that query, allowing **restore** to automatically continue.

Table 15-4: Operations and Options for restore

If you need to restore an entire file system, you would use restore with the **-r** option. You can restore the file system to any blank formatted hard disk partition of adequate size, including the file system's original partition. If may be advisable, if possible, to restore the file system on another partition and check the results.

Command	Description
add [*arg*]	Adds files or folders to the list of files to be extracted. Such tagged files display an * before their names when listed with **ls**. All subfolders of a tagged folder are also extracted.
cd *arg*	Changes the current working folder.
delete [*arg*]	Deletes a file or folder from the extraction list. All subfolders for deleted folders will also be removed.
extract	Extracts files and folders on the extraction list.
help	Displays a list of available commands.
ls [*arg*]	Lists the contents of the current working folder or a specified folder.
pwd	Displays the full pathname of the current working folder.
quit	Exits the restore interactive mode shell. The **quit** command does not perform any extraction, even if the extraction list still has items in it.
setmodes	Sets the owner, modes, and times for all files and folders in the extraction list. Used to clean up an interrupted restore.
verbose	In the verbose mode, each file is listed as it is extracted. Also, the **ls** command lists the inode numbers for files and folders.

Table 15-5: Interactive Mode Shell Commands for restore

Restoring an entire file system involves setting up a formatted partition, mounting it to your system, and then changing to its top folder to run the **restore** command. First, you should use **mkfs** to format the partition where you are restoring the filesystem, and then mount it onto your system. Then you use restore with the **-r** option and the **-f** option to specify the device holding the file system's backup. In the next example, the user formats and mounts the **/dev/sda5** partition and then restores on that partition the file system backup, currently on a tape in the **/dev/tape** device.

```
mkfs /dev/sda5
mount /dev/sda5 /mystuff
cd /mystuff
restore -rf /dev/tape
```

To restore from a backup device located on another system on your network, you would have to specify that hostname for the system and the name of its device. The hostname is entered before the device name and delimited with a colon. In the following example, the user restores a file system from the backup on the tape device with the name **/dev/tape** on the **rabbit.mytrek.com** system:

```
restore -rf rabbit.mytrek.com:/dev/tape
```

16. Shells

Terminal Window

The Command Line

History

Filename Expansion: *, ?, [ ]

Standard Input/Output and Redirection

Listing, Displaying, and Printing Files: ls, cat, more, less, and lpr

Managing Folders: mkdir, rmdir, ls, cd, pwd

File and Folder Operations: find, cp, mv, rm, ln

The shell is a command interpreter that provides a line-oriented interactive and non-interactive interface between the user and the operating system. You enter commands on a command line; they are interpreted by the shell and then sent as instructions to the operating system (the command line interface is accessible from Gnome and KDE through a Terminal window. You can also place commands in a script file to be consecutively executed much like a program. This interpretive capability of the shell provides for many sophisticated features. For example, the shell has a set of file expansion characters that can generate filenames. The shell can redirect input and output, as well as run operations in the background, freeing you to perform other tasks.

Shell	Web Site
`www.gnu.org/software/bash`	BASH Web site with online manual, FAQ, and current releases
`www.gnu.org/software/bash/manual/bash.html`	BASH online manual
`www.zsh.org`	Z shell Web site with referrals to FAQs and current downloads.
`www.tcsh.org`	TCSH Web site with detailed support including manual, tips, FAQ, and recent releases
`www.kornshell.com`	Korn shell site with manual, FAQ, and references

Table 16-1: Linux Shells

Several different types of shells have been developed for Linux: the Bourne Again shell (BASH), the Korn shell, the TCSH shell, and the Z shell. All shells are available for your use, although the BASH shell is the default. You only need one type of shell to do your work. Red Hat Enterprise Linux includes all the major shells, although it installs and uses the BASH shell as the default. If you use the command line shell, you will be using the BASH shell unless you specify another. This chapter discusses the BASH shell, which shares many of the same features as other shells.

You can find out more about shells at their respective Web sites as listed in Table 16-1. Also, a detailed online manual is available for each installed shell. Use the **man** command and the shell's keyword to access them, **bash** for the BASH shell, **ksh** for the Korn shell, **zsh** for the Z shell, and **tsch** for the TSCH shell. For example, the command **man bash** will access the BASH shell online manual.

The shell refers to folders as directories and subfolders as subdirectories. Those terms will be used in this chapter and the next.

Terminal Window

The Terminal window allows you to enter Linux commands on a command line (Applications | System Tools | Terminal). It also provides you with a shell interface for using shell commands instead of your desktop. The command line is editable, allowing you to use the backspace key to erase characters on the line. Pressing a key will insert that character. You can use the left and right arrow keys to move anywhere on the line, and then press keys to insert characters, or use backspace to delete characters. Directories, files, and executable files are color coded: black for files, blue for directories, green for executable files, and aqua for links. Shared directories are displayed with a green background.

The Command Line

The Linux command line interface consists of a single line into which you enter commands with any of their options and arguments. From GNOME or KDE, you can access the command line interface by opening a terminal window. Should you start Linux with the command line interface, you will be presented with a BASH shell command line when you log in.

Note: You can find out more about the BASH shell at **www.gnu.org/software/bash**. A detailed online manual is available on your Linux system using the **man** command with the **bash** keyword.

By default, the BASH shell has a dollar sign (**$**) prompt, but Linux has several other types of shells, each with its own prompt (like **%** for the C shell). The root user will have a different prompt, the #. A shell *prompt*, such as the one shown here, marks the beginning of the command line:

```
$
```

You can enter a command along with options and arguments at the prompt. For example, with an **-l** option, the **ls** command will display a line of information about each file, listing such data as its size and the date and time it was last modified. In the next example, the user enters the **ls** command followed by a **-l** option. The dash before the **-l** option is required. Linux uses it to distinguish an option from an argument.

```
$ ls -l
```

If you wanted only the information displayed for a particular file, you could add that file's name as the argument, following the **-l** option:

```
$ ls -l mydata
-rw-r--r-- 1 chris weather 207 Feb 20 11:55 mydata
```

Tip: Some commands can be complex and take some time to execute. When you mistakenly execute the wrong command, you can interrupt and stop such commands with the interrupt key—CTRL-C.

You can enter a command on several lines by typing a backslash just before you press ENTER. The backslash "escapes" the ENTER key, effectively continuing the same command line to the next line. In the next example, the **cp** command is entered on three lines. The first two lines end in a backslash, effectively making all three lines one command line.

```
$ cp -i \
mydata \
/home/george/myproject/newdata
```

You can also enter several commands on the same line by separating them with a semicolon (**;**). In effect, the semicolon operates as an execute operation. Commands will be executed in the sequence they are entered. The following command executes an **ls** command followed by a **date** command.

```
$ ls ; date
```

You can also conditionally run several commands on the same line with the **&&** operator. A command is executed only if the previous one is true. This feature is useful for running several dependent scripts on the same line. In the next example, the **ls** command is run only if the **date** command is successfully executed.

```
$ date && ls
```

TIP: Command can also be run as arguments on a command line, using their results for other commands. To run a command within a command line, you encase the command in back quotes.

Command Line Editing

The BASH shell, which is your default shell, has special command line editing capabilities that you may find helpful as you learn Linux (see Table 16-2). You can easily modify commands you have entered before executing them, moving anywhere on the command line and inserting or deleting characters. This is particularly helpful for complex commands. You can use the CTRL-F or RIGHT ARROW key to move forward a character, or the CTRL-B or LEFT ARROW key to move back a character. CTRL-D or DEL deletes the character the cursor is on, and CTRL-H or BACKSPACE deletes the character before the cursor. To add text, you use the arrow keys to move the cursor to where you want to insert text and type the new characters. You can even cut words with the CTRL-W or ALT-D key and then use the CTRL-Y key to paste them back in at a different position, effectively moving the words. As a rule, the CTRL version of the command operates on characters, and the ALT version works on words, such as CTRL-T to transpose characters and ALT-T to transpose words. At any time, you can press ENTER to execute the command.

For example, if you make a spelling mistake when entering a command, rather than reentering the entire command, you can use the editing operations to correct the mistake. The actual associations of keys and their tasks, along with global settings, are specified in the **/etc/inputrc** file.

The editing capabilities of the BASH shell command line are provided by Readline. Readline supports numerous editing operations. You can even bind a key to a selected editing operation. Readline uses the **/etc/inputrc** file to configure key bindings. This file is read automatically by your **/etc/profile** shell configuration file when you log in. Users can customize their editing commands by creating an **.inputrc** file in their home directory (this is a dot file). It may be best to first copy the **/etc/inputrc** file as your **.inputrc** file and then edit it. **/etc/profile** will first check for a local **.inputrc** file before accessing the **/etc/inputrc** file. You can find out more about Readline in the BASH shell reference manual at **www.gnu.org/manual/bash**.

Command and Filename Completion

The BASH command line has a built-in feature that performs command line and file name completion. Automatic completions can be effected using the TAB key. If you enter an incomplete pattern as a command or filename argument, you can then press the TAB key to activate the command and filename completion feature, which completes the pattern. Directories will have a / attached to their name. If more than one command or file has the same prefix, the shell simply beeps and waits for you to enter the TAB key again. It then displays a list of possible command completions and waits for you to add enough characters to select a unique command or filename. For situations where you know there are likely multiple possibilities, you can just press the ESC key instead of two TABs.

Movement Commands	Operation
CTRL-F, RIGHT-ARROW	Move forward a character
CTRL-B, LEFT-ARROW	Move backward a character
CTRL-A or HOME	Move to beginning of line
CTRL-E or END	Move to end of line
ALT-F	Move forward a word
ALT-B	Move backward a word
CTRL-L	Clear screen and place line at top
Editing Commands	**Operation**
CTRL-D or DEL	Delete character cursor is on
CTRL-H or BACKSPACE	Delete character before the cursor
CTRL-K	Cut remainder of line from cursor position
CTRL-U	Cut from cursor position to beginning of line
CTRL-W	Cut the previous word
CTRL-C	Cut entire line
ALT-D	Cut the remainder of a word
ALT-DEL	Cut from the cursor to the beginning of a word
CTRL-Y	Paste previous cut text
ALT-Y	Paste from set of previously cut text
CTRL-Y	Paste previous cut text
CTRL-V	Insert quoted text, used for inserting control or meta (Alt) keys as text, such as CTRL-B for backspace or CTRL-T for tabs
ALT-T	Transpose current and previous word
ALT-L	Lowercase current word
ALT-U	Uppercase current word
ALT-C	Capitalize current word
CTRL-SHIFT-_	Undo previous change

Table 16-2: Command Line Editing Operations

In the next example, the user issues a **`cat`** command with an incomplete filename. When the user presses the TAB key, the system searches for a match and, when it finds one, fills in the filename. The user can then press ENTER to execute the command.

```
$ cat pre tab
$ cat preface
```

The automatic completion also works with the names of variables, users, and hosts. In this case, the partial text needs to be preceded by a special character, indicating the type of name. A listing of possible automatic completions follows:

Filenames begin with any text or /.

Shell variable text begins with a $ sign.

Username text begins with a ~ sign.

Host name text begins with a @.

Commands, aliases, and text in files begin with normal text.

Variables begin with a **$** sign, so any text beginning with a dollar sign is treated as a variable to be completed. Variables are selected from previously defined variables, like system shell variables. Usernames begin with a tilde (~). Host names begin with a @ sign, with possible names taken from the **/etc/hosts** file. For example, to complete the variable HOME given just $HOM, simple enter a tab character.

```
$ echo $HOM <tab>
$ echo $HOME
```

Command (CTRL-R for listing possible completions)	Description
TAB	Automatic completion
TAB TAB or ESC	List possible completions
ALT-/, CTRL-R-/	Filename completion, normal text for automatic
ALT-$, CTRL-R-$	Shell variable completion, $ for automatic
ALT-~, CTRL-R-~	User name completion, ~ for automatic
ALT-@, CTRL-R-@	Host name completion, @ for automatic
ALT-!, CTRL-R-!	Command name completion, normal text for automatic

Table 16-3: Command Line Text Completion Commands

If you entered just an H, then you could enter two tabs to see all possible variables beginning with H. The command line is redisplayed, letting you complete the name.

```
$ echo $H <tab> <tab>
$HISTCMD $HISTFILE $HOME $HOSTTYPE HISTFILE  $HISTSIZE $HISTNAME
$ echo $H
```

You can also specifically select the kind of text to complete, using corresponding command keys. In this case, it does not matter what kind of sign a name begins with.

For example, the ALT-~ will treat the current text as a user name. ALT-@ will treat it as a hostname, and ALT-$, as a variable. ALT-! will treat it as a command. To display a list of possible completions, use the CTRL-X key with the appropriate completion key, as in CTRL-X-$ to list possible variable completions. See Table 16-3 for a complete listing.

History

The BASH shell keeps a list, called a history list, of your previously entered commands. You can display each command, in turn, on your command line by pressing the UP ARROW key. The DOWN ARROW key moves you down the list. You can modify and execute any of these previous commands when you display them on your command line.

Tip: The capability to redisplay a previous command is helpful when you've already executed a command you had entered incorrectly. In this case, you would be presented with an error message and a new, empty command line. By pressing the UP ARROW key, you can redisplay your previous command, make corrections to it, and then execute it again. This way, you would not have to enter the whole command again.

History Events

In the BASH shell, the history utility keeps a record of the most recent commands you have executed. The commands are numbered starting at 1, and a limit exists to the number of commands remembered, the default is 500. The history utility is a kind of short-term memory, keeping track of the most recent commands you have executed. To see the set of your most recent commands, type **history** on the command line and press ENTER. A list of your most recent commands is then displayed, preceded by a number.

```
$ history
1 cp mydata today
2 vi mydata
3 mv mydata reports
4 cd reports
5 ls
```

A record of your history commands is saved in the **.bash_history** file in your home directory.

Each of these commands is technically referred to as an event. An event describes an action that has been taken—a command that has been executed. The events are numbered according to their sequence of execution. The most recent event has the highest number. Each of these events can be identified by its number or beginning characters in the command.

The history utility enables you to reference a former event, placing it on your command line and enabling you to execute it. The easiest way to do this is to use the UP ARROW and DOWN ARROW keys to place history events on your command line, one at a time. You needn't display the list first with **history**. Pressing the UP ARROW key once places the last history event on your command line. Pressing it again places the next history event on your command. Pressing the DOWN ARROW key places the previous event on the command line.

You can use certain control and meta keys to perform other history operations like searching the history list. A meta key is the ALT key, and the ESC key on keyboards that have no ALT key. The ALT key is used here. ALT-< will move you to the beginning of the history list; ALT-N will search it. CTRL-S and CTRL-R will perform incremental searches, display matching commands as you type in a search string. Table 16-4 lists the different commands for referencing the history list.

History Commands	Description
CTRL-N or DOWN ARROW	Moves down to the next event in the history list
CTRL-P or UP ARROW	Moves up to the previous event in the history list
ALT-<	Moves to the beginning of the history event list
ALT->	Moves to the end of the history event list
ALT-N	Forward Search, next matching item
ALT-P	Backward Search, previous matching item
CTRL-S	Forward Search History, forward incremental search
CTRL-R	Reverse Search History, reverse incremental search
fc *event-reference*	Edits an event with the standard editor and then executes it **Options** **-l** List recent history events; same as **history** command **-e** *editor event-reference* Invokes a specified editor to edit a specific event
History Event References	
!*event num*	References an event with an event number
!!	References the previous command
!*characters*	References an event with beginning characters
!?*pattern***?**	References an event with a pattern in the event
!-*event num*	References an event with an offset from the first event
!*num***-***num*	References a range of events

Table 16-4: History Commands and History Event References

Tip: If more than one history event matches what you have entered, you will hear a beep, and you can then enter more characters to help uniquely identify the event.

You can also reference and execute history events using the **!** history command. The **!** is followed by a reference that identifies the command. The reference can be either the number of the event or a beginning set of characters in the event. In the next example, the third command in the history list is referenced first by number and then by the beginning characters:

```
$ !3
mv mydata reports
$ !mv my
mv mydata reports
```

You can also reference an event using an offset from the end of the list. A negative number will offset from the end of the list to that event, thereby referencing it. In the next example, the fourth command, **cd mydata**, is referenced using a negative offset, and then executed. Remember that you are offsetting from the end of the list—in this case, event 5—up toward the beginning of the list, event 1. An offset of 4 beginning from event 5 places you at event 2.

```
$ !-4
vi mydata
```

To reference the last event, you use a following !, as in **!!**. In the next example, the command **!!** executes the last command the user executed—in this case, **ls**:

```
$ !!
ls
mydata today reports
```

Filename Expansion: *, ?, [ ]

Filenames are the most common arguments used in a command. Often you may know only part of the filename, or you may want to reference several filenames that have the same extension or begin with the same characters. The shell provides a set of special characters that search out, match, and generate a list of filenames. These are the asterisk, the question mark, and brackets (*****, **?**, **[]**). Given a partial filename, the shell uses these matching operators to search for files and expand to a list of filenames found. The shell replaces the partial filename argument with the expanded list of matched filenames. This list of filenames can then become the arguments for commands such as **ls**, which can operate on many files. Table 16-5 lists the shell's file expansion characters.

Matching Multiple Characters

The asterisk (*****) references files beginning or ending with a specific set of characters. You place the asterisk before or after a set of characters that form a pattern to be searched for in filenames.

If the asterisk is placed before the pattern, filenames that end in that pattern are searched for. If the asterisk is placed after the pattern, filenames that begin with that pattern are searched for. Any matching filename is copied into a list of filenames generated by this operation.

In the next example, all filenames beginning with the pattern "doc" are searched for and a list generated. Then all filenames ending with the pattern "day" are searched for and a list is generated. The last example shows how the ***** can be used in any combination of characters.

```
$ ls
doc1 doc2 document docs mydoc monday tuesday
$ ls doc*
doc1 doc2 document docs
$ ls *day
monday tuesday
$ ls m*d*
monday
$
```

Common Shell Symbols	Execution
ENTER	Execute a command line.
`;`	Separate commands on the same command line.
`` `command` ``	Execute a command.
`$(command)`	Execute a command.
`[]`	Match on a class of possible characters in filenames.
`\`	Quote the following character. Used to quote special characters.
`|`	Pipe the standard output of one command as input for another command.
`&`	Execute a command in the background.
`!`	History command.
File Expansion Symbols	**Execution**
`*`	Match on any set of characters in filenames.
`?`	Match on any single character in filenames.
`[]`	Match on a class of characters in filenames.
Redirection Symbols	**Execution**
`>`	Redirect the standard output to a file or device, creating the file if it does not exist and overwriting the file if it does exist.
`>!`	The exclamation point forces the overwriting of a file if it already exists.
`<`	Redirect the standard input from a file or device to a program.
`>>`	Redirect the standard output to a file or device, appending the output to the end of the file.
Standard Error Redirection Symbols	**Execution**
`2>`	Redirect the standard error to a file or device.
`2>>`	Redirect and append the standard error to a file or device.
`2>&1`	Redirect the standard error to the standard output.

Table 16-5: Shell Symbols

Filenames often include an extension specified with a period and followed by a string denoting the file type, such as **.c** for C files, **.cpp** for C++ files, or even **.jpg** for JPEG image files. The extension has no special status and is only part of the characters making up the filename. Using the asterisk makes it easy to select files with a given extension. In the next example, the asterisk is used to list only those files with a **.c** extension. The asterisk placed before the **.c** constitutes the argument for **ls**.

```
$ ls *.c
calc.c main.c
```

You can use `*` with the **rm** command to erase several files at once. The asterisk first selects a list of files with a given extension, or beginning or ending with a given set of characters, and then it presents this list of files to the **rm** command to be erased. In the next example, the **rm** command erases all files beginning with the pattern "doc":

```
$ rm doc*
```

Tip: Use the `*` file expansion character carefully and sparingly with the **rm** command. The combination can be dangerous. A misplaced `*` in an **rm** command without the **-i** option could easily erase all the files in your current directory. The **-i** option will first prompt the user to confirm whether the file should be deleted.

Matching Single Characters

The question mark (**?**) matches only a single incomplete character in filenames. Suppose you want to match the files **doc1** and **docA**, but not the file **document**. Whereas the asterisk will match filenames of any length, the question mark limits the match to just one extra character. The next example matches files that begin with the word "doc" followed by a single differing letter:

```
$ ls
doc1 docA document
$ ls doc?
doc1 docA
```

Matching a Range of Characters

Whereas the `*` and **?** file expansion characters specify incomplete portions of a filename, the brackets (**[]**) enable you to specify a set of valid characters to search for. Any character placed within the brackets will be matched in the filename. Suppose you want to list files beginning with "doc", but only ending in *1* or *A*. You are not interested in filenames ending in *2* or *B*, or any other character. Here is how it's done:

```
$ ls
doc1 doc2 doc3 docA docB docD document
$ ls doc[1A]
doc1 docA
```

You can also specify a set of characters as a range, rather than list them one by one. A dash placed between the upper and lower bounds of a set of characters selects all characters within that range. The range is usually determined by the character set in use. In an ASCII character set, the range "a-g" will select all lowercase alphabetic characters from *a* through *g*, inclusive. In the next example, files beginning with the pattern "doc" and ending in characters *1* through *3* are selected. Then, those ending in characters *B* through *E* are matched.

```
$ ls doc[1-3]
doc1 doc2 doc3
$ ls doc[B-E]
docB docD
```

You can combine the brackets with other file expansion characters to form flexible matching operators. Suppose you want to list only filenames ending in either a **.c** or **.o** extension, but no other extension. You can use a combination of the asterisk and brackets: `*` **[co]**. The asterisk matches all filenames, and the brackets match only filenames with extension **.c** or **.o**.

```
$ ls *.[co]
main.c  main.o  calc.c
```

Matching Shell Symbols

At times, a file expansion character is actually part of a filename. In these cases, you need to quote the character by preceding it with a backslash to reference the file. In the next example, the user needs to reference a file that ends with the **?** character, **answers?**. The **?** is, however, a file expansion character and would match any filename beginning with "answers" that has one or more characters. In this case, the user quotes the **?** with a preceding backslash to reference the filename.

```
$ ls answers\?
answers?
```

Placing the filename in double quotes will also quote the character.

```
$ ls "answers?"
answers?
```

This is also true for filenames or directories that have white space characters like the space character. In this case, you could either use the backslash to quote the space character in the file or directory name, or place the entire name in double quotes.

```
$ ls My\ Documents
My Documents
$ ls "My Documents"
My Documents
```

Generating Patterns

Though not a file expansion operation, **{}** is often useful for generating names that you can use to create or modify files and directories. The braces operation only generates a list of names. It does not match on existing filenames. Patterns are placed within the braces and separated with commas. Any pattern placed within the braces will be used to generate a version of the pattern, using either the preceding or following pattern, or both. Suppose you want to generate a list of names beginning with "doc", but only ending in the patterns "ument", "final", and "draft". Here is how it's done:

```
$ echo doc{ument,final,draft}
document docfinal docdraft
```

Since the names generated do not have to exist, you could use the **{}** operation in a command to create directories, as shown here:

```
$ mkdir {fall,winter,spring}report
$ ls
fallreport springreport winterreport
```

Standard Input/Output and Redirection

The data in input and output operations is organized like a file. Data input at the keyboard is placed in a data stream arranged as a continuous set of bytes. Data output from a command or program is also placed in a data stream and arranged as a continuous set of bytes. This input data stream is referred to in Linux as the standard input, while the output data stream is called the standard output. There is also a separate output data stream reserved solely for error messages, called the standard error.

Because the standard input and standard output have the same organization as that of a file, they can easily interact with files. Linux has a redirection capability that lets you easily move data in and out of files. You can redirect the standard output so that, instead of displaying the output on a screen, you can save it in a file. You can also redirect the standard input away from the keyboard to a file, so that input is read from a file instead of from your keyboard.

When a Linux command is executed that produces output, this output is placed in the standard output data stream. The default destination for the standard output data stream is a device—in this case, the screen. *Devices*, such as the keyboard and screen, are treated as files. They receive and send out streams of bytes with the same organization as that of a byte-stream file. The screen is a device that displays a continuous stream of bytes. By default, the standard output will send its data to the screen device, which will then display the data.

For example, the **ls** command generates a list of all filenames and outputs this list to the standard output. Next, this stream of bytes in the standard output is directed to the screen device. The list of filenames is then printed on the screen. The **cat** command also sends output to the standard output. The contents of a file are copied to the standard output, whose default destination is the screen. The contents of the file are then displayed on the screen.

Redirecting the Standard Output: > and >>

Suppose that instead of displaying a list of files on the screen, you would like to save this list in a file. In other words, you would like to direct the standard output to a file rather than the screen. To do this, you place the output redirection operator, the greater-than sign (**>**), followed by the name of a file on the command line after the Linux command. Table 16-6 lists the different ways you can use the redirection operators. In the next example, the output of the **ls** command is redirected from the screen device to a file:

```
$ ls -l *.c > programlist
```

The redirection operation creates the new destination file. If the file already exists, it will be overwritten with the data in the standard output. You can set the **noclobber** feature to prevent overwriting an existing file with the redirection operation. In this case, the redirection operation on an existing file will fail. You can overcome the **noclobber** feature by placing an exclamation point after the redirection operator. You can place the **noclobber** command in a shell configuration file to make it an automatic default operation. The next example sets the **noclobber** feature for the BASH shell and then forces the overwriting of the **oldarticle** file if it already exists:

```
$ set -o noclobber
$ cat myarticle >! oldarticle
```

Although the redirection operator and the filename are placed after the command, the redirection operation is not executed after the command. In fact, it is executed before the command. The redirection operation creates the file and sets up the redirection before it receives any data from the standard output. If the file already exists, it will be destroyed and replaced by a file of the same name. In effect, the command generating the output is executed only after the redirected file has been created.

Command	Execution
ENTER	Execute a command line.
;	Separate commands on the same command line.
command\ *opts args*	Enter backslash before carriage return to continue entering a command on the next line.
\`*command*\`	Execute a command.
Special Characters for Filename Expansion	**Execution**
*	Match on any set of characters.
?	Match on any single characters.
[]	Match on a class of possible characters.
\	Quote the following character. Used to quote special characters.
Redirection	**Execution**
command > *filename*	Redirect the standard output to a file or device, creating the file if it does not exist and overwriting the file if it does exist.
command < *filename*	Redirect the standard input from a file or device to a program.
command >> *filename*	Redirect the standard output to a file or device, appending the output to the end of the file.
command **2>** *filename*	Redirect the standard error to a file or device
command **2>>** *filename*	Redirect and append the standard error to a file or device
command **2>&1**	Redirect the standard error to the standard output in the Bourne shell.
command **>&** *filename*	Redirect the standard error to a file or device in the C shell.
Pipes	**Execution**
command **|** *command*	Pipe the standard output of one command as input for another command.

Table 16-6: The Shell Operations

In the next example, the output of the **ls** command is redirected from the screen device to a file. First, the **ls** command lists files, and in the next command, **ls** redirects its file list to the **listf** file. Then the **cat** command displays the list of files saved in **listf**. Notice the list of files in **listf** includes the **listf** filename. The list of filenames generated by the **ls** command includes the name of the file created by the redirection operation—in this case, **listf**. The **listf** file is first created by the redirection operation, and then the **ls** command lists it along with other files. This file list output by **ls** is then redirected to the **listf** file, instead of being printed on the screen.

```
$ ls
mydata intro preface
$ ls > listf
```

```
$ cat listf
mydata intro listf preface
```

You can also append the standard output to an existing file using the **>>** redirection operator. Instead of overwriting the file, the data in the standard output is added at the end of the file. In the next example, the **myarticle** and **oldarticle** files are appended to the **allarticles** file. The **allarticles** file will then contain the contents of both **myarticle** and **oldarticle**.

```
$ cat myarticle >> allarticles
$ cat oldarticle >> allarticles
```

The Standard Input

Many Linux commands can receive data from the standard input. The standard input itself receives data from a device or a file. The default device for the standard input is the keyboard. Characters typed on the keyboard are placed in the standard input, which is then directed to the Linux command. Just as with the standard output, you can also redirect the standard input, receiving input from a file rather than the keyboard. The operator for redirecting the standard input is the less-than sign (**<**). In the next example, the standard input is redirected to receive input from the **myarticle** file, rather than the keyboard device (use CTRL-D to end the typed input). The contents of **myarticle** are read into the standard input by the redirection operation. Then the **cat** command reads the standard input and displays the contents of **myarticle**.

```
$ cat < myarticle
hello Christopher
How are you today
$
```

You can combine the redirection operations for both standard input and standard output. In the next example, the **cat** command has no filename arguments. Without filename arguments, the **cat** command receives input from the standard input and sends output to the standard output. However, the standard input has been redirected to receive its data from a file, while the standard output has been redirected to place its data in a file.

```
$ cat < myarticle > newarticle
```

Redirecting the Standard Error: >&, 2>, |&

When you execute commands, it is possible for an error to occur. You may give the wrong number of arguments, or some kind of system error could take place. When an error occurs, the system will issue an error message. Usually, such error messages are displayed on the screen along with the standard output. Error messages are placed in another standard byte stream called the standard error. In the next example, the cat command is given as its argument the name of a file that does not exist, **myintro**. In this case, the **cat** command will simply issue an error. Redirection operators are listed in Table 16-6.

```
$ cat myintro
cat : myintro not found
```

Because error messages are in a separate data stream from the standard output, this means that if you have redirected the standard output to a file, error messages will still appear on the screen for you to see. Though the standard output may be redirected to a file, the standard error is still directed to the screen. In the next example, the standard output of the **cat** command is redirected to the file **mydata**. The standard error, containing the error messages, is still directed toward the screen

```
$ cat myintro > mydata
cat : myintro not found
```

Like the standard output, you can also redirect the standard error. This means that you can save your error messages in a file for future reference. This is helpful if you need to save a record of the error messages. Like the standard output, the standard error's default destination is the display. Using special redirection operators, you can redirect the standard error to any file or device that you choose. If you redirect the standard error, the error messages will not be displayed on the screen. You can examine them later by viewing the contents of the file in which you saved them.

All the standard byte streams can be referenced in redirection operations with numbers. The numbers 0, 1, and 2 reference the standard input, standard output, and standard error respectively. By default an output redirection, **>**, operates on the standard output, 1. You can modify the output redirection to operate on the standard error by preceding the output redirection operator with the number 2, **2>**. In the next example, the **cat** command again will generate an error. The error message is redirected to the standard byte stream represented by number 2, the standard error.

```
$ cat nodata 2> myerrors
$ cat myerrors
cat : nodata not found
```

You can also append the standard error to a file by using the number 2 and the redirection append operator, **>>**. In the next example, the user appends the standard error to the **myerrors** file, which then functions as a log of errors.

```
$ cat nodata 2>> myerrors
$ cat compls 2>> myerrors
$ cat myerrors
cat : nodata not found
cat : compls not found
$
```

To both redirect the standard output as well as the standard error, you would need a separate redirection operation and file for each. In the next example, the standard output is redirected to the file **mydata**, and the standard error is redirected to **myerrors**. If nodata were to exist, then **mydata** would hold a copy of its contents.

```
$ cat nodata 1> mydata 2> myerrors
cat myerrors
cat : nodata not found
```

If, however, you want to save a record of your errors in the same file as that used for the redirected standard output, you need to redirect the standard error into the standard output. You can reference a standard byte stream by preceding its number with an ampersand. **&1** references the standard output. You can use such a reference in a redirection operation to make a standard byte stream a destination file. The redirection operation **2>&1** redirects the standard error into the standard output. In effect, the standard output becomes the destination file for the standard error. Conversely, the redirection operation **1>&2** would redirect the standard input into the standard error. In the next example, both the contents of the standard error and the standard output will be saved in the same file, mydata.

```
$ cat nodata 1> mydata 2>&1
```

Pipes: |

You may find yourself in situations in which you need to send data from one command to another. In other words, you may want to send the standard output of a command to another command, not to a destination file. Suppose you want to send a list of your filenames to the printer to be printed. You need two commands to do this: the **ls** command to generate a list of filenames and the **lpr** command to send the list to the printer. In effect, you need to take the output of the **ls** command and use it as input for the **lpr** command. You can think of the data as flowing from one command to another. To form such a connection in Linux, you use what is called a pipe. The pipe operator (**|**, the vertical bar character) placed between two commands forms a connection between them. The standard output of one command becomes the standard input for the other. The pipe operation receives output from the command placed before the pipe and sends this data as input to the command placed after the pipe. As shown in the next example, you can connect the **ls** command and the **lpr** command with a pipe. The list of filenames output by the **ls** command is piped into the **lpr** command.

```
$ ls | lpr
```

You can combine the **pipe** operation with other shell features, such as file expansion characters, to perform specialized operations. The next example prints only files with a **.c** extension. The **ls** command is used with the asterisk and ".c" to generate a list of filenames with the **.c** extension. Then this list is piped to the **lpr** command.

```
$ ls *.c | lpr
```

In the preceding example, a list of filenames was used as input, but what is important to note is that pipes operate on the standard output of a command, whatever that might be. The contents of whole files or even several files can be piped from one command to another. In the next example, the **cat** command reads and outputs the contents of the **mydata** file, which are then piped to the **lpr** command:

```
$ cat mydata | lpr
```

Linux has many commands that generate modified output. For example, the **sort** command takes the contents of a file and generates a version with each line sorted in alphabetic order. The **sort** command works best with files that are lists of items. Commands such as **sort** that output a modified version of its input are referred to as filters. Filters are often used with pipes. In the next example, a sorted version of **mylist** is generated and piped into the **more** command for display on the screen. Note that the original file, **mylist**, has not been changed and is not sorted. Only the output of **sort** in the standard output is sorted.

```
$ sort mylist | more
```

The standard input piped into a command can be more carefully controlled with the standard input argument (**-**). When you use the dash as an argument for a command, it represents the standard input.

Listing, Displaying, and Printing Files: ls, cat, more, less, and lpr

One of the primary functions of an operating system is the management of files. You may need to perform certain basic output operations on your files, such as displaying them on your screen or printing them. The Linux system provides a set of commands that perform basic file-management operations, such as listing, displaying, and printing files, as well as copying, renaming, and erasing files. These commands are usually made up of abbreviated versions of words. For example, the **ls** command is a shortened form of "list" and lists the files in your directory. The **lpr** command is an abbreviated form of "line print" and will print a file. The **cat**, **less**, and **more** commands display the contents of a file on the screen. Table 16-7 lists these commands with their different options. When you log into your Linux system, you may want a list of the files in your home directory. The **ls** command, which outputs a list of your file and directory names, is useful for this. The **ls** command has many possible options for displaying filenames according to specific features.

Command or Option	Execution
`ls`	This command lists file and directory names.
`cat` *filenames*	This filter can be used to display a file. It can take filenames for its arguments. It outputs the contents of those files directly to the standard output, which, by default, is directed to the screen.
`more` *filenames*	This utility displays a file screen by screen. Press the SPACEBAR to continue to the next screen and **q** to quit.
`less` *filenames*	This utility also displays a file screen by screen. Press the SPACEBAR to continue to the next screen and **q** to quit.
`lpr` *filenames*	Sends a file to the line printer to be printed; a list of files may be used as arguments. Use the **-P** option to specify a printer.
`lpq`	Lists the print queue for printing jobs.
`lprm`	Removes a printing job from the print queue.

Table 16-7: Listing, Displaying, and Printing Files

Displaying Files: cat, less, and more

You may also need to look at the contents of a file. The **cat** and **more** commands display the contents of a file on the screen. The name **cat** stands for concatenate.

```
$ cat mydata
computers
```

The **cat** command outputs the entire text of a file to the screen at once. This presents a problem when the file is large because its text quickly speeds past on the screen. The **more** and **less** commands are designed to overcome this limitation by displaying one screen of text at a time. You can then move forward or backward in the text at your leisure. You invoke the **more** or **less** command by entering the command name followed by the name of the file you want to view (**less** is a more powerful and configurable display utility).

```
$ less mydata
```

When **more** or **less** invoke a file, the first screen of text is displayed. To continue to the next screen, you press the F key or the SPACEBAR. To move back in the text, you press the B key. You can quit at any time by pressing the Q key.

Printing Files: lpr, lpq, and lprm

With the printer commands such as **lpr** and **lprm**, you can perform printing operations such as printing files or canceling print jobs (see Table 16-7). When you need to print files, use the **lpr** command to send files to the printer connected to your system. In the next example, the user prints the **mydata** file:

```
$ lpr mydata
```

If you want to print several files at once, you can specify more than one file on the command line after the **lpr** command. In the next example, the user prints out both the **mydata** and **preface** files:

```
$ lpr mydata preface
```

Printing jobs are placed in a queue and printed one at a time in the background. You can continue with other work as your files print. You can see the position of a particular printing job at any given time with the **lpq** command, which gives the owner of the printing job (the login name of the user who sent the job), the print job ID, the size in bytes, and the temporary file in which it is currently held.

If you need to cancel an unwanted printing job, you can do so with the **lprm** command, which takes as its argument either the ID number of the printing job or the owner's name. It then removes the print job from the print queue. For this task, **lpq** is helpful, for it provides you with the ID number and owner of the printing job you need to use with **lprm**.

Managing Directories: mkdir, rmdir, ls, cd, pwd

You can create and remove your own directories, as well as change your working directory, with the **mkdir**, **rmdir**, and **cd** commands. Each of these commands can take as its argument the pathname for a directory. The **pwd** command displays the absolute pathname of your working directory. In addition to these commands, the special characters represented by a single dot, a double dot, and a tilde can be used to reference the working directory, the parent of the working directory, and the home directory, respectively. Taken together, these commands enable you to manage your directories. You can create nested directories, move from one directory to another, and use pathnames to reference any of your directories. Those commands commonly used to manage directories are listed in Table 16-8.

Creating and Deleting Directories

You create and remove directories with the **mkdir** and **rmdir** commands. In either case, you can also use pathnames for the directories. In the next example, the user creates the directory **reports**. Then the user creates the directory **articles** using a pathname:

```
$ mkdir reports
$ mkdir /home/chris/articles
```

Command	Execution
mkdir *directory*	Creates a directory.
rmdir *directory*	Erases a directory.
ls -F	Lists directory name with a preceding slash.
ls -R	Lists working directory as well as all subdirectories.
cd *directory name*	Changes to the specified directory, making it the working directory. **cd** without a directory name changes back to the home directory: **$ cd reports**
pwd	Displays the pathname of the working directory.
directory name/filename	A slash is used in pathnames to separate each directory name. In the case of pathnames for files, a slash separates the preceding directory names from the filename.
..	References the parent directory. You can use it as an argument or as part of a pathname: **$ cd ..** **$ mv ../larisa oldarticles**
.	References the working directory. You can use it as an argument or as part of a pathname: **$ ls .**
~/*pathname*	The tilde is a special character that represents the pathname for the home directory. It is useful when you need to use an absolute pathname for a file or directory: **$ cp monday ~/today**

Table 16-8: Directory Commands

You can remove a directory with the **rmdir** command followed by the directory name. In the next example, the user removes the directory **reports** with the **rmdir** command:

```
$ rmdir reports
```

To remove a directory and all its subdirectories, you use the **rm** command with the **-r** option. This is a very powerful command and could easily be used to erase all your files. You will be prompted for each file. To simply remove all files and subdirectories without prompts, add the **-f** option. The following example deletes the **reports** directory and all its subdirectories:

```
rm -rf reports
```

Displaying Directory Contents

You have seen how to use the **ls** command to list the files and directories within your working directory. To distinguish between file and directory names, you need to use the **ls** command with the **-F** option. A slash is then placed after each directory name in the list.

```
$ ls
weather reports articles
$ ls -F
weather reports/ articles/
```

The **ls** command also takes as an argument any directory name or directory pathname. This enables you to list the files in any directory without first having to change to that directory. In the next example, the **ls** command takes as its argument the name of a directory, **reports**. Then the **ls** command is executed again, only this time the absolute pathname of **reports** is used.

```
$ ls reports
monday tuesday
$ ls /home/chris/reports
monday tuesday
$
```

Moving Through Directories

The **cd** command takes as its argument the name of the directory to which you want to change. The name of the directory can be the name of a subdirectory in your working directory or the full pathname of any directory on the system. If you want to change back to your home directory, you only need to enter the **cd** command by itself, without a filename argument.

```
$ cd props
$ pwd
/home/dylan/props
```

Referencing the Parent Directory

A directory always has a parent (except, of course, for the root). For example, in the preceding listing, the parent for **travel** is the **articles** directory. When a directory is created, two entries are made: one represented with a dot (`.`), and the other with double dots (`..`). The dot represents the pathnames of the directory, and the double dots represent the pathname of its parent directory. Double dots, used as an argument in a command, reference a parent directory. The single dot references the directory itself.

You can use the single dot to reference your working directory, instead of using its pathname. For example, to copy a file to the working directory retaining the same name, the dot can be used in place of the working directory's pathname. In this sense, the dot is another name for the working directory. In the next example, the user copies the **weather** file from the **chris** directory to the **reports** directory. The **reports** directory is the working directory and can be represented with the single dot.

```
$ cd reports
$ cp /home/chris/weather .
```

The `..` symbol is often used to reference files in the parent directory. In the next example, the **cat** command displays the **weather** file in the parent directory. The pathname for the file is the `..` symbol followed by a slash and the filename.

```
$ cat ../weather
raining and warm
```

Tip: You can use the **cd** command with the `..` symbol to step back through successive parent directories of the directory tree from a lower directory.

File and Directory Operations: find, cp, mv, rm, ln

As you create more and more files, you may want to back them up, change their names, erase some of them, or even give them added names. Linux provides you with several file commands that enable you to search for files, copy files, rename files, or remove files (see Tables 16-5). If you have a large number of files, you can also search them to locate a specific one. The commands are shortened forms of full words, consisting of only two characters. The **cp** command stands for "copy" and copies a file, **mv** stands for "move" and renames or moves a file, **rm** stands for "remove" and erases a file, and **ln** stands for "link" and adds another name for a file, often used as a shortcut to the original. One exception to the two-character rule is the **find** command, which performs searches of your filenames to find a file. All these operations can be handled by the desktops, like GNOME and KDE.

Searching Directories: find

Once you have a large number of files in many different directories, you may need to search them to locate a specific file, or files, of a certain type. The **find** command enables you to perform such a search from the command line. The **find** command takes as its arguments directory names followed by several possible options that specify the type of search and the criteria for the search; it then searches within the directories listed and their subdirectories for files that meet these criteria. The **find** command can search for a file by name, type, owner, and even the time of the last update.

```
$ find directory-list -option criteria
```

Tip: From the GNOME desktop you can use the "Search" tool in the Places menu to search for files. From the KDE Desktop, you can use the find tool in the file manager. Select find from the file manager (Konqueror) tools menu.

The **-name** option has as its criteria a pattern and instructs **find** to search for the filename that matches that pattern. To search for a file by name, you use the **find** command with the directory name followed by the **-name** option and the name of the file.

```
$ find directory-list -name filename
```

The **find** command also has options that merely perform actions, such as outputting the results of a search. If you want **find** to display the filenames it has found, you simply include the **-print** option on the command line along with any other options. The **-print** option is an action that instructs **find** to write to the standard output the names of all the files it locates (you can also use the **-ls** option instead to list files in the long format). In the next example, the user searches for all the files in the **reports** directory with the name **monday**. Once located, the file, with its relative pathname, is printed.

```
$ find reports -name monday -print
reports/monday
```

The **find** command prints out the filenames using the directory name specified in the directory list. If you specify an absolute pathname, the absolute path of the found directories will be output. If you specify a relative pathname, only the relative pathname is output. In the preceding example, the user specified a relative pathname, **reports**, in the directory list. Located filenames were output beginning with this relative pathname. In the next example, the user specifies an absolute pathname in the directory list. Located filenames are then output using this absolute pathname.

```
$ find /home/chris -name monday -print
/home/chris/reports/monday
```

Tip: Should you need to find the location of a specific program or configuration file, you could use **find** to search for the file from the root directory. Log in as the root user and use **/** as the directory. This command searched for the location of the **more** command and files on the entire file system: **find / -name more -print**.

Searching the Working Directory

If you want to search your working directory, you can use the dot in the directory pathname to represent your working directory. The double dots would represent the parent directory. The next example searches all files and subdirectories in the working directory, using the dot to represent the working directory. If you are located in your home directory, this is a convenient way to search through all your own directories. Notice the located filenames are output beginning with a dot.

```
$ find . -name weather -print
./weather
```

You can use shell wildcard characters as part of the pattern criteria for searching files. The special character must be quoted, however, to avoid evaluation by the shell. In the next example, all files with the **.c** extension in the **programs** directory are searched for and then displayed in the long format using the **-ls** action:

```
$ find programs -name '*.c' -ls
```

Locating Directories

You can also use the **find** command to locate other directories. In Linux, a directory is officially classified as a special type of file. Although all files have a byte-stream format, some files, such as directories, are used in special ways. In this sense, a file can be said to have a file type. The **find** command has an option called **-type** that searches for a file of a given type. The **-type** option takes a one-character modifier that represents the file type. The modifier that represents a directory is a **d**. In the next example, both the directory name and the directory file type are used to search for the directory called **travel**:

```
$ find /home/chris -name travel -type d -print
/home/chris/articles/travel
$
```

File types are not so much different types of files as they are the file format applied to other components of the operating system, such as devices. In this sense, a device is treated as a type of file, and you can use **find** to search for devices and directories, as well as ordinary files. Table 16-9 lists the different types available for the **find** command's **-type** option.

You can also use the find operation to search for files by ownership or security criteria, like those belonging to a specific user or those with a certain security context. The user option lets to locate all files belonging to a certain user. The following example lists all files that the user **chris** has created or owns on the entire system. To list those just in the users' home directories, you would use **/home** for the starting search directory. This would find all those in a user's home directory as well as any owned by that user in other user directories.

```
$ find / -user chris -print
```

Copying Files

To make a copy of a file, you simply give **cp** two filenames as its arguments (see Table 16-10).

Command or Option	Execution
`find`	Searches directories for files according to search criteria. This command has several options that specify the type of criteria and actions to be taken.
`-name` *pattern*	Searches for files with the *pattern* in the name.
`-lname` *pattern*	Searches for symbolic link files.
`-group` *name*	Searches for files belonging to the group *name.*
`-gid` *name*	Searches for files belonging to a group according to group ID.
`-user` *name*	Searches for files belonging to a user.
`-uid` *name*	Searches for files belonging to a user according to user ID.
`-size` *num***c**	Searches for files with the size *num* in blocks. If **c** is added after *num,* the size in bytes (characters) is searched for.
`-mtime` *num*	Searches for files last modified *num* days ago.
`-newer` *pattern*	Searches for files modified after the one matched by *pattern.*
`-context` *scontext*	Searches for files according to security context (SE Linux).
`-print`	Outputs the result of the search to the standard output. The result is usually a list of filenames, including their full pathnames.
`-type` *filetype*	Searches for files with the specified file type. File type can be **b** for block device, **c** for character device, **d** for directory, **f** for file, or **l** for symbolic link.
`-perm` *permission*	Searches for files with certain permissions set. Use octal or symbolic format for permissions.
`-ls`	Provides a detailed listing of each file, with owner, permission, size, and date information.
`-exec` *command*	Executes command when files found.

Table 16-9: The `find` Command

The first filename is the name of the file to be copied, the one that already exists. This is often referred to as the source file. The second filename is the name you want for the copy. This will be a new file containing a copy of all the data in the source file. This second argument is often referred to as the destination file. The syntax for the **cp** command follows:

```
$ cp source-file destination-file
```

In the next example, the user copies a file called **proposal** to a new file called **oldprop**:

```
$ cp proposal oldprop
```

You could unintentionally destroy another file with the **cp** command. The **cp** command generates a copy by first creating a file and then copying data into it. If another file has the same name as the destination file, that file is destroyed, and a new file with that name is created. By default, Red Hat Enterprise Linux configures your system to check for an existing copy by the same name (**cp** is aliased with the `-i` option). To copy a file from your working directory to another directory, you only need to use that directory name as the second argument in the **cp** command. In the next example, the **proposal** file is overwritten by the **newprop** file. The **proposal** file already exists.

```
$ cp newprop proposal
```

You can use any of the wildcard characters to generate a list of filenames to use with **cp** or **mv**. For example, suppose you need to copy all your C source code files to a given directory. Instead of listing each one individually on the command line, you could use an * character with the **.c** extension to match on and generate a list of C source code files (all files with a **.c** extension). In the next example, the user copies all source code files in the current directory to the **sourcebks** directory:

```
$ cp *.c sourcebks
```

If you want to copy all the files in a given directory to another directory, you could use * to match on and generate a list of all those files in a **cp** command. In the next example, the user copies all the files in the **props** directory to the **oldprop** directory. Notice the use of a **props** pathname preceding the * special characters. In this context, **props** is a pathname that will be appended before each file in the list that * generates.

```
$ cp props/* oldprop
```

You can, of course, use any of the other special characters, such as `.`, `?`, or `[]`. In the next example, the user copies both source code and object code files (**.c** and **.o**) to the **projbk** directory:

```
$ cp *.[oc] projbk
```

When you copy a file, you may want to give the copy a different name than the original. To do so, place the new filename after the directory name, separated by a slash.

```
$ cp filename directory-name/new-filename
```

Moving Files

You can use the **mv** command either to rename a file or to move a file from one directory to another. When using **mv** to rename a file, you simply use the new filename as the second argument. The first argument is the current name of the file you are renaming. If you want to rename a file when you move it, you can specify the new name of the file after the directory name. In the next example, the **proposal** file is renamed with the name **version1**:

```
$ mv proposal version1
```

As with **cp**, it is easy for **mv** to erase a file accidentally. When renaming a file, you might accidentally choose a filename already used by another file. In this case, that other file will be erased. The **mv** command also has an **-i** option that checks first to see if a file by that name already exists.

You can also use any of the special characters to generate a list of filenames to use with **mv**. In the next example, the user moves all source code files in the current directory to the **newproj** directory:

```
$ mv *.c newproj
```

If you want to move all the files in a given directory to another directory, you can use ***** to match on and generate a list of all those files. In the next example, the user moves all the files in the **reports** directory to the **repbks** directory:

```
$ mv reports/* repbks
```

Note: The easiest way to copy files to a CD-R/RW or DVD-R/RW disc is to use the built-in Nautilus burning capability. Just insert a blank disk, open it as a directory, and drag and drop files onto it. You will be prompted automatically to burn the files.

Copying and Moving Directories

You can also copy or move whole directories at once. Both **cp** and **mv** can take as their first argument a directory name, enabling you to copy or move subdirectories from one directory into another (see Table 16-10).

Command	Execution
cp *filename filename*	Copies a file. **cp** takes two arguments: the original file and the name of the new copy. You can use pathnames for the files to copy across directories:
cp -r *dirname dirname*	Copies a subdirectory from one directory to another. The copied directory includes all its own subdirectories:
mv *filename filename*	Moves (renames) a file. The **mv** command takes two arguments: the first is the file to be moved. The second argument can be the new filename or the pathname of a directory. If it is the name of a directory, then the file is literally moved to that directory, changing the file's pathname:
mv *dirname dirname*	Moves directories. In this case, the first and last arguments are directories:
ln *filename filename*	Creates added names for files referred to as links. A link can be created in one directory that references a file in another directory:
rm *filenames*	Removes (erases) a file. Can take any number of filenames as its arguments. Literally removes links to a file. If a file has more than one link, you need to remove all of them to erase a file:

Table 16-10: File Operations

The first argument is the name of the directory to be moved or copied, while the second argument is the name of the directory within which it is to be placed. The same pathname structure used for files applies to moving or copying directories.

You can just as easily copy subdirectories from one directory to another. To copy a directory, the **cp** command requires you to use the **-r** option. The **-r** option stands for "recursive." It directs the **cp** command to copy a directory, as well as any subdirectories it may contain. In other words, the entire directory subtree, from that directory on, will be copied. In the next example, the **travel** directory is copied to the **oldarticles** directory. Now two **travel** subdirectories exist, one in **articles** and one in **oldarticles**.

```
$ cp -r articles/travel oldarticles
$ ls -F articles
/travel
$ ls -F oldarticles
/travel
```

Erasing Files and Directories: the rm Command

As you use Linux, you will find the number of files you use increases rapidly. Generating files in Linux is easy. Applications such as editors, and commands such as **cp**, easily create files. Eventually, many of these files may become outdated and useless. You can then remove them with the **rm** command. The **rm** command can take any number of arguments, enabling you to list several filenames and erase them all at the same time. In the next example, the user erases the file **oldprop**:

```
$ rm oldprop
```

Be careful when using the **rm** command, because it is irrevocable. Once a file is removed, it cannot be restored (there is no undo). With the **-i** option, you are prompted separately for each file and asked whether to remove it. If you enter **y**, the file will be removed. If you enter anything else, the file is not removed. In the next example, the **rm** command is instructed to erase the files **proposal** and **oldprop**. The **rm** command then asks for confirmation for each file. The user decides to remove **oldprop,** but not **proposal**.

```
$ rm -i proposal oldprop
Remove proposal? n
Remove oldprop? y
$
```

Links: the ln Command

You can give a file more than one name using the **ln** command. You might want to reference a file using different filenames to access it from different directories. The added names are often referred to as *links*. Linux supports two different types of links, hard and symbolic. *Hard* links are literally another name for the same file, whereas *symbolic* links function like shortcuts referencing another file. Symbolic links are much more flexible and can work over many different file systems, whereas hard links are limited to your local file system. Furthermore, hard links introduce security concerns, as they allow direct access from a link that may have public access to an original file that you may want protected. Links are usually implemented as symbolic links.

Symbolic Links

To set up a symbolic link, you use the **ln** command with the **-s** option and two arguments: the name of the original file and the new, added filename. The **ls** operation lists both filenames, but only one physical file will exist.

```
$ ln -s original-file-name added-file-name
```

In the next example, the **today** file is given the additional name **weather**. It is just another name for the **today** file.

```
$ ls
today
$ ln -s today weather
$ ls
today weather
```

You can give the same file several names by using the `ln` command on the same file many times. In the next example, the file **today** is given both the names **weather** and **weekend**:

```
$ ln -s today weather
$ ln -s today weekend
$ ls
today weather weekend
```

If you list the full information about a symbolic link and its file, you will find the information displayed is different. In the next example, the user lists the full information for both **lunch** and **/home/george/veglist** using the `ls` command with the `-l` option. The first character in the line specifies the file type. Symbolic links have their own file type, represented by an **l**. The file type for **lunch** is **l**, indicating it is a symbolic link, not an ordinary file. The number after the term "group" is the size of the file. Notice the sizes differ. The size of the **lunch** file is only four bytes. This is because **lunch** is only a symbolic link—a file that holds the pathname of another file—and a pathname takes up only a few bytes. It is not a direct hard link to the **veglist** file.

```
$ ls -l lunch /home/george/veglist
lrw-rw-r-- 1 chris group 4 Feb 14 10:30 lunch
-rw-rw-r-- 1 george group 793 Feb 14 10:30 veglist
```

To erase a file, you need to remove only its original name (and any hard links to it). If any symbolic links are left over, they will be unable to access the file. In this case, a symbolic link would hold the pathname of a file that no longer exists.

Hard Links

You can give the same file several names by using the `ln` command on the same file many times. To set up a hard link, you use the `ln` command with no `-s` option and two arguments: the name of the original file and the new, added filename. The `ls` operation lists both filenames, but only one physical file will exist.

```
$ ln original-file-name added-file-name
```

In the next example, the **monday** file is given the additional name **storm**. It is just another name for the **monday** file.

```
$ ls
today
$ ln monday storm
$ ls
monday storm
```

To erase a file that has hard links, you need to remove all its hard links. The name of a file is actually considered a link to that file—hence the command `rm` that removes the link to the file. If you have several links to the file and remove only one of them, the others stay in place, and you can reference the file through them. The same is true even if you remove the original link—the original name of the file. Any added links will work just as well. In the next example, the **today** file is removed with the `rm` command. However, a link to that same file exists, called **weather**. The file can then be referenced under the name **weather**.

```
$ ln today weather
$ rm today
$ cat weather
The storm broke today
and the sun came out.
$
```

17. Shell Configuration

Four different major shells are commonly used on Linux systems: the Bourne Again shell (BASH), the AT&T Korn shell, the TCSH shell, and the Z shell. The BASH shell is an advanced version of the Bourne shell, which includes most of the advanced features developed for the Korn shell and the C shell. TCSH is an enhanced version of the C shell, originally developed for BSD versions of Unix. The AT&T Unix Korn shell is open source. The Z shell is an enhanced version of the Korn shell. Although their Unix counterparts differ greatly, the Linux shells share many of the same features. In Unix, the Bourne shell lacks many capabilities found in the other Unix shells. In Linux, however, the BASH shell incorporates all the advanced features of the Korn shell and C shell, as well as the TCSH shell. All four shells are available for your use, though the BASH shell is the default.

The BASH shell is the default shell for most Linux distributions. If you are logging in to a command line interface, you will be placed in the default shell automatically and given a shell prompt at which to enter your commands. The shell prompt for the BASH shell is a dollar sign (**$**). In the desktop interface, such as GNOME or KDE, you can open a terminal window that will display a command line interface with the prompt for the default shell (BASH). Though you log in to your default shell or display it automatically in a terminal window, you can change to another shell by entering its name. **tcsh** invokes the TCSH shell, **bash** the BASH shell, **ksh** the Korn shell, and **zsh** the Z shell. You can leave a shell by pressing CTRL-D or using the **exit** command. You only need one type of shell to do your work. Table 17-1 shows the different commands you can use to invoke different shells. Some shells have added links you can use the invoke the same shell, like **sh** and **bsh**, which link to and invoke the **bash** command for the BASH shell.

Features	Description
bash	BASH shell, **/bin/bash**
bsh	BASH shell, **/bin/bsh** (link to **/bin/bash**)
sh	BASH shell, **/bin/sh** (link to **/bin/bash**)
tcsh	TCSH shell, **/usr/tcsh**
csh	TCSH shell , **/bin/csh** (link to **/bin/tcsh**)
ksh	Korn shell, **/bin/ksh** (also added link **/usr/bin/ksh**)
zsh	Z shell, **/bin/zsh**

Table 17-1: Shell Invocation Command Names

This chapter describes common features of the BASH shell, such as aliases, as well as how to configure the shell to your own needs using shell variables and initialization files. The other shells share many of the same features and use similar variables and initialization files.

Though the basic shell features and configurations are shown here, you should consult the respective online manuals and FAQs for each shell for more detailed examples and explanations.

Shell Initialization and Configuration Files

Each type of shell has its own set of initialization and configuration files. The TCSH shell uses **.login**, **.tcshrc**, and **.logout** files in place of **.profile**, **.bashrc**, and **.bash_logout**. The Z shell has several initialization files: **.zshenv**, **.zlogin**, **.zprofile**, **.zschrc**, and **.zlogout**. See Table 17-2 for a listing. Check the Man pages for each shell to see how they are usually configured. When you install a shell, default versions of these files are automatically placed in the users' home directories. Except for the TCSH shell, all shells use much the same syntax for variable definitions and assigning values (TCSH uses a slightly different syntax, described in its Man pages).

Filename	Function
BASH Shell	
.bash_profile	Login initialization file
.bashrc	BASH shell configuration file
.bash_logout	Logout name
.bash_history	History file
/etc/profile	System login initialization file
/etc/bashrc	System BASH shell configuration file
/etc/profile.d	Directory for specialized BASH shell configuration files
TCSH Shell	
.login	Login initialization file
.tcshrc	TCSH shell configuration file, sets prompt
.logout	Logout file
Z Shell	
.zshenv	Shell login file (first read)
.zprofile	Login initialization file
.zlogin	Shell login file
.zshrc	Z shell configuration file
.zlogout	Logout file
Korn Shell	
.profile	Login initialization file
.kshrc	KORN shell configuration file

Table 17-2: Shell Configuration Files

Configuration Directories and Files

Applications often install configuration files in a user's home directory that contain specific configuration information, which tailors the application to the needs of that particular user. This may take the form of a single configuration file that begins with a period or a directory that contains several configuration files. The directory name will also begin with a period. For example, Mozilla installs a directory called **.mozilla** in the user's home directory that contains configuration files. On the other hand, many mail application uses a single file called **.mailrc** to hold alias and feature settings set up by the user, though others like Evolution also have their own, **.evolution**. Most single configuration files end in the letters **rc**. **FTP** uses a file called **.netrc**. Most newsreaders use a file called **.newsrc**. Entries in configuration files are usually set by the application, though you can usually make entries directly by editing the file. Applications have their own set of special variables to which you can define and assign values. You can list the configuration files in your home directory with the **ls -a** command.

Aliases

You use the **alias** command to create another name for a command. The **alias** command operates like a macro that expands to the command it represents. The alias does not literally replace the name of the command; it simply gives another name to that command. An **alias** command begins with the keyword **alias** and the new name for the command, followed by an equal sign and the command the alias will reference.

Note: No spaces can be around the equal sign used in the **alias** command.

In the next example, **list** becomes another name for the **ls** command:

```
$ alias list=ls
$ ls
mydata today
$ list
mydata today
$
```

If you want an alias to be automatically defined, you have to enter the alias operation in a shell configuration file. On Red Hat Enterprise Linux, aliases are defined in either the user's **.bashrc** file or in a **.bash_aliases** file. To use a **.bash_aliases** file, you have to first uncomment the commands in the **.bashrc** file that will read the **.bash_aliases** file. Just edit the **.bashrc** file and remove the preceding **#** so it appears like the following:

```
if [ -f ~/.bash_aliases ]; then
    . ~/.bash_aliases
fi
```

You can also place aliases in the **.bashrc** file directly. Some are already defined, though commented out. You can edit the **.bashrc** file and remove the **#** comment symbols from those lines to activate the aliases.

```
# some more ls aliases
alias ll='ls -l'
alias la='ls -A'
alias l='ls -CF'
```

Aliasing Commands and Options

You can also use an alias to substitute for a command and its option, but you need to enclose both the command and the option within single quotes. Any command you alias that contains spaces must be enclosed in single quotes as well. In the next example, the alias **lss** references the **ls** command with its **-s** option, and the alias **lsa** references the **ls** command with the **-F** option. The **ls** command with the **-s** option lists files and their sizes in blocks, and **ls** with the **-F** option places a slash after directory names. Notice how single quotes enclose the command and its option.

```
$ alias lss='ls -s'
$ lss
mydata 14   today  6   reports  1
$ alias lsa='ls -F'
$ lsa
mydata today reports/
$
```

Aliases are helpful for simplifying complex operations. In the next example, **listlong** becomes another name for the **ls** command with the **-l** option (the long format that lists all file information), as well as the **-h** option for using a human-readable format for file sizes. Be sure to encase the command and its arguments within single quotes so that they are taken as one argument and not parsed by the shell.

```
$ alias listlong='ls -lh'
$ listlong
-rw-r--r--    1 root    root    51K  Sep  18  2008 mydata
-rw-r--r--    1 root    root    16K  Sep  27  2008 today
```

Aliasing Commands and Arguments

You may often use an alias to include a command name with an argument. If you execute a command that has an argument with a complex combination of special characters on a regular basis, you may want to alias it. For example, suppose you often list just your source code and object code files—those files ending in either a **.c** or **.o**. You would need to use as an argument for **ls** a combination of special characters such as ***.[co]**. Instead, you can alias **ls** with the **.[co]** argument, giving it a simple name. In the next example, the user creates an alias called **lsc** for the command **ls.[co]**:

```
$ alias lsc='ls *.[co]'
$ lsc
main.c main.o lib.c lib.o
```

Aliasing Commands

You can also use the name of a command as an alias. This can be helpful in cases where you should use a command only with a specific option. In the case of the **rm**, **cp**, and **mv** commands, the **-i** option should always be used to ensure an existing file is not overwritten. Instead of always being careful to use the **-i** option each time you use one of these commands, you can alias the command name to include the option. In the next example, the **rm**, **cp**, and **mv** commands have been aliased to include the **-i** option:

```
$ alias rm='rm -i'
$ alias mv='mv -i'
$ alias cp='cp -i'
```

The **alias** command by itself provides a list of all aliases that have been defined, showing the commands they represent. You can remove an alias by using the **unalias** command. In the next example, the user lists the current aliases and then removes the **lsa** alias:

```
$ alias
lsa=ls -F
list=ls
```

```
rm=rm -i
$ unalias lsa
```

Controlling Shell Operations

The BASH shell has several features that enable you to control the way different shell operations work. For example, setting the **noclobber** feature prevents redirection from overwriting files. You can turn these features on and off like a toggle, using the **set** command. The **set** command takes two arguments: an option specifying on or off and the name of the feature. To set a feature on, you use the **-o** option, and to set it off, you use the **+o** option. Here is the basic form:

```
$ set -o feature        turn the feature on
$ set +o feature        turn the feature off
```

Features	Description
$ set -+o *feature*	BASH shell features are turned on and off with the **set** command; **-o** sets a feature on and **+o** turns it off: **$ set -o noclobber** *set noclobber on* **$ set +o noclobber** *set noclobber off*
ignoreeof	Disables CTRL-D logout
noclobber	Does not overwrite files through redirection
noglob	Disables special characters used for filename expansion: *****, **?**, **~**, and **[]**

Table 17-3: BASH Shell Special Features

Three of the most common features are **ignoreeof**, **noclobber**, and **noglob**. Table 17-3 lists these different features, as well as the **set** command. Setting **ignoreeof** enables a feature that prevents you from logging out of the user shell with CTRL-D. CTRL-D is not only used to log out of the user shell, but also to end user input entered directly into the standard input. CTRL-D is often used for the Mail program or for utilities such as **cat**. You can easily enter an extra CTRL-D in such circumstances and accidentally log yourself out. The **ignoreeof** feature prevents such accidental logouts. In the next example, the **ignoreeof** feature is turned on using the **set** command with the **-o** option. The user can then log out only by entering the **logout** command.

```
$ set -o ignoreeof
$ CTRL-D
Use exit to logout
```

Environment Variables and Subshells: export

When you log in to your account, Linux generates your user shell. Within this shell, you can issue commands and declare variables. You can also create and execute shell scripts. When you execute a shell script, however, the system generates a subshell. You then have two shells, the one you logged in to and the one generated for the script. Within the script shell, you can execute another shell script, which then has its own shell. When a script has finished execution, its shell terminates and you return to the shell from which it was executed. In this sense, you can have many shells, each nested within the other. Variables you define within a shell are local to it. If you define a variable in a shell script, then, when the script is run, the variable is defined with that script's shell and is local to it. No other shell can reference that variable. In a sense, the variable is hidden within its shell.

You can define environment variables in all types of shells, including the BASH shell, the Z shell, and the TCSH shell. The strategy used to implement environment variables in the BASH shell, however, is different from that of the TCSH shell. In the BASH shell, environment variables are exported. That is to say, a copy of an environment variable is made in each subshell. For example, if the **EDITOR** variable is exported, a copy is automatically defined in each subshell for you. In the TCSH shell, on the other hand, an environment variable is defined only once and can be directly referenced by any subshell.

In the BASH shell, an environment variable can be thought of as a regular variable with added capabilities. To make an environment variable, you apply the **export** command to a variable you have already defined. The **export** command instructs the system to define a copy of that variable for each new shell generated. Each new shell will have its own copy of the environment variable. This process is called exporting variables. To think of exported environment variables as global variables is a mistake. A new shell can never reference a variable outside of itself. Instead, a copy of the variable with its value is generated for the new shell.

Shell Variables	Description
BASH	Holds full pathname of BASH command
BASH_VERSION	Displays the current BASH version number
GROUPS	Groups that the user belongs to
HISTCMD	Number of the current command in the history list
HOME	Pathname for user's home directory
HOSTNAME	The hostname
HOSTTYPE	Displays the type of machine the host runs on
OLDPWD	Previous working directory
OSTYPE	Operating system in use
PATH	List of pathnames for directories searched for executable commands
PPID	Process ID for shell's parent shell
PWD	User's working directory
RANDOM	Generates random number when referenced
SHLVL	Current shell level, number of shells invoked
UID	User ID of the current user

Table 17-4: Shell Variables, Set by the Shell

Configuring Your Shell with Shell Parameters

When you log in, Linux will set certain parameters for your login shell. These parameters can take the form of variables or features. See the previous section "Controlling Shell Operations" for a description of how to set features. Linux reserves a predefined set of variables for shell and system use. These are assigned system values, in effect, setting parameters. Linux sets up parameter shell variables you can use to configure your user shell. Many of these parameter shell variables are defined by the system when you log in. Some parameter shell variables are set by the shell automatically, and others are set by initialization scripts, described later. Certain shell variables are set directly by the shell, and others are simply used by it. Many of these other variables are application specific, used for such tasks as mail, history, or editing. Functionally, it may be better to think of these as system-level variables, as they are used to configure your entire system, setting values such as the location of executable commands on your system, or the number of history commands allowable. See Table 17-4 for a list of those shell variables set by the shell for shell-specific tasks; Table 17-5 lists those used by the shell for supporting other applications.

A reserved set of keywords is used for the names of these system variables. You should not use these keywords as the names of any of your own variable names. The system shell variables are all specified in uppercase letters, making them easy to identify. Shell feature variables are in lowercase letters. For example, the keyword **HOME** is used by the system to define the **HOME** variable. **HOME** is a special environment variable that holds the pathname of the user's home directory. On the other hand, the keyword **noclobber** is used to set the **noclobber** feature on or off.

Shell Variables	Description
BASH_VERSION	Displays the current BASH version number
CDPATH	Search path for the **cd** command
EXINIT	Initialization commands for Ex/Vi editor
FCEDIT	Editor used by the history **fc** command.
GROUPS	Groups that the user belongs to
HISTFILE	The pathname of the history file
HISTSIZE	Number of commands allowed for history
HISTFILESIZE	Size of the history file in lines
HISTCMD	Number of the current command in the history list
HOME	Pathname for user's home directory
HOSTFILE	Sets the name of the hosts file, if other than **/etc/hosts**
IFS	Interfield delimiter symbol
IGNOREEOF	If not set, EOF character will close the shell. Can be set to the number of EOF characters to ignore before accepting one to close the shell (default is 10)
INPUTRC	Set the **inputrc** configuration file for Readline (command line). Default is current directory, **.inputrc**. Most Linux distributions set this to **/etc/inputrc**
KDEDIR	The pathname location for the KDE desktop
LOGNAME	Login name

MAIL	Name of specific mail file checked by Mail utility for received messages, if MAILPATH is not set
MAILCHECK	Interval for checking for received mail
MAILPATH	List of mail files to be checked by Mail for received messages
HOSTTYPE	Linux platforms, such as i686 or x86_64
PROMPT_COMMAND	Command to be executed before each prompt, integrating the result as part of the prompt
HISTFILE	The pathname of the history file
PS1	Primary shell prompt
PS2	Secondary shell prompt
QTDIR	Location of the Qt library (used for KDE)
SHELL	Pathname of program for type of shell you are using
TERM	Terminal type
TMOUT	Time that the shell remains active awaiting input
USER	Username
UID	Real user ID (numeric)
EUID	Effective user ID (numeric). This is usually the same as the UID but can be different when the user changes IDs, as with the **su** command, which allows a user to become an effective root user

Table 17-5: System Environment Variables Used by the Shell

Shell Parameter Variables

Many of the shell parameter variables automatically defined and assigned initial values by the system when you log in can be changed if you wish. Some parameter variables exist whose values should not be changed, however. For example, the **HOME** variable holds the pathname for your home directory. Commands such as **cd** reference the pathname in the **HOME** shell variable to locate your home directory. Some of the more common of these parameter variables are described in this section. Other parameter variables are defined by the system and given an initial value that you are free to change. To do this, you redefine them and assign a new value. For example, the **PATH** variable is defined by the system and given an initial value; it contains the pathnames of directories where commands are located. Whenever you execute a command, the shell searches for it in these directories. You can add a new directory to be searched by redefining the **PATH** variable yourself so that it will include the new directory's pathname. Still, other parameter variables exist that the system does not define. These are usually optional features, such as the **EXINIT** variable that enables you to set options for the Vi editor. Each time you log in, you must define and assign a value to such variables. Some of the more common parameter variables are **SHELL**, **PATH**, **PS1**, **PS2**, and **MAIL**. The **SHELL** variable holds the pathname of the program for the type of shell you log in to. The **PATH** variable lists the different directories to be searched for a Linux command. The **PS1** and **PS2** variables hold the prompt symbols. The **MAIL** variable holds the pathname of your mailbox file. You can modify the values for any of them to customize your shell.

Note: You can obtain a listing of the currently defined shell variables using the **env** command. The **env** command operates like the **set** command, but it lists only parameter variables.

Using Initialization Files

You can automatically define parameter variables using special shell scripts called initialization files. An *initialization file* is a specially named shell script executed whenever you enter a certain shell. You can edit the initialization file and place in it definitions and assignments for parameter variables. When you enter the shell, the initialization file will execute these definitions and assignments, effectively initializing parameter variables with your own values. For example, the BASH shell's **.bash_profile** file is an initialization file executed every time you log in. It contains definitions and assignments of parameter variables. However, the **.bash_profile** file is basically only a shell script, which you can edit with any text editor such as the Vi editor; changing, if you wish, the values assigned to parameter variables.

In the BASH shell, all the parameter variables are designed to be environment variables. When you define or redefine a parameter variable, you also need to export it to make it an environment variable. This means any change you make to a parameter variable must be accompanied by an **export** command. You will see that at the end of the login initialization file, **.bash_profile**, there is usually an **export** command for all the parameter variables defined in it.

Your Home Directory: HOME

The **HOME** variable contains the pathname of your home directory. Your home directory is determined by the parameter administrator when your account is created. The pathname for your home directory is automatically read into your **HOME** variable when you log in. In the next example, the **echo** command displays the contents of the **HOME** variable:

```
$ echo $HOME
/home/chris
```

The **HOME** variable is often used when you need to specify the absolute pathname of your home directory. In the next example, the absolute pathname of **reports** is specified using **HOME** for the home directory's path:

```
$ ls $HOME/reports
```

Command Locations: PATH

The **PATH** variable contains a series of directory paths separated by colons. Each time a command is executed, the paths listed in the **PATH** variable are searched one by one for that command. For example, the **cp** command resides on the system in the directory **/bin**. This directory path is one of the directories listed in the **PATH** variable. Each time you execute the **cp** command, this path is searched and the **cp** command located. The system defines and assigns **PATH** an initial set of pathnames. In Linux, the initial pathnames are **/bin** and **/usr/bin**.

The shell can execute any executable file, including programs and scripts you have created. For this reason, the **PATH** variable can also reference your working directory; so if you want to execute one of your own scripts or programs in your working directory, the shell can locate it. No spaces are allowed between the pathnames in the string. A colon with no pathname specified references your working directory. Usually, a single colon is placed at the end of the pathnames as an empty entry specifying your working directory. For example, the pathname **//bin:/usr/bin:** references three directories: **/bin**, **/usr/bin**, and your current working directory.

```
$ echo $PATH
/bin:/usr/sbin:
```

You can add any new directory path you want to the **PATH** variable. This can be useful if you have created several of your own Linux commands using shell scripts. You can place these new shell script commands in a directory you create and then add that directory to the **PATH** list. Then, no matter what directory you are in, you can execute one of your shell scripts. The **PATH** variable will contain the directory for that script, so that directory will be searched each time you issue a command.

You add a directory to the **PATH** variable with a variable assignment. You can execute this assignment directly in your shell. In the next example, the user **chris** adds a new directory, called **bin,** to the **PATH**. Although you could carefully type in the complete pathnames listed in **PATH** for the assignment, you can also use an evaluation of **PATH**—**$PATH**—in its place. In this example, an evaluation of **HOME** is also used to designate the user's home directory in the new directory's pathname. Notice the last colon, which specifies the working directory:

```
$ PATH=$PATH:$HOME/mybin:
$ export PATH
$ echo $PATH
/bin:/usr/bin::/home/chris/mybin
```

If you add a directory to **PATH** while you are logged in, the directory will be added only for the duration of your login session. When you log back in, the login initialization file, **.bash_profile**, will again initialize your **PATH** with its original set of directories. The **.bash_profile** file is described in detail a bit later in this chapter. To add a new directory to your **PATH** permanently, you need to edit your **.bash_profile** file and find the assignment for the **PATH** variable. Then, you simply insert the directory, preceded by a colon, into the set of pathnames assigned to **PATH**.

Specifying the BASH Environment: BASH_ENV

The **BASH_ENV** variable holds the name of the BASH shell initialization file to be executed whenever a BASH shell is generated. For example, when a BASH shell script is executed, the **BASH_ENV** variable is checked, and the name of the script that it holds is executed before the shell script. The **BASH_ENV** variable usually holds **$HOME/.bashrc**. This is the **.bashrc** file in the user's home directory. (The **.bashrc** file is discussed later in this chapter.) You can specify a different file if you wish, using that instead of the **.bashrc** file for BASH shell scripts.

Configuring the Shell Prompt

The **PS1** and **PS2** variables contain the primary and secondary prompt symbols, respectively. The primary prompt symbol for the BASH shell is a dollar sign (**$**). You can change the prompt symbol by assigning a new set of characters to the **PS1** variable. In the next example, the shell prompt is changed to the **->** symbol:

```
$ PS1= '->'
-> export PS1
->
```

You can change the prompt to be any set of characters, including a string, as shown in the next example:

```
$ PS1="Please enter a command: "
Please enter a command: export PS1
Please enter a command: ls
mydata /reports
Please enter a command:
```

The **PS2** variable holds the secondary prompt symbol, which is used for commands that take several lines to complete. The default secondary prompt is **>**. The added command lines begin with the secondary prompt instead of the primary prompt. You can change the secondary prompt just as easily as the primary prompt, as shown here:

```
$ PS2="@"
```

Prompt Codes	Description
`\!`	Current history number
`\$`	Use **$** as prompt for all users except the root user, which has the # as its prompt
`\d`	Current date
`\#`	History command number for just the current shell
`\h`	Hostname
`\s`	Shell type currently active
`\t`	Time of day in hours, minutes, and seconds.
`\u`	Username
`\v`	Shell version
`\w`	Full pathname of the current working directory
`\W`	Name of the current working directory
`\\`	Displays a backslash character
`\n`	Inserts a newline
`\[ \]`	Allows entry of terminal specific display characters for features like color or bold font
nnn	Character specified in octal format

Table 17-6: Prompt codes

Like the TCSH shell, the BASH shell provides you with a predefined set of codes you can use to configure your prompt (see Table 17-6). With them, you can make the time, your username, or your directory pathname a part of your prompt. You can even have your prompt display the history event number of the current command you are about to enter. Each code is preceded by a \ symbol: **\w** represents the current working directory, **\t** the time, and **\u** your username; **\!** will display the next history event number. In the next example, the user adds the current working directory to the prompt:

```
$ PS1="\w $"
/home/dylan $
```

The codes must be included within a quoted string. If no quotes exist, the code characters are not evaluated and are themselves used as the prompt. **PS1=\w** sets the prompt to the characters **\w**, not the working directory. The next example incorporates both the time and the history event number with a new prompt:

```
$ PS1="\t \! ->"
```

The default BASH prompt is **\s-\v\$** to display the type of shell, the shell version, and the $ symbol as the prompt. Some distributions, including Red Hat Enterprise Linux, have changed this to a more complex command consisting of the user, the hostname, and the name of the current working directory. A sample configuration is shown here. A simple equivalent is shown here with @ sign in the hostname and a $ for the final prompt symbol. The home directory is represented with a tilde (~).

```
$ PS1="\u@\h:\w$"
richard@turtle.com:~$
```

Red Hat Enterprise Linux also includes some complex prompt definitions in the **.bashrc** file to support color prompts and detect any remote user logins.

Specifying Your News Server

Several shell parameter variables are used to set values used by network applications, such as web browsers or newsreaders. **NNTPSERVER** is used to set the value of a remote news server accessible on your network. If you are using an ISP, the ISP usually provides a Usenet news server you can access with your newsreader applications. However, you first have to provide your newsreaders with the Internet address of the news server. This is the role of the **NNTPSERVER** variable. News servers on the Internet usually use the NNTP protocol. **NNTPSERVER** should hold the address of such a news server. For many ISPs, the news server address is a domain name that begins with **nntp**. The following example assigns the news server address **nntp.myservice.com** to the **NNTPSERVER** shell variable. Newsreader applications automatically obtain the news server address from **NNTPSERVER**. Usually, this assignment is placed in the shell initialization file, **.bash_profile**, so that it is automatically set each time a user logs in.

```
NNTPSERVER=news.myservice.com
export NNTPSERVER
```

Configuring Your Login Shell: .bash_profile

The **.bash_profile** file is the BASH shell's login initialization file. It is a script file that is automatically executed whenever a user logs in. The file contains shell commands that define system environment variables used to manage your shell. They may be either redefinitions of system-defined variables or definitions of user-defined variables. For example, when you log in, your user shell needs to know what directories hold Linux commands. It will reference the **PATH** variable to find the pathnames for these directories. However, first, the **PATH** variable must be assigned those pathnames. In the **.bash_profile** file, an assignment operation does just this. Because it is in the **.bash_profile** file, the assignment is executed automatically when the user logs in.

Exporting Variables

Any new parameter variables you may add to the .bash_profile file, will also need to be exported, using the **export** command. This makes them accessible to any subshells you may enter. You can export several variables in one **export** command by listing them as arguments. The **.bash_profile** file contains no variable definitions, though you can add ones of your own. In this case, the **.bash_profile** file would have an **export** command with a list of all the variables defined in the file. If a variable is missing from this list, you may be unable to access it. The **.bashrc** file contains a definition of the HISTCONTROL variable, which is then exported. You can also combine the assignment and **export** command into one operation as shown here for **NNTPSERVER**:

```
export NNTPSERVER=news.myservice.com
```

Variable Assignments

A copy of the standard **.bash_profile** file, provided for you when your account is created, is listed in the next example. Notice how **PATH** is assigned. **PATH** is a parameter variable the system has already defined. **PATH** holds the pathnames of directories searched for any command you enter. The assignment **PATH=$PATH:$HOME/bin** has the effect of redefining **PATH** to include your **bin** directory within your home directory so that your **bin** directory will also be searched for any commands, including ones you create yourself, such as scripts or programs.

.bash_profile

```
# .bash_profile

# Get the aliases and functions
if [  -f  ~/.bashrc ]; then
          .  ~/.bashrc
fi

# User specific environment and startup programs
PATH=$PATH:$HOME/.local/bin:$HOME/bin
export PATH
```

Should you want to have your current working directory searched also, you can use any text editor to modify this line in your **.bash_profile** file **PATH=$PATH:$HOME/.local/bin:$HOME/bin**. You would insert a colon **:** after the last **bin**. In fact, you can change this entry to add as many directories as you want to search. Making commands automatically executable in your current working directory could be a security risk, allowing files in any directory to be executed, instead of in certain specified directories. An example of how to modify your **.bash_profile** file is shown in the following section.

```
PATH=$PATH:$HOME/.local/:$HOME/bin:
```

Editing Your BASH Profile Script

Your **.bash_profile** initialization file is a text file that can be edited by a text editor, like any other text file. You can easily add new directories to your **PATH** by editing **.bash_profile** and using editing commands to insert a new directory pathname in the list of directory pathnames assigned to the **PATH** variable. You can even add new variable definitions. If you do so, however, be sure to include the new variable's name in the **export** command's argument list. For example, if your **.bash_profile** file does not have any definition of the **EXINIT** variable, you can edit the file and add a new line that assigns a value to **EXINIT**. The definition **EXINIT='set nu ai'** will configure the Vi editor with line numbering and indentation. You then need to add **EXINIT** to the **export** command's argument list. When the **.bash_profile** file executes again, the **EXINIT** variable will be set to the command **set nu ai**. When the Vi editor is invoked, the command in the **EXINIT** variable will be executed, setting the line number and auto-indent options automatically.

In the following example, the user's **.bash_profile** has been modified to include definitions of **EXINIT** and redefinitions of **PATH**, **PS1**, and **HISTSIZE**. The **PATH** variable has the ending colon added to it that specifies the current working directory, enabling you to execute commands that may be located in either the home directory or the working directory. The redefinition of **HISTSIZE** reduces the number of history events saved, from 1,000 defined in the system's **.bash_profile** file, to 30. The redefinition of the **PS1** parameter variable changes the prompt to just show the pathname of the current working directory. Any changes you make to parameter variables within your **.bash_profile** file override those made earlier by the system's **.bash_profile** file. All these parameter variables are then exported with the **export** command.

.bash_profile

```
# .bash_profile

# Get the aliases and functions
if [  -f  ~/.bashrc ]; then
          .  ~/.bashrc
fi
PATH=$PATH:$HOME/.local/:$HOME/bin:

HISTSIZE=30
NNTPSERVER=news.myserver.com
EXINIT='set nu ai'
PS1="\w \$"
export PATH HISTSIZE EXINIT PS1 NNTPSERVER
```

Manually Re-executing the .profile Script

Although the **.bash_profile** file is executed each time you log in, it is not automatically re-executed after you make changes to it. The **.bash_profile** file is an initialization file that is executed whenever you log in. If you want to take advantage of any changes you make to it without having to log out and log in again, you can re-execute the **.bash_profile** file with the dot (**.**) command. The **.bash_profile** file is a shell script and, like any shell script, can be executed with the **.** command.

```
$ . .bash_profile
```

Alternatively, you can use the **source** command to execute the **.bash_profile** initialization file or any initialization file such as **.login** used in the TCSH shell or **.bashrc**.

```
$ source .bash_profile
```

System Shell Profile Script

Your Linux system also has its own profile file that it executes whenever any user logs in. This system initialization file is simply called **profile** and is found in the **/etc** directory, **/etc/profile**.

This file contains parameter variable definitions the system needs to provide for each user. A copy of the system's **profile** file follows. RHEL7 uses a **pathmunge** function to generate a directory list for the **PATH** variable. Normal user paths will lack the system directories (those with **sbin** in the path). The path generated by users with administrative access and for the root user will include both system and user application directories, adding **/sbin**, **/usr/sbin**, and **/usr/local/sbin**.

```
# echo $PATH
/usr/lib64/qt-
3.3/bin:/usr/local/bin:/usr/local/sbin:/usr/bin:/usr/sbin:/bin:/sbin:/home/richar
d/.local/bin:/home/richard/bin
```

If your system has installed the Kerberos clients (**krb5-appl-clients** package), then the PATH includes for Kerberos tools directories.

```
# echo $PATH
/usr/kerberos/sbin:/usr/kerberos/bin:/usr/lib64/qt-
3.3/bin:/usr/local/bin:/usr/local/sbin:/usr/bin:/usr/sbin:/bin:/sbin:/home/richar
d/.local/bin:/home/richard/bin
```

The **USER**, **MAIL**, and **LOGNAME** variables are then set, provided that **/usr/bin/id**, which provides the User ID, is executable. The **id** command with the **-un** option provides the user ID's text name only, like **chris** or **richard**.

HISTSIZE is also redefined to include a larger number of history events. An entry has been added here for the **NNTPSERVER** variable. Normally, a news server address is a value that needs to be set for all users. Such assignments should be made in the system's **/etc/profile** file by the system administrator, rather than in each individual user's own **.bash_profile** file.

Note: The **/etc/profile** file also executes any scripts in the directory **/etc/profile.d**. This design allows for a more modular structure. Rather than make entries by editing the **/etc/profile** file, you can just add a script to **profile.d** directory.

The number of aliases and variable settings needed for different applications would make the **/etc/profile** file much too large to manage. Instead, application- and task-specific aliases and variables are placed in separate configuration files located in the **/etc/profile.d** directory. There are corresponding scripts for both the BASH and C shells. The BASH shell scripts are run by **/etc/profile**. The scripts are named for the kinds of tasks and applications they configure. For example, **colorls.sh** sets the file type color coding when the **ls** command displays files and directories. The **vim.sh** file sets the alias for the **vi** command, executing **vim** whenever the user enters just **vi**. The **kde.sh** file sets the global environment variable **KDEDIR**, specifying the KDE Desktop applications directory, in this case, **/usr**. The **krb5-appl-clients.sh** file adds the pathnames for the Kerberos application directories to the **PATH** variable. Files run by the BASH shell end in the extension **.sh**, and those run by the C shell have the extension **.csh**.

/etc/profile

```
# /etc/profile

# System wide environment and startup programs, for login setup
# Functions and aliases go in /etc/bashrc

# It's NOT good idea to change this file unless you know what you
# are doing. Much better way is to create custom.sh shell script in
# /etc/profile.d/ to make custom changes to environment. This will
# prevent need for merging in future updates.

pathmunge () {
    case ":${PATH}:" in
        *:"$1":*)
            ;;
        *)
            if [ "$2" = "after" ] ; then
                PATH=$PATH:$1
            else
                PATH=$1:$PATH
            fi
    esac
    }

if [ -x /usr/bin/id ]; then
    if [ -z "$EUID" ]; then
        # ksh workaround
        EUID=`id -u`
        UID=`id -ru`
    fi
    USER="`id -un`"
    LOGNAME=$USER
    MAIL="/var/spool/mail/$USER"
fi

# Path manipulation
if [ "$EUID" = "0" ]; then
    pathmunge /usr/sbin
    pathmunge /usr/local/sbin
else
    pathmunge /usr/local/sbin after
    pathmunge /usr/sbin after
fi

HOSTNAME=`/bin/hostname 2>/dev/null`
HISTSIZE=1000
if [ "$HISTCONTROL" = "ignorespace" ] ; then
    export HISTCONTROL=ignoreboth
else
    export HISTCONTROL=ignoredups
fi

export PATH USER LOGNAME MAIL HOSTNAME HISTSIZE HISTCONTROL
```

```
for i in /etc/profile.d/*.sh ; do
    if [ -r "$i" ]; then
        if [ "${-#*i}" != "$-" ]; then
            . $i
        else
            . $i >/dev/null
        fi
    fi
done

unset i
unset -f pathmunge
```

Configuring the BASH Shell: .bashrc

The **.bashrc** file is a configuration file executed each time you enter the BASH shell or generate any subshells. If the BASH shell is your login shell, **.bashrc** is executed along with your **.bash_login** file when you log in. If you enter the BASH shell from another shell, the **.bashrc** file is automatically executed, and the variable and alias definitions it contains will be defined. If you enter a different type of shell, the configuration file for that shell will be executed instead. For example, if you were to enter the TCSH shell with the **tcsh** command, the **.tcshrc** configuration file would be executed instead of **.bashrc**.

The User .bashrc BASH Script

The **.bashrc** shell configuration file is actually executed each time you generate a BASH shell, such as when you run a shell script. In other words, each time a subshell is created, the **.bashrc** file is executed. This has the effect of exporting any local variables or aliases you have defined in the **.bashrc** shell initialization file. The **.bashrc** file usually contains the definition of aliases and any feature variables used to turn on shell features. Aliases and feature variables are locally defined within the shell. But the **.bashrc** file defines them in every shell. For this reason, the **.bashrc** file usually holds aliases and options you want defined for each shell. As an example of how you can add your own aliases and options, aliases for the **rm**, **cp**, and **mv** commands have been added. For the root user **.bashrc**, the **rm**, **cp**, and **mv** aliases have already been included in the root's **.bashrc** file.

```
# .bashrc
# User specific aliases and functions

alias rm='rm -i'
alias cp='cp -i'
alias mv='mv -i'

# Source global definitions
if [ -f /etc/bashrc ]; then
        . /etc/bashrc
fi
```

You can add any commands or definitions of your own to your **.bashrc** file. If you have made changes to **.bashrc** and you want them to take effect during your current login session, you need to re-execute the file with either the **.** or the **source** command.

```
$ . .bashrc
```

The System /etc/bashrc BASH Script

Red Hat Enterprise Linux also has a system **bashrc** file executed for all users, called **/etc/bashrc**. Currently, the **/etc/bashrc** file sets the default shell prompt, as well as instructions for checking whether a user is authorized to use a command. If in an interactive shell, **/etc/bashrc** file will determine the default prompt. If not in a login shell, it will then determine the PATH and run any **profile.d** scripts.

The BASH Shell Logout File: .bash_logout

The **.bash_logout** file is also a configuration file, but it is executed when the user logs out. It is designed to perform any operations you want to occur whenever you log out. Instead of variable definitions, the **.bash_logout** file usually contains shell commands that form a kind of initial logout procedure. These are actions you always want taken before you log out. As with **.bash_profile**, you can add your own shell commands to **.bash_logout**.

.bash_logout

```
# ~/.bash_logout
```

Table Listing

Figure Listing

Index

A

D

H

I

J

Q

R

S

T

X

Y

Z